SHIP OF FOOLS

BOOKS BY KATHERINE ANNE PORTER

FLOWERING JUDAS

KATHERINE ANNE PORTER'S FRENCH SONG BOOK

PALE HORSE, PALE RIDER

THE LEANING TOWER

THE DAYS BEFORE

SHIP OF FOOLS

Katherine Anne Porter
SHIP OF FOOLS

An Atlantic Monthly Press Book
Little, Brown and Company • Boston • Toronto

LIBRARY OF CONGRESS CATALOG CARD NO. 62-9557

SEVENTH PRINTING

Earlier versions of some scenes from this novel have been published in
*Accent, Atlantic Monthly, Harper's, Mademoiselle, Partisan Review, Sewanee
Review* and *Texas Quarterly.*

ATLANTIC—LITTLE, BROWN BOOKS
ARE PUBLISHED BY
LITTLE, BROWN AND COMPANY
IN ASSOCIATION WITH
THE ATLANTIC MONTHLY PRESS

*Published simultaneously in Canada
by Little, Brown & Company (Canada) Limited*

PRINTED IN THE UNITED STATES OF AMERICA

FOR BARBARA WESCOTT

1932: Paris, Rambouillet, Davosplatz, Salzburg, Munich, New York,
Mulhocaway, Rosemont :1962

The title of this book is a translation from the German of *Das Narrenschiff*, a moral allegory by Sebastian Brant (1458?-1521) first published in Latin as *Stultifera Navis* in 1494. I read it in Basel in the summer of 1932 when I had still vividly in mind the impressions of my first voyage to Europe. When I began thinking about my novel, I took for my own this simple almost universal image of the ship of this world on its voyage to eternity. It is by no means new — it was very old and durable and dearly familiar when Brant used it; and it suits my purpose exactly. I am a passenger on that ship.

K. A. P.

Contents

Contents

Characters

On board the North German Lloyd S.A. *Vera*, between Veracruz, Mexico, and Bremerhaven, Germany, August 22–September 17, 1931.

German

Ship's Captain Thiele.

Dr. Schumann, ship's doctor.

The purser, and a half dozen young ship's officers.

Frau Rittersdorf, who keeps a notebook.

Frau Otto Schmitt, recently widowed in Mexico.

Herr Siegfried Rieber, publisher of a ladies' garment trade magazine.

Fräulein Lizzi Spöckenkieker, in the ladies' garment business; from Hanover.

Herr Professor Hutten ⎫ Former head of a German school in Mexico, and his
Frau Professor Hutten ⎬ wife; traveling with them is their white bulldog
                      ⎭ Bébé.

Herr Karl Baumgartner ⎫
Frau Baumgartner   ⎬ Lawyer from Mexico City — hopeless drunkard;
Hans Baumgartner   ⎭ his wife Greta, and their eight-year-old son.

Herr Karl Glocken, a hunchback, who has sold out his little tobacco and newspaper stand in Mexico, and is returning to Germany.

Herr Wilibald Graf, a dying religious enthusiast who believes he has the power of healing.

Johann, his nephew and attendant.

Herr Wilhelm Freytag, "connected with" an oil company in Mexico, returning to Germany to fetch his wife and her mother.

Herr Julius Löwenthal, Jewish manufacturer and salesman of Catholic Church furnishings, returning to his home in Düsseldorf for a visit with his cousin Sarah.

Swiss

Herr Heinrich Lutz ⎫ A hotelkeeper from Mexico, returning to Switzerland
Frau Lutz   ⎬ after fifteen years, with his wife and their daughter,
Elsa Lutz   ⎭ eighteen years old.

Spanish

A zarzuela company, singers and dancers who call themselves gypsies, returning to Spain after being stranded in Mexico.

Women: Amparo, Lola, Concha, Pastora.

Men: Pepe, Tito, Manolo, Pancho.

Children: Ric and Rac, Lola's twins, boy and girl, six years old.

La Condesa, a déclassée noblewoman who has lived many years in Cuba; political exile being deported from Cuba to Tenerife.

Cuban

Six Cuban medical students on their way to Montpellier.

Mexican

The bride and groom from Guadalajara, Mexico, on a honeymoon trip to Spain.

Señora Esperón y Chavez de Ortega, wife of attaché of the Mexican Legation in Paris, traveling with her newly born son and Indian nursemaid Nicolasa.

Father Garza ⎫
Father Carillo ⎬ Mexican Catholic priests on a journey to Spain.

Political agitator: Fat man in cherry-colored shirt, who sings.

Swedish

Arne Hansen, at feud with Herr Rieber.

American

William Denny, from Texas, a young chemical engineer going to Berlin.

Mary Treadwell, a woman of forty-five, divorced, returning to Paris.

David Scott ⎫
Jenny Brown ⎬ Two young painters living together, on their first voyage to Europe.

In Steerage

Eight hundred and seventy-six souls: Spaniards, men, women, children, workers in the sugar fields of Cuba, being deported back to the Canaries and to various parts of Spain (wherever they came from) after the failure of the sugar market.

Cabin Mates

Frau Rittersdorf	Wilhelm Freytag
Frau Schmitt	Arne Hansen
Mrs. Treadwell	David Scott (David darling)
Fräulein Spöckenkieker	William Denny
Jenny Brown (Jenny angel)	Karl Glocken
Elsa Lutz	Wilibald Graf
Father Garza	Johann, his nephew
Father Carillo	

Herr Rieber
Herr Löwenthal
Señora Ortega
Nurse and baby
La Condesa (alone)
Bride and groom
Herr Lutz
Frau Lutz
Professor Hutten
Frau Hutten
Bébé the bulldog

Herr Baumgartner
Frau Baumgartner
Hans Baumgartner
The six Cuban students
  occupy two adjoining
  cabins.
The zarzuela company:
  Manolo and Concha
  Tito and Lola, with
    Ric and Rac
  Pepe and Amparo
  Pancho and Pastora

PART I

Embarkation

Quand partons-nous vers le bonheur?
BAUDELAIRE

August, 1931 — The port town of Veracruz is a little purgatory between land and sea for the traveler, but the people who live there are very fond of themselves and the town they have helped to make. They live as initiates in local custom reflecting their own history and temperament, and they carry on their lives of alternate violence and lethargy with a pleasurable contempt for outside opinion, founded on the charmed notion that their ways and feelings are above and beyond criticism.

When they entertain themselves at their numerous private and public feasts, the newspapers publish lyric prose saying how gay an occasion it was; in what lavish and aristocratic — the terms are synonymous, they believe — taste the decorations and refreshments; and they cannot praise too much the skill with which the members of good society maintain in their deportment the delicate balance between high courtesy and easy merriment, a secret of the Veracruz world bitterly envied and unsuccessfully imitated by the provincial inland society of the Capital. "Only our people know how to enjoy themselves with civilized freedom," they write. "We are generous, warmhearted, hospitable, sensitive," they go on, and they mean it to be read not only by themselves but by the polyglot barbarians of the upper plateau who obstinately go on regarding Veracruz as merely a pestilential jumping-off place into the sea.

There is maybe a small sign of uneasiness in this pugnacious assertion of high breeding; in this and in the methodical brutality of their common behavior towards the travelers who must pass through their hands to reach the temporary haven of some ship in harbor. The travelers wish only to be carried away from the place, and the Veracruzanos wish only to see the last of them; but not until every possible toll, fee, extortion, and bribe due to the town and its citizens has been extracted. It is in fact to the passing eye a typical port town, cynical by nature, shameless by experience, hardened to showing its seamiest side to strangers: ten to one this stranger passing through is a sheep bleating for their shears, and one in ten is a scoundrel it would be a pity not to outwit. In any case, there is only so much money to be got out of each one, and the time is always short.

In the white heat of an early August morning a few placid citizens of the white-linen class strolled across the hard-baked surface of the public square under the dusty shade of the sweet-by-night trees, and seated themselves at leisure on the terrace of the Palacio Hotel. They stretched out their feet to cool their shoe soles, greeted the soggy little waiter by name, and called for iced limeades. They had all grown up together in the several generations, married each other's cousins or sisters or aunts, knew each other's business, told all the gossip they heard, and heard all they had told repeated to them; had assisted indeed with the intimacy of midwives at the making of each other's histories: and still they met here almost every morning on the way to their shops or offices for a last hour of repose and to catch up on the news before beginning the serious day's work.

The square was deserted except for a small, emaciated Indian sitting on a bench under a tree, a country Indian wearing weathered white cotton drawers and a long shirt, a widely curved old straw hat over his eyes. His feet with their ragged toenails and cracked heels, in sandals fastened with leather thongs broken and knotted together again, lay meekly together on the gray earth. He seemed to sleep, sitting upright, arms folded. With a drowsy motion he pushed back his hat, took out of his twisted blue cotton belt a roll of cold tortillas and ate, eyes roving or fixed on distance, setting his square teeth into the tough bread resolutely, chewing and swallowing without enjoyment. The men at leisure on the terrace did not notice him except as a part of the scene, and he seemed unaware of them.

The beggar who came to the terrace every morning in time for the early traffic appeared around the corner shambling and crawling, the stumps of his four limbs bound in leather and twine. He had been in early life so intricately maimed and deformed by a master of the art, in preparation for his calling, he had little resemblance to any human being. Dumb, half blind, he approached with nose almost to sidewalk as if he followed the trail of a smell, stopping now and then to rest, wagging his hideous shock head from side to side slowly in unbearable suffering. The men at the table glanced at him as if he were a dog too repulsive even to kick, and he waited patiently beside each one for the sound of the small copper coins dropped into the gaping leather bag around his neck. When one of the men held out to him the half of a squeezed lime, he sat back on his haunches, opened his dreadful mouth to receive the fruit, and dropped down again, his jaws working. He crawled then across the street to the square, and lay down under the trees behind the little Indian, who did not turn his head.

The men watched his progress idly without expression as they might a piece of rubbish rolling before the wind; their gaze then roved still idly but with expert observation to the working girls walking in groups to their jobs, all dressed in flimsy light-colored cotton dresses, with bright pink or blue celluloid combs in their black hair; and to the upper-class girls in formal church attire, black gauzy dresses and fine black lace mantillas over high tortoise-shell combs, going slowly, already opening their wide black fans, into the church across the square.

When the last girl had disappeared, the eyes of the lolling men wandered then to the familiar antics of creatures inhabiting the windowsills and balconies nearest them. A long gray cat huddled watchfully in the window of his own house, staring at his enemy the parrot, that interloper with the human voice who had deceived him again and again with an invitation to come and get food. The parrot cocked his bronze-agate eye towards the monkey who began jeering at him every morning at sunrise, and jeered at him all day long in a language he could not understand. The monkey, from his neighboring balcony rail, leaped the length of his chain at the parrot, who screamed and fluttered, tugging at his leg-leash. Bored with this, the monkey sidled away, and the parrot settled down to cursing monotonously and shaking his feathers. The smell of cracked coconuts in the vendor's basket on the sidewalk below tempted the monkey. He leaped downwards towards them, dangled in frenzy by his delicate waist, and climbed again up his own chain to safety.

A woman reached her bare arm out of the window to the parrot and gave him a rotten-ripe banana. The parrot, with a little croak of thanks, took it in one claw and ate, fixing a hard dangerous eye on the monkey, who chattered with greed and fear. The cat, who despised them both and feared neither because he was free to fight or run as he chose, was roused by the smell of the raw, tainted meat hanging in chunks in the small butcher's stand below him. Presently he slid over the sill and dropped in silence upon the offal at the butcher's feet. A mangy dog leaped snarling at the cat, and there was a fine, yelping, hissing race between them to the nearest tree in the square, where the cat clawed his way out of danger and the dog, in his blindness of fury, stumbled across the abused feet of the Indian on the bench. The Indian seemed hardly to move, yet with perfect swiftness and economy swung his leg from the knee and planted a kick with the hard edge of his sandal in the dog's lean ribs. The dog, howling all the way, rushed back to the butcher's stand.

One of the men yawned freely, shaking out the newspaper lying rumpled before him, and examined again the page-sized photograph of the shattered, disemboweled corpse lying near a small crater made by the exploding bomb, in the patio of the Swedish Consulate, against a background of potted plants and wicker bird cages. It had been a young Indian servant boy, the only person killed, after all. The face had not been damaged and the wide-open eyes were peacefully melancholy; one hand lay spread delicately upon a lump of clotted entrails beside him. A man at a near table got up and leaned over to look also at the photograph, and shook his head. He was an older man with an oily dark face, his white linen clothes and soft collar were sweated limp.

"A bad business, though," he said rather loudly, "a mistake, as usual!"

"Of course, and the newspaper says so, in so many words," said the younger man, agreeing with both. They began reading the editorial notice. The editor was quite certain that no one in all Mexico, and least of all in Veracruz, could wish to harm a hair of the Swedish Consul, who had proved himself a firm friend of the city, the most civilized and respectable of all its foreign residents. The bomb in fact had been intended for a rich, unscrupulous landlord who lived next door; by some fatal error never to be too severely reprobated, the explosion had taken place in the wrong house. By such mischances, the editor was well aware, international incidents of the utmost gravity might be brought about. The city of Veracruz therefore hastened to offer its most profound and heartfelt apologies to the Consul, to the great and peaceful nation which he represented, and indeed, was prepared to make any and all reparations required by civility between governments in such cases. Most fortunately, the Consul himself had been absent at the time, enjoying his afternoon aquavit and lime juice with members of his household at the home of a friend. It was the hope of every citizen of Veracruz that the Swedish Consul would consent to overlook and forgive the tragic error, since these were stern days, with danger lurking everywhere for all. In the meantime, the lamentable incident might even so have its good uses if it should serve as a warning to the heartless, shameless exploiters of honest Veracruz tenants that the Revolution had indeed arrived in its power, that the workers were adamant in their determination to put an end to social and economic wrongs, as well as to avenge themselves fully for wrongs already done them.

The younger man turned the page, and the two read on together. The editor wished to explain a further circumstance. It was clearly the fault of no one that the festival planned in celebration of the bombing had taken place after all, in spite of the awkward failure of aim in those dedicated to the work of destruction. The preparations had been made at some expense and trouble, the fireworks had been ordered and paid for eight days before, the spirit of triumph was in the air. It would have been inglorious to the last degree to have disappointed the merrymaking workers of Veracruz, their charming ladies, and their children growing up in the new world of freedom for all. That the life of an honest young boy, a humble member of the downtrodden proletariat, had been extinguished so prematurely was of course a cause for public mourning. An immense, honorable funeral was being planned for his remains, as a martyr to the great cause of liberty and justice; ample material compensation as well would be extended to his grieving family. Already two truckloads of floral offerings had been provided by voluntary contributions from every labor union in the city; there would be five bands to play funeral marches and revolutionary songs from the Cathedral door to the graveside, and it was expected that every working man and woman able to walk would be in the great procession.

"Whew, it's getting hot around here," said the younger man, running his handkerchief into the back of his collar. The older man said, lowering his voice almost to a whisper, speaking with very little movement of his lips, "These swine are going the whole way, that's plain. I haven't collected a peso of rent from any of them for more than a year, I may never collect another. They sit there in that block of thirty-five houses in the Soledad section scratching their lice at my expense —" The two looked each other quietly in the eye. "They don't seem to realize that this kind of thing can be made to work both ways."

The younger one nodded. They moved away together out of earshot of the waiters. "My shoemakers have struck four times in seven months," said the younger man. "They talk almost in my face about taking over the factory. On the day they try it, the whole plant will burn down, I promise you. Everything is well insured."

"Why do we wait?" asked the older man, a compulsive violence bursting suddenly through his guarded tone. "Why hadn't we got fifty machine guns to turn on that celebration last night? They don't own the army yet — why didn't we send for troops? Fifty machine guns? Why not five thousand? Why not a carload of hand grenades? What is the matter with us? Are we losing our senses?"

The younger man stared before him intently as if some exciting spectacle were taking place in his mind. "It's just begun," he said with a smile of relish. "Let it work up a little more to something worth doing. Don't worry, we'll smash them to pulp. They never win. They're such cattle they don't even know they are just fighting for a change of masters. . . . Well, I'm going to be master for a while yet."

"Not if we just sit and let them swarm over us," said the older man.

"They never win," said the younger man. They walked on.

Those left behind began to drift slowly away from the terrace, leaving their newspapers on the tables. The streets, they observed with distaste, were again beginning to crawl with the latest lot of people in town for the next boat, birds of passage from God knew where, chattering their ungainly tongues. Even the Spanish was not the Spanish of Mexico. As for the women among them, except for the occasional soft beauty of some real Mexican girl, they were always the same, no matter of what freakish nationality: middle-aged painted scarecrows too fat or too thin: and young flat-chested loud-voiced things with cropped hair striding around in low-heeled shoes, their skirts shortened to show legs never meant to be seen by any eye but God's. If any exceptions to these rules occurred, they were quite simply ignored; all strangers as such were odious and absurd. The people of Veracruz never tired of the pastime of ridiculing the looks of the foreign women, their costumes, their voices, their wild unwomanly ways — the North American ones more especially. Rich and important persons sometimes arrived and departed by those boats; but being rich and important, they hardly showed themselves except in swiftly moving motors, or in lordly pauses among their clutter of expensive luggage on dock or platform. Their looks did not so much matter, anyway; they were ridiculed on other and higher grounds. *They* — all unconscious and at ease as they seemed, surveying a world made for them and giving orders to everybody in sight without turning a hand themselves — *they* were marked for destruction, so the labor leaders told their followers, and could already be regarded with some curiosity as a disappearing race. The new crowd, the watchers decided, was regular — no better, no worse, but there were always a few amusing variations.

The clerk of the hotel came out for a glimpse of daylight, and the waiters in their stained rumpled white jackets began slapping dust and crumbs off the tablecloths in preparation for lunch. They observed with contempt that their particular share of the day's travelers was straggling in again for a rest after swarming all over the town all morning.

Certainly the travelers were not looking their best. They had crept off the train which brought them from the interior, stiff from trying to sleep fully clothed in their chairs, sore in their minds from the recent tearing up of their lives by the roots, a little gloomy with some mysterious sense of failure, of forced farewell, of homelessness no matter how temporary. Imperfectly washed, untidy and dusty, vaguely not-present in eyes dark-circled by fatigue and anxiety, each one carried signed, stamped papers as proof that he had been born in a certain time and place, had a name of his own, a foothold of some kind in this world, a journey in view for good and sufficient reasons, and possessions worth looking into at international frontiers.

Each hoped that these papers might establish for him at least a momentary immunity from the hazards of his enterprise, and the first thought of each was that he must go instantly, before the rest of that crowd could arrive, and get his own precious business settled first at the various bureaus, consulates, departments of this and that; it was beginning to resemble not so much a voyage as an obstacle race.

So far they were all alike, and they shared a common hope. They lived individually and in mass for the sole purpose of getting safely that same day on board a German ship then standing in dock. She had come from South America the long way round and she was going to Bremerhaven. Alarming rumors had sped to meet the travelers even before they left Mexico City. There were serious hurricanes all along the coast. A revolution or a general strike, time must decide which, was going on at top speed in Veracruz itself. A light epidemic of smallpox had broken out in several coastal towns. At this piece of news, the travelers had all rushed to be vaccinated, and all alike were feverish, with a crusted, festering little sore above the knee or elbow. It had been said also that the German ship might be delayed in sailing, for she had lost time getting stuck for three days on a sand bar off Tampico; but the latest word was that she was in harbor and would sail on time.

They were to travel, it appeared, more than ordinarily at their own risk, and their presence in Veracruz proved that necessity and not the caprices of a pleasure voyage drove them to carry out their intentions in face of such discouragements. They were all of them obviously in circumstances ranging from modestly comfortable to uncomfortably poor, but each suffered from insufficiency in his own degree. Poverty was instantly to be deduced by a common anxiety about fees, a careful opening of wallets and handbags, a minute counting of change with wrung brows and precise fingers; a start of terror by a man who put his hand into his inside coat pocket and feared, for one shattering instant, that his money was gone.

All believed they were bound for a place for some reason more desirable than the place they were leaving, but it was necessary to make the change with the least possible delay and expense. Delay and expense had been their common portion at the hands of an army of professional tip seekers, fee collectors, half-asleep consular clerks and bored Migrations officials who were not in the least concerned whether the travelers gained their ship or dropped dead in their tracks. They saw too many of the kind all day, every day, with that disturbing miasma of financial and domestic worry rising steamily from their respectable-looking clothes. The officials did not care for the breed; they had enough such troubles of their own.

For almost twenty-four hours the anonymous, faceless travelers, their humanity nearly exhausted, their separate sufferings, memories, intentions and baffled wills locked within them, ran doggedly (for there was a taxicab drivers' strike), sweating, despairing, famished (there was a bakers' strike, and an icemen's strike), from hotel to Migrations to Customs to Consulate to the ship's side and so once more back to the railway station, in a final series of attempts to gather up the ragged edges of their lives and belongings. Each one had his luggage seized by a porter at the station, who took charge at once with a high hand, laying down the grimly one-sided laws of the situation;

these fellows all then disappeared with the property into thin air, and where had they gone? When would they come back? Everybody began to miss his hairbrush, clean shirts, blouses, pocket handkerchiefs; all day grubbily they ran, unrefreshed even by clean water.

So the travelers fretted, meeting up with each other again and again in all the uncomfortable places where they were all fated to be, sharing the same miseries: almost unbearable heat, a stony white rage of vengeful sunlight; vile food, vile beyond belief, slapped down before their sunken faces by insolent waiters. All of them at least once had pushed back a plate of some greasy substance with a fly or a cockroach in it, and had paid for it without complaint and tipped the waiter besides because the very smell of violence was in the air, at once crazed and stupefied. One could easily be murdered for an irrelevant word or gesture, and it would be a silly end. All had taken to a diet of black coffee, lukewarm beer, bottled synthetic lemonade, damp salted biscuits in tin boxes, coconut milk drunk directly from the shell. Their porters came back at unexpected times to heckle them, giving wrong advice and demanding more tips for correcting their own errors. The steady trivial drain upon their purses and spirits went on like a nightmare, with no visible advance in their pressing affairs. Women gave way to fits of weeping, men to fits of temper, which got them nowhere; and they all had reddened eyelids and badly swollen feet.

This common predicament did not by any means make of them fellow sufferers. On the contrary, each chose to maintain his pride and separateness within himself. After ignoring each other during the first feverish hours, there crept into eyes meeting unwillingly, for the twentieth time, a look of unacknowledged, hostile recognition. "So there you are again, I never saw you before in my life," the eyes said, flickering away and settling stubbornly upon their own matters. The travelers witnessed each other's humiliations, rehearsed their private business in everybody's hearing, answered embarrassing questions again and again for some sticky little clerk to write down once more. They paused in small groups before the same sights, read signs aloud in chorus, asked questions of the same passers-by, but no bond was established between them. It was as if, looking forward to the long voyage before them, they had come to the common decision that one cannot be too careful of chance-met, haphazard acquaintances.

"Well," said the desk clerk to the waiters nearest him, "here come our burros again!" The waiters, dangling their greasy rags, aimed spiteful stares meant to be noticed at the badly assorted lot of human beings who took silent possession of the terrace, slumping about the tables and sitting there aimlessly as if they were already shipwrecked. There, again, was the unreasonably fat woman with legs like tree trunks, her fat husband in the dusty black suit and their fat white bulldog. "No, Señora," the clerk had told her with dignity the day before, "even if this is only Mexico still we do not allow dogs in our rooms." The ridiculous woman had kissed the beast on his wet nose before turning him over to the boy who tied him up in the kitchen patio for the night. Bébé the bulldog had borne his ordeal with the mournful silence of his heroic breed, and held no grudges against anybody. His owners now began at once to explore the depths of the large food basket they carried everywhere with them.

A tall thin young woman — a leggy "girl" with a tiny, close-cropped head waving on her long neck, a limp green frock flapping about her calves — strode in screaming like a peahen in German at her companion, a little dumpling of a man, pink and pig-snouted. A tall loose-boned man with unusually large hands and feet, with white-blond hair clipped in a brush over his intensely knotted forehead, wandered by as if he did not recognize the place, turned back and sat by himself, relapsed into a trance. A delicate-looking red-haired boy of perhaps eight years was heaving and sweating in a Mexican riding costume of orange-colored leather, his brassy freckles standing out in the greenish pallor of his skin. His sick-looking German father and sad, exasperated German mother urged him along before them. The little boy was saying monotonously, "I want to go, mother — I want to go," and he wriggled all over.

"Go where?" asked his mother, shrilly. "What do you want? Speak clearly. We are going to Germany, isn't that enough for you?" "I want to go," said the little boy dismally, appealing to his father. The parents exchanged a glance, the mother said, "My God, my brain is giving way!" The father took the boy's hand and hurried him through the cavern of the lobby.

"Figure these tourists," said the clerk to a waiter, "dressing a child in leather in August, making a monkey of him!" The mother turned her head away at these words, flushed, bit her lips, then quietly hid her face in her hands and sat there, perfectly still for a moment.

"Speaking of monkeys, what do you call *that?*" asked the waiter, with a barely perceptible flip of his rag towards a young woman, an

American, who wore dark blue cotton trousers and a light blue cotton shirt: a wide leather belt and a blue figured bandanna around her neck completed her outfit, which she had lifted without leave from the workday costume of the town-dwelling Mexican Indian. Her head was bare. Her black hair was parted in the middle and twisted into a bun at the nape of her neck, rather old-fashioned-looking in New York, but very appropriate still in Mexico. The young man with her wore a proper-looking white linen suit and an ordinary Panama hat.

The clerk dropped his voice, but not quite enough, and spoke the deadliest insult he knew. "It's a mule, perhaps," he ventured. As he moved away he observed with satisfied spite that the Americans understood Spanish also. The young woman stiffened, the young man's handsome nose turned white and pinched, and they stared at each other like enemies. "I told you to put on a skirt here," said the young man. "You do know better."

"Hush," said the young woman, in a weary, expressionless voice, "simply hush. I can't change now until we get to the boat."

Four pretty Spanish girls, dark-skinned, long-necked, with an air of professional impudence, their sleazy black skirts too tight around their slender hips, their colored petticoat ruffles showing shabbily over their graceful legs, had been all over the square, back and forth, up and down and sideways in the narrow streets between the low soiled white plaster walls pocked with bullet holes. They had rushed in and out of shops, they sat on the terrace in a huddle eating fruit and scattering the rinds, their urgent Spanish chatter going on noisy as a flock of quarreling birds. They were accompanied by an equal number of dark slim young men with silky black hair oiled to their narrow skulls, wide belts cinched to their tapering waists; and a pair of sallow precocious children, male and female, twins, perhaps six years old. They were the only travelers who had come out and taken part in the show of fireworks and dancing the evening before. They cheered when the rockets went up, they danced with each other in the crowd, and then had gone off a little way by themselves and danced again, the jota, the malagueña, the bolero, playing their castanets. A crowd had gathered round them, and at the end one of the girls had gone among them collecting money, holding her skirt before her to catch the coins, and swishing her petticoat ruffles.

The affairs of this company had required an inordinate amount of arranging. They ran in a loose imperfectly domesticated group, calling to the young, who disobeyed them all impartially and were equally slapped about and dragged along by all. Distracted with shapeless, loosely wrapped parcels, their eyes flashing and their hips waving in all directions, they grew more disheveled by the moment, but their spirits never flagged. Finally, rushing upon the terrace, they clustered tightly around one table, beat their fists upon it and shouted at the waiter, all screaming their orders at once, the children joining in fearlessly.

An inconspicuous slender woman in early middle age, conventionally dressed in dark blue linen, with a wide blue hat shading her black hair and small, rather pretty face and intent dark blue eyes, regarded the Spaniards with some distaste while raising the short sleeve over her right arm, to glance again at the place where the beggar woman had pinched her. A hard knot had formed in the soft arm muscle, already blotchy with purple and blue. The woman felt a wish to show this painful bruise to someone, to say lightly as if she were talking about someone else, This is surely not a thing that really happens, is it? But there was no one, and she smoothed down the rumpled linen. That morning she had set out from the hotel after a cold bath, and plenty of hot coffee beastly as it was, feeling a little less ghastly after sleep, for another visit to the Migrations Bureau. The beggar woman was sitting, back to the wall, knees drawn up in a profusion of ragged skirts, eating a hot green pepper rolled in a tortilla. She stopped eating when she saw the American woman, transferred her food to her left hand, scrambled up and came towards her prey with lean shanks flying, her yellow eyes aimed like a weapon in her leather-colored face.

"Give me a little charity at once in God's name," the beggar woman said threateningly, rapping the foreign woman sharply on the elbow; who remembered the pleasant, clear little thrill of righteous anger with which she had answered in her best Spanish that she would certainly do nothing of the sort. It was then that the beggar woman, fiercely as a pouncing hawk, had darted out her long hard claws, seized a fold of flesh near the shoulder and wrung it, wrung it bitterly, her nails biting into the skin; and instantly had fled, her bare feet spanking on the pavement. Well, it had been like a bad dream. Naturally things like that can't happen, said the woman in the blue dress, or at least, not to me. She drooped, rubbed her handkerchief over her face, and looked at her watch.

The fat German in dusty black and his fat wife leaned their heads together and spoke secretly, nodding in agreement. They then crossed the square with their lunch basket and their dog, and seated themselves on the end of the bench opposite the motionless Indian. They ate slowly, taking glazed white paper off huge white sandwiches, drinking turn about from the cover of a large thermos bottle. The fat white dog sat at their feet with his trusting mouth turned up, opening and closing with a *plop* over the morsels they gave him. Solidly, gravely, with dignity, they ate and ate, while the little Indian sitting near them gave no sign; his shrunken stomach barely moved with his light breathing. The German woman wrapped up what was left of the broken food with housewifely fingers and left it lying on the bench near the Indian. He glanced at it once, quickly, and turned his head again.

The Germans with their dog and their basket came back to their table and asked for one bottle of beer with two glasses. The maimed beggar rose from under the tree sniffing, and crawled towards the smell of food. Rising a little, he embraced the bundle with his leather-covered stumps and brought it down. Leaning against the bench, he hunched over and ate from the ground, gobbling and gulping. The Indian sat motionless, looking away.

The girl in the blue trousers reached out and patted the white bull-dog on the head and stroked him. "That's a sweet dog," she said to the German woman, who answered kindly but vaguely, not meeting the stranger's eyes, "Oh, my poor Bébé, he is so good," and her English was almost without accent, "and so patient, and I am only afraid sometimes he may think he is being punished, with all this." She poured a little beer on her handkerchief and wiped his big face, tenderly, and almost tenderly she ignored the unsightly, improperly dressed American girl.

The crop-haired young woman in the green gown startled everyone by leaping to her feet screaming in German, "Oh, look what is happening! Oh, what are they doing to him?" Her long arms flurried and pointed towards the great tree in the square.

A half dozen small Indian men came padding across from out the shadow of the church. They carried light rifles under their arms, and they moved with short light steps, not hurrying, towards the Indian sitting on the bench. He watched them approach with no change of expression; their faces were without severity, impersonal, secret. They stopped before him, surrounded him; without a word or a glance or pause he rose and went away with them, all noiseless in their ragged sandals and white cotton drawers flapping around their ankles.

The travelers watched the scene with apathy as if sparing themselves a curiosity that would never be satisfied. Besides, what happened to anyone in this place, yes, even to themselves, was no concern of theirs. "Don't trouble your head," said the pig-snouted man to the green-clad girl, "that is nothing unusual here. They're only going to shoot him, after all! Could be he stole a handful of chilis! Or it might be just a little question of village politics."

This remark roused the gaunt blond man with the huge hands and feet. He unfolded his long body, uncrossed his legs and ranged his fixed scowl upon the pudgy man. "Yes," he said in German with a foreign accent, his big voice rolling, "politics it may well be. There is nothing else here. Politics and strikes and bombs. Look how they must even bomb the Swedish Consulate. Even by accident as they say — a lie! Why the Swedish Consulate of all places, may I ask?"

The pig-snouted man flew into a rage and answered in a loud common voice, "Why not the Swedish Consulate, for a change? Why should not other people sometimes have a little trouble, too? Why must it be always the Germans who suffer in these damned foreign countries?"

The long rawboned man ignored the question. He sank back, his white eyelashes closed over his pale eyes, he drew the limeade before him through the straw in a steady stream. The Germans about stirred uneasily, their features set hard in disapproval. Untimely, unseemly, their faces said prudishly; that is the kind of German who gives us all bad reputations in strange lands. The little man was flushed and swollen, he seemed to be resenting some deep personal wrong. There followed a long hot sweaty sunstricken silence; then movement, a rising and pushing back of chairs, a gathering up of parcels, a slow drift towards dispersal. The ship was to sail at four, it was time to go.

Dr. Schumann crossed the deck with the ordered step of an old military man and stood firmly planted near the rail, relaxed without slackness, hands at his side, watching the straggling procession of passengers ascending the gangplank. He had a fine aquiline nose, a serious well-shaped head, and two crookedly healed dark dueling scars on his left cheek. One of these was a "beauty," as the Germans call it, the enviable slash from ear to mouth perfectly placed that must once have laid the side teeth bare. Healed all these years, the scar still had a knotty surface, a wide seam. Dr. Schumann carried it well, as he carried his sixty years: both were becoming to him. His light brown eyes, leveled calmly upon a given point where the people approached and passed, were without speculation or curiosity, but with an abstract goodness and even sweetness in them. He appeared to be amiable, well bred and in perfect possession of himself, standing against a background of light-haired, very young, rather undersized ship's officers in white, and a crew of big solid blunt-faced sailors moving about their duties, each man with the expressionless face and intent manner of a thoroughly disciplined subordinate.

The passengers, emerging from the mildewed dimness of the customs sheds, blinking their eyes against the blinding sunlight, all had the look of invalids crawling into hospital on their last legs. Dr. Schumann observed one of the most extreme forms of hunchback he had ever seen, a dwarf who, from above, appeared to have legs attached to his shoulder blades, the steep chest cradled on the rocking pelvis, the head with its long dry patient suffering face lying back against the hump. Just behind him a tall boy with glittering golden hair and a sulky mouth pushed and jostled a light wheel chair along, in which sat a small weary dying man with weak dark whiskers flecked with gray, his spread hands limp on the brown rug over his knees, eyes closed. His head rolled gently with the movement of the chair, otherwise he gave no sign of life.

A young Mexican woman, softened and dispirited by recent childbirth, dressed in the elegant, perpetual mourning of her caste, came up slowly, leaning on the arm of the Indian nurse who carried the baby, his long embroidered robe streaming over her arm almost to the ground. The Indian woman wore brightly jeweled earrings, and beneath her full, gaily embroidered Pueblo skirt her small bare feet advanced and retreated modestly. A nondescript pair followed, no-colored parents of the big girl walking between them, taller and heavier than either of them, the three looking about with dull, confused faces. Two Mexican priests, much alike in their grim eyes and blue-black jaws, walked briskly around the slow procession and gained the head of it. "Bad luck for this voyage," said one young officer to another, and they both looked discreetly away. "Not as bad as nuns, though," said the second, "it takes nuns to sink a ship!"

The four pretty, slatternly Spanish girls, their dark hair sleeked down over their ears, thin-soled black slippers too short in the toes and badly run over at high heels, took leisurely leave, with kisses all around, of a half dozen local young men, who had brought flowers and baskets of fruit. Their own set of four wasp-waisted young men then joined them, and they strolled up together, the girls casting glances full of speculation at the row of fair-haired young officers. The twins, smeary in the face, eating steadily from untidy paper sacks of sweets, followed them in a detached way. An assortment of North Americans, with almost no distinguishing features that Dr. Schumann could see, except that they obviously could not be other than Americans, came next. They were generally thinner and lighter-boned than the Germans, but not so graceful as the Spaniards and Mexicans. He also found it impossible to place them by class, as he could the others; they all had curiously tense, preoccupied faces, yet almost nothing of their characters was revealed in expressions. A middle-aged, prettyish woman in dark blue seemed very respectable, but a large irregular bruise on her arm below her short sleeve, most likely the result of an amorous pinch, gave her a slightly ribald look, most unbecoming. The girl in blue trousers had fine eyes, but her bold, airy manner spoiled her looks for Dr. Schumann, who believed that modesty was the most beautiful feature a young girl could have. The young man beside her presented a stubborn, Roman-nosed profile, like a willful, cold-blooded horse, his blue eyes withdrawn and secretive. A tall shambling dark young fellow, whom Dr. Schumann remembered as having embarked at some port in Texas, had gone ashore and was now returning; he lounged along in the wake of the Spanish girls, regarding them with what could only be described as a leer.

The crowd was still struggling upward when Dr. Schumann lost interest and moved away, the officers dispersed, and the dock workers who had been loading the ship without haste began to shout and run back and forth. There remained luggage, children and adults not yet on board, and those on board wandered about in confusion with the air of persons who have abandoned something of great importance on shore, though they cannot think what it is. In straying groups, mute, unrelated, they returned to the docks and stood about idly watching the longshoremen hauling on the ropes of the loading cranes. Shapeless bundles and bales, badly packed bedsprings and mattresses, cheap-looking sofas and kitchen stoves, lightly crated pianos and old leather trunks were being swung into the hold, along with a carload of Pueblo tile and a few thousand bars of silver for England; a ton of raw chicle, bundles of hemp, and sugar for Europe. The ship was none of those specialized carriers of rare goods, much less an elegant pleasure craft coming down from New York, all fresh paint and interior decoration, bringing crowds of prosperous dressed-up tourists with money in their pockets. No, the *Vera* was a mixed freighter and passenger ship, very steady and broad-bottomed in her style, walloping from one remote port to another, year in year out, honest, reliable and homely as a German housewife.

The passengers examined their ship with the interest and the strange dawning of affection even the ugliest ship can inspire, feeling that whatever business they had was now transferred finally to her hold and cabins. They began to move back towards the gangplank: the screaming girl in green, the fat pair with the bulldog, a small round German woman in black with sleek brown braids and a heavy gold chain necklace, and a short, worried-looking German Jew lugging a heavy sample case.

At the latest possible moment, a bridal party appeared in a festival flurry at the foot of the gangplank: a profusion of lace hats and tender-colored gauzy frocks for the women, immaculate white linen and carnation buttonholes for the men. It was a Mexican wedding party with several North American girls among the bridesmaids. The bride and groom were young and beautiful, though at that moment they were worn fine and thin and their faces were exhausted with their long ordeal, which even yet was not quite ended. The bridegroom's mother clung to her son, weeping softly and deeply, kissing his cheek and murmuring like a mourning dove, "O joy of my life, little son of my heart, can it be true I have lost you?"

While his father supported her on his arm, she embraced her son, the bridegroom kissed her, patted her heavily rouged and powdered cheeks and whispered dutifully, "No, no, dear sweet little Mama, we shall be back in three months." The bridegroom's mother shrank at this, moaned as if her child had struck her a mortal blow, and sobbing fell back into the arms of her husband.

The bride, in her bridelike traveling dress, surrounded by her maids, stood between her parents, each of them holding her by a hand, and their three faces were calm, grave, and much alike. They waited with patience and a touch of severity as if for some tiresome but indispensable ceremony to end; at last the bridesmaids, recalled to a sense of duty, rather shyly produced each a little fancy sort of basket of rice, and began to scatter it about, fixed smiles on their lips only, eyes nervous and watchful, feeling as they did that the moment for merriment in this affair seemed rather to have passed. At last the bride and groom walked swiftly up the gangplank; almost at once it began to rise, and the families and friends below formed a close group, waving. The bride and groom turned and waved once, a trifle wildly, to their tormentors, then holding hands, almost running, they went straight through the ship to the farther deck. They arrived at the rail as if it were a provided refuge, and stood leaning together, looking towards the sea.

The ship shuddered, rocked and heaved, rolled slowly as the pulse of the engines rose to a steady beat; the barking sputtering tugs nosed and pushed at her sides and there appeared a slowly widening space of dirty water between the ship and the heaving collision mats. All at once by a common movement as if the land they were leaving was dear to them, the passengers crowded upon deck, lined along the rail, stared in surprise at the retreating shore, waved and called and blew kisses to the small lonely-looking clusters on the dock, who shouted and waved back. All the ships in harbor dipped their flags, the small band on deck spanked into a few bars of *"Adieu, mein kleiner Garde-Offizier, adieu, adieu —"* then folded up indifferently and disappeared without a backward glance at Veracruz.

There emerged from the bar an inhumanly fat Mexican in a cherry-colored cotton shirt and sagging blue denim trousers, waving an immense stein of beer. He strode to the rail, elbowed his way between yielding bodies, and burst into a bull bellow of song. *"Adios, Mexico, mi tierra adorada!"* he roared, tunelessly, his swollen face a deeper red than his shirt, the thick purple veins standing out on his great sweating neck, his forehead and throat straining. He waved the stein and frowned sternly; his collar button flew off into the water, and he tore open his shirt further to free his laboring breath. *"Adios, adios para siempre!"* he bawled urgently, and faintly over the oily-looking waves came a small chorused echo, *"Adios, adios!"* From the very center of the ship rose a vast deep hollow moo, like the answer of a melancholy sea cow. One of the young officers came up quietly behind the fat man and said in a low voice, in stiff Spanish, his schoolboy face very firm, "Go below please where you belong. Do you not see that the ship has sailed? Third-class passengers are not allowed on the upper decks."

The bull-voiced man wheeled about and glared blindly at the stripling for an instant. Without answering he threw back his head and drained his beer, and with a wide-armed sweep tossed the stein overboard. "When I please," he shouted into the air, but he lumbered away at once, scowling bitterly. The young officer walked on as if he had not seen or heard the fat man. One of the Spanish girls, directly in his path, smiled at him intensely, with glittering teeth and eyes. He returned her a mild glance and stepped aside to let her pass, blushing slightly. A plain red-gold engagement ring shone on his left hand, the hand he raised almost instinctively as if to ward her off.

The passengers, investigating the cramped airless quarters with their old-fashioned double tiers of bunks and a narrow hard couch along the opposite wall for the unlucky third comer, read the names on the door plates — most of them German — eyed with suspicion and quick distaste strange luggage piled beside their own in their cabins, and each discovered again what it was he had believed lost for a while though he could not name it — his identity. Bit by bit it emerged, travel-worn, halfhearted but still breathing, from a piece of luggage or some familiar possession in which he had once invested his pride of ownership, and which, seen again in strange, perhaps unfriendly surroundings, assured the owner that he had not always been a harassed stranger, a number, an unknown name and a caricature on a passport. Soothed by this restoration of their self-esteem, the passengers looked at themselves in mirrors with dawning recognition, washed their faces and combed their hair, put themselves to rights and wandered out again to locate the Ladies' (or Gentlemen's) toilets; the bar and smoking room; the barber and hairdresser; the bathrooms, very few. Most of the passengers concluded that, considering the price of the tickets, the ship was no better than she ought to be — rather a poor, shabby affair, in fact.

All around the deck the stewards were setting out the reclining chairs, lashing them to the bar along the wall, slipping name cards into the metal slots on the headrests. The tall girl in the green dress found hers almost at once and dropped into it limply. The big-boned man with the frowning brow who had been angry about the bombing of the Swedish Consulate already sprawled in the chair beside her. She waved her little head about, cackled with laughter at him and said shrilly, "Since we are going to sit together, I may as well tell you at once my name. I am Fräulein Lizzi Spöckenkieker, and I live in Hanover. I have been visiting with my aunt and uncle in Mexico City and oh, with what delight I find myself on this good German boat going back to Hanover again!"

The bony man without moving seemed to shrink down into his loose, light clothes. "Arne Hansen, at your service, my dear Fräulein," he said, as if the words were being extracted from him with pincers.

"Oh, Danish!" she shrieked in delight.

"Swedish," he said, flinching visibly.

"What is the difference?" screamed Lizzi, tears rising mysteriously to her eyes, and she laughed as if she were in pain. Hansen uncrossed his long legs, braced his hands upon his chair arms as though he would rise, then fell back in despair, his eyes almost disappearing in his knotted frown. "It is not a good ship," he said glumly, as if talking to himself.

"Oh, how can you say that?" cried Lizzi. "It is a beautiful, beautiful — oh, here again is Herr Rieber, look!" and she leaned far out and flung both arms above her head as signal to the advancing pig-snouted little man. Herr Rieber returned the salute gallantly, his eyes mischievously twinkling. He speeded up at sight of her, his trousers stretched tight over his backsides hard and round as apples, and over his hard high belly. His pace was triumphant, he was a little short-legged strutting cock. The afternoon light shone on the stubby light bristles of his shaven skull full of ridges. He carried a dirty raincoat, with a folded newspaper in one pocket.

Herr Rieber, giving no sign that he had ever seen Hansen before, choosing to ignore the little scene on the terrace at Veracruz, stopped and peered at the card above Hansen's head and spoke, first in French, then in Russian, then in Spanish and at last in German, saying the same thing in each language: "I am sorry to trouble you, but this is my chair."

Hansen raised one eyebrow, wrinkled his nose as if Herr Rieber smelled badly or worse than badly. He unfolded himself and rose, saying in English, "I am a Swede," and walked away.

Herr Rieber, very pink in the face, his snout quivering, shouted after him valiantly, "So, a Swede? Is that a reason why you should take my chair? Well, in such things, I can be a Swede too."

Lizzi cocked her head at him and almost sang: "He did not mean you any harm. You were not sitting in your chair, after all."

Herr Rieber said fondly, "Since it is next to yours, I want it always to be free for me." Grunting a little, he eased himself down, took the old copy of the *Frankfurter Zeitung* out of the raincoat pocket and shuffled it about restlessly, his underlip pursed. Lizzi said, "It is not a nice way to begin a long voyage, quarreling."

Herr Rieber put down his paper, shoved the raincoat away. He eyed her sweetly, roguishly. "It was not, and you well know it, about the chair that I quarrel with that big ugly fellow," he told her. Lizzi instantly grew more roguish than he.

"Ah, you men," she screamed joyously, "you are all alike!" She leaned over and whacked him three times on the skull with a folded paper fan. Herr Rieber was all ready for a good frolic. How he admired and followed the tall thin girls with long scissor-legs like storks striding under their fluttering skirts, with long narrow feet on the ends of them. He tapped her gently on the back of her hand with his forefinger, invitingly and with such insinuation she whacked him harder and faster, her teeth gleaming with pleasure, until the top of his head went florid.

"Ah, what a wicked girl," he said, dodging punishment at last but still beaming at her, unvanquished — indeed, quite stimulated. She rose and pranced along the deck. He rolled out of his chair and bounced after her. "Let's have coffee and cake," he cried tenderly, "they are serving it in the bar now." He licked his lips.

Two inordinately dressed-up young Cuban women, frankly ladies of trade, had been playing cards together in the bar for an hour before the ship sailed. They sat with crossed legs in rolled-top gauzy stockings to show their powdered knees. Red-stained cigarettes sagged from their scarlet full mouths, smoke curled towards their narrowed eyes and heavily beaded lashes. The elder was a commanding beauty; the younger was smaller, thinner, apparently in frail health. She observed the other attentively and played her cards as if she hardly dared to win. The tall shambling young Texan, whose name was William Denny, came in and sat in a corner of the bar and watched them with a wary, knowing eye. The ladies ignored him; though they paused in their game now and then to sip their pousse-cafés and glance haughtily about the comfortably crowded bar, they never once glanced at Denny, who felt it as a personal slight. He rapped sharply on the bar as if calling the barman, still staring at them, a mean cold little smile starting in his face. Chili Queens. He knew their kind. He had not lived most of his life in Brownsville, Texas, for nothing. They were no treat to him. He rapped again, noisily.

"You have your beer, sir," said the barman. "Anything else, please?"

The ladies glanced at him then, their contemptuous eyes fixed upon him as if he were a drunken hoodlum making trouble in a bar. His gaze quivered, his smile vanished; he dived into his mug of beer, drank, lighted a cigarette, leaned over and examined his own shoes intently, fumbled for his handkerchief, which wasn't there, and at last he gave up and broke for the open air, like a man on urgent business. There seemed nowhere to go, though, and nothing much to do, unless he went back to his cabin to start unpacking a few things. Might as well try to settle down.

Already he was beginning to feel exhausted from his efforts to maintain his identity among strange languages and strange lands. Challenged as he felt himself to be, to prove his own importance in every separate encounter, he was badly confused as to what appearance that importance should assume. The question presented itself not for the first time but most sharply when he reached Veracruz. In the small town on the border where his father was a prominent citizen, mayor for many years and rich from local real estate, the lower classes consisted of Mexicans and Negroes, that is, greasers and niggers, with a few polacks and wops but not enough to notice; and he had always relied simply on his natural superiority of race and class, backed by law and custom. In Veracruz, surrounded by a coastal race of Negro-Indian-Spanish, yellow-eyed, pugnacious people, whose language he had never troubled to learn though he had heard it all his life, he had taken the proper white man's attitude towards them and they had responded with downright insolence. He had begun by feeling broad-minded: after all, this was their country, dirt and all, and they could have it — he intended to treat them right while he was there. He had been made to realize his mistake almost at once: when he was polite to them, they thought he was patronizing them; when he was giving a perfectly legitimate order, they let him see he was trying to treat them like slaves; if he was indifferent and let things go, they despised him and played tricks on him. Well, damn it all, they *are* inferior — just look at them, that is all you need. And it won't do to let the bars down for a minute. At the Migrations, he had called the little clerk Pancho, just as back home he would have called a taxi driver Mac or a railway porter George, by way of showing good will. The little nigger — all those coast Mexicans had nigger blood, somebody had told him — stiffened as if he had been goosed, his face turned purple and his eyes red. He had stared at Denny and said something very short and quick in his own lingo, then in good English had asked Denny to sit down, kindly, for a few minutes until the papers could be filled out. Denny, like a fool, had sat there streaming with sweat and the flies buzzing in his face, while the clerk looked after a whole line of people who had come in later than he. It came over him slowly that he was being given the hot-foot. That taught him something though. He had got up and gone to the head of the line and shouldered in towards the clerk and said very distinctly and slowly, "I'll take those papers now," and the clerk instantly produced and stamped them and handed them over without even a glance at Denny. That was what he should have done in the first place and the next time he'd know.

Opening the door of his cabin, he noted three names instead of two. Herr David Scott, said the sign, Herr Wilhelm Denny, and surprise Herr Karl Glocken. He looked in upon a crowded scene. The tight-faced medium-sized young man he had seen running around Vera-cruz with that bitchy-looking girl in the blue pants was cleaning the washhand basin with something that smelled like carbolic acid. There were two strange suitcases and a battered leather bag on Denny's berth, the lower. His ticket called for the lower, and he was going to have it; no use starting out letting himself get gypped. The young man raised his eyes briefly, said, "How do you do?"

"Fairly," said Denny, moving inside one step. The young man went on washing the basin. Seated upon a footstool, Herr Glocken was fumbling among the contents of a clumsy duffel bag. He was the most terribly deformed human being Denny had ever seen, except perhaps the maimed beggar in the square at Veracruz. Bending over as he was, his body was so close to the floor his long arms could stretch further than his out-spread legs. He got up with an apologetic air, and stood almost four feet tall, his long sad face cradled in a hunch high as his head, and backed into that end of the lower berth not occupied by the luggage. "I'll be out of here in just a minute," he said, with a pained smile. He then eased himself down upon the edge of the mattress among the luggage and appeared to faint. David Scott and William Denny exchanged unwilling looks of understanding; they were obviously stuck with this fellow, and there was nothing to be done about it that either could see at the moment.

"We'd better call the steward," said David Scott.

Herr Glocken opened his eyes and shook his head, waving one long hand limply. "No, no," he said, in a dry flat voice, "don't trouble yourselves. It is nothing. I am only resting a little."

"Well, so long," said Denny, backing away, "I'll be in later."

"Here, let me move these," said David, laying hold of the suitcases. There was no place for them under the berth. Denny's luggage was already there. The closet was too small to hold them. He put them on the divan bed for the present.

Herr Glocken said, "I have no right here, I belong in the upper berth, but how am I to get there?"

David said, "You take the divan and I'll take the upper."

"I don't know how I'll sleep there, it's so narrow," said Herr Glocken, and David, measuring the curve of the monstrous body by the width of the couch, saw painfully what he meant. He looked away from both and said, "Better stay where you are, then — don't you think?" he said to Denny.

There was silence while David looked for a glass to hold his toothbrushes.

Though his ticket called for berth number one, plainly, Denny, with a decency that surprised David, offered the lower berth to Herr Glocken, and Herr Glocken accepted with eager thanks.

Herr Glocken fell asleep almost at once. He lay on his side, facing the light, knees drawn up to chin, near the edge of the bed to make room for the curved spine. His thin dry hair was rumpled like sunburned corn silk, the great misshapen face closed in deathly melancholy. The toes of his shoes turned up, there were patches in the soles.

David observed the clutter of small articles belonging to Denny that already took up most of the small shelf above the washbasin. Denny had hastened to wash and comb on coming aboard, and had left as much disorder as if he were at home. "Eats yeast," said David silently, and disgust was added to his deep sense of wrong. He had been assured by the ticket clerk in Mexico there would be only two passengers to a cabin. "Smokes a pipe, and reads improving literature." He removed from the couch a fully illustrated clothbound book entitled

Recreational Aspects of Sex as Mental Prophylaxis, with a subhead, *A Guide to True Happiness in Life.* "Jesus," said David.

The smell of disinfectant could not down the other fetid smells of unclean human garments, the rancid smell of Herr Glocken's shoes, the old mildewed smell of the cabin itself. The ship rolled a little as she met the first waves of the sea outside the harbor. David saw his face in the mirror. He looked greenish, he felt qualmy, the floor visibly upended under him and his gorge heaved spontaneously. He rushed for the door, almost falling over Herr Glocken's duffel bag, and made for the upper deck. Another outrage: he had been promised a cabin on the promenade deck, but he was actually on Deck C, with a porthole instead of a window.

The warm slow winds were clean and sweet and so moist they blew like soft steam against his face. The deeply slanted late afternoon sun cast long shafts of light into the sea, dark blue in the depths, clear green fluted with white at the surface. David saw Jenny Brown strolling towards him, the first time since they had separated to find their cabins. She had changed from the blue trousers to a white linen dress and white leather sandals, with no stockings; she was walking with a man, a strange man — David had never seen him before — as if he were an old friend. He noted with a pang that the man was good-looking in a detestable sort of way, like a sports jacket or whiskey advertisement, with a typically smug, conceited German face. Where and how had Jenny picked him up in this short time? He stood at the rail and pretended not to see them, then turned casually, he hoped, as they drew near.

"Why hello — David?" said Jenny absent-mindedly with a vague air of imperfect recognition. "Are you all right?" and they moved by without pausing.

Her wide light hazel eyes had the look of blind diffused excitement he knew best; she was probably talking already about the most personal things, telling her thoughts such as they were: for even when Jenny seemed intelligent, or sincere, he still distrusted her female mind, crooked and cloudy by nature: she was no doubt asking questions designed to lead the man to talk about himself, meaning to trap him into small confidences and confessions that later she could use as a weapon against him when needed. Already David felt she was building up a case against this fatuous foreigner which she would have well prepared when the time came to quarrel. He watched her small, neat figure, harmonious as a little classic statue; the round head with the knot of black hair, the rather stiff, modest walk, which managed to conceal or misrepresent everything he believed he knew about Jenny. She might, by that walk, be a prim little schoolteacher who kept in mind that she must carry her shoulders straight and her hips smoothly.

David looked at his watch and decided it was time for the first drink of the day, the hour towards which he lived of late, and went in the bar, feeling all at once surrounded and smothered by the sea, which he hated, and which now filled him with a quiet deep horror. There was no place, no place at all to go.

This whole wild escapade to Europe was Jenny's idea; he had never intended to leave Mexico at all, but he had let her lead him by the nose, as usual. Still, not altogether, he reflected, when the first slug of whiskey had begun to take hold. She planned, taking his assent for granted, to go first to France; he at once determined, if he went anywhere at all, to go to Spain. They had two or three violent quarrels about it, and then compromised on Germany, which neither of them wanted to see. That is, they drew one from three named straws of different lengths — he held the straws and Jenny drew one — and the shortest straw, named Germany, came out. They were both so bitterly disappointed they quarreled again, and then drank a little too much, and then made love fiercely half the night as if in a revengeful rage against whatever it was that kept them apart; and all of it had settled nothing. They both stuck obstinately to the chance decision, so here they were — yet even so, Jenny had her plans. She came in one afternoon announcing gaily that in case they changed their minds, they could still get visas for France from the French Consul at Vigo. The German ship's agent at North German Lloyd's had sworn to her that this was a fact.

"What about just being allowed to get off at Vigo for Spain?" asked David.

"I'm not going to Spain, remember?" said Jenny.

Well, if she felt better with an ace up her sleeve, let her. She might go to France if she liked. He would go to Spain. She'd find out in time whether she was going to have it all her own way.

"Bitte," said Mrs. Treadwell, timidly, thinking she might as well begin brushing up on her German, to the small round woman with the glossy braids and the gold necklace who was having tea at a small table by herself. Opposite her was the only empty chair. The bar was crowded, it looked festival enough, but the silence was rather odd Even those persons obviously related in whatever way sat mute as if with strangers.

An amiable but vacant little smile spread over the plump fresh face with its soft features. A competent white hand was lifted, palm out, gently. "No, no," she said, "don't trouble yourself. I speak English for years now. I taught English even — do sit down please — in the German school in Guadalajara. My husband taught there also. But mathematics."

"Tea, please," said Mrs. Treadwell to the steward. She had changed from dark blue to pale gray linen, with still shorter sleeves, and the disgraceful-looking big blotch on her arm was quite livid.

"I am Frau Otto Schmitt," said the round woman, stirring her tea and dropping more sugar in it. "I was from Nürnberg in my youth and I am returning there at last. It was to have been my great happiness, my husband's long-looked-for joy, but now it is only grief and disappointment after all; and I am tempted though I know it is a sin sometimes to ask myself — what is life but that, after all?" She spoke in a low voice without complaint, but as if she wished even the merest chance acquaintance to identify her at once with her grief as the only fact of any importance to be known about her. Her pale blue eyes asked frankly for pity.

Mrs. Treadwell shuddered with a painful twinge of foreboding. "Even here," she thought. "How inevitable. I shall spend this voyage listening to someone's sorrows, I shall sit down and have a good cry with somebody, no doubt, before this trip is over. Well, this is a fine beginning."

"Where are you going?" asked Frau Schmitt, after a sufficient pause in which the expected question leading to the story of her afflictions had not been asked.

"To Paris," said Mrs. Treadwell, "back to Paris."

"Ah, you were only visiting in Mexico?"

"Yes."

"You have friends there?"

"No."

Frau Schmitt's water-blue gaze transferred itself to Mrs. Treadwell's arm. "You have bruised yourself badly," she said, with mild interest.

Mrs. Treadwell said, "The astonishing fact is, a beggar woman pinched me."

"Why?"

"Because I would not give her an alms," said Mrs. Treadwell, thinking for the first time how unusually selfish and stupid that refusal sounded, just told flatly. No decent person refused a beggar in Mexico; like everyone she knew, she carried by habit a handful of copper coins meant only for them. This was no beggar, but an impudent gypsy — the rap on the elbow! Still, the whole thing was somehow shameful to her; how could she have let a low creature like that stupefy her so? The thing was not to be explained, even to herself. "Naturally I don't expect anyone to believe it," she said, selecting a thin dry wafer with her tea.

"Why not?" asked Frau Schmitt, childishly.

"Well, anything can happen, I know that," said Mrs. Treadwell, "but I always find myself thinking, *not to me.*" Now why had she said that? It gave such an opening for more whys and why-nots. Uneasily she glanced about, and saw instantly that, on the other side of the bar, with cocktails before them, the American girl Jane Brown was already seated with the only presentable-looking man on the boat. She turned back to the dull little thing across from her, accepting this voyage and this society as a long boredom like any other, not to be denied, opposed or ignored, but to be fled from, lightly from point to point; moment by moment she would find a split second of relief from boredom in the very act of flight which gave her the fleeting illusion of invisibility.

"Anything at all can happen to any of us at any time," said Frau Schmitt with easy certainty. "My husband — how long has it been that we have hoped to go back to Nürnberg together? But now I am going alone, though his coffin is in the hold of this ship. Oh it smothers me to think of it! My husband died six weeks and two days ago today at seven o'clock this morning . . ."

It is always death, thought Mrs. Treadwell, for this sentimental kind it can never be less than death. Nothing else could pierce through that fat to a living nerve. Still I must say something. "That is a very terrible thing," she said, and was dismayed to find that in spite of her unfriendly thought, she really meant it, she pitied this woman's sorrow; and that death, there beside them at the table, death was what they had in common.

Frau Schmitt's soft mouth turned down at the corners. She stirred her tea and said nothing. Her eyelids turned pink. She was quite alone all at once in her own private luxury of grief, once she had devoured the pink-iced teacake of sympathy. Mrs. Treadwell, leaving half her tea, quietly made her first escape of the voyage.

On her way to her cabin she spoke and smiled, in the same tone and the same smile for each, to the ship's doctor, noting his fine old *Mensur* scar; to the taffy-haired young officer whose name or rank she did not know and would never trouble to learn (though before the voyage was over, she would be kissed, seriously, by that very young man); to an earnest-faced, stiffly laced stewardess; and to a browbeaten little cabin boy, who stared back in silence with offended eyes. The name below hers on her cabin door struck her as too funny not to be unlucky: Fräulein Lizzi Spöckenkieker: Spookpeeper? — and she wondered rather lightly which of the numerous unpromising-looking females on board she might be.

Presently as she was arranging her things on the narrow shelf of her small closet, smoothing multicolored tissue paper over perishable-looking wear, shaking out pleated silks and setting gold and silver and satin slippers in a row, she smiled again into the garments and said *"Grüss Gott"* without turning when she heard someone come in. It was the tall girl with the shrill voice — playmate of that dreadful little fat man. Mrs. Treadwell had a thin tremor of nerves all over, a slight cold shudder from head to foot. She smiled even more amiably, unseen, and became very absorbed in her occupation.

After a brief whirl about the room, during which a cloud of musky cologne water mingled with the thick air, Fräulein Spöckenkieker took herself away, leaving the door open. Mrs. Treadwell closed it, shutting out the sound of voices in the cabin just off hers at an angle, where the name plate read Baumgartner.

The woman Baumgartner was scolding vigorously a complaining, weak-voiced little boy. Ah, family life, good wholesome German family life, thought Mrs. Treadwell cheerfully. The very notion was so suffocating Mrs. Treadwell put her head out of the porthole and breathed deeply.

"Mother," said Hans again, as soon as he dared, sitting on the edge of the divan trying to keep out of her way, "Mother, may I take off my clothes?"

Frau Baumgartner closed both hands into fists and shook them above her head. "Have I not *told* you," she said, in fresh exasperation, "that you cannot take off your clothes until I give you something else to put on? And I have not time now. Don't ask me again."

The child in his prison of stitched and embroidered buckskin, a Mexican riding dress meant for the cold mountain country, writhed with the itching of heat rash and salt sweat. "You may keep on what you've got until I open your luggage," she told him, stubbornly, going on with her search for her husband's shirts. "I have everything to do and I cannot do everything at once." She loosed her wrath upon him. "Be quiet, or I'll punish you!" She raised her hand, flat and threatening.

He collapsed sobbing, streaming; there were dark wet streaks in the wrinkles of his leather trousers. "I'm dying," he told her, in a fainting voice, his freckles looking like spots of iodine on his pale skin.

"Dying!" said his mother contemptuously. "A big boy like you talking such nonsense. Wait till your father sees you like this." She rummaged, orderly even in her haste and discomfort, through the layers of folded things, stopping to push her damp hair off her forehead. She was pale too, flabby and wet down the spine and in the armpits; she could feel the sweat running down her legs, her arms shone wetly through the thin dark stuff of her dress. "I suppose you think your mother is not tired and suffering too? Do you think you are the only one? Instead of whining and complaining and making my troubles worse, get up from there and stop sniveling and help me with these suitcases."

"Mayn't I just take off my jacket?" he persisted hopelessly, wiping his nose on the back of his hand, shedding tears again in spite of himself.

"So — take it off then," she said. "I see you are still just a baby and I shall give you a bottle to nurse — a bottle with a rubber nipple, with milk and sugar, and you shall have nothing else for your supper," she went on, beginning to enjoy her cruelty, the pleasant feeling that she could hurt his pride even if he had won in the matter of the jacket. He had no pride whatever — he stripped off the jacket instantly, the air from the porthole blew over him and the gooseflesh rose all over him deliciously. His face cleared, and he gazed at his mother gratefully with a deep sigh of bliss.

"Wait till I tell your father how you worry me," she said, but in a softer voice, "and if I see you being a crybaby again, you know what you will get."

He waited timidly in the corner at the head of the divan, yearning for kindness, hoping his beautiful good mother would come back soon. She vanished in this frowning scolding stranger, who blazed out at him when he least expected it, struck him on the hands, threatened him, seemed to hate him. His head drooped, his hands hung beside him, he gazed from under his scanty light brows, not afraid, but waiting. She got up, pulled her skirts straight, saw him clearly, and was filled with pity and remorse.

"Well, my little one, my Hans," she said tenderly, and kissing her finger she laid it gently on his forehead. "Now wash your face and hands, wash well, wrists and neck too! and put on your knit jumper and shorts and we will go and have some cold raspberry juice. But hurry. I will wait outside." As if she had never been cross, she smiled upon him most lovingly. In the confusion of his feelings, Hans could have wept again, but the cold water on his face stopped his tears.

Frau Rittersdorf, on Deck A, took advantage of the absence of her cabinmate to establish her prior rights and privileges as to space and choice of bed. Her ticket specified the upper berth, but Frau Rittersdorf had taken a good look at little Frau Otto Schmitt, and saw at once that the situation would be easy to control. She called for vases and set out carefully the two enormous floral offerings she had sent herself, one of pale pink roses, one of gardenias, bought in Veracruz, wrapped in wet cotton, and carrying cards attached by silver ribbons: *"To my dearest Nannerl, from her Johann." "To the gnädige Frau Rittersdorf with greetings. Karl von Ettler."*

They looked well, and it was not really a deception as those interesting friends would have been happy to send her flowers on this as on many another occasion, except for the lamentable circumstance that they were both dead — yet again, so recently departed both of them, she still could not quite realize their loss, and these flowers did almost give her the feeling that they were still alive. In the old days they had sent more than flowers, God remember them both. She crossed herself several times although she was a Lutheran. It was a gesture she felt becoming to her, and it warded off bad luck.

She set out two silver and cut-crystal bottles of perfume, "Garden of Araby" and "Souvenir d'Amour," and fastened a quilted silk contrivance for containing her silver-backed brushes and mirror, comb, nail file and shoehorn on the righthand side of the washbasin, the most convenient spot. She did her hair well, and dressed slowly. She had come on board early to avoid the nuisance of mingling with the crowd, which appeared to be rather inferior in tone. Taking her mirror, she regarded her profile with approval. She had many times been called a beauty and she deserved it. She was beautiful *now*, say what you like. Sitting a moment, she opened a large notebook of red and gilt Florentine stamped leather with a gold pencil attached and began to write:

"So in a way, let me admit, this adventure — for is not all life an adventure? — has not ended as I hoped, yet nothing is changed for the worse. Indeed I may yet see the all-guiding Will of my race in it. A German woman should not marry into a dark race, even if the candidate is of high Spanish blood, of the ruling caste, of sufficient wealth . . . There are those fatal centuries in Spain when all too insidiously Jewish and Moorish blood must certainly have crept in — who knows what else? That I entertained the notion for a moment is no doubt a weakness of which I should be ashamed. Yet, surrounded as I was by foreign influences, soft persuasions of friends, good Germans whose counsels I respected, alone as I am in the world and somewhat reduced in means, perhaps I should not be too severely censured. After all, I am a woman, I need the firm but tender guidance of a husband, whose authority shall sustain me, whose principles shall be my —"

Frau Rittersdorf paused. Inspiration had ceased, the next word would not come. She knew well there is ever and always only one true way of looking at any question, and she had always looked at everything exactly as she should, as she had been taught. She had said and thought all this so many times, why say and think it again? She closed her eyes and fell into a daydream of the long, dark, severe yet benign face of Don Pedro, with its air of remote nobility; hair graying slightly at the temples; around his presence the aura of Spanish wealth and Spanish pride, based soundly on a large Mexican brewery — oh why should this all rise again to plague her? Why had it seemed so likely at one time that he would ask her hand in marriage? Her cousins in Mexico City, also brewers, had believed that he would; her dear friend Herr Stumpfen the Consul had been certain of it; she herself had gone so far as to choose — in her mind — the style of her announcement cards. . . . She clenched her teeth slightly, opened her eyes, closed the book. The dinner bugle sounded with a fine martial clamor as if calling heroes to the battlefield. Frau Rittersdorf rose instantly, a girlish eager light in her eyes. She would of course be seated at the Captain's table.

"Ah, my God, there goes the bugle, we shall be late," said Frau Professor Hutten to her husband, but she continued to hold a bath towel under Bébé's chin. Herr Professor Hutten with torn newspapers was wiping up a mess in the near corner rather ineffectually. Bébé, his big white bulldog face the very picture of humiliation, rolled his eyes and heaved again into the towel.

"My God, my God," said Frau Hutten in patient despair, "seasick already, what shall we do?"

"He was seasick before, when we went to Yucatán, nearly all the way, and from the first moment, if you remember," said the Professor, rolling up the soiled newspapers and standing there before her in majestic benevolence, as if he were getting ready to address his classes. "We need not look for any radical change in his organic constitution as time goes on. As a puppy, you remember, he was easily upset, he could not keep his bottle down if he was in the least agitated; and so he is now, and so," concluded the Professor, "no doubt he will continue with perhaps some increasing symptoms of the sort, to the end."

His wife's distress was if anything increased by this prospect. "But how can I leave him in this condition?" she inquired. She was sitting on the floor, a solid mound of flesh, Bébé sprawled beside her, and they were both equally helpless. "I cannot get up until you come back, either," she reminded him, "my knee —"

"You are in no circumstances to forgo your dinner," the Professor told her, firmly. "I will take your place at his side, and you are to have your food, which otherwise you will miss greatly later in the evening."

"But my dear, you will starve instead, think of that," said Frau Hutten, gazing up at him gratefully.

"A small matter," said her husband. "In fact, I shall not in the least starve, dear Käthe; one does not starve for missing only a meal; one merely goes a bit hungry, which is not always the greatest misfortune. In fact it is possible for man to go without nourishment for forty days; we now have scientific confirmation of the word of Holy Writ. More especially so, I dare say, if the subject has flesh to spare, plenty of water, and perhaps a little stimulant of some kind at intervals. . . .

However, none of this will be necessary. At the worst, you might have them send me a little something on a tray. Better, if we should fold a fresh towel under Bébé's head, with plenty of newspapers underneath, he will do very well by himself for let us say an hour."

Frau Hutten nodded. She lifted Bébé's head and examined him. He seemed more at ease. "Don't think your little Vati and Mutti are deserting you, my precious one," she told him in round maternal tones. "We are only going for a little while." The Professor hooked both his forearms under her armpits, from the back, hauled her up with the expertness of long practice, steadied her while she got her balance, and then carried out his own proposed measures for the care of Bébé, who seemed very little interested in them or in his surroundings.

"Ah," sighed his wife, leaning her head briefly on his bowed shoulder, "it is all very difficult."

"We will find ways and means," said the Professor, reassuringly. Bébé was going to be a problem, though, if not a complete nuisance, as always, he could see that. A hard thought which the Professor rebuked himself for innerly, but could not deny. "Away with us before the soup is cold," he exclaimed with the false gaiety of a guilty conscience.

The big girl Elsa Lutz and her parents Herr and Frau Heinrich Lutz were taking their first stroll in dull leisure around the deck. Elsa towered over her rather weedy elders, but walked between them, their obedient child, holding each by a hand. They stopped and peered downward through an iron grating which rewarded them with a sight of the steerage feeding quarters. There were rows of narrow trestles loaded with food, and long benches ranged beside them. Cooking smells rose warmly, the people were coming in slowly and seating themselves. They recognized the billowing back and bowed head of the fat man in the cherry-colored shirt, already deep in his dinner, helping himself freely from large platters of substantial food in a half circle round his plate.

"Well, God bless us," said Herr Lutz in some surprise, and he put on his spectacles for a closer look. "Why, how can they make any profit if they set a table like that?" He was a Swiss, descendant of a long line of hotelkeepers, and he had run a hotel of his own in Mexico; his interest was entirely professional.

"Fried potatoes," he murmured, "there must be a pound of them on his plate. A whole braised pig's knuckle, with fried onions, red sweet-sour cabbage and split-pea purée — well, true it's none of it on the expensive side, yet it all costs something. And coffee. Fruit besides, and *Apfelstrudel* — no, they can't keep it up and break even. Look how that fellow eats! It makes me hungry to watch him."

His wife, a dumpy plain woman with a roll of faded dry hair bristling with wire hairpins, observed the scene with her habitual expression, long ago settled into a blend of constant disapproval and righteous ill-humor. "It is only to make a show in the beginning," she remarked. "They will begin to economize on all of us before the trip is over. A new broom," she said, "sweeps clean."

"Ha, ha," laughed her husband, "you mean a new customer eats clean." His daughter joined his laughter dutifully but a little uneasily; his wife treated the joke with the contempt it merited, keeping her face still long enough for him to see exactly what she thought of his nonsense. He continued his laughter long enough to let her see that he could enjoy his little joke without her.

"But Papa," said Elsa, leaning again over the grating, "hadn't you noticed another thing? The third class is empty, almost, only a dozen passengers, and yet they would not sell us third-class tickets. Don't you think it was very wrong of the clerk in Mexico City to tell us there was no room in third class for us?"

"Well, yes," admitted her father, "in one way. In another, very good business. Here we are, first-class tickets and all, they have made already more than three hundred fifty dollars on us; you turn that into reichsmarks now and you have some real money. . . ."

"But there must be some other reason besides," said Elsa.

"Oh yes, there are always a lot of good reasons and they know them all, for cheating us," said Frau Lutz. "I wish you might have learned some of those reasons for your own use," she told her husband, and long years of deeply cherished, never-to-be-settled grudges lay in her tone. The three walked on, a family clumsiness in their movements, eyes straight ahead and dull with small anxieties.

"Answer me one thing, my poor wife," said Herr Lutz in a mild, reasoning voice which he knew exasperated his wife more than anything else. "Did we do so badly in Mexico after all? In any sense of the word? Did we by any stretch of your imagination fail? I think not."

"I no longer care what you think," said Frau Lutz.

"Even for you, that is going a little far," said Herr Lutz. "And just the same it doesn't keep me from thinking. And sometime maybe when you happen to be thinking you might think about how we're going home, all in good health, with enough money, honestly earned, to start our own little hotel in St. Gallen."

"Yes, after all these years," said his wife, drearily. "Yes, now when it is too late, when nothing will be the same, when Elsa is grown up and a stranger to her own people — oh think what trouble we had to keep her from speaking Spanish first, before her mother tongue! Yes, now of course, we can go back in style, and set up in business and feel important. What for?"

"As for feeling important," said Herr Lutz, "let us wait and see."

"Mama," said Elsa timidly, trying to change the subject, "my cabin mate is that American girl who came on board with that light-haired young man. I thought they were married, didn't you? But he is in one cabin and she another."

"I am sorry to hear all this," said her mother, severely. "I had hoped you might be with an older woman, somebody respectable. That girl, I don't like her looks or her ways. Pantaloons in the street, imagine! And is she really traveling with a man who is not her husband?"

"Well," said Elsa, uncertainly, seeing that this topic was a failure also, "I suppose so. But she is in a separate cabin, after all."

"I hardly see the difference," said her mother. "I am very sorry. Now listen carefully to me. You are to be always very reserved with that girl. Do not take her advice or follow her example in the smallest thing. Treat her with perfect coldness, don't take up with her at all. Never be seen on deck with her. Don't talk to her or listen when she talks. You are in very bad company, and I shall try to have your cabin changed."

"But who would I be with then?" asked Elsa. "Another stranger."

"Ah, yes," sighed her mother, looking about her at various women passing them or walking near them. "My God, who knows? One may be worse than the other! Just you obey me, that is all!"

"Yes Mama," said Elsa, attentively and submissively. Her father smiled at her and said, "That is our good little girl. You must always do as your mama says."

"But Papa, when she changed to a skirt, she looked like anyone else, she looked very well, not like an American at all."

"Let her alone, just the same," said Frau Lutz, shaking her head. "She is an American, don't forget that. No matter how she looks."

The bugler stepped out on deck sounding his merry call for dinner. Instantly the Lutz family faced inward and hastened their steps. At the top of the stairs they were almost overwhelmed from the back by the troupe of Spanish dancers, who simply went through, over and around them like a wave, a wave with elbows. The Lutzes were so outdistanced the Spaniards were already seated at a good-sized round table near the Captain's and the six-year-old twins were tearing at a dish of celery before a waiter could find the small table set for three — against the wall, to be sure, but happily near a porthole.

"I am glad to see they have washed their faces," said Frau Lutz, beginning to read her dinner card with an eye of foregone disillusion, "but it would look better all around if they washed their necks, too. I saw very distinctly: their necks are gray and stiff with old dirty powder. Elsa, you wonder why I always say to you, wash your neck. And your wrists, too, and as for powder — I hope you will never be so foolish."

Elsa glanced down her own nose, where the shininess was refracted into her eyes. She rubbed her nose with her handkerchief, carefully refrained from sighing and said nothing.

The dining room was clean and well polished. There were flowers on the tables and an adequate display of fresh white napery and tableware. The waiters seemed refreshed and stimulated by the beginning of another voyage, and the famished faces of the new set of passengers wore a mollified, expectant air. The Captain was absent, but at his table Dr. Schumann greeted the Captain's guests, and explained to them that it was the Captain's custom to dine on the bridge during the serious first hours of voyage.

The guests all nodded in generous agreement and acknowledgment of the Captain's heavy task of getting them safely to sea; and all was sedate remark and easy understanding among the chosen ones: Herr Professor and Frau Hutten, Herr Rieber, Fräulein Lizzi Spöckenkieker, Frau Rittersdorf, Frau Otto Schmitt, and the "presentable" young man whom Mrs. Treadwell had seen sitting with Jenny Brown. His name was Wilhelm Freytag, he said several times over in the round of exchange of names when the company had sat down. Within three minutes Frau Rittersdorf had ascertained that he was "connected" with a German oil company in Mexico, was married (a pity, rather) and was even then in that moment on his way to Mannheim to bring back his young wife and her mother. Frau Rittersdorf also decided instantly that Herr Rieber bounced and chuckled rather vulgarly and was hardly up to the rest of the Captain's table. Frau Schmitt and the Huttens were at once well disposed to each other when it came out that they were all former teachers in German schools, the Huttens in Mexico City.

Herr Rieber, in top spirits, twinkling irrepressibly at Lizzi, but decently subdued by the society in which he found himself, proposed by way of a good beginning that he might be allowed to offer wine to the whole table. This was received with the best of good will by the others. The wine was brought, real Niersteiner Domtal of the finest label, so hard to find in Mexico, so expensive when found, so missed by them all, so loved, the beautiful good sound white wine of Germany, fresh as flowers. They sniffed their chilled goblets, their eyes moistened and they beamed at each other. They touched brims lightly, clinking all about, spoke the kind round words of health and good fortune to each other, and drank.

Nothing, they felt, could have been more correct, more charming, more amiable than that moment. They fell upon their splendid full-bodied German food with hot appetites. They were all going home, home at last, and in this ship they had in common for the first time the feeling that they had already set foot upon a mystic Fatherland. Restored, fortified, they paused now and again to wipe their teeming mouths, nodding at each other in silence. Dr. Schumann ate with the moderation of an abstemious man who could hardly remember when last he had been really hungry. The guests gave him admiring glances as they ate and drank. The highest kind of German good breeding, they could see, with the dignity of his humane profession adding still more luster; and his fine scar, showing that he had gone to a great university, that he was brave and coolheaded: so great a scar so perfectly placed proved that he had known the meaning of the *Mensur*, that measure of a true German. If he seemed a little absent, thoughtfully silent, that was his right; it belonged to the importance of his duties as ship's doctor.

"Pig's knuckles, David darling," said Jenny Brown, restoring his private particular name to David Scott for the first time in three days.

His own mood was not so easy — he reflected that she probably would not become Jenny angel to him for several days more — if ever. How much simple fraying of the nervous system can love survive? How many scenes?

"I'm boning up on German from the water taps and all the little signs about, but nearly all these people speak English or French or both. Do you see that fellow I was walking with? Over there — the Captain's table. The one with the invincible haircut. I didn't even know he was German until he told me —"

"With that face?" asked David.

"What's wrong with his face?"

"It looks German."

"David darling, shame on you! Well, I wanted to practice my German on him, but after the first sentence he simply couldn't bear it, and I must say, he speaks better English than I do — awfully English, in fact. I thought maybe he had been brought up in England, but no, he learned it in school in Berlin. . . . Well, my Swiss girl — did I tell you I'm stuck in the same cabin with that big Swiss girl? She wears a white linen corset cover with tatting around the edges. I'll bet you never saw one . . ."

"My mother used to wear them," said David.

"David! You mean you peeped while your mother was dressing?"

"No, I used to sit in the middle of the bed and watch her."

"Well," said Jenny, "my Swiss girl speaks Spanish and French and English and a kind of dialect she calls Romansh — besides German — and she's barely eighteen. And she will speak only English to me, though I certainly do as well at Spanish as she does. I don't see an earthly chance to pick up any language, if this is the way it's going to be."

"These people aren't typical," said David, "and neither are we. Just roaming around foreign countries, changing money and language at every border. We do the same. Look at me, even learning Russian —"

"Yes, look at you," said Jenny, admiringly. "But you even learn the grammar, from the book, a thing that would never occur to me. I can't learn grammar, that's flat, but then, I don't feel the need of it."

"If you could hear yourself sometimes," said David, "you'd feel the need. You say some really appalling things, in Spanish I mean."

"You look pretty as a picture in that blue shirt, darling," said Jenny.

"I hope that doesn't appall you. My God, I'm starving! Wasn't Vera-cruz deadly this time? What came over that town? I had the tenderest memories of the place and now I hope I never see it again."

"It seemed to me as usual," said David, "heat, cockroaches, Vera-cruzanos and all."

"Ah no," said Jenny, "I used to walk about there at night, after a rain, with everything washed clean, and the sweet-by-night and jas-mine in full bloom and the colors of the plaster walls very pure. I would come on those unexpected squares and corners and fountains, all of them composed, just waiting to be painted, and none of them looking the way they did in daylight. All the windows would be open and pale yellow light streaming out, with clouds of white mosquito netting over the big beds, and half-dressed half-asleep people moving about already in a dream; or sitting out on the little balconies just for the pleasure of breathing. It *was* lovely, David, and I loved it. The people seemed so friendly and easy — everybody. And once there was a terrible glorious thunderstorm and lightning hit the elevator shaft in my hotel about twenty feet from my room and knocked me out, almost. It was fun! It was real danger and yet I was alive."

David protested this memory coldly, doubtfully. "You never told me this before," he said.

"I hope not," she said. "Wouldn't that be dull? But you never be-lieve any memory that is pleasant, I wonder why? You must let me re-member it in my own way, as beautiful at least once." After a light pause she added, "I am sure that if you had been there it would all have looked very different." She watched with clinical attention his smooth, tight-skinned face that gave absolutely no sign when he was hit.

"Who was with you then, that it was all so delightful?"

"Nobody," she said softly. "I was there by myself and I saw it in my own way with no one to spoil it for me."

"And no boat to catch."

"No, I had come off a boat from New York. Nine lovely days when I didn't know a soul on board, and spoke only to my waiter and my stewardess."

"They should have been flattered," said David darling, meanly. But it gave him no satisfaction.

Jenny straightened her knife and fork and took a sip of water. "I don't know," she told him gravely as if she were considering deeply an important question. "I really don't know whether I am going to be able to sit at this table with you the whole voyage or not. At least I am glad we have separate cabins."

"So am I," said David, instantly, a cold fire in his eyes.

They both fell silent then, dismayed at how suddenly things could get out of hand; knowing as always there was no end to it, because there was no real beginning. The quarrel between them was a terrible treadmill they mounted together and tramped round and round until they were wearied out or in despair. He went on doggedly with his food, and she took up her fork again. "I'll stop if you will," she said at last. "How does it begin? Why? I never know."

David knew that her yielding was half fatigue, half boredom, but he was grateful for the reprieve. Besides, she had got in a good blow at him, and must be feeling easier.

He did not forgive her; he would take her by surprise someday in turn, as he had done often before, and watch her face turn pale; she always recognized revenge for what it was, yet admitted its barbarous justice. At least she had some little sense of turn and turn about, she didn't expect always to be allowed to get away with murder, and he would make it part of his business to see that she did not. Feeling within him his coldness of heart as a real power in reserve, he smiled at her with that sweetness which always charmed her, reached out and laid his hand over hers warmly.

"Jenny angel," he said. Instantly she felt her heart — she believed firmly that her heart could feel — melting just a little, timidly and distrustfully: she knew what David could and would do to her if she let herself be "caught soft" as he described it. Yet she could not stop herself. She leaned forward and said, "You old thing, you! Oh, let's try to be happy. Let's not spoil our first voyage together, it could be so gay. I'll try, really David darling, I promise — let's try. Don't you *know* I love you?"

"I wonder," said David with the most insidious gentleness. Mysteriously she seemed on the verge of tears, which she controlled, knowing that David regarded her weeping as simply another female trick shaken out of her sleeve at the useful moment. He watched with a reserved little smile to see if she would give way; she had never made a scene in public yet. She smiled back at him, instead, took up her glass of wine and held it out to touch his. "*Salud,*" she said. "*Salud,*" said David, and they emptied their glasses in one breath.

They were both ashamed of the evil natures they exposed in each other; each in the first days of their love had hoped to be the ideal image of the other, for they were desperately romantic, and their fear of exposing themselves, of showing and learning unlovely things about each other, made them dishonest and cruel. In their moments of truce both believed that the love between them was very pure and generous, as they wished it to be; there needed only to be . . . needed only to be what, exactly, they both wondered, secretly and separately, and found no answer. Only in such short moments as this, when they drank the wine of peace together, their bodies grew limp and calm, they breathed easily in the air of reconciliation, and made vague vows to themselves and to each other, to keep faith — faith with what? to love each other, to *try* — But David at least still knew that for himself, trying to be happy was perhaps half their trouble, or the cause of half of it. And the other half — ?

"To happiness then," he said, touching her glass again.

Though it was still broad daylight, the August sun, dipping into the far horizon, threw a burning track over the waters which ran like oil in the wake of the ship. The ladies of trade appeared on deck in identical black lace evening gowns, their fine smooth backs gleaming to the belt, their jeweled sandals flashing. They paced about slowly and came face to face with the two priests, who were pacing slowly also, their dark trap mouths locked, their relentless eyes fixed on their breviaries. The ladies bowed respectfully, the fathers ignored or perhaps did not see them. William Denny followed them at a safe distance once around, pausing now and then to appear interested in something in the depths of the sea, his Adam's apple bobbing ever so slightly. The bride and groom sat together in their extended chairs, watching the sunset in silence, their eyes tranced and mystified, their hands clasped lightly.

The Mexican Indian nurse brought the newly born baby to his mother, who received him rather helplessly in her inexperienced arms. Frau Rittersdorf, passing, took the liberty of a true woman who, though childless herself and never ceasing to be thankful for it, still appreciated instinctively the glorious martyrdom of motherhood as enjoyed by others. With a smile of intimate sympathy for the mother, she dropped silently on her knees to adore the divine mystery of life for a few seconds, admiring his feathery eyebrows and tender mouth, the complexion to the last degree enviable. His mother looked on with a formal, unwilling smile, thinking her son was spoiled enough already, she wished people would let him alone; remembering how he woke and yelled in the night and pulled on her like a pig when she was tired to tears and wanted only to sleep.

"Such a splendid man-child," said Frau Rittersdorf. "Is he your first?"

"Ah, yes," said the mother, and there was a shade of terror in her face.

"A fine beginning," said Frau Rittersdorf, "a perfect little general. El Generalissimo, in fact!" She had been told by her German friends that every second male Mexican was a general, or intended to be one, or called himself one, at least.

The mother could not after all quite resist the flattery, however crude, however German in its style. El Generalissimo indeed! How vulgar; still, she knew her child was superb, she loved to hear him praised, even in Spanish with such an atrocious accent. Somehow Frau Rittersdorf led the talk from infant to mother; began to speak pretty passable French, which delighted the Mexican woman, who prided herself on her command of that language. Frau Rittersdorf learned with great satisfaction that Madame was the wife of an attaché in the Mexican Legation in Paris, she was even now on her way there to join her husband; it had been impossible — "Well, you can see why," said the mother — for her to accompany him. Frau Rittersdorf was soothed in her highest social sense to find a lady in diplomatic circles among the passengers; there would be someone to associate with, after all. Señora Esperón y Chavez de Ortega for her part seemed to sink rapidly in mood, to become a touch distrait, perhaps only natural in her new situation. El Generalissimo opened his eyes, waved his fists and yawned divinely in Frau Rittersdorf's face. His mother frowned just perceptibly and pleaded, "Oh, *please* don't wake him. He has only just got to sleep. If you could imagine the trouble we have with him — colic and all!"

Feeling rebuffed, Frau Rittersdorf rose instantly and took her leave with such exaggerated politeness it hardly stopped short of rudeness. The little Mexican woman was after all probably not particularly intelligent, perhaps not even particularly well bred. It was rather difficult to judge of the standards of the dark races, though no doubt they had them; even Don Pedro in Mexico, whose failure to ask for her hand in marriage after what had seemed irreversible overtures — was there not something sinister in his nature? And yet — could it have been the fact of his owning a great brewery? — he had at times seemed to her so human, so Germanized, she had been quite lulled and led astray. She walked on faster, in a small chill of fright, shaking her head.

After dinner all the desks in the small rooms off the bar were occupied by absorbed letter writers, last words to Mexico to be mailed at Havana. Only the Spanish dancing women patrolled the deck, living in the moment. They had no friends in Mexico and very few in Spain, and this did not trouble them in the least. It was fairly noticeable that romance of a sort seemed to be simmering around them. Their skins breathing forth musk and amber, wearing fresh flowers in their hair, they were to be seen about in shadowy spots, each involved more or less with one of the blond young ship's officers.

The officers were all poor, perfectly disciplined, dedicated to their calling, saving up their scanty earnings to be married: they all wore plain red-gold engagement rings on their left hands, and, bound to their narrow world always in motion, never set foot in any port. It was expensive, it could lead to international complications, and besides there were too many ports. They had clearly defined and not always onerous duties towards female passengers, such as dancing with them in the evenings if they seemed to lack partners, slighting no one, making themselves agreeable in a decorous way. They had no privileges, such as carrying an affair too far, but it was not to be supposed that any one of them should not avail himself of opportunities freely offered so long as appearances were preserved. In this particular case of the Spanish ladies, appearances obviously could not be preserved but must be disguised if possible.

Their experiences with many female passengers on many voyages to out-of-the-way ports had intimidated most of them to a certain extent. So, warily one by one the young officers in immaculate white, with gold or silver insignia at their collars and shoulders, found themselves on the first evening, in instructed gallantry but with also a good deal of pleasant excitement, each with an arm around a surprisingly muscular but slender Spanish waist, looking with mild expectation into the burning depths of eyes that meant business and nothing else.

Something always occurred to throw them off; mysteriously the combinations separated, re-formed with different partners, until at last, early in the evening, all seemed to be over — a question of money no doubt, decided Wilhelm Freytag, who had got into talk over beer with Arne Hansen. They had been watching the little scenes here and there.

"What else could it be," asked Arne Hansen, and he watched one of the girls especially, his choleric blue eyes softened to simple admiration. She was indeed very beautiful, and though of a type with the others, Hansen could see a difference in her, even if he could not point it out to another eye. They all had fine dark eyes, shining black hair smoothed over their ears, their round small hips swayed as they walked in a self-conscious *meneo*, their narrow, high-arched feet were stuffed without mercy into thin black pumps. They all painted, with dark red grease paint, large square brutal mouths over their natural lips, which were thin and hard: but the one he preferred was called Amparo, he had found that out. Already he faced in his thoughts the first obstacle: he spoke very little Spanish and Amparo, so far as he knew, spoke nothing else.

"I can't imagine what they do," said Wilhelm Freytag, "besides of course what they are doing now. They look like a set of gypsies. I saw them dancing and collecting money in the streets at Veracruz."

Hansen could tell him about that. They were a zarzuela company from Granada, gypsies maybe, or pretending to be. They had got stranded in Mexico as such outfits always did, the great Pastora Imperio herself had just barely got out with the clothes on her back, he had heard — and the Mexican government was sending them home, as usual, at its own expense. Freytag considered they looked a tough lot, the four men especially, oblique-looking characters with their narrow skulls and thugs' eyes — a combination of table-top dancer, pimp, and knife-thrower.

Hansen studied them. "I think not dangerous," he judged, "unless it was fairly safe." He settled back comfortably in his powerful frame and stretched his long legs under the table.

The men of the dancers' troupe were sitting in the bar with the children, obviously keeping out of the way while their ladies practiced their arts. They were silent, entirely too graceful in their few movements, and watchful as cats. Sitting over a series of cups of coffee, they smoked constantly; and the children, who were subdued in a way they were not when the women were present, finally leaned their heads and arms on the table and went to sleep.

Frau Baumgartner sat head on hand wearily at a small table with her husband, who had begun his long evening of methodical drinking to ease his constant pain. His hair already was damp and plastered to his temples. For just a short time after taking food, he felt relief in his stomach, but he could not face the beginning of pain again, and hurried to his first glass of brandy and water. These pains had begun about two years before, when Herr Baumgartner lost three important cases in the Mexican courts. His wife knew why he had lost them: he was drinking so steadily he could not properly prepare his arguments, he could not make a good impression in court. Back of that was the sad mystery — why had he begun to drink? He could not explain and he could not resist his longing for brandy. From hour to hour throughout the day and into the evening, he drank — without pleasure, without any lightening of spirit, without relief, without will, in helpless suffering of conscience, his hand still stole out to the bottle and he poured into his glass quite literally in fear and trembling.

On those few days at long intervals when his wife persuaded him not to drink, he would take to his bed with frightful pains in his stomach, writhing, groaning, until the family doctor was called to give him an opiate. They called in specialists, each of whom made his own guess corresponding to his field of interest: ulcers, mysterious entanglements of his intestines, acute (or chronic) infections of one kind and another: one had even hinted at cancer: but none had been able to bring him any ease. He seemed to grow no worse, but he never improved, either. Frau Baumgartner to her own constant self-reproach no longer believed that her husband's illness was real. She did not know what she believed, indeed she believed nothing: and her unbelief was formless, a darkly moving cloud of suspicion that her husband's trouble, once known, would prove to be some kind of terrible reproach upon her. Whenever a marriage was unhappy, or the husband failed in his business, everybody knew it was the wife's fault. She would have to blame herself, too, for as she often said, her husband was the best and kindest of men. He had given her love of the kind she understood as love: faithful and pleasant every day, every day in the year, and thoughtful. Until he began to spend his money recklessly on drink, they kept a good comfortable house and saved money; and the savings were, she thanked God, safely invested in Germany since the mark was restored and business was flourishing and all promised well in that country. Her husband had fought all through the war, and had come out without a scratch — a miracle in itself for which he should be grateful, but no — he never spoke but with bitterness of his sufferings in that time. They were married after the war and went to Mexico, a new land of promise for Germans . . . Oh, what could have happened, what did she do, that their lives had come to this? All had seemed to go so well. . . .

"Oh, Karl, don't take another, that will be four already and it is not two hours after dinner."

"I can't bear it, Gretel, I can't bear it, you cannot understand what this pain is like!"

The same old cry. His face drew together, his mouth twisted and trembled; his bright empty blue eyes grew fierce with suffering.

"Karl, how can it help? Tomorrow it will be the same thing."

"Please, Gretel, be patient a little longer. With one more, I promise to get through the night." He bowed over in grief, in shame. "Forgive me," he said and his humility made her blush for him.

"Don't, my dear," she said. "Go on and take it, if it will make you feel better." She leaned over and gazed at the tablecloth to avoid seeing his face knotted in the expression of pain he made no attempt to conceal or control. The doctors had said he must go home, it might work a cure. She had hoped that the peaceful long voyage, the easy safe life of the ship, away from the false friends who drank with him, away from the place where he had failed, would be a good beginning. It was not going to happen. Herr Baumgartner drained the last drop from his tall glass.

"Now, my dear," he said, in a tearful voice, "now, if you will help me." He rose wavering and she stood close beside him. He leaned upon her heavily as they moved away through the crowded bar, and Frau Baumgartner, her eyes fixed straight ahead, felt sure that everybody was staring with contempt at her drunken husband who was pretending to be an invalid.

Herr Löwenthal, who had been put at a small table by himself, studied the dinner card, with its list of unclean foods, and asked for a soft omelette with fresh green peas. He drank half a bottle of good white wine to comfort himself (the one hardship of travel was this question of finding something he could eat in a world almost altogether run by the heathen) and ate the small basket of fruit brought him for dessert. Afterward he hung around searchingly for a while, first in the salon, then in the bar, then out on the decks, wandering and disturbed; but no one spoke to him and he therefore spoke to nobody. He peered here and there, at every face he saw, a quick glance and away, trying to pass unobserved himself, yet hoping to see one of his own people. It was hardly to be believed. In all his life it had never happened to him, but here it was, the thing he feared most was upon him: there was not another Jew on the whole ship. Not one. A German ship, going back to Germany, and not a Jew on board besides himself. Instantly his pangs of instinctive uneasiness mounted to positive fright, his natural hostility to the whole alien enemy world of the Goyim, so deep and pervasive it was like a movement of his blood, flooded his soul. His courage came back on this tide, incomplete, wavering, but bringing its own sense of restored good health of the mind. He made the rounds once more, this time with a bolder eye and a well-composed air which concealed his worry — but no, of course, why look any longer? If there had been another, they would have seated him at the same table. Two Jews would have recognized each other before now. Well, there would be nobody to talk to, but just the same, it wouldn't cost him anything to be friendly with these people; he intended to get along as well as possible on the voyage, there was no percentage in asking for trouble. He sat down in the bar near a rather decent-looking pair of middle-aged fat Gentiles with a white bulldog at their feet, thinking that if they spoke to him he might pass a half hour in some sort of sociability — better than nothing, and that was barely all it could be. But he never liked to speak to Gentiles first, you might run into anything, and they did not turn their heads his way. After two beers he decided he was tired, ready for bed.

The cabin was empty except for the other passenger's luggage. Herr Löwenthal put his sample case out of the way, laid out his modest toilet articles, got into the lower berth and said his prayers, wondering what sort of cabin mate he had drawn. Perhaps the fellow would be quite pleasant. After all, in a business way at least he had known some very decent Gentiles. Maybe this would be one. He lay there with the light on, unable to settle down, waiting and watching for what kind of man would open the door. At last, at the sound of entry, he lifted his head eagerly. "*Grüss Gott,*" he said, almost before he got a glimpse of the fellow.

Herr Rieber stopped short. Almost instantly a deep look of repulsion set itself upon his snubby features; he drew his brows down and pursed his lips.

"Good evening," he said, with immense, cold finality of dismissal.

Herr Löwenthal fell back upon his pillow, knowing the worst as if he had always known it. "My God, the luck! and for such a long voyage," he mourned. "And yes, there is no doubt, he looks like a pig even more than a Gentile." But he would be careful, he could look out for himself, he would see that that fellow did not get the advantage of him. "Let's just see what he does next, after this start. Now I know what to expect, I should be ready for him. I know most of their tricks . . . he can't surprise me."

So he worried and fretted, turning over and over, suppressing sighs; yet he slept after a while, his brows still knitted, but very deeply and restfully in spite of Herr Rieber's snores.

By nine o'clock the lighted decks were empty, the bar and writing rooms nearly deserted. No life was apparent except some movement on the Captain's bridge and a few calm-faced sailors going about their routine duties. In the depths of the ship, the bakers began setting, kneading, rolling and baking the breakfast bread; and still lower, in the engine room, stout fellows labored and sweated freely all night keeping the ship to her regular speed of twelve knots. She would do a little better when the Gulf Stream got behind her.

Life on shipboard in only two days had begun to arrange itself with pleasant enough monotony, but on the third there was repeated the excitement of being in port again, in Havana. This time, the travelers had nothing to worry about, nothing to do for once but to enjoy the scene so far as they were able. Fresh hot-weather dress appeared on all shapes and sizes, and there was a rush for the gangplank before it had fairly settled.

Even Herr Glocken went ambling down the dock by himself, wearing a gay necktie frayed at the knot, smiling like a gargoyle as he dodged with practiced quickness a bold young woman who darted forward to touch his hump for luck.

The ladies of trade, arriving at home from their business trip to Mexico as casually as though returning from a day's shopping in town, walked away together in white linen backless dresses and fine wide-brimmed Panama hats. William Denny, a discreet distance behind, followed them determinedly, to find out if possible what sort of roof sheltered these haughty creatures on their native heath. He was soured and baffled by their resolutely unbusinesslike behavior towards him. "Women peddling tail don't usually carry it so high, where I come from," he remarked to David Scott. "It's just cash on the barrelhead and no hurt feelings."

David merely remarked that he thought that could easily be a bore. So Denny set out by himself, resolved to track them down to their lair and boldly invite himself inside. Along a narrow street of shops one of them turned about unexpectedly to look into a window, saw Denny, nudged the other. They both looked back then, and breaking into high girlish screams of derisive laughter, they darted through a narrow shop doorway and disappeared once for all. Denny, scalded bitterly, let a pale sneer cover his face for the benefit of some possible witness, and an ugly short epithet form in his mouth for his own satisfaction; then, like a man who had plans of his own, he took a small map meant for tourists out of his pocket and began a search for Sloppy Joe's.

Though it was only four o'clock in the afternoon, the troupe of Spanish dancers appeared dressed for the evening, in serviceable black of daring cut, the gentlemen wearing wide pleated red silk belts under their short jackets, the ladies gallantly exposed as to breast and shoulder. Amparo's ear lobes were half again their natural length, trailing the weight of immense imitation rubies. They all limped a little in their cruel footgear as they set out stubbornly in discomfort and bitter bad temper for an evening of professional gaiety. The twins, left on the ship, at once began to shriek and hoot and run circles in a kind of demon dance around the wheel chair of the small sick man, until the golden-haired boy pushing the chair drove them away with loud curses in German. They then ran to the rail, climbed up and leaned out and screamed desperately, "*Jai alai,* Mama! Mama, *jai alai!*" A good distance away, at the sound all four of the women whirled about, and the one they called Lola shouted harshly, "Shut up!"

"Let's be real tourists this once," said Jenny angel to David darling, for so they were feeling towards each other for the moment. "I have no prejudice against tourists — I consider that a low form of snobbism. I envy them savagely, lucky dogs with money to spend and time on their hands, all dressed up and on their way! I always have to work. If I wasn't on a job I wouldn't *be* there, wherever I am: I'm doing a job or running an errand for some editor . . . even in Paris if I ever get there, I'll still have to do those silly drawings for somebody's foul little stories. Now David darling, don't tell me I'm riddled with self-pity . . ."

"You always say that, I never have said it."

"All right, you liar," said Jenny, tenderly, "but just the same never in my whole life since I was a child have I ever gone anywhere merely to look at the scenery. Now is the moment; let's take a Fordito and see the sights, such as they may be. I've passed through Havana this is the fourth time and it may be the last, and I've never seen the beach and that famous Drive, what's its name?"

David lapsed into what Jenny called his speaking silence; she saw by the expression drifting over his face that the notion appealed to him. They had not far to seek, for there on the first corner was an aged Negro with a crippled Ford car — "a real Fotingo if there ever was one!" said Jenny fondly — it was a Mexican popular name for such a vehicle — and he was waiting and hoping for just such as they. The Negro's skin was the color of brown sugar; he had one light gray eye and one pale tan eye, he believed that he spoke English, and he had a high-flown speech of solicitation made up and learned by heart. They waited politely to the end before nodding their heads; he settled them at once in the back seat where the door rattled on its hinges and the stuffing was coming out in lumps. Setting off instantly with an impressive roar and clatter of mechanical locomotion, he gained an appalling speed almost at once, and began another set speech which flew back to them in fragments of loud croaks and low mutters as they whirled along the splendid white road beside the sea.

"We are passing . . . Monument," he shouted, as they rushed by an incoherent mass of bronze, "WHICH COMMEMORATES . . ." he pronounced largely and carefully, then fell to a mutter. Then, "This," his voice rose again, ". . . the war of . . . year of Our Lord . . . and afterwards," he said clearly, "the Sons of Cuban Independence erected this noble monument for the view of strangers." Mutter, mutter, mutter. "We are now passing . . ." and they spun perilously around a long curve, "the building called . . . erected for the view of strangers . . . TO YOUR LEFT!" he called warningly, and Jenny and David craned to the left instantly, but the spectacle was already far behind, "you see a tragic Memorial erected by the Sons of . . . for the view of strangers."

They slowed down with dizzying suddenness, stopped with a hard jolt. Their guide pushed back his cap and pointed to a vast, nondescript edifice shining through tall palms and heavy treetops in a small park. "And there," he said, in rather smugly censorious tones, "is the famous Casino, where rich North Americans gamble away, before the eyes of the starving poor, hundreds of thousands of dollars every night."

His passengers gawked as they were expected to; then David said to Jenny in an aside, "I don't think so much of our touring, do you?" and in Spanish to the guide, who seemed to be regarding them with a certain possessiveness, "Now let's just drive back the same way, very slowly."

"I understand English perfectly," said the guide in Spanish. "Your touring is not a success yet because you have not seen all. There are monuments of the utmost grandeur and sentiment the whole length of this noble Carrera, some of them more expensive and important than those you have seen. You are paying to see them all," he said virtuously, "I do not wish to defraud you."

"I think our touring is perfect," said Jenny. "It is just what I expected. Let's see them all!" They leaped away like a kangaroo in flight, saw all the monuments in shapeless flashes, and were set down again, wind-blown and flushed with sunburn, under palms on a fine terrace freshly washed and steaming, with great wicker bird cages along the wall and a banana tree in the patio. The waiter brought tall glasses of iced tea with rum in it.

"More and more," said David, feeling again for a few moments that repose of pure sympathy and well-being he had with Jenny now and then — not long enough or often enough for any continuous illusion, but good when it happened — "more and more I am convinced it is a great mistake to do anything or make anything for the view of strangers."

"Let's not ever," said Jenny, in a glow still from their foolish escapade along the beach. "Let's have a wonderful private life that begins in our bones, or our souls even maybe, and works out."

She hesitated and then spoke the word "soul" very tentatively, for it was one of David's tabus, along with God, spirit, spiritual, virtue — especially that one! — and love. None of these words flowered particularly in Jenny's daily speech, though now and then in some stray warmth of feeling she seemed to need one or the other; but David could not endure the sound of any of them, and she saw now the stiff, embarrassed, almost offended look which she had learned to expect if she spoke one of them. He could translate them into obscene terms and pronounce them with a sexual fervor of enjoyment; and Jenny, who blasphemed as harmlessly as a well-taught parrot, was in turn offended by what she prudishly described as "David's dirty mind." They were in fact at a dead end on this subject.

After a dismal pause, David said carefully, "Yes, of course; always that precious private life which winds up in galleries and magazines and art books if we have any luck at all — should we go on trying to fool ourselves? Look, we live on handouts, don't we? from one job to the next, so maybe we should look at all this monument stuff like this — every one of them meant a commission and a chance to work for some sculptor."

"But *what* sculptors," said Jenny intolerantly, "such godforsaken awful stuff. No, I'll do all the chores I can get, but there is something you can't sell, even if you want to, and I'm glad of it! I am going to paint for myself."

"I know, I know," said David, "and hope that somebody else likes it too, likes it well enough to buy it and take it home to live with. There's simply something wrong with our theory of a private life so far as work is concerned."

"You are talking about public life," said Jenny. "You're talking about the thing on the wall, not when it's still in your mind, aren't you? — I want good simple people who don't know a thing about art to like my work, to come for miles to look at it, the way the Indians do the murals in Mexico City."

"That was a great piece of publicity all right," said David, "you good simple girl. These good simple Indians were laughing their heads off and making gorgeously dirty remarks; then they went out in the Alameda and scrawled pubic hair on the copy of Canova's Pauline Bonaparte — that elegant marble dream! Didn't you ever notice any of this? Where were you?"

"I was there," said Jenny, without resentment. "I expect I was looking and listening for something else — I saw and heard a lot of other things, too. I don't blame the Indians really. They have something better of their own, after all."

"Better than what? Canova? All right. But better than Giotto let's say or Leonardo? It's not better than a lot of things, even things they've done themselves. It's debased all to hell now — after all, they find their really good stuff in buried cities. But I do like it, too, and it's plain they prefer it to anything else. But look, Jenny angel, what good does all this do us? We are on our own; let's not go fake primitive, we couldn't fool even ourselves . . ."

"David, just because I don't do any underdrawing is no sign I'm trying to be primitive . . . Now don't say that again! I love the Indians, I've got a weakness for them," said Jenny. "I feel certain I learned something from them, even if I don't know yet what it is."

"But they didn't love you," said David, "and you know it. We keep on liking them one by one, as we do each other, but they hate us in a bunch simply as members of the other-colored, oppressor race. I get damn sick of it. And the only thing in this world they wanted from you was your broken-down old Fotingo, last year; and my cigarette lighter; and the portable phonograph. We love their beautiful straw mats because we don't have to sleep on them, and they want our spring mattresses. There's nothing to blame them for, but I'm sick of this sentimental yap about them."

Jenny laughed because she felt very melancholy and baffled. "I wasn't looking for a new religion, either," she said. "I suppose you're right so far as you go, but there is something else. . . . I know I'm much too simple to be a good primitive."

"I don't think they are any more complicated than we are," said David. "They tie a different set of knots, that's all."

"That *isn't* all, by any means," said Jenny. "That is *too* simple."

David, hearing the thin edge in her voice, said no more, but reflected that no matter how he tried to explain his point of view to Jenny, about anything at all, he seemed always to go off at a tangent, or in a circle, or to get bogged down in a spot he had never meant to be in, as if Jenny's mind refracted his thought instead of absorbing his meaning, or even his feelings about certain things — Indians, for example. He would give up from now on talking to Jenny about Indians, or about her painting, either; she was sentimental about the one, and obstinate about the other; let it go.

They finished their second tea and rum in a comfortable-looking silence, wondered what time it was, had to ask the waiter because they complicated their lives on principle by refusing to wear watches; and strolled back toward the harbor.

The heat was overwhelming, the life of the streets wandered torpidly in a sluggish dream, the charge of daylight was almost staggering, and sweat broke from every pore of every human being; the tongues of dogs streamed, and Jenny and David, in their cool-looking linen, were wet and streaked and almost gasping by the time they reached the dock. At the entrance to the long shed through which they must pass to the ship, they saw first a large thick cluster of people with frowzy dark heads and ragged clothing. There was no space to pass among them, for their bundles wrapped in hemp fiber sacks tied with rope lay on the ground, filled their arms and bulged from their shoulders. There were men and women of all ages, in every state of decay, children of all sizes and babies in arms. They were all unbelievably ragged and dirty, hunched over, silent, miserable. Several of them, seeing the two strangers, quietly pushed and nudged at each other and at their bundles in signal, until a narrow way was cleared.

"Pass if you please," they murmured in Spanish, and "Thank you, thank you," said Jenny and David, edging through carefully. The crowd thinned a little then, but the whole huge shed was filled with them. They sat huddled on the ground, they stood formlessly bowed, they leaned in tired arcs against the walls.

The air was not air any more, but a hot, clinging vapor of sweat, of dirt, of stale food and befouled litter, of rags and excrement: the reek of poverty. The people were not faceless: they were all Spanish, their heads had shape and meaning and breeding, their eyes looked out of beings who knew they were alive. Their skins were the skins of the starved who are also overworked, a dark dirty pallor, with green copper overtones, as if their blood had not been sufficiently renewed for generations. Their bare feet were bruised, hardened, cracked, knotted in the joints, and their hands were swollen fists. It was plain they were there by no will or plan of their own, and in the helpless humility of complete enslavement they were waiting for whatever would be done to them next. Women nursed their starveling infants; men sat fumbling among their wretched possessions, tying them up more firmly; they picked at their feet or scratched in their hair; or they sat suspended in uneasy idleness, simply staring. Pale anxious children, miserable, uncomplaining, sat near their mothers and gazed at them, but asked for nothing.

Several officious-looking men were moving among them, counting them with pointing fingers, writing down something over each one, consulting with each other and steadying themselves as they felt their way between bodies by laying a hand upon the nearest head as if it were a newel or a doorknob. The strangest silence was over the whole scene — strange, thought Jenny, because the misery is so great and something so terrible is happening to them, you might think they would all be howling and crying and fighting to escape. "David, what can it be?" she asked, but he shook his head. They came out into the open air, and there was the ship looming up, the gangplank ready.

Almost everyone on shipboard forgot his reserve for the moment, and strangers were asking each other questions and getting answers full of rumor and conflicting theories. The young officers found themselves under a rapid fire of curiosity about the beggars on the dock who now seemed to be coming on board the *Vera*. The officers could only shake their heads. They were sorry, but they had no idea who the steerage passengers were, nor why there were so many, nor what their situation was precisely, except that anyone could see they were of the lowest class. No doubt everything would be known in time.

This answer raised greater curiosity all around. Professor and Frau Hutten, who had persuaded their seasick bulldog Bébé out for a breath of air on solid earth, had been told by someone in town that the strange people were political malcontents and were being deported as dangerous and subversive elements. Professor Hutten, observing them carefully, remarked that they seemed to be quite harmless though unfortunate people. Herr Lutz, the Swiss hotelkeeper, told the Professor that he had heard that the people were returning to Spain because of a new sudden demand for labor in that country: since the Spanish had thrown the king out, Spain, it was said, was lining up for progress, catching up with the modern world. "Same old story," said Herr Lutz, "the grass looks greener in the next pasture until you get there. It is the first I have heard of prosperity in Spain."

Herr Rieber and Lizzi Spöckenkieker pranced onto the deck, and Lizzi screamed out to little Frau Otto Schmitt, whose tender heart was plainly to be surmised in her soft pink face: "Oh, what do you think of this dreadful fellow? Can you guess what he just said? I was saying, 'Oh, these poor people, what can be done for them?' and this monster

—" she gave a kind of whinny between hysteria and indignation — "he said, 'I would do this for them: I would put them all in a big oven and turn on the gas.' Oh," she said weakly, doubling over with laughter, "isn't that the most original idea you ever heard?"

Herr Rieber stood by smiling broadly, quite pleased with himself. Frau Schmitt went a little pale, and said in a motherly, severe tone, "There may be such a thing as too much originality — for shame, I don't think that is funny!" Herr Rieber's face fell, he pouted.

Lizzi said, "Oh, he did not mean any harm, of course; only to fumigate them, isn't it so?"

"No, I did not mean fumigate," said Herr Rieber, stubbornly.

"Well, then, you are not very nice," said Lizzi, in a tone so indulgent, indeed more than forgiving, he braced up again at once; she smiled at him and he smiled back, and they left the atmosphere of Frau Schmitt's moral disapproval for the freedom of the bar.

At last the afternoon papers appeared on deck, and there was the whole story, quite straight, and nothing so unusual after all. It had something to do with the price of sugar in the world market. The bottom had fallen out, it seemed. Cuban sugar, because of international competition, had fallen in price until the sugar planters could no longer afford to gather and market their crops. There had been strikes and riots too, and demands for higher wages at the very moment of crisis as always, due to the presence of foreign labor agitators among the workers. The planters were burning their crops in the fields, and naturally this had thrown thousands of sugar workers in the fields and refineries out of employment. A great number of these were Spanish, mostly from the Canaries, Andalusia, the Asturias, who had been imported during the great days of Cuban sugar.

This policy of importation, to which there had been in the beginning some local opposition, had turned out to be a farsighted one, for if these laborers had been Cubans, what could have been their fate except reliance on charity, beggary, or a temporary haven in the public jails and hospitals? As it was, the government had acted with speed and good judgment to forestall the inconvenience of so many idle foreigners on the island. Arrangements had been made to send them back to their native land, their fares had been raised by public subscription, everything was being done for their comfort, and the first lot, consisting of exactly eight hundred and seventy-six souls, were already safely on their way. Thus, the newspaper stories and editorials agreed,

Cuba was setting an example to the world in disposing of its labor problems in the most humane yet practical manner.

The eight hundred and seventy-six souls formed a straggling procession and moved across the gangplank leading to the steerage, while a dozen or more first-class passengers lined up above to watch them. Herded carefully on either side by sailors and the officious men who had been counting them, the people came on with some nervous jostling, thumping of feet, hesitations when the whole mass would be agitated, clotted in one spot; then it would smooth out and go forward. Among the watchers a new uneasiness rose, and Frau Rittersdorf mentioned it first.

"There is great danger of infectious disease among such creatures," she said to Herr Baumgartner at her elbow. "I am wondering — should we not complain to the Captain? After all, we did not engage to travel on a cattle boat."

Herr Baumgartner's pained face leaped into new lines of anxiety. "My God," he said, "I was thinking the very thought. I was thinking, you can almost smell the diseases among them. No, it is not right. We should have been warned."

Professor Hutten remarked to his wife, "I was told by the purser the steerage contains accommodations for only three hundred and fifty, and yet look, still they come. I am interested to see what accommodations can possibly be made for such a number. Infants, too," he said, and clicked his tongue in deprecation. His wife sighed and shook her head, accepting once more the sad truth that there is no cure for the troubles of life, no peace nor repose anywhere. Her comfortable fat quivered with some intimation of suffering, but she could not bear to think of it. "Come," she said, "let's not spy upon them. Suppose they should look up and see us gazing?" She moved away, her face tender and vacant. Bébé, somewhat improved in spirits, followed on a loose leash.

William Denny, who had made his way safely to Sloppy Joe's and had there swallowed rapidly several daiquiris with increasing depression of mood, leaned on the rail and spoke at random in loud indignation. "Poor devils, they don't deserve it," he said, almost tearfully. "After all, why should they be kicked out? They're not dirty Reds, the papers said so."

Mrs. Treadwell, who had found herself once or twice in some passing talk with the young man, whom she considered odious, was standing almost next to him; she knew well that no matter what he thought or felt it was none of her affair, but spoke just the same on impulse, which she also knew very well was not her style, and always got her into some kind of difficulty.

"Why always 'dirty' please," she said in her light agreeable voice, "and why always 'Red' and what do you really know or care about it?"

Denny's head rolled a trifle; he stared at her as if he had never seen her before. "Are you a Red?" he asked. Without removing his folded arms from the rail he slid along toward her, turned sideways and inspected her as if she were a horse he was thinking of buying. His gaze ran like a hand to her ears, her neck, over her breasts, down her thighs, and his mouth was bitter as if he did not like what he saw, but could not control the roving of his eyes. Mrs. Treadwell made a determined effort to catch and fix his gaze with hers, but he would not look at her face, where a rather too-girlish prettiness lingered under the mask of middle age.

"Do you know the meaning of the word?" she inquired coldly, moving from him along the rail as he approached. She regretted now the three planters' punches she had drunk with Wilhelm Freytag in Havana; for to tell the truth, she did not know the meaning of the word herself — it was just that she resented that stupid Denny to the point where she could have enjoyed slapping him. She had never known a Red and did not expect to know one ever.

"I know what I'd do to them if I were running the government," he said, in a heavy rage, peering into the front of her blouse. Mrs. Treadwell pulled herself together resolutely. How typical — here she was, about to get into an altercation with a drunken stranger, *une espèce de type* at that, on a topic of which both of them were totally ignorant, and she at least hadn't the faintest desire to learn anything. She turned her head aside, wheeled about and walked away, smiling into the air and trying not to hurry.

The ship, full of fetid port air and swarming with mosquitoes, got under way late in the evening. A fair number of new passengers had been added to first class, and were rather regarded at first as interlopers by the original voyagers, who had got already a proprietary interest in the ship. A half dozen noisy, mongrel-looking Cuban students made themselves conspicuous until a late hour. Several married pairs brought with them an assortment of normally troublesome children. After dinner the students formed a parade and marched around deck chairs containing soberer folk who wished only to be left in peace, through the ship where people were reading or playing cards, around deck dozens of times past windows of people trying to sleep, bawling verse after verse about *La Cucaracha*, the poor little cockroach who could not run about any more because she had no marihuana to smoke, second because she had no money to buy it, third because she had no feet anyway, fourth because nobody loved her, and endlessly the students rehearsed her misfortunes as they tramped in a line, hands on each other's shoulders. They ranged in height from short to tall, but they were all very stringy. They all wore baggy "Oxford" trousers, rather lumpy below the knees, identical in cut but of fascinating variety in pattern: tartans, stripes, squares, zigzags, and improbably tinted tweeds. They wore tennis shoes and T shirts. Occasionally they wove sinuously in line, imitating a serpent. Again, they leaped rhythmically in turn, beginning at one end of the line and working forward or backward in an ocean wave effect.

Wilhelm Freytag watched their antics for a while, decided they were no doubt going to be a complete nuisance for the whole voyage, and wondered if he had ever been so puerile, so callow, so absurd. He was thirty now, five years married, and life was getting to be a pretty tough business, a good deal more than he had bargained for; but then, he had not been looking for a bargain, after all. But could he ever have been such a fool as any one of these in that crowd? He remembered well that he had been, indeed; but he had not reached the age of sentimental reminiscence of youthful imbecilities: he had just come to the place where he shuddered to be reminded of them. He now did in fact shudder and walk on hunched a little, like a man facing a blizzard.

He paused on his way to bed and glanced into the dim pit of the steerage. The deck was covered with huddled figures, their heads resting on bundles, with only the floor under their bones. A few men were in hammocks, a few women with young babies sleeping on their stomachs were leaning back in canvas chairs. The rest slept piled upon each other like dirty rags thrown out on a garbage heap. He stood and contemplated the inviolable mystery of poverty that was like a slow-working incurable disease, and there was nothing in his own mind, his history or his temperament that could even imagine a remedy for it. He had been comfortable all his life in the way of his middle class; and to them, though they furnished largely to all the professions

and esteemed them warmly, money-making was the career undisput-
edly theirs, to them the most becoming of all occupations for a well-
brought-up, well-trained young man. He was not yet rich, but it had
not until lately occurred to him that there could be any obstacle to
his getting as rich as he liked. And it would be very rightly — after
giving due thanks to his father and mother for his education — very
rightly all due to his own efforts; if he failed it would be through
some weakness in himself that he had not suspected. He had a moral
aversion to poverty, an instinctive contempt and distrust of the swarm-
ing poor spawned like maggots in filth, befouling the air around them.
Yet, he thought, moving on with a reluctant tinge of pity, they are
necessary, they have their place, what would we do without them? And
here they are, being sent from a place they are not wanted to a place
where they cannot be welcome; they are going from hard labor and
hunger to no labor and starvation, from misery to misery — what kind
of creature would endure this except a lower order of animal? He
shook off his pity as hateful to him, and went back to his own dilemma,
and realized that the chill of horror the sight of the wretched people
gave him was for himself, his own fears taking monstrous shapes in
his imagination. He, a German of a good solid Lutheran family, Chris-
tian as they come, against terrible opposition from both families, against
his own better judgment, against all common sense and reason, had
married a Jewish girl with a beautiful exotic name, Mary Champagne.
The family had come from wherever Jews did come in the Middle
Ages, and had dropped Abraham ben Joseph or whatever it was,
named themselves for the district and settled down for a few hundred
years. Some of them turned Catholic or married Gentiles and were
kicked out, and changed their names once more and became really
French; but Mary's branch were diehards and they started roaming
again, through Alsace into Germany, God knows why. Pretty poor
judgment it seemed to him. But they kept the fine French name they
had picked for themselves. And they all made a point of broad-minded-
ness and liberality, and mingled socially with Gentiles, if they were of
the right class and would still have them. Yet he and Mary fell in love,
and so honestly and surely in love, it was like knocking down a hor-
net's nest. They had patiently fought the battle to a finish with his
family and connections as well as with hers; in the end they had got
married in a Lutheran church, with wails and sobs of *Oi oi oi oi!* rising
from one spot in the small group on the left-hand side of the main

aisle. . . . His parents could not conceal their relief when he announced he was going to Mexico, plainly they were grateful to have an impossible situation cleared up so simply. Mary's mother, a widow, did not consider her daughter as married at all, except perhaps legally, but she was rather a worldly gay woman, not especially religious, being at times no more Jewish than she felt suitable to the occasion: what people didn't know wouldn't hurt her, she argued; whose business is it but mine what I am? What she had feared in the marriage was scandal and ostracism from her family and friends, and she got plenty of both, poor woman. In the end she had come over to her daughter and son-in-law, cast in her fate with theirs and was prepared to live and die with them — bless her! he thought with gratitude, what a good heart. And he remembered they had all three begun to be proud of themselves and each other for being able to throw off stupid prejudices and live like free people, making a good life for themselves in an open world. "Oh, *God*," said Wilhelm Freytag, almost aloud. Then he smiled to himself a little grimly. "God of Israel," he added, "where are You?" and turned into the passage leading to his cabin.

Jenny Brown and Elsa Lutz, in their stuffy little cabin, were brushing their hair and preparing for sleep in an amiable silence. They were getting on very well, with small talk about life on the ship, mild gossip and harmless opinion. Elsa in spite of her mother's warnings was quickly disarmed by her cabin mate's gentle, rather orderly ways, and sat by fascinated while Jenny did up her face with sweet-smelling waters and layers of ointment like whipped cream. The roar and tramp of the students passed for the third time on the deck just over their heads; the noise, rising above the sea and the engines, poured through the portholes. Again Elsa lifted her head to listen, with thoughtful face.

"The ship is full of boys now," she said, almost hopefully.

"Very," said Jenny. "It will be nice if they happen to know more than one song."

They both were startled by an unusual noise in the passageway just beyond their door: they listened, staring at each other, to a violent confused rushing and stumbling about, like a struggle of some sort, ending with a heavy soft thud as if a sandbag had been hurled against the panel. Two voices, male and female, in which they recognized members of the Spanish dancing troupe, rose in a fierce quarrel. The quarrel was about money. They screamed hotly in a ragged duet about money, calling each other by name, Concha and Manolo. Manolo wanted, he wanted instantly with no more talk, the seven Cuban pesos he knew Concha had got that evening. He had seen the man give her the change after paying the barman. Concha denied it brazenly, she was shrewish and fearless. Jenny, following the logic of the fight, realized that Concha did not for a moment question Manolo's right to the money if she had it to give. She took what might seem the easy way out and denied she had it. It was not going to be easy.

"I saw it," said Manolo, fiercely. "Give it me or I'll rip your lying tongue out!"

Concha screamed that he could rip her entrails out if he liked, he would not find the money. Their voices joined again and crashed like breaking crockery, then stopped dead to the sound of a ringing slap. An instant's pause and Concha began to weep, helplessly, tenderly, submissively as if this was what she had been waiting for, and Manolo's voice purred as softly as if he were making love, "Now will you give me the money, or do you want me to —"

Jenny glanced uneasily at Elsa to see how much of Manolo's threat she understood. The voices faded around the corner into the main corridor.

"Well, did you ever?" asked Elsa in English. Her big childish mouth, eyes, nostrils were wide open. "Now what kind of woman is that? He doesn't sound like her husband to me."

"They're in the same cabin, you know," said Jenny.

"But you do not occupy the same cabin with your husband," said Elsa, "so how can one ever tell?"

"We are not married," said Jenny, beginning to file her nails.

Elsa waited hungrily for more. There was no more. Her cabin mate smiled at her pleasantly and went on with her filing.

"Well," said Elsa in disappointment, "I don't understand a woman who lets a man treat her like that. She must be from the lowest class. No woman is expected to put up with such things."

"It's part of her business," said Jenny, yawning. "Are you ready to have the light out?"

"Her business?" Jenny saw that Elsa was sincerely shocked, confused, even pained.

"Never mind," she said, uncomfortably. "I'm talking nonsense. I expect they're just a married pair fighting over money. They often do, you know."

"Oh yes, I *do* know," said Elsa.

In the darkness, when Jenny was growing drowsy, Elsa spoke from her divan bed under the portholes, an important confidence. "My father, all my life, told me to believe in love, and to be loving, and it would make me happy; but my mother says it is all just make-believe. Sometimes I wish I knew — I love my mother, but it seems to me that my father knows more."

"He very probably does," said Jenny, rousing a little. "Good night."

"Good night," said Elsa. "My father is gay by nature, he loves to have a good time. But my mother cannot laugh, she says only fools laugh, that life is not a thing for anybody to laugh at. . . . Once when I was little I remember . . . I remember so many things; but this time I was with my father and mother at a party — in Switzerland in the country they used to take all the children, even the little babies, to the parties — and my mother would not dance the first dance with my father, so of course, my father could not dance with anyone else. So he said to her, 'Very well for you, all right, I'll find a nicer partner than you'; and he got a broom and danced with that, and everybody but my mother thought it was very funny. She would not speak to him for the rest of the evening. So my father drank too much beer and was very gay, and on the way home he said suddenly to my mother, 'Now you are going to dance,' and he took her by the waist and swung her round and round until her feet were whirling off the ground, and she cried. I could not understand my mother. Really it was no harm, it was funny. But my mother cried and then I cried too; and my poor father walked along with us then very quietly, and I think now he wished to cry. She never has laughed at a single one of my father's jokes, and yet he will keep making them. Some of them are awful, don't think I don't know that. Oh," said Elsa, her voice in the night slow with grieved wonder, "I am afraid I am like my mother; I cannot be funny and amusing to people, I would be ashamed to call attention to myself, but sometimes it is hard just to sit; and I think there must be something wrong with me or the boys would ask me to dance."

"There's almost nobody on this ship you'd want to dance with," said Jenny. "You wouldn't look at them if you were at home."

"But I am not at home," said Elsa, "and I have never been, for in

Mexico the boys there, the ones I was allowed to go with, don't like my style. . . . My mother said just like you, 'Don't worry, Elsa, in Switzerland they will think you are just exactly the right kind of girl, a real Swiss girl, the kind they like there, don't worry, it will be all right when we get home.' She thinks love is all nonsense, but she wants me to get married. She says it is what women are expected to do. But I am not in Switzerland yet, and I hardly remember it though my mother took me back for a visit when I was nine years old. But oh, it seemed such a strange place! I shall speak Swiss-German like a foreigner, because I spoke so much French and English and Spanish in Mexico. I was never at home in Mexico, but now maybe I shan't be at home in Switzerland, either. Oh, I am so sad about going there . . ." The small monotonous plaint went on like rain at midnight, and Jenny listened, touched and attentive. She thought she knew real trouble when she heard it.

"My mother said all this time, it is not fair to Elsa, we must take her home in time so that she can marry a Swiss, here it is no good for a Swiss girl. I hope she is right, I hope they like me in Switzerland."

"Of course they will like you, you will be the new interest, the girl from a far country," Jenny told her, and she felt an anxious tenderness, as if she had been asked for help which she was not able to give. What hope was there for the discouraged young face with its double chin, the crease of fat like a goiter at the base of the throat, the oily skin, the faded gray eyes without the light of spirit, the dull thick hair, the heavy haunches, the gross ankles. Good nose, good mouth, good enough forehead, these were all; no sparkle, no lift at all in that solid mound of not very appetizing flesh. And inside, there groped blindly, the young innocence and the longing, the pained confused limited mind, the dark instincts winding upon themselves like snails.

Jenny said, "This time, I feel your mother is right. Let me tell you I never knew a girl who wanted to marry who didn't get married, sooner or later."

"Oh, I have," said Elsa, rejecting the half-truth and the pity it offered with bitter pride and honesty. "I have . . . I think sometimes that if I had different clothes," she said, "or maybe a permanent wave. Maybe if I had one of those. But my mother says young girls must be perfectly natural and pure in every way. No curls, even. They must wait for everything until they get married, even to use perfume. . . . But suppose I never get married?"

Jenny said, "To marry properly, you must first, yourself, fall in love. Were you never in love?"

"Why no," said Elsa, in a startled voice. "Never. But my mother says I must wait until a man shows interest in me first."

"Interest!" said Jenny, rousing a little. "Listen," she said, trying to sound very wise and final, for she could not stay awake much longer, "I'm frightfully tired, aren't you? It doesn't in the least matter who falls in love with who first, but first there must be falling in love and then marriage will take care of itself."

"But what happens," asked Elsa, with patient persistence, "if I never fall in love?"

"Well then, just hope madly that someone will fall in love with you," said Jenny, feeling that she had got on a slow-moving merry-go-round. "Don't you see? It's really all so simple, Elsa!"

"But suppose," said Elsa, "no one falls in love with me, what happens then?"

"Nothing, I expect," admitted Jenny at last, completely cornered.

"That's just it," said Elsa, a despairing satisfaction in her tone, and she said no more.

PART II

High Sea

Kein Haus, keine Heimat . . .
SONG BY BRAHMS

Ric and Rac, Lola's twins, got up early and dressed themselves quietly before Lola and Tito were awake. They were badly buttoned and frowsy-haired; their wary black eyes gave their sallow sharp faces a hardened, precociously experienced look; awake, they were up to mischief, and asleep, they dreamed of it. They did a song and dance act in the show, in bullfighter and Carmen costume, and tore each other's hair in the dressing room afterward through jealousy of the applause and sheer nervous excitement. Otherwise they were of one mind and spirit, and lived twined together in a state of intense undeclared war with the adult world — or rather, with the whole world, for they did not like other children, or animals, either.

They were christened Armando and Dolores, but they had renamed themselves for the heroes of their favorite comic cartoon in a Mexican newspaper: Ric and Rac, two lawless wire-haired terriers whose adventures they followed day by day passionately and with envy. The terriers — not real dogs of course, but to their idolaters real devils such as they wished to be — made fools of even the cleverest human beings in every situation, made life a raging curse for everyone near them, got their own way invariably by a wicked trick, and always escaped without a blow. They were in short ideal characters and the first the children had ever admired and longed to emulate. Ric and Rac they became to themselves and it gave them secret strength.

The decks were still damp and steaming lightly under the morning sun, and only a few sailors were moving about slowly. Ric and Rac went into one of the writing rooms and there silently, as if by previous plan, Ric took the cork from an ink bottle and turned the bottle on its side. For a moment they watched the ink pour out over the clean blotter and onto the carpet, then silently they went out on the other side of the ship, where Rac, seeing a small down pillow which Frau

Rittersdorf had left in her deck chair, without a word took it up and tossed it overboard. Soberly they watched it bob upon the waves, wondering why it floated so long. A sailor appeared just back of them, and they fled with such obvious signs of guilt, he frowned and looked about him carefully to find what they had been up to; saw nothing, shook his head, went about his business, while the evidence slowly sank far in the wake.

Ric and Rac climbed the rail in the stern above the steerage deck and gazed down upon a fascinating sight. Hundreds of people, men and women, were wallowing on the floor, being sick, and sailors were washing them down with streaming hose. They lay in the film of water, just lifting their heads now and then, or trying to roll nearer the rail. One man sat up and held out a hand to the sailor nearest him, and the sailor turned the hose down to a light drizzle and washed the man's face and head, then turned the water on plentifully and washed his clothes, there on him, just as he was.

Another man lay on his face and groaned and gurgled as if he were drowning. Two sailors picked him up out of his own sickness and carried him to the lowest step of the stairway to the dark steerage quarters and there set him down. He fell over on his side at once. "Let's make him get up," said Ric, the male twin, and taking off his loose heavy brown sandal, he threw it by the toe. It missed and struck a young woman sitting near with a baby in her arms. Her skirts were sopping wet and her bare feet were black with filthy water. She looked up at them and clenched her fist, shouting a wonderful string of dirty words — which they knew — at them, and added a few they had not heard, but they knew the meanings. They smiled for the first time at each other with an expression of discovery, then listened with all their ears, watching her dirt-streaked face work and crumple in hatred and helpless fury.

A sailor on deck below picked up the sandal and tossed it back so accurately he hit Ric in the chest, and almost at the same instant the twins were seized by an arm each from the back, and a stern voice of absolute authority said, "What are you doing here?" They were hauled downward so strongly they had not time to stiffen their spines, but they refused to meet the cold eye of the young officer, who shook them quite freely and said, "If you do such things again you will be locked up for the rest of the voyage. Now remember!" He gave them a little push, and they ran in silence, with impudent faces.

They almost collided with the dying man in the wheel chair being pushed along like a baby in a carriage by the tall angry-looking boy. "Get out of my way," snarled the boy in Spanish, and they dodged around him, putting out their tongues.

The man in the chair sat among his pillows and coughed, as he did nearly all day and all night, his weak little beard agitated, his eyeballs mustard-yellow.

"Stop here," he said to the boy, and they paused while he craned feebly to see the people on the lower deck, a sick pity in his face in the presence of so much misery. Some of the men were getting on their feet by then; they stood jammed together along the walls of the ship and at the rail while the sailors went on hosing down the filth of their sickness into the sea. They then piled back upon each other, on the wet canvas chairs in their wet clothes, and in the abominable heat a strange mingled smell of vegetable and animal rot rose from them.

Herr Graf said in a low voice as if talking to himself: "I can think only of how all that sinful flesh must suffer before it shall be allowed to die. We must all earn the blessing of death at a great price, Johann." At the sound of his name Johann's mouth quivered with rage and disgust. He did not reply. The dying man spread one hand out in the direction of the steerage in a gesture of blessing. "God, heal them, give them health and virtue and joy. . . . If only I could touch them. Johann," he said to the boy his nephew, in a weak but natural voice, "you must help me down there among them, to touch some of those sick; they must be eased, it is not right to let them suffer."

Johann's sulky mouth curled with exasperation, his hands jerked on the chair: "You know you will not be allowed to go down there. Why do you always talk nonsense?"

In silence they moved on, the chair creaking faintly. "I forgive you, nephew Johann, I forgive you your hard heart and evil will. You cannot harm me by any means, but I might help you if you would let me."

"You can help me by dying and letting me go free," said Johann in a low shaking voice, giving the chair a sharp swerve. "You can die and let me go home!"

His uncle considered this awhile, and then said in a reasonable tone as if in ordinary conversation: "I promised I would leave you the money, Johann, if you would come with me and see me safely to Germany once more, for a last look. Is that not worth considering?"

"When?" asked Johann wearily. "When?" and the chair wheels rattled a little.

"It should not be long, Johann, in the very nature of things. Do you expect me to set the exact date for you? But I told you in the beginning that if you would come —"

"Don't go over that," said Johann, "I know all about it."

"And your mother my poor sister, she was glad of the chance for you. I renew my promise to leave you everything in my will, though you do not deserve it, you have not merited it; for charity and kind behavior were part of your agreement. But leaving all that aside, you may now finish your education in Germany; you may not have to go back to Mexico at all; I hope not."

"I will go where I please," he said bitterly. "And what did my mother care what happened to me? She wants only the money."

"It is perhaps true, my dear nephew," said Herr Graf, choking and beginning to cough. "Yet in fact the money will be yours and not hers." He spat into a folded paper box which he produced from under his light rug. "I can see that you are my sister's own child. She was never like the rest of us. She had a cold nature, a hard heart, from the beginning."

"It is time for me to go and ask for your breakfast," said Johann. He broke out suddenly as if he were near tears. "Why can't I have my meals with the others in the dining room? It is making me sick to eat always with you in that nasty cabin. Why can't you sit up here on deck by yourself for an hour and let me breathe? You are a beast of selfishness, Uncle, I say it to your face. So."

Herr Graf groaned and hid his face in both hands. "My God," he said, "go, go and leave me. Yes, leave me alone. God will take care of me. He will not let me suffer by your cruelty. Stay as long as you like. But remember, I have made my will in your favor, and you shall have everything. Be sure of that. The rest is between you and your conscience."

Johann gave a great explosive sigh and pushed the chair very fast. He was ravenously hungry, ah, he would sit in the pleasant bright dining salon among the lively young people and maybe get into a conversation with one of those pretty girls. He would get away from death for just an hour, the smells, the praying, the phlegmy rattle in the throat, the smothering air of old age, sick and whining and clutching . . .

{ 7 4 }

"You will be all right, I will fix everything and you can read for a while," he said, and he felt cold and determined. No, not for any money could he bear another day without relief, a little freedom, just a few turns on deck by himself before he lost control and smashed something. No, not for any money. He eased the chair downsteps with unusual gentleness, turned expertly through the cabin door, opened the porthole; and feeling the half-fainting gaze of his uncle heaping untold reproach upon him, he bounded out again. Half a dozen paces away he was whistling gaily a doleful little tune: *"Das gibt's nur einmal, das kommt's nicht wieder,"* as if his heart would break for joy.

David Scott, who slept on the narrow bunk against the wall, was wakened by Denny climbing out of the upper berth. David, after a quick glimpse, pretended to sleep. There seemed nothing much wrong with Denny except he was a bore. His mind seemed to run monotonously on women, or rather, sex; money, or rather his determination not to be gypped by anybody; and his health.

He got up early every morning and took a dose of effervescent laxative salts, making the same nauseated face after the draught. Then he ate a cake of yeast, nibbling it little by little as he shaved. He would dash cold water in his face and examine the whites of his eyes apprehensively. He had small, mattery pimples on his neck and one cheek, like a boy of fourteen. He had, by a long roundabout arrangement through German friends of his father, got a chance to work with a great chemical manufacturer's firm in Berlin, and now and then he made a vague reference to his future as a chemical engineer. But as David displayed not only an utter ignorance of the subject but a total indifference as well — and Denny thought David meant signboards or houses when he called himself a painter — their topics of conversation had narrowed almost to nothing unless Denny's three preoccupations could be called topics.

Herr Glocken said little, but after a few days' rest he seemed in fair health, and began to show himself at moments to be rather a good-humored twinkling little man in the friendly male atmosphere of the cabin, with the two young fellows who never seemed to notice that his back was not like theirs. Sometimes they talked German together, gossiping about the affairs of the ship, and the young men never made Herr Glocken feel that their general experience of life was particularly different from his own. Herr Glocken was at ease. He slept well, and kept the curtains drawn in the morning until he could emerge fully dressed, saving them the sight of his unseemly frame except under the best disguise he could manage.

At that moment there was no sign of movement behind his curtain. David did not stir, but was outraged to observe that Denny proceeded to strip and give himself a sponge bath from the communal washbasin. But I have to wash my face in that, he thought, and viewed with horror and repulsion the naked brown flesh of the other, like badly tanned leather, all overgrown with sparse curly hair which came off on the soapy cloth and stuck to the sides of the bowl in a light scum. If he does that again, I'll stuff him through the porthole, resolved David, seething. Still he said nothing and realized that probably he never would. He would wait until the fellow was gone and scrub the bowl with disinfectant. Hot and nervous, he sat up and felt for his straw sandals with his wriggling toes.

"Hello," said Denny in a cautious voice, "I'll be the hell out in a minute. It's a tight fit in here."

David, feeling that for him it would be a tight fit anywhere that he had to put on his shoes before a stranger, or speak to anyone except perhaps Jenny before he had had his coffee, said, "I'll try to get in the shower, don't hurry yourself."

Herr Glocken's head appeared between the long curtains, his thin confused hair all on end. His long face with its pseudo-Hapsburg jaw was a network of fine wrinkles. "Good morning," he croaked, though not gloomily. "Would you be so kind as to hand me that little flask?" and he pointed towards it, standing beside his water glass. "And some water, if you will please."

David gave him both, and noticed that the flask was marked "Every three hours or when required," and it occurred to him that perhaps Herr Glocken was never altogether without pain. Herr Glocken, reaching out, parted the curtains more than he intended, and David noted with intense surprise that he wore a bright red silk pajama coat. Profusion of color in anything was offensive to David; it offended more than his eye — he distrusted it on moral grounds, and nowhere more so than in dress. His own neckties were black knitted strings he bought by the half dozen from sidewalk peddlers, his socks were black cotton, his suits were mottled gray, dark gray, light gray, Oxford gray and blue-gray, besides the chaste white linen and canvas he wore in summer. His favorite palette was a mixture of grays, browns, ochers, and dark blues with a good deal of white; and his favorite though not original theory was that persons who "expressed themselves" by wearing color were merely attempting to supply its inner lack in their own natures, adding a façade that fooled nobody.

A great deal of this he knew had been aimed at Jenny, who had been brilliant as a macaw when he first fell in love with her, wearing for her own delight high, cool colors, and splashing her little canvases recklessly with geometrical designs in primary colors like fractured rainbows. She had seemed quite serious about it, too. Little by little he had succeeded in undermining her confidence in this nonsensical way of painting. Her palette lowered in tone; gradually, too, she had taken to dressing in muted colors or black and white, with only now and then a crimson or orange scarf, and she was not painting much, but working almost altogether in charcoal or India ink.

Deeply he hoped she would give it up altogether — there had never been a really great woman painter, nothing better than some superior disciple of a great man; it disturbed him to see a woman so out of place; and he did not believe in her talent for a moment. The best she could hope for was to be a good illustrator, and that she despised. But there was something in her whole nature that obstructed the workings of his own: when she was painting, he could not; just as when she was in a loving tender mood, he felt himself beginning to grow cold and defensive, to hold her off and deny her.

Jenny was like a cat in her fondness for nearness, for stroking, touching, nestling, with a kind of sensuality so diffused it almost amounted to coldness after all, for she almost never wanted to make love outright as he did, suddenly, violently, grimly, and have it over with. She would drink from his cup and share a fruit with him, bite by bite: she loved to tell him how much she loved him, though she was getting over that; but she was never happy with him, and when they slept together, they quarreled. David in the wave of repulsion he suffered at the sight of Herr Glocken's red pajamas hated Jenny for a violent moment, as he did often, and oftener. As for Glocken — on deck in daytime, except for his silly bright neckties, his clothes were shabby and dull, his shoes broken. Almost everyone avoided him. He scared people off; his plight was so obviously desperate they were afraid some of it would rub off on them. At night, behind that curtain, in the dark, wrapped in his red silk, what did he dream about himself?

Denny was pulling on his trousers, his face thoughtful. "Say," he remarked suddenly to David, "you know that little one with the red ruffles on her skirt they call Pastora? Well, she looks to me hot as a firecracker. And she has been giving me the eye, from time to time. What do you suppose it would cost?"

David said, "I suppose about whatever the traffic will bear."

"Well, traffic's jammed right now, so far as I'm concerned. But I think I'll prospect around a little. We're going to be on this boat nearly a month, you know. That's a long long time. I'm beginning to worry about the future."

David said, "You'd better try to keep on ice until you get to Berlin where they're government-inspected, or you may have to go to see Dr. Schumann before you get to Bremerhaven."

"I know," said Denny, turning a little pale, "I've thought of that. But there are all kinds of things you can — well, I think I can take care of myself."

"Things might work and they might not," said David. "They can talk all they like, there aren't any sure ways."

"God," said Denny, sincerely. He got up and looked at himself in the mirror and took a last swipe at his hair with the brush. "But she certainly looks all right, healthy and everything."

"You never can tell," said David, with malice.

"Well," said Denny, "we aren't there yet. If I can ever get her cut out from the herd," he said. "They run together so close you can't get a word in between them."

Bébé, Frau Hutten decided, was recovering. She brought him food when she came from breakfast, and after consulting with her husband, fed Bébé, who made out a very good meal. "The dear blessed one," said Frau Hutten, watching him eat with pleasure, "with his so fine instincts and feelings, eating his food humbly face downward like any animal; it is a great pity. He is too good for that."

"He does not mind in the least, dear Käthe," said her husband. "He is more comfortable in that posture, on account of the construction of his frame. It would not be natural or right for him to sit up to his food. I have seen children with unconscious cruelty try to train their pets to eat at table, and it was so much labor lost, besides the suffering of the animal. No, I think our good Bébé does very well, and misses nothing that he should have."

Frau Hutten, her confidence restored and her mind set at ease as always by her husband's words, fitted on Bébé's leash and the three went for a good fast walk. Seven times around the deck was, Professor Hutten calculated, just the right distance for a proper constitutional. But Bébé, who started briskly enough, began to lag on the third lap, and midway of the fourth he stopped in the grip of his familiar convulsions and disgraced himself most hideously then and there. Professor Hutten knelt and supported his head, while Frau Hutten went to look for a sailor who could bring a bucket of water.

A few feet away, she heard a shout of laughter, a raucous chorus with no gaiety in it, and recognized with a chill the voices of the Spanish dancing troupe. They had a way of sitting together, and without warning they would laugh dreadfully, with mirthless faces, and they were always laughing at somebody. They would look straight at you and laugh as if you were an object too comic to believe, yet their eyes were cold and they were not enjoying themselves, even at your expense. Frau Hutten had observed them from the first and she was afraid of them.

Without looking, she felt that they had seen her husband and her poor Bébé; and she was right. They came on in a pack, sweeping around the forlorn tableau, and as they passed her, their unfriendly eyes took her in from head to foot. Their teeth were disclosed and they were making those gruesome sounds of merriment. She felt her fatness, her age, her heavy ankles; the Spaniards' slenderness and youth cast contempt on her and on all that she was, in one bitter, mocking glance.

She found a sailor, a nice big boy with a good square face who was used to seasickness. He brought water, washed up after Bébé and went away. The Huttens laid Bébé beside their deck chairs, folded bathtowels under his head, and sat together in massive silence, feeling themselves figures of fun to those debased creatures, real hoodlums who should never have been allowed to travel first class at all. There were many good people, Frau Hutten was sure, in the steerage who better deserved to be on first deck.

In Mexico they had been accustomed for years to an easy atmosphere, among Germans of the solid cultured class who lived well and were treated with great consideration by Mexicans of the corresponding class. They had never been sneered at for their shapes nor their habits. But as for these *Gachupínes*, these low Spaniards, the Mexicans knew how to treat them! The Huttens remembered a Mexican saying that the Germans in Mexico were never tired of repeating: Mexicans loathe

the Americans, despise the Jews, hate the Spaniards, distrust the English, admire the French and love the Germans. An immensely clever Mexican gentleman had composed this saying at a dinner party, and it had spread like wildfire among their little circle. It was the kind of thing that almost reconciled one to living in a foreign country with mixed races and on the whole rather barbarous customs.

Herr Professor for years was the head of the best German school in Mexico City, where the little boys carried their school packs on their backs and wore round student caps; and the little girls wore black pinafores over their sober-colored frocks, their hair shining in smooth blonde braids. Now and again, standing at the window of his classroom in the big solid Mexican-French house which the German colony had bought and remodeled in the seemly German style, Professor Hutten watched the children walking sedately yet vigorously in small groups, their faces and their simple clothing so immaculate; observed the meek looks and good manners of the German young, heard them speak their mother tongue with good accent and pure diction, and fancied that he might almost imagine himself to be in Germany. Oh, that the whole world of men might be so orderly, so well arranged, so virtuous in its basic principles. This hope, coming as it did to him at long intervals, making him feel he was a part of a great universal movement towards the betterment of mankind, had no doubt, as he confessed to his wife, kept him alive. But they had their private grief, their personal loss. They were childless, and would always be so.

The white bulldog Bébé for nine years had lived with them, sharing their lives. He ate sitting on the floor beside the table, taking food from their hands. He had slept at their feet when he was a helpless crying puppy afraid of the dark and missing the comfort of his mother's milk. Professor Hutten admitted in his heart that he was fond of Bébé, in fact with his wife he loved Bébé warmly and tenderly and constantly, in spite of the trouble he gave them. To them, there was nothing absurd in their feelings; Bébé, of a nobly disinterested nature, deserved their care and repaid them with devotion. His wife was cut to the bone, he could see in her face, by the jeers and laughter of the particularly base kind of Spaniards on the boat. Professor Hutten shared her grief, mixed with indignation and it must be said a touch of shame. He did not feel it was unmanly of him to have held Bébé's head, but it was careless of him not to have a proper regard for appearances, and to have exposed himself to the ridicule of those coarse-natured persons. It was a consolation to remember that Bébé was an English bulldog of champion stock, of distinguished if not absolutely flawless ancestry; he had been awarded blue and purple ribbons without number in very creditable shows. Now he was a trifle aged perhaps and out of training, but he was still able and willing to defend his master and mistress and incidentally himself against all attacks. If the word was said to him it was still in Bébé to spring like a trigger, seize and hold one of those jeering little black people by the throat, never letting go until his master gave the command. Professor Hutten leaned over the sleeping Bébé and said in a low, urgent voice, "Attack, Bébé, attack!"

Bébé rose drunkenly, scrambled on his feet trying to get a balance, his eyes rolling. He uttered a deep ominous growl, tottered, and pitched forward on his blunt nose, spread out flat. "What are you doing?" asked Frau Hutten, in wonder. "If we do not keep him quiet, he will be sick again."

"It came over me to test the permanence of his training," said the Professor, with a gratified air. "No, he has forgotten nothing. Ah, Käthe, how blood and training do form and sustain character. Look at the good animal: he will never fail us."

Frau Hutten said, "How he reminds me of the past, of our life, now we are going home again." She gazed at Bébé with tenderness, but her thoughts were disturbed with looking backward and looking forward, for nothing in the past seemed properly related to the future. She was almost afraid to hope, for things in the old country must be very much changed, and in ways she could not be prepared for. She said as much to her husband.

"Where we are going," he reassured her sweetly, "people and things and ways change slowly. We will be among those of our own age, our own way of thinking and feeling; they were the friends of our childhood and youth, they cannot now be strangers to us — or so we may only hope," he added, bravely.

Frau Hutten was silent, remembering when the whole German colony in Mexico City went to a theater to see the moving picture of the funeral of the Kaiserin Augusta Viktoria. They rose in silence as the great hearse appeared, surrounded by its horse guard of helmeted soldiers. Like brothers and sisters reunited at the graveside of their mother, they all wept together, each turned and embraced the one nearest him. Aloud they had wept together in broken sobs and gulps, until the whole theater was a place of mourning, full of the sound of this homesick, heart-soothing sorrow. They had sung "A Mighty Fortress," "O Tannenbaum" and "The Watch on the Rhine," with tears still on their faces. How near to the homeland they had seemed at that moment, but never to be so near again, because of what they had lost: the good, the gentle, the long-suffering Empress who had been symbol of all they revered in home and family life, the generous hearthstone around which their best memories clustered.

"What will it be like now, I wonder?" she wanted to ask her husband again, but she knew he could not answer except with hopes; and she did not wish to trouble him.

Professor Hutten was sunk in his thought too: how he had worked all these years, hoping against all reason that the day of his honorable retirement with savings and pension would come, and God in his goodness would let him see again the house where he was born in the Todmoos country of the Black Forest; and now it had come, he was full of misgivings. What would it be like? He buried his face in his hands, leaning forward in the deck chair, and almost instantly a qualm caught him in the pit of the stomach, and a surge of most awful sickness chased out his comfortable piety. He raised his head, streaming with sweat. "Käthe," he said in a low despairing voice, "help me. For God's sake quickly before anyone sees."

It happened Frau Rittersdorf saw. But she was much too occupied searching for her goose-down pillow, pure white goose down covered with cream-and-pink striped taffeta, which had been sent to her from Germany all the way to Mexico as a Christmas present from her dear dead husband's dear mother. How she could have misplaced it, have forgotten it for a moment, Frau Rittersdorf was unable to explain to herself. It was really indispensable to her comfort, as the deck chairs were unusually hard, or seemed to be so at any rate on this ship where everything was undeniably more than a little on the second-rate side. In any case, since no doubt she had left it in her chair, it was the plain duty of someone — the deck steward for choice — to have salvaged and returned it at once to her stateroom.

She advanced upon the steward firmly though kindly. He was a most polite and attentive fellow who spoke with an Austrian accent . . . "*meine Dame,*" he called her, which she rather preferred to the homelier-sounding *Frau,* "it cannot be lost, it is only misplaced for the moment, and I shall find and return it to you. After all, this is a small ship, and it cannot have got overboard by itself! So do please, dear lady, be at your ease and I shall bring it to you very presently."

Frau Rittersdorf, winding her green veil closely about her head and knotting it over one ear, noticed those two awful Spanish children standing a few feet away, simply staring at her with animal curiosity. She returned their attention with a slit-eyed disciplinary face, such as had always proved effective with her English charges when she was a governess with a country family in England.

"Have you lost something?" asked the little girl in a high bold treble.

"Yes, have you stolen it?" inquired Frau Rittersdorf, sternly.

At this they seemed strangely agitated; they wriggled somewhat, exchanged wicked glances; the little boy said, "Who knows?" Then they both cackled with unchildish laughter and ran away. Frau Rittersdorf, considering exactly what she would do with them if they were in her power, moved over to the deck rail near that pair of young people, obviously American — what was there about Americans that made them so obviously *only* that? the gradual mongrelization of that dismaying country by the mingling of the steerage sweepings of Europe and the blacks had resulted only in a mediocrity of feature and mind impossible to describe! — yet she wondered what they could find to talk about so constantly, as they spent at least half their time in each other's society, and one might think they should finally have exhausted topics for conversation. They were leaning together companionably, both pairs of eyes fixed on the glittering stretches of water, talking idly, with short pauses.

Frau Rittersdorf did not hope to overhear much, for she was slightly deaf, nor to observe details except at short distances, for she was extremely nearsighted. At the right distance, however, considering these disadvantages, she leaned upon the rail next the young man, and bringing her vision into focus swiftly, ascertained that he was younger than she had thought. His light hair was nicely cut, he had a good thin high nose and a well-shaped mouth, and a general though no doubt misleading air of good upbringing. His pale gray shirt was quite fresh but his white linen suit was ready for the wash.

The young woman wore a short-sleeved, belted no-colored frock that appeared to have been fashioned from hop sacks. Her face was pale and too thin, with high cheekbones and a sharp pointed chin that gave her a vixenish look. She had fairly good light eyes and black hair parted plainly in the middle — one of these advanced, emancipated young women of the Bohemian world, no doubt. Frau Rittersdorf noted that in repose his face was sulky and hers impatient. Suddenly they both lifted their heads and laughed together, and their faces were instantly gay, good-humored, a little reckless. She smiled involuntarily at the fresh, pretty sound of youthful happiness; they both saw her smile. Their expressions grew a little blank and cool, and they turned their faces away.

Frau Rittersdorf had seen quite enough to convince her that this was an odd outlandish pair; there was something about them she could not understand and did not like at all. They were not the sort of persons she would care to cultivate as traveling companions. She returned to her chair, arranged her skirts carefully about her legs, leaned back, missing her soft little pillow, and got out her notebook.

She had a poor memory and a passion for recording every minutest detail of her daily existence — even to the very moment in which she carelessly spooned her soup too hot or forgot to stamp a letter — mingled with scraps of philosophy, observations, reminiscence and meditation. For years she had filled notebook after notebook with tiny jottings in a sharp cultivated little handwriting, and as they were filled, she put them away neatly and never looked at them again. Shaking her gold-banded fountain pen, she wrote in English:

"These young Americans have the affectation of addressing each other always by their full names, perhaps the only formality they maintain between themselves, and a very *gauche* sort of thing it is, or perhaps it's the only hope they have of making themselves known to the public. There is a faint atmosphere of moral slackness in their manner, their dress — I cannot quite place or describe it. It is more of an *effluvium*. The names are musical, if somewhat sentimental: Jenny Angel — the real name is, I suppose, Jane, Johanna Engel it would be, and much better, in the German — and David Darling. The latter is a common surname as well as a usual term of affection among Americans, I believe; much less among the frozen English naturally, though it does seem to be a corruption of the word *Dear*, Dearling, the diminutive; this would sound as if pronounced Darling, since the English have a slovenly way of speaking certain words to which, frankly speaking, I could never accustom myself during those seven long penitential years in that country. Naturally I learned English perfectly at school in Munich, and had always heard it spoken well, and the English manner of speech seemed very crude to me after that. Ah, those years of bitter exile! Ah, those frightful two-faced English children whose affection I could never win, and who could never learn German by any means. *Deyahling*, the English would call it after all, and the Americans, who seem to learn their language phonetically, or by ear, as they say, because of their distaste for reading, would add the sound of R, a letter they seem fond of to excess. It is all quite interesting in its limited way."

Reading this over, she decided it was too good to hide, but would go well in a letter to her dearest friend and schoolmate of long ago, Sophie Bismarck, highly connected, unhappily married and living in luxury in Munich. Stupid little Sophie's head would spin as always, trying to follow her brilliant schoolmate's mind. She made a note in the margin, *"Für liebe Sophie,* to be translated in case she has forgotten her English,"* dropped the book into her large flat handbag and got up to take her walk, nine times around the deck. Exercise warded off seasickness, kept down liverishness, gave one an appetite, indeed there was everything to be said for it, dull as it might be; and the boundless rolling waters of the mighty deep inspired noble thoughts.

Her dear husband had taught her all this. He was a man of endless activity, and believed firmly — how right he was — that good health was necessary to good morality. How many times he had fairly dragged her up and down during their Channel crossings, even in the worst weather — indeed he welcomed the worst weather as the most exhilarating test of courage — when they had to cling to any available support as if they were drowning, the waves dashing over them. Somewhere in the calm blue sky above she felt that her dear Otto, dead in his manly strength and beauty at the battle of Ypres, was looking down approvingly at his good, obedient Nannerl, walking — yes, and alone, Otto, alone! — round and round the deck for the sake of her health, as he would have her do.

On the seventh lap, feeling her arches fail her in her three-inch heels, she rested provisionally on the arm of her chair and took out her notebook again: "If those young American persons are not married, they ought to be. But in that monstrous country all the relations of life are so perverted, more especially between the sexes, it is next to impossible to judge them by any standards of true civilization."

Reading this over, she decided it was unworthy of her. Where had her mind been wandering all this time? She struck out the whole passage, and wrote in above the thick black line: "Divine weather, if a little too warm, and a heavenly stroll with the pure sea air on my face, thinking of my dear Otto and of the blessings of our happy though all too brief marriage. R.I.P. August 25, 1931."

She went on, piously to finish the two laps — what were fallen arches in comparison to the blissful sense of keeping faith with Otto? — carrying the journal between her hands as though it were a prayer book. She met the bride and groom also strolling, their clasped hands swinging lightly, both very beautiful in pure white; looking, too, astonishingly fresh and carefree considering the newness of their honeymoon. As they neared, she perceived that the bride, though serene-looking, was rather pale, with darkening smudges under her eyes; even a little ill, perhaps? And quite properly, Frau Rittersdorf answered herself with matronly approval. One had well-founded suspicions of those brides who remained unchanged in appearance and manner after marriage. Even with all the happiness of the new state, still one does not step from virginity to the strains and stresses of married life without visible sign. Say what you will, it is not all roses! She considered this thought for a while and decided it was leading her mind into forbidden areas: "Even during the most passionate of her husband's embraces, a pure woman never permits herself an impure thought," her Otto had instructed her more than once: a hard saying, but no doubt true. Resolutely she turned her mind to higher things, putting the memory of Otto back once more in the sacred potpourri of the past.

Jenny had coffee early, on deck, in the cool morning light bluetinctured between sea and sky, and began making sketches with a fountain pen: the canvas wind-funnel like a conventional ghost with outspread arms over the grated pit of the steerage eating place; Bébé the white bulldog, apparently recovering from his seasickness, sprawled weightily on his belly; Elsa, her cabin mate, from memory, big arms raised, doing her hair; a passing sailor with a bucket; furtively, after a quick glance around, a hasty outline of Herr Glocken's harmonious, interesting deformity. Jenny, sitting at ease in her own neatly pretty small body which gave her very little trouble except for its long famine of love, rather idly wondered what it might be like to live in such a hideous shape as Herr Glocken's. The thought frightened her so much she started sharply and dropped her pen, in a flash of blind terror and suffocation, a child again locked in her grandmother's bedroom closet narrow as a coffin. She shut her eyes so tightly that when she opened them she saw Wilhelm Freytag through a rainbow dazzle of light, taking a long rather graceful stride toward her, holding out her pen.

He stopped before her then, receiving her thanks, looking very sunny and amiable, waiting to be invited to sit with her. She moved her legs aside and made room for him on the footrest of her chair.

"But if you are doing something — ?" he said.

"This is just idleness," Jenny told him. "A form of solitaire. I'd much rather gossip a little." She leaned toward him, feeling again how her habitual mood of resentment, the growing bitterness and melancholy of her mind when she was alone, could so quickly be dispersed in the sound of voices and the nearness of others, no matter if the voices had nothing to say to her, if the presences were strangers indifferent to her. Women spoil this fellow, she thought: his charm is perhaps slightly overconfident — and then reflected that the society of someone with no troubles of his own might be a rest for her after her thorny progress with David.

Freytag was cheerfully ready for gossip, and happy to tell her there was a mysterious stranger aboard, a real political prisoner, being deported from Cuba, it was said, in connection with the student riots that led to the closing of the University — to be confined in cabin for the whole voyage, finally to be put off ship at Santa Cruz de Tenerife.

"In chains, I suppose," said Jenny. "What did he do?"

"It's a woman."

"Would that make any difference?"

"I hope so," said Freytag. "But then, besides that, she is a Spanish countess, and to the Captain, let me tell you, that alone makes all the difference possible. He has given orders all around that she is to be treated with the utmost consideration, and sends messages to her himself asking her what she would like. No, our prisoner isn't going to suffer. She has a whole stateroom on Deck A to herself — more than I was able to get!"

"I would be a prisoner myself for that," said Jenny.

"Yes, indeed. I like space above everything, but I have that seven-foot Swede Hansen for cabin mate, and he sleeps in the upper berth with his feet stuck out so that I bump my head on them every morning."

❧{ 87 }❧

"My cabin mate is on the ample side, too," said Jenny, "but a very nice girl and we don't elbow each other much."

"Why, I thought you were with your husband," said Freytag, and there danced in his eyes a curiosity so instant and so candid it was almost appealing.

"We are not married," said Jenny. She scratched a few lines on the drawing of the wind-funnel and stopped herself sternly from adding, "We are just friends who happened to take the same boat." Could she fall so low? No, there *were* limits, and she believed she still knew where some of them were. And that was not altogether an innocent question on Herr Freytag's part, either. She took a good, considered look at him. Perhaps not innocent at all, but a blunder and he knew it. Did his face contract for a moment in strain and embarrassment or was she giving him more credit for sensibility than he deserved? He picked up her drawings and turned them about and she saw by his look that he cared very little about them. He lingered over the sketch of Herr Glocken and said finally, "It's terribly like. I wonder what he would think of it."

"He'll never see it," said Jenny, taking the drawings back and putting them in the folder. Freytag said, "I didn't know you were an artist," and Jenny gave her usual answer to that, "I am not, but maybe I shall be someday."

The evil little moment blew over, but there would be an endless series of them from now on out no matter where. She was beginning to see too clearly what she had let herself in for when she took up with David. At this point she was losing confidence in her whole life, as if every step of it had been merely one error leading to another, back to the day she was born, she supposed — no, that is too much! I'm not going to let this business throw me off track completely. That poor Elsa thinks there is something wrong with her; she would feel better if she could know about me. Yet I wanted to live in clean air and say Yes, or No, mean what I said and have it understood and no nonsense. I hate half-things, half-heartedness, stupid false situations, invented feelings, pumped-up loves and hand-decorated hates. I hate people who stare at themselves in mirrors and smile. I want things straight and clear or at least I want to be able to see when they're crooked and confused. Anything else is just nasty and so my life is nasty and I am ashamed of it. And I have an albatross around my neck that I didn't even shoot. I simply don't know how he got there.

Freytag offered her a cigarette. "Would you like to walk a little?"

"Oh, yes, I suppose it is time to start tramping around the deck saying '*Grüss Gott*' to everybody."

"It's a pleasant Christian greeting," said Freytag amiably. "But I like better the way the country Indians say '*Adios*.' Still," he said, nodding slightly towards a group of the Spanish company strolling by, "I'm afraid it wouldn't be suitable for those."

"They're really tough, aren't they? An *Adios* would bounce off them like a rubber ball on a sidewalk."

"They're attractive-looking, though," said Freytag, "and perhaps a little dangerous."

"They are exactly as dangerous as we allow them to be," said Jenny; "why flatter them? Really all we need to do is watch our pocketbooks. Otherwise they are bores, I think — all that dingy picturesqueness. Such weather," she remarked, "isn't it merry?" and stared upward with a melancholy face.

They walked slowly, nodding to various passing figures by now more or less recognizable on fiftieth sight. They exchanged amused glances when they saw Arne Hansen walking with big Elsa, her small parents following half a dozen steps behind with tactful feet and discreet faces. Elsa wore an absurd white beret much too small, and she was stiff with shyness. Hansen was silent, his eyes fixed straight ahead.

Jenny and Freytag fell into a kind of half-confidential talk about themselves with the ease of travelers who hardly expect to know each other better; that near-candor which comes of the possibility of future indifference. German as he was, he told her, he had a great deal of English and Scottish in him, also Hungarian, on his Austrian grandmother's side. That branch of the family had been reckless marriers, the more farfetched the match, the better. Beyond that, God knows what — it seemed better not to inquire. In turn, Jenny recited her mixed ancestry of which she was rather proud: "Western broth," she said. "No Tartar, no Jew, no Chinese, no Bantu, just the old home mixture: Dutch, Scotch-Irish-English-Welsh, French and one great-great-grandmother with a Spanish name who was just the same half-Irish — no Hungarian even," she told him, "and above all no German. No German at all."

He wanted to know how, among so many nations, all blood-cousins as they were, she could be so certain — did she dislike Germans? Because of that beastly war? That had been everybody's fault, everybody had suffered, the Germans most of all; if the Americans had taken the part of Germany in that war, the whole future of the world would have been changed for the better! His eyes kindled, he grew quite eloquent. Jenny smiled a little: no matter whose fault it was, she was glad her country had not gone with the Germans. But at once she had a twinge of conscience, and said, "No, not even the war." She had, she told him, no prejudices of any kind. She had been partly brought up by her grandmother and grandfather, her father's parents, for her mother had died young: and these grandparents were old-fashioned eighteenth-century rationalists, just simple descendants of Diderot and d'Alembert, her grandfather used to say; and to them nothing could have been more vulgar and unenlightened than even the faintest shade of disapproval of anything or anybody on grounds of nationality or religion. All this was concerned with manners as related to morals. "Negroes came to the back door, of course," said Jenny, "and I never saw a Red Indian or even a Hindu at our dinner table, and all sorts of persons were excluded for this and that reason, mostly on the grounds that they were underbred, or bores; but this was mere observance of local custom, they told me, or they were exercising their natural right to choose their own society — both an important part of the manners of good breeding. Oh," said Jenny, "what a museum piece of an upbringing it was! Yet I loved it, I believed every word of it, I still do . . . so I've never caught up with my generation. I'm bogged down in a whole set of ideal precepts and nowhere to practice them! My radical friends look upon me as a youthful fossil. They can pronounce 'lady' as if it were an indecent word; and one of them said, 'Listen to the way she pronounces "Chantilly" — wouldn't you *know?*' "

"How did you come to pick up radical friends?" asked Freytag. "The only ones I ever saw had dirty fingernails and needed haircuts, and they cadged cigarettes from anybody and then stubbed them out in their coffee cups. Do your radical friends behave like that?"

"Some of them," said Jenny, rather reluctantly, "but they some of them have very interesting minds."

"They'd better," said Freytag. "Is your friend Mr. Scott a radical?"

"Sometimes," said Jenny, "for the sake of the argument. It all depends on which side the other person takes."

Freytag laughed at this and Jenny joined in a few notes. After a moment's silence he spoke of his wife, as he always did sooner or later in any conversation. He described her coloring, very dear to his taste:

wheat blonde, rosy-faced, true Rhine-maiden sort of girl; and told again her charming name. "Mary Champagne," he said, fondly. "I think I fell in love first with her name," he said. It came out this time that she selected his clothes and did rather better for him than he could do for himself, he believed; and he looked perfectly satisfied with himself. In another sort of person, Jenny decided, all this could be a horrid complacency. She told him she thought it took a special kind of self-confidence for a woman to choose a man's neckties for him. She herself would never dare. He thought it depended entirely on the man.

"I have a fantastic respect for my wife's taste and judgment in everything, or nearly," he said. There was another vacant pause while Jenny brooded on David's dull black knitted strings. David's kind of conceit was really much worse than Freytag's kind, which had a little warmth and generosity in it: poor David! sitting in himself like a hermit in a cave, peering out, determined not to share the parings of his nails with *any*body.

"My wife is visiting her mother in Mannheim," said Freytag. "I am going to bring them both back with me to Mexico. We have decided to live there."

His air of satisfaction and repose in happiness deepened until it was a positive radiation, like fine health or the mysterious enchantment of beauty. Jenny felt that his pleasure in himself was not vanity, after all, but came of something in his state of being: something he possessed, something he had found or that had been given to him. He is lucky in some way, she thought; lucky, and he knows it. As they rounded the bow, she leaned toward him slightly, gaunt and empty and famished, to breathe in the air of good fortune.

The bride and groom were sitting stretched at ease in their chairs. She was a beautiful creature, with the grace and silence and naturalness of a fine shy wild animal. The other passengers glanced at them quickly whenever they appeared, glanced away again. Dazed and smiling, the bride sat or walked all day with her husband, her narrow curved hand lying loosely in his. He was, Jenny thought, a quietly merry person; she liked his witty, irregular features, thin and quick; he would be the intelligent one of the two, with the undisputed moral upper hand from the beginning.

"Aren't they lovely together, really?" said Jenny, and hoped there was no forlorn envy in her voice. "Something to look at, aren't they?"

"All brides should look like that," said Freytag. "She has just the right look, somehow. I don't know exactly what it is, but I know it when I see it. Eden just after the Fall. That little interval between the Fall and the driving out by that tricky jealous vengeful old God," he said. "Anyone who doesn't know that, once in a lifetime, once anyway — and maybe it doesn't happen oftener — is unlucky, no matter what else good may happen to him."

"I suppose so," said Jenny, dryly.

"You will call that German sentimentality," he said, and smiled as if he were smiling to himself about something he knew that pleased him, something he need not tell anyone.

"I haven't the faintest notion what it is," said Jenny, "but it sounds very attractive." Her tone did not match her words, and her answer struck him unpleasantly as having a flinty little edge on it. He felt again that odd contraction of dislike for her he had felt when he first saw her, before they had even spoken to each other. He put the width of another step between them and said nothing.

Jenny saw this and was curiously chilled by it. You are perhaps purposely making yourself very attractive with this light conversation about the Fall, as if you know something you could teach me that I need badly to learn. Maybe I shall fall in love with you, maybe I am in love with you already, the way I fall in love: always with utter strangers and as if I were going under water, and I'll fall out again as if I were falling off a cliff. I'm glad I don't know anything about you, except that you have the kind of looks I like — one kind, anyway — and that you are married and anxious for me to be sure that you love your wife. Don't insist — I am happy to believe you. And if I knew you better I might not like you at all — in fact I don't even like you now. And I can tell *you* now that you aren't ever going to like me — you will hate me in fact. There would be something about the whole thing I shouldn't be able to put up with at all. It doesn't matter what it might be, and I can't even imagine what it is. . . . If we could sleep together without too much trouble and lose ourselves together for a little while, I'd be easy again, I'd be able to see better. It's only — how did it happen? I'm just starved and frozen out; my man won't share with me, he wants everything to himself. What is that Spanish saying — "Is this bread good or is it my hunger?" And what's the other — "What dog will refuse meat that is thrown to him?" But that one of course will be for you.

They had come round to her chair again. "I'll stop here," she told him, and no longer troubled herself to pretend any interest in his company. He could not consent to be dismissed so offhandedly.

"Maybe you would like your morning beer," he offered. "I'm quite ready for mine." She shook her head with a shade of a grimace of distaste, without looking at him. He turned away instantly and within three steps' distance had joined up with the Huttens and Bébé, who seemed all three delighted to see him. Jenny knew they would sit down comfortably over their big steins together with nothing in particular to explain or conceal; each well nourished and self-sufficing on his own peculiar food. They would loll cool and at ease, with no starved animal sitting by feeding on the wind of a daydream, with a sorry monologue gnawing away silently in the brain; or talking nonsense aloud at a tangent — a stranger, a real death's-head, peering out at them through natural-enough-looking flesh.

She took up her drawing and went on with it. Her attention flickered away from what her fingers attempted on the page, and back and away, while she worried along in monotonous confusion and indecision, about Europe, about David — what a rotten sense of proportion! A man and a continent simply can't have the same importance, or not the same kind, or they shouldn't have — that's getting entirely the wrong kind of things mixed up, she decided, enslaved as she was to her notions of what life *should* be, her wish to shape, to direct, to make of it what she wished it to be; and if she let David spoil Europe for her, she must be even a greater fool than she had feared. Leaning back in her chair and dropping her papers into her lap, dry-eyed and staring up into the pure blue light of a day fit for the joy of angels, she gave way and despaired quietly and awfully.

It was very hard to admit to herself that she was a fool, but everything in reason pointed to that fact. Time to put on the hair shirt, her guardian demon prompted her. Time to say your prayers. Don't be a lost soul, it's so stupid, such a dull occupation. Jenny answered herself, for her colloquies with this other self took place with real words and a face-to-face encounter: I'm not lost, I never have been, I never will be, unless this is being lost here and now. No, I'm not lost, I can't get out of it that easily. It's only I don't know just how I came here or how I'm going to get out again, but I know where I am all right! Rehearsing for blowing bubbles through boiling pitch later on! It's the wrong place altogether, I never meant to be here, and I believed I was on my way somewhere else altogether different — maybe there never was any such place, or anyway, not for me. Never mind, my girl, pull yourself to-gether — we aren't going to stay here.

She examined the drawings she had just made — bad, unfinished, half-made, half-seen, not felt at all. All her feeling had gone into self-indulgence, self-pity, and she had done nothing but dull hard lines, enclosing perfect emptiness. What nonsense! Her dishonest remark to Freytag about her drawing being a form of solitaire rounded on her and became true with crushing suddenness.

In self-defense she abandoned herself to fury and hatred against David. She crumpled her drawings in both fists cruelly as if they were live things and she could hear them scream, went swiftly to the rail and tossed them overboard and turned away without another glance at them. Black and white — no more of that for her. She would draw directly on the canvas with brush and colors as she had done before, and damn David's advice. I sold out, she said, for a mess of pottage and I didn't even get that. Well, good God, can you imagine? I was letting that fellow tell me how to paint. But not for long, remember.

She stretched out in her chair and pulled her dark blue scarf over her eyes to shut out the hateful day, but for a good while a part of her unhappy guilty mind went on with its dialogue with another part. She explained and justified her mistakes, her hopeless errors, as well as she could to her indwelling enemy, who answered her always with the same cold unbelief, the same finality, saying still, No that won't quite do either. You know what you are doing, you know what is going on, how it must end — come out with it, why did you choose this particu-lar kind of sordid mess? Speak up, woman, let's have the truth for once, if you think you can finally admit what it is. . . . The nagging voice went on, oafish and devilish at once, until at last, wearied out with self-torture, Jenny turned her face aside and fell asleep heavily, with sick eyelids twitching under the scarf when it moved lightly in the wind; her terror followed her in her sleep and gave her bad dreams and would not forgive her for anything or let her rest for a moment.

Lizzi Spöckenkieker, running as if pursued and looking back over her shoulder, dashed full tilt into Captain Thiele, who had chosen to show himself on deck that morning. He was unmistakably the Captain even to the most landlubberly eye. In stiff immaculate white with bits of gold braid and lettering disposed hieratically upon his chest, collar and shoulders, he bore himself rigidly, and his face was that of a pompous minor god: a god who had grown somewhat petulant and more than a little mean in his efforts to maintain his authority. Every feature of his face was ill-humored, from the narrow forehead, the little eyes close-set and crafty, to the long sharp nose casting its shadow over the tight mouth and stubborn chin. It was as if his own nature had shaped his face to match itself: and there he walked, alone, returning the respectful salutations of the passengers with reluctant little jerks of his head, upon which sat a monumental ornate cap, white as plaster.

Lizzi almost overturned him in her career, slipped, and would have fallen if the Captain had not braced himself with instant presence of mind and balance. He threw an arm about her stiffly, his face a dark furious red; and Lizzi, blushing, whinnying, cackling, scrambling, embraced him around the neck wildly as if she were drowning. Then she let go and backed away, crying shrilly, "Oh Captain Thiele, how frightful of me — oh I *beg* of you — good heavens, how could I be so awkward?"

The Captain glared at her bitterly, said, "It is nothing, dear Fräulein, nothing," and moved on majestically annoyed, biting his underlip. When Herr Löwenthal rather nervously ventured to salute him the Captain looked straight through him. Löwenthal, thinking himself snubbed, was cut to the marrow, his heart broke, the very nerves of his back teeth began to ache, and this state went on for hours. He went to the stern of the ship and leaning his head on his arms he brooded over the water in silence and wished for death, or thought he did. He retired into the dark and airless ghetto of his soul and lamented with all the grieving wailing company he found there; for he was never alone in that place. He sat down there head in hand and mourned in one voice with his fated people, wordlessly he bewailed their nameless eternal wrongs and sorrows; then feeling somewhat soothed, the inspired core of his being began to search for its ancient justification and its means of revenge. But it should be slow and secret.

When a shadow fell upon his shoulder, he moved away without turning his face, not wishing to meet another blank hostile eye. A flat American voice said in ordinary tones: "Is this your first trip over?" and Löwenthal, cheered almost instantly, was able to say with pride: "I make this trip twice a year now for ten years; I have a little international kind of business, I go everywhere." The American was Herr Denny. He lounged over and seemed perfectly friendly and harmless.

"Golly," said Denny, looking really interested, "you do?"

"South America," said Löwenthal, "all parts of Europe, Spain, and of course, Mexico. Mexico is headquarters: less taxes, cheaper labor, cheaper rent, less overhead all around, cheaper materials, and those peons, they turn out high-class articles out of nearly nothing, so you should see what they can do when you give them good stuff to work on. Anywhere there is a Catholic church," said Löwenthal, "I can make money. Rosaries, plaster and wooden saint statues, some of them painted and decorated with real gold and silver; altar furnishings of all kinds. There's money in it. Indians not got enough to eat will buy a saint statue! I'd like to show you my samples: rosaries alone," he said, "I got every grade from just plain wooden ones up to handmade silver ones. Some I designed myself and they're really pieces of jewelry already, with opals and amber and even that Mexican jade. I even tried some of that obsidian, but it don't pay to work it — too hard. But there's a market for all this stuff, never fails."

He stopped; for over Denny's face there was moving an unpleasant, prejudiced look. Deeply disturbed, mystified, Löwenthal watched it grow. Then Denny said, "If there's one religion on this earth that I despise, it's those Catholics. I don't like anything about 'em. Where I come from, only the lowest kind of people, greasers and wops and polacks, are Catholics, and I say they can have it — it's good enough for 'em."

Löwenthal smiled, his thick curly lips and heavy-lidded eyes formed a grin that drew all his features to the center of his face. With relief he seized upon this common sympathy between them, and they spent a profitable few minutes putting the Catholic Church in its place. The conduct of priests towards young women in the confessional, the secrets of monasteries and convents, the sale of Masses for the dead, the worship of images, all these failings were aired again and denounced thoroughly. Löwenthal even expanded to the point where he told how his sweet old grandmother from Cracow — "finest woman I ever knew," he said, "the best —" had warned him many times when he was a little boy, never in his life to pass a Catholic church at midnight, for at that hour the doors opened and the ghosts of all the congregations who had died that year would pour forth in the shape of swine and they would eat him, then and there. For years his hair stood up in fright when he passed a Catholic church, even in daytime. He remembered his revered grandmother's exact words: "The dirty cannibal

Goyim — they even eat their own brothers — the pigs! Then they turn into pigs when they die and eat little Jewish boys!"

Denny frowned at this, slanted an eye at Löwenthal as if remembering something suddenly from the back of his mind, and said with a touch of censoriousness: "I wonder why you are in that business if you feel like that about them. I think that one religion oughtn't to make fun of another. I don't believe in any of them so I can say what I please. I just happen specially to hate Catholics, that's all, and I wouldn't want to handle their goods."

Löwenthal, excited, flung up his hands palms upward and said, "The way I look at it, it's a business. There is nothing personal in it at all. The way I look at it, the business is there, and if I don't sell them, somebody else will. So why not I sell them? It's got nothing to do with religion, anyway, from my standpoint. From my standpoint, it's not a religion. What I say is, well, it's just straight business and there's nothing personal in it."

Denny, stirring himself as if about to move on, agreed halfway. "Oh yes, I can see that. Business is business. But just for myself, I wouldn't like it."

Löwenthal watched him go with a feeling that the conversation had been a failure, after all; maybe he said something wrong, or maybe the fellow didn't like his looks — Löwenthal hadn't much liked Denny's either, but that was another matter. At any rate, he went on feeling baffled and sore; he had taken no pleasure in Denny's society, yet still thought they might have gone on and had a drink together. Maybe his mistake was in not offering him a drink. . . . Well, next time, maybe better luck.

His feelings about the Captain came back, but in the shape of anger this time. That swine. And the steward, putting him at a table by himself. And the dirty things they offered him to eat — he had to live on eggs, fruit, and broiled herring. On many boats he had been able to get kosher food. Ah, he needed to be more careful and clever than he was — he suffered waves of fright sometimes because he feared he was not clever enough, they would play him a trick someday and he would not know until it was too late. It occurred to him often that he was living in a world so dangerous he wondered how he dared to go to sleep at night. But he was sleepy at that very moment.

Rolling steadily and balancing on his short legs, feet turned out and slapping the deck lightly, he went to his chair and settled himself, sighing, full of shapeless worries, running his hand over his hair crisped in tight waves and standing up in a ridge at the crown of his head. He would sleep and forget his troubles. He would sleep until lunchtime, and then there would be eggs or fish, sometimes fish from a tin. He longed for Düsseldorf and his cousin Sarah's good comfortable house and the good solid clean food.

Elsa's mother gave her a firm kind motherly talk early in the morning, before breakfast, telling her there was no need for her to be too stiff in her manner towards the men. Naturally she was not expected even to glance at those terrible Spaniards or those crazy students from Cuba, but after all there were some nice men on board. Herr Freytag even if married was a good dancer, there was no harm in a little modest dancing with a good partner, married or not; Herr Denny, though American, might do; at least she could try him once. Then there was Herr Hansen, no objection whatever to him. "When I say to you, be modest, be discreet, I don't mean you are to sit without a word, or a look around you, Elsa, and Herr Hansen is a man I would trust. He is the kind of man a girl may depend upon to be a gentleman in whatever circumstances."

Elsa said with surprising spirit, "I don't like his looks, he's too cross."

"I would never pick a man for looks," said her mother. "Handsome men are often deceitful. When you think of marrying, you must look for one who has a firm character who could be the head of his own house. A steady, real man. I do not think Herr Hansen is cross, he is just serious. As to most of the others on this boat, I think I never saw a worse lot — all those male dancers, la de da deda! with all those loose dancing women — it is a scandal."

"Herr Hansen never takes his eyes off the one they call Amparo," said Elsa, hopelessly. "If he likes her, Mama, you know he can never like me. I saw them standing very close together this morning, and he was giving her money; I am sure it was that."

"Elsa," said her mother, shocked. "What do you mean? Do you know what you are saying? You are not supposed to see such things!"

"I couldn't help it," said Elsa, with a grieved face. "I was just coming out of my cabin and there they were, in the passage, not ten feet away, I had to walk right past them. They did not pay any attention. But I cannot believe that Herr Hansen will like me."

"Never you mind, my dear little girl," said her mother, "you have your own virtues and qualities, never you be afraid of wicked women. Men always come back to the good ones at last. You will have a fine husband someday when she will be in the ditch. Don't you worry."

Instead of raising Elsa's spirits, this conversation seemed to dampen them completely. The prospect of following Amparo in Herr Hansen's affections somehow was not attractive. She drooped and folded her hands on her knees. Her mother said, after a sad little pause, "Look, if it will make you happier, I will buy you a box of face powder when we get home. After all, it is perhaps time for you to be a real young lady, now that we are going to be among our own kind once more. Yes, you shall have face powder, any shade you prefer."

"They have it for sale in the barbershop here," said Elsa, timidly, "all kinds, some of it perfumed with lily of the valley. It is Rachel number one, just my shade exactly. I just happened to notice it when I was having my hair washed . . . I . . ." she trailed off, losing courage.

"How much did it cost?" asked her mother, opening her purse.

"Four marks," said Elsa, and she stood up stammering with amazement and joy. "Oh, M-M-Mama, d-do you m-mean I am really to have it?"

"Didn't I say so?" asked her mother, and put the money in her hand. "Now go and make yourself pretty and come to breakfast."

Elsa threw her big arms around her chubby mother and hugged and squeezed her and kissed her face, her eyes trembling with tears. "No, no, now, that's enough," said her mother, "don't act like a big baby."

All the way to the barbershop Elsa fought to control her tears. She appeared at breakfast with her hair fluffed out under a child-sized white beret, her face, neck, arms and hands covered smoothly with a thick coat of flesh-colored powder. She had also ventured a tiny crooked smear on her lips with one of Jenny's lipsticks. Her mother said censoriously, "I did not say paint, Elsa — that is going a little far — but let it be for the present."

Elsa blushed and her father said, "Ah, so that is why my Elsa is looking so pretty this morning. Now, there remains only to get your hair wound up on bobbins, and the next thing you know —" He beamed and wagged a finger at her. "Ah ah now, be careful!" Elsa smiled in quiet rapture and ate a fine breakfast.

Arne Hansen hardly knew how it happened, but as he left the dining room the Lutzes were with him, he was walking beside Elsa, and

Frau Lutz was saying that a short turn around the deck might be very pleasant in the morning air — would he join them? He glanced back at Amparo like a man expecting the worst. She, with elbows on table, managed an impressive display of pantomime at high speed: pity for him or perhaps his stupidity, contempt for the Lutzes, warning, insult, false commiseration, and finally, just simple ridicule.

He turned away and lunged forward. The big plain girl at his side hung her head with her eyes so cast down she seemed to be asleep. The gay little procession advanced, but after one lap around Herr Lutz moved up abreast of Herr Hansen, and Frau Lutz walked with her daughter, it being quite clear that the young people were not making any headway in conversation.

Herr Lutz, whose mind, when not exercising its peculiar form of humor, stuck pretty consistently to the practical considerations of life, always led off his first talk with any stranger by inquiring how he got his living. The more unpretentious and immediate the means proved to be, the sooner the stranger established himself in Herr Lutz's esteem. He learned with delight that Herr Hansen had been in the dairy business in Mexico. "Ah ha," he exclaimed, "we go well together. I deal in bread, you in butter. I ran an inn near Lake Chapala, but you see, we have thought better of that. And how did you find the dairy business, in Mexico?"

"I found it so poor," said Hansen, "I sold out and am going back to Sweden. However, I made enough on the deal to start again at home, and there at least I shall know the tricks and know how to look out for them. In Mexico, they change the rules every day."

"Oh, there is only one rule everywhere," said Herr Lutz, expansive as if he were bringing a pleasant piece of news. "The big fish eat the little ones, and the little ones eat seaweed, maybe."

"Well do I know that," said Herr Hansen, joining Herr Lutz in a moderate laugh.

"I tell you what," said Herr Lutz, warmed by the young man's wonderful sense of humor, "let's all have one more little cup of coffee in the bar. Or maybe Elsa would like a glass of beer, eh?" he said slyly teasing. Frau Lutz frowned, Elsa turned dark red under her powder, and Hansen said quickly, "No, please let me invite you."

There followed a sociable little contest all the way to the table, but finally it was as Herr Hansen's guests that the Lutzes sat down to the morning beer.

"You being Danish," said Herr Lutz affably, after the first fine swig, "naturally you would be in the dairy business."

"I am Swedish," said Herr Hansen, patiently weary of this lifelong dullness on the part of foreigners who could not tell a Dane from a Swede or a Norwegian from either. "There is a slight difference."

"So? Well, myself being Swiss, naturally I am in the hotel business. From my great-grandfather to me, we had the same hotel in St. Gallen. But I was restless, a good living was not good enough for me, I must go and run a hotel somewhere else besides Switzerland. Switzerland, for me, was too peaceful. Ah, beautiful, picturesque, peaceful Switzerland, as the travel books say. That's true enough. But almost every week I got in the mail guidebooks and pamphlets from Mexico inviting solid businesslike foreigners to come to Mexico, invest their money and make their fortune."

"So did I," said Hansen. "Some of it was true."

"Not enough of it, though," said Herr Lutz. "Not a word about politics, not a whisper about revolution. Just all about beautiful scenery, beautiful weather, beautiful tourists with pockets bursting with beautiful money. Now then," he asked in some surprise, "wouldn't you think that I, a man weaned on those very things, would have said to myself, Why, we have all that here already. But only one thing wrong: there are many tourists in Switzerland, but also there are many, many too many hotels. The tourist trade did not always go around. We had dead seasons. There came those times when we were all prepared to hand out lavish hospitality and almost nobody came. In Mexico, the pamphlets said — serious, official, from the proper departments of government — all was better. No seasons, the suckers just poured in the year round. Cheap food, cheap labor, cheap rent, cheap taxes, cheap everything except the tourists. They were nearly all North Americans and you could charge them just what they were used to paying at home or even more. You could give them almost anything, they wouldn't know the difference. . . . Of course the pamphlets did not say this in so many coarse words, but I, a good hotelkeeper, could read between the lines. Even now, it sounds like Paradise on earth — well, we all know there is no such place. In Switzerland it was the Germans and the British and the French and the Spanish and the Central European Jews and oh, my God, in the old days the Russians who drove us to our graves. Also the political refugees from everywhere who arrived looking rich without a franc in pocket who were always expecting tomorrow huge sums of money . . . So, we started out, my wife and I with this Elsa here, who was a lump of a thing this high, in 1920 —"

Elsa fidgeted and clutched her beer glass. Hansen glanced at her briefly as if she were an inanimate object of no interest whatever, and away. Her mother tried anxiously to catch her father's eye, but failed. Herr Lutz was wound up in his story and talked only to Hansen.

"We told our families we were coming back millionaires, and they believed us. We promised to send back money in the meantime and make everybody rich. Truth is we never sent a centime. We were a year getting started, with finding a suitable place, arranging things with the government, bribing here and there, struggling with native labor — too long to tell, and you know all of it, anyway. But we did get a presentable little inn going, and yes, it was true, the tourists did come and they did pay well for everything. In 1920 there was revolution. Likewise in 1921, 1922; then counterrevolution in 1923 and '24: and so, revolution again, and so on, until now. At last we decided to go back to peaceful Switzerland. So you see? Well, maybe we can talk a little business. Send me tourists from your country and I will buy a few pounds of your best butter. We have butter too — we have everything in Switzerland but not quite enough . . ."

Herr Hansen then talked a little, obligingly, in turn, about the export business in butter and cheese, also eggs and bacon, strictly and minutely from the standpoint of the hazards and profits to be expected from it. Elsa, discouraged, was sure that Hansen did not talk about the butter business to Amparo. Well, it was a good thing he really did look crossgrained and hard to get along with. And he was as tiresome to listen to as her father. She was glad she did not like him, never had; she did not want him to like her, either, yet she was deeply wounded by his neglect, which seemed as if he meant to insult her. He was too old, anyway — at least twenty-eight.

She drew a deep weary breath and straightened up and turned her eyes away to the morning light on the glittering, dancing sea. Quietly she worked up in her mind a sound grudge against him, his poor manners, his awkward long legs and huge feet and furry light eyebrows. No, she wanted another kind of man altogether. Surely now her mother would be able to see that Herr Hansen, even without Amparo, would never be the right one. Not even just to dance with on a ship. No, she would never dance with him even if he asked her. But of course he never would . . .

There was a tall thin black-haired young student, with a dangerous eye as if he feared nothing and nobody on earth, who went leaping madly around the deck at the head of the line, shouting mysterious Spanish phrases — some kind of slang she could not make out. Once he had looked at her and leaned out towards her as they passed, smiling on one side of his face as if they had a secret together. His glance had shot like arrows into her eyes and he had gone on leaping and singing. That was the one for her. She leaned her face on the palm of her hand, hiding from the others, fearing that the warmth and sweetness that poured into her heart would show on her face.

"Elsa," asked her mother, anxiously, "what is the matter? Do you feel badly?"

"No, no, Mama, thank you," said Elsa, without taking her hands from her face, "the light is blinding."

That very student, as if Elsa had conjured him up, appeared in the bar; he was not leaping or shouting, but walking lazily with two others of his crowd. He was talking, though, and his voice carried to her buzzing ears. "La Cucaracha Mystica," he was saying, with a flourish of theatrical inflections, "the mystical cockroach herself, the queen of insects, is on board this ship, the very figure of rampant idealism. I saw her. She is here, pearls and all, a prisoner."

"La cucaracha, la cucaracha," chorused the others, as instinctively malicious as monkeys. They were halfway through the first verse, leaning towards each other and making dreadful harmonies, when the bugle sounded for the second breakfast sitting. With famine-stricken comic faces they turned as one and charged towards the dining room. As by then everyone on shipboard lived for food, there was the usual crowd milling at the top of the stairs, thinning out gradually into a procession.

At lunch, the Captain was seated at the head of his table, his napkin tucked into his collar and spread neatly over his rigid chest. Dr. Schumann, seated at the opposite side, was turning his water glass about absently. At sight of the ladies of the party they both rose. The Captain withdrew his napkin, made a deep bow and seated himself once more, tucking the napkin back under his chin.

Lizzi Spöckenkieker, at his left, giggled and blushed, eying him with coy intimacy. "Dear Captain, we met this morning, I believe!" she said, indiscreetly.

"We did indeed, my dear Fräulein," responded the Captain, with extreme formality. On his right, Frau Rittersdorf gave Lizzi a guarded look of warning and social censure, then turned her most charming smile upon the Captain, who rewarded her with a glimpse of his two front teeth and slightly upturned mouth corners. The others ranged round him, faces bent towards him like sunflowers to the sun, waiting for him to begin conversation.

"It is not usual for me to appear at table so early in the voyage," stated the Captain, as if he were reading an address, "since all my energies and attention must be devoted to the affairs of my ship. But I am happy to be able to say that in spite of a thousand difficulties and inconveniences which added together amounted to a state of emergency, never have I been able so swiftly and so effectively to dispose of them all. On a ship, no detail is trivial; the slightest laxity at any given point may lead to the gravest consequences. For this reason," he said, "usually I must deprive myself at intervals of the good company I enjoy at my table. But it is in the cause of your safety and comfort that I deprive myself," he told them, putting them forever in his debt.

Little Frau Schmitt blushed at her own boldness but managed to utter in a tiny voice, "Even if it is for our own good, we are also deprived."

Frau Rittersdorf was annoyed at this speech, which should have been made, certainly, but in much more elegant terms, with more manner, and not by Frau Schmitt, who by no means took precedence at that table. The Captain however seemed pleased. He bowed gently to Frau Schmitt. "You are very kind," he said, approvingly.

Herr Professor Hutten, without changing the conversation from its prime subject, the presence and authority of the Captain, shifted the emphasis from the feminine to the masculine domain by speaking in general terms of the importance of the science of navigation: "Of which, frankly I can do no less than admit, I know nothing," with the manly generosity of one who knows himself to be an authority in his own field, "yet it is of never-failing interest to me to observe how all science, as all art, is based firmly, immovably, upon mathematics. Without mathematics, where should we be for music, for architecture, for chemistry, for astronomy, above all for the scientific art of navigation, both on the sea and in the air? One may safely set it down as a rule that the better the mathematician, the better the navigator, the better the composer of music. Do you, my dear Captain, from the point of view of practical experience, find yourself in agreement with this rule?"

The Captain almost modestly admitted that his native aptitude for higher mathematics had been of great value to him as seaman. Professor Hutten went on to expand his ideas somewhat, from the purely philosophical view, while the others, more especially the ladies, listened in respectful silence, all except Frau Rittersdorf having lost the thread of discourse some time ago.

A slight but welcome interruption occurred when Wilhelm Freytag was heard again as usual to refuse the delicious Westphalia ham as appetizer. "Deviled eggs, then, sir?" asked the waiter, "or perhaps liver pâté?"

"Herring in sour cream," said Herr Freytag, "I think."

"Oh, Herr Freytag, are you a vegetarian?" asked Lizzi. "How interesting! How can you give up all these delicious sausages and bacon for breakfast and this delicious ham. You must try it with a slice of melon sometime. It is divine!"

Freytag, helping himself to a fine mound of fresh peas, said rather flatly, "Oh, no, I never eat pork at all," at which Frau Rittersdorf exchanged a lifted eyebrow first with the Captain, then with Frau Hutten, then with Herr Rieber, and her fleeting thought was returned to her in the quick gleam of their eyes from all three. Herr Rieber smiled broadly, wagged a finger at Freytag and remarked, "Aha! Observing the dietary laws, I suppose." At this improbable notion — or was it? — everybody laughed heartily and beamed upon Herr Freytag as a man who could take a friendly joke. They then exchanged a few customary remarks about the Jews and their incomprehensible habits, a sort of small change of opinion which established them once for all as of the same kind of people without any irreconcilable differences; and they settled down together comfortably prepared to change the topic; but their attention was directed to a rather noticeable commotion at the students' table.

The boys rose from their chairs and bowed in the direction of the stairs, and one of them shouted "*Viva!*" explosively. The woman who came in made them a formal little bow, very old-fashioned and learned in courtesy, then followed the steward to a small table where she sat alone with her back to the students. They sat down again exchanging odd malicious glances, elaborately wiping away smiles under their napkins.

She was perhaps fifty years old and she had been a fine beauty not so long ago. Her face was smooth and wax-colored, her small round mouth was painted bright red, the small, clever-looking black eyes were sketched in and lengthened with dark blue smudges, her lightly tinted reddish hair was cut short and curled around her forehead and ears. She was slender except for a lazy little belly, and her clothes were very expensive-looking; shabby as they were, they were still much too elegant for her present occasions. She wore enormous pearls in her ears, around her throat, on two fingers of her left hand. On her right she wore what appeared to be a light-colored much-flawed emerald, big as a robin's egg and surrounded by small diamonds. These hands, very narrow, fine, heavily veined, and old-looking, were in constant movement. Thumbs turned in lightly to the palm, the hands moved aimlessly from the edge of the table to her lap, they clasped and unclasped themselves, spread themselves flat in the air, closed, shook slightly, went to her hair, to the bosom of her gown, as if by a life of their own separate from the will of the woman herself, who sat quite still otherwise, features a little rigid, bending to read the dinner card beside her plate.

Everybody in the room turned to stare at her.

"But where," inquired Frau Rittersdorf of the Captain, "*where* does she come from? No one saw her come on board, nor in the town before that," she said, doubtfully, looking around the table, "at least, none of *us*."

"And no wonder," said the Captain, importantly. "That lady — she is a Spanish condesa — was brought on board quietly, hours before the other passengers, by two police officers who attempted at once to escort her to the steerage, under the impression that I was going to put her in chains for the voyage, or at least confine her to a cabin. I could not treat a lady so, no matter what she had done," said the Captain, and his eyes rested gently upon his passenger; indeed, they feasted themselves upon that personage, a real member of the nobility, a species seen all too rarely upon his modest decks. "I should somehow have managed to provide for her properly; but fortunately, friends of hers reserved her stateroom by cable to Mexico, when it was learned that she would sail on this ship."

"Her hands!" exclaimed Lizzi. "What is she doing with them?"

"She is in a highly wrought nervous state at the moment," said Dr. Schumann. "Pardonable in her situation, perhaps. She will feel better shortly." His tone and glance were dryly professional.

"A little on the faded side," said Herr Rieber, and instantly repented his tactlessness when seven pairs of eyes fastened upon him in rebuke.

"She is not young, true," said Dr. Schumann, "and her troubles are rather complicated — all completely unnecessary perhaps, but still . . ."

"Would I not be a dupe," asked the Captain, glancing sharply from face to face, "to take these Latin-American politicals seriously? I was told she is a dangerous revolutionist, an international spy, that she carries incendiary messages from one hotbed of sedition and rebellion to another, that she incites to riot — you would hardly believe all the nonsense. My own opinion is, she is one of these idle rich great ladies who like excitement, who get into mischief and make more mischief without in the least understanding what they do — this is always true of women in politics of any kind! — and she has got her fingers badly burnt. Well," his voice softened, "this will teach her a lesson, it is not for us to add to her penalties. She is only going to Tenerife, in any case. That is not so bad, and in the meantime, I wish her a pleasant voyage."

"Those students who greeted her with such apparent respect," said Herr Professor Hutten, thoughtfully, "resemble very little the revolutionary type as I have learned to recognize it in Mexico. I should have said of these that they are the lamentably overindulged sons of well-to-do parents who have not taken their parental duties very seriously. It is a type all too prevalent in Mexico, indeed, in all the Americas. One of our most constant problems," he said, "was to protect our German youth from their influence in our schools. I am happy to say, relying as we did on the infallible combination of German character and German methods of discipline, we enjoyed a modest success."

"In Guadalajara also," rejoined Frau Schmitt, "how often I have heard my dear husband deplore a state of affairs where our beautiful German children were exposed to the pernicious foreign customs."

"I had never imagined a revolutionist wearing such pearls," said Frau Rittersdorf, who had been thinking her own thoughts. "If, indeed, they are real, which is doubtful."

"When such a lady wears pearls," said little Frau Schmitt, respectfully, "I think we may be confident they are real."

"The students," said the Captain to Herr Professor Hutten, heading off this dangerous feminine diversion of the topic, "are on their way to complete their studies in Montpellier, since on account of the recent disturbances the University in Cuba has been closed over their heads.

It is all disorder of the most senseless kind, naturally, and should have been suppressed long ago without hesitation and with every necessary severity. As for revolutionists, they are a species of animal I am not acquainted with. I leave them gladly to those whose business it is to deal with them." Leaning his head low over his plate, ducking up and down rhythmically, he began to gulp his dinner.

The subject seemed closed, or suspended satisfactorily, on exactly the right note.

Jenny, who felt refreshed and good-tempered after her nap, in spite of her disturbing dream, told David what she had learned about La Condesa, and was surprised at his look of lively admiration as he watched the lady, who had grown calmer and was peering nearsightedly into her salad. "Who told you all this?" he asked, unwilling to believe anything Jenny said, however entertaining it might be.

"Wilhelm Freytag, this morning while we were walking around deck," said Jenny.

"Is it a habit by now?" asked David.

"This is only the second time," said Jenny. "I wish you'd look at the zarzuela troupe. Aren't they simply weird?" For some reason she could not admit the human existence of the Spanish company. They seemed to be life-sized dolls moved by strings, going gracefully through a perpetual pantomime of graceless emotions. Their frowning faces, their gestures of anger, ill-humor, mockery, contempt, all seemed too far-fetched and overrehearsed to be probable; she did not believe that any of it came out of living organisms.

The Spaniards had hardly removed their several gazes from La Condesa since she appeared, and their eyes were charged with staring, bitter resentment. They nudged each other and whispered, their mouths sullen; as they ate, or turned their heads, their eyes moved and maintained their gaze.

"If they're planning to rob her," said Jenny, "they will give themselves away long before the deed. That fellow they call Pepe hasn't been able to tear his eyes from her pearls once. And I really don't blame him — look, David darling, aren't they lovely?"

"They seem all right," said David, "but they could be pearls from the ten-cent store and I wouldn't know. I never saw a real pearl close up."

"Darling, you make yourself sound as if you'd had a pathetic childhood. Did you?"

"Yes, I damned well did."

"Well, you might at least admit they are beautiful."

"I'm not sure I think so," said David, "I'm so blinded with prejudice against people who can afford to buy pearls. They may be wonderful. I don't care."

"It's handsome of you to concede that much," said Jenny. "Really handsome."

"I'd perhaps like them better if I knew they weren't real," said David, idly, losing interest.

"Yes, darling," said Jenny, with sudden gaiety, "I know, that is just the kind of fellow you are — but would you like a sawdust woman instead of one with live insides? It is really strange," she said, "but I can love you and real pearls too — now how can that be?"

She smiled at him, he watched the smile change her face altogether for the better, and smiled back at her lovingly. They seemed beautiful to each other. "Are you calling me a fake?" asked David. Jenny said, "Besides, maybe she didn't buy them at all. Maybe she inherited them, or they were given to her by a lover."

"Maybe," said David, and a pleasant silence settled between them.

At the Captain's table, Frau Hutten observed that her husband was not eating well; indeed, he was manipulating his knife feebly, raising an ill-laden fork from time to time for appearance's sake only. His face was stern and pale, a light effusion appeared on his forehead. When the talk, rather aimless, drifted around to the Professor, it paused there uncertainly, went around him and was taken up on the other side. Halfway through her own lunch, which she was enjoying, Frau Hutten in one flash of a thought was annoyed with her husband — so reasonable a man where the problems of others were concerned, so wise and all-seeing in abstract ideas, he was no more than a willful child when it came to a question of his own good. She had helped him to their cabin two hours before, he had allowed her to stretch him flat and put cold towels on his head, and he had, in his temporary weakness, promised that he would be quiet and allow her to nurse him back to health.

Then without warning he had roused himself, had thrown away the towel and sat up, exclaiming in a loud, martial voice, "No, Käthe, this is a weakness of which I must be ashamed . . . it wants only a small effort of the will, and this shall be conquered . . ."

Frau Hutten, seeing that one of his stubborn fits was on the way, had tried to head it off, as if it were an escaping animal. "Ah, no!" she protested. "Here, Will does nothing for you. Let your Will rest for the moment, and make yourself comfortable. This is no time for the exercise of the higher faculties."

Her husband had not troubled even to answer such heresy. He had risen, squared his shoulders, drawn his brows together over his nose, and, at the sound of the bugle, had taken her arm firmly under his.

"Forward," he said, "let us breathe the fresh air and take our food as usual, and leave all such nonsense as seasickness to our good Bébé who has no intellectual resources to speak of — *il est chien de coeur*," he said, archly; they then both laughed, jovially, and went away laughing, and arrived in triumph at the table.

Now, unless they got away quickly, God knew what might happen. Losing her appetite so suddenly it left a great void that filled promptly with nausea, she did the one thing necessary to deceive her husband and persuade him from the table. "Excuse me," she said, standing up without looking at anyone, nodding around the table slightly. "My dear," she appealed to the Professor, "will you please go with me, I don't feel very well."

Herr Professor Hutten rose at once, backing stiffly away from his place, overturning his chair, which he hardly noticed. Frau Hutten had to brace herself strongly to support the weight of his assisting arm. There remained nothing to do but to go, as swiftly as possible, without another word. Not until their cabin door had closed upon them safely did Herr Professor Hutten fetch a loud hollow groan. He fell face downward on the couch, retching. Bébé crawled out of his corner towards him and licked his fallen hand more in duty than in pleasure; and Frau Hutten, overcome by the revolting sight, felt a dreadful chill down her spine. She fell back too, upon the bed, eyes closed.

"Käthe," called her husband, hoarsely, "Käthe, help me."

"Let me alone," she said heavily, through stiffened lips. By means of a slow surging movement, she rolled over and reached for the bell, which she pressed down and held steadily, not letting go until the door was opened and she heard sounds of rescue in the room. Conscience, duty, attentiveness, obedience — all the granite foundations of her marriage, her wifely career slid from under her without a sound, and she sank into a hideous luxury of moral collapse. Let somebody else wait on him hand and foot for a change. Let him do something for himself.

Let somebody even, for once, do something for her! She was sick of the world . . . she was sick to death of people . . . in a harsh gulping voice she demanded relief of the stewardess, whose rather amiably stupid, absent-minded face instantly chilled into hostility; and the hand that poked spoonfuls of crushed ice into Frau Hutten's open mouth was anything but gentle.

Dr. Schumann, strolling about the deck after lunch, paused to glance at the horse races, set up for the first time since Veracruz, and was indignant when he saw that, in spite of his express orders, the boy with the floating kidney had been put again at the job of moving the toy animals along the track. A small number of passengers were sitting about comfortably, their faces smooth and at ease, eyelids relaxed behind dark glasses, enjoying the sunlight and the sea air; but the boy sweated as he stooped and rose, straightening his lame back slowly, stooping again, with dark lines around his pale gray mouth, his eyes strained. The other boy was tough and able, but he kept his eyes down as if he were ashamed of his childish occupation.

Further along, Dr. Schumann saw the tall shrill girl and the little fat man, who seemed to be inseparable, playing ping-pong violently, and several persons were splashing about in the small canvas swimming tank set up on the lower deck. On the port side Dr. Schumann stepped carefully around a game of shuffleboard without observing the players, but nodding Good day in their direction; and saw, at the same time, almost without seeing, Ric and Rac, the two Spanish children, beguiling the ship's cat, a fine tiger tom, with back strokings and ticklings under his chin. The cat arched, his face full of sophisticated pleasure, and allowed himself to be picked up between them.

He was heavy, loose, ungainly in his surrender, and in his sensual trance he did not grasp the nature of their intentions towards him until it was almost too late. With sharpened faces and urgent hands, Ric and Rac lifted him to the rail and tried to push him overboard. He stiffened, dug his foreclaws into the rail, braced and clawed fiercely with his hind feet; his back went into a bow, his tail became a wild plume. Silently, desperately, he fought with all his weapons.

Dr. Schumann fairly leaped forward and seized the children back from the rail. They brought the cat with them in their rush; he fell out of their clutches and tore his way across deck straight through the shuffleboard game — a thing he would not ordinarily have done, for he was a polite cat. The children stared upward at Dr. Schumann, their bare arms, striped with long bleeding scratches, going suddenly limp in his hands.

Dr. Schumann, holding them firmly but with practiced gentleness, examined the depths of their eyes for a moment with dismay at their blind, unwinking malignance, their cold slyness — not beasts, though, but human souls. Oh yes, human, more's the pity, thought the Doctor, loosening his hold.

Instantly they wriggled free, their fierce little faces exactly alike except for the mysterious stigmata of sex, turning towards each other with their instinctive complicity; then they ran, their thin legs jutting at the knees, their tangled hair flying. He supposed they should have, as a matter of form, at least a few drops of iodine on those scratches, but he felt they would probably do as well without it.

He sat down carefully in the nearest chair, breathing as lightly and deliberately as he could, holding himself together with intent stillness. He had a very ordinary kind of heart trouble and might drop dead at any moment. He felt his pulse softly with two fingers, but he knew the count already; he knew exactly what was happening, what always did, or could, happen at the slightest shock or sudden movement: he had been over this rather dull case so often in the past two years there was nothing new to say or think; above all, alas, nothing new to be done.

He had always tried to avoid diagnosing and treating himself, he made a habit of consulting doctors he believed more able than he, he wished to believe in their procedures in his case, but he had not needed to be told what his trouble was. In the end, there was nothing in medical science related in his mind to what he knew about himself as physician, and what he felt about himself as a man in danger of death from one moment to the next. He sat with the fated calm of a man caught in a thunderstorm in an open space, rather humorously counting on a scale of chance he knew to be mythical. At last, cautiously, he felt in his inside pocket and brought out the small phial of crystal drops.

. . . The thing he could never explain to himself about this incident was this: knowing about himself such a simple daylight fact, with his orderly plan to live as long as he could on whatever terms he could make with his disease, he had endangered his life to save the life of a cat, a kind of animal he disliked by temperament; he was devoted to dogs. Given a moment for reflection, would he have leaped so and risked the stopping of his heart to save — even his wife? He had never been required to face that emergency, and the idea was an absurdity, of course — of course the answer was clear, that question had been settled long ago, or so he hoped. He smiled inwardly, with a composed face, at the thought of the cat, that supposedly most astute and self-possessed of all animals, being seduced within an inch of his life by a tickling of his nerve endings, the pleasant crackle of his own electricity along the fur of his spine. Nothing in his celebrated instincts had warned him that those stroking hands were willing to give him a moment of his private pleasure so that they might the more easily seize him by the scruff for their own satisfaction.

Perhaps that should not be surprising. It happened to others besides cats. Love! said the Doctor, surprised that the word should have popped into his thoughts. He put it out again at once, with a proper regard for its true meaning. He had spent the best years of his life — after all, he had prepared well for it, how else should he have spent them? — patching up the deceived, the foolhardy, the willfully blinded, the lover of suffering; and the most deadly of them all, the one who knew what he was doing and what he was bringing upon himself, and yet could not for anything resist one more fling at his favorite hot thrill of the flesh — drink, drugs, sex, food — whatever his particular concupiscence might be, though it might be his own death.

His own death, or my own death, I know it is of no importance, Dr. Schumann told himself, especially my own if I have made peace with it; he touched his wrist again with two fingers and waited. He longed so deeply to live, even merely to breathe, to move within his familiar body, to stay safely within himself, a place he knew as home, he could not control the warm wave of excitement which ran all through him as if he had drunk hot spiced wine. "My God," he said, and fixed his eyes attentively on the deep waves of the sea, turning upon each other endlessly, without thought, without feeling, moved by a power they obeyed in universal harmony. "My God, my God!"

Dr. Schumann believed in God, the Father, the Son and the Holy Ghost, and the Blessed Virgin Mother of God finally, in a particularly forthright, Bavarian Catholic way; and having spoken the Name which included all the rest, he closed his eyes, gave himself over to the hands of mercy, and became soothed and quiet. Deliberately he removed his fingers from his pulse, ignored the beat of his heart upon his eardrums, and for a few seconds his whole being reconciled itself almost completely to the prospect of death, despising briefly, but with satisfaction, the cowardice of the flesh. He realized then that the drops were working, as they had worked before, as they might again and again work; that the attack, a light one, was passing over; he had escaped once more. He opened his eyes and crossed himself unobtrusively, noticing at the same time an arresting scene about twenty feet away.

La Condesa was talking to a young sailor. He was a very attractive-looking fellow, with a fine show of manly muscles in shoulders and arms, his cap sitting forward over an ingenuous sunburned face with a broad mouth and slightly snubbed nose. He stood perfectly straight with his hands at his sides, but his head was inclined away, and he looked past La Condesa with an occasional quick, uneasy glance at her. His back was to the rail, he was almost touching it, and La Condesa stood before him, talking very intently but slowly, spreading her arms as if she would bar his way. Her thumbs were turned in flat to her flattened palms, which moved in a monotonous beat; her eyes were like agates, and she swayed from side to side, stretching her neck, trying to force the boy to look her in the face. His head turned from her, far to one side and then in a slow swing back again, nodding slightly always as if in deferential agreement, but full of shame and confusion. La Condesa patted him on the arm, at which he leaped as if touched by a live electric wire-end. His hand flew to his cap in automatic salute, he stepped past her and seized his bucket and brush, and made off in a long stride, his ears a burning red, leaving La Condesa standing. After a moment she walked slowly in the same direction, her neck and spine very straight, her hands clenched at her sides.

Dr. Schumann, finding himself of at least three minds in the matter, that is, simple human curiosity at this freakish behavior, an unwilling admiration for the woman, who struck him as unusually beautiful, and that professional interest which had become second nature in him, rose and followed her at a good distance, keeping the appearance of being on a casual promenade.

Within the next hour, the Doctor had seen enough to make him very thoughtful. Wherever she saw a man alone, any sort of man so long as he was young, the Doctor observed with a good deal of moral disapproval, whether sailor or officer or passenger, she backed him into a corner, or against a wall, or rail, and somehow managed to pin him there, standing before him and talking always in the same intimate way, as if she were imparting some agonizing secret with which they would be bound to sympathize.

The effect on the several different young men was astonishingly similar. They began with polite listening expressions deepening rapidly to surprise, pained embarrassment, then to utter restlessness. Their faces would freeze in strange smiles, their eyes would begin to roam seeking a way out. At last in some pause in her uneasy flow of words, or suddenly as if signaled from afar, they would break away, no matter how.

Dr. Schumann never came near enough to hear what she was saying, but her gestures shocked him deeply, modest man that he was. She stroked her own breasts and thighs, patted the face of her listener, laid her hand upon his heart. Yet the expression of her face was grief-stricken, her words seemed grave and hopeless. "Perhaps I am not young enough to attract her eye," Dr. Schumann thought a little acidly, "I am no doubt much too far from the cradle for her," but he decided deliberately to put himself in her path. He had a powerful sense of time and its effects on the human organism, and he felt that man owed it to his own dignity to live with philosophy within the limitations of his own time in the world.

All other considerations aside, he reflected, there was something scandalous and perverse in older persons, especially women, who at their very best showed always disturbing signs of innate perversity, turning back to youth for sexual satisfactions: unnatural parents devouring their own young — a species of incest, in short, to put a severe word upon it. . . . Well, he would see. It was obvious the woman suffered from some acute form of nervous disorder; she should not be traveling alone, her situation as prisoner itself proved her irresponsibility, and she must be friendless indeed. That was the first, the most dreadful effect of even a simple "breakdown" — the loss of human love and sympathy, the literal alienation from the common life of one's fellow beings. Madness, he considered, having never separated the practice of his medical science from his theological beliefs, was the temporary triumph of Evil in the human soul; he had never seen mania assume any but ignoble shapes. Let science do what it might, there was a mystery in the destiny of man beyond fathoming except in the light of divine revelation; at the very bottom of life there is an unanswerable riddle, and it is just there, concluded Dr. Schumann, his softened eyes still observing La Condesa, just there, where man leaves off, that God begins.

La Condesa disappeared, walking rather fast, around the upper end of the deck, and Dr. Schumann turned through the bar and emerged on the opposite side intending to approach her slowly. But at sight of her, three of the Cuban students left their shuffleboard and swarmed about her. She put on a new air for them, gentle, graceful, indulgent. They fell in step with her and with each other, and fairly outdid themselves in deference and attentiveness to her. She was talking as they passed Dr. Schumann, and he caught a few words in her frail, complaining voice: "Hunted like beasts, my children, my children, my lovely ones, and they ran away to sleep in the woods . . . and I could only wait and suffer, suffer and wait — I could not lift a hand for them —" Her hands flew up and described a whirling ring around her head. "But they were right to revolt, they were right, my children, even if they die for it, or I must die, or be in exile. . . ."

The students put on faces of exaggerated melancholy. She smiled at them blindly with frowning brows. One of the students fell back a pace or two, and boldly with crassest impudence he winked at Dr. Schumann and swiftly tapped his forehead with a forefinger. He got in return a stare of such stony severity it abashed even him and he made haste to catch up with his gang. Dr. Schumann looked at his watch, drew a careful slow breath, feeling oppressed in flesh and spirit, and decided to lie down quietly for the rest of the afternoon.

Lizzi Spöckenkieker and Herr Rieber were having a very fast game of ping-pong, which had begun lightly and at once developed into a duel. They smashed the little ball back and forth over the net, crack pop pop crack, their strokes speeding up shorter, faster, their faces darkening with blood, until both grimly, silently, struck like automatons. It was a matter of life or death to win and they were smiling no longer. La Condesa with her three students who were singing "La Cucaracha" bore down upon them suddenly at Lizzi's back, sailed by her without a pause or glance; but Lizzi faltered, her eyes flashed aside, and Herr Rieber won, at last.

"Ah, shame!" screamed Lizzi, and running around the table with long strides she cracked the triumphant Herr Rieber over his bald head with her little paddle. "Ah, if it had not been for that crazy woman and those stupid boys — they — they — Oh why must things like this always happen to me?"

Herr Rieber ducked and sidestepped; indulgently he soothed her: "Come now, even the best of us must lose sometime. Let's not mind so much. Remember, it is the playing of the game that counts, not winning!"

"You can talk," cried Lizzi, lifting her paddle again. Deftly he seized her wrist, brought her hand down to his mouth and imprinted a large, juicy kiss upon it. "There now," he said, "what a quick pretty hand it is and it shall be much quicker the next time. Don't mind not winning from me. I am ping-pong champion of the *Sportsverein* in Mexico City now three times over."

"I can believe it," said Lizzi, calming down a little. "I am not used to losing at this game."

Herr Rieber twinkled instantly with immense meanings. "At what game then *do* you lose?"

Lizzi shook his elbow violently. "If you talk like that I shall leave you!" she threatened, tossing her head like an unmanageable mare. "No, I shan't listen to such things or answer them."

"Clever girl," cried Herr Rieber, "nothing escapes you. Now suppose we take a little swim and cool off, unless of course you want to beat me *again*," he said with infinite slyness, "at ping-pong or at any game at all — any game you choose?" He squeezed her arm with such warmth that Lizzi blushed.

"No no, let's swim," she said, her voice rising, "ah, we must have a race!"

At six o'clock a steward brought Dr. Schumann a message from La Condesa, saying she was ill and must see him at once. A stewardess, waiting outside La Condesa's cabin, knocked rather loudly when she saw the Doctor approaching, and moved as if to follow him in.

"You may go, thank you," said La Condesa to the stewardess, in the metallic quiet distant voice of a woman skilled in handling servants whom she hated and who hated her, and she looked a shade to the right of the stewardess as if she were already not there. The woman, trained in the same school, backed out at once with her eyes fixed on a point in air about the height of the washbasin.

The air of the cabin was thick with Turkish cigarette smoke, a mixture of heavy scents, and ether. Expensive-looking, badly worn luggage was spread about open, with shoes, evening wraps, improbable hats, wrinkled soiled fine gloves, and pale-colored unbotanical flowers of crumpled silk and shattered velvet tumbling out on all sides in a confusion past ordinary remedy. La Condesa was in bed, a faded pink satin bedgown falling off her white shoulders, barely veiled in thin violet-colored stuff. She sat up staring, opened her mouth without speaking, her clasped hands snapped apart and flew backward, forward, backward again, and she gasped at last, "You must help me, I believe I am going to die!"

Dr. Schumann summoned his calmest and most reassuring air, laid his palm on her forehead as though she were a child, and said, "I don't think so, at least not just yet."

She bowed her head upon her raised knees and broke into a kind of sobbing, a crying complaining voice full of incoherent words, but, Dr. Schumann observed, without tears. He sat beside her and began to remove various contrivances from the black instrument case he carried. She stopped crying and peered into its depths with instant curiosity. He took advantage of her silence to ask her some plain necessary questions about her bodily functions and she answered plainly and sensibly. When, however, he asked her to take off her bedgown and lower her nightdress over her shoulders and back, she simply sat and looked at him with a provocative flicker in her black eyes, and began to smile with sly glee; she sat quite still, smiling so, while he removed them himself. She lifted her arms to help him with the sleeves, but that was all.

He counted her pulse and listened to her heart and breathing, setting his ear firmly to her breast and shoulder blades, noting her long thin delicate bones. He flashed small white lights into her eyes, and took her blood pressure. He caused her to breathe deeply and say oh and ah several times while he peered down her throat with another little light. He tapped her ribs front and back rather sharply with two fingers, kneaded her stomach in careful exploration, fetching a slight sigh from her. "Clench your fist, please," he told her, and took some blood in a tiny glass pipe from the thin blue vein of her inner arm. Her dilated eyes gradually became calmer, she lay back at last with hands and shoulders flat and still, gazing at him as if she were rather pleasurably hypnotized, and said in an entirely changed voice, "All these charming attentions are making me deliciously sleepy, dear Doctor. Perhaps I only needed a human touch after all those interrogations and those military police. They are very heavy-handed."

She breathed out lightly with her mouth open, and the smell of ether on her breath was very strong. The Doctor leaned towards her to speak, concealing his moral disgust at the discovery he had made in the first few seconds of the interview.

"You don't need stimulants," he said gravely, taking one of her wrists and holding it lightly, "nor narcotics, either. Whatever you may need," he said, his forehead gathering in a frown, "it is not ether. What a debased sort of habit for a woman like you! Why do you waste my time calling for me? So far as I am able to see, you are not sick at all," he told her, severely; "you are in enviably good condition, organically quite sound. How old are you?"

"Old enough as you can see," she said. "Much too old."

"Perhaps fifty?"

"When you guess so well," she said, "you deserve to be told you are right. Fifty, then."

"That does not seem so great an age to me now," said Dr. Schumann. "I should be pleased enough to be fifty again."

"Ah, I would not be a day younger for anything. Believe me, there is not one day of my dreadful life I would live again . . . or so I think now. What shall I do? Where shall I go? What is to become of me? I am exiled," she said, sitting up again, and beginning to weave and sway, "my husband is dead . . . my husband, thank God, is dead," she repeated without levity, "but my two sons, my children, they are fugitives somewhere — here, now, while we are here talking comfortably, sheltered in this mean ship, but sheltered! my sons are . . . where do they sleep at night, who befriends them, who gives them food, where are they — when shall I see them again? My house was burned too," she went on in a lifeless voice as if she were reading a dull page aloud, "and my beastly servants all ran away, looting as they went — money, silver, clothes, furs, anything, whatever they had coveted; they scattered out of the gates like the cattle they are. Every face I saw then was the face of someone who no longer regarded me as a human being. . . ." Her hands began to dance, her lips drew back over her teeth, she struggled to get out of bed and knocked the instrument case to the floor.

"Wait," said Dr. Schumann. He rose, picked up the black case, and began to prepare a small hypodermic needle. She became silent at once and watched him with her air of easily distracted attention.

"This for tonight," he explained, "only. And you must not take any more ether. Where do you hide it? I shall take it away with me."

She motioned towards one of the sprawling pieces of luggage. "It is all there somewhere."

He pinched up the flesh of her arm, and at the slight stab of the needle she shuddered and said, "Ah, how delicious. How I love drugs, any kind of drug, to wake me or to make me sleep, I adore them all. You should praise me a little, because I do not, ever, take all the kinds of drug I should like. It would be so easy, so easy . . ."

She dropped back among the pillows, and Dr. Schumann rummaged carefully among the disorder of the suitcase, bringing up a flask of ether.

"Is this all?" he asked. "I expect you to tell me the truth."

She prolonged her silence, waiting to be cajoled, but he said nothing more. He went over to the washbasin and emptied the flask. The fumes rose in his face and he coughed. "You have taken too many drugs of one kind and another," he said, "say what you please."

"Don't scold," she said, "you have not told me what is to become of me, with or without them."

"With your good health," said Dr. Schumann, "I could wish you a sufficient settled income and some reconciliation with society. And nothing more could happen to you."

"How dull," she said, blankly.

"Maybe," said Dr. Schumann, "for one of such specialized tastes."

"Here is the difference between you and me. I do not intend to reconcile myself with a society I despise. Yet it was not I who quarreled with society, but my sons — I was content to despise it. It was my sons who turned me out into this world. . . . Look, I have such good health as you say. But no income at all. A prisoner on her way to a dreary island in the Canaries . . ."

"I do not find Santa Cruz de Tenerife so bad," said the Doctor, comfortingly.

"You have not been deported there," said La Condesa. "Cuba, God knows, is dull enough, but Santa Cruz! No, don't try to console me. . . . You know what? You sound to me like a man with money in the bank, entire personal freedom, all you want — and your health is perhaps not so good? How right am I?"

"Right enough," said Dr. Schumann, sitting beside her again. "Where is the rest of the ether?"

"You can see how useless, how unkind really, it will be for you to give me good advice," she said, stroking his hand that lay on his knee near her. "But don't stop giving it. Don't go away. I love your good advice, I love to hear you scold and see you frown straight into my eyes, as if you meant it just for me — as if you cared what happened to me. I should like being dull for a little while. I promise to stop taking ether, at least for this voyage. I do this for you, not for myself. I know I will begin again afterward. . . . I tried everything, anything at all, in the end ether seemed best, vulgar as you seem to think it! A lovely excitement without pain. Have you ever taken it?"

"No."

"You must try it sometime," she said, in a drowned voice. "The other flask is in the red leather dressing case."

"It is time for you to sleep," said Dr. Schumann, and he laid her hand back at her side. "I shall send the stewardess now, and I shall see you again tomorrow."

"What is this heavenly drug I have now?" asked La Condesa, her eyes closing slowly. "I don't recognize it; is it something new?"

Dr. Schumann gave a short laugh, at which she opened her eyes shining with delight upon him. "Do you expect me to tell you?" he asked, as if he were speaking to an obstinate child.

"You laughed," she said, tenderly, "I never heard you laugh before! But never mind, I'll try to guess this drug, or maybe you will give it to me again. . . . I adore you," she said, "you are such a preposterous good moral dull ridiculous man, but charming, charming!"

Her eyes closed again, she lifted both hands and slowly stroked her small breasts upward, and her expression, especially about the mouth, quite startled Dr. Schumann. He shook her shoulder with careful violence. "Look at me," he said sternly, "stop that nonsense!" Her hands fell back and her face turned to one side. He stood almost holding his breath watching her sink into sleep as into the bottomless pit — he touched her pulse lightly, and almost feared to leave her. He gathered up his black case and turned away resolutely, stopped himself from saying "Good night," and opened the door.

The dank air of the passageway struck upon him as a fresh breeze after the fetid sweetness and rot of the cabin. He instructed the waiting stewardess and returned to his quarters, feeling unpleasantly exhausted and freshly apprehensive about his own condition. He lay down with his rosary in his fingers, and began to invite sleep, darkness, silence, that little truce of God between living and dying; he put out of mind, with deliberate intention to forget forever, the last words of that abandoned lost creature; nettles, poisoned barbs, fish-hooks, her words clawed at his mind with the terrible malignance of the devil-possessed, the soul estranged from its kind.

On the second evening out from Havana, with twenty-odd days to go, the ship's commissary began doling out the modest pastimes and amusements of the voyage in the attempt to make life on shipboard resemble a perpetual children's party on land. Dinner was "gala," so the dinner card read, and fresh flowers appeared on every table. Be-side every plate were small gilded paper snappers with noise-making machines inside, and comic paper hats for everybody. Several of the women wore dinner gowns; beer foamed in great steins; waiters twirled bottles of Rhine wine in ice pails, with a flourish.

Herr Glocken and William Denny, sitting together, put on their clownish hats first, grinned around vaguely and received a vague grin or two in return. Hats then bloomed on many heads; small colored balloons floated about over tables, tossed from hand to hand, now and again exploding to the noise of rattles and tin whistles. The band struck up "Tales from the Vienna Woods," and continued with Strauss waltzes to the end. Dinner was going to be treated as a social event, so the voyagers seemed to agree, even if on the most provisional terms. There was a great deal of laughter and calling out of toasts between tables, and the Spanish dancing troupe leaned over and lifted their glasses to the Captain, who responded with a stony face but an elegant bow, raising his own in acknowledgment, setting it down again and seeming to put the whole thing out of mind.

Herr Baumgartner had got a false beard with his hat, and he sent two small children at the next table almost into fits of joy with his trick of making it waggle up and down, like a goat's beard. The children, a boy of five and a girl of three, were peaceably waiting for food with their parents, Cubans who had embarked at Havana. Hans, the Baumgartners' timid child, was enchanted with these chil-dren, such a change from Ric and Rac, who could terrorize him with just a glance. He had been hanging shyly around these new pas-sengers without daring to speak, but now, by means of his amusing father, he saw his chance to make friends with them.

Herr Baumgartner quite outdid himself with fascinating devices, and the children squealed and giggled and peeped through their fingers most flatteringly. Hans made himself laugh louder and longer than he wanted, to bring himself to their attention. "Eat your dinner, though, Hans," said his mother after a while, "and we shall play some more afterwards."

Her husband disregarded this hint. He pushed the beard up to the middle of his forehead, parted it like a curtain and said "Boo!" The children screeched with delight and the parents smiled indulgently. Herr Baumgartner pulled the beard down under his chin and pushed the paper hat far back on his head. The children still laughed. Frau Baumgartner took a morsel of food and set about cutting up the roast duck on Hans's plate. She did not altogether trust his table manners in public for such things. Nearly eight years old and yet so awkward with his knife and fork — it made her feel that she was not a good mother. "Eat while it's hot," she told him. Observing her husband uneasily, she reflected that his great weakness was a lack of the sense of propriety, or the limits of things. He simply never knew when to stop — drinking, making faces, anything. Her heart sank as she perceived that now in a split second he would go too far, and he did. He pushed the beard up under his eyes, dragged his hat forward, agitated the beard fiercely, growled like a lion, maybe, or a bear, and it was too much. Hans, his mouth half-open to receive food, stopped and smiled uncertainly; the other little boy laughed in a quavering artificial tone; but the baby girl was too young to pretend anything, and she gazed in growing terror, then burst into tears. Lamentably she wept "Ay, ay, ay," her flooded eyes fixed unbelievingly on the sight that had been so jolly suddenly turned dreadful without warning. The young mother, with a quick sharp exclamation at Herr Baumgartner, took the child on her lap and pressed the crumpled face against her breast; the young father leaned forward to lay a tender hand upon his frightened baby.

Frau Baumgartner said, "Oh, I am so sorry," and her tone, her manner, shut out her husband. Her eyes signaled to the other woman, You see how it is, please do not blame me . . . as woman to woman, as a mother who knows all that can happen, I beg of you. . . .

The young mother gave her back the guarded look of an indifferent stranger, refused confidences, rejected implied kinship of feeling, and managed a deprecating small smile and nod as if to say, This is nothing — and thinking all too clearly, Except perhaps a little stupid, and what trouble you are making for us!

Herr Baumgartner swept the hat and beard from him, cast it utterly away to the floor like a man in a play, his face tormented with remorse. "Oh dear sir!" he addressed the father in German, "I meant only to amuse the little ones." The young father nodded, made a light gesture of waving away all misunderstandings, then exchanged a troubled glance with his wife, for they knew no German. Herr Baumgartner would have persisted, in Spanish, but his wife halted him. "Don't," she said, "don't. You have said and done enough. They understand perfectly, and if they choose to pretend they don't at least please keep your dignity."

This completed the ruin of what was left of Herr Baumgartner's self-esteem. "Ah, good God," he said, "has it come to this with me, that I cannot even play with a little child without frightening it? Hans, you were not frightened, were you? Your poor father hoped only to hear you laugh!"

"I laughed," said Hans, with a manly air, comforting his father. His mother said, "Of course you laughed, because it was very funny. Little babies always cry for everything. You cried when you were a little baby," she told him, so convincingly Hans forgot for a moment all the crying he had done since.

His father ate in silence as if his food were bitter medicine to him, and the three of them fell silent. Hans felt that his mother was being particularly gentle and that she smiled at him too tenderly, too often. It worried him to have to smile back every time, for he felt he was taking her side against his father, and he did not want to take sides. His father went on looking at him so kindly too, with his familiar sad face, poor good Vati; until Hans could bear it no longer, but turned his head from them both, unhappy and lonely and lost. The children at the next table had forgotten the whole thing and were playing with their balloons and rattles and hats while their mother and father fed them from spoons and forks and buttered their bread for them, and none of them gave Hans another look or thought. The little crybaby of a girl was having the best time of all.

The festival spirit seemed to go on thriving more or less. The diners followed the band on deck, where the Strauss waltzes sang to the stars above the sound of the waves. The ship rolled gently, the heavy cooling winds whipped skirts and scarfs about, hair became ruffled but faces were smoother, and the slow great waves folding back from the ship's side were alive with lazy green fox fire. A gauzy new moon sailed downward swiftly.

"It's so *heavenly*, David," said Jenny. "How I wish you would dance."

But David did not dance, and he had a not-heavenly name for dancing, a byword of contempt which offended Jenny, who had danced a distance perhaps twice around the globe. "And my mind was never purer than then," she told him; "I wish I had worn one of those measuring things on my ankle — then I could tell you exactly how many miles I have traveled when I was happiest!"

They enjoyed the light of the starry sky and the glow of the seaweed-colored deck, and breathed in the fine weather, but Jenny was restless, wanting to dance; so David, with a tight, obstinate face, left her and went in the bar. A few minutes later he looked out and it was as he had expected: she was dancing with Freytag.

The whole scene was filled with spinning figures whirling like cheerful dervishes in the Viennese style. Mrs. Treadwell, dressed in some kind of airy yellow stuff, was dancing with a young officer; Arne Hansen with the Spanish dancer they called Amparo. The absurd Herr Rieber clung as usual to the tall, awkward, ugly Lizzi; he was as light as a rubber ball on his feet, and spun and whirled with the equilibrium of a top, guiding Lizzi in rings around the others. These others were married pairs mostly, though the Lutzes and the Baumgartners sat the evening out. Two of the Cuban students danced with Pastora and Lola, while the male Spanish dancers sat in the bar and kept out of their way.

David's attention was fixed on those who were not dancing: the born outsiders; the perpetual uninvited; the unwanted; and those who, like himself, for whatever sad reason, refused to join in. He ranged himself with all of them; they were his sort, he knew them by heart at sight. That big Elsa for one, sitting with her parents, drooping, unable to conceal her yearning, her disappointment, her fear of being left out. "I would dance with you," he told her, but she would never hear him say it. Herr Glocken, huddled on the foot of a deck chair near the band, his face in his hands, his paper hat over one eyebrow, sat motionless listening but not seeing.

The dying man in his chair was drawn to the rail, wrapped in shawls and rugs to the throat, asleep perhaps; the boy Johann, his nephew who attended him, leaned his arms on the chair handle, with the look of an outcast dog for longing and hopelessness. David felt he knew all of them well. For himself, he refused to join in, to take part, because he knew well there was no place for him and nothing that he wanted anywhere — not at that price, he said, loathing the milling herd whirling past the window.

The Mexican bride and groom, he noticed, were not dancing. They were strolling together, came upon the scene and paused there, amiable, distant, like charmed visitors from another planet. They did not dance or put on paper hats or drink or play cards or grin at other people. They did not even talk much to each other; but they were paired, that was clear. This silence, this isolation, this ceremonial exclusion from their attention of all but their love and their first lessons in each other, seemed natural, right, superb to David. He surmised in them gravity and severity of character; under their beauty there lay the promise of dryness and formality in time; but the marriage would last, they were joined for good. As he imagined their characters and the nature of their marriage, which was the kind he believed he would want for himself, Jenny went dancing by again with Freytag. They were spinning gaily as one body, but their faces were only two fatuous masks. David, who considered sexual jealousy as a piece of nonsense beneath his notice, felt again that familiar hot wave of repulsion against Jenny's lack of discrimination, her terrible gregariousness, the way she was always ready to talk to anybody anywhere, join up with any sort of party, go anywhere she was invited, take up with the most gruesome assortment of loons and clowns and thugs and drunks and perverts, and male model types like this Freytag. "To hell with it!" said David aloud, feeling more bitterly trapped than usual.

He returned to the bar and drank a whiskey neat, then another. Denny was there, and David had seen him hanging around uneasily on the edge of things too, but he could not take Denny into his sympathies. No, Denny was on the outside for the wrong reasons. He would follow and leer at the Spanish dancing girls — or rather, at Pastora — but none of them would have him. They had found him out. He would not buy them drinks, he would not come to any terms with them — he wanted his pleasures for nothing, the kind of man who should be whipped with scorpions and made to pay well for it. He honed and hankered, that was obvious, but not to the extent of a five-dollar bar bill, which might lead to nothing, or to more expense in the long run, and nothing gained either. The girls had got in the way of snapping their eyes at him in contempt as they passed; a little more and they would be flipping their petticoats from the back at him, they had so low an opinion of him. They also fully intended that one of them, no matter which one, should certainly pick his pockets clean before the voyage ended.

Denny was drinking steadily with a firm purpose. "I aim to be stinkin' before this here night is done," he promised solemnly. "Come on and get in the game."

"It's as good as any," said David; and for a fact, Denny was just the one to get drunk with. No pretensions, no fooling around, no chatter, just a slow deliberate premeditated wallow to the finish. Fine, that would be just fine. David downed his third whiskey, and the small nagging dig of uneasiness, not quite pain, in that blank hungry spot just between his forward ribs, began to ease up a little. He intended to drink until no matter what happened he shouldn't be able to remember one thing tomorrow morning.

Arne Hansen and Amparo ended their dance, a rather monotonous swing-around accommodated to Hansen's awkwardness, within arm's reach of Elsa, and Elsa gazed from under puzzled eyebrows at Amparo, trying to find the secret. There was no secret that Elsa could see, or admit: Amparo was beautiful in a slatternly too-dark sort of way, but she made no smallest attempt to be agreeable; she had a sulky, unsmiling face, she hardly spoke, she seemed even a little bored and out of temper. Hansen, Elsa observed with satisfaction, danced like a bear. He kept his attention set upon Amparo as if she might disappear if he looked aside for a moment. Amparo carried and waved freely a black lace fan with a red cotton rose pinned over a torn place. Anybody with eyes in his head could see why the rose was there — anybody could see! Amparo, her hips rocking, walked over and said something to Pastora, who left the deck and went in the bar to take a message to Pepe. Then Amparo walked away slowly without looking back, and Hansen took off after her with long steps. Frau Rittersdorf, who had just danced with the purser, a hugely fat, fatherly-looking fellow with a dumpling face and walrus mustaches, found herself standing near Mrs. Treadwell. She nodded, her mouth prim, towards the retreating figures. Hansen had overtaken Amparo, had seized her arm, they were hurrying away together.

"I don't think that is a very pretty sight," she observed. Mrs. Treadwell turned a too-innocent face upon her and asked, "Why not? I think they look very well together!"

Pepe sat late alone, over a half bottle of red wine. Ric and Rac, Tito, Pancho, Manolo, Pastora, Concha, and Lola had finally deserted him. The band stopped playing, the dancers dispersed, lights were dimmed in the salon and on deck; sailors came out with their buckets and brushes; the man at the bar was obviously closing up for the night. Cigarette ends were stacked high in the tray before him, though the waiter had emptied it twice. Swallowing his last drop of wine, Pepe lighted another cigarette and strolled outside once around, and then, cautiously as a cat, descended into the depths of the ship. Lingering there, patrolling the corridor, at last he saw Arne Hansen come out looking as if he had dressed in a hurry, enter the passage almost at a run and disappear around the far corner as if the police were after him.

Pepe advanced then softly, opened the cabin door, and found Amparo as he expected, in her black lace nightgown, counting her money, in substantial-looking American banknotes, and a sizable lot of them. He put out his right hand palm up, rubbing thumb and forefinger together humorously as if this were an old joke between them. Instead of giving them to him as she usually did, she tossed them into the washbasin, where he had to pick them out for himself.

David Scott and William Denny woke from drunkenness with shattering headaches, eyes that would not focus properly, and sunken stomachs. Herr Glocken in a trembling voice was asking for his morning medicine and water as if he had been asking at intervals for a good while. Denny groaned loudly and thrashed about in the upper berth. David rolled off the couch and ministered to Herr Glocken, whose hand shook as it closed round the tumbler. Instantly his medicine was down, he gave David a proud, lopsided smile. "I drank too much," he said, and dropped back behind the curtain.

David, brushing his hair, noted with sickening anxiety the thin line of glossy skin at the top of his forehead where, at twenty-six years, his hairline was slowly but fatally, visibly receding. Years might pass before it happened once for all, but there would come a day, an unspeakable day, when he would be bald, as his father and his grandfathers and his great-grandfathers were before him. No earthly power could avert it. He knew because he had tried everything. He had been guilty of buying every kind of hair tonic and salve and fancy shampoo and massage device any barber wished to sell him. At great damage to his Pennsylvania Quaker conscience, he had committed methodically the two greatest sins possible (or so he had understood it as a child, from precept and example): he had spent on frivolities money meant for better purposes, and he had pampered his bodily vanity. Not that he gave a damn, as he was fond of assuring himself; but those tight-mouthed, tight-handed, tight-souled old gaffers had left some kind of poison in his blood that kept him from ever really enjoying his life, and besides, he was going to be bald. Still he blushed at having been such a dupe as to think, for example, that a hairbrush operated by electricity was going to destroy the genes of all those bald-headed ancestors. His inevitable baldness, then, he jotted down as one more grudge against his mother, who had never shown any judgment as a mother, certainly, and least of all in her choice of the father of her children. His father had not only been prematurely bald, he was flighty, irresponsible, unfaithful openly in low ways, incapable of even the lowest form of loyalty to anything or anybody. He had the Quaker tendency to count his pennies, but that was all. He had finally looped out with a girl half his age, and nobody ever caught up with him, or even ever heard of him, again.

He left his wife a letter, though, saying that this new love was not based on mere physical attraction, as his marriage and many affairs had been, but was a matter of deep spiritual and intellectual interest as well, something too high and beautiful for his wife to understand. He did not expect her to understand it, and was not going to try to explain any further. It was Good-by, and Good Luck!

David was nine years old at the time, and had already thought often how pleasant life could be if it were not for his father being around all the time. Now his disappearance seemed to David no less than a wonderful stroke of divine Providence, the source from which he had been informed all blessings arrived. His mother had taken the whole thing quite differently. "Spiritual!" she had said violently, as if it were an unclean word. Then she said to David, "Here is the kind of father you've got," and read the letter in a high strained voice to him; standing in the middle of the floor with her chin thrown back and her eyes closed with the tears streaming, she had nearly laughed her head off. Then she sat down and almost embarrassed him to death by seizing him, a big bony lank boy, and dragging him onto her lap, where she cradled him as if he were a little baby, rocking back and forth sobbing as if she would never stop. It had all made him so sick he threw up his supper, and afterward he got very sleepy; but woke in the night with the most terrifying feeling of pure desolation. Quietly, secretly, he cried bitterly too, cried himself to sleep again in his dampened pillow smelling of old feathers.

In the midst of brushing his hair, David vomited suddenly into the washbasin. Furtively with shame he scrubbed the bowl, thinking that his hair tonic was as bad as Denny's patent medicines and laxatives and sleeping pills. He turned away from the sight of his hangdog face in the mirror, and the dreadful muddled feeling of moral self-reprobation which Jenny called a Methodist hangover clutched him, not for the first time, in the vitals.

He had done something ridiculous last night, what was it? He remembered Jenny's face somewhere along the evening, her eyes very brightly cold; she was closing a door in his face — what door, and where, and why? A great thunderous gap of darkness existed in his mind between a last series of drinks with Denny at the bar, and Jenny's glittering eyes at the closing door. But she would remember, she would be glad to give him a full account. He had only to wait until they met at breakfast or on deck. She would tell him a story to please herself, half invention, half true, he would never know which was which, and she would be certain to add something like: "Don't feel badly about it, darling. I'm probably making it all sound much sillier than it really was. I wasn't quite sober myself, remember," she would say with purest hypocrisy: for Jenny was a sober little creature who didn't depend upon alcohol for anything. The thought of Jenny's mere existence at that moment was a fresh accusation against him. He should marry Jenny, or offer to marry her, anyway: they should have got married before they left Mexico — this way everything was plainly going to be a mess. But Jenny was not the wife he wanted if he wanted a wife, which he certainly did not want now: in fact, he faced it coldly, he would never in the world marry Jenny, he did not intend to marry at all; marriage was a bad business, a mug's game

On reaching this candid conclusion, his spirits improved somewhat: he felt able to face Jenny on her own terms.

Herr Professor and Frau Hutten opened their eyes, moved their heads experimentally and asked in duet, "How do you feel, my dear?" Comparing notes, they decided their seasickness was past, they must rise and face the day. Bébé, seeing them stirring, took heart and walked about confidently, and when Frau Hutten kissed him on the nose, he responded with a hearty lap on her chin.

The Indian nurse waked Señora Ortega gently and tucked the baby to her breast for the morning nursing. The mother drowsed and waked deliciously to the steady warm mumbling of the ravenous mouth, the long forward rolling surge of the ship, the sleepy beat of the engines. Her pains and fatigues were gone at last. Folded together, mother and baby slept as one in soft animal ease, breathing off sweet animal odors, cradled both like unborn things in their long dark dream. The Indian woman, who slept in her white chemise and full white petticoat, filled her palms with cold water, washed her eyes and smoothed her hair, slipped into her embroidered wool skirt, put on her earrings and neck- laces, and lay down again, her meek bare feet, pointed and delicate, close together; and dozed. Now and then she twitched a little, and opened one eye. A voice she did not recognize, but believed to be her dead mother's, often called her name in a tone of warning as she slept. "Nicolasa," the voice said very tenderly as if she were a child again. But it meant to tell her the sad news that she was needed, she must break her night's rest, she must all day long be silently ready to do whatever was required of her. She often wept in her sleep because she lived her whole life among strangers who knew only her christened name, not a word of her language, and who never once asked her how she felt. "Nicolasa," said the soft voice, urgently. She sighed and sat up; saw that her poor little baby was still asleep and the poor mother also, but perhaps they would be quieter, sleep longer and more deeply, if she kept watch over them. She drooped on the edge of her bed, smil- ing vaguely at mother and child; then dropped to her knees and took her rosary out of her pocket. A charm of dried herbs in a cheesecloth bag was attached to the rosary, and she kissed this charm before she kissed the crucifix.

Wilhelm Freytag woke feeling a fresher, cooler wind blowing upon his face. The round bit of horizon shone through the porthole, not clear but a thick cloudy blue. They were six days out, yes, this was Sunday and the ship had settled to her speed such as it was in a beeline across the waters, already, he noticed, putting out his head, a little troubled. It was real sea air, dense yet sweet and mild, with long sooty streamers of cloud trailing from deep blue thunder banks to the east. It seemed late; perhaps he had missed breakfast. The ship's bell clanged. Eight o'clock; time enough if he speeded up a little. Hansen would miss it, though. The breathing of deepest slumber stirred behind the curtain, and Hansen's huge feet, with smooth glossy soles and assertive great toes standing apart from the others, stuck out of the upper bunk as usual. Freytag wondered how he managed in cold weather, and remembered being half wakened by the noise of Hansen scrambling into bed at what must have been a very late hour. . . . Probably up to no good with that Spanish woman he had been dogging from the first.

While he shaved he riffled through his ties and selected one, thinking that people on voyage mostly went on behaving as if they were on dry land, and there is simply not room for it on a ship. Every smallest act shows up more clearly and looks worse, because it has lost its background. The train of events leading up to and explaining it is not there; you can't refer it back and set it in its proper size and place. You might learn something about one or two persons, if you took time and trouble, but there was not time enough and it was not worth the trouble; not even that American girl Jenny Brown was interesting enough to try to know better. By herself, a nice enough person, he believed; good dancer and full of lively talk and odd random humor that amused you at the moment, though you could not remember a word of it afterwards. But that strange young man she was traveling with gave her own personality a dubious cast: such as that odd behavior of his last night, when he came between them abruptly during a waltz, seized Jenny Brown by the elbow and snatched her away, and had performed a few steps with her of a kind usually seen only in the lowest dance halls. Jenny Brown had to fight her way out of his clutches, and she succeeded for a moment; turned to wave good night to Freytag, and then David Scott had seized her arm and she had given up and walked away with him. It was all pretty cheap and stupid, from Freytag's viewpoint, and it illustrated the danger of getting involved with strangers and their messy situations.

What he, Freytag, preferred from strangers was a friendly indifference, a superficial pleasantness. This was quite enough for any voyage, any evening at all among strangers, but it is just these things that too many persons know nothing about, he said, now beginning to carry on a silent, internal conversation with his absent wife Mary. People on a boat, Mary, can't seem to find any middle ground between stiffness, distrust, total rejection, or a kind of invasive, gnawing curiosity. Sometimes it's a friendly enough curiosity, sometimes sly and malicious, but you feel as if you were being eaten alive by fishes. I've never been on a boat, remember, said Mary in his mind. Ah, but you will be soon, you will be. You'll see for yourself then. Would you believe, I danced with a girl, her name was Jenny something-or-other, had a drink with her, and a young man she was traveling with, rather a common sort of chap I think he must be, made the oddest scene about it. Traveling with? He realized at once that such an episode was not the kind of thing he could tell Mary. It had no meaning, no importance, it was outside of their lives altogether, he would have forgotten it by the time he saw her again. And then too, if Mary heard such a story, she might say slyly, as she had said before when he told her of his travel adventures, often rather charming, he thought: "More Goyim, I expect?" And he always had to say, "Yes." And she would remark, "It's so strange that you never meet any Jews when you travel alone!" Once when he had tried to show her why he felt that this was an outrageous thing for her to say, they had almost quarreled; she would not at these times accept a fact she knew well: that it was the Jews who drew the line and refused associations and friendship. But the subject was dangerous ground between them, and he had learned to avoid it. He felt his own life within him thriving safe and sound, something intact with a smooth surface very hard for the fishes to get their teeth in. He would keep away from that Jenny Brown and her private affairs, whatever they were. She was evidently at loose ends, ready for a little excitement. Her way of talking was too intimate, too personal; she asked questions; she wished to confide and explain about herself. She was not so interesting as her vanity led her to suppose.

There was nothing he wished to confide or explain to anyone but Mary. He was very simply transporting himself, like something inanimate sent by freight, stored in the hold, until, from the house he had taken and begun to prepare for Mary in Mexico City, he should set himself down in the house where Mary was waiting for him in Mannheim. In that interval nothing concerned him, he had no business with strangers. When they returned together, the ship and the passengers would still not matter, for it would be the voyage of their lives. They would never see Germany again, except for a miracle. Mary must be his native land and he must be hers, and they would have to carry their own climate with them wherever they went; they must call that climate home and try not to remember its real name — exile. A vision of Mary playing and singing at the piano formed in his memory, and he whistled along with her the song she was singing: *"Kein Haus, keine Heimat. . . ."*

That was the way it would be. And what would it be like to know always, to carry the knowledge like a guilty secret, that they had not come to any given place of their own free happy choice, but had been driven there; that they were in flight, harried over one frontier and then another, without power to choose their place or to refuse what shelter might be offered? His pride sickened. What a shameful existence for any man, what a doubly shameful existence for a German! No matter what he might say for the sake of politeness about his mixture of nationalities, he knew he was altogether German, a legitimate son of that powerful German strain able to destroy all foreign bloods in its own veins and make all pure and German once more; and the whole world had been for him merely a hunting ground, a foraging place, a territory of profitable sojourn until the day should come when he would go home for good, having never been away in his soul. Wherever he had been, he had felt German ground under his feet and German sky over his head; there *was* no other country for him, and how was this taken away from us, Mary? You are no longer a Jew, but the wife of a German; our children's blood will flow as pure as mine, your tainted stream will be cleansed in their German veins —

Freytag pulled himself up with a sharp turn, and wiped his streaming face. His reveries had turned to a painful rhapsody, some fearful daydream had taken hold of him, he was talking his madness even while the solid earth was slipping from underfoot, the house shaking overhead, the long flight was beginning, and he could not even imagine the end. The future was a vast hollow sphere, strangely soundless, uninhabited, without incident or detail; yet he knew that, visibly, nothing might be changed for a great while; perhaps things would change so slowly he might hardly be aware of change until one day it would be too late. No doubt he would continue as a minor executive in the

German oil company until the time came to look about for something else in a firm where nobody would mind that he had married a Jewish girl. He dreaded introducing Mary to his circle in Mexico City — they would never be deceived by that blonde hair and her little tip-tilted nose. He had been deceived, but then he had loved her on sight, literally; she had told him almost at once, but he had not cared, and he could see no signs of Jewishness in her — but those colonial Germans in Mexico City, they would know what she was instantly and as far as they could see her. He had seen it happen in Germany, in all sorts of places, restaurants, theaters, all kinds of company — well, there it was, beyond belief and beyond help, and he could only hope that by the time the thing caught up with them he would have found another job as good or better, somewhere else. He might go in business for himself, in Mexico or South America, perhaps even in New York, but only as a last resort.

Facing the perpetual question as he did, his mind turned dry and practical. He could not feel fated, destined for catastrophe; actually he could not imagine himself being driven out of a place, or in peril of his life; surely he and Mary would never be put on a ship, penniless, prisoners, to be thrust into still another country that did not want them either — like that unbalanced Spanish countess prisoner with her wild tale of terror. Poor woman, he found himself thinking with impersonal pity, but his own worry was such he was unable to care deeply for her fate. Leaning over the rail, he looked again into the steerage deck.

Dr. Schumann was nearby, observing the steerage passengers also with a very thoughtful face. He greeted Freytag mildly and shook his head.

"They seem to be more comfortable this morning," said Freytag. The people were moving sluggishly, but they were moving, busy with their hands, putting things to rights as well as their means afforded. Some of the men were smoking, and the huge fat man in the cherry-pink shirt, who had sung as the ship left Veracruz, stood among them, legs apart, roaring another song, a few scattered words rising on the wind. The other men, rolling up their bundles or opening canvas chairs, stopped now and then to listen, smiling broadly, joining in for a phrase or two. The women had managed to wash a few garments, faded shirts and baby rags; a long line of them flapped from a cord hung so low everyone crossing the deck had to stoop under it. There appeared to be somewhat more space, and nobody was actively sick.

"They will do well enough if we don't run into weather," said Dr. Schumann. "Broken arms, legs, heads, maybe necks," he said, brooding over them. "They have no place to make themselves secure — there are too many of them — it's a disgrace to the ship. I am hoping the weather holds at least to the Bay of Biscay, when more than half of these will be left at Santa Cruz de Tenerife."

"It is always rough in the Bay of Biscay," said Freytag. "Well, at least these people are lucky in one way — they are all going home."

"So they are," said Dr. Schumann. "I hope only we can get them there without further suffering for them." He seemed rather gloomy and under the weather himself, and barely nodded when Freytag moved away.

In the areaway leading into the dining room, the bulletin board was a morning gathering place. David saw Jenny, looking very smooth and fresh, standing before the board with Mrs. Treadwell. He went straight up and joined them, meaning to take Jenny away at once and have it out with her.

"Why, hello, David darling," said Jenny, easily, and slipped her arm through his. He gave it a small pressure, at the same time pushing her away. She let go at once and moved away a step from him. Mrs. Treadwell nodded a greeting, and together they read the thin array of pastimes, already somewhat frayed with repetition: religious services in the morning, a variation because this was Sunday; horse races at two o'clock, swimming at all hours, music on deck at five, tea in the bar, a band concert after dinner, dancing on deck later.

The little flags on pins, stuck every day in the map to mark the progress of the ship, were marching in a curve across the blue field of the Atlantic. "We are really getting somewhere," said Mrs. Treadwell to David. "I can't sight land anywhere with my strongest glass." From the Caribbean to the Canaries would be fourteen days; from the Canaries to Vigo, to Gijón, to Southampton, to Bremerhaven, eight days more or ten perhaps. "We can begin to look forward to the end of this voyage," said David. News dispatches were rather nautical in character and the movements of ships unknown to landlubbers were thought worth mentioning, with passing references to dockworkers' strikes almost simultaneously in San Francisco, New York, Lisbon, Gijón. Passengers advertised on little thumbtacked slips of paper that they had lost or found jeweled combs, down pillows, tobacco pouches, small cameras, pocket mirrors, rosaries. The ship's pool was there with the name of yesterday's winner.

Mrs. Treadwell traced with a bright red varnished fingernail the ship's course on the blue map. She spoke, perhaps to David. "It's true," she said, "we do not stop at Boulogne." Her face was amiable, timid, composed into a smile. He watched her sparkling fingernail glide into port, into Boulogne. "And that happens to be the only place I wish to go," she told him, speaking into the air.

"Then why did you take this ship?" asked David. He waited confidently for some preposterous feminine explanation. She was undoubtedly a woman who lost her keys, missed trains, forgot her engagements, and mailed letters full of indiscreet gossip to friends in the wrong envelopes. But no, she had a reasonable answer.

"The man at the North German Lloyd in Mexico City sold me a ticket for Boulogne and said the ship stopped there," she said carefully, without indignation or complaint. It was, she added, nothing unusual or surprising. Ticket agents often did that. "My ticket reads . . ."

She opened her handbag and rummaged among the contents delicately with a forefinger. David glanced over her elbow at a clutter of expensive trifles in gold, silver, leather and tortoise shell. Mrs. Treadwell removed a flat envelope of red ostrich skin bound in gold, her passport case. "It should be here," she said, without expectation. "Wherever do things go?" she asked herself aloud. "At any rate, it said Boulogne, clearly."

"You haven't lost your ticket?" asked Jenny, alarmed.

"I haven't it with me, but it's about somewhere. I am not the only passenger for Boulogne. Those Cuban medical students . . ."

"Montpellier, yes, I know," said David.

"I wonder what they mean to do there, what possibly?" asked Mrs. Treadwell. "Surely not to study medicine?"

"Poor Cuba!" said Jenny, idly.

David asked how they would get there, in the first place. Mrs. Treadwell supposed they would be put off, all of them and herself, at Southampton and from there —

"It would be nice," remarked Jenny, "if the Captain might just put them off in a leaky lifeboat, with two oars maybe, and a small keg of old water with tadpoles in it and a few biscuits full of weevils — I'd love seeing them start out and I bet you anything they'd get there."

"But what about me? I want to go to Boulogne too; from where I stand, that's the shortest route to Paris."

"Ah, so do I want to go to Paris," said Jenny. "The more I think of it, the more I hate going to Germany. That same man in Mexico told us if we changed our minds about Germany, we could always get a visa from the French consul at Vigo, and that is my one hope now."

Mrs. Treadwell turned smiling to David and saw with amazement that his face was pale and tight and he seemed silently enraged. "How nice," she told him, saying what she had meant to say before she saw his face. "Do you wish to go to Boulogne too?"

"Not in the least," he said, "I am going to Spain."

"And I am going to Paris," said Jenny, sharply.

Mrs. Treadwell felt quite suddenly that she was standing between two persons throwing stones at each other. She stiffened and smiled, and almost furtively began to edge away, covering her retreat with little haphazard statements about the beautiful morning and a mention of breakfast. Could it have been possible they were ready to quarrel there before her? The notion filled her with embarrassment and fright. As she hurried along, the smile must have remained on her face, for Wilhelm Freytag asked her what she was looking so gay about so early in the morning? She had no idea, she told him, and watched his gaze resting on Jenny and David, who drifted past together, both a little pale and strained in the brilliant light; they exchanged sketchy nods. Freytag, with the stupid incident of the evening before fresh in mind, felt a certain lightly malicious satisfaction in his belief, his knowledge indeed, that no matter — no matter at all — what kind of appearances they chose to keep up, the match was no good; they were not in the least happy together and would never be; it couldn't go on. He turned as if for a last look at the retreating figures to fix an image in his memory even then changing and disappearing; and before he could stop it, suppress it, before he even realized he had thought the fearful thought, it formed in actual words shockingly in his waking mind: "If that were Mary walking yonder, even at this distance, at first glance, anybody — even I! — anybody would know she is a Jew. . . . What have I done to us both, Mary, Mary . . . what shall I do now?"

It was all in a fraction of a second that his image of his whole life split apart. He turned back to Mrs. Treadwell with an amazed face, and suggested in a slightly raised voice that they breakfast together on deck. "Delightful," she agreed, after thinking about it. They settled themselves and hailed the steward. The sunlight poured upon them, the waves glittered. Coffee was brought, the trays with smoking broiled lamb chops, honey and hot rolls and butter. The big white napkins reflected softened light on their faces, their momentary well-being cast a brief pleasant glow forward over the whole unpromising day.

As their fellow voyagers passed, Mrs. Treadwell noticed that at least half of them did not salute each other, not from distaste but from indifference; she remarked to Freytag that the party last night had not seemed to change things much. Freytag said, in what sounded to Mrs. Treadwell a very good humor, that a few little incidents had happened, just the same, that might make changes in the long run. Mrs. Treadwell privately considered the few little things she had observed and decided that silence perhaps would be, as usual, best.

Herr Lutz, alone and at his ease, stopped to peer down at their trays. "Ha," said he, wagging his head at them, "eating again, eh? Three times a day for a hundred years if we are lucky, what?"

Mrs. Treadwell's plate seemed to her at once too full, the food somewhat coarse; not the first time she had felt the coarsening effect of Herr Lutz's presence on everything around him. Freytag was piling honey and butter on half a roll. "How true," he said cheerfully, and engulfed the hearty morsel. Too handsome in that wrong kind of German way, Mrs. Treadwell decided, too carefully dressed, too healthy entirely, not an idea in his head, and it was a sad fact that too often the very nicest Germans wolfed their food. It had been noticed and mentioned by travelers through the ages; she herself had never known one who was not a glutton. Freytag turned to her innocently, his mouth stuffed, enjoying his breakfast, and encountered her eyes for the first time fixed on him in a bland gaze, slender dark eyebrows lifted lightly, head on one side, a look that said nothing in particular but which threw him off center for an instant. He turned away and swallowed laboriously. When he looked at her again, her face was towards the sea.

"I like breakfast best of all," he told her. "At home we used to have it English style, with all kinds of hot things, chops and scrambled eggs and broiled mushrooms and little sausages and muffins on the sideboard where you helped yourself, with a big urn of coffee steaming away. My wife —"

English style of course for breakfast, and French style for dinner no doubt, and other imported styles for other occasions, with just now and then a comfortable lapse into the native *Eisbein mit Sauerkohl* and beer. "What a hard-trying race it is," thought Mrs. Treadwell, "and all their style, whether their own or imported, comes out in lumps just the same. '*Ich bin die fesche Lola*,'" she hummed, imitating Marlene Dietrich's broadest lowest style. Freytag laughed gaily, and joined in with the line about the pianola.

"Where did you learn that?" he asked. "It's my favorite of all."

"In Berlin, when I was there last," said Mrs. Treadwell. "I loved her best when she was being comic in her wonderful bull-contralto. How much nicer she was when she wasn't being the romantic heroine in the movies."

He agreed, and added, "My wife collects that kind of disk, we have hundreds of them, all nationalities, all delightful low types, we love them." He went on to say what a knack his wife had for making everybody around her comfortable, and gay too. "Life, in fact," he said, "goes on better wherever she is." And for a moment he was re-assured by the sound of his own words. His imagination began picking up the pieces of his shattered image and putting it together again; it did look almost the same. It was true, or had been — it could still be. It was Mary herself who made the difference to his whole life, her qualities were changeless, what had possessed him to fall into a fright about their future? The rest of the world would be no worse than it had been in Germany, maybe not so bad. He was sunk in shame and contrition for his abject disloyal thoughts; he must be careful not to be-tray anything of his doubts to Mary, who for all her gaiety and worldly smartness was easily upset and nervous: she woke screaming in nightmares and clung to him pressing her face under his arm as if she were trying to hide inside him; but she could never tell him what had frightened her in her sleep. And there were times when she re-treated from him, from life itself, and would sit nerveless and sunken for a whole day, her face hidden in her hands. "Let me alone," she would say, tonelessly, "I must go through it. Wait." And he had learned to wait.

Mrs. Treadwell tried without much interest to imagine his life, a moment-by-moment affair, no doubt, running along night and day be-tween four walls, with much hearty love-making under the feather quilts, and bushels of food; with a smooth rosy calm wife on the large scale, pouring out comfort and fun like thick crusty soup into deep bowls, her light hair in a braided crown. There would be an occasional opera or theater party; frequent visits to cabarets and variety shows to hear the latest comedians and bawdy singers. Plenty of wine and beer drinking at all times, and very special celebrations on birthdays and wedding anniversaries. She pondered his manifest contentment, based no doubt on lack of imagination and the family custom of hearty English-style breakfasts; and gnawed her lamb chop lightly, finding it delicious.

For all the money she had spent, and the things she had bought, and the places she had visited, she could hardly remember ever having been comfortable. Beggars pinch me, she reminded herself, and never for any price will I be able to buy a ticket that will set me down in the place I wish to be. Maybe the place does not exist, or if it does, it's much too late to go there. And my husband preferred sleeping with any chance slut rather than with me, though I tried hard to be slut enough to please him — and he talked day and night about how he loved me! Especially he talked about it to other people. And if there is a dull man on board ship I am certain to fall into conversation with him. Yet this one looked promising enough when Jenny Brown was hanging on his words.

Freytag had been saying something, and she emerged from her warm bath of self-pity in time to catch the tag of his sentences: ". . . my wife is Jewish, you know — and we are leaving Germany for good —"

"But why?" asked Mrs. Treadwell.

"I suppose there is no real hurry," said Freytag almost apologetically, "but I prefer to make my own arrangements and to leave while there is time."

"Time?" asked Mrs. Treadwell, without thinking. "What is happening?" Then her heart jumped, for she already knew the answer and did not want to hear it spoken.

"Oh, same old signs and portents," said Freytag, already regretting his words, for the intelligent-looking, attractive woman beside him seemed remarkably obtuse and apathetic. "Warnings of one kind or another. Nothing too serious, I suppose, but we" (We? he asked himself) "have a habit of watching the weather," he ended, and wondered at his weakness in having spoken so carelessly to this stranger.

"Oh, you needn't tell me," said Mrs. Treadwell hastily. "I once knew a Russian Jew who remembered a pogrom he was in when he was a child. He was six when it happened," she told him in a light, gentle voice, "and he remembered absolutely everything — he gave terrible details — everything, except how he got away alive. That he did not

❧ 141 ❧

know at all. Isn't it strange? He was rescued and adopted and brought to New York by some people he had never seen until the pogrom, and he does not remember anything about any of it. He was a very sane, kind, learned man, a teacher of languages, all sorts; he looked as if he had never had a trouble in his life. Don't you think that's pretty beautiful?"

Freytag was silent for so long that she turned her amiable smile, somewhat brighter than usual, upon him. He was picking at his thumbnail and looking as if he had got a blow over the head. "I shouldn't have tried to talk about it," he said, with some underlying resentment, "I should never say anything about it."

"Perhaps you are right," said Mrs. Treadwell, thinking, What do you expect of me? What can I do? She moved to put her tray aside. He took it from her and set it on the deck beside his own. They rose.

"That was lovely, having breakfast here," she told him, "it was wonderful of you to think of it." "Charmed, I am sure," said Freytag, in a rather stagy manner. Mrs. Treadwell moved away again, from the threat of human nearness, of feeling. If she stayed to listen, she knew she would weaken little by little, she would warm up in spite of herself, perhaps in the end identify herself with the other, take on his griefs and wrongs, and if it came to that, feel finally guilty as if she herself had caused them; yes, and he would believe it too, and blame her freely. It had happened too often, could she not learn at last? All of it was no good, neither for confidant nor listener. There was no cure, no comfort, tears change nothing and words can never get at the truth. No, don't tell me any more about yourself, I am not listening, you cannot force my attention. I don't want to know you, and I will not know you. Let me alone.

Through David's blurred eyes and rather seedy morale, Jenny had seemed so fresh and fair at the bulletin board before breakfast, and her manner to him had been so misleadingly sweet, his anger against her began to simmer again; it was indecent for her to look and behave like that after what had happened, whatever *had* happened, last night. Jenny for her part was in a fine state of mind, and for a strange reason. She had wakened early out of a nightmare, and even after her eyes were open she was holding her breast in horror, afraid to take her hands away because of the blood on them. Then her brain cleared and the vision dispersed like smoke, she was able to explain quite logically the whole train of her dream and its connecting links. Of course. The night before, David had stayed in the bar until he was glassy-eyed drunk, then had followed her and Freytag about, skulking along very like a private detective collecting evidence for the suspicious husband. Freytag had seen it all too soon, but pretended not to notice. They danced again, and hoped to escape, but David had pushed in between them and seized her by the arm with a foolish mean look on his face. After trying to free herself, she gave way and went with David, who kept his hard clutch on her arm. She had seen at a distance that he was utterly drunk; he would be stubborn, silent, unmanageable, a lunatic in fact; at such times she was afraid of him; it was best to walk along with him and work her way towards his cabin, where she could manage to leave him. She realized very soon that his intentions were otherwise. He was leaning upon her shoulder and regarding her with a glazed, wandering, but lustful eye, and their direction was towards her cabin, not his. She turned cold with anger and disgust; at the door, she wrenched her arm free, taking him by surprise, swung through and turned instantly to close it in his face. He braced against the panel with his shoulder, and she strained with all her strength on the other side. He stopped instantly when Elsa, who had started up in terror, cried out, "Who is it? What are you doing here?" The door closed then and Jenny slipped the bolt.

"Don't be nervous," she said, her voice shaking. "He is only drunk and a little confused. He forgot you were here."

Oddly enough, Jenny thought, Elsa connected the sordid little episode somehow with love. She wanted to talk about love. She confessed she was afraid she might fall in love — she drooled the word rather, Jenny noticed, which is perhaps the right way — in love with the wrong man, with that beautiful Cuban student, the tall one who sang and danced so well.

"But I dare not let my mother suspect," said Elsa, with something very like a tremor of delight in her tone. "Can you imagine what she would say?"

"Oh yes, I can," said Jenny, "and you had better be careful. That Cuban will make you nothing but trouble."

Elsa thought this over for a while, then ventured, "But I have always been told that love makes trouble — that is what it is for. Trouble." She drew a deep quivering happy sigh. "I shouldn't mind!" Then she ventured rather timidly: "I think it must be divine to have a man so much in love with you. It seems to me so sad that you must shut him out."

"Sad?" said Jenny, surprised at the bitterness of her feelings. "No, that isn't exactly the word for it."

After a long time of lying still in the darkness, listening to Elsa turn and sigh, Jenny slept and lived through again in her sleep something she had seen once in broad day, but the end was different as if her memory had patched together two or three unrelated bits and pieces to contrive a meaning for the whole which the separate pieces lacked. During the first month after she began to live with David, she had gone by bus from Mexico City to Taxco, to look at a house there. At noon of the burning bright day they had slowed down in passing through a small Indian village with the little thick-walled windowless houses sitting along the road, the bare earth swept before each door. The dust was bitter to taste, the heat made her long for sleep in a cool place.

Half a dozen Indians, men and women, were standing together quietly in the bare spot near one of the small houses, and they were watching something very intensely. As the bus rolled by, Jenny saw a man and a woman, some distance from the group, locked in a death battle. They swayed and staggered together in a strange embrace, as if they supported each other; but in the man's raised hand was a long knife, and the woman's breast and stomach were pierced. The blood ran down her body and over her thighs, her skirts were sticking to her legs with her own blood. She was beating him on the head with a jagged stone, and his features were veiled in rivulets of blood. They were silent, and their faces had taken on a saintlike patience in suffering, abstract, purified of rage and hatred in their one holy dedicated purpose to kill each other. Their flesh swayed together and clung, their left arms were wound about each other's bodies as if in love. Their weapons were raised again, but their heads lowered little by little, until the woman's head rested upon his breast and his head was on her shoulder, and holding thus, they both struck again.

It was a mere flash of vision, but in Jenny's memory it lived in an ample eternal day illuminated by a cruel sun, full of the jolly senseless motion of the bus, the deep bright arch of the sky, the flooding violet-blue shadows of the mountains over the valleys; her thirst; and the gentle peeping of newly hatched chickens in a basket on the knees of the Indian boy beside her. She had not known how frightened she was until the scene began repeating itself in her dream, always with some grotesque variation which she could not understand. But this latest time, she had been among the watchers, as if she were at a play, and the two narrow white-clad figures were unreal as small sculptured altar pieces in a country church. Then with horror she saw that their features were changing, had changed entirely — the faces were David's and her own, and there she was looking up into David's blood-streaming face, a bloody stone in her hand, and David's knife was raised against her pierced bleeding breast. . . .

In her relief at waking, and her melancholy in remembering that time when she had been enchanted with David and had believed in their love, she almost wept. The tears rose back of her eyes and dried there. She still believed she loved David, but whatever it was that he understood as love was a mystery to her. She believed she thought of love as tenderness and faithfulness and gaiety and a true goodness of the heart to the loved one; she wanted David to be comfortable, she wished to be easy within herself, and though David seemed coldly to devour everything, yet it was as if he were alone, he would not take her into his confidence, he would give nothing back. He sulked when she was painting and could not do his own work, but wandered about aimlessly. He disliked her friends, and made none of his own. He would not listen to music with her, he would not dance, he would not share her moods or allow her to share his, or to make some sort of life of his own that she might share, if he could not take part in hers; he lived like a willful prisoner within himself, he would not let the door be unlocked.

Lying there with her arms under her head, her list of accusations grew. They had agreed in the beginning not to marry because they must be free, marriage was a bond cramping and humiliating to civilized beings: yet what was this tie between them but marriage, and marriage of the worst sort, with all the restraints and jealousies and burdens, but with none of its dignity, none of its warmth and protection, no honest acknowledgment of faith and intention. Ah, it was high time to think a little. She had fallen in love with him recklessly, on sight (why?), and she went over the hurdle at once because she did not dare to hesitate, to think of anything. Once they were together, she no longer felt reckless, but happy and right in her feelings and strangely bound to David. She had believed he felt the same, for a year at least she had been certain the bond was real and would hold fast. They were going to make a splendid life together.

Little by little she had been dismayed by his stubborn resistance to love, as if it were an evil force outside of them both, instead of a force of life they both possessed and exchanged with each other, and by his refusal to take part in any plan that would engage him for even the nearest future. She had believed that his recurring fits of long silence were evidences of strength and reserve power of character; but when he was drunk he was vulgar and silly, as if the binding strings of his character were cut and he fell apart. She had believed that his contemptuous dismissal of all her friends was the sign of a discriminating taste and judgment superior to her own. Now it seemed to her that David watched and listened so narrowly for the fallacy, the blind spot, the small but certain marks of weakness and vulgarity in others because finding them soothed his own fear, lulled his deep uncertainties about his own qualities. She wanted to cry out, "Oh David darling, there's nothing to be afraid of! It's only this world! Let's not mind it!" Had he always been like this, or was it his defense against her? And why should he defend himself? And had he been like this all along and she could not see it because she had been so much in love? But what was there to love in him, then? How could she have loved him?

She began to wash and dress with a wonderful exhilaration. The long fight was over, the question had been asked, and it carried its own answer — not the answer she had expected — what had she expected, then? — but it was an answer and she would accept it. We will go on for a while, and it will be worse and worse, and we will say and do more and more outrageous things to each other, and one day we will strike the final death-giving blows. There is nowhere to go back and begin again with this . . . there is no place to go. The past is never where you think you left it: you are not the same person you were yesterday — oh where did David go, I wonder? The place you are going towards doesn't exist yet, you must build it when you come to the right spot. Oh, God, don't let me forget any more what really happened to me. Don't let me forget. Please help me!

When Jenny saw David a few minutes later at the bulletin board, she felt very tenderly towards him, after the purging of her bitterness. If she could possibly help it, she would not quarrel with him any more. She was going to separate from him at the dock in Bremerhaven,

and go straight to Paris, and he could go to Madrid as he wanted; and
meantime —

The very first words she spoke to him were full of provocation; she
could hear them as they must sound to David. She could not stop her-
self. As she poured his coffee she glanced about the dining room and
greeted almost everyone who entered. "I see that all the drunks and
seasicks are up and tottering about," she said, "even your cabin mates.
Do you ever get lonely in there, darling? Ever feel like coming in to
spend the night with Elsa and me?"

David turned a pallid green and braced himself. "Was that it?" he
asked. "I knew it was something good. Go ahead and tell me."

"That's all," said Jenny, "unless you can remember something more
— something interesting you did when I was not there? You never
remember what happens when you're drunk, do you? I think that must
be superbly convenient."

He gazed into his plate and said nothing. She studied the very fine
clear modeling in the outer corners of his eyes, and the touching inner
corners with their thin blue veins in the lids. The nose was especially
fine. The set of the ears. The whole head, long and narrow. She had
made dozens of sketches of his head, trying to catch exactly what she
saw, but none of them were ever enough like to please her; maybe
she could bring it out in color. The face was a curious mixture of sensi-
bility, with some elements very hard, and others very petty — perhaps
it was in the mouth. David ate as if there were no God, and he never
gained an ounce; there was a starved look about him. She had never
even heard of anybody who could sleep as David did, like a dead man;
sometimes it was terrifying. She would go back on tiptoe to have an-
other look at him, listening to his breathing. On Sundays and holidays
he slept for sixteen hours on end. He would wake looking tired as if
he never hoped to catch up on his sleep. He loved to loll in water
without ever having learned to swim, and he could lie on a mat sun-
ing himself for hours, idle as a dog. When he drank whiskey, de-
liberately he went on with it until he was in a stupor. He practiced all
these dull excesses in a methodical, uncommunicative frenzy of cold
yet sensual enjoyment; and when he made love, Jenny knew he forgot
who she was. Yet he still managed to look like an innocent young
monk during Lent. He had told her once that his mother had not been
able to keep him after she was deserted by his father — he had a nasty
younger brother who cultivated asthma as a means of getting his moth-

er's whole attention — and she had turned him over to be brought up by three dreadful, sour-smelling old great-aunts who never gave him enough to eat. Hunger was in his bones, in his soul. Vague maternal feelings of the kind she abhorred in herself welled up in Jenny.

"David," she said, in a soft, blurred voice, and he saw with surprise again the now familiar change in her face, just when she had been in her most difficult and perverse mood, the gentle blinded look of abject tenderness, mysterious but real for the moment, touching and believable.

"What is it, Jenny angel?" he asked very gently, and waited for her to repent of something, to offer some concession he had not asked of her, which later she would take back and deny when her mood had changed and hardened again. He was tired of trying to understand her, and he knew by now that he could not depend upon her for anything at all.

"I am glad you have decided to go to Spain," she said. (A lie, thought David, you are anything but glad!) "Let's go there first. I've always wanted to go to France, I shall always want to go. Any time at all. And one day I shall. It will always be there. I have time. But you want to go to Spain now. So let's. I wish we had never drawn those straws."

"It was your idea," said David, relentlessly. "I have a notion we'll land up in France, after all."

"Oh no!" cried Jenny, though her eyes lighted at hearing the mere words. "No! We are going to Germany, God help us, unless we can get a visa at Vigo, and if the ship stops at Boulogne, after all. Those Cuban boys are saying there is an old maritime law the Captain is bound to put you down at the port you have paid passage to. But the purser told Mrs. Treadwell that the fare is the same to every port beyond Gijón onward, and the Captain isn't bound to stop anywhere he doesn't please between Gijón and Bremerhaven. And the Captain has said positively he doesn't please to stop at Boulogne. So darling — when we get to Bremerhaven, let's toss a coin, *once:* heads for Spain, tails for France; and let's buy our tickets then and there before something else happens to start us off on another tack." She became very gay at the prospect of settling a question. "Oh, David, let's just do this and end the worry. This would be such a nice voyage if only we knew where we were going!"

David could not or would not make the decision. "Let's wait," he said, after a long uneasy pause. "I don't know yet where I want to go."

He was annoyed at the situation getting out of his hand, rather; he had meant to quarrel with her about her carryings-on with that preposterous Freytag; for once he had her fairly in the wrong. She had intended to turn the thumbscrews hard, and give him a comic and cruel account of his behavior of the evening before. But there was nowhere to start, no common ground — their separation had begun, the distance between them had widened without warning. There is no moment of peace, thought David, except in that split second of hope, of belief even, that now, now you have it. If we go on together, she is going to be unfaithful to me, she is going to have "affairs" as she did before. Why go to Spain with her? Why should we go anywhere together? Her life, or her version of it to him, had been a disordered history of incoherent events, apparently meaningless wanderings. "Oh, no," Jenny would protest, "it all meant something marvelous to me," but what the marvel was she never said. She could never explain her real reasons for having been in certain places, or what she was doing there. "Why, I was painting, David. And I had no home any more. My grandparents were dead, and the house was sold, and they had almost nothing to leave me — I had to make a living, didn't I? And I wasn't very good at it — I'm still not, but I do try! I had a *job* there." A man, or men, always seemed to lurk in the background. "Good heavens, David, of course there were men. What do you take me for?" . . . "Why no, David, of course I never married anybody, why should I?"

She would never admit that she had loved any man but David, and more curious still, she would never admit that any man, except perhaps David, she would wait and see, had ever loved her. "None of it meant anything at all, David darling," she assured him over and over with earnest innocence, "nothing lasted. It was just for the excitement, David. It wasn't love, it was fox fire." She could never understand why, for him, the whole wrong lay precisely there. It should have been love, it was a disgrace to her that it was not love; and, he told himself with bitterness, it isn't love again, I expect. Maybe it will never be anything but fox fire.

It was Sunday morning, after all, as the godless were reminded by a sight of the godly wearing Sunday faces going each one to his own kind of worship. At six o'clock Father Carillo was down on the steerage deck, saying Mass before a portable altar adorned with small lighted candles and limp red paper flowers. The people knelt and rose and knelt again, huddled shoulder to shoulder, with bowed heads and moving lips, their hands fluttering constantly in a complicated series of signs of the Cross. Among them all, only six women were in a state of grace. They crawled forward on their knees, their heads shawled in black, to receive Holy Communion. Raising their chins and closing their eyes, they opened their mouths wide and thrust forth their pallid tongues to inordinate lengths to partake of the Angelic Bread. The priest went through the ceremony severely and hastily, placing the wafers on the outstretched tongues expertly and snatching back his hand. He ended the Mass in due form but at top speed, and almost instantly began to pack up his altar as if he were removing it from a place of pestilence.

At the farthest end of the deck from the altar, a considerable group of men who had stood throughout the ritual with their backs to the priest now faced about and began to disperse. In silence, without any other demonstration, they expressed contempt and anger even in the movements of their hands, exchanged scornful derisive smiles. The fat man in the cherry-colored shirt seemed to be the ringleader. He walked deliberately against a man who was still kneeling, his ragged cap in hand, almost knocking him over. The man got to his feet, put his cap on slouchwise and squared up to the other, who stopped short, looking down his nose with exaggerated disdain.

"Wipe that dirty look off your face in the presence of the Host," said the man who had been jostled, with extraordinary ferocity.

"In the presence of what?" asked the fat man. "I see a eunuch with a bread pill."

They struck at each other's mouths almost at the same instant; the smaller man leaped and tripped the fat man, they crashed to the deck together and fought with deadly fury for a few seconds, when half a dozen men seized and separated them by force, holding them intently, while the women scattered, crying out and stumbling over chairs and bundles.

Father Carillo picked up his altar and made for the stairs without even a glance towards the unseemly disturbance. When the men who had fought were freed and standing, there was blood on their faces and their torn clothes. Their eyes, quite murderous and calculating, met for an instant in a promise that this was not the end; then they walked away from each other in silence, each mopping his face with a dirty rag, each surrounded by his own friends, or guards as they had become.

At seven, in the small library off the main salon, Father Garza said Mass attended by the troupe of Spanish dancers, the bride and groom, Dr. Schumann, Frau Otto Schmitt and Señora Ortega, who was pale and blotchy so early in the morning, and who leaned upon the shoulder of her Indian nurse. All knelt upon the carpeted floor, missing their padded prayer stools, the soft hot wind bringing out drops of sweat on their foreheads. The Spaniards knelt closely together, their bitter faces closed smugly, their dingy slender hands twiddling with their rosaries.

Frau Schmitt, observing that the bride and groom knelt at a discreet distance from each other and did not even once exchange a glance, approved this delicacy of behavior. She then covered her face with her hands to shut out all distractions, and gave herself up to soft emotions, remembered blisses of mingled love and prayer, a melting sweet, ageless vision of divine joys to come. Lamb of God who takest away the sins of the world only in Thy grace shall my soul be healed. Holy Mary, Mother of God, pray for us sinners now and at the hour of our death.

Near her, Amparo stirred, rustling her petticoats and rattling her beads, hissing her prayers under her breath, exuding from every pore a warm spermy odor mixed with the kind of perfume only the lowest sort of woman would ever use. Frau Schmitt, disturbed by the sounds and the smells, body odors and stale hair oil added from all sides, moved away a few paces on her knees, then stopped, feeling foolish. Her happy mood was shattered. She sat back on her heels, resigned and dull, opened her eyes and followed Father Garza's formal gestures as he murmured in a low voice. She knew it all by heart, but feeling cheated of her rapture, she stole glances now and then at the Spaniards, who had cheated her.

They were peculiarly repellent to her; how could anyone call such swarthy people beautiful? The presence of Dr. Schumann, the good and wise man, was comforting to her. She felt she knew him well, ah, he was the kind of man she understood and who would understand her. A tender, sunny memory of her honeymoon at Salzburg rose like a little painting framed in gold in her mind — her new, wonderful, ever-to-be-wonderful husband with her in their first room together in the White Horse Inn at St. Wolfgang's; the lovely green summer light everywhere; the small white steamer coming in from a trip around the lake, and everyone going down to a wharf no larger than a school platform, to meet it as if it came from across the sea . . . and the little gilded globes dancing in the fountain spray at Hellbrun, and the darling little dwarfs and gnomes in glazed colored crockery peeping out from hedges and flowerbeds! Ah, those Spaniards with their harsh faces and hating eyes, if ever they had seen the white marble statue of the martyred Empress Elizabeth at Hellbrun, they would understand what beauty is . . . This was a sad voyage, her last in this world maybe, and what a pity most of the people around her were so unpleasant. She was so bitterly lonely for her husband, one night she had put herself to sleep imagining that she might get up and go down into the hold, and just sit there by his coffin in the dark, for the dear company of it. Then in her sleep she had gone down, and there at the door stood her husband shining like moonlight on the sea, and he had said, waving his hand, "Go back, go back, go back," just that and nothing more, three times; and had disappeared. She had waked in a fright, turned on her bed light and begun to say her rosary; and now she had only to resign herself to not seeing him again in this poor world, and to try not to let her heart be hardened against the poor and the unfortunate — for surely those dreadful Spaniards were both. She had always believed so deeply that human beings wished only to be quiet and happy, each in his own way: but there was a spirit of evil in them that could not let each other be in peace. One man's desire must always crowd out another's, one must always take his own good at another's expense. Or so it seemed. God forgive us all.

Herr Löwenthal, wandering moodily alone, after having put on his phylacteries and said his morning prayers, was brooding hopelessly on Herr Rieber's treatment of him. It was not a matter of rude words, for Herr Rieber would hardly speak to him, and if Herr Löwenthal asked a civil question he got only a grunt for answer: the trouble was that Herr Rieber behaved as if he were alone in the cabin, and had all the rights and space there. He pushed Löwenthal's belongings around as if they were mere trash in his way. Once he had deliberately swept all of Löwenthal's toilet things off the shelf to the floor, breaking a good bottle of shaving lotion, and he had not even the decency to pretend it was an accident.

If Herr Löwenthal hung his pajamas in the small locker near Herr Rieber's garments, Herr Rieber, with a nasty fastidious expression, handling the pajamas between thumb and forefinger, would remove them and let them drop to the floor. And all this, mind you, in the most confident insolence, as if he knew he could dare venture to any lengths without fear of consequence.

Herr Löwenthal, accepting all this without present protest, making up his mind painfully to endure in silence and wait as patiently as he could for the end of this monstrous situation, spent a good deal of his time trying to find a place of his own to stow his property that could not possibly be claimed by Herr Rieber. He repacked his suitcase and sample cases, put his new supply of toilet articles in a bag, and set them all in the corner opposite the bunks, at the foot of and under the couch. Once he found them all in the middle of the floor again, and once piled helter-skelter in the lower bunk. There would be no end to it, that was clear. Herr Löwenthal with some wry humor began to think of Herr Rieber as that fabulous German household sprite of mischief, the poltergeist. No poltergeist could have been more persistent in malice. All this so soon, what would not Herr Poltergeist think of to make himself tiresome before they reached Bremerhaven?

This dark question in mind, Herr Löwenthal on deck glanced through the window into the small library and saw the Mass going on. He restrained his impulse to spit until he had passed beyond the line of vision of the worshipers; then, his mouth watering with disgust, he moved to the rail and spat like a landlubber into the wind, which blew it back in his face. At his curse being thus returned to his very teeth, his whole body was suffused with superstitious terror, it scurried like mice in his blood, it shook his nerves from head to foot. "God forbid," he said aloud, with true piety, and dropped shuddering all over in the nearest deck chair.

Father Garza came out in a few minutes, looking very refreshed and good-natured after the performance of his religious duties, lifting his cassock skirt and plunging his square bony hand into his trousers pocket to fetch forth a packet of cigarettes. Father Carillo joined him. They both beamed amicably upon Herr Löwenthal, whose gaze was fixed unseeing upon them. "Good morning," said the fathers, affably, in very bad German, and Father Garza added, "It's a beautiful day we are having." They paced on slowly, and Herr Löwenthal in his pit of misery did not even hear them until they were gone. He pulled himself up laboriously. "*Grüss Gott*," he said forlornly, to the empty air and the bitter rolling sea.

There being no Lutheran minister aboard, the Captain assumed leadership of the religious observances suitable to the day. At eleven o'clock all the guests at his table except Dr. Schumann and Frau Schmitt gathered in the main salon, and were joined there by Herr Wilibald Graf and his nephew, Herr Glocken and the Lutz family, the Baumgartners and their son Hans. Even Wilhelm Freytag, who happened to be already present, stayed on for the service. The Captain read a few verses of Holy Scripture in his most commanding voice, and said the appropriate prayers, his congregation listening respectfully with bowed heads. Everybody joined in several fine rollicking hymns, their firm warm voices carrying all through the ship, even out to the bar, where the barman stood listening thoughtfully, with a pleased face, nodding in time and humming under his breath.

Frau Hutten, Frau Rittersdorf and Frau Schmitt retired to the shady side of the deck prepared to sit there in Sunday dullness waiting for their dinner. Herr Professor Hutten took part in a conversation with the Captain and Dr. Schumann, a short distance away. Their voices were low and their manner earnest, so the women gave up trying to overhear, and Frau Hutten, observing that Frau Rittersdorf was writing in her notebook, kept a considerate silence, fumbling absently with Bébé's cropped ears.

"It seems that those young Americans," wrote Frau Rittersdorf neatly, "have quite commonplace names, after all, Scott and Brown. Braun the name no doubt was, and perhaps the young woman is of German origin, though I should detest thinking so. One more un-German in every respect it would be difficult to imagine. Angel and Darling are their love-names for each other. In quite bad taste of course, and much exaggerated besides, as neither of them is in the slightest degree attractive. She is a dry thing like too many American women — even the beautiful ones have no real freshness, but seem either like painted wood or just on the point of fading. This is caused, I am told on good authority, by their almost universal custom of losing their virginity at puberty or even earlier, and thereafter leading lives of the utmost promiscuousness. But this young woman is not beautiful in the least; I should think she might have encountered difficulties in losing her virtue at any age. As for the young man, I suppose she is the best he can do for himself, and indeed, is quite all that he deserves." She tucked her pen in the narrow pocket on the back of the book and leaned back cheerfully, thinking she had well repaid that pair for misleading her in the first instance.

She turned to speak to Frau Hutten, when her attention was arrested by the queer behavior of Herr Rieber and Fräulein Spöckenkieker, engaged in a most unedifying scuffle at the rail. Herr Rieber was wearing the lady's green and white scarf around his neck, and she was rather pulling him about by the ends. Frau Rittersdorf snapped her *face-à-main* upward for an instant. Yes, that girl was pretending to tie a bow under Herr Rieber's chin, but she was really drawing the noose about his windpipe until he clutched for air and his beaming smile almost disappeared in a blue cloud of distended veins. She then loosened the knot, and the good-humored martyr went through a pantomime of coming to life again, gratefully.

His whole attitude was offensive to Frau Rittersdorf. It was unbecoming to the dignity of a man to submit to amorous persecutions from any woman, no matter how irresistible her charms. More properly the other way about, for the crown of womanhood was suffering for the sake of love. A positive thrill of sensual excitement ran through Frau Rittersdorf's frame as she tried to imagine what would have happened if ever she had, no matter how playfully, attempted to strangle her Otto.

"Let us have some beer," shouted Herr Rieber gleefully, stuffing the scarf in his pocket, where it dangled like a tail, and the shameless pair ran away, followed by a row of censorious glances. Frau Rittersdorf remarked to Frau Hutten, in a sweet charitable voice: "If one judged always by appearances, how often one would be obliged to think the worst."

Frau Hutten stirred lazily, and after reflection, answered with indulgence: "Ah well, it seems that neither of them is married. Who knows, it may be a match."

Little Frau Otto Schmitt ventured: "They seem rather oddly matched. I always like to see the man taller than the woman."

The three then noted that Captain Thiele, Herr Professor Hutten and Dr. Schumann were still absorbed in their talk a safe distance away. They gave free rein to their womanly tongues without fear of being overheard by the men, to whom such talk was always trivial, unworthy, and fair game for their male sense of ridicule.

"Fräulein Spöckenkieker is a divorced woman, so I have heard," said

Frau Rittersdorf. "She is, I am given to understand, a woman of business — a lingerie business of sorts, she has three shops and has kept her maiden name in all circumstances. No wonder she no longer has a husband. It may also account for her manners, or lack of them."

"I wished to continue with my teaching after marriage," said Frau Hutten, with wifely pride, "but my husband would not hear of it for a moment. The husband supports the family, he told me, and the wife makes a happy home for them both. That is her sacred mission, he said, and she must be prevented at all costs from abandoning it. And so it was. From that day to this. I have done only housework, except to act as secretary to my husband."

Frau Schmitt blushed. "I taught for years," she said, "in the same school with my husband, who was in poor health, almost an invalid, after the war. He could not carry a full professorship; it was important for him not to be too heavily burdened. We had no children, what else should I have been doing? There was not enough to do in our simple little house to keep me occupied. No, I was glad to help my husband. And we had a happy home as well." Her tone was gently defensive and self-satisfied.

"We can make no fixed rules, after all; it depends always on what the husband wishes," said Frau Hutten. "For me, I lived only to please my husband. Now, whatever life was like in that wild foreign country, we are all going home at last. But it cannot be the same," she told Frau Rittersdorf. "Nothing can be the same. We went out to Mexico in 1912, foreseeing nothing of the disaster that was to overtake our beloved country. Fortunately, the Professor has very poor eyesight, and has suffered since youth with fallen arches: there was never any question of his going to war —"

"Fortunately?" echoed Frau Rittersdorf, her arched eyebrows rising. "Fortunately, my husband was a magnificent, a perfect physical specimen of a man, a Captain, who saw three years' service at the front, in the very thick, I may say, of the battle. He received the Iron Cross for his displays of superhuman courage in action, and he was killed on the field. . . . Is it not strange that war should destroy such men, the brave, the noble-minded, the sound in body, the invaluable fathers, and leave only the defectives to carry on the race? Oh, I have asked myself that question many times in these years since I have been alone, and I can find no answer!"

"The world needs scholars and thinkers as well as soldiers," said Frau

Hutten, mildly. She was proof against this argument, being the sort of woman who admired intellectual attainments and bowed eagerly to moral superiority. "But I quite understand your feelings in the matter."

"My husband," said Frau Schmitt, "was a brave soldier, and a fine scholar, at once. These qualities are not incompatible. My husband . . ."

She stopped, drawing a long breath, which fetched up tears on its return as a pump from a well. Her face quivering, she felt blindly for her handkerchief. "No better than a dead man all those years," she said, choking, "a dead man all those years."

The two women observed her display of feeling with composure and perhaps a slight tinge of satisfaction. Women must weep, each one her own tears for her own troubles, in her own time. Tearless themselves at the moment, their faces wore also a faint expression of disapproval. Frau Schmitt appeared to be making rather a parade of grief, yet they could not help seeing with some adverse criticism that, in spite of her widow's crape, she wore a heavy gold necklace with a large locket — inappropriate, to say the least. Frau Schmitt saw their glances wandering around her neck and throat, and being another woman, guessed their thought. She put her hand over the locket: "My husband's portrait," she said. "I have worn it so long, I cannot be without it!"

In a rather prolonged silence not without edges, Frau Schmitt rose, her small nose and eyelids scarlet. "Excuse me," she said. Balancing herself on her blunt-toed pumps, she edged around them and proceeded uncertainly towards the door. She paused there and stood aside for the sick old man in the wheel chair. Above the yellowed, parchment-colored skull the bright angry face of the young boy hovered, and rudely he attempted to crowd his way through the door, almost before Frau Schmitt could get out of his path.

"Stop," said the sick man, in a hollow voice, holding up his hand, taking hold of Frau Schmitt's sleeve with finger and thumb. She trembled and dared not move, as if a ghost had laid a hand upon her. "Are you in pain, my child?" he asked her. "Let me help you. Come, walk beside me and tell me your trouble."

"Oh, no, no," whispered Frau Schmitt hurriedly. "It is nothing. Thank you, thank you so much. You are very kind."

"It is God who is kind through me, his instrument, his servant," said the sick man. "I, Wilibald Graf, can heal your sorrows by His grace if only you will believe . . ."

"Uncle," said the boy, hoarse with rage, "we are blocking the door-way." He shoved the chair forward violently, and Herr Graf's fingers still clinging slipped from Frau Schmitt's sleeve. "Oh *no*," she said, hurrying by, her body clumsy in flight, "thank you!" The shock of his blasphemous proposal dried her tears, her grief made way for a sound religious indignation, and a few minutes later she was talking to the Baumgartners, who had been sitting in a doleful family isolation in the main salon. Herr Baumgartner was making his daily brief losing fight against his longing for a brandy and soda before his dinner, and his wife was waiting stonily for the moment when he should admit defeat. Hans was kneeling on a chair at the window, watching the sea and waiting for his glass of raspberry juice. His mother would then sit be-tween him and his father, her head on her hand, and she would not let either of them out of her sight for a minute if she could help it. Hans wriggled and sighed, seeing Ric and Rac climbing to the very top of the rail, leaning far out over the water, shouting to each other, wild and free. They saw him and put out their tongues at him. Rac turned her back, flipped up her skirts and showed him the seat of her pants. He shrank down a little at this, behind the upholstered chair, shocked but not unpleasantly. He had never seen a girl do *that* before.

Frau Schmitt said to Frau Baumgartner, "Imagine a man on the edge of the grave . . ." and Frau Baumgartner mentioned, almost shyly, that she had herself known persons, not always in the best of health themselves, who had the power of healing. Indeed, it had sometimes seemed it was their own health they gave away to others, so that they had none left for themselves.

Frau Schmitt shook her head. "His face is not good. He frightened me with the look in his eyes."

Herr Baumgartner frowned with pain, groaned softly, and said, "There were saints in the old days certainly who could heal the body as well as the soul."

"He is a Lutheran," said Frau Schmitt, impulsively, "how could he be a saint?"

Frau Baumgartner stiffened slightly, her tone and manner thoroughly chilled. "We are Lutherans," she said. "We have our saints also."

"Oh dear," said Frau Schmitt, "please believe me when I say I would never willingly offend the religious feeling of anyone — oh, to me, that is an unpardonable thing! I am sure I did not make myself clear . . ."

"I am afraid you did make yourself very clear indeed," said Frau Baumgartner, not ceding an eyelash. "There are saints in every church. But I suppose you Catholics think that nobody exists in God's sight but yourselves — I suppose you could not admit that I am as much God's child as you are . . ."

"Oh please, Frau Baumgartner," cried little Frau Schmitt, who by now seemed ready to swoon away. "Yes, we are all God's dear children together, and I have never dreamed of anything else. When I said you had no saints in your church, it was my ignorance — I did not *know* you had saints, nobody ever told me! I thought only the Catholic church had saints — forgive me!" She held out her hands wrung together. "Who are they?"

"Who are what?" asked Frau Baumgartner, distracted by the expression on her husband's face which meant he was going to order a brandy and soda.

"Your saints?" asked Frau Schmitt, eager to learn.

"Oh good heavens what a question," said Frau Baumgartner, firmly putting an end to the scene. "I never discuss religion with anyone. Come Hans," she called to her son, "we are going to have raspberry juice." With averted face she snubbed Frau Schmitt finally and forever, and left her sitting there feeling deeply, unjustly injured. Even with the best will in the world, with nothing but kindness in your heart, Frau Schmitt felt again for the thousandth time, how difficult it is to be good, innocent, friendly, simple, in a world where no one seems to understand or sympathize with another; it seemed all too often that no one really wished even to try to be a little charitable.

Captain Thiele, in his talk with Herr Professor Hutten and Dr. Schumann, mentioned the trouble in the steerage that morning. He remarked in the easy tone of one whose authority is not to be disputed, if there was any more disturbance among that riffraff, for any cause, he would lay the troublemakers in irons for the rest of the voyage. He loved to see his small brig occupied, and it was now standing empty. Dr. Schumann mentioned he had been told that one man had a broken nose, another a cut chin. On going down to see for himself, he had found them both getting on very well; he had put court plaster on the nose and had taken two stitches in the chin. Herr Professor Hutten was pained to hear that the fight had been about religion.

"Religion?" said the Captain haughtily. "What do they know about that?" And they dismissed the matter. But Professor Hutten thought it interesting enough to mention to his wife and Frau Rittersdorf. Meeting Arne Hansen on deck, Frau Rittersdorf made bold to ask him if he had heard any further details about the riot in the steerage. Hansen, being barely awake, had heard nothing, but he asked a sailor in passing, and the sailor told him it had been a pretty good fight, though short. He had missed it, but he heard they drew knives.

Frau Hutten, airing Bébé, fell in with the Lutz family, and in some agitation told them what she had heard from her husband, what she believed she had heard, and the Lutzes got the impression there had been a full-scale free-for-all scrimmage among dangerous criminals lurking below, with much bloodshed.

Herr Lutz asked Herr Glocken, who was walking, swinging his long arms, whistling a tuneless air, if he had heard of the battle in the steerage, adding his hope that their grievances might be settled to their satisfaction. "Or they'll be up here cutting all our throats," he said, only meaning it halfway. Frau Lutz turned pale at such scandalous levity, and added as her personal opinion that it was probably a food riot: "Our own is not improving, you may have noticed," she remarked.

Herr Glocken was pleased to find Wilhelm Freytag knew nothing of the disturbance. "Odd," Freytag said, "I saw Dr. Schumann just a few minutes ago, and he said nothing of such a thing." But he took the cheerful view. "So they are fighting down there already? Good," he said, "good. What about?"

Herr Glocken did not know. Opinion was divided. People drifted into the bar. Arne Hansen's booming intolerant voice could be heard in English saying bitterly to the company assembled in a line on the high stools: "When they are all starving, in rags, shipped like cattle only not with such good care, can you guess what they find to fight about? Religion. My God. They give each other bloody noses because one man kneels and another does not."

"Maybe religion is the only subject on which they have opinions," said Mrs. Treadwell, gently whirling her stein of beer to make the foam rise again.

"Ach," said the purser, next to her, in distress, "please don't whirl your beer. You will spoil it."

"Sorry," said Mrs. Treadwell, smiling at him and setting down her stein.

Hansen leaned forward, his pale eyes glaring under his knotted brows. "Opinions? What opinions? What do they know to have opinions about? Only the fat man has opinions and the Captain says he is to be put in irons . . . so much for the right to opinions among those people."

"I beg your pardon, sir," said the purser, "the Captain has said only if the fat man makes more trouble he will —"

"And who is to judge what is trouble?" bawled Hansen.

"Why, the Captain, of course," said the purser, readily but a little uneasily as if he were dealing with a lunatic. Hansen nodded his head. "Just so," he agreed, sourly.

"How could anyone have an honest opinion about religion?" intervened David, and Jenny noticed that he spoke with a slight Spanish accent, one of his more irritating habits: pure affectation, she called it, though David denied it bitterly and claimed it was the natural result of speaking Spanish almost constantly for eight years. "All the claims are just prejudice against prejudice; blind feeling fighting for the upper hand. . . . People love the right to hate each other with moral sanction. The real basis of the religious question is political —"

"Just so," boomed Hansen. "All is politics, who said otherwise? Who would give a damn what a man's religion was if religion was not part of politics? Who will go to jail in this case? The man who is against religion. Why? Not because he does not like the Church, but because his acts disturb the government. The Church and the government are like *that!*" Hansen held up two fingers pressed together. "He could knock down altars all day and who would care? Nobody, if it was only a question of religion." He turned his frown upon Freytag as to someone he knew. "Isn't that so?"

Freytag said in a calm reasoning voice: "Perhaps the man whose altar was knocked down might fight for pure religious reasons. His act might be useful to a political party, but his own feelings needn't have any political meaning at all. . . . I don't suppose either of those fellows could give a reasonable explanation of why they hit each other, but on one side at least I like to think it was something better than politics." ("Now I really like you!" Jenny said to herself, and hid her pleased face behind her tilted stein.)

"Better?" asked Hansen, and his heavy voice took on reproach and grief. "You think it is better for religion to make dupes of those poor people so that they fight each other instead of fighting their enemies together?"

His sorrow and indignation were real, but their origins so mysterious to his listeners no one could answer him. The purser only clicked his tongue against his teeth several times and wagged a finger at him, shaking his big head with paternal gravity. Hansen ignored him.

Herr Baumgartner spoke up from his table in a voice of deep emotion. "I am a lost soul, perhaps," he said, "but never would I deny the power of true religion. It is the spiritual source of our civilization, our one hope in eternity. Poor as we may be now, what would we be without it?"

Hansen swung around and glared at Herr Baumgartner under his pale eyebrows. "Which true religion?"

"They are all true," spoke up Herr Baumgartner, stoutly.

"Oh," said his wife in a tiny prolonged scream, "*how can you say such a thing?*"

Herr Hansen paid no attention to Frau Baumgartner. "Civilization," he said, with blunt contempt, "let me tell you what it is. First the soldier, then the merchant, then the priest, then the lawyer. The merchant hires the soldier and priest to conquer the country for him. First the soldier, he is a murderer; then the priest, he is a liar; then the merchant, he is a thief; and they all bring in the lawyer to make their laws and defend their deeds, and there you have your civilization!"

Herr Baumgartner flinched and closed his eyes and seemed about to reply; his wife set her lips and nudged him with her toe; he remained silent.

"What about the artist?" asked Jenny, egging him on. "What about him?"

"He comes last, he pretends everything is what it is not, he is a fake," said Hansen simply, without looking at her. Denny, sitting next to Löwenthal, who kept saying under his breath "Bolshevik, Bolshevik!," had been very gloomy during this exposition of Hansen's views. He now burst into a loud laugh. Nobody laughed with him. He lapsed into red-faced confusion. "Fakes, ha, that's right," he said, at random. "Fakes!"

"I'd like to see what is really going on," said Jenny to Freytag, who had been watching her face. "I think if the fat man is in the brig we ought to picket the Captain and carry banners and make a big day of it . . ."

Freytag followed her, and they watched the people in the steerage for a while, but nothing was happening beyond the ordinary. Men lolled and played cards on the deck, the women nursed their babies or did their washing, the hot sunlight poured over them, there were no signs of uneasiness.

At the other end of the ship, they found the Lutz family, the Huttens, the Cuban students, and Herr Glocken in a row looking down into the pit, where the canvas covering had been removed from the grating to give light and air to the quarters where the steerage passengers ate. The first table was already spread, a reassuring sight. Thick as flies the people were clustered around huge slabs of boiled ox-brisket, dumplings, bowls of cooked apricots, piles of fresh green onions. They fed in devoted silence, reaching out long arms for the chunks of bread scattered along the white oilcloth. They leaned on their elbows and ate, feeling their strength return, feeling their blood and bones renewing themselves, their hopes coming back, their desire to live rousing once more. The six students lined up and shouted something friendly and barbarous in their unfathomable argot; several of the men turned their faces upward, mouths full, cheeks bulging, and jerked a hand at them, good-naturedly. They were sunken hardened faces, but their eyes were the eyes of tired men who had at last slept and eaten.

The sight-seers moved on, a little bored with relief, their eased minds reflected in their slightly vacuous expressions. Murmuring among themselves like pigeons, the Lutzes and the Huttens and Herr Glocken seemed to be vaguely agreed that to mistreat the poor is not right, and they would be the first to say so, at any time. Therefore they were happy to be spared this unpleasant duty, to have their anxieties allayed, their charitable feelings soothed. Those strange foreign people did not appear to be dangerous; they were obviously not being mistreated at all; on the contrary they were enjoying an excellent dinner; and if there were mischief-makers down there, no one need worry — the Captain would know how to quell them.

Jenny and Freytag lingered, some distance apart, then moved closer and stood together, their hands almost touching on the rail. Last night's absurd scene was between them, and David Scott might again appear at any moment behind them, like a ghost returning to confirm his first suspicions of their guilt, or guilty intentions at least. Freytag's belief in his own innocence took the form of an obscure resentment against Jenny: why did she allow that fellow to carry on like a cad, when he so obviously had no rights over her except such as she chose to allow? Freytag in the depths of his mind believed instinctively in legal rights only; marriage tacitly gave to a man the legal right to abuse his wife up to a certain point, and Freytag took rather for granted that the wife had consented to this state of affairs when she took the marriage vow. All this was fermenting in his brain shapelessly, but he was clear about one thing — a woman who allowed a man to mistreat her when he had no legal right to do so was a fool, or worse. His feeling about Jenny, such as it was, lowered and cooled within a few seconds. Could she be in love with that fellow? It seemed most improbable.

Jenny, leaning far over, searched among the crowd in the shadowy grated pit. "Yes, there he is," she said, pointing out the fat man, who had changed to a grass-green shirt, "eating away. Not in the brig at all. So our parade is off, what a pity! No injustice has been done, isn't that a shame?" Her manner was entirely candid, her eyes very clear and gay.

"There is injustice, all right," said Freytag, "but it lies far back and deep down, it is in our grain, incurable — look," he said earnestly, "if there were not injustice how could we even have the idea of justice? An old lecturer I knew as a boy used to say, 'We right Wrong, and wrong Right.' It wouldn't have done any good to picket the Captain."

"Oh, wouldn't it?" cried Jenny. She disagreed with him altogether. She thought he was just sitting down and letting things run over him. Nothing was incurable, not even human nature. And if you waited to get to the root you would never get anywhere. The top surface was quite enough to keep anyone busy! If you wanted things changed — always for the better, of course! — you just kicked over the nearest applecart, spilled the first available bag of beans. She believed warmly and excitedly in strikes, she had been in many of them, they worked; there was nothing more exciting and wonderful than to feel yourself a part of something that worked towards straightening out things — getting decent pay for people, good working conditions, shorter hours — it didn't much matter what. She had picketed dozens of times with just any strikers who happened to need pickets, and she had been in jail several times, and really, it was just a lark! She didn't stay long, anyway. Somebody always came from a mysterious Headquarters with plenty of money, so it was out on bail for everybody and back to the line. She had never held with those hotheads who advised her to bite policemen and kick them in the shins. She had heard gruesome stories of police brutalities to working women, really on strike, on the picket line and in jail, and knowing what she did about people, she could believe it. But she was glad to say she had got along very amiably with her policemen, all of them. She always made conversation and tried to convert them on the way to the station, and they were always quite polite, or at least decent, and impervious. They also knew what they knew and what they believed, and if this picketing stuff wasn't against the law, it ought to be. "And yet," she said, "some of them were quite nice!"

She might have been a young girl talking about the gay parties of her debutante season. Freytag could not take her seriously. She did not say where or when these things happened, nor precisely how she had happened to be mixed up in them — where had an apparently well-brought-up young girl run into such company? — nor what were the beliefs that led her to such acts. Her light running talk was full of omissions and pauses which she seemed to expect him to fill in from his own experience of such events. He knew nothing whatever about them except from a distance: he had seen police breaking up picket lines before cigarette factories in Mexico and had approved of it thoroughly, waiting until the sidewalk was cleared before going about his own business.

He listened, then, not for what she was saying, for it sounded like childish nonsense, or was repellently hard and careless, he could not decide which; but she was full of feminine gentleness in her little person, harmoniously modeled and sweetly rounded. He realized with acute dismay that she seemed beautiful to him, and he remembered well that on first sight she had certainly struck him as nothing out of the ordinary. He shuddered. Out of his past, out of his restless, seeking sentimental youth before he knew Mary, there rose disturbingly a half dozen faces, dimmed, almost forgotten; none of them beautiful before he loved them, none of them beautiful since, some of them hateful even, but each one unbelievably enchanting for that brief time when he was hot after each in turn, bedeviled and blinded with illusion. It was always true love and it was always going to last forever. . . .

He moved away from her abruptly and, frowning a little, leaned on his folded arms and let his eyes rest on the people below. They were milling about, replacing each other at the tables; great heaps of dirty plates were being taken away, the platters of hot food were again being thumped down on the oilcloth. Jenny's face was a little dulled with melancholy; rather suddenly her mood changed for no reason that Freytag could surmise. Amparo and Pepe, with sulky morning faces, paused for a glance into the pit, another glance of calculated insolence at Jenny and Freytag, and passed on, their narrow, highly specialized behinds swaying gracefully.

"Wasn't Hansen funny in the bar just now, with his poor crooked mind trying to straighten out the question of justice?" asked Jenny. "All animals are sad after making love."

"Except women and mares," said Freytag.

"I don't know about mares," said Jenny, "but it seems to make Hansen angry."

"He's an extreme character," said Freytag. "Something is troubling him. He groans and yells and thrashes about at night and gets into fearful scrimmages with some enemy who attacks him in that upper berth."

"A political enemy, no doubt," said Jenny. She enjoyed Freytag's good looks, he was a delight to her eyes. She liked his harmless dandyism; every man she had ever liked except David had been beautiful and vain as the devil. It had been her ruin, she decided, this weakness for handsome men. If a man were sufficiently good-looking she granted him all desirable qualities without hesitation. Freytag was almost too conventionally handsome to draw — David had a much more interesting face, really. Or had he? A clinical expression dawned in her eye: she wanted to see the bones.

"Whatever *are* you looking at?" asked Freytag uneasily, and barely restrained himself from running his hand over his hair, twitching at his necktie. He was not the first man so affected by Jenny's intent but not flattering stare.

"At your head, I like your head," said Jenny. "I wish I could see the brains . . ."

"Oh *God*, what an idea!"

"The brain is most beautifully designed," said Jenny loftily. "Maybe you would let me try to make some drawings of you?" It might mean a few pleasant hours sitting about on deck; she'd like to see David try to make a scene about that.

"Of course, I would," said Freytag, "but—"

"Nothing would happen," she said, cheerfully. Then she took the plunge. "I don't understand David at all," she told him. "I never pretended to, and he is always surprising me by some new glimpse of him. Nearly always when he is drinking. And there is a certain kind of truth in drunkenness. I know that what I do and say when I am drunk is just as true as the other different things I do and say when I am sober. It's just another side of me coming up for air!"

"Do you get drunk?" asked Freytag. "Amazing. You seem a very sober person to me."

"I am sober, even when I'm drunk," she said, anxiously. "It's always by accident and just for fun. But I am apt to say things I'd have sense enough to hide at other times. And I know David does the same thing . . ."

David gives himself away badly, she thought. That is what I am saying now, cold sober. The next step is to apologize for him. Explain that he really is not that sort of man — or not often. That is not at all the kind of thing he usually does. He is ever so much nicer than you might think from what you have seen of him. He's had a terrible kind of life and has to work harder than most people to keep his balance. You must know him pretty well before you can see his true qualities clearly. I do know him well and when I say I don't understand him it's because I am ashamed for him and for me about what happened last night. It was the least important part of David who did that. I know a great deal more about him, I know some lovely things, I love him. Shameful, shameful. The next step would be to break out with what was really hurting her; about that terrible dream last night that just left her nowhere to go but out and away . . .

"When you are in love," she said aloud above the chattering of her thoughts, "it is nearly impossible to make yourself see straight, isn't it?"

"I'm not sure I can agree with that," said Freytag. "Love," he said speculatively, giving the word just so much weight and no more. The nape of her neck was very white and exposed-looking as she turned away her head, but she listened attentively when he talked about love, boasting a little, perhaps.

He told her, as if not making much of a point of it, that he believed love was based on faith, complete loyalty its first attribute. Far from being blind, real love helped one to see clearly perhaps for the first time. Any smallest betrayal of the loved one, whether the act came early or late, was total betrayal from the first, and it destroyed not only the future but the very past itself, for every day lived in confidence had been a lie and the heart a dupe. To be unfaithful even once was never to have been faithful at all . . .

"No," said Jenny, "to be unfaithful once is to be unfaithful once, and you can be repentant and get back in the fold just like an old-fashioned Methodist. I used to have a lover," she said, clearly but without boldness, "who always said he never realized how much he loved me except when he was being unfaithful to me. There's a flaw in that doctrine," she said, beginning to laugh rather sharply, "but I was never able to convince him."

Freytag laughed with her, and agreed that men's techniques of having it both ways had a comic side. Then he went on quietly as if he were talking to himself: Love, he said, was a benevolent passion, full of patient kindness and fostering tenderness, faithful not by choice nor design but by nature, hardy and lasting, full of courage. Flowers crept into his sentences, life, death, even eternity, were mentioned: bread and wine, and the perpetual recurrence of hopeful mornings with no evil memories and no remorses.

Jenny listened as if hypnotized. The dreamy voice was soothing as a cradlesong, a song her own wishful deluded heart sang to itself. It mingled with the soft dance of light on water and the fresh wind on her face. She heard a strange voice, now with the faintest trace of a German inflection in it, echoing not what she knew in her bitter mind, but her feelings; it seemed sick and sentimental and false. At the last word her eyes flared open, and she cut through his maunderings.

"I think it is a booby trap," she said, with a violence that made her shake all over. "I hate it and I always did. It makes such filthy liars of everybody. But I keep falling into it just the same."

"With all the wrong people," he said, flatly, but in a covert tone of triumph which annoyed her at once, "and what you fall into isn't love."

"I know, I know," said Jenny, intolerantly, "it's only Sex, you'll be telling me next. How do you manage to keep True Love and Sex separated?"

"Why, I don't," said Freytag, surprised and indignant, "I don't at all, of course not. It never occurred to me that it was possible!"

"I don't know what I fall into, then," said Jenny, and her face was pale, woebegone, no sparkle or warmth at all, "only that it comes to no good and it could be love." The word fell softly between them and chimed in them both.

"It *might* be," agreed Freytag gently after a moment. "Maybe we get the kind of love we are looking for."

Jenny turned on him in a blaze. "*Stop* tying everything up in your neat little bowknots!" she said vehemently. "That's just a way of side-stepping your own responsibility for the trouble you cause somebody else. 'She asked for it,' you can always say, 'I only gave her what she wanted!' . . . that's just moral imbecility and you know it!"

"Oh come now, Jenny," he said masterfully, using her name for the first time, quite sure of her feeling for him by now, "you're talking nonsense. I won't listen to it. We have no quarrel, none at all. Can't we be friends, can't we be loyal good friends and talk things over sensibly? Isn't there something besides love?"

Oh God, thought Jenny, that's the next gambit.

"Oh yes, of course, and much better as a rule," she said, in order to end the talk, and they stood together in a baffled silence. As for loyalty, thought Jenny, you shouldn't be talking about love to a strange woman on shipboard, nor I to a strange man. It's the narrow end of the wedge. Your wife would hate it and so would David, and they'd be quite right. That's one thing about David. He'll never be mooning around about love to any other woman. He won't even talk about it to me. David hates love worse than I do, even. You've got a roving eye and the sidelong approach. If you belonged to me I wouldn't trust you any further than I could throw you by the ear. I can always trust David. David is going to be mean and tough and stubborn and faithful to death. We aren't going to kill each other because I mean to get away before that happens. But we'll leave dents in each other. When I get through with David, he'll know the difference between me and the next woman, and I'll be carrying David like a pet-rified fetus for the rest of my life. She felt empty and sick and tired enough to lie down.

"Love," she remarked, wrinkling her nose, "this ship is simmering with it. I'm sure it's all Real Love. I must fly," she said, "Elsa's in love, too, and I promised to help her fix her hair in a new way."

Alone, Freytag regretted what he had said to her, or most of it; she was rather plainly laughing at him more than once. No doubt she thought him a touch soft-headed. But she would live to learn better. She might have been lovely before she was maimed and perverted by her disordered life, her false notions of love and reckless waste of her womanly substance. He had known girls like her before, in several countries — wild and confused and lonely, full of mistrust, letting him come nearer with a wary look in their eyes as if they would dash away if he tried to touch them. Their waywardness, homelessness, and lack of scruples had freed him from any sense of obligation to them, they asked nothing of him, and had left him at last free to enjoy a remembering pity and tenderness for them.

But that was all in the past. Such follies as Jenny promised to be belonged to his other life, that life peopled with phantoms and foolish dreams; he knew what they were worth, compared to the solid reality of his marriage. He was certain that he was by nature the most singlehearted and faithful of men, he had needed only to find his Mary, his love, and he had found her. Now, he had been separated from her for nearly three months, and his flesh was uneasy, desirous; he was sleeping as badly as when he was a bachelor, spending far too much time and energy trying to find relief from sex: and accepting too often, he remembered with a chill, some pretty sad versions of it. It was a very bad sign when he began feeling sentimental about the first possibly available woman not a professional whore, at least, who crossed his path in an unlucky moment.

What was he thinking about? He brought himself up short; a slight uncomfortable twinge — could it be guilt? — went over him, almost a tremor of the nerves. This tremor of guilt and the beginning of sexual uproar were hardly to be told apart: his preoccupation shifted without warning from Jenny to one of those available Spanish dancers — Lola for choice, she was the basest-looking of the lot. Something good and dirty and hot — that would do. He gripped the rail and stood there holding himself together resolutely, and trying to get his impulses under control again. The first sign of returning sanity was that he damned Jenny freely for a teasing bitch: invoked the name of his wife fervently and made up his mind to write her a long letter after dinner, and to read all her sweet, passionate, wifely letters again before sleeping.

The Cuban medical students on their way to Montpellier had become more than ever a hermetic society, with ritual greetings, secret handgrips which when applied properly wrung responsive yells of facetious anguish from the initiates, and a jargon so recondite they referred constantly in speech to small typewritten code sheets. They engaged in what appeared to be long, learned debates, carried on with farcical solemnity always where they might be seen, but in such lowered tones their rather bored audiences were in no danger of sharing their secrets.

It became known however that they called themselves *"Les Camelots de la Cucaracha,"* and they published on the ship's press every morning copies of a miniature newspaper bearing in highly visible type the banner *El Pi-pi Diario*. Midmorning they were often seen going into La Condesa's stateroom, and coming out being a little boisterous among themselves later; and one day in the small writing room off the bar, they held a meeting and elected La Condesa president, or Cockroach Extraordinary.

Dr. Schumann, who was sitting outside the window, could not have helped overhearing and in fact had not tried to avoid it; and he was outraged to hear in what lewd and disrespectful terms the students talked about her. They believed her to be insane, that was clear, and the designated object of their monkeyish ridicule, but why they chose to expend their boyish filth upon her the Doctor could not understand. Above all, she was not a fool, but a woman of the world and wise in it, and why would she let herself be made a figure of fun by these particularly crass young men?

Upon her appearance in the dining room, Dr. Schumann observed again that La Condesa seemed to have all confidence in her young admirers, and enjoyed their company. They rose as one, bowed deeply, and escorted her to their own table. Her chair was brought, and she sat among them with her elegant manner and, Dr. Schumann thought, a slightly distracted smile. He continued to watch her while she read their no doubt dreadful little newspaper, and she laughed most unbecomingly, showing gold teeth in the back. Taking first the student on her right, and then the one on her left, by the head with both hands, she whispered things in their ears that set them off with shouts of applause and eager questions from the others. Her hands then flew to her own breasts and she stroked them up and down, her face pained and thoughtful. No doubt she had reserved for herself a third flask of ether, and perhaps a fourth, Dr. Schumann concluded with resignation, and a great temptation to give her up, to make no further attempts to help her.

Captain Thiele, whose standards of behavior for the nobility were of astronomical heights, viewed with pinched mouth and beady eyes the frivolous conduct of his distinguished prisoner. She glanced his way, fluttered her fingers at him and at Dr. Schumann, both of whom returned the salute gravely.

Captain Thiele was suffering from indigestion brought on by frustration of his natural sense of authority, to say nothing of his official rank. Upon hearing of the disturbance in the steerage his first impulse had been to order all the participants instantly confined for the rest of the voyage. He had received the deported workers as so many head of cattle, and to find them at the very beginning of the voyage daring to assert themselves with outright insolence was not to be endured for a moment.

Father Carillo had talked to him, in abominable German, as if the fight were not merely a low brawl; he mentioned several times such terms as syndicalism, anarchism, republicanism, communism, besides atheism, above all atheism, the common root of such pernicious theories; and he seemed very instructed in the fine shades of opinion on all subjects existing among the rabble on the lower deck. According to Father Carillo, the lower classes were being led astray by a thousand evil influences from every direction, and a great many dangerous subversive elements were on the steerage deck. These should be watched carefully, not only for the sake of the first-class passengers, the crew, the ship herself, but for the protection of the innocent poor below, those good and harmless people who wished only to be allowed to obey the law and to practice their religion in peace.

The Tenerifans, for example, were mostly decent pious folk. The trouble would be found among the Asturians and the Andalusians, between whom there existed old enmities at best, and he, Father Carillo, was not surprised to discover that the antireligious faction consisted almost entirely of Asturians, with a sprinkling of Basques. . . . They were then the ones to watch. As for the fat man who had pushed the man still kneeling in prayer, he was of the lowest order of rabble rouser and meanest of leaders, a Mexican on his way to Spain for the sole purpose of making trouble there and linking Mexican labor uprisings with those of Spain. No use to worry with him — he would be arrested the moment he set foot on Spanish soil.

The Captain found himself divided into many sections: he loathed Catholics on principle (he believed that priests without exception took advantage of the privacy of the confessional to seduce their more attractive female penitents), he was violently prejudiced against Spaniards as well as Mexicans, and he felt it was beneath his dignity to take the advice of a priest, as well as to admit any human meaning or importance in the doings of the rabble in the steerage. He thanked Father Carillo stiffly for his information, promised to order a general tightening of discipline, using his favorite phrase about laying in irons the next offenders against the peace, and very shortly after that his breakfast began to disagree with him.

His real trouble was, in the heavily overcrowded condition of the ship, there was no place to confine malcontents, especially if they were so numerous and so slyly threatening as Father Carillo seemed to think. In case of outright revolt, it was possible the crew would not be sufficient to control them. Suppose they should seize such small arms as were in the hold, what then?

The Captain, who had spent his professional career, except for the interval of the war, in the relative calm of merchant passenger ships, small ones on long dull cruises, had a riotous, violent imagination which now took possession of him. He dreamed for a brief moment of a cinematic crisis full of darkness, hand-to-hand struggle, flashes of light and thunderous explosions, broken heads and mangled limbs and pools of blood, screams and yells and incendiary flames lighting the sky, with lifeboats being lowered away into the heaving sea, himself still on the bridge somehow in full command of the situation, and completely calm.

Before actually leaving the bridge, however, in the present broad light of a peaceful day, he issued a hasty order that every man in the steerage — woman too, on second thought — was to be searched for weapons however insignificant, and all were to be confiscated for the duration of the voyage. This done, he felt somewhat restored, and in spite of his gas pains was able to speak of the morning's incident with becoming casualness to Herr Professor Hutten and Dr. Schumann. They had disappointed him by accepting his manner at its face value, and seemed to think the incident of very little importance.

The Captain's mood of disapprobation drifted from La Condesa. She was after all not to be blamed so much, since she was a lady in frail health and in a situation highly unsuitable to her caste; however, her very presence on board in such circumstances was a serious symptom of the disorder abroad in the world. Dimly her conduct reflected upon his authority as much as the impudent brawling among the steerage passengers. He was not thinking only of himself — a deviation from routine, a threat to his established rule, every moment of every day within the range of his orders, was not merely a personal affair. As Captain he belonged to a larger plan, he fulfilled his destiny in his appointed place as representative of the higher law; if he failed in his duty — and the very foundation of his duty was to exact implicit obedience from every soul on the ship, without exception — why, then the whole structure of society founded on Divine Law would be weakened by so much. He could not face such a moral catastrophe, and he need not. He would not.

He gazed fretfully, his underlip pouted, at the irritatingly complacent faces gathered around his board. Herr Freytag — who was he? A man who looked upon a ship as a public conveyance meant only to get him in safety and comfort from one port to another. Herr Rieber, the same. Herr Professor Hutten was a man of learning, but what could a professor know of the stern realities of the sea? In spite of his profound respect for Dr. Schumann, he had felt more than once that the Doctor had no real understanding of the discipline necessary on a ship, no genuine regard for rank. He had to warn him more than once, tactfully, against coddling the sailors when they were in sick bay as if they were his patients at home. There were even times when the Doctor seemed to be enjoying himself, quite as if he were merely on a voyage for his own health. It was true, except for his heart he would never have shipped as doctor, but still: when he returned from the steerage that morning, the Doctor had almost ignored the disturbance at the end of Mass, but had mentioned that during the night two women had babies on the bare deck, and he had arranged for them to have bunks in the same cabin for three or four days at least. It showed a lack of proportion in his mind somewhere, the Captain concluded, an indifference to truly serious things.

Of the women the Captain expected nothing, but their low-voiced babble among themselves annoyed him. Little Frau Schmitt was leaning over and talking across Herr Rieber to Fräulein Lizzi, while Frau Rittersdorf and Frau Hutten leaned towards her from their side of the table. Frau Hutten was shaking her head sadly. The Captain pretended to attack his dinner, but he was hot with irritation and his vitals were stabbing him cruelly.

Frau Schmitt's grief had dried up somewhat after her experience with Herr Graf and her unlucky encounter with the Baumgartners; she wandered out on deck and paused idly, as everyone did sooner or later during the day, to watch, as at the bars of a cage, the strange life going on in the steerage. She found herself near the reserved-looking young American, Herr David Scott, also leaning on his elbows with his collar hunched up around his ears. Her eyes were attracted to a sad sight. A man, very bony and ragged and worn, but perhaps young, it was hard to tell, his tousled hair on end, was sitting, back to the rail, his knees drawn up and his bare toes curling and uncurling with sorrow; he was crying openly and bitterly like a child. He wept and scrubbed his eyes with his fists, his mouth was distorted like a howling dog's, and at his feet were several small objects, Frau Schmitt could not quite make out what they were. The other people paid no attention to him; they sat near him with stony indifferent faces; men stood in groups over him with their backs turned, women almost stepped on him going about their own concerns. He seemed completely alone in the world; there is nothing like trouble to divide the human heart from you, thought Frau Schmitt, her own heart swelling with tears once more, but this time with softer and gentler tears, because they were shed for another's sorrow.

She spoke gently to the listening women.

"So I said to the young man, Oh, wouldn't you think at least some one of them would speak to him? They might ask him what is the matter. The young American then said to me, They know already what is the matter; why should they ask? And then it seemed there had been an order, from whom I do not know, and the officers went among all the people and took away their knives and such little edged tools as they had, and this poor man is a wood carver."

Frau Schmitt, deep in her story, raised her voice a little, forgetting her natural timidity in the interest she saw in the faces around her, and the Captain sat up sharply listening with a gathering frown which Frau Schmitt did not notice.

"Well, the Herr David Scott told me then this man was carving small animals from bits of wood he had brought in his bundle, hoping to sell them to people in first class. Herr Scott had half a dozen in his pocket, and he showed them to me: they were very pretty and childlike; Herr Scott said, He is a fine artist. But you know how these Americans are — they worship primitive things because they cannot understand better. They are corrupted by the Negro, of course — what can we expect? I smiled at him and said nothing; but the poor man in the steerage was in trouble! When the officer asked him for his knife, he somehow thought he was lending it, imagine, and would be given it back in a few minutes. Think of that. The young man told me everything. He had seen and heard. He was very angry in a cold pale way as if he had lost blood. Gone then for good were the hopes of that poor man, gone his happy occupation and his little knife, and so he cried, he cried like a baby."

Frau Schmitt's sensibilities almost overcame her again. She sat back and put her napkin to her mouth.

Frau Hutten clucked softly, deprecatingly. Lizzi said in a high infantile voice, "Oh, I don't think that was very nice, taking the poor little man's property away from him! Make them give it back, dear Captain, please?" Her long arm flew forth and she struck him lightly on the sleeve with her fan. The Captain did not respond with the charmed gallantry she expected. His wattles grew scarlet, he bridled until his chin backed into his collar, and he gave Frau Schmitt a truly awful glare. The perfect victim of his wrath had been delivered into his hands, and he proceeded to make an example of her.

"I am exceedingly sorry, ladies," he began, in a voice of blistering courtesy, and his glance took them all in: their unbalanced female emotions, their shallow, unteachable minds, their hopeless credulity, their natural propensity to rebellion against all efforts of men to bring order and to preserve rule in life. "Oh, very sorry indeed, ladies, to distress your kind hearts, but let me confess that I myself gave the order for the disarming of the deportees. I wish I might trust you to believe me when I say that all my acts are governed by a knowledge of the true situation regardless of sentimental considerations. In the end I alone am answerable not only for your safety but for the very life of this ship; therefore, please do allow me to advise you that I act from the gravest motives of responsibility. A little discretion, please, dear lady," he added sternly to Frau Schmitt, "at least do us the favor not to listen to the gossip and prejudices of foreigners, who naturally are anxious to put the worst possible light on anything at all done by a German. Or if you must listen to such rubbish, above all do not repeat it to anyone!"

This unexpected climax to a trying morning crushed Frau Schmitt. She bowed her head, her shoulders drooped, a blush mounted painfully, slowly, from neck to forehead, her hands lay beside her plate and she seemed unable to lift them. From under her eyebrows she saw Frau Rittersdorf's sweet, satisfied smile, yes, just like a cat's. Frau Schmitt

was not comforted to know she would see that smile again in the cab
that evening, and for many days after.

The ship's band did not play in the morning, it being Sunday, but
after dinner the elevating strains of Wagner and Schubert filled the
salon, where the Baumgartners, the Lutzes, the Huttens, in a word the
more respectable element, settled down to the relaxation of cards,
dominoes, and chess. La Condesa disappeared, and later the students
could be heard shouting first at shuffleboard and then in the swim-
ming pool. Mingled with the strains of the band came a harsher
music. The zarzuela company had brought a small gramophone on deck,
and a sharp soprano was raised in urgent obsessive complaint, accom-
panied by the insinuating clack and whine of outlandish instruments.
They danced together, clicking their heels and snapping their fingers
resonantly, revolving about each other with the grace of birds in a mat-
ing dance, but with cold professional faces.

They stopped the music for a few minutes, talked among themselves,
and began again, watching each other sharply. Ric and Rac joined in,
facing each other with narrowed eyes and bared teeth, their small
thighbones strangely agitated. At intervals they stamped and screamed
criticisms at each other without interrupting the rhythm of the dance,
their faces almost touching. Their elders watched them without inter-
fering or offering advice. Then all but Lola sank gracefully to the deck
in a beautifully composed group, and Lola the star began a slow graceful
intense dance.

"Olé, olé, viva tu madre!" they cried in time to the music, clapping
their hands with subtle variations of rhythm as Lola's undulating
skirts almost rose over their heads. The Cuban students came up out
of the pool; reluctantly most of the Germans left their games; sailors
appeared with the air of being there on duty; all were drawn irresistibly
to the charming scene. Freytag, finding himself standing beside Herr
Hansen, said in real surprise, "Why, she's a wonderful dancer!" Herr
Hansen turned like a man brought out of a hypnotic trance. "Eh?
What's that? She's great — she's a great dancer." Not quite that, per-
haps, thought Freytag, moving on, still feeling a little ashamed of his
recent flurry about Lola. He felt a touch of condescension towards a
man so poverty-stricken he must fall in love with the whole zarzuela
and its future for the sake of such an animal as Amparo.

Lola danced grandly and severely, her features fixed in the classic erotic-frowning smile, which fetched forth ritual amorous groans from the males of her assisting company. At her last roulade of clicking heels, the others sprang up. The rehearsal over, they danced in pairs as if for pleasure, but with no pleasure in their faces, and they ignored their audience with well-rehearsed contempt.

Elsa, with her hair in a roll on top of her head, which Jenny had helped her to do and which made her look older, broader in the cheeks, averted her eyes suddenly and stepped backward as if she would hide behind her parents. Excited by the dancing, her face had fallen into a vacant, happy smile. Then alas she saw her student, with only black wool trunks concealing his nakedness, take one of the Spanish girls about the waist and begin dancing with her. Elsa's modesty suffered a shock which caused real pain at the very center of her body; it rippled out in hot waves to her fingertips. She closed her eyes and saw in fiery darkness what she refused to see by daylight — the flexing muscles of his back, the thin beautiful ribcage, the long slender legs with boyish bony knees, and worst of all, the long fine-muscled arms embracing that girl they called Concha, her body limp and yet in movement against his naked chest. No, she could not bear it. "Mama," she whimpered, "Mama, please, let's go inside."

"Are you sick, Elsa?" asked her mother. "Is there anything wrong with you?"

"No, no, please," said Elsa, in an oppressed, patient voice. "The sun is so hot."

"I give you until tomorrow," said her mother firmly, "until tomorrow to be in better spirits, and then I shall give you a good purge. That is no doubt what you need. Here on this ship, with the lack of exercise, the indigestible food — yes, I could have a headache myself, easily. A good purge, that is what you need. But now control yourself, and come finish the dominoes with your father. As to your hair, Elsa, I don't like it so. This evening you must put it back in the old way. And never change it again without asking me."

"Yes, Mama," she said, meekly, and sat down with her father again. Dominoes and checkers with her father, housework that she hated under the constant advice, direction and reproof of her Mama, never to be able to call even her hair her own, to be left on the shelf an old maid at last, yes, that would be her fate, she could feel it deep within her. Her heart sank and then rose again in her and began to knock desperately against her ribs as if it were a prisoner beating against the bars, as if it were not part of her but a terrified stranger locked up in her, crying crying crying "Let me out!"

Her father, noticing her forlorn face, pinched her cheek with tenderness and said jovially, "Maybe our Elsa is in love with somebody — maybe that big solemn Swede Hansen. No, Elsa, my treasure? Tell your papa and mama. We know best."

Elsa said even more meekly, placing a double six after long hesitation, "No, no, Papa, not that."

Frau Lutz, glancing up from her knitting, saw for a moment framed in the doorway against the bright horizon a sight which caused her to frown warningly at her husband, indiscreet as he ever was, thoughtless as usual. Arne Hansen was dancing with Amparo. She seemed to be instructing him in the mysteries of her native dances. They passed and repassed the doorway, Hansen following as awkwardly as a dancing bear, with Amparo treating him as if indeed he were that animal and she the trainer. She seemed to be scolding and laughing at him; they would pause swaying and she would take him by the elbows and shake him. In all seriousness he would begin again, his big hands and feet getting in the way, his wet shirt sticking to his pink skin. He seemed like a man bewitched, utterly indifferent to the scandalous figure he presented to the eyes of the world.

Frau Lutz, amazed at this instance of failure in her judgment of men, a subject in which she considered herself an expert, was pleased to note that her daughter's back was turned towards this unedifying scene. She never ceased to worry, night and day, at the unbelievable hardships a mother encountered in her efforts to preserve the innocence of a daughter. Everywhere you turned, unsavory sights, immoral situations, disreputable characters, shameless behavior on the part even of those in whom you had some reason to place a little hope. Men!

Her gaze rested upon her husband with baleful intensity. He was talking his usual foolishness to Elsa, playing his game without a care, understanding no better than ever the deadly seriousness of life's problems; joking with Elsa about love, of all things. What would have become of them if she had been unwise enough to depend upon him in anything for a moment? Ah, she would find a very different kind of husband for Elsa, she had made up her mind to that.

Johann, pushing his uncle's wheel chair, heard the Spanish music and went a little faster, then slowed down again as he came in sight of Lola, turning and clicking her heels. His sullen fair-skinned face, with its scanty blond stubbles of beard shining, lighted up so tenderly he looked for an instant like a young angel. He turned the chair to the rail and stopped to watch the delightful show.

"Go on, Johann," said his uncle, for the slight joggling of the chair soothed him, and the movement against the wind helped his breathing. His shriveled flesh and his very bones were old and tired and lonely; they cried day and night for a little pity and ease and comfort. In the hospital in Mexico the nurses had rubbed him with sweet-smelling witch hazel all over, their firm young hands pressing lightly into the weariness of his shriveled muscles; they had fed him warm milk and cool fruit juices, papaya, pomegranate, lime; he sucked them through a glass tube, half asleep as if he were a baby again. In the night when he groaned and called out, a Mexican nun in her white face bands and gauzy white veil would come and minister to him, and she would swing the mattress softly on its light springs as if it were a cradle, saying under her breath, "*Ave Maria . . .*"

Now in the miserable cabin, Johann touched him with loathing, he would hand him a dripping cold cloth and say viciously, "Wash your own dirty face." He set down trays of coarse revolting food beside him and went away without giving him so much as a spoon for the soup. In the long nights, when he would be in pain to ease nature, he might call and call until his throat closed and the pain in his chest shot through him like fire before Johann would rouse to bring him the vessel. The humiliation of the helpless flesh was punishment enough, without that hard, unforgiving face above him, averted in loathing.

"Johann," he wanted to cry, "child of my hopes, what has become of you? Where did you go? Pity, a little pity, in God's name." But there was no pity in that child. His soul was sicker than any flesh could be. Herr Graf trembled to think of its fate before God's judgment.

"Can't you see there is no room to pass?" asked Johann, stubbornly lingering. "Let me alone a minute, can't you?"

"Turn back, then, Johann," said Herr Graf, calmly, "turn back."

The chair was whirled about so sharply he was thrown to one side. "Don't try to kill me, Johann," he said in an ominous voice. "My God has promised me that I shall see Germany again. Defy Him if you dare!"

"Keeping me penniless as a beggar," Johann burst out in a fury. "Where is the allowance you promised me? Why must I ask you for money even to go to the barber?"

"What would you do with money on this ship, Johann? It would be only another temptation set in your way. I will provide the necessaries, nephew, but I will not nourish your lusts and appetites. Your soul is too precious to risk in such a way, Johann. I know too well what use you would make of money here." He drew a long, rattling sigh, the bloody phlegm came up in his throat and he spat into his paper box.

"That's what you get for gabbing all the time," said Johann, "you miserly old Jew."

Herr Graf looked at his hands, emaciated, the knuckles mere knobs, the fingers so weak and limp they lay flat or curved as they fell, and thought how not so long ago they would have had the strength to thrash this boy as he deserved. For such as he there was only one remedy — to mortify the flesh until the hard knot of the will was reached and dissolved — ah, a task he might have done so well, and would have so delighted in, the saving of this now ungovernable soul. But God, who was taking away his life little by little, meant for him to suffer all affliction, all possible abasement of mind and flesh to balance the great gift he had conferred upon his spirit. From the very moment he had learned that his body was beginning in earnest to die, like a stream of pure light the divine knowledge had descended upon him that, as recompense for his death, God had given him the power of healing others. In this power his soul had been eased of its fears. To his shame now he remembered that he once feared death, he had cringed abjectly as a condemned criminal at the sight of the ax, he had prayed endlessly and incoherently, begging God to reverse his inalterable law in his, Wilibald Graf's favor; to send a miracle; to punish him for his sins in any other way, no matter how cruel, but only to let him live, even as he was, in pain, in decay, in despair — to let him live.

He, a philosopher and teacher of philosophy, lecturer in universities and before learned societies, had done this terrible thing. When? In his other world, his other life. All his false wisdom had dropped away from him like soiled, outworn rags, he had stood naked as the newly born in the steady stream of cleansing light, and the softest most loving voice he had ever heard, he had not dreamed of such love in a voice, spoke within his ear. "Heal the sick," the voice had said, with the simplicity and directness which is the language of true revelation. And from that day he had gone about his work, knowing the truth; so long as he was able to keep upon his feet, he was to go among the sick and touch them and counsel them and heal them in God's name.

It had not been easy, for the perverse human wills of his family and friends had put every obstacle in his way. It seemed almost — and this was so dreadful a thought he hardly dared give it room in his brain — as if they bore some malice or evil intention toward the dying, as if they did not wish the sick to be healed and well again, like themselves. A friend of his sister's, a willful woman, would not allow him to touch her little grandson who was suffering from bowel complaint. "He needs his rest, he must not be disturbed," she said angrily, and the child had died. But he had saved his sister's servant, an Indian woman who had been in labor for three days, until her eyes were mere pits in her face, and her lips were blackened and dry. "It is not decent for an Indian woman to let a man see her having a baby," they told him. "A modest woman would rather die!" At last he had gone in boldly, pushing them aside, asserting a man's authority over them, and they gave way before him as God meant them to. He had laid his hands upon the distorted suffering belly where the child kicked and heaved in his struggles to be born, called upon God to admit this new soul to life and to His heaven at last, and the child was born safely with three tremendous tearing pains in a very few minutes. He had breathed secretly into the mouth of an infant drowning with pneumonia, and from his own ruined lungs had poured life into the child's.

Oh, there were many: after he had been sent to the hospital, he had been forced to do good by stealth, for the doctors were bitterly jealous of his power, and hindered him by rules, forbidding him under pain to visit the dying in order to touch them and give them life again. But God guided him. He knew from God in what place and at what hour he might find the one who needed him most, and no one was afraid of him because he always said at once, "God bless you, and make you well," and then he touched them lightly, just barely with the tips of his fingers, and was away before some prowling nurse or interne should discover him and put an end to his work. Rarely in the hospital did he have the joy of seeing his dear resurrected ones in health and strength — he was watched too closely, he could not risk a second visit. But there was one: the girl with the red hair in two braids lying behind the death screen with eyes fixed upward, her face livid and mouth half-open, burning to his touch like living fire.

"God will make you well, do you believe?" he asked her, and from the scorched mouth scarcely moving he heard the words, "I believe." Oh blessed child of faith. He had seen that girl, recognizable by her two long red braids flying and shining in the sun, leaving the hospital with her happy family not a week later. "The doctors will think they did it, but we shall know the truth," he had told her.

These were his memories, and this his recompense, and what were his own sufferings but a divine grace since they had been made useful to others? What was death? Why had he been afraid? There remained the greatest reward of all: immortality for the suffering bewildered soul. Immortality. It is not a matter of belief, what is there to believe? How can anyone form even an idle wish around anything so infinitely formless? It is a matter of faith — no, a *hope*, a fixed changeless longing for a continued existence in another place, under another appearance, in a different element; continued existence at least until all questions are answered, and all unfinished things are done. Is it not fairly a certainty that this is a divine impulse sent from God to guide us to Him? . . . And yet, this longing may prove to be merely a motive power of man's present existence, an intellectual concept related to his animal instinct of self-preservation; man loves himself so dearly he cannot relinquish willingly one atom of himself to oblivion. Perhaps the whole idea then originates in the will, that source of self-love, and is simply one more of its various and deluded activities. And what about the four-footed beasts, the feathered, the finny? Perhaps they have a corresponding source of vitality in them; or better, they do not even suspect they shall not live forever precisely as they are. Ah, there's happiness for you, there is the lucky state of being.

Herr Graf opened his eyes with a leap of the nerves, thrilling with pain all through: he must have dozed and dreamed, there was some terrible nightmare at the edge of his memory. Weakness and despair almost overwhelmed him. "Johann, Johann," he muttered, his tongue thick, "water, water," and then, "My God, my God," but the prayer, whatever it was, stopped on his lips. He did not dare to pray, he did not know what to pray for. The soul after death may discover, may wake in morning radiance, to a bliss it is now unable to imagine, and no matter how mysterious its longings now, it will understand everything then. Ah, maybe heaven itself is only this: that Wilibald Graf may never once remember he was Wilibald Graf, miserable lost pilgrim in this terrible world. Is that what is meant, perhaps, by the blessed words "forgiveness of sins"?

"Water, water, Johann, my sweet child," he said again, but there was no answer. He felt the slight swaying motion of the chair being wheeled again smoothly after a long pause. As they turned the corner the dark shadow of his nephew's head and shoulders fell across his own, lay upon his knees and stretched before them upon the deck. The silence stretched too until it broke with the strain of its own hatred.

"You want water?" asked Johann, with false solicitude, mimicking the tone of kindness with elaborate cruelty. Gathering himself, he spat out his poison: "Well, wait until you get it, you stinking old corpse."

"Shame on you, Johann," said his uncle calmly. "I leave you to God."

Without warning, in silence, Johann spun the chair around violently, guided it swiftly through the main salon, down the stairs and through the long passageway into their cabin with its bitter smells. At the door he simply gave the chair a shove through; it rolled to the opposite wall and fetched up with a bump. Herr Graf had not protested, nor even turned his head. The chair slithered a little sideways, and in a flash of fearful hope Johann saw his closed eyes and dropped jaw like a newly dead man's. Slamming the door behind him, he raced back to the deck, his stomach so sunken and tight between fury and terror, his heart pounding so heavily he could hardly hear, his eyes dancing so that he was nearly blinded. Yet he could see Concha, not clearly, but enough. He halted then and moved to the rail and stared at her; she stared back in perfect stillness, meaning with her look to motion him to her. He did not move, and with his hot, fixed eyes he resembled uncommonly a famished tiger regarding its prey, lips drawn back, teeth bared. Concha had seen this look often and had never been dismayed by it. On the contrary, it exhilarated her, lightened for her often her rather dull occupation, to find a young one full of fire and awkward eagerness. She was young too, the youngest of her company, not yet hardened altogether, and she was not at all deceived by this unhappy boy, standing there gazing at her like something lurking behind a bush, slouched over a little, hands in pockets, trying to carry it off, longing to be a man.

Concha walked towards him smiling, and without hesitation held out her arms to him while she was not yet within reaching distance. Johann took one bound towards her, seized her waist accurately at arm's length, and strode away with her in the dance, still with the look of one caught between flood and fire. Concha put her nose to his chest inside his open shirt front and took a deep luxurious breath. He smelled like a clean baby, with rich undersmells of a real male. She took a good hold of him then; her breast rose high under her thin shabby black dress, her neck arched; she preened and strutted and murmured like a pigeon. Head back, eyes raised and shining, she smiled at him deeply, gave him a long heart-shaking look, then dropped softly against him the full length of her body, and rested her pale cheek on his chest as if she slept. Meanwhile, asleep or not, her neatly rolling little hips kept tireless rhythm, she stepped and swayed and spun in the perfection of her delicate art. Little by little Johann's desperate face smoothed and softened, he rested his cheek on her sleek black hair and danced too with closed eyes.

A rather routine performance perhaps, Freytag was thinking. Considering all the uproar it can cause, the instrument is strangely limited; a mere reed flute with a few monotonous notes — but this girl does have style. She may teach him something he'll never be sorry for knowing. He could see that Concha was not just running through her repertory like a wound-up doll, as she had done at the rehearsal with the company, but was putting her heart, or whatever stood for her heart, into the matter, with perfect effectiveness. It was easy to see that she had reduced that glittering-haired boy, who had struck him as no great specimen of wit at best, to a state of bliss bordering on idiocy, in this sudden half-relief from the hopeless ferocities of his desire which was, if only he could have known, so simple, so usual, and at his age and in his prime condition, so easily satisfied. Why could he not put on a cheerful grin, and jingle a few coins in his pocket? However, in his situation, obviously under the thumb of his dying old uncle, the lack of money was no doubt the main reason why he could not put on the cheerful grin. That too was a commonplace. Freytag, having somehow recovered his own self-approval, left them dancing and walked on.

Jenny, who had borne all she was able of David's silence and sulkiness, and tight, white-ringed mouth at dinner, after a day of sitting or strolling about with him, the air between them twanging painfully at every passing breeze, disappeared into her cabin to write letters to several members of her family. Though David never believed it, no matter what she told him, Jenny had, in a mid-Southern state, a small but pertinacious family of brothers, sisters, aunts, uncles, cousins, even a small niece and nephew, the quite most conventional assortment, really; and she was fond of them all, in a baffled, detached sort of way. As she began "Dear . . ." she thought again that it did not matter which of the lot she addressed the letter to, for they presented to her the impermeable front of what she called "the family attitude" — suspicion of the worst based on insufficient knowledge of her life, and moral disapproval based firmly on their general knowledge of the weakness of human nature. Jenny couldn't possibly be up to any good, or she would have stayed at home, where she belonged. That is the sum of it, thought Jenny, and wouldn't their blood run cold if they could only know the facts? Ah well, the family can get under your skin with little needles and scalpels if you venture too near them: they attach suckers to you and draw your blood from every pore if you don't watch out. But that didn't keep you from loving them, nor them from loving you, with that strange longing, demanding, hopeless tenderness and bitterness, wound into each other in a net of living nerves.

It was no question at all whether they were the kin you would have chosen, would have preferred, at any rate; they were the family you belonged to, and there you were, stuck for good, for life and for eternity itself, no doubt. At this point in her half-conscious meditations with her pen hesitating above the paper, Jenny dropped the "you" form, and stopped thinking in words, only knowing in her bones that she could not live near her family because she was afraid of their weaknesses and faults — they were also her own; and most of their virtues repelled her even more than their faults. She had spent years of strategic warfare trying to beat those people out of her life; then more years trying to ignore them; to forget them; to hate them; and in the end she loved them as she knew well she was meant in simple nature to do, and acknowledged it; it brought her no peace, and yet it put a certain solid ground under her feet. She did not turn to them at last for help, or consolation, or praise, or understanding, or even love; but merely at last because she was incapable of turning away. They were the family and she was the stray sheep; they never let her forget it, they were full of malice and resentment they could not hide, and they invented little slanders about her among themselves to justify their view of what they called her "desertion."

And moreover, they couldn't be fooled for a moment with all that nonsense about wanting to paint, to be an "artist." A young woman of good family leaves her home and place for only one reason: she means to lead a shameless abandoned life where her relatives and her society cannot restrain or punish her. Artist indeed! What was to stop her painting at home in the back garden?

With all this and a good deal more running not exactly in her mind but in her bloodstream, Jenny was writing, "Dearest Cousin or Brother or sweet Nephew or Aunt . . . weather is beautiful, getting cooler . . . I am in wonderful health . . . looking forward to Paris . . . let me hear from you . . . yours, yours and yours with my love . . ." yours indeed, with my love, my devilish dear family! She was folding up the last when Elsa came in from the moving pictures, with traces of tears in her eyes, yet cheerful and ready to talk.

She sat on the side of her bed and began letting down her hair. "Mama doesn't like it this way," she told Jenny, shyly.

"I don't either, really," said Jenny, "the other is prettier."

There had been moving pictures for the first time, and when Jenny had suggested to David that they see them, David had said he couldn't imagine a reason for passing an evening in such a stupid way, and Jenny had retorted at once that she couldn't imagine anything more stupid than the way they were passing it now. That had settled the question and ended the talk, and they spent the evening apart, Jenny writing letters.

Elsa, it came out, had a lovely time. The pictures were just the kind she liked best, the kind one saw so seldom in Mexico, where they were always about bandits fighting on horseback in the mountains, and burning ranches; and low women always after men; and all sorts of ugly people playing bad tricks on each other. No, these two pictures were very different. They were German, and so sweet. As she sat getting ready for bed, she remembered the plots utterly. There was one about the miller's beautiful daughter who was loved by two rich gentlemen, real lords — father and son. She will not have the father, who forbids her to have the son, whom she loves. By a vile plot, she is seized by two villainous servants of the old lord, while she is picking flowers by the millstream, and taken to the lodge of the gamekeeper, and there she is heartlessly married off to that low person, who is a widower with a daughter her own age, the old lord standing by giving the orders for everything in the most cruel way!

"Where was the son?" asked Jenny, stamping envelopes.

"He had just happened to go on a journey," said Elsa. "But the gamekeeper's daughter thought of a way to help her. She pretended to go with the bride to her room to help her undress, but instead she tied sheets together and let her down out of the window and the new bride ran home through the woods — oh it was beautiful with the moonlight shining in the treetops — and the wicked gamekeeper sets out after her; but his foot slips on the bridge of the millstream — it is an act of God, you understand — and he is drowned. And just at that moment the young lord comes home and learns everything; and the girl is restored to him a virgin widow!"

"What became of the old lord?" asked Jenny.

"He repented and gave them his blessing," said Elsa. "The last scene was the wedding in a great church full of flowers and music, and then a dance on the village green. I wish they would show more pictures like that . . . the girl was so pretty, and the young man was so handsome, and they were so happy together!"

"It's a fine big wedding cake with plenty of icing and sugar birds and roses," said Jenny, "like the one you'll have someday."

"Oh, I hope so," said Elsa, but doubtfully as ever. "The second picture was nice too . . ."

Jenny reached for a light wrap, laid it across her knees, and sat waiting for the end. "It was a little hard to follow because there was so much happening all the time, but there was a handsome young Archduke who wished to marry only for love, and he would not wed the Gräfin von Hohenbrecht sight unseen, out of obedience to his dear parents, who arranged the marriage for his own good — you know how parents are," said Elsa, with a surprising lapse into everyday common sense, "and the poor old people, who want him to be happy, make a plot with the Gräfin's father and mother to bring them together in some way so that they are both disguised and take each other for simple peasants. You will understand that the Gräfin, too, is romantic and has also refused even to meet the Archduke, for she wants to marry only for love. Well, the Gräfin's parents tell her it is time for her to know something about life and how to run a castle, and that she is to dress like a laundry maid and go with servants to the river for the washing day. But she doesn't do any work, you know, she just orders the others around. Meantime they have arranged for the Archduke, disguised as a forester, to be hunting in that part of the woods with some of his men. He sees the beautiful maiden, she sees him, they fall in love on sight, of course! that's the point; and the young Archduke tells his parents he has met the true love of his whole life, and will marry only the laundry maid and no one else. Then the two families have a great time carrying on the joke and making difficulties until they are sure the love is real. Meantime the Archduke and the Gräfin put on their disguises and run away to meet each other in the forest every time they can manage. This goes on for a long time, until finally everything comes out; and there is a great wedding, in a cathedral, and afterwards a gay ball at the castle, and the servants all dance on the castle green. Oh," said Elsa, suddenly, "you'll think I'm just silly. I know already that life is not like that, I don't expect any such thing. And yet," she said, "I don't understand those Cuban students. Even that tall nice-looking one who sings so well — you remember the one I like? — well, he was just like the rest. All through, in the love scenes and even the sad parts, they jeered, and whistled, and yowled like cats and behaved so badly a steward asked them for silence. So they all got up and went away with that Condesa, you know the prisoner, and she was making fun too. I can't understand people being so hardhearted — they were sweet pictures full of lovely scenes —"

"The trouble with those students is simply that they haven't been born yet," said Jenny, severely. "They are just their parents' bad dreams. Elsa, you should try to forget about that boy."

"How can I forget him," asked Elsa, a trifle fretfully, "when I see him every day? But my mother says La Condesa is a disreputable woman, title or no title, and that I must on no account even speak to her. How can I speak to an older woman unless she speaks to me first? And yet, how I should love to know what it is like to be that kind of woman!"

Jenny said, smiling, "But Elsa, you *are* coming on, fast. What an idea . . . what would your mother say? Now tell me, after this merry evening at the movies, why were you crying?"

"I am so happy sometimes, and then so miserable," confessed Elsa, simply, and she wiped her eyes where the tears began to form again.

"That's all right then," said Jenny hastily, "if it's nothing more serious than that. I'm not sleepy. I'll take a turn around the deck and look at the moon; good night."

"Good night," said Elsa, in a pacified voice; and the long confusions of her day slipped into easy dreams.

Frau Otto Schmitt was still feeling somewhat intimidated by her recent encounters with a world of male unaccountability which she found dismaying in her new and tender state of widowhood. She was beginning to realize with astonishment that she had never really known any man but her husband; no women except wives of her husband's friends, or old maid teachers as remote from her womanly confidences as if they belonged to another species. For years she had hardly seen anyone, outside of her classrooms of younger students, except in the company of her husband: indeed, she had lived her married life almost literally in his presence. His state of health after the war had made it seem at times almost as if he were her child; in better times, a kind sympathetic brother; yet always her husband, after all. And oh, what a poor preparation for her life without him he had given her! Where could she turn, to whom could she speak, sure of a gentle human response?

Almost she took it as an answer to prayer when Dr. Schumann appeared alone at the head of the deck and stood at the rail. She approached him as nearly as she might without, she hoped, appearing to ambush him, but she longed to be near him if only for a moment, for he soothed and reassured her sense of all that was right, good, and appropriate in every way.

The left side of his face was turned towards her, and she could have worshipped that noble *Mensur* scar. Her husband's scar, quite as impressive as the Doctor's, had been her life's pride. It reminded her of salutary facts: that his family had been superior to her own, that his university dueling had further enhanced him socially; that altogether he could have made an advantageous marriage, a rich one. But no, he had chosen her, with her tiny dowry, and her brothers who had never touched a foil; and had never, he told her, regretted it for a moment; for which she never ceased to be grateful to him. The Doctor's scar was as perfectly placed as could be: for if a student flinched, turned his head or lowered his chin, he was apt to be slashed even on the forehead, or the cheekbone — she had seen too many such scars — and it was a disgrace to him, unless it could be blamed on the awkward swordsmanship of the other — and how does one go about explaining *that*, all one's life? Frau Schmitt had grown a little tired of hearing Frau Rittersdorf boast that her husband was a bold dueler, always the challenger, always the victor, with four scars on his left cheek, every one a beauty, a split to the teeth, and not a quarter-inch apart! Well, she suspected Frau Rittersdorf of exaggeration, at times. Besides, one good scar well placed was enough — what was it for, after all? A token in the living flesh, another kind of medal bestowed for proved courage. Having achieved it, a gentleman might then go about his other concerns and occupations.

In her shy adoring mood she almost crept towards the Doctor, who turned and gave her that serious smile she admired in him, and seemed about to speak, when the raucous chorus of "*Cucaracha*" broke upon the evening air. La Condesa, in a flowing white dress and green sandals, sailed out of the salon in her swarm of grotesque courtiers, riffled her fingers and smiled charmingly at the Doctor, and walked on swiftly, her skirts flying, the students howling their song and keeping time in a rumba step. One of them, a stringy boy in purple tweed Oxford bags, like tucked-up skirts, lolloped in the rear a safe distance, mimicking her frail complaining voice: "Ah, youth, beautiful youth, she's not having any, thank you."

He even had the impudence to wink outright at Frau Schmitt, who scarcely believed her eyes. She turned in dismay to Dr. Schumann, and could only gasp, "Well! . . . but did you ever?"

Dr. Schumann moved nearer, and they stood together watching the students — their convulsed gait, their apelike grimacing, the flying impudent gestures of their hands, in the graceful wake of La Condesa. How could she, who seemed so acutely aware of herself and all around her, tolerate for a moment such effrontery? He suppressed a huge sigh, turned back to the sea, and said to Frau Schmitt, in a melancholy voice: "It is hardly to be believed, the malignance of the young. We hear a great deal, do we not? spoken against the middle-aged, and too much of it is true — about our growing faults of sloth, of selfishness, of complacency, of despair —"

"I hope not despair, dear Dr. Schumann," said Frau Schmitt, uneasily.

"Above all, despair," said the Doctor firmly. "But the real wickedness," he said, "is in youth. We sin, we older ones, and we know we sin; some of us try hard to repent, to make reparation. But they —" he inclined his head towards the students — "they sin and they do not even know it; or they know it and they glory in it. They are shameless, cruel, and proud . . . they love themselves with a passion unknown to age — perhaps exhausted," he added, with some sudden touch of humor, "in age . . . but still, they sin all day long against all that exists, from the human heart to the Holy Ghost, and when they are tired of sinning they lie down and sleep like newly washed lambs. All that ignorant scorn and mockery," said the Doctor, "all that senseless cruel jeering against a lady who is suffering, and who has never harmed them!"

Frau Schmitt said, with naïve, gentle wonder: "But Doctor! This is the first time I ever heard you speak harshly!"

"I mean to be harsh," said the Doctor, calmly. "I am the voice of rebuke itself lifted in the wilderness, or over the waste of waters! I wish my words were stones that I might throw them to crack the heads of those savages."

"Or their hearts," said Frau Schmitt.

"No, they have no hearts," said the Doctor.

Frau Schmitt was silent, feeling that she had been drawn beyond her depths, and yet, such depths as she longed to be drawn to. Ruefully she watched his gaze as it followed the figure of La Condesa disappearing around the stern; saw what she saw, read it in her own way, thought her own simple thoughts. What a pity such a good man should fall in love with such a woman. And at his age too, and married, and all! Oh, it was frightening, and it happened all too often. Her faith in the Doctor wavered, sank, recovered somewhat, but never in its former glory. She felt newly wounded, left out of things again, life was going to pass her by. She wished only to say her rosary and place herself in God's hands, and go to sleep and forget. There was never again to be anything pleasant or good in this world for her. After a stricken moment, she murmured a little formal phrase proper to leave-taking, and went on her way.

Dr. Schumann wondered at himself, reflected somewhat on his words, and regretted them as immoderate: that is, spoken out of place, with undue emphasis, at the wrong moment, and to the wrong person — indeed, they should never have been spoken at all, he concluded, the feeling which inspired them being itself suspect. He made a little Act of Contrition in the depths of his mind, stretched himself in the nearest deck chair, and closed his eyes. The deck was dimly lighted and deserted for the moment, all silence except for the lulling sound of the waves. Dr. Schumann, who before had been playing with the notion of signing up for another voyage, then and there in a flash of insight knew that this voyage was to be his last. In his relief at being given a glimpse of the certain end of a journey that was proving to be, mysteriously, a surprisingly trying time for him, the Doctor fell into a gentle sleep.

When he opened his eyes, La Condesa was stretched beside him in the neighboring chair to his right, quite at her ease, wide awake, pensively beautiful, regarding the darkened sea as if she were waiting for a curtain to rise. He was so amazed he almost stammered:

"W-what have you done with those terrible young men?"

"They can be a little dull at times, that's true," she told him calmly. "They got tired of playing the monkey, and said they were going to play dice. You were sleeping enviably. How do you do it?"

Dr. Schumann sat up, feeling refreshed and restored to his center. He said almost merrily, "A clear conscience, of course!"

"Of course," said La Condesa. "I can see that you are a man who could not live without a clear conscience."

"There are worse things to have," said the Doctor, sturdily, being by now well aware that he must begin to take a firmer hand with this erratic lady who was after all his patient. "Tell me, have you nothing to reproach your own conscience with just now?"

"I know nothing about a conscience," said La Condesa. "I have instead just the faintest sense of honor which does almost as well . . . intermittently! But as to my promise to you, I have kept it until now — can you not see? But it does not make me happy; no, it causes me acute anguish, I have cactus in my veins, and why do I do it? For you, as I told you; why do you ask more?"

"I did not even ask that," said Dr. Schumann, "that least of all. Indeed, I never would have made so bold as to dream of such a thing."

"I know," said La Condesa, almost with tenderness. "I need badly something to help me sleep. I cannot endure any longer."

"Try just a little longer to do without," said the Doctor, "and I promise to help you when the time comes."

"I detest martyrdom in all its forms," said La Condesa. "So unbecoming to me. I cannot be heroic — I detest that even more. Yet, see — here I am promising to be both because you think it may be good for me — good for what, my soul?"

"Your soul as well, no doubt," said the Doctor, amiably.

"Do you expect some great change in me because of this strange voyage, so unexpected, so unlike anything I have ever known?" asked La Condesa. "A miracle of some kind?"

The Doctor began to speak, and at that point they both noticed the rather comic pair, the scrawny Lizzi and the little fat Herr Rieber, ascending to the boat deck, followed rather furtively at a little distance by Ric and Rac, the twins. Neither La Condesa nor the Doctor mentioned these apparitions, or hardly noticed them, and went on with their conversation, pleasantly.

Ric and Rac, after skulking about the boat deck, keeping well out of sight of the objects of their attentions, whose habits and designs they knew well, heard at last a confusion of most promising sounds coming from behind the second great funnel, a fairly dark and private place: a light scuffling, slipping boot heels, frantic smothered feminine yaps and hisses, a male voice gleefully gurgling and crowing. Ric and Rac could not understand the words, but they knew in their bones the lingua franca of gallantry. Discreetly as little foxes they approached, holding each other back, for fear the other would get the first glimpse, exchanging shrewd glances, the whites of their eyes gleaming, their pointed red tongues running round their open mouths. The wind whistled past their ears and whipped their hair against their cheeks; their stringy garments flattened against their meager frames as they leaned upon the funnel and slid round towards the enticing noises.

In greedy silence and stillness they observed the expected scene. Lizzi and Herr Rieber were huddled together on the deck, backs to the funnel, fighting, laughing, wrestling. He was trying to play with her knees, and she was pulling down her skirts with one hand and pushing feebly at him with the other. Ric and Rac waited for something more interesting, but the bony girl broke away and shoved the fat man almost over on his back. The front of her blouse was open almost to the belt and the children remarked with distaste that there was really nothing to see. Tossing her head about, squealing, the girl's wild eyes pointed suddenly at Ric and Rac. She gave a shrill, new kind of scream, "Oh, look, oh look, oh — " waving her long arms at them.

Herr Rieber sobered at once, and as Lizzi sprang upright in an instantaneous unfolding movement like a jackknife, he got to his feet by squatting first, then supporting himself on a coil of rope and at last heaving himself up with a laborious groan. Ric and Rac merely took a step backward around the funnel, still gazing, balanced for flight if necessary.

"*What* are you doing here, you shameless creatures?" asked Herr Rieber, taking a somewhat choked but severely paternal tone.

"Watching you," said Rac, pertly, putting out her tongue; and Ric joined in, "Go on, don't stop. We'll tell you if anybody's coming."

Herr Rieber, honestly shocked by such early cynicism, rushed at them snarling, with ready hands, but they leaped out of his reach.

"Out of here!" bawled Herr Rieber, almost beside himself. Ric and Rac danced, actually clapping their hands for pure glee, as Herr Rieber bounded here and there after them, aiming blows which landed in air and turned him right about. Ric and Rac pranced savagely around him, shouting, "A peso, a peso, or we'll tell — a peso or we'll tell — a peso — "

"Monsters!" cried Lizzi hoarsely. "You horrible little — "

"A peso, a peso!" chanted Ric and Rac, still sliding around Herr Rieber and avoiding his blows with perfect ease. Herr Rieber stopped, panting, head down like an exhausted bull in the ring. He reached in his pocket. A peso rang on the deck and rolled. Ric put his foot on it. "One for her too," he said, "one for her." His face was sharp and cool and wary. Herr Rieber cast away another peso. Ric snatched them both and clutching them in one hand he motioned to Rac, who followed him instantly.

Running, they collided somewhere at the head of the steps, and both of them saw the same thing at once and had the same notion about it. The canvas covering of one of the lifeboats was partly unfastened, it hung loose and could easily be opened further. They tried the fastenings, which gave way surprisingly; they raised the flap and wriggled into the boat, Rac first, Ric following, without a word.

The boat was very much deeper than they had thought. With a good deal of scrambling about, they managed to bring their faces up to the opening in the flap, where they listened attentively, faces touching, for some moments. Then the fat man and the scrawny girl passed by them, she buttoning her blouse and both of them very angry-looking. Ric lost his balance and made a scrabbling noise; the girl turned her head and peered toward them without seeing; then she stumbled on the steps and the fat man took her arm. "Careful, my beautiful," he said softly.

"Stop that," she said, bitterly, snatching away from him.

Ric and Rac fell back into the boat, all tangled up giggling in the darkness. "Give me my peso," said Rac fiercely, clutching Ric in the ribs and digging her nails in. "Give me my peso or I'll tear your eyes out."

"Take it," said Ric, in the same tone, clenching his fist over the money. "Go on, take it, just try!"

Locked in what seemed to be a death grapple, they rolled to the bottom of the boat and fought furiously, knees in ribs, claws in hair; the pain they inflicted on each other had a strong undertow of pleasure. Little by little they fell quiet and then began to giggle again. A young officer passing stopped to listen, his face very thoughtful. Stepping forward, he snatched back the canvas, and whatever he saw there appeared to turn him to stone for a second. Then, throwing himself over the side and bending down nearly head first, he seized them and dragged them both over the side of the boat. They were as light as if their bones were hollow, and they came out limp and dangling as broken dolls.

La Condesa and Dr. Schumann remained at ease in their long chairs, watching the ship's lights dance in the darkened sea, and the Doctor was saying: "One has no new weaknesses, no new strengths, but only developments, accentuations, diminishments, or perversions of original potentialities. These may at times be so abrupt and powerful they give the illusion of radical change, but it is only illusion, I am afraid. As one grows older, one is more conscious of the shifting, unstable elements in one's temperament. One attempts to keep accounts, to assume control, you might say. One realizes at last, simply and perhaps with some dismay, that what one was told in childhood is after all true — one is immortal certainly, but not in this flesh. One . . ." He paused.

"One, one — one," said La Condesa lightly. "Who is this One you are always talking about? Let's talk about us — you and me, precisely."

"Myself, I have a very ordinary weakness of the heart; so I ship as doctor for a voyage or two, following the prescription I have so often given others, hoping for a little repose, imagine. Now if only I can live long enough once more to see my wife chasing the chickens out of our country kitchen with a broom, and scolding steadily, I shall ask no more of this world. How much that dear woman has scolded me, and everybody and everything, all her married life, at least, with such good reasons always, and for everybody's good, for truly she is nearly always right — and what has it come to?"

"Well," said La Condesa gaily, "for you at least, it has come to an end for a little while."

Dr. Schumann chose to smile only a little at this and looked away over the rail to the waters. "Imagine me, a doctor, after all these years in quiet Heidelberg thinking I should find repose from the world on a ship. I am astonished at myself for thinking, now maybe I shall learn something new about myself or the people I live with; but no such thing. I have seen all this before, over and over, only never until now did I see it on a ship. These people I have seen them all before, only in other places, under different names. I know their diseases almost by looking at them, and if you know what sickness is in a man you very often can tell what form his vices and his virtues have taken."

"Now talk about me," said La Condesa, clasping her long hands lightly about her knee and bending forward from the leg rest of her chair.

There appeared at the upper end of the deck an unusual group in a state of violent action. A young officer with his cap knocked crooked was struggling with those dreadful Spanish twins. Yet in spite of all, the officer continued to advance firmly and managed a kind of ragged progress toward Dr. Schumann and La Condesa, hauling his captives, who were trying to bite his hands.

"More mischief," said Dr. Schumann, his serenity fading away. "I have yet to see those children in a situation where they are not making trouble for somebody." He called out to the young officer, "What is happening?"

The young officer blushed at the question. He planted himself before the Doctor and renewed his grip on Ric and Rac, who suddenly gave up struggling and stood stock-still, sullen eyes gazing at nothing. The young officer began: "Sir, these children, these unspeakable —"

Ric and Rac made a concerted bolt for freedom in opposite directions so that his arms flew wide but he did not lose hold of them. His blush deepened until his ears seemed about to burst into flames. He turned his head from side to side, mouth opening and closing in silence, appealing to them both wordlessly that in the presence of a lady he could not continue.

"I am a mother," said La Condesa encouragingly, giving him a most unmaternal smile; her bright red mouth rounded and softened, her eyebrows went up. "I can guess the very worst and truly I must say I do not find it so bad. What do you think, Doctor?"

"I agree that no matter what they did, they are little monsters," said Dr. Schumann, bending his head to observe them without hope, "and entirely outside any usual mode of discipline."

"They were in a lifeboat," said the young officer, stuttering slightly. "They had unfastened the edge of the canvas top and had crawled in —"

"And were amusing themselves?" asked La Condesa. "Well, *il faut passer la jeunesse* . . . infancy is a great bore, I find, one's own first, and then other peoples' . . . my poor children were not in the least monstrous, on the contrary almost disconcertingly normal — but they were quite simply bores until they were eighteen years old. Then they became charming young men to whom one could talk. I do not know how this miracle occurs. And so," she added, "we must wait and have patience with such phenomena as these," and she smiled enchantingly at the children, who stared back with utter malignance.

"Nothing of the sort will happen with these," said Dr. Schumann. "Their evil is in the egg of their souls." And then to the young officer: "Can't you just hand them over to their parents?"

"Their parents, my God!" said the young officer, in a spurt of contempt and despair. "Have you not seen them, sir?"

"Then," said La Condesa, "I see nothing for it but to let them go — or," and she looked tenderly into the burning eyes of the two little criminals, "perhaps we should save time and trouble for everybody if we threw them overboard?"

"Yes, Madame, a good idea," said the young officer, bitterly, "and a pity it cannot be carried out."

"Oh, you take everything too seriously," she said. "They're only children."

"Devil-possessed, though," said Dr. Schumann. La Condesa studied his friendly benevolent face now overcast with an almost military severity. "What an old-fashioned sort of man you are," she said, admiringly.

The Doctor's eyelids flinched once. "Yes, I know — a little dull, no doubt."

"But charming!" she said, and reached for his hand.

The young officer, whose moral sense was in a particularly tender, inflamed state, was almost as shocked by this gesture as he had been by the sight of Ric and Rac in the boat. So all the rumors he had heard about La Condesa were true! He saw himself abandoned to his dilemma with Ric and Rac — very well, they were no worse than their elders. Let them do as they pleased. He loosed them as if he were throwing off vipers; they broke instantly into their long, shambling run up the deck. He then bowed with a courtesy as false as he dared to show to La Condesa and the Doctor, straightened his cap and moved on.

La Condesa glanced after him and laughed, in a fresh, joyous tone, her eyes glistening. "Poor, nice young man," she said, "he's still too young — too young to remember his own childhood. Dear Doctor, I have never understood the dogma of Original Sin. Children are only perfectly natural little animals before they are brought under the whip — why be shocked at them?"

"There is nothing discoverable of good in these," said the Doctor. "Never these. Why deceive ourselves with hope? They will come to no good end."

"They are not in such a good state now," said La Condesa. She leaned back and drew a long breath. "What kind of childhood had you?"

"An innocent one," said Dr. Schumann, in perfect good temper again, "or so I like to think."

"Ah, so you like to think and maybe it is true," cried La Condesa. "But can't you remember anything interesting at all? Did nothing gay ever happen to you?"

Dr. Schumann meditated in silence for a few moments, began to smile rather reluctantly, then decided to make a clean breast of it.

"Innocence," he began, "our highly debatable innocence . . ."

"So you do have some amusing memories," said La Condesa, laying her silky hand over his, the blue veins standing up branched like a little tree. "Well, truth — to encourage you — I was never innocent, never. I had not the opportunity, for one thing, surrounded as I was by attractive cousins, boys of the most adventurous temperament, like mine. I had no aptitude for it, above all, never the wish. I could never endure to think that any secret or any pleasure was being kept from me. I surmised without help, everything, very early. From there to experience, it was only a step; from experience to habit a matter of moments. I cannot be sorry for anything except that I did not always make the most of my chances!"

"I *was* innocent," said Dr. Schumann, "as a calf; full of hopes and animal spirits, a simple soul without a care, believing everything I was

taught, an obedient loving child . . . I could be kissed into anything,"
he said. "But still, it is true that at the age of five I seduced my little
girl cousin aged three, and at six I was in turn seduced by a little girl
playmate aged nine. In our ignorance, we did preposterous things —
not even parodies," he said. "Both of my playmates were very nice,
charming, virtuous girls who turned out well, married happily, and
spanked their own children thoroughly for the least thing. Yet I say,
the impulses that drove us were grounded in Original Sin, in which I
believe as I do the Real Presence. . . ."

"I believe in neither," said La Condesa, without emphasis.

"Still you must allow me my beliefs," said the Doctor, gently. "As
for innocence, does anyone know what it is? For I remember guilt
and pleasure, always associated, yet never seeming to touch that part
of my life and those acts founded on the moral law and which seemed
real to me and not a fable, or a mere daydream, and which I do believe
were innocent."

"I shall not try to follow this," said La Condesa. "Are we not talking
for pleasure? Theological discussion fills me with gloom. I had all the
joys of sinning as you call it, without guilt," she said, with a certain
complacency. "But you must have been a most charming little person.
I should have adored you, even then. Some of my crimes were of a base,
unimaginative order, I am sorry to say. When I was four I persuaded
my little brother to drink lye-water used for cleaning drains, telling
him it was milk. He took a mouthful, spat it out, ran shrieking. He
was rescued at once, his mouth scrubbed out; I was punished, beaten
black and blue; otherwise nothing came of it. And indeed, I meant no
harm — I was only curious to see whether it would kill him. But older
people do not understand these things."

"Ah, childhood," said Dr. Schumann, "time of the tender bud, the
unfolding leaf." They both laughed pleasantly and sat back in their
long chairs.

"Truth is, it was not so bad," said La Condesa. She lifted the
Doctor's hand and slipped her fingers between his, knitting them to-
gether.

"I love you," she said, gently and unexpectedly. "Not so much you,
perhaps, though you are very nice, but I love what you are. I like
gravity and seriousness and strong principles in a man. There is noth-
ing more repellent to me than a frivolous, timid, vacillating man, who
does not know his own mind and his own heart. And why? Because

then he cannot ever know the mind and heart of a woman. Were you ever unfaithful to your wife?"

"Well!" exclaimed Dr. Schumann. "What a question!"

"Oh yes, I know, you have to be surprised and even a little shocked. It is quite proper, you are always right. But think a moment. It is not just curiosity and impertinence in me. Partly that, of course, but there is something more besides, and it is that something more I want you to believe — "

Dr. Schumann untangled his fingers from hers, took her hand in his, and then slipped his fingers to her pulse.

"How does it do?" she asked. "Is it settling down?"

"Very well," he said, "perhaps better than mine just now. But then I have told you," he said, and yet could not help mentioning again his unsteady heart. "At any moment," he told her, and laid her hand down again.

"I think it is enviable to know how you will die," she said, "and that it will be sudden and not ugly. I wish I knew, because I am afraid of long suffering and disfigurement. I don't want to leave a hideous body behind me — "

"You are just hopelessly vain," said Dr. Schumann, and it sounded as if he were praising her. "I know that nothing is more precious than beauty to the one who has it. And it is hard to come into the world in beauty and to go out in ugliness. And it is like any other gift or quality in the least worth having, you must be born with it, you cannot acquire it, and you should treat it as it deserves."

"But you find me beautiful now?"

"Of course," said the Doctor. After a short pause he said, "I will answer your question truthfully. I was never unfaithful to my wife."

"How charming of you," said La Condesa, sympathetically. "It must have been dull at times."

Dr. Schumann, who had always viewed himself as the soul of reserve, found himself possessed by a demon of frankness. "It was," he answered simply, amazed at himself, "but she was faithful to me, and that could have been a little dull for her, too, at times."

"Were you really so very good because you wished to be, or was it your weak heart?"

"My heart was sound until about two years ago," said Dr. Schumann with a faint trace of resentment, feeling that his confidence was being abused, and that perhaps he deserved it.

"But you love me just a little, don't you?"

"No," said Dr. Schumann, "not at all. Not at all if I know in the least what love is. I know what I should say, I know that is not very gallant, but I am not a man who can afford to say what he does not mean; and would you wish to hear it? There is perhaps not time for that sort of thing."

La Condesa took his chin between thumb and fingers and kissed him on the forehead twice. Her round mouth left two shiny red smears on his face. Dr. Schumann looked very pleased but quite calm.

"You are delicious," she told him. "You are exactly right. I love you." She added, "Let me wipe your dirty face." She touched her wet tongue to her small lace-bordered handkerchief and scrubbed away the red spots and said, "If anyone saw us now, they would think we were the most devoted married pair."

"Someone has already seen us," said Dr. Schumann, "the very one of all people who would enjoy it most."

They sat in silence, hands folded, heads inclined towards the sea, faces tranquil, as Frau Rittersdorf strolled by alone. "Such divine weather for sitting out," she informed them in a high clear voice, full of the most intimate sympathy and comprehension. She paused, shivered a little, and wrapped her thin scarf about her bare arms. "Perhaps one should be careful of the night air, especially at sea," she said, smiling gaily. She bent over and peered into their faces with the most ravenous inquiry. They gazed back calmly. A second's hesitation and Frau Rittersdorf moved on slowly, tossing back over her shoulder, "After all, rheumatism and arthritis lurk in night air and we're only young once."

"What a museum piece," said La Condesa, also in a high, clear sweet voice, aimed at Frau Rittersdorf's undulating shoulder blades.

"Oh come now," said Dr. Schumann mildly, "do leave that sort of thing to her," and he seemed ruffled and uncomfortable.

La Condesa gave a little saw-edged trill of laughter. Then she fell silent again for a moment, and her face was grieved and weary.

"I loathe women," she said, in a tone of flat, commonplace sincerity such as the Doctor had never heard in her voice. "I hate being one. It is a shameful condition. I cannot be reconciled to it."

"That is a pity," said Dr. Schumann, who in his heart knew that he quite agreed with her. But he did his manly duty of reassuring her. "And you are quite wrong. It may be a misfortune to be a woman, so many of you seem to think so, but there is nothing shameful in it — it is a destiny to be faced, like any other. Truth is," he told her earnestly, "you are a more than ordinarily perverse sort of being, and a change of sex would do nothing for you. There are many men of your temperament and of your habits; if you were a man, you would still be a mischief-maker, a taker of drugs, a seducer."

La Condesa rose lightly as a cloud, opened her arms wide as if to embrace him, leaned over him smiling and exhilarated. "Naturally!" she said with delight, "but think with what freedom, and more opportunity, and no scolding from mossy old souls like you!"

Dr. Schumann rose deliberately and stepped back from her hands that were about to rest on his shoulders. "I am not scolding," he said, in pure forthright anger, "and you are talking like any foolish woman!"

"And you sound like a husband," cried La Condesa over his shoulder, for he had turned and was leaving her, "like *any* foolish man!" and her terrible peals and trills of laughter followed him, blowing like a cold rain down his collar as she ran after him, came abreast, slipped her arm around his elbow, folded her hand in his. "You are adorable and you *can't* shake me off," for Dr. Schumann was trying to reclaim his arm without losing at least the appearance of dignity.

She loosed him then and stepped before him, and he saw that her eyes were wild and inhuman as a monkey's. "Stop," she said, her laughter threatening to slide into tears. She held his hands and laid her head on his shoulder lightly for an instant. "Oh, can't you see? I am tired, I am crazy, I must sleep or die . . . You must give me a *piqûre*, a huge one that will make me sleep for days . . . Oh, don't leave me, you can't — you shan't, I won't let you go! . . . Oh, quiet me — put me to sleep!"

Dr. Schumann gripped her hands and held her off, searching her face shrewdly, hoping to be able to refuse her; but what he saw decided him at once. "Yes," he said, "yes."

She turned at once, dropping her hands at her side, and they walked together through the ship towards her cabin. "Ah," she said, and raised to him under the mottled light of the passage a ravaged and desolate face, unbelievably changed, "ah, you are so good. Oh, never believe I am not grateful . . . and now I can keep my promise not to take any more ether!"

"Ether," said the Doctor, on a rising note of diciplinary severity. "You still have ether? You did keep back a flask, then?"

"Of course," she said, responding instantly to his tone of voice with a faintly contemptuous impatience. "When will you learn not to trust me in anything?"

Dr. Schumann stopped short and turned to face her. "Even now?" he asked.

"Even now," she said boldly. Before the expression in his face as he studied hers for the space of a breath, she lowered her eyelids and glanced aside.

"Well," he said at last, in a dry distant voice, "you shall have your *piqûre* just the same. Go on by yourself," he said, turning off towards his own cabin. "I will join you in a few minutes. You may trust me, as you know well enough," he said, and was amazed at his own bitterness. She turned and went her way as if she had already forgotten him, as if his given word could be so taken for granted she could treat it lightly — which was true, he admitted to himself with a wry little grimace of humor, or had been true until now. As he was selecting and arranging the ampules for the *piqûre*, the doctor began to think fairly clearly and in a more or less straight line, with the reasonable, cooler part of his mind. He had not failed, he thought, in his responsibility to her as her physician. Yet he could not deny that his personal feelings for her had intervened and helped to create a situation very unbecoming to him — to her, also, he admitted with reluctance. But all these shocks and upsets — her constant turning of every meeting between them into scenes which left them both prostrated; the constant danger of his having another heart attack; her reckless disregard for appearances, which could so easily make the kind of scandal the Doctor shuddered even to think about — ah, well, it all must end. He called upon not only the reserves of his authority as ship's physician, but, if she resisted, upon the Captain's final word, and resolved that this unruly relationship should be put in order at once. She must be treated like a hysterical woman with no control over her own acts. She could have been the death of him with her silly melodramas. Nonsense, and there was to be no more of it. Yet, he intended to be merciful and consign her to a narcotic limbo, which was, after all, her notion of Paradise.

"Oh," said La Condesa, sitting up at sight of him, her face shining with relief from anxiety, "I am so happy to see you again! I was so afraid you would not come!"

"What?" said Dr. Schumann, amazed. "When I had just assured you that I would not fail you?"

"Ah," she said, "it is just then one should begin to doubt! The eternal vow — ah, that is the one that is always broken!"

"I did not make any such vow, remember," said Dr. Schumann, "it was only a little promise for this very evening." He resisted the slow ripple of apprehension that ruffled his own nervous system and disturbed the marrow of his bones; here at any moment, if he did not act with speed and decision, was the beginning of another scene.

"I am keeping here and now the promise I made you," he told her, "and the only one I did make." As he approached the side of her bed, needle poised, she dropped back on her pillows and gave him a melting glance of confidence. They smiled at each other lovingly as he took hold of her upper arm.

Mrs. Treadwell sat in the middle of her narrow bunk as if it were an island, and played an intricate game of solitaire with miniature cards on a folding chessboard. She drank wine in slow occasional sips from a small glass; when it was half empty she would pour a little more from a bottle of Burgundy standing on the floor beside her.

She wore a nightgown of smooth white satin, with a buttoned-up collar and full bishop sleeves. Her hair was brushed back from her forehead and bound with a white ribbon, in the Alice in Wonderland style she had worn in bed since she was four or five. Yet viewed from without by an impartial eye, the scene, she decided, would be completely disreputable. The lack of a table and tray for the bottle and glass, the bottle itself even, in the circumstances; Lizzi's clothes lying about in heaps just as she had stepped out of them; the rank smell of Lizzi's stale mingled scents all based on musk; perhaps above all her own occupation, or pastime, contributed to an effect, oppressive to the last degree, of female disorder, hysterical solitude and general forlornness.

Mrs. Treadwell had been in a pleasantly self-sufficient mood when she left the boredom of the upper deck for what had then seemed a reasonable prospect of silence, seclusion, an evening with her own thoughts, such as they were, and early sleep. Lizzi's habits were fairly dependable. She stayed out usually until after midnight with that wretched little fat man; they were to be seen dodging about from one shadowy recess to another, with a great deal of giggling and squealing and not too furtive fumbling. Then Lizzi would come in, steaming hot, knocking against objects, her awkward stride accommodating itself too late to the confined space, clicking on the light and revealing herself with her hair like electrified strings, and her pupils excited as a cat's in the small mean-looking irises. She would step out of her shoes and kick them into a corner, step out of her flimsy frock and expose her long bony legs in their short pink pants and flesh-colored stockings. Dropping her brush and picking it up, without fail she would say in her insolent imitation of courtesy, "So sorry. I hope I didn't wake you," in that voice which affected Mrs. Treadwell's nerves like the sound of a file on metal. It was absurd to pretend to go on sleeping after that.

The woman was, Mrs. Treadwell decided, the most entirely unattractive animal she had ever seen. Undressed, her ugliness was shocking. Yet she was possessed by the mysterious illusion that she was a beauty, as she sat before the spotty little looking glass of the washhand stand, looking deeply into her own eyes, the corners of her mouth twitching. She painted and powdered her face half a dozen times a day, putting on her mask as carefully and deliberately as an actress preparing to face her audience. Upon her head as if in baptism she poured her musky cologne out of a large square bottle, drenched her underarms until the liquid ran down her lean ribs, a flickering, self-absorbed smile on her face, her nostrils working like a rabbit's. All her talk ran on about perfume, about clothes, about her shops, and men. "Friends," she called them. "A man I know in Hamburg, a real gentleman, very rich — a friend," she would say coyly, and rear the undersized head on the long neck with the cords in it. "I almost married him, but now I am glad I did not," because it turned out he had lost his money.

These friends however were not all so unfortunate, and they paid her at all times the most expensive attentions, the most overwhelming compliments; she had them at her beck and call. Only the difficulty had been that there were so many of them. "One must choose somewhere, *nicht wahr?* One can't marry them all, that's a pity!" Little by little though the truth leaked out; most of them were married already, but that was a detail of no consequence; they were all of them prepared to break up their domestic arrangements at any moment if she said the word. But she loved her freedom too well, that was her trouble. "When I left my husband, he accused me of going away to another man. 'Ha,' I told him, 'what do you take me for? There are five of them.'" She would writhe with laughter at passages like this, flapping her hands. "Well of course, you know that was not quite true, there were only three or four, and none of them serious. But believe me, I am finished with marriage. I mean to amuse myself, but no more marriage!"

Mrs. Treadwell gathered up her playing cards and fitted them into their case. She folded the chessboard and set it aside, smoothed the slightly rumpled sheet and light blanket. There was a new chill in the air; she shivered and closed her eyes. Why could she not remember what traveling was like in these out of the way places and on horrid little boats? Why hadn't she sense enough to stay in Paris the whole year round, yes even August — Paris was delicious in August — where she was always so safe from the sort of people she seemed to meet up with almost anywhere else? The faces and figures of her fellow passengers, if they could be called that, were all in a muddle with the wrong names attached, and the very thought of them confused and oppressed her mind. Lizzi gossiped about them perpetually, her dreadful voice grating along, with an affected superior little air.

"Oh now, imagine — that Spanish Condesa, the prisoner, you know her? — well, they say she is sleeping with every one of those students by turns. They are always in her cabin, sometimes two or three of them, and they say it is quite fantastic what goes on there. They say the Captain is outraged by it, but what exactly can he do? Should he put a spy under her bed? . . . and here is a marvelous thing; you know that little sick man in the wheel chair? Well, if you don't watch carefully, he will reach out and touch and stroke you — that is, if you are a woman. He will pretend he is curing you of whatever ails you. The old hypocrite, at his age, and with one foot in the grave! And do you know that miserable Jew they put by mistake with Herr Rieber? Well, the other day he asked Herr Rieber, 'What time is it? My watch has stopped,' and Herr Rieber said, 'Time to stop all Jew watches.' Herr Rieber is very witty. He says the look on his face would have done anybody good."

Mrs. Treadwell threw off the gabbling Fury-like echoes, got up suddenly shaking out her long gown and went to the porthole. The pure cool air bathed her face, she opened her mouth to breathe more freely, feeling soiled by what she had listened to in that cabin. The sea and the sky were almost one in the vast darkness, the waves just beneath rolled and washed back upon themselves in white foam in the rayed lights from the ship. What am I to do, she asked herself, where am I to go? Life, death, she thought in cloudy fear, for she was not able to face the small immediate situations which might demand decision, action, settlement no matter how temporary. Her very vagueness frightened her, for life and death, rightly understood, were ominous dreadful words, and she would never understand them. Life, as she had been taught in her youth, was meant to be pleasant, generous, simple. The future was a clear space of pure, silvery blue, like the sky over Paris in good weather, with feathery playful clouds racing and tumbling in the lower air; all clean and crisp as the blue tissue paper in which all the white things of her childhood had been folded, to keep them white, to make them whiter, to give them icy-blue whiteness. She was always going to be gay and free, later, when she was rid of nurses and school was over, and there was always to be love — always love.

Well, well, she said, drawing in her head, Life has been in fact quite disagreeable if not sordid in spots. If anybody called me a lady tramp I hope I should not have my feelings hurt. Nasty things have happened to me often and they were every one my own fault. I put myself in their way, not even knowing they were there, at first. And later when I knew, I always thought, But this is not real, of course. This is not Life, naturally. This is just an accident, like being hit by a truck, or trapped in a burning house, or held up and robbed or even murdered maybe — not the common fate of persons like me. Was I really ever married to a man so jealous he beat me until I bled at the nose? I don't believe it. I never knew a man like that — he isn't born yet. It's something I read about in a newspaper . . . but I still bleed at the nose if I am frightened enough at anything. Would murder seem real, I wonder? Or would I just say, Oh, this isn't happening either — not to me!

Yet, here I am cooped up in a dingy little cabin with a vulgar woman who will come in presently and begin talking about her "affairs." She is a woman I would never have in my house except to dress my hair or to fit a new frock; and I sit here smelling her horrible perfumes and sleeping in the same room with her; and I have drunk too much wine and played thirty games of solitaire without winning once. Because otherwise life — this life, this is life, this beastly little business here and now — would be too dreary and disgusting to be got through with another moment. . . .

She turned the covers down, smoothed them out again, and went back to bed; drew her nightgown about her legs, shook her sleeves down into pretty folds, and poured another glass of wine, all her movements very calm and orderly, like a convent-bred girl. Maybe her ruinous childhood was to blame for everything. A doctor had told her once, years ago, that sometimes it was as disastrous for a child to be loved too much as too little. How could a child love, or be loved, too much? She thought the doctor was silly. Her childhood had been very bad for her on the whole, no doubt, and very lovely. The memory seemed to be in her blood, alive and breathing in her. The old house in Murray Hill was a beautiful ample house, she realized later; then it had been merely her home. In her blood still were all those years of softness and warmth and safety, the easy procession of days, the luxury she had not known was luxury, everyone she knew lived so. And the gentleness of the voices and hands around her every day — her nurse's voice, "I declare, this child is almost *too* meek!" and her mother answering, "No, not meek at all — just very good-tempered."

Later she knew so many women who envied her because she had traveled in France and Italy every year of her childhood, and because she had been brought up in her girlhood in French and Swiss schools. She had not thought it so grand — mostly she remembered the discomforts of those schools, the stuffiness of the mistresses, the cold water, the tasteless food, the niggling rules, the constant chapel, the horrors of examination papers; and the strange pleasure of weeping or rejoicing with her roommate over the letters and little gifts from home. Each of them could weep or rejoice quite as freely over the other's news and presents as her own. What was that girl's name? Her name, her roommate? As if it mattered. As if she could even invent a regret for a bond that had no more substance than a drift of cigarette smoke. She turned the light on and took a cigarette and tried to break through the senseless melancholy blur of her thoughts.

All those parties and dinners and dances and flowers of the year of her coming-out had whirled into one soft shimmer; could they have been anything like so joyous as she remembered them now? No dream of war — no dream of change. Her memories of that life — of her nurse who had in time become her maid, and always her near friend and confidante, how much more about her did this old nurse know than any parent or kin — had become a warm soothing mist, a rosy cloud moving in her head, she had long got in the way of putting herself to sleep with them; she had in this memory the happiness she had expected, had been taught to expect, in first love.

Time had juggled everything, time was a liar and a cheat, but it could not touch anything that lay on the other side of that first love which had cut her life in two, leaving all that had happened before it enclosed and changeless, and true, so far as she could see, for all she had been able to learn. Keep it, keep it, her heart said, it is yours whether it was true or not. What if her father and mother could not recognize her now if they saw her? In her flesh they slept serenely, loved and loving, not as remembered faces, nor in any arrested act or posture, but as her blood running softly in her veins, as the beat of her heart and the drawing of her breath. It was all real, it had happened, it was hers. Until she was twenty, life — life, what a word! — had been believable, for the more wonder in it, the more she could believe; oh it had been anchored fast yet always in slow movement, like a ship in harbor. She had fallen in love with the wrong man, how wrong her parents never knew, for they never saw him, and she never went home afterwards — and the long nightmare had set in. Ten years of a kind of marriage, and ten years of divorce, shady, shabby, lonely, transient, sitting in cafés and hotels and boats and trains and theaters and strange houses with others transient as herself, for half her life, half her life, and none of it had really happened. Only one thing real had happened in all that time — her parents had been killed together in a motor accident, and she had not gone home to see them buried. For all the rest, she denied it, not a word of it was true.

Not a word. If it were I couldn't bear it, she said, and sat up again. I can't bear it. I don't remember anything. Oh my dears, she said to her parents as if they were in the room with her, if you had known you wouldn't have let it happen. Oh why didn't I come home? Why didn't I tell you?

She reached for the wine bottle and held it up to the light. There was nearly half the bottle left. That will be enough, she decided, if I drink it fast. She poured steadily into the glass, smiling. After all, soon she would be in Paris. In Paris there would be somebody — a dozen names and faces trailed through her mind — somebody to sit with her at the Flore, or we'll go and play roulette at the Cosmetics Queen's Husband's Polite Gambling Hell. We can lose our money, what there is of it, until it is time to go to Les Halles for onion soup. We can drive through Paris after midnight with the horse's feet going clop-clop, echoing in the dim houses, and watch the vegetables coming in on the little old-fashioned train running straight through town like a child's toy. We shall go again, again to the flower stalls and find one of those poisonous-looking flowers, what's its name? like a bleeding tongue on a pike, and drive home again with the sun just turning the sky opal colors, the clouds and the houses all gray and rosy, and the workmen beginning to drop into the cafés for coffee and cognac.

We'll drop in too, and we will kiss each other because we've had such a good time together — who will it be first, I wonder? — and are such good friends. And we will watch the sun come up as if we had never seen it before, and vow to get up early every morning, or stay up all night to see it because sunrise is much the prettiest sight in the world. These are the simple kind of human pleasures I love, the kind I can do with, the things one can just naturally do if one is a resident tourist in Paris. I don't really live there any more, I'm really no better than those American drunks at the Dôme I used to sneer at with my French friends.

I want to live there again. I want to live in that dark alley named l'Impasse des Deux Anges, and have those little pointed jeweled blue velvet shoes at the Cluny copied, and get my perfumes from Molinard's and go to Schiaparelli's spring show to watch her ugly mannequins jerking about as if they were run with push buttons, hitching their belts down in back every time they turn, giving each other hard theatrical Lesbian stares. I want to light a foot-high candle to Our Lady of Paris for bringing me back, and go out to Chantilly to see if they've turned another page in the Duke's Book of Hours. I'd like to dance again in that little *guinguette* in rue d'Enfert-Rochereau with the good-looking young Marquis — what's his name? descended from Joan of Arc's brother. I want to go again to la Bagatelle and help the moss roses open; in cold springs, they get stuck, poor things, halfway — all you do is loosen one outer petal and there it opens, before your eyes! I want to do that again. I'll go again to Rambouillet through those woods that really do look just as Watteau and Fragonard saw them. And to St. Denis to see again the lovely white marble feet of kings and queens, lying naked together on the roof above their formal figures on the bier, delicate toes turned up side by side.

I never saw such rainbows as I saw over the city of Paris, I never saw such rain, either. . . . I wonder if that Catholic society in Montparnasse still gives dowries to poor but honorable girls in the parish. I wonder if the little novices who used to climb ladders and go to the top of the apple trees to pick the apples — in that old convent garden under my window — oh I wonder if they have grown sober and sad living on greens, and apples and prayer? . . . I'm going again to St. Cloud next May to see the first lilies of the valley. . . . Oh God, I'm homesick. I'll never leave Paris again, I promise, if you'll let me just get there this once more. If every soul left it one day and grass grew in the pavements, it would still be Paris to me, I'd want to live there. I'd love to have Paris all to myself for even one day. Slowly, with strangely blissful tears forming under her closed lids, she drifted from her waking dream to quiet sleep.

"I can't see quite why it gets so stuffy in here," said Lizzi, dropping her hairbrush and picking it up. "So sorry. Did I disturb you? When there's a whole ocean full of the most divine air outside."

Mrs. Treadwell opened her eyes, shut them painfully and turned on her side towards the wall. "It's the way they build ships," she said drowsily. "Little cubbies with little holes in them and all kinds of smells. . . . Sometimes they build houses the same way," she said, feeling very reasonable and remote. "Very few houses are fit to live in either, it's the world makes it so, didn't you know? Who are you?"

"You were asleep with the light on," said Lizzi, her glance darting over the wineglass and bottle on the floor. Lowering her voice somewhat, she added confidentially, "I had some delicious *Schaumwein*, with Herr Rieber. Are you awake? You sounded still asleep, somehow? Every day I learn new things about him. Just to think he is a publisher. I had not known that!"

"How fascinating," murmured Mrs. Treadwell, from the depths of her pillow.

"Yes, in Berlin. It is a new weekly devoted to the garment trade, but it has literary and intellectual features besides. One of these is called the New World of Tomorrow, and he engages the very best writers to contribute, all on one topic, to be examined from every point of view. The idea is this: if we can find some means to drive all

Jews out of Germany, our national greatness will then assert itself and tomorrow we shall have a free world. Is that not marvelous?"

Mrs. Treadwell deliberately kept silence. Perhaps the worst thing about her undesirable cabin mate was the extraordinary vulgarity of her talk about Jews. The word haunted her speech, it cropped up no matter what the topic, a most unpleasant obsession, and the sound of it gave Mrs. Treadwell again a creeping chill of distaste.

"He is very intellectual, Herr Rieber, in spite of the fact," Lizzi smirked, leaning into the looking glass and brushing her hair as if she would scrub it off, "he is so very playful at times. He is part of the movement to restore German publishing, more especially in the trades and professions; it has been almost destroyed by the Jews. They are poisoning German thought, Herr Rieber says. And I quite agree, I know that in my business, lingerie, they are everywhere, making prices, cutting prices, tampering with fashions, bargaining, cheating, trying to control everything and everybody. You do not know what it is to try to deal with them in business. No trick is too low."

"Isn't all business low?" asked Mrs. Treadwell, turning again, and yawning. "Doesn't everybody cheat?"

"Oh, Mrs. Treadwell, that is the way the old-fashioned socialists talk; all business is graft and corruption. No, not at all! In Germany at least, it is only the Jews. That is what is the matter with German business and finance, Herr Rieber was saying only last evening, at dinner."

"It must be wonderful to have intellectual companionship," said Mrs. Treadwell, sweetly, in German.

Lizzi turned upon her the eyes of puzzled, dawning suspicion. Mrs. Treadwell's eyes were closed, her features looked quite innocent.

"Oh yes, naturally," said Lizzi, after a stiff pause. Then, "You have really such an American accent I could hardly understand you at first. The best German of course is spoken in my own city of Hanover; you were never in Hanover, I imagine?"

"Only in Berlin," said Mrs. Treadwell, patiently.

"Oh, you will never learn good German if you go only to Berlin," said Lizzi, oiling her hands freely and drawing on a pair of large soiled cotton gloves "Perhaps you cannot hear the difference, but for example, Frau Rittersdorf for all her airs and graces speaks a vile Münchener accent; the Captain speaks Berliner style, atrocious; the purser speaks Plattdeutsch, the worst of all except some of those sailors from up around Königsberg who talk like mere Baltic peasants!"

Mrs. Treadwell's head swam slowly, the darkness behind her lids was full of fiery sparks. What she wanted to hear, God let her live to hear again, was Parisian in every street and alley and *place* and park and terrace in Paris, all of it, from Montmartre to Boulevard St. Honoré to St. Germain to Ménilmontant; from the students on Mont-Ste.-Geneviève to the children in the Luxembourg — the speech of Paris, and in every accent from the Haute Savoie and the Midi to Rouen and Marseille. She wished she might be unconscious until she got there, she wished she might sleep the voyage out or be dead drunk all the way. Would that bloodcurdling voice go on all night?

"Even Herr Rieber," said the voice, now coming from the berth above, "even he comes from Mannheim and his accent is a little provincial — only a little."

The sounds came nearer, and Mrs. Treadwell opened her eyes to see the shadowy little nubbin of a head waving like a cobra's in the air over the berth side, the face a blur dropping its words with mincing elegance, Hanover style. "As for that high and mighty Herr Wilhelm Freytag, he prides himself on his Oxford English, but as for his German — well, it is hard to explain, but he has some odd little turns of speech, not really German. Also, words, perfectly proper in meaning, you will understand, but in a dreadful dialect . . . Herr Rieber says he thinks it is Yiddish, can you imagine? And it is true, he does not eat pork in any form, nor oysters. . . . When we speak of Jews we have observed a certain expression on his face. It is not the right expression for a good German. And so in a word, Herr Rieber and I think — and we are not the only ones — that he is a Jew. *And at the Captain's table!* Could anything be more scandalous?"

"Easily," said Mrs. Treadwell, "many things. I can think of a great number in fact." Through her maze of wine and sleep and boredom she suddenly came wide-awake, feeling thoroughly competent to clear up at least one small area of confusion in this woman's afflicted mind, senseless and restless as a caged monkey's. "You are entirely wrong. It is Herr Freytag's wife who is Jewish, not he. He told me this himself. He is very much in love with her. So you see," she said, sweetly, with satisfaction, "you are in no danger of contamination."

"He told you this himself?" asked Lizzi in a shocked hoarse whisper. "You are on such terms with him? Well! — may I ask you one little question. Do you like Jews?"

"Not particularly," said Mrs. Treadwell, watching the porthole swimming like a blue globe filled with the dark, hypnotic sky. "Should I? Is there something about them?"

"*Should* you? Oh, my dear Frau Treadwell, how amusing you can be, like a little child," cried Lizzi, and she fetched up two nervous hiccups to prove it. "Oh, you Americans who go through the world and never understand anything! Should you? Oh, what can you mean?" Waiting, head cocked for an answer, she heard at last a sigh of resigned weariness from the berth below. After which, the silence continued until morning.

After dinner Captain Thiele, still unsettled in his midriff and full of generalized, unsatisfied indignations, took a ceremonial, solitary tour of the main deck. He had said a short grace before soup and then sat in bitter patience waiting for the others to finish eating, successfully concealing, he hoped, his disgust at the gluttonous spectacle his guests were making of themselves. A breath of fresh air was what he needed before turning in early.

The unexpected and therefore annoying sounds of singing, and dancing, or rather a rhythmic thumping of feet, brought the Captain to the stern overlooking the steerage deck. Those people down there who had still seemed half-dead that very morning were now, he decided, showing a touch too much spirit. They had fetched from their abject bundles not clothing or household gear, of course not, thought the Captain with deepened contempt; but battered guitars and decrepit accordions, and numerous worn leather dice boxes and ragged packs of cards. The women and children, dark and shapeless as heaps of refuse, had moved back into a closely massed circle, in perfect silence; the old men were seated in another circle in front of them; and the center was a varied sports arena.

Graceful, light-boned, underfed boys, who the Captain admitted grudgingly seemed to have some sort of training in the art, wrestled among themselves so lightly it was more like dancing; but they were urged on as if it were a blood-combat with impassioned cries from the witnesses and beseechments to murder each other, and at once!

Older men danced strange outlandish dances in a ring, or facing each other in two lines; creaky in the joint, stiffened in the foot, yet they raised their heads and chests proudly and moved together with the rhythm and incessancy of a drumbeat, their faces solemn. Still others crouched over their slow, fatal gambling games, each man putting down his greasy card as if his head went with it, tossing the dice as if his life were on the cast; and each man bet what he had, from a frayed neckcloth to a packet of matches.

Little boys who knew better than to open their mouths were allowed to sit in front of the women, but at a respectful distance from their elders to observe and take serious notes on the conduct becoming to the state of manhood. Harsh toneless voices were raised in songs of despair almost beyond lamentation, while the sweet-toned guitars mocked them with their frivolous, heartbreaking irony; occasional boot heels tapped and rattled and cackled and clacked like gossip on mar· ket day.

The Captain, whose favorite composer was Schumann, and who admitted no dance but the true Viennese waltz to his graces, felt his ear and his nervous system being most impudently imposed upon; for there was, no doubt about it, something strange in those savage rhythms that moved the blood even against all efforts of the will; indeed, he recognized it for what it was, the perpetual resistance of the elemental forces of darkness and disorder against the very spirit of civilization — that great Germanic force of life in which — and the Captain began to feel a little more cheerful — in which Science and Philosophy moved hand in hand ruled by Christianity. Gazing downward, he despised these filthy cattle, as he should; yet, viewing the scene as a whole, he could not but in all fairness admit there was a kind of shapeliness and order in it; not even his rightly censorious eye could find any real harm, other than the harm of allowing such people any liberties at all; and harm of some sort was naturally, constantly latent in any human situation. It was possible that the spirits of the rabble in the steerage had been elevated by liquor. A limited quantity of beer had been made available for sale to them, though with what coin they were supposed to buy it, the Captain could not imagine. He had been told that not a man in the lot had more than ten Cuban pesos on him. Still, rumors had gone abroad, after the fight at Mass, that the fat man who had started the row was not only a labor agitator and atheist, but an unlawful seller of hard drink; he was said to have brought on board at Havana a large supply of a vile cane-juice concoction, you could hardly call it rum; and was dispensing it secretly and cheaply, hoping to attract followers and disciples. A search for this contraband ended in failure; perhaps the rumor had been only that, the Captain decided. Still it boded no good for these creatures, little better than four-footed animals — indeed it was a question whether they were not lower — to be showing so much energy all at once. The voyage was still new, Santa Cruz de Tenerife seemed a long way off; in fine, it always disturbed the Captain, annoyed him, put him off, to see the lower classes enjoying themselves; and never more so than in his own steerage. The premonitions of the day suddenly returned to him full force — this was no time for rosy optimism. Glancing at his watch, he decided on a reasonable step. His order given from the bridge was passed on until it came to the right man, who put out the lower deck lights, except for the essential two, fore and aft, two hours earlier than the usual time.

This measure did not have the desired effect at once; the people in the steerage were not used to lamps in the evening. They had played cards by moonlight often, it was not the first time they had danced by the light of the stars. The still-weary, more delicate ones gave way at last and slept, face downward on the edge of the crowd. A few mothers sighed with relief, sank limply into their canvas deck chairs, and shifted the weight of their babies to more restful positions. Gradually there was less shouting, and more singing, lower-toned; at last only the plaintive notes of the guitars, like sleepy birds in a far-off wood.

This died away; and a small group gathered around a bony, shambling shape with the loose weathered clothes of a scarecrow, his *boina* pulled to a rakish tilt over one jutting ear. He opened his great toothless mouth in his furrowed narrow face and lantern jaw, and began to sing improvised couplets on words suggested to him by his audience. They cleared a good circle for him, and clapped their hands as he sang a wandering tune in a strong deep voice, head bent, eyes fixed on his own feet. Someone would call out a theme, or word; he would mutter to himself for a moment, then break into a long cry, sing his verse, and wind up with a slow, flatfooted dance, backwards and forwards, stamping to the rhythm of the accompanying hands. His listeners would shriek for joy and shout merry double meanings at him, which he would pick up and improve upon.

This performance went on and on; and the young officer whose duty it was, and who had been peering down upon this scene as into a bear pit, decided that, until further orders, he could safely ignore the whole thing. Though his naval training and the practice of his vocation rested securely on the dogma that disobedience to his superior officer equaled disobedience to God — and was considerably more dangerous — still, in the farthest, deepest, darkest, most suppressed reaches of his being, there lay vast quicksands of reservations which now took partial form in a fleeting, heinous thought: the Captain took alarm at some very odd things and a little too easily? And he had a somehow amusing vision of the Captain breaking into a sweat at the thought of those harmless poor devils in steerage.

In this moment he noticed some night-prowling first-class passengers, and took himself off with the speed and silence of a ghost. He had got a bellyful of passengers for that day. These particular ones had no designs on him, if only he could have known — Jenny Brown and the Huttens with their bulldog Bébé; Jenny fighting restlessness and anxiety, the Huttens and Bébé fighting seasickness and insomnia; all looking for relief from themselves and from each other in the fresh winds from the sea and the lulling darkness. To the young officer it was not so much a matter of fleeing their designs to intrude upon his privacy, his few free moments of solitude in a long crowded day — though that was a never-absent threat. It was their mere presence he had learned by experience to deplore, to resent, and to avoid by flight whenever possible. He had no use for male landlubbers; he found his right and proper friendships with young officers of his own rank and class; and as for women traveling alone, he feared them, for no matter how amiable they might seem at first, if they once grappled they developed claws like a crab's. He realized that all this was quarreling with his bread and butter. Ship's passengers were like that, just hopelessly what they were and no help for it; and if they refused to sail on his wretched ship — for he was ashamed of the honest *Vera*, and schemed constantly to get a better berth — his noble calling, as he had once been taught to regard it, could not even survive. But the fact remained, he detested the very sight of passengers, all sorts: there was no point in pretending anything else.

Yet there was on board a rather prettyish American woman of maybe forty, a Mrs. Treadwell, who looked nice enough. He had begun little by little to feel a certain friendliness towards her, and he knew why — she had never even glanced at him, she did not know he was alive. That was the way he liked his women passengers: not like that high-smelling Spanish woman who kept trying to corner him. He was engaged to be married and glad of it, to a girl he had known all his life who would never be able to surprise him, or so he hoped; there should be some safe place to go when a man is on land. What he did not know, could not have imagined, and would have been displeased to know, was that Jenny and the Huttens were also entirely unaware of his existence. Indifference and reserve were his prerogatives — not theirs.

At this unexpected encounter, Frau Hutten was disposed to be a little more friendly to the American girl who, no matter what she said or did — indeed, even when just sitting silent with her hands folded — would always seem odd, unaccountable, unacceptable to her; but her natural amiability would not be suppressed altogether. After all, as her husband had reassured her earlier in the evening, this voyage was a thing that would end. Jenny was all sympathy for the family seasickness.

"It is nothing much, our own indisposition — but ah, our poor Bébé," said Frau Hutten. "First he is a little better, and then he is worse," she said in wonder, as if this phenomenon were entirely outside nature. Jenny showed no surprise but leaned over and patted Bébé between the ears. As she straightened up, she glanced right and left, and saw, first, David seeming to lurk on one side of the deck, while Herr Glocken, approaching from the other side, obviously had seen them and was hurrying to join them. Jenny tried to pretend to herself that she had not seen either of them, or rather, that it did not concern her.

Herr Glocken, suffering more than usual, drowsy and dazed with his narcotic but unable to sleep, drew near them hopefully as if he expected some sort of relief and help from them. They all greeted him pleasantly, and when he said that such air and such a sea and such moonlight should never be wasted in sleep — "Above all," agreed Jenny, "in such stuffy little dens." Out of curiosity Herr Glocken turned his attention to Jenny, for that strange young man David Scott, her lover, had treated her much more like a wife or a sister than a mistress: he had never once mentioned her to his cabin mates. While he spread his arms and rested his chin on the railing, Jenny repeated that one should never waste moonlight in sleep anywhere, especially not on a ship — above all not in the Atlantic . . . She had never voyaged anywhere except in the Caribbean, among the summer islands, and to Mexico; didn't he find the Atlantic much more impressive? The very ship seemed to know she was in bigger waters, and was sometimes playful as a dolphin, et cetera, et cetera; she babbled on as if talking to herself, now and then glancing away, to her left. Herr Glocken understood easily that she was not talking to him, that she was not going to let him say a word, nor would she say anything to him that could possibly call for an answer at any future time; so when she paused for breath, he said, "Ah, yes, quite, Mees Brown," in English; and Jenny, turning to look at him, realized what she had done when she saw the dwarfish shape make her a bow, with a slight click of the heels, and swing away without hesitation.

"Oh, I am afraid I hurt his feelings!" she said almost in a whisper to Frau Hutten, who drew away and seemed confused. Herr Professor Hutten intervened with words of reassurance. "You need not distress yourself too much, my dear Fräulein," he said, addressing her kindly over the slightly bowed head of his wife. "Persons with incurable physical defects, especially of a congenital nature, invariably and always show an excessive sensibility to the attitudes of others, more particularly in situations of a social character, and peculiarly so in all that concerns the other sex . . . you can hardly avoid wounding such persons at one time or another, no matter how unintentionally. . . ."

"I just didn't want him near me," said Jenny, almost in tears. "I have a kind of horror of him!"

"I should think he'd be used to that by now," said Frau Hutten, gently. She tightened the leash on Bébé, took her husband's arm, and said, as they moved away slowly, "Ah, well, we must try again to sleep a little! Good night."

"Good night," said Jenny, noticing for the first time that Frau Hutten limped slightly. Jenny felt a little pang of fright: had Frau Hutten been born to a limp, or was it an accident? And she thought she must be changing in some evil way: she had never been repelled by deformity, or any affliction, before. What was happening to her? And did David think she was flirting with Herr Glocken, as well as with Herr Freytag, and for that matter, anything on board ship in trousers? She walked slowly in the direction where she had last seen David, meaning if she saw him to put her arms around his neck and kiss him and say, "Good night, darling," for she could not in the least control her terrible rushes of tenderness for him. But resolutely she left the deck and walked through the ship and down the long corridor to her cabin, hoping that Elsa was safely asleep.

David, after his appalled glimpse of Jenny and the new company she appeared to be keeping, went back to his cabin, lay down in his clothes, turned out his light, and crossed his hands palm upwards loosely over his eyes. Who wouldn't she take up with, he wondered. She'd run off with just anybody — if a band passed playing in the street, she'd fall in step and march with them . . . would say just anything she pleased to the merest stranger — did she ever really see a stranger? Listens to just anybody, as interested in the idlest silliest chatter as she is in the most intelligent talk — more so, damn it! Can't pass a beggar without handing out; her house full of stray cats and dogs — given away at last, when she left, to people who didn't want them. She would sit and listen with an eager look to that big dull Elsa mumbling along — as if Elsa were telling the most marvelous thing in the world. Get out and picket with strikers without even asking what they were striking for, or even where they worked. "Tobacco factory, I think," she said one night, when he came in and found her very exhausted, in bed drinking hot milk. "I lost five pounds today," she told him, bragging.

"Whatever for?" he asked. "For fun," she said, not bothering to try to explain anything to him. Yet there had been a time when he felt so close, so nearly identified with Jenny, so tenderly in love with her, she could have done anything with him, have made him understand anything no matter how preposterous: or so he believed now; and why had she refused to become that part of him which was missing, which would have made him whole — why had she been so strange and wild and made their life together so impossible? It occurred to him bitterly for the first time that, in fact, Jenny seemed to get along on the simplest terms with anybody, everybody, but himself. The notion, too, of that Glocken prying into his private affairs, getting on terms with Jenny, made his blood run cold. He was astonished to find that he disliked Glocken intensely. God knew what Jenny would say to him, what impression he would get of her; he could imagine Glocken turning a low, mean opinion of Jenny over in his warped little mind —

The light flashed on and there was Herr Glocken, grinning like a complacent gnome. "Ah, awake still?" he asked, and added almost at once in what David took to be an intolerably intimate tone: "I cannot rest until I tell you what an entirely charming young lady your fiancée is . . . We talked a little on deck just now," he said. "She is delightful."

David had a singular gift of hardening instantly into silence that extended long after the speaker had ceased to expect an answer, expressing disapproval and disagreement in terms much stronger than words. The air of the cabin froze with this silence now as David rose, undressed deliberately — though omitting to wash his teeth as being an act too ridiculous to perform before this detested stranger — put out his light again and turned his face to the wall, every nerve humming and every fiber dancing in outrage. It was long before he gave way and slept, in his sleep contracting convulsively again and again; but longer still for Herr Glocken, bewildered, stung, mystified. He had thought that being on speaking terms with Jenny, even though she had snubbed him so rudely — who need ever know that? — would have meant a pleasant friendship with her lover. He had felt very elegant and worldly and correct in substituting the French "fiancée" for the less musical if more exact German word he had in mind; but everything had gone wrong between him and these young people, and he must be more careful. He had not known many Americans, and those only in Mexico; he could never make them out, nor had he tried particularly. But these had seemed a little different, because they spoke Spanish and were obviously living in a Bohemian style. Just the same she was an attractive young woman, no matter about her poor manners, and Herr Glocken wondered what she could see in that cranky, bad-tempered young man. Finally he slept. In the morning, feeling very poorly, he asked Herr Denny, by name, please to hand him his medicine.

The sailors were out again washing down the decks, which rolled gently as the *Vera* set out resolutely for the Canaries, with only a head or two looking out of her portholes to watch the eternal love affair between the moon and the sea. Pepe, again turned out of his stateroom for Arne Hansen, began to look at his watch, deciding that even for the money, Amparo was giving the fellow too much time. She had done that before, with other men, often, and no amount of beating had cured her of the habit. However, he would try it again, but not until they landed at Vigo, where she could scream as much as she liked without attracting attention. He stepped tiptoe around the sailors' buckets and brushes, and stood on the coping of the deck rail looking into the steerage deck. Everybody seemed to be settled down and sound asleep; the very sight caused him to yawn heavily. Some of them lay stretched in canvas chairs, some were flattened out on hard bare benches, others were curled like snails in hammocks. One man in blue overalls lay stretched crosswise in his hammock, his head hanging over one side, his great crooked dirty bare feet over the other. Pepe knew all of them well, he was an Asturian, and just like them; yes, there were times when he even felt kinship with an Andalusian, but not with any of those down there! If he had been as stupid as they, he would have been sleeping among them or in the fleas and lice of some hovel in Spain. He shuddered fiercely as if a snake had crawled over his bare foot. All those shouting, singing, dancing, fighting, cursing Asturians as he remembered the people of his childhood, now lay, most of them, among the quieter Andalusians and Canary Islanders, in the attitudes of well-disposed corpses; under the ghostly white moonlight, the muffling sheets gave them the look of bodies waiting to be taken to the morgue. Pepe selected the man hanging at both ends out of his hammock and deftly flicked his lighted cigarette into the folds of dry cloth which muffled his middle. That might wake him up!

Three shapes sprang instantly to their feet, and one of them, the huge fat man Pepe remembered as singing like a bull, found the cigarette and ground it between his fingers. He shook his fist at the slender figure above still leaning over the rail. "*Cabrón!*" he shouted furiously in his comic Mexican accent, even as he recognized one of the pimps he had seen floating about on the day of sailing. He changed his tone to a heavy jeer. "*Puto!*" he said. "Come down here and we'll —"

Then others woke and joined in, making a clamor. Pepe, glancing back uneasily, saw that the sailors had heard the noise. One of them was coming toward him, of course not threateningly, but solidly, calmly, striding like a horse, just in line of duty to find out what was going on. Pepe stepped off the coping and sailed gracefully as a swan but much faster in the opposite direction.

He found Amparo brushing her tangled hair, her lipstick badly smeared over her bitten-looking mouth, and the lower berth was in a tumble as usual. "Well?" he said. In sulky silence she nodded backward. He picked up one of the stale-smelling pillows and found the firm green notes there. "More dollars, good," he said, smoothing them out and counting them.

Amparo frowned and said, "They are not so easy to get, let me tell you. That fellow keeps saying, 'Five dollars more for one more time!' and he wants his money's worth." She turned the tap in the basin.

"What are you doing?" asked Pepe, beginning to undress.

"I'm going to wash," she said, still frowning. "I'm filthy."

"Don't be too long about it," he said, and at his tone as at a signal she shivered a little, her flesh rippled with excitement. She soaped a cloth and began washing herself and he watched without curiosity, yet following her hands intently as they moved over her body. He stripped to the skin and lay down.

"You were a good while at it," he said, "even for the money."

"Let me alone," she said, "I've told you how it is."

"Let you alone?" he asked, smiling. He got up very swiftly and quietly and gave her a solid openhanded blow on the flat of her shoulder blade where it would sting but not bruise. Then he grabbed her by the nape of the neck with one hand and shook her hard, his other hand stroking down her spine and ending with a blow of his fist. Her eyelids drooped, her mouth became full and moist, her nipples stiffened. "Now hurry," he said.

"I won't hurry," she said with bitter coquetry, powdering herself with a very dirty eiderdown puff. "I'm tired."

"Not too much of that," he said, taking the puff and tossing it away. "So you let him have everything did you, pouring your stuff down the gutter again? Do you want me to break every bone in you?"

"He is just an ox," she said. "What do you take me for?"

She was standing near the berth. Seizing her by one wrist, with a light turn of his arm he threw her off balance and she fell easily full length upon him. Their supple dancers' legs writhed together for a moment like a nest of snakes. They sniffed, nibbled, bit, licked and sucked each other's flesh with small moans of pleasure, exploring for odors and savors and sensations in all its parts, their bodies going obediently through a repertory as complicated as a ballet, in the rhythms of a slow-motion film. He never wished to make love to her except when she had just come from another man, full of strange smells and heats, roused and disturbed, ready for him and his special ways with her. Since she had known him he was the only man who could please her in the least, and to please her she had only to let him please himself. She saved herself like a miser in the dull plungings and poundings of those men who were her business, and spent herself upon Pepe, who was tricky as a monkey and as coldly long-lasting as a frog. Pepe beat her often, for jealousy, he said, when he suspected her of some feeling for another man. But often after he beat her the hardest he made love to her for hours afterwards until it would seem their bones would dissolve in delicious exhaustion. He could beat her as much as he pleased, for she never tired of the pleasures he gave her.

Pepe was hard as nails about getting every last peso, franc, dollar, no matter what, from her, because he was saving to open a little place of his own, in Madrid, where Amparo, as long as she lasted, would be the main attraction as dancer; he had often, in a cold still fury, threatened to kill her in such ferocious ways she knew he did not really mean it; but she was saving too. All through the bad times in Mexico, and here on this boat, Amparo was holding back part of her money from Pepe, who would undoubtedly strangle her at least if he knew. But he did not know; and Amparo meant one day to be a star all by herself, traveling everywhere and getting rich and famous like the great Pastora Imperio.

The Captain was increasingly annoyed by the slow drift of rumors that came to his ears he hardly knew how; crosscurrents of gossip he could scarcely realize he had heard at all until in his solitary hours on the bridge they began to move and mingle in his head. The most persistent of these were murmurs about the life of La Condesa in her private stateroom, if private it could be called any longer, with those students making free of it at all times. The Captain turned over rather sourly in his mind the notion of putting a stewardess in there as guard; but he knew well there was no stewardess to spare for such duty. He thought now and then halfheartedly of keeping her confined to her stateroom for the rest of the voyage, but he had no means of doing it short of force, the very idea of which horrified him. He had heard from someone — was it that Frau Rittersdorf? a very strait-laced woman — that La Condesa had been seen clinging in hysteria to Dr. Schumann, who had great trouble in controlling her. Well, Dr. Schumann was her doctor for this occasion, let him take his luck. The Captain could not think it too hard a fate to be embraced and wept upon by a beautiful noble lady, no matter how hysterical. When the Captain had asked Dr. Schumann, as discreetly as he was able, how his patient was doing, Dr. Schumann said, "Very well indeed. She has decided to keep to her bed for a few days. She is reading."

The Captain hoped he concealed his surprise. "Reading? She? What, I wonder?"

"*Romans policiers*," said the Doctor. "The students bring them to her from the ship's library. She tells me there is a fine collection on board."

The Captain said, in some pique, "I cannot imagine how they came there, unless they were left by passengers."

"Possibly," said Dr. Schumann. "I am grateful to whoever did leave them. She was very overwrought the other evening, and I have decided to put her on a régime. She reads her detective and murder mysteries, then she plays chess with one or another of those students, and I give her a sedative at night. . . . I am much more hopeful of her condition than I was."

The Captain said warily, "Then you think the presence of the students at all hours does not upset her nerves?"

"For some mysterious reason," said the Doctor, "they amuse her. They are rowdy, noisy, disrespectful, ignorant —"

"I have heard them mention Nietzsche, Goethe, Kant, Hegel, Schopenhauer," said the Captain, "in those loud discussions at table."

"Oh yes," said the Doctor, "they have all been to the university."

The Captain occasionally invited the Doctor for an afternoon coffee or an after-dinner schnapps in his quarters, and a little pleasant, if always reserved, conversation with one whom he could, in a way, regard as an equal. The Captain did not really care for the society of his equals — he got on best looking down his nose, or up under his brows. He had hoped to find the Doctor a source of information as to any disorders or strangenesses among the passengers, which he himself would hardly have occasion or opportunity to observe. For example, it appeared that an odd thing had occurred — nobody's fault, he supposed, unless the purser's, and yet! no, not even his . . . the first time in his whole experience as a seafaring man, indeed, the first time in his whole life, so far as he could know, he believed that he was sitting daily at the same table with a Jew. Had Dr. Schumann, by any chance, heard anything about this?

Dr. Schumann said easily that yes, he had heard something of the sort two or three days ago, but from a source he considered very unreliable; his tone seemed to say, "The ladies, God bless them, of course, but don't listen to them." He did not even have to restrain himself from saying he was not in the least concerned whether Freytag was a

Jew or not, and that he thought the whole question beneath contempt. He regarded the unbridled expression of opinion on all topics and at all times as mere self-indulgence, if not actually the mark of a mischievous nature. Also Dr. Schumann had been all over this rather dreary subject many times before with too many persons long before he had come on this ship, and he was a little tired of it; he no longer felt able to fight with those strange senseless states of mind, as shapeless and uncapturable and real as smoke.

The Captain understood the Doctor's detachment as his professional unwillingness to take sides: after all, everybody on board was his potential patient, he could not choose any on personal grounds. Yet tactfully as he could, he hinted to the Doctor that in his special situation he must learn a great deal about all sorts of persons. "Priests, lawyers, doctors," he said, cordially, "how many secrets must be unloaded on you! I don't envy you, really," and the hint was rather broad that the Doctor would find a way to pass on to the Captain any scandals, queernesses, indecorums which might need to be corrected. The Doctor did not pretend to misunderstand: he simply ignored the suggestion, amiably refused a second cup of coffee, shifted the topic almost imperceptibly, and very soon took his leave. The Captain, newly flushed, uneasy, irritable, resolved that no later than tomorrow he would proceed to settle this dubious and unbecoming state of affairs, whatever it was. The Doctor had left with him an uncomfortable impression that he, the Captain, was listening to women's gossip. Well, this was a question to be settled strictly between men, and the first thing to be done was to get the women out of it, and keep them out. The unsavory fact remained that women had started the whole thing: that American Mrs. Treadwell had told Fräulein Lizzi Spöckenkieker some confidence she had got from Herr Freytag, and Lizzi had told Herr Rieber, who had passed it about freely until it had come to the ears of the Captain, who now, as a matter of social duty and his own dignity, must at once take steps. He shook his head as if in a swarm of gnats, and decided to dine alone that evening.

Freytag was a few minutes late to the dinner table. Everybody was present except the Captain; Dr. Schumann conveyed the Captain's regrets to his guests for his unavoidable absence, which were received in form. Freytag slipped into his chair with a smiling nod of greeting all around, which was returned not so smilingly — or was it his own state of nervous exasperation which caused him to imagine all these rather dull strangers were looking at him with a kind of furtive curiosity, except Dr. Schumann, whose air of benevolent detachment was beginning to annoy Freytag somewhat, as being a little patronizing; and Frau Hutten, who gazed in her plate, as usual.

The steward presented him with the appetizer, Westphalian ham folded delicately beside a slice of melon. He shook his head, and the steward asked, "What would you like instead, sir? Smoked salmon? Herring in sour cream?"

"Either will do nicely," said Freytag. "The herring."

Herr Professor Hutten, observing Herr Freytag's lack of conformity in choice of food, as usual, remarked almost absent-mindedly, as if his thoughts had taken off from some very distant point of origin: "The condition of Jewishness offers to the Western, more especially the Christian, mind an endless study in spiritual and moral contradictions, together with a mysterious and powerful emotional and psychological cohesiveness. Nothing can equal the solidarity of the Jew when attacked from the outside, by the heathen, as they say; nothing can exceed the bitterness of their rivalries in every field among themselves. I have asked many in all scholarly seriousness and philosophical detachment, 'Tell me, please — what is a Jew?' and not one of them has been able to give me an answer. They call themselves a race, yet that is absurd. They are just a tiny fragment of a branch of the white race, like ourselves!"

"Oh, not Nordic!" squealed Lizzi, "not that! Since when?"

"Are they Hamitic then?" answered the Professor, turning upon her witheringly." "Mongolic? Or Ethiopic?"

"They are everything, utter mongrels to the last degree, from every dregs of every race and nation!" said Herr Rieber, suddenly losing his merry temper and turning quite scarlet. "And so they were from the beginning of time . . ."

"In that sense," said Wilhelm Freytag, putting down his fork, "we are all mongrels by now, I expect . . ."

"Oh, speak for yourself, dear Herr Freytag," said Frau Rittersdorf, and she leaned forward to smile at him with her teeth closed. "But I am astounded. How can you, a German of the purest type, blond, tall, gray-eyed —"

". . . and I ask them, 'What is a Jew?' and I ask them, 'Are you a nation?' — No. — A race? — No. — Are you then only a religion? —

No. — Do you practice your religion, do you observe dietary laws? No." Herr Professor Hutten raised his voice and chanted, silencing Frau Rittersdorf and forging on determinedly to his little joke, which he would not be denied. "So then, I ask them — and I would have you remember that I choose only those who could easily have been mistaken for pure Germans, anywhere — I ask them, 'On what grounds then do you call yourself a Jew?' And without a single exception, every one of them said with perfect obstinacy, 'Still, in spite of all, I *am* a Jew!' — So then, I say to them, 'Ah, so! it is clear that Jewishness is a state of mind!'" He beamed under the approving smiles of his hearers.

"It is their claim of Chosenness that annoys me," said Frau Rittersdorf. "It makes God look so stupid, don't you think?"

There was a shocked silence, as if no one dared to deal with this mixture of good sense and something too near blasphemy for comfort. Frau Rittersdorf instantly perceived her mistake and tried to right it. "I only mean," she began, "I — I —"

Herr Professor Hutten rushed to her rescue kindly. "That mistaken idea, born of tribal vanity, is of such an extreme antiquity I think we may safely say it was a most primitive kind of god who chose that peculiar people. Or rather, let us say more precisely that they chose him — not an ignoble concept at the time," he added, generously, "when we consider the nature of certain other gods equally ancient. By comparison at least, on the whole Old Jahweh does not come out so badly."

"You are right!" cried Herr Rieber, swallowing and wiping his mouth. "It was Jahweh who chose the Jews, and he can have them —"

"Imagine a handful of people, a few little millions among nearly two billion others, having such impudence!" cried Lizzi. "I think it is that makes me most furious. Besides their manners, their tricks, their —"

"The divinely inspired truth of a God of Justice, Mercy, and Grace, the Holy Trinity, Father, Son and Holy Ghost, the great truth which Christianity brought to the world," began Herr Professor Hutten, by now faintly discouraged, "proves . . ."

Frau Rittersdorf, while conscious of the social inferiority of Herr Rieber, yet in justice, swallowing her prejudice, agreed with him. "You are right, Herr Rieber," she said, with condescension. "It is only their god who chose them, we must remember. We are under no obligation to emulate his poor taste . . ."

"I am not interested in the religious question," said Herr Rieber, who never dreamed that Frau Rittersdorf was condescending, "I am anxious only that the German nation, the bloodstream of our race, shall be cleansed of their poison."

"But you are a real anti-Semite!" cried little Frau Schmitt, suddenly, as if frightened. "I don't know any Jews, but I don't dislike them —"

"I am not an anti-Semite at all," said Herr Rieber, contentiously. "How can you say that? I am very fond of the Arabs, I lived among them once and found them very good people . . ."

Frau Rittersdorf turned her smile upon Dr. Schumann. "You have said nothing, dear Doctor! What do you think about Jews?"

Dr. Schumann said mildly and precisely, "I have nothing to say against them. I believe that we worship the same God."

"But Doctor," said Lizzi, leaning forward and waving her head, "you are a Catholic, are you not? Do not Catholics worship the Virgin Mary first, and then God?"

"No," said Dr. Schumann, crossing his knife and fork in the form of an x, laying down his napkin carefully, and rising without emphasis. "Allow me to be excused, if you please," he said, and left them.

"He is subject to heart attacks," said Frau Hutten to her husband. "Do you suppose we should send to inquire after him?"

"He is a doctor," said the Herr Professor, "he does not need our attentions or advice."

"Schumann," said Rieber, pouting his underlip, "is that not a Jewish name?"

"There is no such thing as a Jewish name in the German," said Herr Professor Hutten, who seemed a little on edge and spoke rather abruptly, for him. He observed that Herr Freytag had sat in stiff silence throughout the talk, now and then moving a morsel on his plate from one point to another with his fork, but not eating; and his face was so fixed and pale one might suspect oncoming seasickness. "There are only German names adopted by Jews in medieval times and later, when they decided to drop their ancient style — Isaac ben Abraham, let's say — a good old custom, and a pity they abandoned it; and these by lineal descent have become associated with Jewish families. Schumann is one of them, and Freytag, may I venture, is another. Is that not so, Herr Freytag?" He spoke directly across the table, unexpectedly, and Freytag raised cold gray furious eyes. "Have you never been troubled by discovering Jewish branches of your old German family name?"

"I do not know any Jews named Freytag," he said, and the tremor of his rage got into his voice, "that is, except one — my wife," he said, and he raised his voice and steadied it. "She is Jewish and her name is Freytag, and she does it honor."

The instant he heard the words pronounced he knew he had let himself be trapped again into temper, into melodrama, into a situation as false as it was unnecessary. His mother-in-law had spotted this weakness in him. A little mockingly she advised him: "Remember the rules! Never tell your family business. Never say what you are expected to say. Answer one question with another." She said it with laughter, but he noticed that she practiced it seriously. He had felt again and again that he was living between two armed and irreconcilable camps, deserter from one side, intruder in the other, the turncoat nobody trusted. How often, when he had found himself alone among Jews, after he married Mary, they had attacked him, from all sides at once, some of them with open contempt, or a genuine personal dislike; others told Jewish jokes against the Goyim, and they used in his hearing the disrespectful names for Christians they used in their private talk. And now his own side — he turned his eyes slowly along the faces at the table, and there was not one he did not find detestable — his own side, for these were his people, were getting another chance at him; they would never let up on a German who had degraded himself so. He decided he had had enough; with his hands against the edge of the table he pushed back his chair.

Lizzi cried out in shrill excitement, so that he stopped on the point of standing up. "Oh, Herr Freytag, how strange! We some of us thought *you* were the Jew — how could we have been so blind? — and only a few evenings ago, I was talking to that odd American woman who shares my cabin — you know her? Mrs. Treadwell? and she told me something I simply did not believe — that no, it was your *wife* — just as you say!"

"Mrs. Treadwell?" repeated Freytag, shocked. "She said that?"

"Of course, am I not saying so? But — please don't misunderstand me — she was a little — you know, she drinks — sometimes she is very vague . . ." She looked for understanding in the faces now all pointed towards her with exact attention. Nothing however disreputable they could hear about the Americans on board could surprise them. Lizzi ended: "Well, more than once, a whole bottle of wine, by herself, after dinner!"

Freytag got up decisively at this point, favored his circle of compatriots with a nasty smile, and spoke like an actor giving the curtain line: "Well, I leave Mrs. Treadwell to your tender mercies!" and did not wait for an answer. And may they pull you into pieces, he wished hotly, noticing her seated alone at her small table, eyelids lowered, the living image of innocence, eating ice cream. He was struck with a wish to have a table to himself. He would speak to the head steward about it tomorrow. He could not stick that crowd at the Captain's table much longer. One more round of remarks about the Jews and he would slap their faces, once each. Yes, even Dr. Schumann, old hypocrite, who had got out without committing himself. And instantly upon this blaze of fury came a chill straight from the grave — he was going even now to Mary's relatives, those of them who would still call on Mary's mother, or come for dinner: to listen to jokes about the Goyim, jokes that had burnt acid-holes in his memory, and in his feelings for all of them. He leaned on the rail and gazed into the darkening water, by now no longer the pleasant novelty it had been. "Can I be thinking of suicide?" he asked himself after a short interval of rigid blankness; for all the time when he believed his mind was empty, he had seen himself going smoothly as a professional diver head-first in the depths, sinking slowly and slowly to the very ocean floor, and lying there flat, for good and all, eyes wide open, in perfect ease and contentment. He pulled up with a shudder, blinked several times, and began to walk. The image had been so clear it unnerved him almost. But no, nothing to worry about. That easy way out was not for him. His way was clear — the road ran all the way in, and through, and out again on the other side; all he had to do was to keep going, and not lose his head, and not let Jew or Christian bedevil him into losing his temper and playing into their hands. In the meantime, he'd like just a word with that Mrs. Treadwell; but no hurry.

The Captain left his second cup of dinner coffee and went out to grant, on the bridge deck, not in his private quarters, a curt interview to Fräulein Lizzi Spökenkieker, who embodied to the last trait and feature everything the Captain found most positively repellent in womankind; and to her besotted admirer Herr Rieber, who must surely be lacking in some indispensable male faculty, such as taste or judgment where women were concerned. They had requested to see him in writing, which gave an urgency no doubt spurious to their occasion. What business could they have with him that would not wait until lunch tomorrow, if not even to the judgment day? He suppressed a belch and eyed them sternly, meaning to warn them even at this late moment that he was not to be disturbed frivolously.

Both of his visitors were breathless at their own daring, the honor being done them, and the importance of their errand. Their message was simple but cogent. Not only the Captain's own guests, but many other German passengers, had almost from the first their suspicions that there was one person at the Captain's table who had no right to be there. Perhaps not a Jew himself — though they had no proof that he wasn't except his own word — but he was known — indeed, he declared it at table before everybody — that he had Jewish connections of a most intimate nature — in fact a wife! Oh how Fräulein Lizzi and Herr Rieber regretted to cause unpleasantness of any kind, but they were so certain the Captain should know, would indeed wish to know of such an unheard-of mischance at his table. They understood well that such details properly belonged to his subordinates, and yet — yet —

The Captain, instantly sensitive to the faintest implication that a subordinate of his should dare to be remiss in duty however slight — indeed, there was no such thing as a *slight* duty on his ship — now bridled haughtily and said, "Of course, I am very grateful to you for your thoughtfulness. I agree it is a most unusual occurrence." Lizzi added impulsively, stretching her long neck at him and cackling in her highest voice, that the dear Captain had done so much for all of them and they could do so little for him, it was a divine pleasure to be of even the smallest service to him. The Captain, whose irritations invariably translated and expressed themselves in a knife-edged grinding and growling of his bowels, now began to feel his familiar distress. With many more thanks and compliments, even taking three steps forward with them to speed them on their way in the right direction, he dismissed them — they had been standing all the time on the well-lighted bridge deck under a starry sky — and burning, went to look for his bismuth. Changing his mind, he gulped down the last of the coffee and swallowed a drink of schnapps. This eased him at least for the moment, and with no period for reflection, he did not need it, he set in motion at once a train of events that would shortly result in a slight but significant rearrangement of the seating order in the dining room.

This done, the Captain's mind turned to relatively happier topics. La Condesa — ah, the right thought occurred at once. He would send her a little present of wine, an attention no lady could find fault with. She reminded him of his university days — he had hung around stage entrances and yearned after strange idols, great wax dolls so painted, laced, covered and disguised in the hieratic dress of their calling, he had offered his modest flowers and wine, his shy boyish itch of sex, his dirty little dreams without ever daring to get within arm's reach. He had never been able to imagine one of them undressed, and he had never even once confused any of them with any living women he had known. Yet he loved his dream of them, and La Condesa somehow brought it all back. The Doctor was right, though — it would not do to be too lenient with her. She must be kept in order, perhaps reminded from time to time that she was his, the Captain's, prisoner. He sent her two bottles of well-chilled sparkling white wine, with a gallant little note: "Dear Madame: We Germans no longer use the word 'champagne' nor indeed, drink that rather pretentious wine any longer. So I am happy to say this modest offering is not French, but only good *Schaumwein* from an honest German vineyard, sent to you by one who wishes you well in the cordial hope that it may bring you an evening's refreshment and enjoyment. In the meantime, please do me the great favor to obey your doctor's orders and keep to your stateroom for so long as he thinks necessary for the good of your health." And he was, so to speak, entirely at her service.

When Dr. Schumann called on La Condesa to administer the last hypodermic for the day, he found her in a fit of laughter, sitting up in bed with a red damask bedgown falling off her shoulder, her curly reddish hair somewhat too youthful for her face, standing up in tendrils waving like little serpents. She held a note open in her hand, and beside her were two bottles of German champagne.

"Ah," she called out in delight, "you are just in time to share my wine and my love letter from the Captain! Oh, come and laugh with me please?" She gave him the note, and as he stood looking at it uncertainly, the stewardess, obeying Dr. Schumann's latest instruction always to be present at the giving of the narcotic, knocked and entered.

"What are you doing here," demanded La Condesa, "did I send for you?"

"Let her stay," said the Doctor. "I cannot read this letter, I am sure the Captain does not mean anyone but yourself to see it."

"As if it mattered what the Captain means!" cried La Condesa. "It concerns you too! I am ordered to obey you and keep to my stateroom — in a word, I am in jail again!"

Uncomfortably, Dr. Schumann held the paper nearly at arm's length as if distance might lessen the fault of reading something not meant for him to see, while the stewardess began to pull at the bed coverlets and reached for the pillows to plump them. "Wait until you are told to do these things. Don't come near me unless I send for you," said La Condesa. The stewardess backed away with a scarlet face and stood near the doorway.

"No, you exaggerate. And you distrust the Captain, who wishes to protect you, and I, who wish to help you, and yet look at your amiability, your confidence, in those mannerless students who should treat you with the regard due a mother, and yet! — I cannot repeat to you the disrespectful things they have been heard to say about you, but please take my word for it, they say them! Tell me, why do you let them make you a laughingstock?"

"Do they?" said La Condesa, and she reached out to stroke his hand. "On this ship? Well, that amuses me. You have heard someone laughing? Do not all boys speak disrespectfully of women of any age?" She laughed, holding her head. "I am not their mother! If I were, they might have better manners, better family, better minds, more imagination, and I think, I am almost certain, they would be somewhat better-looking too. No, I am attached to them because they were schoolfellows of my sons, my charming young madmen who must go running off after something they called the Revolution!" She turned to him with a face of distress, her hands beginning to dance. "Where are they now? I hid them for a day and night under the altar in the chapel, and the soldiers and the ruffians were everywhere, yet not one thought of looking under the altar! Then they set the whole hacienda on fire, cane fields and all . . . and my sons escaped, but I was taken away —"

Her voice had lapsed into the monotonous complaining light chant he had heard that first day out on shipboard, but she wrapped her arms around her knees and looked at him very reasonably. "It is over," she said. "They are gone. They will never come again."

"How do you know?" asked Dr. Schumann. "Can you not wait a little patiently for news? This need not be the end! I think you make everything unnecessarily difficult," he told her. "Have we not troubles enough as it is?"

"We? You have troubles, too?"

"You are my trouble," he told her, "but I shall help you if I can!"

"Do," she said, lightly, her arms falling away to her sides. "Do try!"

"Captain Thiele has not sent you a command, but a recommendation; I hope you will take his advice as well as mine. He is an honorable man."

"I shall always take yours, always," she said, with her habitual gesture of reaching for his hand, which this time he quite openly evaded. She drew hers back instantly and laughed again. "*Schaumwein!*" she said in mocking delight, making it an absurd sound. "Oh, how ineffably German! I'm sure the Captain's honor is just as good an imitation as this," and she flourished one of the bottles.

"Please," said Dr. Schumann, feeling a new sort of sting of anger against her that made him sound touchy and quarrelsome. "If you please, remember I am German, too —" and he stopped himself just short of saying something as ridiculous as "and proud of it."

"Ah, yes," said La Condesa, and she sighed with real weariness, "too true. It's an incurable malady, isn't it? As hopeless as being a Jew."

"Or a woman," said Dr. Schumann with malice, "you said so yourself."

"It is not the same," said La Condesa almost gaily, "I am not going to listen to you any longer, I have something better to do." She threw back the covers and swung her delicate white feet, legs bare to the knees, over the side of the bed, let her bedgown fall away, and stood up in a limp blue silk shift that hardly covered her thighs. She picked up the two bottles of the Captain's *Schaumwein* and went to the washhand stand. She wrapped each in a towel neatly, then stood back at the right distance and crashed them, one and then the other, against the metal edge of the bowl. The jagged glass flew from the bottom of the towels and the wine foamed up through the cloth and splashed the walls, the looking glass and the carpet. Leaving the debris, she nodded to the stewardess. "Now you will have something to do," she said, pleasantly.

The stewardess moved sideways along the wall, somewhat as if she had found herself caged with a dangerous beast. Dr. Schumann did not wait for La Condesa to get back in bed, but seizing her by the upper arm as she passed plunged the needle abruptly into the soft muscle. She shuddered deeply with pleasure, her eyes closed, and reached up to breathe in his ear warmly: "What a bad-tempered man you are, and what shall I do without you?"

He glanced at the stony-faced stewardess on her knees mopping up *Schaumwein* and back to La Condesa, frowning. He dropped her arm and summoned the principles of his whole life to rebuke her immodesty and her utter lack of regard for appearances.

"Oh Madame, good night, and do try to compose yourself!" he said, sternly, hearing how feeble his words were compared to what she deserved. He waited to see her cover her nakedness; lie flat and turn her head on the pillow to smile at him drowsily. "Sleep," she said, in a drowned voice, "sleep, poor prisoner."

Turning the corner in the corridor a few steps from her door, he almost collided with two of the Cuban students, one carrying a bottle of wine, the other a chessboard. They bowed and stood to the wall to allow him to pass, but he stopped also, and spoke to them abruptly without any attempt at ceremony: "Gentlemen, I have been many times astonished at your lack of consideration for Madame, and I must now insist that your attentions cease at once. Madame is my patient, and I forbid all visits in the evening, and none in the day without my special permission. I am sorry," he said, with a good deal of bitter satisfaction.

They bowed again with effusive good manners — a slight parody of good manners, the Doctor thought — and one of them said, "Of course, dear Herr Doctor, we understand perfectly." The other said, "Oh, perfectly," and they turned ahead of him, outdistanced him and disappeared almost at once. The Doctor dismissed them from mind with a swift impression of their coarse-grained, thick-looking skins and the muddy whites of their eyes — a slight touch of the tar-brush, no doubt — what matter? His nerves were shaken again, and he permitted himself a brief vengeful meditation on the crockery-smashing sex, the outraged scullerymaid, the exasperated housewife of the lower classes, the jealous mistress — the sex that brought confusion into everything, religion, law, marriage; all its duplicities, its love of secret bypaths, its instinct for darkness and all mischiefs done in darkness. Who was La Condesa smashing, he wondered — himself, or the Captain, or both? Or another man, or other men in the past who had resisted her, restrained her, baffled her, denied her, and finally evaded her? Or was she used to easy conquests, eager dupes? The Doctor halted at this point, said suddenly under his breath, "Mother of God be my refuge!" and crossed himself, and instantly felt his head clear a little, as if the demons had fled. Quietly, as if he were thinking about someone else's misfortune, he faced his own: this bitterness had tinged his sinful love from the first, for he had loved her from the first before he admitted it was love; as his guilt deepened, his wish to ease her sufferings was changing slowly into a wish to cause her suffering, of another kind, in which she would be made to feel his hand and his will . . . why did his love wish to degrade her? He knew well she was no enraged servant, no jealous mistress; she had chosen the simplest most direct way in the world, even touching in its simplicity and directness, to express her contempt and her defiance of the Captain, of the Doctor, and of all the powers that held her prisoner. Her face had been composed, her eyes when she turned them towards him had been shining with amusement; she had swung the bottles as if she were christening a ship. As for her immodesty, walking about in her nightgown, showing her bare legs so carelessly — there was something in it very disrespectful to him, as if he were not even present, or was not really a man with whom she should exercise a little prudence . . . as if he were harmless, impotent. This was a familiar trick of women, every man knew it well, but — and the Doctor's heart gave a leap and started beating too fast — it was intolerable, just the same! He slowed down, unnerved, and reached in his inner pocket for the little phial. "Love," he said with hatred, as if someone could hear him and answer, "to call this baseness love?" He walked slowly once around the deck, making up his mind to look for one of those priests and go to confession, and to receive Holy Communion in the early morning. For the first time in a great while, he felt not the right contrition, that good habit of the spirit, but a personal shame, a crushing humiliation at the disgraceful nature of what he had to confess. Folly, folly, at his age, a married man, running in his mind after that strange woman as if he were one of those pimple-faced students, yet denying his feelings to himself, blaming her for everything, and hating his own evil in her. . . .

He drew a good breath and squared his shoulders when he saw striding down upon him, cassock flapping, the sterner, more trap-jawed of the Spanish priests, no doubt taking a constitutional before turning in. He stepped in his path a few paces away, and put out an arm in signal.

"Father . . ." he said, and Father Garza stopped before him.

Late next morning Freytag, still sulky and uneasy after a nearly sleepless night listening to Hansen's loud quarreling with his nightmare in the upper berth, drank coffee alone in the bar. He was ravenously hungry after his spoiled dinner the evening before, but his resentment had hardened, and he was resolved to ask for a change of table before he ate again. When he saw the drift of familiar figures beginning the morning round of the deck, he went to look for the head steward.

The head steward's love of authority was second only to the Captain's. Freytag expressed his wish to be seated alone for the rest of the voyage in the easy tone of a man reserving a table in a restaurant with the headwaiter. The head steward consulted his seating chart as if there might be some doubt in the matter. Then he tapped his palm with the head of his pencil and said, most politely, "*Mein Herr*, there will be no difficulty. In fact, it has already been arranged for you, I am happy to say."

"Arranged?" repeated Freytag, and stopped himself just in time from asking "Who arranged it?"

"Your request made to the purser was conveyed to me, sir," said the head steward, in a voice full of respect, his face full of guarded insolence. Freytag said at once, "Thank you," and turned away. He felt quite light and hollow with rage, and hardly knew how he reached the upper deck again; when that doleful little Baumgartner family, with its sickroom air, walking in a huddle, murmured among themselves at him "*Guten Morgen . . . Grüss Gott . . . Haben Sie gut geschlafen?*" he rudely passed them by, and hurt their feelings badly, and never knew it, and would not have cared if he had known; such abject bores did not really exist, they had no right to feelings. Or at least, no right to intrude them on him. He thought he could trace the snail's trail of events quite clearly; there was nothing subtle about either that pig Rieber or that half-witted rattle Lizzi; they would go to the purser, or even straight to the Captain himself; the Captain would do the rest, at the proper godlike distance — oh it was all plain enough! Except for certain details, it was not even anything new, not the first time since he married Mary that he had been refused a table in places where before he had been welcome. But this never had happened except when Mary was with him. Smart and beautiful and golden and trim and smiling a little, eyes averted, Mary would stand beside him in silence while the headwaiter explained that he was sorry, but there was no record of a reservation: "Our mistake, no doubt, we regret it deeply, but as you see —" and it was true, every unoccupied table in the place would have a large card saying: "Reserved." He would rage and storm along the street and in taxicabs and back at home, but Mary never lost her strange patience. "I am used to it," she told him, "and you are not. But didn't I tell you my love how it would be? I know where *We* may go and where not, please will you not listen to me?"

"I will listen, Mary," he promised her now. "If you can't come with me, I will go with you!"

At lunch Freytag advanced into the dining room without hesitation, as if he knew where he was going. A steward ran towards him as if he were heading him off, and in a wheedling murmur directed him towards a small table set near the service entrance against a blank wall, where, Freytag had noticed a good while ago, the Jew Herr Löwenthal sat by himself. He was sitting by himself at that moment. The steward bowed Herr Freytag to his chair, drew it out, seated him, unfolded his napkin and handed it to him, and offered him the lunch card before Herr Löwenthal finished choosing his own lunch and glanced up. "Good afternoon," he said, in the tone of a man in the door of his own house greeting a stranger, perhaps a dubious one.

"Good afternoon," said Freytag, with neutral blandness, considering that he had fought this battle out with himself, and was going to control the situation by sheer calm and will power. "I hope I am not intruding."

"And could we help it if you were?" asked Löwenthal, raising his shoulders and eyebrows. "Did anybody ask us?" He did not seem offended, but merely was mentioning an obvious fact.

Freytag's raw nerves prickled. "I asked the head steward for a table by myself," he said, in a carefully easy tone. "There has been some mistake." He could not help seeing at much too close a range Herr Löwenthal's smooth oily face, his large heavy lids over chocolate-colored lightless eyes, the unpleasantly thick mobile lips that squirmed as he chewed or talked. Freytag knew the type too well — overfamiliar if you made the mistake of being pleasant to him; loud and insolent if he suspected timidity in you; sly and cringing if you knew how to put him in his place. No, this one won't very well do as the hero of a Cause, Freytag decided. He's not the one all the row is about. Even other kinds of Jews don't like him. He's the kind that comes to the side door peddling trash; Mary's mother would set the dog on him! He recalled all the queer comic names the Jews made up for each other, names of contempt and ridicule, and the worst of them were meant for fellows like this.

Löwenthal was looking about him with skeptical eyes, a sour twist on his mouth. "You didn't look around before you asked? Where did you see a free table?"

Freytag, to his intense irritation, found himself answering earnestly, "There is one on the far side, near a porthole."

"That is for that big raw German boy with the sick uncle," said Löwenthal. "Only he's like a prisoner yet; and there's that Condesa, only not for days now; and that American shicksa, the widow — she never misses! What I mean is, you got to sit with somebody — so why not somebody else? Why me? Why not one of the ladies, or that boy you won't have to see much?"

"The purser used his own judgment, I expect," said Freytag, "such as it is."

A sarcastic grin positively discomposed Herr Löwenthal's features. "At the Captain's table?" he asked unbelievingly. "And you want to be moved? Only Allrightniks eat with the Captain — so you don't appreciate all that high society? Well, excuse me, no kikes wanted, hein? So we are in the same boat, hein? No, no, don't tell me, let me guess!"

Here it comes again, from the other side, thought Freytag, in a second of pure panic. I can't sit here, either. His stomach squeezed into a tight knot, his right hand clenched until he forced it to open to pick up the lunch card. "Vegetable broth, salmon with cucumber," he told the waiter, and then added in nearly the same tone to Löwenthal, "I am almost sorry to have to say it, sorry for my own personal reasons, but you are mistaken, if I understand what you seem to be saying. I am not a Jew."

Varying contradictory expressions rippled over Löwenthal's face like pond water on a windy day. "Something new every moment," he said, at last, "that I should live to hear this from a *Krist!*" The waiter set before him a plate of hard-boiled eggs and raw cabbage salad. He took half an egg in his mouth, added a heap of cabbage, and chewing a while, went on: "You don't have to say it to me. What you want to do about that is positively your business, I got nothing to add. There's been times when I was tempted, God forbid, to say it myself. But I couldn't get away with it — not with this map. Why, babies barely able to talk yell 'Sheeny' at a hundred feet. I will say this, you don't look it — I got a sharp eye, and I never took you for one of the Chosen People, and that's a fact. But in Germany there's all this mixed marriage, good Jewish boys chasing out after these towheaded shicksas, they should be ashamed, so a lot of us look more like the blockheads than we should. In Germany you see Jews with no back head already, and that's not natural. Plenty of the lowest-down anti-Semites I know don't have to look further back than their grandfather to find the good old blood . . . but they don't look if they can help it —"

Freytag, trying to eat, nodded pleasantly as if in agreement. Löwenthal was doing all the talking, and that made the right appearance. Freytag was seated with his back to most of the room; if he had turned his head halfway round he could have looked directly at the Captain's table, though a good distance away. He felt that he was the object of stares, whispers, scandals, mean bits of gossip; let them see then that he was listening to Herr Löwenthal's talk with amiable interest, nothing in the least disagreeable or even conspicuous was to happen; he intended to preserve the very best of appearances to the end. Sitting there feeling as if the blood were about to burst through his pores, suffering the tortures of a prisoner being crushed in the boot, he listened to Löwenthal.

"Sometimes it gets tough, I don't have to tell you," he went on, "but I don't know — I don't know," he said with a sudden deep sigh, "if I could turn on my own people . . . I'd feel strange, being taken for anything else. Why, what else could I be?" He seemed bewildered, as if he had never thought of this before. "But as I say, if you've got your reasons, and you can get away with it, why, I don't blame you. Me, I'm a Jew, and if sometimes I think that's hard luck, why I just try to imagine being a Goy. Yarrrr," he ended, with a look of nausea.

Freytag's tone was so patient it visibly roused Löwenthal's resentment. "My wife is Jewish," he said, "but I am not." Being under compulsion to keep the talk going for the mere look of the thing, he decided he might as well bring the question out in the open. "She belongs to one of the very oldest Jewish families . . ."

Löwenthal's manner changed again at this. His mouth pouched out and down at the corners, he expressed disgust and disapprobation all over his face, his very ears moved, and he said rudely, "All Jewish families are old. Everybody descended from Abraham, at least. Question is, was her family Orthodox?"

"No, Reformed, for the last two or three generations."

"Jewish boys can marry Gentiles, that's all right, who cares, what does it matter?" said Löwenthal, shrugging. "But a nice Jewish girl to marry a Goy! Tell me, what kind of a family is it?"

"Rich," said Freytag, "most of them. Father a lawyer. Dead now. Two rabbi grandfathers!" he boasted to this poor thing before him descended obviously from a long line of peddlers.

"That makes it worse," said Löwenthal. "A low-life woman running out I can understand, for her it's too good, maybe, but a girl from a rabbinical family — that I can't take!" He leaned forward and said in a deliberately loud voice he hoped might be heard at the nearest tables, or at least by the waiter: "That's the kind of Jewish girl that makes disgrace for all the rest of us. Any Jewish girl marries out of her religion ought to have her head examined! . . . I never laid a finger on a Gentile woman in my life, and the thought of touching one makes me sick; why can't you Goyim leave our girls alone, isn't your own kind good enough for you? . . . When I want woman company, I look for Jewish! When I got any money to spend for an evening I take out a good Jewish girl who appreciates it; and when I marry, I marry Jewish — and nothing else do I understand! Be ashamed, Herr Freytag — when you wrong a Jewish girl, you wrong the whole race . . ."

"Shut your foul mouth!" said Freytag with odd ferocity, "or I'll knock you away from this table!" His whole body prepared itself instantly to deliver the blow, yet stopped in time, arrested by Löwenthal's sudden silence, and complete stillness.

He was not intimidated; he was aware, attentive, and ready; he did not even seem surprised at Freytag's sudden violence. Freytag, horrified at what he had almost done, searched Löwenthal's face. It was curiously impassive, grave, the only sign of strain the twitching of the small muscles around the eyes, which regarded Freytag with a look very near curiosity, as if he were a species of animal it was necessary to understand to learn to handle.

Löwenthal broke the silence and in some sort the tension by asking one of his perpetual questions that was no question at all, but a statement; and his voice was reasonable: "Look, let me ask you one thing — what did I ever do to you? To you, or any of yours? What did I ask of this trip but only to get through it without trouble, or making trouble for anybody? Did I ask you to come here? This table they sat me down to by myself without asking me; where do I sit if not here? They put me here by myself because I am the only Jew — why then must a Gentile come pushing in and make threats because we don't agree on religion? Why must . . ."

Freytag said, "Wait a moment. Let me explain . . ." Haltingly, bitterly, he tried to tell what had happened at the Captain's table, and he added, "It was the insult to my wife I could not endure . . . then I come here, and you . . ."

"It is not insult to say a Jewish girl should not forsake her people," said Löwenthal, still in his reasonable tone. "That I do not dream is insult." And Freytag saw that in that closed mind there was not one trace of sympathy or understanding of his plight, or Mary's. He gave up in defeat, and at once felt stronger: it was not defeat at all, he would simply move the whole question to another ground and go on fighting from there. He admitted his errors; he had been wrong all the way, he had talked stupidly to stupid people, and he was being nicely paid out for it. He would take another grip on his affairs, and keep his mouth shut.

"I am very sorry I lost my temper," he said, handsomely, leaning forward a little stiffly. "I wish to offer you my apology."

There was a short pause, during which Freytag felt cold sweat forming on his forehead. Löwenthal wiped his mouth with his napkin, and leaned forward a little too, with an expectant air. He said nothing. Freytag pulled himself together.

"I have said, I should like to apologize," he repeated, very formally.

"Well, then," said Löwenthal, matter-of-factly, "why don't you? I'm waiting to hear what you've got to say."

"No dessert, please," said Freytag to the waiter, hovering over them. He got up, and nodded slightly to his table companion. "I've said it," he remarked, almost cheerfully, "all I'm going to say." And he took himself out of the dining room at the proper speed without a glance around him.

Captain Thiele, having, in the Freytag crisis, improved his opportunity to perform still another of those little acts of authority which mount up finally into a base of solid power, showed up for his midday meal with an air not exactly of good humor so much as a kind of mollified ill-temper. He could do no better. His big clean cotton napkin snapped like a flag as he unfurled it and tucked it under his collar. He stretched his neck, turning his chin from side to side until his wattles were comfortably disposed, and his gaze ran around his circle of guests as if expecting their gratitude. With a tight smile full of crafty meanings, and a busy series of stiff nods, he said, "I am sure you are all much more comfortable now that we are less crowded and there are no discordant elements. Now," he said, lifting his right hand as if blessing them, "I have got rid of that person who was here under false pretenses, and we are all the right sort of people together. I hope we shall enjoy the rest of our voyage."

The circle applauded this graceful little speech, patting their palms together with genteel restraint, smiling at the Captain until their cheekbones rose, their eyes narrowed and foxy.

"The test of true strength," remarked Herr Professor Hutten, "is in action, sudden, decisive and, naturally, successful action, perfectly timed, directed, and taking the enemy by surprise. In this case, my dear Captain, any hesitation on your part — and may I say, that is quite unimaginable — would have resulted in a state of affairs false to our true spirit, and weakening to the whole fabric of our society. It might seem quite an unimportant incident," he went on, earnestly, to his listeners, "but it is these apparently minor decisions that help to remind us most clearly of our principles, and to see whether or not we are in harmony with the great pattern of our tradition . . ."

"And *so* tactfully done, too," said Frau Rittersdorf. "Naturally! After all, style, manner, ah, how very important they are."

The Captain smirked and shook his head gallantly at Frau Rittersdorf, who, encouraged, was about to speak again, when Lizzi leaned over, stretched her long thin arms towards him and patted him rapidly, violently on the arm. "You were wonderful the way you received us yesterday evening —" She glanced at Herr Rieber, who smiled until his eyes almost disappeared. "You are always wonderful, but with one word — one! — to end as you did this horrid business that was worrying all of us. I envy such power!"

The circle applauded again, and from the Spanish dancers' table, some little distance away, but still too near to please the Captain, Manolo said in a low but carrying voice: "I know! They have thrown out that Jew and are celebrating. Well, let us celebrate too!"

"Bravo!" called Amparo, clapping her hands and smiling and trying to attract the Captain's attention. Instead of looking their way, he frowned straight ahead of him. "Bravo!" all of them called to him, softly. Ric and Rac beat on the table with their knife handles and were instantly quelled on all sides by the others, who still smiled and fluttered their fingers towards the Captain's table.

"What business possibly can it be of theirs?" he inquired at random, scowling. "Do you suppose they have been eavesdropping, or have picked up some gossip which makes them venture on such liberties?"

"Those tramps," said Herr Rieber, severely. "Except for the ladies present, I would name them more exactly. But what do you expect of them, after all? Gypsies!"

"Gypsies? With those beaks?" asked Lizzi.

"Why not?" asked Herr Rieber. "They are supposed to be a remnant of the lost tribes of Israel . . ."

"That notion, I believe," began Herr Professor Hutten, "has been relegated to the domain of myth, or folklore . . ."

"They are Catholics," ventured little Frau Schmitt, happy to contribute something to this animated conversation.

"Just very low-class Spaniards masquerading as something else," said the Captain, firmly. "In my home place, we have a saying, 'Scratch a Spaniard, bleed a Moor'; which says all!"

At this moment Dr. Schumann joined them, and they greeted him as if he were returning from a long absence. He was amiable and distant, said to the waiter, "Just a little clear soup, please, and coffee." When Frau Hutten said to him, "We have missed you!" with the new tone of familiar friendship established in his absence, he inclined his head towards her, but in some surprise. "Now," she went on, including the Doctor in the charmed circle, "we are just seven — seven, for good luck."

This was the kind of puerile nonsense her husband had never been able wholly to eradicate from her mind, and had long ago learned to pretend not to notice. He now addressed the Captain: "Such as *They*," he pronounced, nodding towards the spot where Wilhelm Freytag was seated with Herr Löwenthal, "such as They should have special quarters on ships and other public conveyances. They should not be allowed the run of things, annoying other people."

"But yesterday you seemed to defend them, I was astonished," said Frau Rittersdorf.

"I was defending nothing, dear lady — I spoke in the light of the history and the religious superstitions of an ancient people; I find them remarkably interesting, but I must say, their descendants a good deal less so, do you agree, my Captain?"

"Let me say at once that if I had my way in the matter," said the Captain, "I should not allow one even on board my ship at all, not even in the steerage. They pollute the air."

He closed his eyes, opened his mouth, turned the point of his large spoon spilling over the thick pea soup and fried crusts towards him, plunged it deeply into his mouth, clamped his lips over it and drew the spoon out empty, chewed once, gulped, and instantly set about repeating the performance. The others, except Dr. Schumann, who drank his broth from a cup, leaned over their plates also, and there was silence for a time except for gurgling, lapping noises while everybody waded into the soup, and stillness except for the irregular rhythm of heads dipping and rising. The ring was closed solidly against all undesirables, ally as well as enemy. All the faces were relaxed with sensual gratification, mingled with deep complacency: they were, after all, themselves and no one else: the powerful, the privileged, the right people. The edge being taken off appetite, they fell to being charming to each other, with elegant gestures, and exaggerated movements of their features, as though they were in a play; making a little festival to celebrate their rediscovered kinship, their special intimate bonds of blood and sympathy. Under the gaze of aliens as they believed — in fact no one, not even the Spaniards, was paying any attention to them — they set an example of how superior persons conduct themselves towards each other. Herr Professor Hutten ordered wine and they exchanged toasts all around. They smacked their lips and said, "*Ja, ja!*"

Even little Frau Schmitt, who had wept when the Captain chastised her publicly, though for her own good, and who suffered at the very thought of the miseries of the world; who wished only to love and to be loved by everybody; who shed tears with sick animals and unhappy children, now felt herself a part of this soothing yet strengthening fellowship. After all, no matter how right her sympathies may have been, she was wrong to talk with that American Herr Scott about the poor woodcarver in the steerage. The memory of the Captain's rebuke, so well merited, she now accepted with pride, and it gave her courage. For a moment she forgot her long life of petty humiliations, her fear of her superiors, her feeling that she was only a humble poor woman — even if a teacher and a professor's wife — that the butcher could cheat and the clerks in shops could snub: a creature of no importance that anyone could impose upon. No more of this! She was tired of being crowded and fobbed off with the second choice in everything. She glanced at Frau Rittersdorf with narrowed eyes, and resolved that she would claim her rights in the cabin. She would teach that woman a lesson! Her heart expanded, and swam easily on the warm wave of blood kinship with her great and glorious race, even though she might be its smallest, its least considerable member. Yet, observe her many privileges.

She continued to beam mildly at the Captain, adoring him because he was stern, strong, relentless, instant in administering justice, a visible present incarnation of the mystical male force which rules not only the earth and all its creatures but indeed, as God the Father, the universe. On every face around her she thought she saw the same reflected light of glory.

She spoke. "After all, my Captain, one must often do severe things in self-defense?"

"Defense?" the Captain echoed briskly. "What nonsense, my dear Frau Schmitt. To put people in their proper places and keep them there cannot be called severity, nor defense. It is merely observing and carrying out the natural order of things."

She winced but managed to smile bravely. "Wrong, I am always wrong," she murmured. The Captain gave her a sharp little grimace of approval — women were almost first among those who must be kept in their place. She warmed and palpitated under the male dominance of his eyes; still smiling, she bowed her smooth little head and took a mouthful of Hasenpfeffer.

Herr Rieber, after the first few moments of merriment, began to grow more and more thoughtful. As he ate, the cold sweat formed on his temples; it collected in small rivulets on his bald head and ran into his collar. His breath began to come short and agitate his tight round stomach. He stopped eating and pushed back his plate, thinking hard, his underlip pursed out like a sulky child's. Wriggling a little, he wiped his face and head with his napkin and stuffed it in his pocket. Taking it out again at once he folded it neatly as if he were at home, crossed his knife and fork carefully; knife across, fork up and down; his grandmother had taught him he must leave the sign of the Cross on his empty plate as a mark of gratitude to Our Lord for his food, and he never forgot.

"Please excuse me," he muttered in fussy haste, sidling away and breaking into a short-legged canter as he neared the stairway. Action, quick decisive — yes, the Herr Professor was right. And he, Siegfried Rieber, had through his own carelessness, yes through his own weakness, allowed himself to be put in a false position on this ship, unworthy of his dignity as a German: he was sharing his cabin with Löwenthal, and this should never have been allowed to happen in the first place. It was an inexcusable offense against that natural order of things which he, as well as the Captain, was bound to obey and to see that others obeyed. What could people have been thinking about him all this time? That he was perhaps privately fraternizing with that Jew, treating him as an equal? Herr Rieber was as embarrassed and confused as he remembered to have been in nightmares, where he found himself in a public place, in a crowd, conspicuous for his nakedness in a clothed world; or worse, found himself hideously exposed in some grotesque forbidden act which had drawn upon him the condemnation of a horde of ghostly spectators, not one face of which he recognized, though they every one knew him well, all his vileness, his shameful history . . .

Ach, Gott! ach Gott! he told himself, speeding up as he approached the purser's office, this can't go on, no, no — this must be set right at once, all this must be changed *now!*

The purser was leaning back in his deep chair eating a large piece of spicecake he had brought away from the table, a third piece of cake he had seized guiltily as he was leaving. He was enormously fat and getting fatter all the time, and hunger gnawed his vitals night and day. When he saw Herr Rieber peering in upon him, he made a motion to hide the cake under some papers, thought better of it and stuffed the whole chunk in his mouth.

"Come in, then," he said grumpily, blowing cake crumbs and choking on his mouthful. He swallowed heavily twice and repeated, "Well, come in, please," with some emphasis on the last word. He felt undernourished and regretted his cake. He had meant to enjoy it slowly, and he resented Herr Rieber's intrusion. He had never liked the fellow anyway, from the very first day out, and he resolved to do as little as he could for him, no matter what his business.

Herr Rieber went at once to the point. The purser, he was sure, would see the situation at once and clearly. "I have felt the honor of being seated at the Captain's table," he said. "The Captain is a man very particular in his choice of company. If he will not allow a Jew to sit there in his presence, why then must I share my cabin with one? I must ask you to regulate this mistake at once."

"He is not a Jew," said the purser mildly. "It's his wife. I have heard about it." He pretended to be, if not exactly sympathetic, at least willing to fulfill his duties as purser, part of which consisted of listening to the complaints of fellows like this one. He must not give the little nuisance any cause for thinking he was being neglected. "You are right. I shall see what can be done. There is only one proper place for Freytag, of course; with Löwenthal. If I had known, I would gladly have made that arrangement. But I think now," said the purser, "in the present case, we shall have to ask Herr Arne Hansen to change into the cabin with you, since he is now quartered with Freytag."

Herr Rieber heard a dim roaring in his ears at these words. "Hansen no!" he almost shouted, then lowered his voice. "No, that would be almost as bad."

"Why?" asked the purser, who knew why. Hansen and Rieber had disliked and avoided each other ever since the first day on deck, when they had some sort of silly argument over deck chairs. The purser took no interest in this kind of nonsense — it was merely part of his job to know such things. Herr Rieber said, "That is a fellow I would not want to have around me, that's all."

"Well, leave it to me," said the purser, "I will see what can be done. Come back in an hour, please."

Promptly Herr Rieber returned and the purser, looking very cheerful, had only bad news. Merely for the sake of leaving nothing undone, he had spoken to Herr Hansen about Herr Rieber's predicament. "After all," said the purser, soothingly, "a Swede is at least a human being." "Not that one," said Herr Rieber, gloomily. However, Herr Hansen was not uncomfortable, in fact he expressed very friendly feelings for Herr Freytag, and would remain where he was — so that part was settled. But if Herr Rieber would be willing to move into a cabin with three occupants, no doubt Mister Denny or Mister Scott would be willing to go with Löwenthal, and Herr Rieber could then share the cabin with one or the other and Herr Glocken the hunchback. Herr Rieber objected violently. "No, I could never do that!"

Very well. Then let Herr Glocken move in with Herr Hansen, who would never refuse, the purser was certain. Then Freytag could move in with Löwenthal, and Herr Rieber could move in with Mister Scott and Mister Denny. Herr Rieber thought this over for a while, and at last with deep reluctance decided that such an arrangement might be the least objectionable of the whole series of painful choices. Considering the change as good as made, he went to pack his belongings. Löwenthal was not there; he had got in the habit of spending all but his sleeping hours on deck. When Herr Rieber returned once more to the purser's office, he received a brutal setback.

Under no circumstances whatever, said the purser, evidently repeating verbatim, would Mister Denny or Mister Scott consent to any change at all. Herr Glocken, they said, was a very small man who took up almost no room, they were used to him and he to them, they were nicely shaken down and doing fine and saw no reason to disturb themselves.

The purser then leaned towards Herr Rieber and said in an insinuating manner: "Let me tell you they were really anything but agreeable, oh, I don't mean angry, or anything of that sort — no, just the opposite. You must have heard Americans make fun of people — you know, they always laugh. That makes it worse. Well, that Scott fellow said something in American slang, I think, I couldn't understand it, but at any rate they both laughed — a jeer it is, you know, not really a laugh, and it freezes the blood. I should try to kill anyone who laughed at me like that! — well, at any rate, you don't want to get in there with them. God knows what would happen. I do not trust Americans — they all have Indian, or Negro, or Jewish blood — mongrels and savages. They kidnap little children for money, and then murder them," said the purser, on the verge suddenly of tears. "Imagine, even if you give the money, they murder them just the same!"

Herr Rieber, who had been listening with his whole head on fire, watching the purser's face with intent blinking eyes, was outraged by this sudden detour from the subject. He suspected the purser of all evil. It was no time to be sniveling over kidnapped children — Americans at that! No doubt he was in collusion with Freytag, who was determined with the effrontery of his race to push himself in among his betters whether they wanted him or not; for though Herr Rieber knew the facts, he would not admit that Freytag was a Christian. He had married a Jew and he *was* a Jew, that settled it . . . or maybe he was in criminal conspiracy with those foul Americans, who were probably part Jewish themselves. As for Arne Hansen, that big nose of his was not Nordic, let him call himself a Swede if he liked. The purser, at any rate, was clearly a traitor with Jewish sympathies himself; perhaps that Löwenthal had bribed him in the first place for the privilege of sharing a cabin with a German. Herr Rieber fumed himself into a fury, his face swelled and grew scarlet, and he shouted at the purser, "So I am to be called names and laughed at by those guttersnipes and you do not say one word to them?"

"What shall I say?" asked the purser. "I am not responsible for their manners."

"You let them insult Germans on a German boat, do you? Well, the Captain shall hear of this, we'll see what he has to say to such goings-on on his ship."

The purser raised one hand mildly. "I advise you earnestly not to mention any business of mine to the Captain," he said. "Take my word, you will find he does not take kindly to any passenger mingling in the affairs of the ship. I say this to spare you embarrassment," he added, kindly. And indeed, Herr Rieber seemed to be subsiding into something like despair. "They talk, they do stupid things, what do we care?" asked the purser, largely, and somewhat vaguely. "Try to control yourself, Herr Rieber, this is not such a bad situation, it will all end in a few days! Things can't be settled in a day!" he reminded him, with an air of discovery. "We may yet think of something. Now come," he said, with fatherly cordiality, "let's have a good glass of beer, and ideas may occur to us." Herr Rieber revived a little at this, and seemed willing to cultivate patience for a time.

The purser heaved himself up and stood, breathing heavily. It was the hour for his nap, and yet he must be humoring this fool. He said politely, "Let us go," and restrained, no doubt to his own permanent moral injury, a very pure, laudable impulse to spread his huge fat hand over Herr Rieber's red, sweating face and push, hard.

It was Mrs. Treadwell's birthday, not the first she had spent alone on a train or a ship; she was feeling her age, forty-six, as a downright affront to her aesthetic sense. All the forties were dull-sounding numbers, but forty-six was so hopelessly middle-aged, so much too late to die young, so much too early to think of death at all. The last day of August was a nondescript time to be born, anyway — the coarsened, sprawling sunburnt afternoon of summer, not becoming to her at all; and yet, here she was arrived at that age in human life supposed most to resemble this insect-riddled month . . . when nothing blooms but weeds in earth, and the soul puts out rank growths, too, according to dreary popular opinion. The lower instincts take alarm for fear they have missed something, are hot for marginal enjoyments. Hearts grow hard and cold, they say, or go overripe and pulpy; women especially, one is told, so often lose their modesty, their grace. They become shrill, or run to fat, or turn to beanpoles, take to secret drinking or nagging their husbands; they get tangled up in disreputable love affairs; they marry men too young for them and get just what they deserve; if they have a little money, they attract every species of parasite, and Lesbians lurk in the offing, waiting for loneliness and fear to do their work; oh, it is all enough to scare anybody, said Mrs. Treadwell, shaking her head and taking up her magazine again.

She was half reclining in her deck chair, partly reading an old copy of *L'Illustration* in a comfortable drowse, partly thinking about her age, which had never really worried her before, when without any warning at all she felt Time itself as a great spider spinning a thick dusty web around her life, winding and winding until it covered all — the light is shut out and the pulse shrivels and the breath is slowly smothered off — Death, death! she said, and her fright was as simple and overwhelming as her fear of the dark when a child. Oh how absurd, she told herself, and stood up, throwing aside the magazine, remembering how her elders talked long ago some pleasant nonsense about growing old gracefully; she had told them firmly then and there that she was never going to grow old at all, no matter how gracefully. And she had believed it — that was what being a child meant. But had she grown up at all, then? Had she simply gone without knowing it from childhood to age, without ever becoming — unattractive word — "mature"? Well, everybody knows that melancholy brooding and a tendency to dwell in the past are most certain signs of growing old. She left her chair and walked to the rail — such a little ship, like a prison almost, so few places to go — and leaned there breathing in the sweet cool wind, assuring herself that this late-summer day in mid-Atlantic was not going so badly — she could easily remember worse birthdays. The heat was lessening gradually, the sunshine was paler; for the past two evenings great motionless columns of cloud had reared up and shone red over the far waters, full of muttering thunder and broad slow lightnings; they were beginning to form again, on a sky-filling scale. "I wish I knew somebody to watch clouds with," she said, and decided that she did not want a cocktail before dinner.

The thought of dinner reminded her of her tiresome cabin mate Lizzi Spöckenkieker, who had gone on excitedly making great mystification about something that had happened in the dining salon, something about a most significant change in seating arrangements. "But it happened yesterday!" cried Lizzi. "I was waiting for you to speak!"

"What about, though?" asked Mrs. Treadwell, idly, not caring.

"What, you really did not see *anything?*" demanded Lizzi. "And something so much before your very eyes?"

"I didn't look," said Mrs. Treadwell.

"I am dying to tell you, but no, you must find out for yourself."

"Does it really concern me, or am I supposed to be peeping?" asked Mrs. Treadwell.

"It concerns all of us," said Lizzi in an exalted lilting voice. "It is something so wonderful it makes me happy and I want to laugh." She did laugh and Mrs. Treadwell heard it wondering, thinking that if a hyena suffered from hysteria it would laugh like that. This was the moment she had left the cabin and decided on fresh air and the French magazine for the rest of the afternoon. What had Lizzi called out to her as she closed the door after her? "Ask Herr Freytag — he'll know." In remembering it, Mrs. Treadwell heard an insinuation in the tone she had not noticed before. Why not then look for Herr Freytag, who had been quite pleasant during their hour in Havana over the planter's punch, hear the newest scandal over cocktails, ask the band to play *"Ich bin die fesche Lola,"* and maybe even dance a little after dinner? She began a search which ended in one of the writing rooms, with Freytag just getting up from a desk with a sealed envelope in his hand. He stood stock-still at sight of her, but she spoke too quickly, before she had got a clear sight of his face.

"Do come out and watch the clouds with me," she said. "This is my birthday."

He came towards her, pale and frowning, and asked in utter incredulity, *"What* did you say?"

"Well, what *have* I said?" she asked. "Herr Freytag, what is wrong?"

"Mrs. Treadwell, will you please tell me what you want? What are you doing here, after your mean treachery to me, betraying my confidence, gossiping about my wife to that hag Spöckenkieker, making me all this stupid trouble . . . ?"

His words were exploding in hot puffs of breath in her very face; she shrank and began to tremble, not for fear but for dismay of conscience, for she remembered everything and knew what Freytag was talking about, saw that she had fallen into the trap Lizzi had set for her. "Oh, tell me what has happened," she said, in a low shaking voice, and she spread her two hands flat, palms out, before her breast. "She said you would know!"

"How stupidly cruel you are!" he burst out again, incandescent with fury. "Do you mean to ridicule me besides what you have already done? Can you pretend — look, don't you know that — that —" he stumbled on the brink of a foul name for Lizzi, drew back — "that she babbled at the table before everybody, how you were drunk . . ."

Mrs. Treadwell sat with a slight stagger on the nearest chair, holding her head.

"— Drunk and oh shame on you repeated what I had told you in confidence . . . and that swine of a Captain, that stinking swine —"

"Don't call ugly names," said Mrs. Treadwell, raising her voice a little, shaking her head as if she could rid her ears of his clamor. "And I was not drunk, that is a slander —"

"He is not only a swine, but the worst sort of swine, the self-satisfied swine who cultivates and loves his own swinishness; he boasts of it, he imposes it on those around him; he thinks and talks like a swine, he gobbles and guzzles like a swine, he is swinishness itself, he would look much better and be more comfortable on four feet —"

Mrs. Treadwell stood up again and put her hands over her ears. "I won't listen any more," she called through the words pouring like a rockslide, "unless you tell me what he did."

"He put me at the table with the Jew!" shouted Freytag in a climactic mystical spin of outrage, and stopped as if a hand had been laid on his mouth.

"Is that so bad?" asked Mrs. Treadwell, gently, as if she were humoring a madman. "Do you really mind?"

Freytag, still furious and colorless, quieted somewhat, but stuck to his point, which was to force her to see, acknowledge, and accept the fact that she was to blame for the whole thing. She could sidestep and throw him off track as long as she liked, but he was going to tell her the facts.

"What I mind is your treachery," he said. "The Captain meant to insult me, and to insult my wife through me, but he cannot insult us. He is capable only of impudence, the filthy —"

"No," said Mrs. Treadwell, shaking her head, "not that again."

"If you had been a dear friend," Freytag said, his voice now hoarsened and full of pathos, "or a member of my family, or anyone I had loved and trusted, what you did would not have surprised me. But how could I expect such treachery, such malice, from a stranger?"

Mrs. Treadwell was silent as a prisoner on trial, turning this unanswerable question over in her mind rather coldly, wishing the talk might end, but knowing it must go on until the suffering man, her accuser, had cleared his mind of her.

"Of course I do not mind Löwenthal, and I am sure he does not mind me," said Freytag, and was hypnotized almost into calm by the quite civilized relationship he began inventing between Löwenthal and himself. "We would probably bore each other to death if we tried to talk, so I imagine we won't try it. He is obviously of low origin, but I prefer him to the Captain and that dull crowd at his table — at least he has decent feelings and —" he hesitated a moment — "and really, quite good manners —"

Here he paused, unable to go on with his fiction. Mrs. Treadwell had sat down again, and was listening intently. Freytag sat down too, and leaned towards her to speak again, when she said, "But he sounds rather nice!"

Freytag seemed to collapse as if he could no longer contest with such an impermeable being. "My God, nice!" he said finally. "No, he is not nice, and I don't like him, and not because he is a Jew; if he were seven times a Christian I should still not like him because he is the kind of man I don't like. Can you understand that?" he asked her with some curiosity, as if he were trying out a strange language on her. "It is true, he is not even the kind of Jew I like, or is that going too far?"

Mrs. Treadwell heard the stagy sarcasm and decided she had let him be rude long enough, out of deference to his sense of wrong against her. Now she went back to the subject.

"I can't defend myself at all," she told him, choosing her words. "But why did you give me your confidence? I did not want it. I did not even imagine it was a confidence. If you had told me — but you accuse me of such ignoble motives —" She stammered, repelled by the almost unbearable, shameless pathos in the now puzzled mournful anger of his face. He looked as if his teeth were on edge; he had frowned until a new set of wrinkles was already fixed between his eyebrows. He looked as moody as Arne Hansen. He now turned this alienated face straight to her as if it helped him listen better, but the pale gray eyes with their sick look avoided hers at last.

". . . not because I had any motive," she went on, rapidly, "but exactly because I *hadn't*. I wasn't your friend, how could I be? If I had been your friend I would have known about your life and there would be no occasion to talk about it to anybody. What did you expect of me? I was not your enemy either. I just hadn't thought of you at all."

"Thank you," he said, with bitterness. "You were quite right."

"Don't be childish," said Mrs. Treadwell. "I meant nothing personal. I mean only to say, I didn't know enough about you to guard your secret — though why you look upon it as one at this point I can't understand."

Freytag said in perfect simplicity, "When I travel alone, I go as a Christian. When my wife is with me, things are different: we never quite know . . . maybe you don't know Germany? Things are very uncertain there for us, and getting worse . . ."

"But if your secret was so important to you, why did you give it to me?"

"It was on my mind, you seemed sympathetic. I spoke without thinking of consequences."

"Ah, so did I," said Mrs. Treadwell, "and I will confess something. I had drunk a whole bottle of wine that evening. Out of boredom, out of stupor, out of indifference . . ."

"You are worse than a treacherous friend," he said suddenly, harshly. "You are worse than a worst enemy. Out of your boredom! What right have you to be bored? Indifference — what right have you to live in this world and care nothing for the human beings around you? You did a mean treacherous thing to someone who trusted you and never harmed you, and then you don't even care — oh you don't even *know*, what you have done."

Mrs. Treadwell felt anger flashing all through her. She would not be bullied any longer about this absurd episode.

"You betrayed yourself first," she told him, with a light, glib inflection, "and you are carrying all this very much too far and you are quite wrong. I do really, with all my heart," she said, wondering at herself for the phrase, "care about what has happened to you —"

"About what you *did*," he persisted, maddeningly. "Remember, it was you, it was what you *did* that . . ."

"I have been amazed enough at myself," she said, "and perhaps you are right, and you may blame me as much as you please; but you make it easy for me to be frank with you now and tell you that, yes, you are right again — I simply do not want to be annoyed with this business, I do not intend to worry about it at all, and I shall not talk about it any more."

She rose and turned away a few steps, then faced about again, waiting for whatever he might want to say. Surely in such a case, the last word was his privilege. She was trembling deeply with resentment; the face before her was repulsive in its hardened expression of self-absorbed, accusing, utter righteousness.

"With all your heart," he said, "you have no heart. And you do not understand what is happening. It is not just this one thing — no no, it is a lifetime of it, it is a world full of it — it's not being able ever to hope for an end to it — It is seeing the one you love best in the world treated like dirt by people not fit to breathe the same air with her! If you could see her, you would know what I am talking about. Mrs. Treadwell, she is a little golden thin nervous thing, most beautiful and gay in the morning, she is innocent, innocent, she makes life charming where she is, when she talks it is like a bird singing in a tree!"

He came very near to her and spoke urgently, so near that she could feel his breath again, his face strained in anxiety, his eyes bright with tears. Mrs. Treadwell, taken terribly by surprise, without in the least intending to and with no warning from her own feelings, gave way and consented to see him in his own light, understood his sufferings as real and terrible, admitted her fault, and took on as a penance her share not only of this pain but whatever other shapeless, nameless endless human anguish chose to search her out and accuse her. She dropped her hands to her sides and retreated a step. Of course it was her fault.

"Don't!" she said. "Don't say any more. Listen to me. Listen to me for just a moment." She drew a deep breath. "I want to be forgiven. You must try to forgive me."

It was his turn to be surprised, to be reversed with a jolt, rather unpleasantly. He had been enjoying the scene, easing the pressure of his baffled fury on her; he had meant to insult her enough to satisfy his desire for revenge, and to leave her well cut up without letting her say a word. And now almost instantly, in spite of himself, a generous warmth of feeling came over him, and he said, "Oh, no, please not," almost in embarrassment, "don't say it. I am sorry, too. We will have to forgive each other if we go on like this —"

"The thing that is so frightening," said Mrs. Treadwell, her voice shaking a little, "is this. Here we are talking about this as if it were real, and I expect it is, but it seems to me like a horrid dream, I cannot believe it —"

"It's real, though," he said, and now he wished to console her. "Oh no, surely you are not going to cry?"

"How absurd," said Mrs. Treadwell, quite in her usual manner. "I never cry." She gave a bubbling little laugh and burst into enormous, helpless tears. Freytag, with the presence of mind of a married man used to feminine emergencies, glanced round to see if any witness had entered the writing room, moved between her and the door to provide a screen, and offered her a large white linen handkerchief. "Now, now," he said soothingly while she wiped her eyes and blew her nose. "Oh that's better. Do you know what I think? What do you say we have a good drink, a big cocktail?"

Mrs. Treadwell said, "Wait a minute." She took a little looking glass and powder puff and lipstick out of her handbag, and for the first time in her life applied make-up in public. One witness was as damning as a crowd. She did not care. She was exhausted, serene, unnerved, all at once, this melodrama was the kind of thing she abhorred — oh, the dowdiness of making scenes, and she did not trust Freytag for a moment, he was obviously a born scene-maker — yet, no matter how it came about, she felt just for a moment, knowing even then it could not possibly last, an airy lightness of heart. In recklessness, or something like it, she said, "I'd love a cocktail, a huge one," and they emerged into the passageway together like two amiable well-disposed persons apparently on the best of terms.

Freytag said, "I don't know if I am going to be able to sleep tonight, thinking about what fun it would be to throw the Captain overboard, drown the little rat off his own bridge. But I'll resist temptation now, thanks to you."

"Why? I shouldn't mind what you do to the Captain."

"You've cooled my mind, somehow. I have got to go to Germany and leave again with my wife and her mother, and that's all I have to think about, and I must do it without attracting any attention. Drowning the Captain indeed," he said, "a pleasant daydream, but I mustn't give way to it. I must work things out."

When they were seated, he asked, "Is it really your birthday? Is that what you said when you came in?"

She nodded. "The forty-sixth, imagine!" He was obscurely offended at her unfeminine frankness, and to hide it, he said, "How charming! Many, many more."

"Not too many, please. I'll let you know if I want another."

He surveyed the bar, now beginning to be crowded. Jenny Brown and David Scott, climbing on stools, greeted him Mexican fashion, right hands raised face-high, palms out, fingers fluttering. He responded with the same gesture, and Mrs. Treadwell said, "I think it's pretty." Freytag said, "They say it means 'Come nearer,'" and continued to move his look from face to face, as if he expected each one to notice his presence, though he had never thought of such a thing before. The Lutzes and Baumgartners in turn caught his glance, and nodded to him: the dullest of all the dull people on board, of course — they probably wouldn't have worldly sense enough to understand what had happened. Everybody from the Captain's table was there, apparently unconscious of his existence. Those appalling Spaniards, not even they turned an eye towards him, though one of the girls, the little young Concha, had been following him about lately, as if she had something on her mind. Even the young Cuban pair ignored him, though he had played games with their small children, tootling on paper flutes, letting them shoot at him with water pistols, walking around the deck with one straddled on each shoulder; even the hunchback, even that ridiculous fellow from Texas, Denny, somehow failed to see him; it did not occur to him to speak to anybody first, nor did he remember that ordinarily he hoped that his fellow passengers so-called would keep away from him.

"I forgot," he said, his frown deepening, "but do you want to be seen with me? I'm a pariah here, remember."

"Are you sure? Have you counted your friends?"

"I hadn't got any to begin with that I know of," he said, quickly irritable. "It was rather more than enough to be on speaking terms."

"Then why do you care now whether anyone speaks to you or not?" she asked, and her feelings were slowly very surely retreating to their hiding place. "I have done it again," she reminded herself, and thought quite coldly, holding the stem of her cocktail glass and fixing her eyes at a point just under the knot of Herr Freytag's necktie, that this man was as impossible in his way as that tiresome Denny was in his. Still, she added at once, for fear he would suspect her change of mind and heart, that she had found several pleasant persons on board — she did not name them — yet it was quite true, she would be as happy if not a soul even looked at her for the rest of the voyage.

"I don't care at all either," he said, "certainly not. But remember, it can be a very different thing when people, and especially people you despise, suddenly feel themselves capable of snubbing you."

"Quite," she said, and finished her drink and ate the olive.

"Another?" he asked, and without waiting, "Do please. I'd like another."

"Of course," she said. While they were waiting, Mrs. Treadwell rested her cheeks in the palms of her hands, elbows on table, and said in her usual voice of one making conversation to scatter silence, and of which one need not bother to remember a word: "Imagine, I used to think you were a man without a single trouble in the world — perhaps the only one; and if only I had not said that silly thing to that awful Lizzi, I should still like to be able to believe it. It would amuse me, and I shouldn't have to think of you. And now, I suppose, we have a kind of bond, we must be friends in a way, and speak to each other carefully whether we are in the mood or not, just so all these strangers that we shall never see again, or I hope not, will see that we are not at each other's throats in spite of Lizzi and Rieber and the Captain and all the rest . . ."

Freytag was listening, and her words dismayed him to a degree. It had already crossed his mind that a scene so intimate as that in the writing room might lead in her mind to notions of further intimacy. She must have been a very pretty girl, she was not bad-looking now in a discreet, rather too delicate style, but the very thought of going to bed with a woman forty-six years old gave him such horror he was afraid it would show in his face. The one sure way to bring upon yourself the inescapable devotion of a dog was to beat him regularly. Certain kinds of women were not so different. This one had taken a good thrashing in the proper spirit — she had earned it — but was he now going to be, as the Americans say, "stuck" with her? He must find out if he could.

"But we are friends, are we not?" he asked, warily.

He was to find later that he need not have feared her persecutions, and was to be surprised at his own annoyance about it; but her answer to his question did nothing to quiet his present uneasiness. Mrs. Treadwell, however, was herself again, wearing her way smilingly through the second cocktail, waiting for the moment of escape.

"Naturally," she said in a tone of such reassurance he could not dream that she meant just the opposite.

He decided that he needed only to be reasonably discreet, a little watchful, to keep out of her way. He finished his drink in a gulp and set the glass down and pushed it away from him. Mrs. Treadwell set hers down unfinished. When they parted he was again in doubt: he did not want her at all, and he was not willing to let her get away altogether. "This has been delightful," he said, "after all the unpleasantness. I feel we know each other a great deal better?"

She smiled in his direction, looking through him as through a pane of glass. "Oh, much better, I'm sure," she said, and drifted away. Anger against her rose in him again, but a different kind, not fury, but still a lively resentment. He had so many reasons for anger in all directions he could hardly fix upon the real, the main reasons. One of them, though, was the way his hand had been forced by the Captain, and that woman — whose flat hips and slender legs, he noticed, as she retreated from him, moved almost invisibly within her perfectly fitted, expensive-looking linen frock — had been to blame for the whole thing. In spite of her brief tears he did not believe she felt any true remorse; in spite of what he had said, a bitter desire rankled in him to humiliate her further, to put her to shame in some public way, to teach her a good lesson. . . . At this point, Herr Löwenthal came in by himself as usual and stood at the bar and beer was brought to him. Freytag felt his throat closing as if he might choke on his sense of injury; one thing certain, he would not sit at the table with that Jew. . . . No, he explained to himself as if arguing with a disapproving stranger, No, it is not because he is a Jew. It is because of what has been done to *both of us*. But he will never acknowledge that any wrong has been done to anyone but himself. The thought was like a flash of light in his mind — I have no prejudice against Jews — how could I? Mary is one, Mary — but why must he worry about this wretched little man, with his comic trade — he would just be a laughingstock anywhere: "Has he got any fragments of the True Cross, I wonder?" Jenny had asked, and Freytag had been maliciously cheerful to be able to answer, "I've been told he has, in tiny hand-carved ivory reliquaries, set with a piece of magnifying glass — and a sliver of wood no bigger than a hair!"

"I can't quite say why, but I find that revolting," said Jenny. "Just suppose a Christian tried to sell him a sliver of the Ark of the Covenant, or a fragment of the Wailing Wall, or Abraham's toenail cuttings?"

"He'd know better," said Freytag. "He'd say, 'I'm overstocked with that line myself!'" They had laughed easily, but now Freytag felt corroded with guilt, heaping ridicule on one of Mary's people with this shallow girl. But that had happened before he had been kicked away from the Captain's table. He reminded himself fiercely that he must put up with Löwenthal, must treat him decently no matter what he said or did — if for no other reasons, he owed it to Mary. He also owed it to his own self-respect . . . I will have meals sent to the cabin, he decided; I will eat on deck sometimes. I will speak to him when I have to.

Herr Löwenthal was in better spirits and a calmer frame of mind since his encounter with Herr Freytag. He always felt safer, indeed at times there came over him a simmer of elation, when at last, and always sooner or later, no matter where, the lurking enmities, the evil designs, the formless miasmas of hatred took on shape, color, direction, language; and Persecution by the heathen world, his unescapable destiny as Jew, the one unanswerable argument for his chosenness, was once more under way, with no more doubts, no more waiting and watching. It always turned out not to be so bad as he had feared; even though he was never able to imagine the actual form the persecution would take, yet he found he was never really surprised by anything — never twice alike and always the same, yet no real danger, nothing that could not be handled after all — words, what are they? Insults, threats, names, low jokes — what of it? They couldn't touch him; he wanted only one thing from them, and that he had already — their trade. Why not sell graven images to the heathen if that's what they want? And get good prices for it too. He was making money, and he would make more; he knew well how many desirable places he could buy with money. It would be a positive pleasure someday just to see how far he could buy his way into places where they wouldn't dare to throw him out! His mood grew almost festive; he gulped down his beer and asked for another; he looked forward to seeing Herr Freytag at his table that evening, and he would make him feel that it was his, Löwenthal's, table, and that Freytag was there on sufferance. . . . Herr Löwenthal lighted a good cigar and settled down over his stein. He had heard about how that pig Rieber had tried to get him thrown out of the cabin, and had failed, because nobody wanted Herr Rieber either! That would be something to tell Cousin Sarah when he finally thank God got to Düsseldorf. When later at dinner Herr Freytag did not appear, and he had to eat his dull tinned fish alone, he was a little let down, disappointed. He must persuade him back, if only for the look of the thing. He would say to him sometime on deck, before a lot of people, loud enough for them to hear: "You mustn't take wrong what I said, Herr Freytag. You're more than welcome to sit at my table, if you haven't got any place else." He'd like to hear his answer to that!

He was considerably put out and disgruntled when the steward, answering his question, said simply, "Herr Freytag prefers to dine alone, later."

Lizzi giggled and trilled at sight of Mrs. Treadwell, who was sitting on the side of her berth fastening her sandals, dressing for the evening. Mrs. Treadwell glanced up, without inquiry, and Lizzi said rashly, "Oh, I must hear what Herr Freytag had to say when you asked him your question!"

"Nothing much," said Mrs. Treadwell easily. She stood up and shook out her silvery pleated gown, slipped into it, and moved towards the door, fastening her belt as she went. "He seemed to feel, on the whole, that it was a great change for the better — the company, he seemed to mean . . ." She gathered up her skirts and closed the door after her gently.

"David," said Jenny, as they touched their cocktail glasses together, "*Salud*, David darling! Don't you find that business about Freytag being put away from the Captain's table — do you know, imagine all the things he has told me, and he never told me such an important thing as that about his wife! But he thinks she hung the moon! — don't you find it is the most utterly disgraceful episode you ever heard of?"

"No, I've heard of worse," said David, "and so have you. But it's pretty nasty."

"I think we ought to speak to Freytag and let him know how we feel!"

"Go ahead," said David darling, with blazing eyes and an icy voice. "Since when do you need an excuse?"

"You are getting simply intolerable on this subject, David," she said, in a low distressed voice. "You know perfectly well he is a married man crazy about his wife, he is sociable and lonesome, there aren't too many people on this ship to talk to — oh, the whole thing is so silly I'm ashamed to be talking about it! I can't understand. You were never jealous before . . ."

"Wasn't I?" asked David, cutting in like a razor blade. "Are you sure?"

"Well, you were wrong," said Jenny, "and you're wrong again — but I don't care, if only —"

"If only what?" asked David gently, for they both felt the same treacherous tenderness, that melting of the heart that would lead them further astray. "Can't you just be a little flattered if I am jealous? It must be that, don't you think? Any other explanation of my conduct is silly."

"No, I'm not flattered," said Jenny, "but do you know what I had in mind? You'll be furious, David. I thought you might invite Freytag to sit with us, he must be horribly uncomfortable sitting with that funny little man . . ."

"No, I'm not furious," said David, "I am just overwhelmed at the clear and beautiful workings of your mind. Maybe Löwenthal is unhappy too."

"Why of course, David, why shouldn't he be? But he was doing very nicely before by himself, and if Freytag comes to us Löwenthal will be just where he was — perfectly comfortable."

"What makes you think Freytag would enjoy our society and our conversation any more than he does Löwenthal's?" asked David. "How do we know he isn't perfectly contented with Löwenthal?"

"I thought you could find out," said Jenny. "I was going to leave it to you."

"Why? He's your friend. I've never spoken a dozen words to the man."

"We ought to have friends in common," said Jenny. "We ought to try to like the same people. But it's your place to ask him."

"I don't quite know what you've got in mind," said David, and his nose grew pale and sharp, "but I think you're trying to treat me like a husband."

"I never had one," said Jenny, "so I don't know how they expect to be treated."

"Invite Freytag to our table if you like," said David. "And I'll be delighted to go over and sit with Löwenthal."

Their hearts hardened again with a suddenness surprising to them both. They exchanged glances of cold bitter obstinacy, each quite determined that the other should pick up the pieces if any pieces were to be picked up. On the other side of the bar, plainly to be seen by them both, the object of their quarrel, or rather the pretext for it, Freytag, was having cocktails with Mrs. Treadwell, the two of them quite untroubled and good-looking, asking for nobody's officious help or pity. Jenny's composure, her assurance, her belief in her own view of things, vanished at this sight. She turned back to David and stooped and picked up the first piece of whatever it was they had broken, and then another, and began trying to put them together in whatever shape they had been before.

"David darling, I'd like another drink — I'd like a lot of drinks. Every day I learn about something else that is none of my business!"

The Baumgartners with their little son Hans were sitting near the largest table in the bar, entirely occupied by the Spanish dancing company, who were devouring great wedges of cake and swallowing pints of coffee with milk and sugar. Frau Baumgartner could not refrain from mentioning this circumstance, with an appropriate moral reflection.

"What really sober people they are," she remarked, with a glance at her husband's nearly empty goblet of brandy and water. "Look, this whole voyage, nobody has seen them take anything stronger than table wine, and nearly always coffee!"

"There are coffee addicts as well as other kinds," Herr Baumgartner reminded her. "There are also those who are gluttons for cakes and pastries, to the detriment of their health!" He flicked a shrewd look over the assorted pastries with whipped cream on her plate. "Those Spaniards are not people whose morals can be judged by their diet, my dear, whatever it may be. What good does mere abstinence from alcohol do people who are so sunk in every other vice?"

"How do you know?" asked Frau Baumgartner. "I love to watch

them dance, and if the women do flirt, why, they are gypsies, after all."

"Flirt!" said Herr Baumgartner, with infinite meaning. "Now then my dear Hans, no more raspberry juice before dinner, it will spoil your appetite."

He ordered another brandy, and a small cherry cordial for Frau Baumgartner, who smiled at him reproachfully, then sat smelling the liquor now and then, and taking a drop on her tongue. But no, the pleasure had gone out of it . . . ah yes, the pleasure had gone out of everything in life!

Frau Rittersdorf had the deck steward raise the back of her chair to a comfortable position, drew her red chiffon veil somewhat further over her eyebrows for the double purpose of letting the slanting sunlight throw a rosy glow on her face and to insure against intrusion while she posted up her diary, neglected of late.

"Though it is no exaggeration to say there is not a moment of my existence, waking or sleeping, yes even in my deepest dreams, that I do not miss the company and conversation of my Otto, yet in the past few days I have missed him if possible yet more keenly than ever because of a certain little episode we should have so enjoyed together — a comic situation good enough for a play: The Christian man married to a Jewish wife being set by mistake at the Captain's table! A most misleadingly presentable young man he is, too — one can only regret his appalling lapse of taste. Yet this is no time for making allowances in such questions — quite simply, he must be rejected utterly from decent German society. We at the Captain's table were of course of the most charming unanimity that he should be sent to his proper place, at the table with the Jew. I hear this has created some little commotion among some of the other passengers. Those dreadful Americans, together with the vulgar Lutzes (Swiss!) and the even more vulgar Baumgartners (Bavarians, I believe), are showing ostentatious sympathy for him. I am not surprised at the Americans, nothing too base for them, let them find their own level; but even the lowest of Germans — one would think their *blood* would make the proper responses to a thing of this kind, without having to reflect for an instant. Alas, this is not always so. In Mexico I found it quite disturbing. I knew there the purest Germans of correct society who invited — not often, true — their Jewish clients or business associates to dine in their own homes. They excused themselves to me — 'Oh, it's only a question of business,' they said; or 'You know we would not think of such a thing in Germany. Here, what does it matter?' But it does indeed matter, I told them; I feel that God sees us, and our dead heroes are looking down upon us in distress and amazement! My Otto had written this to me once after a defeat in battle, and I shall never forget it. How unerring his instincts in everything! It was his boast that no Jew had ever set foot in his father's house, to the farthest known generations. But I must not dwell on this — it is all too bittersweet.

"There is some light scandal about Herr Rieber having been put in the same cabin with this Jew, and now he must stay there, because there is no other place to put him, imagine. I cannot much care what happens to Herr Rieber, hopelessly coarse and common as he is — it is a mystery why he is at the Captain's table, except that he is a publisher of some kind, and I suppose merits consideration in this respect — yet I cannot be cruel enough to say he deserves this. The purser is being blamed for everything of course; he in turn blames the ship's agent in Mexico City who gave incomplete or misleading data on many of the passengers. I blame no one; but merely allow myself to be amused at this small diversion which provides a tiny respite from this voyage, which must undoubtedly be described as somewhat on the dull side."

Frau Rittersdorf pushed back her veil, closed her fountain pen, and leaned forward stretching her neck and arms discreetly to ease the strain of writing, unfortunately just in time to attract once more the attention of one of those male Spanish dancers, the one they called Tito, the supposed husband of Lola — the "star" of the zarzuela, the putative father of those indescribable twins, though it was improbable that they were of human origin; rather, little demons one expected to blow up with a smell of brimstone and disappear before one's eyes. Still, this Tito — two evenings ago, when she had finished a delightful dance with a most charming young ship's officer, this Tito with ineffable impudence had come boldly up and asked her to dance with him! Whenever she remembered what happened next, and she had not been able to forget it for an instant, she began to blush, turning blood-red all over and breaking into a sensation of heat rash. She tried again hard not to remember, resolutely she had omitted all mention of it from her diary, and turned from the thought: she even repeated all the prayers she could remember, rapidly over and over as an incantation against evil.

Instead of refusing him quite in the easy friendly tone she would have used to a gentleman, so that he should not suspect her horror at his indecent proposal, she stood transfixed, lips parted, unable to breathe a syllable, with his black eyes like a snake's gleaming wickedly only a few inches from hers; and had felt herself taken without her consent and spirited away like a cloud, in the lightest, surest, gentlest embrace she had ever known, in such a dance as she had not even dreamed of since her innocent girlhood, herself again a pure sylph of the most gauzy lightness — oh no, Frau Rittersdorf almost moaned to herself, could I have done such a thing? Oh, did I really allow that to happen?

When it was ended, he kissed her hand quickly and darted away, leaving her standing alone, dazed; Lizzi Spöckenkieker whirling by like a merry-go-round with that puffball of a Herr Rieber called out mockingly, "Where are your castanets?" The young officer returned then and asked once more to dance, and though he had seemed so graceful and easy before, now they trundled along and could hardly catch step together; and though he said rather gaily, "I dare not leave you alone for a second, a gypsy will kidnap you!" she knew she was being warned and rebuked at once. As she reflected on her unheard-of behavior, and what would have been the retribution visited upon her by her Otto, never a man to withhold justice, for one blinding moment she was almost grateful for his absence. Instantly right feelings reclaimed her; she realized that if Otto were alive, oh if only he were alive, she would be far from this wretched ship, far from this mean society. She had always had the look and deportment of a lady, and her husband had been proud of her in any company! Now she must make certain by her manner that that Lizzi shall not dare to mention this incident of the Spaniard's presumption at the Captain's table, nor would she tolerate any familiarity on the subject from anyone else. She grew quite rigid; but it had not been necessary. No one mentioned it — no one seemed even to have heard about it. Even Lizzi had never presumed to give her a little conspiratorial smile the next day. This in the end had made it all the worse — their ignoring might be a form of criticism of her conduct or morals — yet, she asked herself, what could possibly have been said or done by anyone to make it better?

She must simply forget, as she was forgetting Don Pedro, as she was forgetting the miseries of being a girl of a poor family who must educate herself to be a governess in England; as indeed sometimes she feared she was forgetting Otto. Whenever she thought of him, and it was very often, he was no longer solid remembered flesh and blood with a resonant voice still speaking in her ear, no; he now appeared a shining image a few feet off the ground like a visitant angel, in pure white and gold uniform (though he had been an army officer, field artillery, never the navy), with a rainbow aureole around his head that quite obscured his features. She had not been able to remember his look for years; and now she often had to strive to see and feel again that wonderfully shaped golden head that she had cradled in her arms and kissed and sung to as if he were her little child, rocking him to sleep, both of them molten with tenderness. . . .

Frau Rittersdorf had a sensation of drowning, she closed her eyes and gasped, her head swam and rolled; she opened her eyes again and there was Tito bending over her gracefully in his tight black dancing dress, red waistband, bolero, frilled shirt and all: and he was saying — what on earth was he saying? He was carrying what looked like a sheaf of small tickets of some kind in his left hand; he slipped one out and held it towards her, and he was not smiling but holding her gaze with his as if he meant to hypnotize her. Frau Rittersdorf reached out her hand to take the ticket, at which it was withdrawn and he said, "Not yet. Let me tell you something . . ."

Frau Rittersdorf's head cleared, she sat up and listened attentively, expecting to hear something sinister, forbidden, or at the very least disreputable. Instead it was disarmingly, childishly simple. The zarzuela company wished to promote a little fiesta in which everyone on board could take part; a specially festive dinner in which everybody would appear masked and change places at table. There would be special music, dancing for all, and the zarzuela company itself proposed to give a full evening's show from the most elegant numbers in its repertory: then there would be a drawing of numbers for beautiful prizes; the prizes were to be purchased at shops in Santa Cruz de Tenerife, a place known for its refined arts and handiworks. It was all to be offered as homage to the Captain, the evening before the ship should reach Vigo, where the zarzuela company would disembark.

"We have said it is a pity to spend such a long voyage without one public fiesta," said Tito, seriously, as one in all good faith. Frau Rittersdorf's head cleared another degree: her mercantile instincts took charge. "But you sound so businesslike, for an artist," she told him. "How can you be so practical?"

"I am the manager of this company," he told her, "also the director, and my wife is my assistant."

"Lola?" asked Frau Rittersdorf, with condescension.

"Yes, Doña Lola," he corrected her, haughtily.

The mists cleared from Frau Rittersdorf's mind at his tone. "You must let me think a little," she said languidly, making motions as if she would open her diary once more. "I am not a devotee of games of chance in any form —" Her eyes wandered and she saw that Lizzi Spöckenkieker had taken up her station two deck chairs away, with a large-leaf magazine she was not pretending to read. This sight was so annoying to Frau Rittersdorf she sat up and spoke with perfect firmness.

"How much are these tickets for your game of chance?" she asked, briskly.

"Four little marks," said Tito, curling his lip to show what a contemptible sum they must both think it.

"I would not mind the money," said Frau Rittersdorf, noting with some distress that this scene could hardly be more conspicuous. People were beginning to go by on their before-dinner parade. The bride and groom, oblivious of course; Dr. Schumann, oh dear! The Cuban students, somewhat more subdued these days, but full of mischief, with evil tongues, you might be certain; the dull Lutzes with their dull daughter, nothing to think about but gossip! The two priests — she had always made a point of bowing to them, but now she wished she were invisible. That dreadful American Denny with his mean sneer and evil eyes — the whole shipload of first-class passengers seemed to have taken advantage of her predicament, which she could never explain; for Tito was bending over her with the air of one very sure of his welcome, as if she were about to accept his invitation to coffee, perhaps. The sheaf of tickets had disappeared from his hand. Frau Rittersdorf summoned all her powers, sat up straighter than ever, noting in the same moment that Lola and Amparo, also in their ruffled dancing costumes, were leaning together at the rail nearby; she spoke firmly.

"I must know more about this from others," she said. "It is a little vague, I do not understand yet precisely what it is you wish me to take part in. What you propose is far from customary. On the best boats you will find no such custom as this offering of a gala to the Captain in mid-voyage, or nearly. The proper moment for the Captain's dinner, you will find I am right, is the second evening before reaching the final destination. Believe me, I have traveled always until now on the finest ships and this is what is done by *le beau monde* . . . at earliest the third evening out depending on the weather and other such things. . . . No, I cannot see the necessity for your rushing this occasion merely because *you* must leave the ship at Vigo; most of us shall continue our journey to the end. Just before we arrive at Bremerhaven, I shall be delighted to join in any little plan to show our gratitude to our good Captain for his pains and troubles with us on this voyage. Not before. You must be so good as to excuse me."

"But we who disembark at Vigo wish also to offer a little correct homage to our noble Captain," said Tito, with great formality and in pretty fair German.

"Persons of the best society do these things otherwise," answered Frau Rittersdorf, now in full stride as mentor, an apostolic light in her pale eyes. "I see no reason for assuming that the Captain will not know the difference if we offer him an entertainment which ignores the accepted forms of social life . . . and also, perhaps you do not know this, there is hardly ever — indeed, I can remember no such occasion, where an element of the commercial or of the lottery has been involved. One does not buy tickets for the Captain's dinner. Indeed, in the very last analysis, I am trying to explain to you that the Captain's farewell gala is by invitation of the Captain himself to his passengers, not the other way around. The food, decorations, favors, music, indeed everything but the champagne is provided from the commissary, for all the passengers as well as the guests at the Captain's table. So," she ended triumphantly, for Tito was listening sharply and she hoped her lesson was sinking in, "you and your Spanish friends must do as you wish about this, privately, without engaging others who have different ideas about such things!"

Tito exchanged a quick glance with Lola and Amparo, who moved a little nearer draping their mantillas over their arms. He gave a good imitation of the German salute, clicking his patent-leather pump heels smartly, and said, smiling, in a rattling fire of Spanish: "Whether you like it or not, you stinking German sausage made of old women's behinds, we are going to have our show and you are going to help pay for it." Lola and Amparo broke into screams of helpless laughter, and applauded his performance. He swung into step with them, they moved away together and stood at some distance laughing, Tito bending over and holding his narrow waist with both hands. Frau Rittersdorf, who had not understood, or could not believe what she had seemed to hear, suspecting the worst, even a little frightened for she had seen in dismay that he really was a *maquereau* capable of anything, flushed a deep painful red and leaned back in her chair.

"God in Heaven," she said, turning towards Lizzi as to a known being who could offer her reassurance, "God in heaven, what can one do with such people?"

"One can always dance with them!" said Lizzi, and Frau Rittersdorf felt her malice flickering out of her very pores like electric sparks.

Seeing Frau Rittersdorf's chin tremble at this, Lizzi went on in a tone of false sympathy. "They really are making fun of you, the little pigs. . . . Look at them, Frau Rittersdorf, did you ever see such impudence? They are all but thumbing their noses at you. What could that fellow have said, I wonder? I did not catch it, but it sounded frightful."

Frau Rittersdorf began at once correcting her terrible error in giving Lizzi such a brilliant opportunity to display her peculiar gifts. "I am not the only one, perhaps," she said. "It may be your turn next, if you have not had it already!"

Lizzi fanned herself with her magazine. "Oh, one of them — not that fellow, the one they call Manolo — and one of the women, I don't know which, approached me this morning — it seems their plan is well under way . . . you really had not heard?"

"No," said Frau Rittersdorf, faintly, "no one told me."

"I was happy to bribe them for peace," Lizzi confessed smugly. "It cost me only four marks to be rid of them. It would have been worth twice as much."

"They can laugh at you for another reason, then," said Frau Rittersdorf. "At least, they cannot make a dupe of me!"

"Do you think I would really go to their low little party?" asked Lizzi. "I gave them the money as I would give it to a beggar."

"I shall not go to their party, either," said Frau Rittersdorf, recovering her spirits slowly. "And I shall not pay a pfennig for my right to stay away!"

The two women fell silent and watched with deep resentment the flying feet of the Spaniards disappearing around the upper end of the deck. Their magpie voices floated back only to deepen the gloom around the two stiff figures stretched in the deck chairs.

Frau Rittersdorf opened her diary and went on with her account of events. After a little thought, pen suspended, she wrote resolutely: "That little mealsack of a Frau Schmitt, my cabin mate, who has not one claim to any consideration whatever from anyone, has within the past few days commenced to show signs of a changed character. She monopolizes the washhand stand and the looking glass. She sits quite coolly and powders her face and dresses that mouse-colored hair of hers in a bun as leisurely as if she were not keeping me waiting. I consult my watch from time to time, remark how late it is getting, and that I, too, must dress. But it has no effect so far. Incapable as I am of rude behavior to anyone, I shall be forced to take steps to correct her bad manners. It is an offense against morality to overlook or condone insolence in an inferior. The effective practice of severity — I learned this with those beastly English children — lies in ceaseless, relentless, utter persistence, never an instant's letdown, but vigilance, vigilance, all the way, or they will be upon you like a pack of hyenas." She considered this, and added: "*Note Bene:* I must be especially on my guard with certain very low elements on this ship, who mean no good to anyone. Vigilance, vigilance." Frau Rittersdorf felt very tired, famished as if she had not eaten for days, she longed for the dear homely sound of the dinner bugle. Her mind was full of thoughts that did not belong there, strange ideas were bumping around colliding and threatening her with a headache. She added a line before closing her diary. "All this can be very wearing, but I must suppose it is necessary, and that the meaning of it will become clear later."

"Those greasers are up to something," Denny remarked to David. "They got a plan on foot." He was examining three new pimples on the underside of his jaw in his shaving glass, which magnified the disasters of his skin fivefold and kept him in a state of perpetual alarm. "My God, *look* at these things!" he said to his cabin mates, holding up his chin.

Herr Glocken was curled up in the lower bunk, waiting for the two young men to change their shirts and ties before dinner. "From here I can't even see them," he said, meaning to reassure.

"Maybe you're nearsighted," said Denny, who did not intend to have anyone make light of his afflictions. Herr Glocken reached in his jacket pocket and put on his spectacles. "Even so," he said, peering keenly, "I can barely make them out."

David, buttoning his shirt, did not turn his head. "What 'greasers'?" he asked. He detested Denny's vulgar habit of calling all nationalities but his own by short ugly names; yet even for his own he had a few favorites — "cracker" for example, but that applied strictly to people of the state of Georgia; "white trash" was another, specifically applied to persons of low social station combined with financial insolvency, and in general to anybody whose attitude towards him or his point of view he found unsympathetic.

"Those Spanish dancing greasers," said Denny, suspecting an implied rebuke in David's tone; Denny suspected often that David Scott disapproved of any number of things, though he could never be quite certain what they were. But this hoity-toity voice about the word "greaser," now —

"Well, what do *you* call 'em?" he asked. "Wops? Dagos? No, that's Italians. Polacks? No. Guineas? No, they're from Porto Rico, ain't they? Or is it Brazil? They're not niggers. Nor kikes. Kike is the name the Jews made up for a low-life Jew. Like that Löwenthal, for instance. But he's not a bad guy. I've talked to him. Did you know I never saw a Jew in my life until I was fifteen and went away to school? Or if I did see one I didn't know what he was. We didn't have a thing against Jews in our town — we didn't even have any Jews!"

"Maybe you were so busy lynching niggers you couldn't take time out for Jews," remarked David in a tone so remote and unheated, Denny's mouth dropped open and he shut it with a snap.

"Where are you from?" he asked, after a loaded pause.

"Colorado," said David. Denny tried to remember what he had ever heard, if anything, about Colorado except silver mines. He could not recall any traits of character of the people of that state, and so far as he knew, they had no nickname, like Hoosier or Cajun. You couldn't hardly call him a Yankee.

"Mining?" he ventured.

"Sure," said David, "timekeeper in a mine in Mexico."

"I thought you said you're a painter," said Denny.

"I am. Timekeeping in a mine was the way I made my living, so I could work," said David. Denny thought this over a while, and then said: "Look, that's something I can't understand — you spend time working at something you can't make a living at, and then you take a job so you can make enough money to go on working at the work you can't live on — it gets me down," he said. "And you call yourself a painter, but why aren't you just as much a timekeeper in a mine? Why can't you call yourself a timekeeper?"

"Because I really am not one," said David, "I just make my living that way, or did. . . . Now I'm going to try to make a living painting, but if I can't, why, I can always get some kind of job, to keep me while I paint."

Herr Glocken uncurled himself, ran his hand over his face and hair before the looking glass, pulled his tie knot a touch to center, gave himself a slight shake to straighten his rumpled clothes, and was ready to go. "Ah well," he said to Denny, "that is the heroic life! That is the way men who trust themselves can afford to live! Me — I never had courage. Me, I run my little stand, my newspapers and magazines and birthday and Christmas cards, yes and ink and pens and writing paper, and every day I have the small change running through my hands, and every night when I close shop I have made my day's living, yes and a little more, and that I invest so a few more pfennigs — *centavitos* — will be coming in always, a little more and a little more, for I have had no life — I only exist! And I have no existence coming except old age, and if I am not careful, I shall die under a bridge, or in a pauper's hospital . . ."

"Maybe I shall too," said David cheerfully, though Herr Glocken's sudden flood of confidences chilled him.

"Maybe," said Herr Glocken. "No man knows his end! But you will not have to die in despair because you never had courage to live! You have taken hold of your own life, for that no man can ever make you sorry!"

He spoke with such fervor the two young, straight-backed, lucky men had perhaps their first emotion in common: a twinge of apologetic shame, as if they owed him some reparation for the misfortune of his body, some explanation of why it was easy for them to have courage — for Denny felt that he too was launching out, taking hold; it was a fact that a trained engineer had forty good jobs waiting for him, but he had the right to choose the one that would take him farthest from home and deepest into adventure — that freedom at least he had. He couldn't see the point in being plain foolhardy, though — David Scott struck him as just being plain foolhardy, and that poor hunchback was buttering him up about it as if he envied him; he spoke up:

"It's not the shape of your body but your mind that shapes your life," he said, and he heard his own philosophical statement with amazed delight — he hadn't known that he thought that. "I'll bet no matter what, you'd have wound up with a newsstand," he said. "I tell you something, I believe we get what we want!"

"Oh!" said Herr Glocken with a groan, and he began moving towards the door. "Oh no, excuse the strong word, it is not for you, but for this so-false belief — it is one of the great lies of life! Ah no, no — for I wanted only one thing in the world —" He paused to make his effect.

"What was that?" asked David, obligingly.

"To be a violinist!" said Herr Glocken as movingly as if he expected them to shed tears.

"But why was that impossible?" asked David.

"You can wonder in such a way, after one look at me?" Herr Glocken's eyes were stricken . . . "Ah, well," he ended, "it is impossible to make one understand. But I had the soul," he said, patting himself lightly on the pointed misshapen ribs of his chest, "and I have it yet, and that consoles me a little." He smiled his painful jester's smile, and vanished.

"Well," said Denny, "that's that, I hope," and not another word was said about Herr Glocken.

"You never did tell me the nickname for Spaniards," said Denny.

"I don't know what they call each other when they want to be insulting in Spain," said David, "but in Mexico, the Indians call them *Gachupín.* It means a spur, really, or a boot that stings like a viper, the Aztec roundabout for the spur."

"Too good for them," said Denny.

"What do you think they're up to?" asked David, returning to the zarzuela company. "I see them about buttonholing people and talking but they haven't come near me yet. The gossip is they're getting up some kind of show, and a raffle with chances, and so on: a kind of old-fashioned *feria* on shipboard, which will be a novelty. I can't say I like their looks or ways . . ."

"That Arne Hansen has blown his top about that Amparo," said Denny, with unconcealed envy. "They've got *something* I could use right now. That Pastora . . ."

He stopped, teetering dizzily on the edge of giving himself away by telling the true story of his encounter that very afternoon with Pastora. He thought better of it, for he wished to maintain the view of his character he hoped he had built up in David Scott's mind, of himself as a man not to be taken in by women, who were every last one of them after nothing in God's world but money. And it should be the positive pleasure of any man in his right mind to see that she didn't get a nickel she hadn't earned the hard way. . . . But he drew back into himself and saw it happen again: Pastora, who had never bothered to hide her contempt for him, met him head-on in the promenade around the deck, and suddenly stretched her arm at full length towards him with a frank graceful gesture, and stopped him in full stride, her hand on his necktie. Her deep eyes wide open, she smiled in the most inviting way, and said in childish English: "Come help us make our fiesta! We will dance, we will sing, we will have games, we will kiss, why not?"

"How much?" he heard himself asking, but he felt like a bird gazing into the eyes of a serpent.

"Oh nothing almost!" said Pastora, winsomely. "Two dollar, three, five — ten — what you like."

Denny had broken into a light sweat, he felt he ought to say, "Make it two dollars then, that'll suit me," but he was afraid if he let this chance slip, he wouldn't get another. "Have a drink?" he asked recklessly. They sat together in the bar for a good while over a bottle of German imitation champagne, at twelve marks a bottle, he noticed; but Pastora sipped with great pleasure, their feet nestled together under the table, and Denny, who thought champagne, even the best, tasted like thin vinegar with bubbles in it, was so wrought up and full of anticipation he could hardly swallow. Pastora also wanted cigarettes. "Have one of these," offered Denny, producing his Camels. Pastora could not smoke that kind of cigarette. She wanted a slender gold-tipped jasmine-scented cigarette in a purple satin box stamped in gilt lettering: "La Sultana." Denny hastily figured out the exchange from marks to dollars — one dollar ninety cents a box of twenty. He bought it. And then Pastora sold him two tickets for the raffle, at five marks a ticket — one mark more than the printed price. Denny paid for them and did not notice the deception until much later. Pastora had slipped her foot out of its narrow black shabby little satin slipper, and her tiny foot ran caressingly up within his trouser leg, the little toes pressing and twiddling delicately as fingers on his calf muscles. "When — when is this party going to come off?" he inquired, trying not to squirm in mingled pleasure and embarrassment. "Oh not until just before Vigo," she told him. "But when are *we* to — to — get together?" he stuttered.

"Why, we are together now," she reminded him, disingenuously.

"Yes, I know," he said, trying to pull himself together, all his deepest suspicions rushing back upon him, "but this can't go on like this, you know perfectly well what I'm talking about . . ."

"I no understand Enlish very well," she told him, "but you mean you want sleep with me?"

Denny was delighted with this turn of the conversation. "You bet," he said, "now you're talking. I want to know when!"

"No," said Pastora seriously, "first, monee, how much monee."

"Well, how much?"

"Twennee dollars." Denny, in the act of swallowing his last mouthful of wine, now choked violently and spewed it back in the air above her head. She was liberally besprinkled, wiped her hair with her paper napkin, and said, with some dignity: "That is not nice. Now I go." Denny took her wrist as she stood up and said, desperately, "Tonight?"

"Not tonight," she said coolly disengaging herself. "Tonight, I am tired."

"Tomorrow?"

"Maybe. Let my arm go. People will think you are going to try to make love to me here on the table." She drew herself away with finality, and left him. It was all he could do to pay the bill and get out with everybody staring at him, or so he believed. He hadn't dared to look around to see.

Now he decided to tell David Scott a reconstructed story of the event. "Cost me a bottle of that lousy champagne," he admitted, rather shamefacedly, omitting to mention the cigarettes and the raffle tickets. "She doesn't drink much, but she wants only the best — I mean, she wants champagne. She's got the cutest little feet I ever saw, no bigger than a baby's and soft as a bunch of feathers. She took off her shoes and we played footie the whole time, like two school kids. But she wants more monee, as she calls it, than she's going to get, from me." And he wasn't going to cross her palm with silver until after the ball was over. He knew better than that, he hoped. A few drinks now and then and he would string her along, but that was all. No bed, no board, that was his policy.

"You sure had better get what you're going to get before you start crossing her palm with silver," said David. "She'll never put out afterward, let me tell you — I know the type."

"Well, in a way, that's fair enough," said Denny. "If I can get it before I pay her, and I'm going to, well, I won't pay her, either!" He brooded on his words a moment, surprised to find he had made this drastic decision. He'd never tried to do a girl out of her money yet. He had always simply been careful not to pay her too much. But there was something about the way this one was trying to play him for a sucker that made him want to get back at her. "Listen!" he said, with indignation as hot and real as if the cheat had already taken place, "if I give her any money before, she'll put out all right or it'll be the last white man she'll ever gyp." David said nothing, and after a moment Denny added, "Up till now I've never had anything to do with anybody but white girls."

"These girls are white," said David.

Denny was plainly baffled. "Well, I mean *white* — American girls."

David, who had spent a long hard apprenticeship learning to be a man among men in the mixed society of the Mexican mining camp, took his bottle of genuine sour mash, Old Cedar Rail, out of the Gladstone bag. "Have one?" he asked. Denny nodded and watched him pouring into the thick cabin tumblers. "Get the champagne out of your mouth," David said.

"One thing," Denny pursued his single idea in a worried tone, after a good swig of his drink, "one thing is, there's no *place* on this boat. She's got that pimp of hers in with her, and of course, I know that Amparo's pimp dodges around the ship all hours of the day and night while Hansen is in their cabin, but that kind of stuff gives me the jitters. It just wouldn't work, that's all. I see Rieber and that long-legged road-runner of his crawling around into dark places on the boat deck and anywhere else, but I don't think they really mean business. I think they just like to tickle each other. And besides, Pastora didn't say a thing practical except about money. She never did say where, or when."

"Why don't you ask her?"

"I did. She said, tomorrow, maybe. But where, that's what's on my mind."

"In the mining camp," said David, pouring another round, putting the stopper back and bracing the bottle between his feet, "up in the mountains of Mexico where I had my first job, the whorehouse, the only one, was just one big room, big as a barn, with rows of cots so close together you could barely squeeze your way in between them, and it was dark in there except for a red light in one corner. You and your girl just fumbled around among the cots until you got one that wasn't busy, just ran your hands along until you didn't feel a leg or a rump, and then you piled in . . ."

"Gosh, I'd a went limp," said Denny, appalled, sitting on the floor and taking off his shoes.

"It wasn't so bad," said David. "In fact, for what it was, it was all right." And slowly there poured through all his veins again that deep qualm of loathing and intolerable sexual fury, a poisonous mingling of sickness and deathlike pleasure: it ebbed and left him as it always had before, merely a little sick. Once in the early days with Jenny, he had confessed to her, haltingly, after their fresh gay love-making in the cool spring morning, the strange times he had lived through in that place; somehow he felt, and expected her to understand, that this aftertaste of bitter disgust had cleansed him, restored him untouched to the wholeness of his manhood. He was glad to be able to say he was sick of the thought of sex for a good while after such nights. He had felt superior to his acts and to his partners in them, and altogether redeemed and separated from their vileness by that purifying contempt.

Jenny, sitting up in bed, had leaned over and taken his face between her hands and said blithely, "Never mind, darling. That's a normal Methodist hangover. Men love to eat themselves sick and then call their upchuck by high-sounding names . . . I . . . Oh, I do hope you won't make yourself sick on me!" He had never forgiven her for that. He never would.

"Another?" he asked, pouring. Denny nodded. "Well," he said, "hot chance there is for any loose piling in bed around this tub!" He inspected his ingrowing toenail with deep alarm. "Gosh," he said, "I think this thing is infected!" He forgot everything else in his search for the iodine.

Until they came on the ship, Hans had never seen his parents dressing and undressing together. He could remember when he was very little, they would take him into bed with them in the morning and play with him. But one day, he did not know just when, his mother said to him, "No, Hans, you are a big boy now, time to stop all this babying." Until then, he had been able to open their door and come in when he pleased. Afterwards when he tried the knob now and then, the door was always locked; his father and mother came instead into his room at night to say evening prayers with him.

In their close, crowded cabin, there was nothing for it, nowhere to go. When the time came, his mother would fold a handkerchief over Hans's eyes, and say, "Now, don't take this off until I tell you! and don't peep!" But he did peep of course. To his disappointment, there was nothing much to see. He could not quite understand what all the mystery was about. With their backs turned to him and to each other, they would remove their clothes a garment at a time, slipping their night clothes on a little at the same time, so they were never really undressed at all, and he caught only an occasional glimpse of his mother's plump shoulder, or his father's lean ribs. This secrecy was all the more mysterious to him because he had many times seen more of them in broad daylight at the beach. So he was certain there was something about undressing for bed that was different from undressing at other times, and he meant to find out what it was if he could. Before Hans could quite see how it happened, they would face about fully covered again, his father in a long skinny nightshirt edged with red cotton braid, his mother in a billowing, long-sleeved white nightgown. She would say "Now!" as if it were a game, and whip the handkerchief from his eyes, and Hans would try to look sleepy.

The air of the cabin was thick, even when the porthole was open; but it was closed at night, for night air was always dangerous, but night air at sea was deadly. While his parents were undressing they loosed smells from their skins that made Hans long to beg to have the porthole opened, but he would never dare — his father's smell, bitter and sharp like the drugstore in Mexico City where his father often went with a little paper his doctor had given him; his mother's smell, sickly sweet, like the mixed-up smells of the fishstalls and the flower stands right next to each other under the hot noon sun of the Merced market. He knew which smell was which, his father's and his mother's, for he often got a whiff of them outside, in the garden in Mexico or at the table, or even on the deck of this ship. It made him sick, it made him feel sometimes that his mother and father were strangers, he was afraid of them, there was something wrong with his father's breath and his mother's armpits, and it made him wonder if there was something wrong with him. Now and then he would turn his head towards his own shoulder and breathe in, or even pull open his shirt front and take a good sniff of himself from below. He always smelt just like himself, nothing wrong at all, and he would feel easier for a while.

His mother knelt beside his bed, and Hans got up and knelt by her. The arm she put around his shoulders smelt of sweet freshly washed linen. His father knelt on the other side, and they said their prayers together in a murmuring chorus. They both hugged him and kissed him good night; and at once he felt so near to them, so full of confidence, he said, sitting up again: "Mama, today Ric and Rac told me they were going to throw me overboard, but I wasn't scared!"

His mother said sharply, "Hans, you are not supposed to talk after you have said your prayers." But his father almost leaped out of his shirt, and said, "What did you say?" and to his wife, "Didn't you hear what he said? That those terrible Spanish children threatened . . ."

"Nonsense," cried his wife, and to Hans, "What do you mean, running off to play with those children? Haven't I told you to keep away from them?"

His father said to his mother, "Well, where were you, that you lost sight of him?"

"I was at the hairdresser's, and I told him to sit still and wait for me in his deck chair. Blame me, of course — I am not to have a moment's peace for anything!"

"Look after your child, and stop tormenting your husband," shouted his father, and Hans saw they had forgotten him entirely.

"I didn't leave my chair," he said almost tearfully, "they came and stood there, and they said, 'We are going to throw you overboard. And everybody else too, and the bulldog.' That is what they said, and it is not my fault. I said 'Go away, or I'll tell my father.' And they laughed and made fun of me . . ."

"Monstrous!" said his mother, deeply shocked. "That good innocent helpless dog? Oh Hans, if you are ever so cruel as to mistreat a poor dumb animal, never let me hear of it."

"I wouldn't hurt Bébé, not for anything," said Hans, piously, having got his mother's attention again.

"I shall speak to them, or to their shameless parents if necessary," said his father. "After all, it is not exactly a joke, they have threatened to throw Hans overboard as well, remember."

"My advice is to say nothing to them, to ignore them as if they do not exist, and Hans, stay near me always and do as you are told — don't let me have to speak twice."

"Yes, little Mama," said Hans in his most submissive voice. The lights were turned out and all was quiet. Hans fell asleep after a short time of worry because his mother had not seemed to hear at all what he was trying to tell her about how very nearly he had come to being drowned off the ship while she was having her hair washed, without a thought for him.

Herr Rieber had wound himself up to a state of decision regarding Fräulein Lizzi Spöckenkieker. First, she was not a Fräulein at all, but a woman of worldly experience; and though Herr Rieber liked nothing better than a proper amount of feminine coquetry and playful resistance, still, carried beyond certain bounds, they became mockery and downright insolence which no man worthy of the name would endure from any woman, no, not if she were Helen of Troy herself! In this frame of mind he took her arm after dinner and guided her for their stroll. While listening to music, he drew her up the stairs to the boat deck, and led her, with the silent intentness of a man bent on crime, to the dark side of the ship's funnel. He gave his prey no warning, no moment in which to smack his face or flee, he seized Lizzi low around her shoulders, hoping to pin her arms to her ribs, and snatching her to him, he opened his mouth for a ravenous kiss.

It was like embracing a windmill. Lizzi uttered a curious tight squeal, and her long arms gathered him in around his heaving middle. Her thin wide mouth gaped alarmingly and her sharp teeth gleamed even in the dimness. She gave him a good push and they fell backward clutched together, her long active legs overwhelmed him, she rolled him over flat on his back and for a moment her sharp hipbones ground his belly cruelly. Herr Rieber had one flash of amazed delight at the undreamed-of warmth of her response, then in panic realized that unless he recovered himself instantly, the situation would be irremediably out of his control.

He braced himself to reverse the unnatural posture of affairs, and attempted to roll into the proper position of masculine supremacy, but Lizzi was spread upon him like a fallen tent full of poles, her teeth now set grimly in his jowl, just under his jawbone. Pain took precedence of all other sensations in Herr Rieber's being; silently with tears in his eyes he fought to free himself. Yet there was a muted exhilaration in the struggle. When, if ever, he got the upper hand of this woman he would have got, he felt, something worth having. Meanwhile she showed no signs of surrender, but gripped him with her knees as if he were an unmanageable horse, her arms folded him in almost intolerably, with long thin tough muscles like a boy's working in them.

Never before had he encountered a woman who would not let herself be overcome properly at the correct moment: her intuition should tell her when! In despair, his jaw by now benumbed, his eyes wandered as if seeking help. The half-darkness showed a white blotch which proved to be the motionless form of Bébé, who had found the Hutten cabin door ajar, and had wandered aimlessly alone until at last he stood there not three feet away from them, openly gazing.

"Lizzi, my dearest," gasped Herr Rieber, "Lizzi, the dog!"

His agonized tone brought Lizzi out of her carnivorous trance. Her teeth parted, she breathed "Where?" Herr Rieber snatched his face out of her reach. Her arms loosened and he seized her wrists, at the same time rolling over until he was at least lying beside her. At last by a series of resolute disentangling movements, for now Lizzi seemed quite inert in his hands, he brought them both to a sitting position once more.

Bébé, balanced on his bowed legs and wavering slightly with the roll of the ship, the folds of his nose twitching, regarded them with an expression of animal cunning that most embarrassingly resembled human knowledge of the seamy side of life. Plainly he could see what they were up to, their intentions were no secret from him, but because of their strange shapes, and the weird sounds they made, he was puzzled — puzzled, and somewhat repelled. Indeed he was not at all sympathetic.

"Go away, get out," commanded Herr Rieber, in as deep a growl as Bébé himself could have fetched up; but because Bébé wore a hairy hide and was on all fours he was therefore sacred, there was no question of using sterner measures. Herr Rieber was the soul of sensibility on this question: as a child, he had cried his eyes out on seeing a horse fall in the icy street, tangled in his harness, prisoner to a beer truck. He wanted to beat, to kill the cruel driver who had let him fall. No tenderness could exceed Herr Rieber's for the entire brute kingdom — indeed, he still believed hanging too good for any person who abused even the humblest member of that mystical world. When for the most unavoidable reasons of discipline he was forced to beat his own dogs, his heart almost broke, every time. He spoke now to Bébé in his most wheedling tone. "Go away, there's a good doggie," he said, looking around hopefully for something weighty to throw at him. "Good doggie!"

Lizzi began to laugh uncontrollably, her head between her hands. "Ah hahaha," she uttered in a voice thin as a twanging wire. Bébé went away then in silence, padding softly on his big feet, dismissed but not minding, full of his own business. He had ruined the occasion, though. Herr Rieber had not the heart to take up again at this perhaps more promising point with a now somewhat chastened Lizzi. He contented himself with taking her hands and saying soothingly, "No, no — there now, there!" She scrambled to her feet talking incoherently, gave Herr Rieber a weak little poke in the chest, and ran ahead of him down the steps without looking back. Herr Rieber followed but more slowly, thoughtfully fingering his jaw. He must not for a moment admit discouragement. After all, this was only another woman — there *must* be a way, and he would find it. He thought with some envy of the ancient custom of hitting them over the head as a preliminary — not enough to cause injury, of course, just a good firm tap to stun the little spirit of contradiction in them.

Earlier in that evening at dinner, Herr Professor Hutten, still lacking his proper appetite, barely refrained from pushing away his loaded plate, rising and seeking fresh air; but his wife was eating well, and though the sight was faintly repugnant to him, still that was no good reason for interrupting her. The other guests seemed as usual, the Doctor amiably silent, Herr Rieber and Fräulein Lizzi exuding their odious atmosphere of illicit intimacy, Frau Schmitt unremarkable as ever; only Frau Rittersdorf was chatting away lightly in the direction of the Captain — a frivolous woman, with what a vanity at her age! — and even if Herr Professor Hutten had no hope of hearing anything in the least edifying or enlightening, he listened in the wan hope of some distraction from his inner unease.

Frau Rittersdorf noted his attention, saw the other faces beginning to take on a listening look; without loosing her hold on the attention of Captain Thiele, she turned clever glances upon the others and raised her voice a little to include them in the circle of those who had been lately amused or annoyed or both with the antics of the zarzuela company and their *outré* notions of the etiquette of social occasions on shipboard — if such a word could be used even remotely in such a connection. There was above all that impudent creature they called Tito, who had tried to sell her some tickets of one kind or another for some sort of petty cheat they had thought up among themselves, who knew what?

"Ah yes," Lizzi broke in, "for a raffle! I bought one and got rid of them."

"You should have told me!" cried Herr Rieber. "For I bought *two* — you must give one of yours away!"

"I'll return it to them and get back my money!" whinnied Lizzi, tossing her head.

"Oh," said Frau Rittersdorf, "that should be something to see, anyone getting back a *pfennig* from those bandits, for I know they are that! No, dear Fräulein, good businesswoman, that you are, everyone knows, but you will want to be better than that!"

"But wonderful dancing partners, don't you find, Frau Rittersdorf?" asked Herr Rieber, gleefully. Lizzi slapped his hand, annoyed, because she had meant to say that herself. "Shame on you," she said, "you are not very kind. Dancing partners are sometimes scarce, one cannot always choose too delicately."

Frau Rittersdorf, shocked at this turn of talk just when she was ready to give a sparkling account of that unusual incident, cried out in a high yet ladylike soprano, "Ah, but there are effronteries so utterly unexpected one is taken off guard, one is defenseless, it is better to follow one's instinct — yes, as well as training! and to behave as if nothing out of the way were happening — how could I dream of such a thing as that?" She sat back and held her napkin to her lips, staring over it in distress at Lizzi, whose laugh was a long cascade of falling tinware.

"Ah, but that is just what ladies are supposed to dream about," called Herr Rieber in delight, leaning forward to make himself heard over Lizzi's clamor. "What is wrong with that, please tell me?"

Pig-dog, thought Frau Rittersdorf, her dismay turning in a flash to a luxury of rage, at least I am not reduced to dancing with you! She bared her teeth at him and lifted her brows and narrowed her eyes: "Are you sure you would know what *ladies* dream about, Herr Rieber?" she inquired, dangerously.

These tactics impressed Herr Rieber, who had got his face smacked more than once by easily offended ladies, and at that moment Frau Rittersdorf resembled every one of them, in tone and manner. A man couldn't be too cautious with that proper, constipated type, no matter how gamey she looked. He wilted instantly, unconditionally.

"I meant it as a pleasantry, *meine Dame,*" he said, with rueful respect.

"No doubt," said Frau Rittersdorf, turning the knife-edge of her voice in his wounded vanity. "No doubt at all."

Herr Rieber could not quite give up, but floundered and floundered. "It was a roundabout allusion to a theory of Freud's on the — ah — the meaning of dreams . . ."

"I am well acquainted with his theories," said Frau Rittersdorf icily, "and I see no connection whatever between them and our present topic!"

Herr Rieber sat back, his underlip pouched, and began loading his fork, sulkily. Frau Rittersdorf turned to the Captain with her most sparkling smile, full of confidence after her plenary chastisement of that presumptuous fellow — Freud, indeed! — and said: "We are all of us taking these Spaniards very lightly, and indeed, we may as well, seeing there is no help for it, we must endure their presence until Vigo, I believe. But tell me, how can it happen that such people are traveling first-class on a respectable German ship? One finds oneself in unheard-of situations which they invent. . . ."

The Captain did not relish hearing his ship called "respectable" in a tone implying she was barely that; he did not like hearing the quality of his passenger list criticized, though privately he respected none of them except La Condesa, and she was turning out to be a grave disappointment in a personal way. His chin jerked forward irritably, he spoke as bluntly as possible: "The Mexican government paid their fares; no doubt it was worth it to be rid of them."

"No doubt at all," agreed Frau Rittersdorf, gaily, "and what a relief it will be, to see them really going ashore at Vigo, and the rest of us going on in quiet and safety . . . for Captain, I believe those people are dangerous criminals. They are evil people, the kind who need to be controlled by the police, they are capable of anything."

Lizzi fired an instant barb out of loyalty to Herr Rieber: "Even to dancing with you?"

A small ripple of shock ran around the whole table — even Dr. Schumann seemed startled at this reckless attack. The Captain intervened instantly as was his right and duty, and dealt the deciding blow. He favored the opened-mouthed Frau Rittersdorf with a glint of steel from the corner of his eyes, and said: "Dear lady, aren't you flattering them? It requires a certain force of character to be really evil, and these seem to me rather ordinary little people of the rubbish-born class, not worth mentioning. My ship, like any other, carries all sorts. I am invested with every disciplinary power. Please, may I beg of you? allow me to be the judge of how dangerous they are."

Little Frau Schmitt could not help but observe with some mild glow of satisfied justice that it was Frau Rittersdorf's turn to flinch amazed, ready to burst into tears, blushing a clear bright becoming red from the edge of her hair to the depths of her modestly exposed front. Yet even as she observed, Frau Rittersdorf straightened up with great dignity, raised her chin, turned her head, and surveyed the other diners haughtily, then returned to her dinner and ate in a mannerly silence, the only sign of discomfiture being that her blush had vanished and left her pale as unborn veal. The silence began to weigh, even on Herr Professor Hutten, who suffered numbly at trivialities of any kind, especially rash unbalanced expression of ill-understood ideas.

He seized a text out of the floating confusion of words, "criminals — evil — capable of anything," and spoke to the Captain with that mild deference and moderation which masked his sense of utter rightness, always soothing to the Captain because he did not have to listen or pretend to reply to the Professor, who was not interested in discussion, but in speaking his own thoughts aloud in company. As a public lecturer, the Professor had long since learned that a silent audience is an attentive one.

"Whole systems of philosophy are based on the premise of the total depravity of mankind," he began, putting the tips of his fingers together before his chest, spreading and flattening them from time to time, then drawing them all together at the very points, "no need to name them, perhaps?" He glanced about him, thinking it would be quite useless. "And I must say some very superior minds have given us some very closely knit arguments in favor of this thesis. It is also undeniable that they can point, by way of powerful illustration, to aspects of mere human behavior proving that human nature is entirely and unredeemably evil. Yet, yet," he said, "in spite of cogent evidence to the contrary, or say, rather, manifestations which the unphilosophical mind (or, minds insufficiently supported by sound religious training) might be impelled to regard as evidence to the contrary, I cannot help but believe unshakably — call it *sancta simplicitas* if you must," and he tucked in his chin and huddled the tips of his fingers together in humility, "unshakably in the fundamental goodness of human nature as a principle; the God-intention, you might call it, irradiating the flesh. Men who do evil, who seem by nature inclined to evil, willfully following evil, are afflicted, abnormal — they are perverted from the Divine Plan; though it does not necessarily follow in the least that they may not be every one redeemed in God's good time. . . ."

Frau Schmitt surprised everyone by speaking up with some firmness. "Only if they repent and ask God's forgiveness," she said. "Any Catholic knows that no man may lose his soul except with his own consent —"

She quailed under Herr Professor Hutten's interruption. "That is not quite what is under consideration, dear Frau Schmitt," he said, with awful blandness. "I was about to say, if men do evil through ignorance, they must not be condemned. It is because their education has been neglected, they were not subjected to good influences in their youth, in such cases, it is often enough only to show them the good, the true, the beautiful — the *Right*, in fact, for them to embrace it eagerly."

Truth is sometimes hideous and bitter, thought Frau Schmitt, it is the truth that my husband is in his coffin in the hold, and I am a widow going home to nothing, and I have tried to be good and love God and what has it got me? For she was apt to stray off into such confusions if she was too long away from her confessor and spiritual adviser. She said nothing more, only thought sadly that she shouldn't be exposed to Lutheran doctrines. Not that they tempted her, no no — it just made her unhappy to think of so many people, really good people like the Professor, going astray like that. In spite of knowing two languages, she had never been very clear about the meanings of words. Truth was anything that had happened, and a fact was anything that existed.

"Very little in my experience," continued the Professor, now in excellent health and spirits, "has occurred to disturb my confidence, founded firmly on the tenets of my childhood faith, in the absolute benevolence of God. . . ."

That is not Lutheran, though, thought the Captain, frowning. I am just as much Lutheran as he is, and even I know better than that. For he had been hearing in spite of all he could do.

"Generally," continued the Professor, "I have found that even the most unenlightened obstinate man may be approached, persuaded, won over to right feeling and irreproachable conduct if only you first demonstrate to him your own intention of dealing honorably with him in every smallest particular. . . . As for children," he went on, his spirits rising with the pleasant thoughts flooding his brain, driving out imaginary ills, his ample face beaming with the virtues he extolled, "they respond most remarkably to the steady hand, the unwavering point of view, the firm but reasonable methods of dedicated teachers, who can nevertheless, when discipline demands it, wield the rod without mercy, for true justice is stern and must be administered sternly. We do better in the long run to leave mercy to God, who alone is powerful and wise enough to use it rightly. Yet I say still, from one day to the next, yes, even from hour to hour, moment to moment, we must lead our little charges in the hard path of virtue and learning."

Frau Hutten flattened her hands at the edge of the table on either side of her plate and twiddled her fingers ever so slightly; her husband's tricks with his hands while talking made her nervous — they always had. Everybody looked as if he were listening to a sermon — a dull one. He was boring them to death again, she could feel it like vinegar in her veins. All in one vast drowning movement she remembered those many years when she had interposed herself, literally, bodily, between her husband and the seamy, grimy, mean, sordid, tiresome side of life that he simply could not endure. All those stupid details, all those endless errands, all that long war with the trickeries and the cheats and the slacknesses of the dishonest, the unscrupulous, the lazy and insolent, the ignorant, the wayward, the greedy people of whom the entire workingclass from top to bottom seemed to consist; she had dealt with them all, with that endless parade of them through the days of her life, without once disturbing her husband or asking for his help. The superiority of his mind, the importance of his profession, required that his energies and dignity be saved for the higher things of life, and so she had saved them. No one had ever seen the professor carry even the smallest parcel in his hand — not even a book to and from the school. She carried everything, his books, paper parcels, suitcases, string bags, and even pushed a market cart before her like a baby carriage. She had done it with pride and love, for everybody who saw her knew that her husband was a distinguished professor and that she was a good devoted wife who did everything well. "The ideal German wife," she had been called by persons she had reason to trust and respect.

Yet — more had been required of her. How often there had been brought in and turned over to her for final discipline the most irreconcilable of the younger students, embittered, tenacious, rebellious beyond their years; and their strength as well, as Frau Hutten had been more than once able to prove to them.

It was her pride — and her weariness — to remember in spite of her resentment at the extra task put upon her, how, once a rebel was in her hands, how entirely she was able to convince him, sooner or later, that his punishment was to be unremitting, tireless, and daily increasing until at last — no matter when, that was his business! — he arrived at a willing, complete, even eager submission. She had never failed to subdue even the most recalcitrant spirit, and she knew well that not one of her initiates ever set eyes on her again without a shudder. Why had this sacrifice been demanded of her? She who had asked God only for children of her own to love and bring up tenderly as birds in a nest? She who would never have beaten or starved or terrorized with threats a child of her own, no more than she could have laid an unkind hand on her poor Bébé. Even as a little puppy he had taken training like an angel, needing nothing but a few simple words and tones of voice, a touch of the fingers, a morsel of biscuit, to guide him in the right direction. So would her children have been loving, intelligent, obedient children — why not? Consider her own character, and her husband's; why should not their children have been noble examples to others?

She knew that her husband was a saint, too good for this world, and she loved him for it. If these stupid people could only listen to him, they would hear something for their good. Ah well — even if through her fault some small crudity got through to him from time to time, he blamed no one, least of all herself, and never remembered anything about it. He even, and this was so sweet the tears almost came to her eyes, seemed honestly to believe they had never had a quarrel. She encouraged him in this. If he had forgotten their first five years, well and good, let him. For herself, she could never forget, for the many lessons taught her then had gone into her blood and bones, and changed her almost beyond her own recognition. By now she remembered these hard lessons dimly and without that secret fury against her bridegroom which even at its hottest she had known for what it was — treachery to her marriage vow. She knew well that upon the woman depends the whole crushing weight of responsibility for happiness in marriage. At times this had seemed to be just one more unbearable burden which fell to the lot of wives. Other moments brief and delightful, such as weddings, birthdays, anniversaries of friends, Christmas, Easter, or even simply days of bright weather, of fine health, or good news, indeed, whenever her husband's face shone with domestic content and enjoyment, she could feel her very soul growing wings. Her constancy would revive, flourish, grow strong, her faith could almost match her husband's, who was unwavering, even stern, in his doctrine of their perfect marriage. Never had he admitted a shadow or a flaw, but always spoke, and taught her to speak, of their past together and their daily life through the endless years with unfailing, lying tenderness.

Frau Hutten leaped innerly as if she had been struck by lightning. Lying? Where in God's name had her thoughts got to? She glanced about her tingling with shock, with the helpless feeling she had known too often, not only in sleep, but in all too waking moments like this, the fear that her thoughts had been exposed in their misshapen nakedness, their puerile infamy, and that public disgrace must follow — her own disgrace and her husband's with her, for how often had he not charged her to remember that any discreditable act of a wife, even the slightest indiscretion, redounded to the discredit of her husband, thereby exposed as a man unable to control his household. "You are responsible to me, my dear," he used to lecture her in those early days when she showed signs of childish rebellion against him, "unless of course in an unimaginable situation you might find yourself in direct conflict with the law itself; but I am responsible to God for you, as well as for myself, and, in many particulars, to the secular law also, founded as it is on divine decree. Ah, my dear child," he would say in those faraway times, tenderly, his voice beginning to thicken and shake, his hands to tremble, "how important it is for you to accept life as it truly is, to understand it, with my help and my love," he would say, with a rush of feeling that broke them down and carried them both away; and where did they end, always, these little scenes, these forever unfinished homilies? In bed, always in bed, melting together in long loves so delicious and shameless it felt sinful, not like marriage at all. She had never dared to confess this to her husband, who in their daylight life never mentioned their dreamlike life of the night, as if they were changed by day into different persons, or that making love was a secret they must keep even from each other. . . .

Frau Hutten began blushing all over, but not with shame, with guilt, with repentance. Oh how could she even for a breath of time have thought the word "lie"? For how well she knew — how had she forgotten? — that this anxious preservative tenderness, this resolute casting out of the flaws and sediments of human nature, this striving for perfection, was the very thing, the only thing, they had made together, it was their child, that child of perfect goodness she dreamed of? In a round soft gesture she lifted her hands, covered her face, and put them down again beside her plate.

"Have you a headache, my dear?" asked her husband, interrupting himself, for he was still talking. "Oh, no," she said, "please don't worry. I am perfectly well."

He turned again, this time to Dr. Schumann. "The problem of good and evil is by definition insoluble. Do they really exist, except as concepts in the human mind? Even if so, how and why did they originate? Philosophically this is unanswerable. I ask it merely for the sake of the argument."

"It is not for me a question of philosophy," said Dr. Schumann, "and even if it were, I am not a philosopher. I rely on the teachings of the Church and I am sorry I cannot argue the matter. I am a poor sinner," he said, good-temperedly and dryly, "who needs divine help every day. I agree with the Captain, it takes a strong character to be really evil. Most of us are too slack, halfhearted, or cowardly — luckily, I suppose. Our collusion with evil is only negative, consent by default, you might say. I suppose in our hearts our sympathies are with the criminal because he really commits the deeds we only dream of doing! Imagine if the human race were really divided into embattled angels and invading devils — no, it is bad enough as it is," he said, crossing his knife and fork, "with nine-tenths of us half asleep and refusing to be waked up." His tone had become slightly muted and apologetic, as he heard his voice drawing out and going on and on, like the Professor's. He drank the last of his wine in silence.

Frau Hutten had not listened particularly to her husband, for she knew his speeches by heart, but for years she had brooded on his theories of human nature, so far removed, so infinitely above and beyond the actual she had never dared to hint to him her conclusions on the subject, after her life's daily battle with evil incarnate in its working clothes.

She spoke aloud, astonished to hear her own voice: "I do know well there are many evil people in this world, many more evil than good ones, even the lazy good ones; evil by nature, by choice, by deepest inclination, evil all through; we encourage these monsters by being charitable to them, by making excuses for them, or just by being slack, as

Dr. Schumann says. Too indifferent to be bothered so long as they do not harm *us*. And sometimes even if they *do* harm us. They don't in the least care that we are being scrupulous to treat them fairly and honestly — no, they laugh up their sleeves at us, and call us fools, and go on cheating us even more, because they think we are too stupid to know what they are doing to us! And we do not punish them as they deserve, because we have lost our sense of justice, and we say, 'If we put a thief in jail, or a murderer to death, we are as criminal as they!' Oh what injustice to innocent people and what sentimental dishonesty and we should be ashamed of it. Or we go on blindly saying, 'If we behave well to them, they will end by behaving well to us!' That is one of the great lies of life. I have found that this makes them bolder, because they despise us instead of fearing us as they should — and it is all our own weakness, and yes, we do evil in letting them do evil without punishment. They think we are cowards and they are right. At least we are dupes and we deserve what we get from them. . . ."

She ran down slowly at this point, in despair and something like prostration, hearing herself with frightful clearness in the clammy silence. The others were thoughtfully arranging their plates and fiddling with their napkins. Dinner was over, they were ready to leave the table, and were waiting for her to finish her talk. Her husband sat like something molded in sand, his expression that of a strong innocent man gazing into a pit of cobras. After her instant glimpse of his face, she dared not look above his hands, folded across his stomach. She thought, Now, I have ruined his life; and it did not occur to her until later what she might have done to her own, which depended so entirely on her husband's well-being. She had offended not even recklessly, just thoughtlessly, so intent on giving out her own opinions she didn't care for anything else, against her husband's main conviction on which everything else in their marriage was based soundly: that a wife's first duty was to be in complete agreement with her husband at all times, no matter on what questions, from the greatest to the smallest; more especially, the faintest shade of public dissent was a most disloyal act. She need not hurry to support him positively — that would give the air of compulsion to her manner. No, hers was the amiable part of that silence which gives consent. In any case, it would never be her opinions that counted. The important thing is her unquestioning constancy to her husband, which often can be shown all the more eloquently without words.

Frau Hutten expelled an enormous charge of breath like the last exhalation of a dying person, straight up from the bottom of her very being. Resolutely then she faced her lifetime of expiation, and her soul seemed to take flight into a region beyond suffering, as if it had escaped the pains of punishment by consenting to them.

"I agree with you," said little Frau Schmitt, unexpectedly, "we must not encourage people to behave badly to us. If we let them run over us, it's our own fault. . . ."

"Oh, I didn't say that!"

"Then what *did* you say?" asked Frau Schmitt, baffled.

Herr Professor Hutten stood up at this, reaching for his wife's arm, and Frau Hutten rose, grateful for being rescued from a foolish discussion with another woman. It was an article of faith with her husband that all associations between women, even of the most casual and passing kind, were unnatural, morbid by nature, hotbeds of complicity against men, leading to divisions between husband and wife. Married women "compared notes" on their husbands' marital practices and faults, and gave bad advice to young girls. A woman's loyalty must not, cannot ever be, to her own sex, but to her men — to father, to brother, to son, finally above all and before all, to her husband. They have no understanding of true friendship in the high noble sense as it exists so naturally between men; they are incapable of it, they are born rivals and not to be trusted with each other. There is always something tainted, hysterical, in the associations of women; nor can they be admitted to the great hermetic male society, for they have no reverence for the Truth, nor for sacred rites. . . . Oh, how often Frau Hutten had listened to her husband expounding these doctrines to a mixed company in her very parlor, while she sat silent under instruction, but with an almost wordless protest — "But there are so many other things about us he doesn't seem to know! This is not all there is to this —" helplessly inarticulate and strangely — this *was* strange, she could never explain it — fearfully lonely. Still, the other women seemed to agree, or submit, and most of the men she knew talked that way, and she had read it more or less in a number of books by respected writers; her father had said it, and so did some ministers of the Gospel. In the end, she was bound to admit that this bitter judgment was just another of those great truths she was by nature unfitted to grasp.

They made their bows and escaped. "Not so fast, please," she said, on the stairs, breathing heavily and limping. Her husband slowed his step immediately. "Ah," she said gratefully, then hurried on to speak before the silence full of danger could widen between them, "my dear, why I spoke as I did, I cannot think!"

The Professor's tone was measured as his step. "Save your breath for the stairs, my dear," he said coldly. "When a wife contradicts her husband, at some length, in public and before strangers, on a subject to which he has devoted some thought, and about which she knows nothing — may I remind you that if she cannot think why she speaks, she may have done better to keep silence?"

"Oh God, oh God!" cried Frau Hutten, falling into a moral huddle before the awful traps of life, her life which was like walking in the dark with wires stretched across the path. "Oh God, I didn't mean it!"

The Herr Professor almost stopped in his tracks, then lunged forward again abruptly. "You did not mean it?" he asked in amazement. "You were then only talking frivolously? Like a woman? When you say such things, it is unpardonable not to mean them. Only a mistaken sincerity can excuse such wrongheadedness! What am I to understand then? That you merely wished for your own reasons to put your husband to shame? What disloyalty!"

"Oh God, no!"

"Disloyalty to my ideas," said her husband, resuming his reasonable tone after his brief outburst of righteous wrath, "to my whole mind, to my humble career as scholar, to the entire inner meaning of my life, which I had so foolishly confided to your hands — merely that," he assured her, with dreadful gentleness, "nothing, nothing at all!"

They were in the passageway leading to their cabin, and both of them saw at once that the door was wide open. Each felt the shock in the other's body. The Professor recovered first.

"How could you have done that?" he asked his wife, still in that reasonable voice which nearly drove her distracted when there was no reason at all in what he was saying.

"I didn't do it," she said, and the tears came up, "why must I always be blamed for everything?"

"This is not a time for self-pity," said the Professor, "you came out after me and closed the door, or so I supposed. I remember your hand on the knob."

"No, I can't bear that," she told him, tremulously, "whenever in your life did you go through a door before me? You know you hold the door for me and close it after us."

At this, the Herr Professor stood and studied his wife's face as if he had never seen her before, and was ready to dislike her on first sight.

"I do that?" he asked with sarcasm. "You are sure I have always been so courteous to you?"

"Yes," she said, "you have always been." She met his eyes with perfect obduracy. The Professor was shaken somewhat — in some devilish way she had got him in an awkward fix, because of course he did observe courtesy with her; habit had become second nature and he no longer remembered his acts; but no doubt he had held the door, and . . .

"Thieves, perhaps," he said, as they entered, and pretended to examine the lock. His wife was stooping over slightly, peering with crinkled lids in every corner.

"He is not here," she said in a small childish voice, "my dear, he's gone. . . . He has wandered out by himself because you left the door open!"

"I forbid you to say that!" he almost shouted.

". . . He is lost and looking for us. He is wondering why we deserted him. Somebody will beat him or kick him if he wanders into some place he shouldn't be. Oh, let's go back quickly and find him, oh why couldn't you think of Bébé when you left the door open? He is like a child, he wants to go everywhere with us . . . Oh how could you?"

"You are still not thinking, that is clear," said the Herr Professor, pulling himself together with a mighty shrug and a sudden upward and outward gesture of his right hand. "Come, let's look for the beast before you become entirely unhinged. Has it not occurred to you that this could be a matter of breaking and entering, theft may have been the object, where are your garnet necklace and your grandmother's diamond earrings?"

"With the purser," answered Frau Hutten, the tears running freely by now. "Please, let's go find him?"

The Professor, hand on knob, stood aside for her to pass, and drew the door closed firmly after him. "Can you not see, my dear, how securely it is closed when I close it?"

"This once," she answered implacably. Not for the first time did the Professor dwell with warm sympathy on the wisdom of the fathers about women: they were merely children of a larger growth, and needed a taste of the rod now and then to keep them in order. In gnawing silence, arm in arm, they set out again, pacing up and down the closed corridors of the lower decks, asking everybody, passengers, sailors, officers, stewards, whether any of them had seen their dog. "Surely you remember him? a white bulldog — the only dog on the ship." Several claimed to remember him, but no one had seen him that evening. They turned and climbed upward once more. Frau Hutten felt her husband's shoulder rise and his elbow thrust out giving her a slight impatient nudge in the side, as if her weight were a burden to him. She was so frightened she almost let go of his arm, and then dared not for fear he would take her sign of wounded feelings as resentment. This new fear caused her to cling tightly, knowing at this point that anything she did, or left undone, would only offend him further.

The after-dinner waltz music was thumping along vigorously on the port-side deck, a beat regular as a clock striking, mingled on the wind with the wandering current of a wilder strain from the accordions below, where the men of the steerage were dancing in circles, clapping hands, snapping fingers, clacking heels, clattering castanets and shouting "Olé!" while the women and children watched in stillness, massed in the shadows.

"Oh, Papa," said Elsa, pleadingly, "I don't want to dance . . . always those same old waltzes . . ."

Her mother said, "Now Elsa, you know that is no reason not to dance. The waltz is very pretty and becoming to a lady. What do you want, to dance that indecent jazz? What would they think of you in St. Gallen?"

"No, Mother, just a fox trot, maybe . . ."

"Well, my Elsa," said her father, "you are just being shy, so now let me tell you that when you go to a dance, you dance first with your escort. Now I am your escort, so you will dance first with me and then, who knows? You haven't danced with your papa since your last birthday dance."

"And then when you are seen dancing," said her mother, "someone else will invite you."

Elsa at her first glance round had seen her student dancing with that Spanish girl called Pastora, and her heart, which felt bruised all the time, was crushed again. She put her hand on her father's arm, dreading the coming ordeal. No matter what the music, her father danced a funny little hopping and whirling dance, swinging her out and bringing her in again on the turns, stamping his feet in pauses while she hung suspended waiting for his next move. She dared not even look around her for fear of seeing people making fun of them both. She was taller and larger than he, and he pranced like a little bantam saying loudly, "Lift your feet, Elsa, my girl, move, move, can't you hear the music?"

Elsa longed to cry out, "I am not a mealsack, I am not a broom, this is no way to dance, you are making us ridiculous, nobody but you would dance like this!" Her father's face was merry and full of love as he stamped and romped and hauled her about against her will, and she went with him, suffering numbly because a girl must obey her father.

One white-clad young officer standing near said to another who was just moving into the fray for the evening: "One of us must do something about that girl. Now which?"

The other took a small coin from his pocket, said, "Heads or tails?"

"Heads," said the other. The coin fell tails. The spinner said, "It is all yours," and picked up his coin. "Your time will come," said the other. They both laughed, and the loser moved in gently at the end of the dance and spoke to Frau Lutz with the deepest respect. "I should so enjoy dancing with your daughter," he said, bowing, "with your permission."

"You may invite her," said Frau Lutz, with the highest elegance as if she were conferring a priceless favor. Alas, Elsa was taller and larger than the dapper little officer, too, and felt it bitterly, and could not catch step with him, either. He felt moisture on the back of his neck, seized her more firmly, asserted himself, pushed her unresisting but unresponsive bulk here and there as long as the music lasted, always managing to avoid her feet and to keep almost in time with the band. At the end, he thanked her profusely and handed her back to her parents and fled. "You see?" said Frau Lutz. "One thing leads to another. We are going in to play chess, but we are not far away. Stay here and enjoy yourself. We will come for you in an hour."

Elsa looked about desperately for a place to hide, or failing that, to sit. The stewards had left several deck chairs about, and one of them was near the chair of the poor sick man, the poor sick man who believed he could cure others even though he was dying himself. She went near to him, timid and uncertain of her welcome, made tender and charitable by her own sufferings and feelings of being shut out from natural life. She was still several steps away from him when he lifted his hand eagerly and motioned towards a chair near him. "Bring it closer," he said, "and let us talk."

She drew the chair towards him, and sat so awkwardly her knees nearly touched his. She veered around and her sad gaze roamed over the dancing pairs: Jenny Brown and Herr Freytag; Mrs. Treadwell and the best-looking of the young officers, a gold-braided one, too; hers had had only silver. Herr Hansen always always with that terrible Amparo — and, hard to believe but there they were, turning and swaying with not a rift of light between them, the sulky boy Johann and that girl called Concha. Nobody for Elsa — nobody, and there would never be; she would always sit and watch her love dancing with someone else, and always someone like Pastora! Her blood surged so hard in her veins she began to ache all over with real pain. Herr Graf saw her distress and asked kindly: "How are you feeling tonight?" before she remembered to inquire about his own health. "Why are you not dancing, a fine young girl like you? You should be dancing with my wild nephew instead of that strange girl he is with . . ."

"I have a sore throat, I think," she said, not knowing very well how to lie fluently. "My mother says it is better for me to be quiet."

"Come nearer still," he said, "lean towards me, I will cure your throat. You need not be sick so long as God lends me His power to heal you." His hand was lifted ready to reach out and touch her. She leaned away instead, slow mind and honest flesh repelled by his corpse-like nearness, death itself —

"But then, first make yourself well," she said, softly but forthrightly.

" 'He saved others, let him save himself,' " Herr Graf rejoined instantly, for he had heard this speech many times before. " 'If he be Christ,' remember? He gave the power of healing to his chosen disciples and apostles, yet not one of them could save himself, either, nor can we of the holy descent, even to this day. Why should I heal myself? God does not will it, and so neither do I. Listen to me, my child — if I could heal myself I should become selfish like the others; I should go about my own pleasures and forget my duty to the suffering ones. God wills it I should stay and suffer with others in houses of pain and death. Only in my own pain am I useful to Him, He has given me His word. It is not so hard," he said in a weak whisper almost drowned by the sound of the waves, the wind blowing past her ears. She inclined deeply to him to catch the words, respectful of the holy speech, and he said, "Don't pity me. It is easy. It is my visitation of God's love."

She was silent, on the edge of tears. The music rose piercingly, the lighted deck looked so festive with its floating dancers, even those dreadful Spanish twins seemed happy for once — the stars seemed so near and the rushing wind was so sweet, so pure, so cool and clean and *good* —

"I must go now," she said, uneasily, "I wish you a very good night, Herr Graf. Thank you for offering to help me . . . but I am not really sick, not really —"

"I have taken the pains of the world, the diseases of all the diseased, upon myself," he told her, "into my own flesh, and so I will take your sore throat, too, and your unhappiness . . . but I must touch you," he said. He drew himself forward, straightening his neck a little, pointed thin beard rising from his chest. "Let me touch your throat," he said, "and say a prayer for you, and you will be truly well, body and soul." Before she dared to draw back, not wishing to be rude, he stretched out his arm and clasped her throat with his long cold bony hand, the curved fingers clung feebly for an instant and slipped away, sliding over her breasts and falling back upon his lap rug. He saw her face of horror, felt the firm flesh shudder keenly. "God forgive you, you hard-hearted girl," he said sternly. She stood up and turned away, but not before she saw the tears sliding out and down his cheeks into the scanty dirty-looking beard. In desperate haste she ran up the deck past the dancers, dodged the white bulldog Bébé, who appeared at that moment coming down the steps from the boat deck, and plunged into the lighted salon. Her father and mother were so engrossed in their chess game they barely nodded to her as she sat down near them. She was gasping a little.

"You seem out of breath, Elsa?" asked her mother. "Have you been dancing so hard as all that?" They both then favored their daughter with beaming warm intimate little family smiles of approval. "Ah, good, good," said her father, "our Elsa must not be the kind of girl who sits against the wall. Now go to bed," he instructed her, "and get your beauty sleep."

Mrs. Treadwell was dancing with her young officer, who had got in the habit of inviting her almost every evening. He had long since mentioned his name, even the name of the town where he was born; at first she had confused them, and then could not remember either of them. When not looking directly at him, she could hardly remember his face, and often did not recognize him at once when he appeared before her. Since her late entanglements with Lizzi and Freytag, she wished more than ever not to touch or be touched, neither with hands or words. Speech of their sort could be a pawing and prying not to be tolerated. She liked her young officer's style of holding her by the mere fingertips, his right hand resting — no, not resting, poised weightlessly at the most neutral spot on her entire person, that harmless area just below the right shoulder blade. Her hand in turn hovered lightly just above his bent elbow, keeping the stipulated distance between bodies which, at school dances, it had been the undivided responsibility of the girl to maintain.

"If you are uncertain whether you are at the proper distance," her dancing teacher told her earnestly, "mentally raise your right arm crooked at the elbow, straight out from your shoulder, and if it barely touches your partner's chest, rest assured you are entirely correct. If your partner seems to be encroaching, simply hold yourself away firmly but gracefully without losing step until he takes the hint. And remember this, if he is a gentleman, he *will* take the hint. If he does not, then you will not dance with him again. . . ." This voice from the pre-Flood era of her youth so delighted her, its ghostly sound drifting through endless spaces of forgetfulness, she turned upon her partner a dazed, tender smile, and came wide awake when she saw him respond with a faintly puzzled, if not quite disturbed, frown. At the same moment his hold tightened ever so slightly, and ever so gently he drew her towards him. Mrs. Treadwell mentally raised her right arm, crooked at the elbow. The young officer slacked his arm at once, and remarked thoughtfully, seeing Bébé blundering about among the dancers, "I wonder what that dog is doing out by himself?" Mrs. Treadwell couldn't imagine, and they drifted along in easy silence and harmony until the music stopped. "Thank you," he said. "Delightful," said Mrs. Treadwell smiling just over the top of his head, "good night," and she left the deck at once.

Amparo, still teaching Hansen to dance, trundled him about joylessly, her face the mere image of boredom. In spite of her efforts to direct him he managed to lunge them into the swiftly spinning Johann and Concha, who veered and flew away like birds. "Oaf," said Amparo intensely, the first word she had spoken to him that evening. "How long do you expect me to keep this up?"

Hansen, who had not spoken at all, said nothing but renewed his oppressive clutch and tramped forward as if he were following a plow, almost running them into the band. "Idiot!" she said. Hansen brooded as he stumbled onward. "I pay you, don't I?" he inquired at length, heavily. "Not for stepping on my feet, no," said Amparo. "Goat!" she said in fury, "watch your big hoofs!"

Freytag and Jenny, who took pains to assure each other that they had met on deck quite by accident, lingered wondering whether they dared to dance together again. David might decide to be awkward at any moment. Jenny had come upon Freytag standing alone, leaning slightly at the waist, one hand in pocket, watching the dancers, or pretending to, his features set in the strange frowning blind stare, the whites of his eyes sometimes showing all round the iris, that look Jenny had seen often by now, at first with perfect belief and indignant sympathy, and of late, always of two minds about it — first that his suffering was real, and second, that he was perhaps being a touch theatrical about it. Yet she could always feel again, as ever, the same light blaze of indignation against the vulgar insult offered him by the Captain. She put the blame squarely on the Captain because he was the only one who could have stopped the nonsense with a word; instead he had given it shape and direction. It was simply cowardly and low to hit someone who had no way of hitting back. Poor Herr Löwenthal was mistreated too, and Freytag never seemed to give this a thought; — that was wrong of him. She believed in hitting back, blow for blow and as many extra as you could manage to get in. — Not to resist and punish an injury, to oneself or to anyone else, was to consent to the wrong, plain moral cowardice in her view, and there was nothing she despised more. Thinking these thoughts, which grew more and more dispersed and vague as she came near Freytag, when he roused himself at sight of her and smiled as if pleased, she forgot them altogether and asked, "Wouldn't you like to dance? I'm tired of catering to David's suspicious mind!" "How flattering," he said, "of course!"

As they swayed together a measure or two then moved into step, he said, "Did I tell you how I first saw my wife? We were in a huge expensive Berlin night club, a kind of high low-life place, where anybody could go." He paused as if he had bitten off the end of that phrase. "That is, if you were dressed right and smelt of money. I was dancing with one of the girls, one of those bare-backed ladies who showed off their figures and agility by playing innocent little games such as handball among themselves between dances . . . and this beautiful little creature who came in with a small party of excessively rich-looking young men and women — I wish you could have seen her then — looks over her partner's shoulder with a face full of mischief and the boldness of a spoiled, well-protected girl and calls out to me as if answering something I had said to her before, 'Why of course you may have the next!' You can imagine that I went looking for her, and I asked her if she meant it."

Brassy little wench, thought Jenny, but it works, it works quite often.

He began again on some equally fatuous souvenir, Jenny listened with patience while he went on tormenting himself, wondering if he realized that at last he was talking about his wife in the past tense. "She was really a quite conventional girl, she didn't do that sort of thing, usually. Later, much later, when I asked her why she had done it, she said she had fallen in love with me on sight, and had made up her mind to marry me before she was near enough even to know the color of my eyes! Quite mad, wasn't it?"

"Utterly," said Jenny, "really suicidal." He seemed somewhat disturbed by this word, but decided to let it pass.

"She was so clever," he said fondly, "she'll be cleverer than her mother when she comes to that age . . . she used to tell me exactly how things would be, she couldn't be fooled, she could just take a breath of air in a place and say, 'Come along, this isn't for us!' Sometimes I didn't believe her or didn't wish to believe, I'd lose patience with her being so self-conscious about her Jewishness and I'd tell her that she was just another persecuted Jew, determined to be hated and persecuted no matter what. She would say in my very face — 'All Goyim hate the Jews and those who pretend to like us are the worst, because they are hypocrites.' And I'd tell her that this notion just made her feel important — one of the Chosen — the most unpardonably conceited and utterly beastly selfish idea that ever got into the brain of man! 'I'd think you'd all be ashamed of yourselves,' I'd say. . . . Not that we quarreled, no, not at all. But these things did come up now and again, and she'd get furious and cry out, 'The same old Goy talk . . . didn't I tell you?' and then we'd fly into each other's arms in a fright, and say, 'Let's not turn on each other!' and it would all blow over, because we were really in love."

His talk went on as if he were hypnotized by the swing of the waltz and the sound of his own voice running along under the music. Jenny wondered if he remembered other things he had said about his wife, all those words of pure admiration, the romantic tenderness, the rosy honeymoon illusions, the protective, defensive, constant praise — why not? It was all true so far as it went; but after one went so far it was always necessary to go back and touch base and start again on a new set of truths. There is a dream and it is one kind of reality; a waking up and that is another kind; or it is all the same reality under its endless aspects. Now she knew that all along he had been talking about his wife as people talk about their dead, and in this constant reminiscence of her, he was visiting her grave with flowers and reading there the inscription he had composed for her himself.

". . . and oh God," he said almost in a whisper, his mouth close to her ear as they drifted easily in a circle near the music, "I wish I could just take her, without her mother, who never lets us forget for a minute that she has lost nearly all her friends on our account, and find a country — there must be one somewhere — to live like human beings — like *other* people, and never to hear the words Jew or Gentile again."

"You might go to Africa," said Jenny, "you might look for one of those fascinating surviving tribes of cannibals and head-hunters where you would both be hated on exactly equal terms, because you're another color. And you could despise them comfortably because they stink horribly and scratch themselves all the time, and bow down to sticks and stones and wear gaudy blankets; and they love and admire themselves with the same passion that all the rest of us adore ourselves, and our color reminds them of ghosts and death and they say our smell turns their stomachs. Would you like that any better?"

Freytag drew back his face a few inches and his offended, self-pitying eyes rebuked her severely. "You are being frivolous," he said, "you are ridiculing a dreadful human tragedy." Their dancing slowed down almost to a standstill.

"I sometimes sound more frivolous than I am," she said. "It's just my unfortunate manner. It has caused nearly all my troubles . . ." Over his shoulder she saw David appear in the doorway a moment, take in the scene at a glance, and disappear without a sign of recognition. "There goes David," she said, without surprise.

"Where?" asked Freytag, turning too late for a glimpse. His face cleared and a curious thin smile tightened at the corners of his mouth. He drew Jenny closer to him with a conspiratorial quick gesture of familiarity and put his cheek against hers. "Is he still there? Is he still jealous? Ah, why didn't we give him something to be jealous about?"

"He doesn't need anything," said Jenny, brightly, repelled by his impertinence, and stiffening against his arm, "he's doing beautifully on his own, thank you."

Freytag laughed outright, and Jenny observed that it was becoming to him. He wasn't meant to be a hero of drama, much less tragedy. "Do you mean, you cruel creature, you are going to leave him shadow-boxing for all the rest of your life together? It's wicked of you not to give him just cause when he needs it so badly —"

"Oh no," said Jenny, "you're quite wrong. He doesn't want me to be unfaithful to him. He only wants to feel there is always the possibility, that I am desirable to other men, and he wants the right to accuse me of things — things that if he really believed, he wouldn't be on this ship with me now! But do you mind? Let's not talk about David. That is one of the things he hates, and I don't blame him!"

"I have talked to you about my wife," Freytag reminded her.

"In not quite this way," said Jenny, feeling she was splitting hairs. They were both of them being quite stupid and vulgar, and for her, that would not matter for one moment if only somehow somewhere on that wretched crowded ship they could find a place to spend a few nights together. She wished nothing else of him, but she wished for that with the quiet fury of high fever, and the abandonment of a dream. She wondered at him — was he so insensible he could not feel her through his pores?

"That's true," he agreed, "not at all the same, but she isn't here, and that makes all the difference. . . . What are you going to do, my dear?" he asked tenderly.

"I don't know," said Jenny, "I only know it must end."

Freytag folded her into his arms with sudden warmth and waltzed her rapidly over to the band. "Play 'Adieu, mein kleiner Garde-Offizier,' please," he called to the man drooping over the rattly little piano, who nodded, soothed at even the smallest acknowledgment that he was alive. When David paused for a second time in another doorway, farther down, he saw them doing a romping improvised dance with long, swooping, drunken steps, both laughing like maniacs. He went back to the bar.

"Oh, take care," said Freytag. "There's Bébé, what's he doing here?" and there he was indeed nearly underfoot. He dodged too, they avoided each other and he wandered on.

Ric and Rac, outside the traffic of dancers, were doing a dance of their own. Facing each other, as always teeth to teeth, their toes almost touching, they clasped hands, and leaning backwards from each other at the farthest possible stretch, they whirled round and round like planets fiercely, the tips of their shoes clattering delicately as castanets. The game was to see which one would be exhausted first, relax his hold and get a good rolling fall. Even better, one would let go of the other, at the same instant throwing himself forward, keeping balance while the other got his head bumped. In fact, however, such triumphs were largely theoretical, since they were evenly balanced in body and soul. When one loosened and hurled himself forward, the other took a firmer grasp and hurled himself forward also; the most that could happen was a head-on standing collision, with, on luckier days, maybe bloodied noses for both.

This was an indifferent day. They did not enjoy their game and they were too stubborn to stop until they succeeded in hurting each other in some way, it hardly mattered how. So they turned on their axis, shoulders far out, chins tucked in, eyes staring into eyes as balefully as two infant Gorgons intent on turning each other to stone. Neither gave way, but whirled more furiously, digging their claws in each other's wrists, stamping carefully on each other's toes, working up to that moment when by perfect unspoken consent they would break and fly apart and see which one got the fall, or the worst one.

Concha, dancing with Johann, shuddered and hid her face as they drew near his uncle's chair, and said: "Ah, God, how dead he looks — let's not go nearer. Take me away. Why is he not dead?"

Johann said bitterly, "God knows I wish he were." He laid his smooth cheek on the top of her beautiful calm-looking little head with its young sleek black bands of hair, his own hair golden and glittering even in the dull light, and Dr. Schumann, passing on his way to the steerage to attend another birth, paused to look at them with pleasure and pure generous joy in their freshness of beauty — how could such beauty come out of such dinginess and poverty as theirs? For he knew their origins, and no doubt their natures were as poor and shabby as their lives, yet there they went, as perfectly formed as champion-bred race horses, the look of longing and uncertainty in their faces as touching as the tears of a wronged child. "It *is* of the Devil," he said finally, turning on his way to help bring another lump of mortal procreation into the world, "of the Devil, that beauty, and he will desert them presently — even now he is going, what a pity!"

When Concha danced with Johann, or any man, she did not just dance close, or press herself against him, she melted softly into him from top to toe, warm, solid, yet without weight; her breath came and went lightly on his cheek with a small simmering sound; she purred warmly in the hollow of his ear, nuzzled him cheek and neck, with the tip of her tongue discreetly and invisibly she left a moist shivering-hot trail of miniature kisses under his jaw. "Stop that!" he said, clutching her desperately around the neck instead of her waist. "Do you want to drive me crazy?"

"Oh, you talk, you talk like that, but you do not really love me — you do not even really want me very badly." She leaned her head far back on his arm and looked up helplessly. "What should I do, then? You say you have no money — well, neither have I. You have your uncle to take care of you, but I have nobody but myself. I have not asked you for much, but I must have something! You are stronger than he is — why do you not just make him give you some money?"

Johann said desolately, "He is nearly dead, that is so. And he is going to leave me his money, and he tells me often it can't be long, for me to be patient. I hate him when he says that — I hate him for knowing all my bad feelings, for talking about it when he knows how miserable he is making me! But he is not dead yet, and I must wait." His voice almost broke, he closed his eyes and gripped her as if she were his one hold on life.

"Not so tight, please," said Concha, with a pretty smile of appreciation of his strength. "Well, do you love me a little, or not? Do you take me for one of those creatures who stand in doorways at night?"

"Aren't you a dancer? Can't you make a living at that?"

"Not a very good one," said Concha, coolly, "not until I am famous. Not enough. But you are shameless — do you want to be my 'manager' instead of Manolo? He beats me if I do not give him all the money. Would you?"

"If he gets all your money, what good does it do you to make it?" asked Johann, his German merchant blood warming to the financial aspects of her trade, curiosity almost overcoming his other feelings.

"He does not get it all, not by any means," said Concha. "And if he did, how are you any better than he? He wants me to sleep with men for money to give to him; you want to sleep with me for nothing — a cheat both ways! And you talk about love!"

"I never did," said Johann, furiously, "I never said that word!"

"Well," said Concha, her light contemptuous laugh stinging him to the marrow, "you are just a coward, after all — you cannot face anything, even the word love. You are just not a man yet. . . ."

"I'll show you, I'll show you," Johann raged, charging forward and pushing her back so rudely they almost lost balance.

"No," said Concha, "that is not what I mean by being a man . . . it is something much better. Yes. Let's dance away from the others and I'll tell you." She pressed the palm of her hand against his cheek and said sweetly, "Don't be angry, my love." Turning in step and rhythm with him, yet guiding him, she said warningly, "Oh, take care!" as they almost stepped on the fat white bulldog wandering aimlessly by himself through the dancers. He sniffed at them and went on indifferently. They leaned on the rail and Concha said, "I cannot think how you can put up with such miseries when none of it is necessary, not in the least. It would be so easy, and so safe, to end it — no danger at all. Look at him —"

They watched Herr Graf for a moment, far down the deck, head on chest, eyes closed — "That big ugly girl is gone," said Concha, "why, he is not really alive even now. He hardly breathes. Just a pillow, a soft one, over his face for a few minutes — *un momentito*," she said, seriously, measuring the smallest fraction of time with thumb and forefinger — "oh, it has been done often successfully. Then you would have the money he carries with him, and when you get home, you will be rich! Ah, have a little courage, my darling. No one would ever know — not even I! If he should die tonight, I shouldn't be surprised, or ask any questions — neither would anybody else. . . ."

What we all wonder about is, Why is he still alive at all? How does he keep on breathing? So you see . . . ?"

Johann, listening in horror, kept turning his head and swallowing as if he were being strangled. He who had so often wished his uncle dead was nearly stunned at the proposal that he should murder him. He could swear that thought had never entered his mind. His ears roared, he felt a great charge of electricity flash through him. He could not in that second even feel the small hand on his wrist, slipping into his sleeve up his arm.

"Do that," she said, with urgent tenderness, breathing upon his face, "do that, and you will know what it is to be a man."

"You mean tonight?" he asked, forcing his voice through his closing throat.

"Why not? Is tomorrow any better?"

"I never dreamed of it," he said with a great burst of anguish, "never, never!"

"It is time you did, then," she said, "and now, oh, how I wish we could celebrate with a bottle of champagne. We must drink champagne together, can't you buy us even one little bottle — even the German kind — this evening?"

Johann groaned in a shame so deep it seemed to poison his bones. "Wait," he stammered in the voice of one begging for mercy, "wait! I haven't a pfennig — tomorrow, I promise, I promise, I will buy you champagne!"

"Well, then, let me buy it for us tonight, and you may pay me back tomorrow. Only, you must do what I tell you, you must not be a timid child any more. Now I will give you the money —" and she reached into the bosom of her flimsy black bodice.

"No!" shouted Johann, the wind carrying his voice over the water. "You will give me nothing. What are you trying to do? Do you take me for that pimp of yours? You will see what kind of man I am . . . do you dare to say such things to me? Well, tomorrow you try saying them!"

"I dare now," she said, leaning lightly upon him and stroking his hand, "and I dare tomorrow. Don't threaten me. I am not afraid of you, how could I be? You will never harm me? I shall be so pleasant to you, you will never want to harm me! Let's not quarrel, it's so dull, let's dance. . . ."

"I don't want to dance," said Johann with honest brutality, "I'm sick of dancing. I want something more, something real, the real thing, you've fooled me long enough. The next time, there'll be something different!"

"Oh, I hope so," said Concha, "or what are we talking about? Are you going?"

"Of course," he said. "It is late and I must put my uncle to bed."

"What will you do?"

"Put him to bed, what did I say?" he asked. "What else do you think?"

"And then you put him to sleep? . . ."

He brushed her hand off his arm and gave it a good wrench as he threw it from him. "If he should die tonight you would accuse me," he said, "you would say I did it. I'll show you, he won't die tonight — you don't get me that easily!"

"Tomorrow night, maybe?" she called after him, as he took off towards his uncle's chair like a man running for his life. She stood watching him pushing the chair through the doorway, rubbing her wrist, her face entirely expressionless. Then she went in the bar, where Manolo sat before a half-emptied bottle of red wine, with two glasses. She sat across from him and their eyes met briefly; she pushed her glass towards him and he poured for her. They lit fresh cigarettes and sat smoking as if each were alone, or they were strangers.

Bébé halted for a moment, and sniffed politely at the extended hand of Herr Graf, who patted him on the head and blessed him as he went by. "We are all God's children, safe in His loving hands," he assured the dog, who wagged faintly in response to the benevolent tone, but shook his head and blew the odor of the hand out of his nostrils as he waddled around the bow and disappeared just as Herr Professor and Frau Hutten emerged from the door of the bar and began inquiring of the dancers, "Have you seen our white bulldog? Do you remember him?"

Ric and Rac, having spun slowly to a stop, bored and ready for a good fight, saw as if with one pair of eyes Bébé's dignified rear end walloping away from the sick man's chair. Without even exchanging glances, they turned and loped through the ship to the deserted lee side to head him off. They ran full tilt updeck to meet Bébé, who saw them coming and stopped uncertainly, his nose working. Ric and Rac whirled down upon him, fell upon him fore and aft, clutching him at random but with utter purpose, and carried him instantly to the rail.

Bébé was again somewhat seasick, he could not resist, but he deeply resented being hauled around in this fashion. He rolled his eyes and growled and muttered under his breath, waggling feebly. They managed to lift him, limp legs dangling, helpless soft belly heaving, up to the rail, where his hind quarters stuck for a moment, but they pushed hard, together, and over he went, with a dolorous yelp. He hit the water like a sack of sand, went down, the sea rolled over him, he came up at once, took a good breath and stayed up bravely, keeping his nose and his frantically working front paws above water.

Denny loitered about pretending to watch the dancers, though his sole constantly baffled aim was to catch a glance from Pastora. One of those Cuban students had latched on to her and they had settled down for the evening together, dance after dance. Denny was forced to admit at last that his prospects were gone, and in his disappointment even the desire for liquor had abandoned him. Getting drunk was not the answer to this one. From mere habit he stood at the bar and absorbed three or four quick ones, then carrying a double bourbon with him he took himself away, to the other side of the ship where he might brood unseen, staring into the monotonous waves streakily lighted from the portholes and decks, sulking corrosively and consoling himself by spitting through his teeth and repeating under his breath short nasty names for women — all women, the whole dirty mess of them, not just Pastora. Why pick on her out of all the millions? One as much a bitch as the other, he decided, noticing a bulky white bundle strike the water about midway of the deck — a bale of garbage from the galley he supposed — as Ric and Rac scurried past with wild eyes and open mouths, tongues strained out of the corners, crazy as ever, he observed; and almost instantly he saw another long dark bundle hit the water near the white one and there rose from the steerage a long hoarse bloodcurdling howl like a pack of coyotes. The sound rose, died down, renewed itself with shrill high women's screams running above it. Denny spilt his whiskey, dropped his glass without noticing, scurried to the rail overlooking the lower open deck and saw the shapeless dark mass huddled and heaped, leaning far out and over, working madly within itself as if the people were all entangled and could not break apart, but the anguished howl had become human and was full of tears, and Denny in his drunken fog was filled with tears too. He put his hand over his mouth and began to cry, and raced back to the side again to see, now falling in the ship's wake, a half dozen life-rings floating near a man and a white dog struggling in the sea, both swimming, the man holding the dog by the collar, a life-boat with small white figures rowing hard towards them, leaping and falling with each bound forward. He felt an abrupt halt in the ship's progress, an internal shock as if her engines had been stopped suddenly. He saw the course changing, felt the ship swinging around with a heavy churning and commotion at her prow, circling slowly around the lifeboat and the floating ring. A hard white searchlight showed the swimming man, still wearing his *boina*, reaching for the nearest ring; he missed and sank once more. The dog was seized over the side of the lifeboat, and as he came up again, the man.

Herr Baumgartner appeared, in more than usual distress, and asked Denny, "Why were those people howling?"

"Man overboard," said Denny with authority, his tears dried. Herr Baumgartner responded with gratifying intensity, grimacing so deeply his ears and scalp moved, slapping himself on the forehead, uttering a loud groan and rushing to view what was left of the spectacle. He was joined presently by Herr Freytag, and then the alarm, or diversion, became general. The dancers left the music, the members of the band put down their instruments, all flocked to the rail to watch the rescue. Officers began moving among them asking them not to crowd the side, to keep away from the boat when it came up, please to stand back, there was, they declared, nothing to see; the rescue had been effected. The passengers glanced about as if they were listening, but no one moved or answered. Frau Hutten, who had been growing more and more frantic in her search, was almost in despair. She began to be resentful of the indifference shown by everyone, nobody sympathized or wished to help her. She was by now dragging her husband along by the arm, her limp had almost disappeared. Seeing that disreputable young Denny, the nearest person to her, she forgot all reserve and rushed upon him, close to tears. "Oh Herr Denny, please — have you seen my good Bébé, my white bulldog Bébé? Oh we cannot find him anywhere!"

Denny turned his head with a leer meant to be full of ridicule, turned back to the sea pointing, and asked, "Is that him, down there?"

Frau Hutten looked down and saw the boat being drawn up with Bébé sprawled in the bottom. She gave a shriek, fell back against her husband's chest so violently he almost toppled, then fell forward as he seized her waist; he could feel by the surge of her body that if he had not been holding her, she would have gone forward full length upon her face.

The sailors lifted the long narrow body of the man over the side, limp as seaweed, his bare feet with crooked toes dangling, the shabby black wool scarf still knotted around his neck; the water streamed from his clothes as they carried him carefully back down to the steerage deck. Two sailors hoisted Bébé into Frau Hutten's opened arms. She tottered under his nerveless weight, let him down on deck, and kneeling beside him, wept aloud like a mother at the graveside of her only child.

"How really revolting," said David Scott to Wilhelm Freytag, who happened to be near. Herr Baumgartner heard and could not refrain from protest.

"But grief is grief, pain is pain, Herr Scott, no matter what the cause," he said, his mouth wan and drooping.

"Ah, the drooling German soul," said Freytag in pure disgust, moving away, remembering with an unpleasant start that this was a phrase of his wife's, and one he had always resented from her. Herr Professor Hutten, in a heavy sweat of humiliation, finally got his wife to her feet, a sailor came forward to help him carry Bébé, and the mournful little group disappeared. At this point it occurred to Herr Lutz to suggest to one of the young officers that perhaps Dr. Schumann should be sent for to attend the nearly drowned man. "They are already giving him resuscitation exercises," said the officer, as a rebuff to officiousness. But he did send for Dr. Schumann as, to be sure, he had intended to do without advice from a passenger.

Dr. Schumann walked slowly down the passage on his way to the main deck, not being able to decide by the sounds what sort of panic or emergency it was, and met La Condesa at the first turning, strolling like a ghost, in a black nightgown and a long old brocade wrap trimmed with monkey fur.

"Ah, there you are," she said in a dreamy childish voice and reached to touch his face with her fingertips as if she did not expect to find him solid flesh. "What is the strange noise? Is the ship sinking?"

"I think not," he said, "what are you doing here?"

"I am walking about, just as you are," she answered. "My stewardess ran away. Why not? The steward told her something was happening."

"Maybe you had better come with me," said Dr. Schumann, taking her arm.

"I'd like nothing better," she whispered. He saw that the drug he was giving her was beginning to lose its effect; by this hour she should have been unconscious — no shipwreck could wake her. His heart gave a perilous leap of rage when he thought of her abandoned there by that cowardly stewardess, and yes — yes, abandoned by him, who had caused her to be made helpless and then had left her to her fate. In this moment of possible danger he had not given her a thought. "God help me," he said, almost terrified at the evil he was discovering in his own nature.

"Let's walk a little faster," he told her, "the ship seems to be turning. There is surely something gone very wrong."

"How can you tell if the ship is turning?" asked La Condesa, moving he thought as if she were already under water. She leaned until her cheek touched his shoulder and spoke in a wavering chant. "Imagine, if the ship should sink, we should go down together embraced, gently, gently to the bottom of the sea, quiet dark love in the cool sleepy water. . . ."

Dr. Schumann's hair moved shudderingly upon his crown, he had a savage impulse to strike her from him, this diabolical possession, this incubus fastened upon him like a bat, this evil spirit come out of her hell to accuse him falsely, to seduce his mind, to charge him with fraudulent obligations to her, to burden his life to the end of his days, to bring him to despair.

"Hush," he said, putting into that mild word a weight of command that arrested her roving attention, and even lighted a small flicker of life in her voice: "Ah yes, I do talk too much, you always said so!"

"I never said such a thing," said Dr. Schumann, flatly.

"Oh never — not in words," she answered, lapsing once more into her half-stupor. On the stairs she roused a little and said, "Isn't that my stewardess coming back?" It was, and behind her came the steward. "You are needed below, sir," he said. "Man overboard, half drowned."

Dr. Schumann said to the stewardess, "Take this lady to her cabin and don't leave her again without an order from me." Returning to his own cabin to pick up his black case, he reflected on the expression on the face of the stewardess as she acknowledged his rebuke — an unpleasant mixture of furtive insolence and false abasement, the all too familiar look of resentful servility. He reflected uneasily that she could not be trusted, and La Condesa, who knew well how to deal with her sort, was now in no condition to control her. His agitation grew as he felt the oppression of the increasing millions of subhuman beings, the mindless grave-stuff not even fit to be good servants, yet whose mere mass and weight of negative evil threatened to rule the world. Sweat broke out on his forehead, he slipped a small white pellet under his tongue, picked up his case, and set out walking as fast as he dared, in the hope of saving a nameless, faceless fool in the steerage who had been stupid enough to fall overboard. "Jesus, Mary and Joseph!" he prayed, to chase away the stinging swarm of his thoughts, and crossed himself openly as he emerged on deck, without caring who saw. Frau Rittersdorf saw, and crossed herself responsively, saying on impulse to the Lutz family, "Ah, the dear good man, going with prayer on his errand of charity!"

"Charity?" inquired Herr Lutz, who considered that Frau Rittersdorf gave herself airs above her station in life — she was no better than he was! "Charity in what way? He is only doing a duty that he is paid for, after all!"

Frau Rittersdorf gave him a bright stare of amused curiosity as if he were a kind of strange insect, and moved away in silence.

Father Garza, surrounded by weeping women and gloomy men huddled on the floor in the stinking cabin beside the bunk where the drowned man lay, rose from his knees and turned when Dr. Schumann stood in the doorway. A weak naked light hung from the ceiling, and a single candle burned on the small collapsible table the priest had brought with him for the Viaticum ceremony. He blew out the candle and assembled the sacred objects, and shook his head.

"Too late, I'm afraid," he said, smiling rather cheerfully, "for materia medica."

"Still," said Dr. Schumann, "there is something to be done," and he advanced with his stethoscope and sat on the edge of the grimly dirty bunk where the dead man, naked to the waist, washed and purified by the salt sea, lay at perfect ease in the state and dignity of his death.

Dr. Schumann in his long experience as unwilling witness of death in nearly all its aspects had never lost his awe and tenderness for that Presence. He felt it now, again, an almost visible shade hovering over them. He knew by all the signs and all his senses that the man was dead, yet he continued for some time to listen intently through his instrument for some flutter or whisper of life in the gaunt rib cage and the sunken famished belly of the long body with its great knotted shoulder joints, the skeleton arms, and big warped hands, now curled inward like a child's. Nothing. He rose and took a last glimpse at the dark melancholy exhausted face now closed in a secretive faint smile. The women, huddled together near the dead man's feet, began praying aloud, their rosaries clicking, and one of the men came forward and crossed the limp hands on the breast, and tenderly covered him up.

"Can you imagine anything more absurd," said Father Garza to Dr. Schumann in his atrocious German as they walked back slowly and took a turn around the deck together, "than this, that a man jumps from a moving ship at night in mid-ocean and is drowned, a deed of carelessness reprehensible to the last degree, not suicide certainly, but a blamable disregard for his life, which is not his to throw away so lightly — Imagine, my dear Doctor? to save the life of a dog?"

Dr. Schumann considered his own rash act in leaping to save the ship's cat from Ric and Rac, and wondered what the priest would think of *that*. He felt he did not have to imagine anything, the man's impulse seemed almost too crudely natural. "I have seen him down there, on the deck, carving little animal figures with his pocket knife," said Dr. Schumann, after a pause. "He was a Basque," he added, as if that might explain some mystery.

"An unbalanced savagely individualist people," said Father Garza, "with their weird untraceable language and their pagan Catholicism . . . what would one expect? His name was Echegaray," he pronounced, rolling the word with sensuous pleasure.

"I must remember," said Dr. Schumann. "Thank you. Sorry, I have a call to make." He turned away, then retraced a step and asked, "Oh Father — who do you think threw that dog overboard?"

"Those devil-possessed children with the zarzuela company, of course," answered Father Garza. "Who else?"

"I wonder if anyone saw them," said Dr. Schumann, pleasantly, "or are they real devils who can take any shape, or make themselves invisible for their deeds of darkness?"

"A sound whipping and three days' penance on bread and water would drive out their devils," said Father Garza, "they are only rather dull little sinners. I do not believe in making them feel self-important by calling them devils. A series of good whippings on an empty stomach is all that is needed."

"I wish it might be so simple," said Dr. Schumann, a lively sparkle of impatience in his eyes. Seeing the priest's frowning glance ahead, and his mouth pursing bitterly to pursue the topic, Dr. Schumann said "Good night" hastily and turned aside.

He found the Huttens kneeling on the floor of their cabin, bowed like a sculptured Pietá over the prostrate form of Bébé, who now and then raised his head, retched and drooled more salt water. They raised their heads towards him with the same burdened, sorrowful air of the men and women beside the dead man, and Frau Hutten, against all her rules of domestic discretion, spoke first: "Oh Doctor, I *know* it is not right to ask you, but oh, what can we do for our Bébé? He is suffering so!"

Dr. Schumann said dryly, "I have dogs at home." He spread his hand under Bébé's head, lifted it, put it down gently and said, "Go on kneading him strongly and keep him flat on his belly. He will recover. But the man," he added, "the man who jumped overboard to save him is dead."

Frau Hutten sat back on her heels and covered her ears flatly. "Oh no no!" she cried out with a note of anger under the shock, then remembered and went back to digging her clenched fists into Bébé's lower ribs and spine, heaving him forward and back, fetching a low grunt from him and a rush of frothy water.

"Let us hear what the Herr Doctor has to tell us," said Herr Professor Hutten with the utmost formality. With some barely disguised struggle he got to his feet and faced the Doctor as man to man, leaving his wife to her humbler duties towards their wretched beast, who, the Professor could not help but see plainly, would become a more and more onerous burden as time went on.

"Do you wish me to understand, sir," he asked, "that a man leapt into the sea to save our dog?"

"I should have thought you knew this," said the Doctor, "there was a rescue with a lifeboat," he said, "with all shipboard on deck. No one told you?"

"I was occupied with my wife, who was on the verge of fainting," said Herr Professor Hutten, almost regretfully. "Yes, I was told, but I did not believe it. Who could be such a fool?"

"He could," said Dr. Schumann. "He was a Basque, his name was Echegaray. He was the man who carved those little animals from bits of wood . . ."

"Ah," said Herr Professor Hutten, "so! Yes now I recall — he was among those dangerous agitators — those whom the Captain ordered to be disarmed . . ."

"They took away his pocket knife, yes," said Dr. Schumann, sighing on a wave of weariness and hopelessness. "He was quite harmless, and entirely unfortunate —"

"Ah, of course he expected a reward!" cried Frau Hutten in a voice of revelation. "We would have been glad to pay him well! What a pity we can never shake his hand and thank him."

"At least," suggested Herr Professor Hutten, consulting gravely with the Doctor, "at least we can offer some little financial relief to his family . . ."

"He has none, or none on this ship," said the Doctor, observing the look of relief that passed like a beam of light across the Professor's face. Frau Hutten's face also lightened as by reflection. "Well, it can't be helped," she said, almost cheerfully, "it is done now, it is out of our hands."

"Yes," agreed Doctor Schumann. "So good night to you. Keep him warm," he said, bending his head towards Bébé, who was showing signs of recovery. "Give him some warm beef broth."

Frau Hutten held up her arms to her husband, who drew her deftly to her feet. She stole out after the Doctor, motioning him to stop as if she had something secret to tell him. Yet she only asked, "What was his name?" something mysterious and wondering in her half-whisper, the fat aging face suddenly childish.

"Echegaray," pronounced Dr. Schumann, carefully, "a very common family name among the Basques."

"Oh," said Frau Hutten, not attempting to repeat the name, "just to think he gave his life for our poor Bébé and we cannot even let him know we are grateful! I can't bear it," she said, her eyes filling with tears.

"The burial will take place tomorrow morning at the first Mass," said Dr. Schumann, "if you wish to attend."

Frau Hutten shuddered and shook her head. "Oh, how can I? But thank you," she said hastily, turning away biting her lips and winking her eyes.

"What did the Doctor say his name was?" asked the Professor, standing where she had left him, his attention fixed not on Bébé, but on some point beyond the cabin wall, beyond the ship, as if somewhere there were bounds, a limit, a shoreline to his perplexity.

"A strange one," she said, "almost comic, outlandish . . . Echege — Echege — "

"Echegaray," said her husband. "Ah yes. I remember several Basques of that name in Mexico City. . . . I confess, my dear, to being deeply puzzled as to the motives of the unlucky man. The hope of reward — of course, but that is almost too simple. Did he wish to attract attention to himself, to be regarded as a hero? Did he — unconsciously of course — long for death, and so took this way of committing suicide without being actually guilty of it? Did he — "

"Oh how do I know?" cried his wife, ready to seize her own hair with exasperation; but Bébé saved her from this rash gesture by starting to retch and vomit salt water again, and went on with it for some time as Frau Hutten and the Herr Professor took turns rubbing him with brandy and drying him with bath towels until the stewardess, beady-eyed and simply crackling with indignation, brought them the beef broth they demanded, a quart of it in an ample bowl. She handed it to Frau Hutten at arm's length and did not wait to witness the desecration of good broth meant for human beings — think of all the innocent starving poor in the world, the little babies — down the gullet of a worthless dog! And who in that stinking steerage was beside him when the man who saved this beast was strangling to death on sea water, what did he get but a little dry wafer from that hypocrite of a priest, and a wicked parody of God's word? The stewardess felt herself strangling too in a wild sea of salt rage; her very joints stiffened with it, she began hobbling like a cripple down the long passageway. Divine Providence sent her the chance to explode her wrath in the face of an undergrown cabin boy rushing somewhere with an armload of linen.

"One should be a dog in this filthy world! A rich man's dog drinking broth made from the bones of the poor. What is the life of a man compared to a dog's, tell me that? A rich man's dog, naturally!"

The fourteen-year-old boy, himself the pallid growth of a lifetime of underfeeding, recovered instantly from his fright when he realized her fury was not directed at himself. "A dog, Fräulein, please if I may ask?" he said with his ritual air of servility towards his betters, which included everybody on the ship, and without any hint of self-respect which they one and all would have taken for pure impudence.

"Broth for that dog!" she broke out again, almost choking. "And the man is dead! Dead to save the life of a dog!" she screamed, lashing out around her with her long flail of an arm. The boy, extremely uneasy, sidled past her and ran, his knees trembling. "I would have let them both drown and you too," said the cabin boy to himself, "you crazy old mule." He liked the feel of the words in his mouth so well he went on repeating them under his breath until his feelings of injury were soothed.

No matter what the efforts of Herr Professor and Frau Hutten, Bébé went on being violently agitated — shudder after shudder racked his awkward frame. He raised himself at last and sat stupefied and passive under their anxious hands. Frau Hutten said, "He makes me feel so guilty!" for he seemed to be asking her a terrible question, with doubt in his bleared eyes. Even his silence seemed to be accusing her of some wickedness against him.

"He is by nature silent," her husband reminded her, "this is not new."

"Oh but it is not the same!" she said, appalled.

She forgot that she had displeased her husband deeply, that she was not in his good graces. She leaned towards him confidingly as ever, head bowed and tears flowing again. She reached for his hand and he responded at once. "He trusted us," she wept, "he was part of our past, our happy past," she said, "of our life together." She sat on the side of the bed, disheveled and forlorn, and her husband moved over and sat beside her. "Mexico!" she cried out, sobbing with a depth he had never heard in her. "Mexico! Why did we leave it? What sent us on this terrible voyage? We were happy there, we were young together there . . . why have we thrown it all away?"

For the first time in years, the tears rolled unrebuked down Herr Professor Hutten's face. "Try not to grieve so, my poor child," he said. "It puts a great strain on your heart, and will seriously upset your nervous system. You are not," he reminded her, drops forming on the end of his nose, "exhibiting your usual characteristics here of late — that discretion, that foresight, that stability of temper which have been the admiration of all who know you . . ."

"Forgive my weakness, forgive me, I need your help. You are goodness itself. I am certain I left the door open, it is all my fault, you are always in the right," she implored; and though the Herr Professor drew out his handkerchief and dried his tears and mopped his brow, resolving to be firm in this crisis, and not let a flood of emotion sweep from his mind the truly important events of the day, and his just grievance against her, yet he could not control or deny some melting in his whole being. The sore spot in his mind was eased, his hurt self-esteem ceased to throb, as if some magic balsam had been poured into the open wound of his soul. Benevolence, magnanimity, Christian charity, uxorious warmth, even human tenderness itself marched in bravely to reoccupy their rightful place in his bosom, all in perfect order and called at once by their right names. The Professor had not known such luxury of feeling in years; a bliss exuded again from this indwelling potpourri of virtues which, in her simple words, his wife acknowledged and invoked once more.

He kissed her full on the mouth deeply, as if she were a bride, thrusting his tongue almost into her throat, and seized her head in the old way, pulling her hair painfully as ever in his eagerness. They began to fumble awkwardly at the more obstructive articles of each other's clothing as if they meant to tear each other apart, and slumped over in a heap grappled together like frogs. After inordinately prolonged labors, floundering, groaning, grunting and rolling in a savage wrestling match, they collapsed melted together into nerveless quivering and long moans of agonized pleasure; then lay joined for a pleasurable time in a triumphant glow of exhaustion, their marriage mended almost as good as new, their feelings fresh and purified.

"My little wife," murmured the Professor, as he had done after the long exhilarating siege of deflowering her on their wedding night. "My husband," she had replied then, with perfect propriety, and by now she spoke the word occasionally as part of a ceremony.

From his rug in the corner, in his haunted sleep, Bébé uttered a long hoarse sobbing terror-stricken howl which brought them out of their sensual inertia with a sickening shock. Frau Hutten began to weep again almost by habit. "Oh, he knows, he knows they tried to drown him," she cried accusingly, "his heart is broken."

The Professor's nervous system, somewhat mangled by his unusual exertions, now rebelled. He groaned again, this time in real anguish. "I forbid you to shed another tear about this matter," he said, resonantly, all his manly authority restored and in working order. "And what do you mean by They? Be careful of reckless speech, my dear." He gave her an affectionate little shake, and she enjoyed pretending to fear his anger, for this never failed to please him even when his anger was real and not pretended as now. It occurred to her that the only time in her life she had ever been afraid of him, just a few hours ago, when she believed she had offended him mortally, she had no power at all over him, no charm for him, no wile to play. How strange, how terrifying — it must not happen again. "Please let me go to him," she said, drying her eyes on his shirt sleeve. "I meant those indescribable children," she told him, in a carefully moderate tone. "Surely only they could do such a thing?"

"I agree," said her husband, "but still we must not say so, for we cannot prove it. And besides, it is perhaps no crime, legally, to drown a dog?"

"Ah, but they caused the death of a man!"

"In what way?" asked the Professor. "Was he forced to his rash act? Did anyone, even those children, dream of that?"

Frau Hutten said no more, but knelt slowly: her knee was paining her again: took Bébé's big sorrowful face between her hands, and said, "It was not us, not your little Vati and Mutti, remember? who did this to you. We love you," she told him earnestly, fondling his ears and chin. "He understands perfectly," she told her husband. "Go to sleep, my darling," she said, laying his head down on his rug.

"Ah, I could sleep too," said the Professor, helping her to rise. They got off the rest of their clothes and into night dress as if they were already asleep, and the movement of the ship under them, so hateful before, was like the rocking of a cradle. Half asleep, the Professor whispered, "What did the Doctor say his name was? Odd now I cannot remember."

"Oh what would be the use?" breathed Frau Hutten wearily. "Let's not try to remember."

Elsa, lying flat, arms under her head, gazed sleepily at the bright blue sky which seemed just outside the porthole. "So early?" she asked without curiosity, seeing Jenny washing and dressing in a hurry. "Oh, I couldn't, I'm too lazy."

"They are going to bury that poor drowned man this morning," said Jenny, "just think of him being left here all by himself."

"Why, he doesn't know," said Elsa, quite sensibly. "So how could he mind? My father said last night it was a very foolish thing for him to do. He said it is stupid thoughtless people like that who make all the trouble for others. He said — "

"He meant saving other stupid people's stupid dogs? Things like that?" asked Jenny in a chilling voice. Elsa sat up, her features gave a little twitch of distress. "My father did not mean that," she said anxiously. "He is a kind man by nature, he would never harm anybody. He did not mean he was not sorry for the poor man. It is something hard to explain — "

Jenny coldly finished doing her hair in silence and let Elsa struggle.

"It is just that he is too practical sometimes, like my mother, almost. He says life is for the living, that the dead need nothing, that we must not let our feelings run away with us when it doesn't do any good! And my mother says — "

Jenny melted into laughter. "Oh Elsa, won't you be glad when school lets out?"

Elsa eyed her distrustfully, as she did more and more often of late. Her cabin mate seemed like anybody else, yet — and she couldn't quite put her finger on it — there was something odd about her. "I am not in school," she said.

Jenny wrapped a dark silk scarf around her head. "Never mind," she said. "I'm going down to say good-by to him when he goes, whether he hears it or not."

The early sunlight reflected in the water danced and glittered in Father Garza's eyes as he stood at the rail on the steerage deck near his altar, but his dazzled glance upward took in the row of curiosity seekers on the deck above — vultures who smelled death and could not keep away from it. Father Garza through a long experience of his own human nature and that of others had learned to doubt the purity of gratuitous sympathy or pity in any form. He dared to venture there had not been a Christian thought among them, nor a prayer uttered. Before him, the body was ready to be sent over the side at the right moment, a long stiff narrow mummy shape wrapped in dark canvas balanced outward on the rail, held in poise by several towhaired young sailors, their rosy faces ceremonially solemn above their white cotton garments. The steerage passengers in their rags and dirt and darkness stood back respectfully, massed and humming like a swarm of bees, rosaries swinging, hands agitated in ceaseless signs of the Cross, eyes fixed, lips moving. Only the fat man, wearing a bright orange shirt, stood somewhat apart with his small party of followers, all of them set and brightly ready for trouble. Now and then the fat man would let out a loud belch, and with spread fingers would make the sign of the Cross with his thumb on the end of his nose. He was quite aware that a number of the men saying their prayers were also watching him closely with murder in their eyes, and it seemed to stimulate him to fresh feats of imaginative blasphemy.

Father Garza saw all this as he saw everything around him in spite of his absorption in the Burial Service, reading it to himself as if it were his breviary. "Come to his assistance, ye Saints of God, meet him, ye Angels of the Lord, receiving his soul, offer it in the sight of the Most High . . . Eternal rest give to him, O Lord, and let perpetual light shine upon him. Receiving his soul, offer it in the sight of the Most High . . . Be merciful, O Lord, we beseech Thee, to the soul of Thy servant Juan Maria Echegaray, for which we offer up to Thee the sacrifice of praise, humbly beseeching Thy Majesty that, by these holy peace-offerings, it may be found worthy to win everlasting rest. Through our Lord."

The rhythmic smash of the waves, the steady drone of massed voices, the nervous perpetual movements of the crowd, the obscenities of the fat man, had no effect on the silence and stillness of the disciplined group gathered around the dead. With every due prayer and ceremony, every movement of respect, with holy water, bell, book and candle, with incense and the sign of the Cross, the sealed and weighted body that had contained a human soul was released, tilted slowly downward, and as it slid forward was given a decisive thrust that sent it clear of the side, falling straight, striking the water feet first and sinking at once without haste even as the ship moved away from it. "God receive his soul," whispered Frau Schmitt, and the young Cubans, and Dr. Schumann, and Señora Ortega the Mexican diplomat's wife, all secretly uttering the same words, and even Frau Rittersdorf crossed herself; and the body was still visible to them a good depth under the water in the long slanting rays of sunlight. Even as it disappeared, the ship had moved far: before Father Garza could reach the upper deck, the dead was left behind.

Pausing only to pocket their rosaries, the devout men fell upon the blasphemous men with fury. They fell in a milling thrashing heap upon the fat man and his friends — though these did not so much matter — and before the sailors had succeeded in dragging them off, they had done a very creditable job of destruction upon the enemies of religion and decency with their bare hands. Only, one man had got hold of a small monkey wrench, where or how nobody ever found out, and he managed to put an end to the active career of the fat man, at least for the voyage, with one well-placed blow on the crown of his head, a little to the fore.

Jenny found David at once, leaning forward on his elbows, coat collar up around his ears, hands cupped over his half-closed eyes, try-ing to bring the scene below into focus. He was extremely nearsighted but could not persuade himself to wear spectacles except when work-ing alone. Yet it was an amiable conspiracy between them that his nearsightedness was becoming to him, and a special advantage. When they walked in the woods he always found the minute strange flower, or the tiny plant that turned out to be a botanical curiosity; on the beach he found shells that gave up their beauties only under the mag-nifying glass; in the Indian markets he went straight to those toys so small they could be made only by the fingers of very young children. He had just lately showed her several times, with possessive pride, his latest treasures — a pocketful of inch-long animals carved in wood he had bought from the man whose funeral was then going forward on the steerage deck. She stood silently by him until he became aware of her, and he said, "Why, Jenny angel!" but it was plain he was locked up in himself, in his own feelings, he would turn to stone if she touched him or uttered a word. She retreated at once, trying to turn her attention away from him, chilled with the familiar famished hol-low in her midriff, suffused with the kind of suffering, so blind, so senseless she despised herself for it, that he could inflict upon her at any moment by his terrible trick of not-being. In her distraction she barely avoided catching Denny's eye, who was hurrying towards them, carrying a stein of beer. Arne Hansen followed, frowning deeply without a glance for anyone; looking, Jenny thought again, as she had often thought, as a man might look if he were alone on a desert island.

Ric and Rac, more than usually savage and unkempt, climbed to the rail and straddled it as if they were riding a tree branch, leaning out perilously to get a better view of things, mouths open, eyes sharp and wild. No one paid any attention to them, not even a sailor passing by took the trouble to order them down. Each pair or individual of the watching group kept strictly apart without any acknowledgment of the others' presence, and each had found a vantage point of his own; yet all of them gazed at a certain spot, like persons being photographed together.

Jenny stood with her hands clasped breast high, and gazed too, at the ritual grouping below, observing the composition of the foreshortened figures with the long bluish shadows running sideways from them, storing it in her mind to sketch the instant she got back to pencil and paper, wondering why she had not brought them with her; and wondering too at her lack of feeling. It was quite unreal, a pantomime by dolls worked with strings, there was nothing that had ever been alive in that dark swaddle of canvas; and even as she wondered at her callousness, she felt her eyes filling with perfectly meaningless tears, tears for nothing at all, that would change nothing, that would not even ease the pain of her emptiness; and through a mist she saw the canvas leap outward and strike the water.

She was so absorbed in trying to follow its path into the depths, she almost missed the commotion of the battle, it happened so quickly and was so summarily ended. While Denny was shouting quite close beside her, "Well, I be dog! They got him! Well, I be dog!" she saw several sailors hauling the fat man into the clear, while others were industriously breaking up the formation of attackers, who fell back easily and made no further disturbance. They could see at a glance their work was done, they were quite eased and satisfied and perfectly ready for all consequences. Arne Hansen raised both fists and shook them in rage, shouting, "Cowards! Fools! Slaves! Kill your enemies, not your friends! Fools! Fools!" he went on shouting convulsively as if he could not stop, and at last the group near him began to exchange uneasy glances. Below deck, several of the attacking crowd glanced up, their faces tough as pickled walnuts, and one of them shouted back contemptuously, "Shut your big mouth, you *cabrón* of a Swede! Keep out of our business!" and all of them burst into galling jeering laughter. Hansen took off in his long lumbering stride, head between his raised shoulders.

The fat man lay sprawled on his back, bleeding sluggishly from a shocking-looking wound that glistened and gaped in the sunlight. Dr. Schumann did not wait to be called for, but appeared almost at once on the lower deck, spoke to Father Garza, who was departing with his characteristic promptness and detachment, but took time to say, "It's nothing serious, Doctor — you won't need me!" with a sardonic hoot that was nearly laughter.

David had come out of his fit of self-absorption rather abruptly, and though his face had not changed expression, his eyes had a curiously pleased, excited fire in them. "Well," he said, "they've done it! I always thought they might." "That's just what Denny said," flashed Jenny in sudden anger. He peered at her closely then and saw the tears not yet dried on her face, and he said bitterly, "My *God*, is there *nothing* you won't try to take part in? What on earth have you got to cry for now?"

"Everything," said Jenny, her voice shaking. "Everything in the whole world. That lets you in, somewhere . . ." She saw in his eyes the beginning gleam of pleasure it gave him to be able to work her up into a temper in which she would say anything and everything and have to be sorry for it afterward. And no matter how sorry she was, she knew she would never be forgiven. It would be just one more thing. Jenny peered at him in turn as if she were as nearsighted as he, and said very sharply in a quick low voice, "No, David, no you don't — not again — not this time!" Rather slowly, so he might see that she was in perfect control of herself, she started to walk away from him, then turned back and said savagely, "Don't you follow me — don't you speak to me!"

"Don't worry," said David, his whole face cold and sharpened, "I shan't."

Ric and Rac, still straddling the rail, began screaming shrilly one word over and over, waving their heads and their arms frantically towards the open sea.

"Whales, whales, whales, whales!" they screamed in pure ecstasy; and so there were indeed whales passing, as everyone present could not help but see in a reluctant glance; there was a common thought in every mind, that this was frivolous, inappropriate: and yet, after that first glance, they all stared with enjoyment: not too far away for a good view, three enormous whales, seeming to swim almost out of the water, flashing white silver in the sunlight, spouting tall white fountains, traveling with the power and drive of speedboats, going south — not one person could take his eyes from the beautiful spectacle until it was over, and their minds were cleansed of death and violence. "*Whales!*" screamed Ric and Rac, rising on their perch, losing their balance, and almost going overboard. They balanced dizzily, teetered, recovered, and dropped to the deck again, unharmed. Not a single hand had been stretched to aid them, though a dozen were near. No one moved. They all regarded the peril of Ric and Rac not precisely with indifference, something a little more positive perhaps, as if their going overboard would have been accepted with entire equanimity as some unexplained but not disastrous freak of natural law. Deeply, deeply not one of them but would have found a sympathetic agreement with all the others that overboard, the deeper the better, would have been a most suitable location for Ric and Rac. Any one of them would have been indignant if accused of lacking any of the higher and more becoming feelings for infancy; but Ric and Rac were outside the human race. They were outside undeniably, and they had known it for a good while; it was where they chose to be and they could more than hold their own. So they recovered their balance, hung on firmly and lithely as monkeys, shouted and screamed and enjoyed themselves; enjoyed their funeral of the man they had killed — the crazy old man in the wheel chair had told them so, to their delight — their fight on deck, their whales. It was a fine day. The only thing lacking was, they had not been able to ride on the whales' backs.

About halfway down the deck Jenny stopped to watch the whales, and forgot her grief. David went straight to her, and took her arm, and said, "Haven't we had enough of this? Let's go get some coffee." "Yes, let's," she said, and as they walked she began, "David darling, I remember once I was swimming far out in the Bay of Corpus Christi, on a beautiful day, and I was coming towards land again, and a whole school of porpoises came straight at me, oh they looked like mountains rising and dipping in the waves, and I thought I might die of fright; but they just divided around me and went on, sweeping out to the Gulf of Mexico. And I was suddenly very happy, and thought, 'Oh, this is the pleasantest thing that ever happened to me!'"

"And was it?" he asked, very tenderly and a little teasingly.

"Nearly," she said.

"No knives, thank God, due to the firmness and foresight of our Captain," Herr Baumgartner was heard to remark in the bar a few hours later.

"They didn't need knives," said the purser, his satisfaction with events making him recklessly indiscreet. Not that he cared what happened to Catholics, their mummery was their own business, but it was high time for somebody to stop that Bolshevik in his tracks, and if the Catholics did it, why, a worthy deed all the same. "They had something as good," he said, smiling deeply into his morning beer. "That Bolshevik — those Catholics! Let them all kill each other — a good thing!"

Father Carillo, normally a lover of peace and an uncontentious man, happy to say his daily Mass and leave the rough work to Father Garza, who enjoyed it, was sitting at a small table some distance from the bar, sherry glass in hand, but he heard the purser's few and foolish words. "He is a very ordinary type of low Spanish syndicalist," he said, "not a Bolshevik at all. That is a careless use of terms on your part," he said, mildly, "a mistake many persons make." His self-possession nearly deserted him, his face was illuminated with fury. "And if you wish others to respect your religion, whatever it may be, you will do better to speak decently of the faith of others." He rose abruptly, left his untasted sherry and walked away.

The purser, dismayed at his own breach of discipline, scrambled off his stool and stood at attention. "I beg your pardon, sir, I beg your pardon," he called after the rigid figure of the priest. "Sir, I am deeply sorry!" But the title *Father* refused to pass his Lutheran teeth, and the priest went on as if he had not heard him. The purser, still standing, turned unusually red and swollen in the face and neck and emptied his seidel down his throat as if it were into a drain.

"To hell with him," said Denny, sympathetically. The purser, who had even a lower opinion of Denny than he had of the Catholic religion, ignored him ostentatiously: it was entirely safe to be rude to *him*. One of his most important duties was, of course, to be impartially polite to passengers, one and all, no matter how disgusting any number of them might be to him personally. It was a sacrificial daily task, for in every voyage for going on thirty years he had fought and conquered the natural deepest impulses of his very being to beat the head off at least twenty persons, all passengers and nearly all of them males. His utter contempt for the female sex, mixed with a dash of wholesome fear and an entire inability to fathom its motives or cope with its vagaries, found expression in a false front of indulgent good humor which deceived or at least placated most women; they all of them only wanted to be flattered, he had found out for himself long ago, and that simplified matters immensely. Without a word but a glare of piglike malice for Denny, and without waiting to order his second beer, which he had been looking forward to pleasurably even while in the middle of the first, he heaved himself into ponderous motion, belly rolling, backsides heaving, the cushion of fat across the back of his neck quivering.

Denny gave a muffled snort. "Kraut!" he said, into his empty stein. He waved it at the barman. "Here!"

Arne Hansen was sitting three stools away, bowed over, head in hands, his beer untouched. He now turned a face of monstrous despair to Denny, and spoke in a low moist growl like a sick bear. "If I believed in a God I would curse him," he said. "I would spit in his face. I would send him to his own hell. Oh, what a foulness is religion! Those people down there in the steerage. They cringe and they bow and they give their money to priests and live like mangy dogs kicked by everybody and what do they get? A string of beads to fumble and a scrap of fish bread in their mouths! . . ." He pulled the hair on top of his head and wrung it. Denny decided this speech was meant for him and he was not only embarrassed but shocked. "Aw, take it easy," he said, for he felt dimly it was all right to curse and damn around as much as you pleased just so long as it was understood that you didn't mean it. It was all right to make jokes about religion, there's a funny side to everything, a man has got to laugh off a lot of things in this world or he'd go nuts, but still that didn't mean he didn't believe in *something*. He had been brought up scared to death of the Old Man With Long Whiskers Up Yonder, a real fire-eater who in the long run sent nearly everybody to hell. There was a heaven of course, but Denny had never heard of anybody going there, or at least not in his time, and not from his community. An older cousin of his, a big bully twice his size and age, grabbed his hand one day and held a lighted match to the palm. While Denny danced and screamed and licked the scorched place, the cousin said, "Well, I just wanted to show you what you're going to get all over, all the time, soon's you die and go to hell!" Denny had yelled back, "You're going to hell yourself!" but it hadn't done him much good. He felt like a boob when he remembered how long that hell business had worried him. He'd got over it though, good; religion was about the least of his troubles, but just the same, funny, he couldn't stand atheists. This fellow sounded like an atheist if Denny had ever heard one. He wasn't joking, either.

"Take it easy," he said, "what you got against religion — I mean, well, *religion*? I don't mean beads and fish bread and mumbo-jumbo, I mean — well, I just don't understand, that's all."

"No, you don't," groaned Hansen. "Do you know what happened this morning at the funeral of that poor man who gave his life for a worthless dog, a pampered pet of those fat middle-class people who —"

"I nearly missed it," said Denny, "I just got in for the scrimmage. Why, hell, man, I was standing right next to you!"

"I did not see you," said Hansen.

"Well, I damned near didn't make it," said Denny, having lost the thread of his argument, whatever it was. Hansen, glowering knottily into his beer, said nothing further and seemed to forget that Denny was there. Herr Löwenthal sidled over to the bar, with a face of distress, and nodded to Denny, one of the few passengers with whom he still felt on speaking terms. He grimaced and laid his flattened hand on his midriff. "It still makes me feel sick," he said. "Think of being sewed up in a sack and thrown overboard like a dog! Makes me sick . . ."

"Well, I can't think what else they could do with him," said Denny, reasonably.

"Why, they could put him in a box with ice and keep him until we got to dry land," said Löwenthal, "and bury him like a human being."

"It wouldn't be practical," said Denny. "Too expensive. And besides, that's a regular custom . . . if you die on board ship you get buried at sea, don't you?"

"I've been back and forth, back and forth, how many times already, and never till now did I see a thing like this. It looks like heathens."

"Well, yes," agreed Denny reluctantly, "those Catholics. But what do you care?"

"I don't," said Herr Löwenthal, "I should worry about what Christians do to each other — I got enough trouble without. But it made me sick."

It was Denny's turn to brood. He was in a bad position. Here was an atheist on one side, talking like a Bolshevik. And here was a Jew on the other side, criticizing Christians . . . that is, Catholics. Well, he didn't like Catholics any more than he did atheists, on the other hand he didn't like the idea of a Jew talking against Christians. Suppose he, Denny, said to Löwenthal, "I think Jews are heathens," how would he take it? He'd accuse him right away of persecuting Jews . . . Denny began to feel tired in the head. He began to look forward to the end of his stay in Germany, and to getting back to Brownsville once more, where a man knew who was who and what was what, and niggers, crazy Swedes, Jews, greasers, bone-headed micks, polacks, wops, Guineas and damn Yankees knew their place and stayed in it. That fat guy in the steerage got what was coming to him, treating a funeral like that, and he acted like an atheist too, but it stuck in Denny's craw that a bunch of those spic-Catholics had conked him. "Wops," he said loudly, to nobody, "just a lot of wops."

"Wops?" asked Herr Löwenthal, uneasily, a red spark glowing deep in his eyes. "What wops?" He did not wait for an answer, but walked away rapidly, carrying his drink. "I don't know any wops," he said over his shoulder.

"Kike," said Denny to himself, in a confidential tone, "that's all."

Freytag and Löwenthal, though they would never know it, or if they had known, would never admit it, shared a common cause for thankfulness in the diversion of the passengers' attention towards such dramatic events as the drowning and burial at sea of the reckless Basque, whose name even now no one remembered, except perhaps an equally nameless few in the steerage. Freytag's rage and resentment at the mean little scandal at the Captain's table had swept him away into postures he had not intended; had exposed him in a peculiarly false, unbecoming light, no less false because the incident was only a variation of many that had happened before, and would happen to him again and again, so long as he was married to Mary. The sinister thing about this episode was, it was the first time any unpleasant thing of this kind had happened to him when he was traveling without Mary. He had to admit that he looked forward to the few occasions that separated them for even a few days, when he enjoyed again, with a great lightness of heart, the privilege — and what a divine privilege it was, how ever had he taken it so for granted in the old days? — of being a member of the ruling class of the ruling race of the world, capable of extending his career as far in any direction as his own talents could carry him; free to rise without challenge to any level of society he chose. Oh, what had he thrown away in this insane marriage — yes, and what had he done to Mary, whose life was as threatened as his own? Suddenly without any care for appearance, for he was sitting in his deck chair, he doubled his fists over his eyes and groaned, "Mary, darling, forgive me." He heard her light pretty voice saying instantly, "Why of course I forgive you — what have you done?"

The whole thing from start to finish was his own fault; he could only accept this hard fact, writhing with wounded pride — how could he trust himself for anything if he made such a fool of himself in this matter of his whole life and Mary's? His rage rose again in its first freshness against everyone who had witnessed his humiliations, those who presumed to pity him, to make apologies — that wretched Baumgartner — and those who presumed to share his wrong — that Jenny Brown, with her sentimental habit of trying to get into everybody's skin. Really, he liked Mrs. Treadwell better, with her complete insensibility. And as for the rest of them, especially the dullards at the Captain's table, who would take pleasure in snubbing him if only they could catch his eye, he wished deeply that Mary were with him: she would have made them positively entertaining with her ruthless humor and charming utterly heartless malice. "Why, Mary!" he said to her once, shocked and admiring, "How can you be so cruel? Don't you belong to the human race?" She had paused briefly, shot him a keen sidelong glance, and said: "No, not really — I am a Jew, remember?"

Löwenthal, in spite of the unpleasant state of affairs — it was nothing new to him — was still quite willing to engage in a little conversation for sociability with almost anybody who came along, just so they kept off the subject of religion — *his* religion, for he did not admit the existence of any other; all religions except his own were simply a lot of heathens following false gods. It didn't matter what they called themselves. He had been reminded more than once by some Goy who wanted an argument that there were something like two billion human beings in the world, all presumably created by the same God, and only a matter of some twenty million Jews. So what had God in mind, showing such unjust partiality? Such nonsense never fazed Herr Löwenthal for an instant. "I got nothing to say on the subject," he would answer, "you should argue with a rabbi. I take his word he knows God's business." But the mere pronunciation of the Name, even in a heathen language, even only the Name which stood for the Name which must never be uttered, made him uneasy. He always changed the subject if he could, or walked away if he couldn't. It didn't matter to him what the Goyim thought of him, whether they liked him or not. He didn't like them, so he was a jump ahead of them from the start. He didn't want them to do him any favors — he would get what he wanted out of them by himself, and no thanks to anybody.

All he wanted in the world was the right to be himself, to go where he pleased and do what he wanted without any interference from Them — what right had They . . . ?

That no race or nation in the world, nor in all human history, had enjoyed such rights made no difference to Herr Löwenthal: he should worry about things none of his business. He simmered and seethed like lava boiling underground, turning upon itself with no way out. He distrusted all Goyim, but he distrusted most of all those who plagued him with talk about how they disapproved of all racial prejudice, how they had none themselves, and how they hated what the Captain had done, and how they had good Jewish friends, and how everybody knew that some of the most talented people in the world were Jews. And so generous — always helping somebody. Herr Löwenthal pursed up his mouth and made a spluttering sound, almost in the very face of that American shicksa who carried a drawing book everywhere, the one traveling with a man she wasn't married to, as if it mattered! Who without even saying good morning came up from the back and started walking along with him, chattering about how she thought the whole thing was a perfect disgrace, and she wanted him to know that she was shocked at it.

"At what shocked?" he asked, not looking at her, feeling his face curl up with distaste at her nearness. She kept bending her neck around trying to look him in the eye, but one quick glance was all she got from him. He couldn't stand shicksas at any distance. "What happened you got shocked?"

She didn't take the hint, but went on saying she couldn't bear for him to think that everybody had felt the same as the Captain, or Herr Rieber or — well, people like them. Nearly everybody she had talked to had hated the whole thing; but the Captain, she pointed out, was running the ship, so what could a passenger do? "I just wanted you to know," she ended, rather timidly, as if that settled something, as if he cared what she thought, as if what she said would make any difference to him. The nerve of her!

He said, "Well, what I got to do with all this? I'm not worrying, I just sit where they put me, minding my own business; maybe Herr Freytag is the one you should sympathize with. He's the one got kicked out, not me. I been out all along," he said, "I got no complaint, I'm used to being a Jew."

The shicksa stopped in her tracks and asked him in a blaze of temper: "Are you always so stupidly rude, or is this a special occasion?" Without waiting for an answer, she spun about and made off in the opposite direction. Herr Löwenthal noted that her legs were like a stork's. In a pleasant glow of satisfaction he lighted a good cigar and stretched out in his deck chair. He snapped his fingers at a passing steward. "Beer," he said, briefly but not unkindly.

One of the Spanish dancing girls stopped beside his chair, and offered two oblong bits of cardboard with printing on them. "Here are your two tickets for our fiesta," she said, her harsh voice toned down to a rough murmur. Herr Löwenthal on inspiration decided to pretend he took them for a gift. "Thanks just the same," he said in a patronizing manner, making a motion to put them in his pocket.

"Two dollars," she said, holding out her palm slightly cupped, rubbing thumb and forefinger together.

"*What?* You selling them? What for?" Herr Löwenthal was in a waggish humor.

"A fiesta."

"What kind of fiesta?"

"We dance, we sing, we eat and drink and then we have a little lottery for beautiful prizes — maybe one of your tickets win? Maybe both! Who knows?"

Herr Löwenthal's good humor lapsed. "Who knows? I know one thing, I got this kind of luck — if I had a winning number in my pocket, by the time I got to the place to claim it, the number would have changed, all by itself . . . Now don't argue," he said, thrusting the tickets back into her hand. "Take these and go away."

"Filthy pig," she said in a Romany dialect.

"Whore," he said in Yiddish.

Manolo bowed to little Señora Ortega, bent over her deck chair offering tickets and a shattering fire of explanations. The Indian nurse, sitting near holding the baby, glanced quickly at the tickets and away again, face calm, eyelids lowered. She could not read words, but she could smell a chance-game at a great distance, she knew numbers when she saw them, and bought a fraction of every lottery that came along, because she knew one more thing very well: for her kind, born on the straw mat, barefoot from dirt floor to grave, there was only one hope of fortune — to hit the lucky number, just once! Her dead mother often spoke to her anxiously in dreams: "Nicolasa, my child, listen now to me carefully — listen, do you hear me, Nicolasa? I am about to give you the winning number for the next lottery. Buy the whole ticket, look until you find the seller who has it. He is in Cinco de Mayo street. His name is . . ." and always, as she began to recite his name, the number, the serial, all, her words would run together, her face grow dim, her voice die away, and Nicolasa, waking in fright, would hear herself calling out, "Oh wait, Mother! Don't go . . . tell me, tell me!"

Señora Ortega smiled at the expression on Nicolasa's face. She knew it well, and what it meant. She bought the two tickets from Manolo and gave them without a word to the Indian girl, who would have kissed Señora Ortega's hand if she had not instantly taken it back. She then dismissed Manolo without a glance at him as if he were a stupid servant, and said to the girl, "Let me hold the baby awhile. He is so sweet this morning." Manolo was touchy and impudent: he had the money and it would take more than a Mexican halfbreed to insult him. In fact he was so elated with success where he had not expected it, he sold tickets to the Baumgartners and to the bride and groom before his spirits flagged; they didn't put up any sort of fight. He observed, however, in the two pairs of eyes, light blue and dark blue, of the American painters a glint of pure, implacable hostility which did not waver as he came nearer. He had no words to express his contempt for this colorless, sexless pair, no more juice in them than a turnip, sitting around with their drawing boards pretending to be artists. He did not pause at their chairs, just the same: he would leave them to Lola or Amparo, especially Amparo, who could tame tigers.

Jenny and David, sitting together amiably, watched Manolo prance by with an extra flip of his behind for their benefit. David said, "I liked them better before they began mingling social consciousness with their blackmail. Did you happen to see the bulletin board this morning?"

"I was so furious with that Löwenthal I couldn't see anything," said Jenny. "What are the dancers up to now?"

"I could have told you not to say anything to Löwenthal," said David. "It's none of your business, to begin with, and even if it were, he wouldn't think so — you're just another Goy, so far as he's concerned, the Enemy."

"I should think he'd be able to see when a person is really friendly to him," said Jenny, and her melancholy expression began to settle on her face.

"You mean you'd think he'd make an exception for you? He just couldn't help seeing how sincere you are? Well, Jenny angel, he might hate you worse for that very thing! Oh, can't you ever see?"

Jenny said carefully, cross-hatching a hasty sketch of Manolo's back view: "I don't think that is what I felt at all. I somehow wanted to have my part in the business straightened out. I wanted him to know . . ."

David said, "Angel, get it in your head that he doesn't want to know. He knows what he knows already."

"All right, David darling," said Jenny, "let's not run this into a quarrel. I feel lovely with you today. Please let me sit here near you and don't scold me. I'm tired of quarreling . . . only, my feelings are real, and my thoughts are part of me, I can't just throw them away; I can't go all my days *not* saying this, and *not* doing that, and *not* feeling what I do feel, anyway, no matter what I might pretend to you — just to keep the peace! Well, I'll see you dead and damned first." She kept her voice low and never stopped drawing.

David went on drawing too, without a word. His face was taking on the paleness and coldness that Jenny dreaded and was seeing more and more often. She loved David's roseate flush, a fresh masculine young tone of coloring, thin-skinned and healthily tough. If he didn't look out, all that food and alcohol would catch up on him someday, he'd wake up some morning to find that fatal ruby network on his nose and cheeks. This treacherous thought having come of itself expanded at once into action. David sat very still and intent on his work, and Jenny, stealing slant-eyed glimpses at him, began a prophetic portrait of David, say at fifty. She draped forty sagging pounds on David's familiar bony framework, added jowls, thinned his hair back level with his ears, doubled the size of his unbelievably handsome acquiline nose, extended his chin so extravagantly he began to resemble Punch, and as a last satisfying luxury of cruelty, she added a Teutonic roll of fat across the base of his skull. She was so happily absorbed and soothed in the execution of her little murder, her features assumed the sweet serenity and interior warm light that David loved to see, and saw only when he surprised her really sunk in work. Of himself, by no means could he bring that look to her face. When Jenny faced him, she was

—

always under tension, poised for the encounter, full of contradictory emotions, her eyes always seeking, wandering, gazing, flickering, dilating and wincing. She had got in the habit of expecting trouble from him, no matter what. He thought grimly, "And she won't settle for less now, won't have anything else. That's what it has come to, it is simply no good any more, no matter if we can fool ourselves into thinking so a little while every day. And what a rotten painter she is! Why can't she see it for herself and give up?" He studied her a few seconds longer. Her knees were drawn up to make a table for her drawing pad, her graceful slender ankles were crossed, and a smile curled delicately at the corners of her mouth, not ecstasy, but something tender and pleasant and happy. He could not resist breaking it up. He reached out abruptly to seize her drawing. Jenny jumped violently, snatched it out of his reach, crumpling it. He rose out of his chair and took hold of the drawing and was surprised at the ferocity of her resistance and would not give it up.

"What is this you're so pleased with?"

"No, David, let go — let go — you shan't see it —"

"Look out, Jenny — you're going to tear it!"

"I mean to." She stuffed the drawing down the front of her dress and held the sketching table over it with her crossed arms. "Do I go peeping and snatching at your papers?"

"Oh," said David, offended, and he gave way sulkily. He detested Jenny's obstinate insistence that there was any comparable connection between his ways with hers and her ways with him. She fought with him bitterly about his habit of opening her letters — he had no such right, she said. "I don't open your letters," she argued.

Certainly not — why should she? "Do you suspect me of getting love letters?" she inquired indignantly. Of course not — or rather, well, no. That was not the point. It was just that he could not admit that Jenny had any privacies he was bound to respect. At least that was her view of the matter. His own boundaries and reserves were inviolable, and Jenny was little by little finding it out; but she had not found out, nothing could teach her, what it was a man really wanted from a woman. At this point, he felt lost in a fog, as usual. A man, a woman, meant nothing to him. Jenny was the question and he could not find the answer. She had got back into her chair, knees up, ankles crossed, hugging her drawing close. She met his eye gaily and cunningly. "This is one thing you'll never see!" she assured him, and burst out laughing all over, shaking from head to foot, wriggling her bare toes in her flat thonged Mexican sandals.

He gave up his grudges and his bad temper as useless, charmed again by Jenny's laugh, always so fresh and merry; you couldn't call it a belly laugh exactly, proceeding from that flat little midriff, but it was right out of the cellar, every time. He said, "Look, tell me the joke, I'd like to laugh, too."

"No, then it wouldn't be funny," said Jenny. Still smiling in high good humor, she said gently, "David darling, if only you could know how beautiful you are to me this minute. Let's never get old and fat."

"All right, grasshopper. Not fat, anyway." They were agreed that to grow fat was the unpardonable sin against all the good in life, from ethics to morals to esthetics and back again. "Not like the Huttens."

"Not like Bébé," said Jenny. "What *was* that you said about those dancers having social consciousness?"

The Cuban students, deprived of the society of La Condesa by her jealous lover the Doctor, somewhat bored with their secret society into which no one had attempted to intrude, and their newspaper, read by no one but themselves, took to chess tournaments and pingpong. Their style however continued the same, implying that fascinating sophisticated secrets were to be read by initiates into their symbolic speech and ritual. It was coming over them gradually that really, nobody cared; they were not annoying anyone enough to make a difference. They decided to attack directly. Where the zarzuela company merely stared bitterly at their victims and uttered their jeering laughter, which never failed to raise a responsive blush of anger or shame, the students thought of a method they believed more subtle and deadly. They consulted with each other gravely, then turned to regard some chosen subject with clinical detachment, saying to each other audibly:

"A serious case?"

"No hope," the other would reply. They would shake their heads, glance piercingly again at their patient, and go on with their chess.

On deck, in passing, they exchanged critical medical views. "Chronic skeletonism," they said of Lizzi, gloating over the instant look of fright in her face. "No hope."

"Congenital albondigitis," they called loudly to each other as the Huttens approached with weighty tread, Bébé waddling laboriously on a leash. "No hope!" Professor Hutten glanced swiftly at his wife to see if she had heard. Of course she had, and her feelings were hurt again. The Professor recalled that from the beginning he had expressed his disapproval of these savage boys, and his astonishment at hearing them bandying about, in their unintelligible gabble, the noble, the revered names of Nietzsche, Schopenhauer, Kant; did his ear mislead him or had they dared also to take in vain the name of Goethe? Besides lesser yet still venerable names such as Shakespeare and Dante. Their faces even in relative repose were never serious, their voices not thoughtfully modulated. They chattered like monkeys while daring to utter the name of Nietzsche, no doubt misinterpreting and dishonoring him to their own base satisfaction. No reverence, no proper humility in the presence of greatness — these were the failings of all the non-Nordic races, Iberian, Latin, Gallic, especially; indeed, frivolity was endemic among them, a plague they had carried with them to the whole New World, truly appalling in its lack of intellectual sobriety. Professor Hutten felt he could despair once for all of the human race if there did not remain some hope of the survival of the old Germanic spirit. Rallying bravely, he tried to comfort his wife.

"Don't listen to them, my dear, they are mere ragamuffins, naturally stupid, and stupidity is always evil, it is not capable of anything else." These words dismayed him, they sounded like an echo — from where? — in his mind. Surely he did not believe that any human being, no matter how sunk in sin, was irredeemable? What had come over him? He could not imagine, but he could not deny either that this strange point of view struck him powerfully as revealed truth. There was such a thing as incurable love of evil in the human soul. The Professor tasted such bitterness in his mouth he wondered if his gall bladder had emptied itself suddenly on his tongue.

"I heard them, though," said Frau Hutten, like a grieved child. "They called us meatballs." She had not expected anything better of them; she was only tired of the unkindness of people to each other.

"In fact," said the Professor, resolutely, "they said, in their low medical student dog-Latin, that we are hopeless cases of congenital meatballitis — an inflamed state, as you know. If you must hear unpleasant things, at least hear them right. In any case, such clownishness can do us no harm."

"I think *they* are clowns," agreed Frau Hutten, gently, "yet I never ridicule them. Why should they ridicule us?"

This was a topic for the Professor to get his teeth into. He took up the whole morning walk, and the round of beer that followed, explaining to Frau Hutten the mysteriously variable distribution of common traits in human nature which created the individual being — yes, in fourfooted beasts, also, and in every living thing, insect, fish, flower, bird — even no two leaves on any tree are exactly alike! — causing all these endless and incalculable points of view and needs and desires, the limitless kinds of personal satisfactions to be fought for even to death, in many instances, ranging from the vilest forms of abuse, cruelty, crime, to the very heights of sainthood and martyrdom itself. This group of Cuban students was a lamentable example of naturally base minds incapable of the higher understanding, exposed to education above their capacities, who naturally could make no good use of it, being constrained with their monkey paws to pull every superior thing down to their own level. They were unable to endure, indeed they hated, the very thought of nobility or greatness on any plane. "They think that if they should spit on Michelangelo's *Moses* they shall have proved it to be no better than they are," he said, triumphantly. "That is their great mistake," he ended, soothingly, "and they will be given their lesson, in time."

Frau Hutten concealed her astonishment at this change in her husband's viewpoint, now so exactly agreeing with her own, and waited a respectful interval of consenting silence before going on with what was on her mind.

"They are publishing some kind of paper again," she told him. "Something for those Spanish dancers. I saw them all reading a printed sheet together and laughing."

Professor Hutten's train of thought was not interrupted. "It does not concern us, that is certain." He went on further to expand and elucidate his convictions on his subject. "Our attitude is indicated clearly, we need have no doubts. We shall ignore their existence as heretofore, do not give them the satisfaction of even the slightest response, neither in word or look. If they persist in their savagery to a point where this is no longer possible or commensurate with our own dignity, then — retaliation, swift, painful, and certain. I shall find a way to let them feel the sharpness of my rebuke. Don't be troubled, my dear. We have dealt with intransigents before."

Frau Hutten fondled Bébé's ears and smiled at her husband. "Of course," she said. She could not help thinking, looking towards the future, that her husband was already beginning to miss his classes and his lecture room. It was obvious that a whole series of new lectures was forming in his mind. She resolved to offer to take them down at his dictation, and began to speculate on the possibility that some special appointment might be found for him in a small educational institution of some kind in the Black Forest, or perhaps even publication in a journal or philosophic magazine. Or maybe when he got back to a desk with his papers and books around him, and she would be so busy with housework, he would be glad to write his lectures for himself and give her a moment's peace. Frau Hutten admitted finally to herself that she was tired to death of Ideas. If she never heard another she would be perfectly happy. She went on petting Bébé and smiling at her husband.

"It is not a fracture," said Dr. Schumann to Captain Thiele, choosing his words for a layman's ears, "but a long and deep head wound, to the skull, with some concussion. He has not regained consciousness."

The Captain stirred his coffee once, took a gulp, and said measuredly, "It will be all for the better if he never does."

Dr. Schumann stirred his coffee but did not drink. "It could be fatal, but not necessarily. He has an enviable heart — like an ox, I should say."

"Such swine always have," said the Captain, falling in easily with the barnyard images appropriate to the subject. "What interests me," he said irritably, "is this. Where did the weapon — "

"The monkey wrench," said Dr. Schumann, helpfully.

"The monkey wrench," said Captain Thiele, accepting the correction with dignity, "where did it come from? Who struck the blow? That is the man we must find."

"The monkey wrench was found lying near the scene of the struggle," said Dr. Schumann. "No one seems to know anything at all about it."

"As if it were of the slightest importance," said the Captain. "Let them decimate each other if they like, but not on my ship. I am astonished that Father Garza, who was so near, did not notice and identify the criminal."

Dr. Schumann smiled and drank his coffee. "Father Garza does not know one face from another," he said. "He sees only souls."

After a moment's consideration, the Captain decided it would not be unbecoming for him to share this pleasantry, since it seemed to contain a slight belittlement of the priestly office.

"He will want sharp eyes to see a soul in that rubbish heap," he said almost cheerfully. He leaned towards the Doctor and remarked as if making some generous concession not required by the rules: "I admit that with the crowded condition of this ship, and the peculiarly hostile elements fermenting in the steerage, with the possibilities of a breakout of the lowest forms of violence and disorder, I am not readily able to proceed with such disciplinary measures as might be most effective."

He thought this speech over for a while and added: "After all, the first-class passengers have rights that must be considered." He considered them with an expression of bitter distaste fleetingly, and went on, "Frankly, I get no help from the priests. My officers have of course done admirably in every way, but they cannot be everywhere at once! The habit of the shiplines overloading their second-class passenger ships in cases like this —"

He stopped, amazed at the word "second-class" hanging in the air before him, at his indiscreet reference to the landlubberly characters who ran the shipping business and had no decent respect for ships or ships' officers — such crosses were his own and none of Dr. Schumann's business. He closed his lips and frowned deeply.

"It is reprehensible in every way," said Dr. Schumann, too readily perhaps.

The Captain shook off the subject. "What shall I do with this scum until I can empty it out into the ports of Spain?" he asked frankly. "My dear Doctor, what do you advise?"

Dr. Schumann said, "I should want a little time, dear Captain, to consider that question fully, but my first thought is to say, Do nothing at all. The worst of this is most certainly over, the one real trouble-maker is disposed of for the voyage. I have no doubt he is a professional agitator of some underdog political movement, the disturbances always occurred where he was. Yet generally, I believe those are good harmless people — nothing at all wrong with them except they are born unfortunate . . ."

"For them to have been born at all is everybody's misfortune," said the Captain. "There is nothing left for us but to conceal them as well as we can and keep their plague from spreading."

The Doctor maintained that silence which the Captain regarded as a dubious way of avoiding honest controversy: at times it had the look of tacit consent to those evils the Captain was so quick to observe and so keen to suppress. In any question of mere discipline, the Captain had long since discovered the Doctor was not a man to be depended upon, and his indifference to graver problems began to impress the Captain as a dangerous moral inertia. Yet he was of the good old Junker class; his instincts, training, natural point of view must surely support the great old society in which both of them were born to take their rightful places, perform their destined duties, reap their timely reward — rigorous, unflinching, Junker to the last.

"When we weaken in our exercise of authority, slacken in our moral fiber, we betray our class and our country," he said, severely.

Dr. Schumann rose. "Quite, quite," he said amiably. "Our responsibilities are endless." Bidding the Captain good night, he absented himself from the scene and the argument — not for the first time, either, the Captain thought, sourly. He remembered too late that he had neglected to inquire about the health of La Condesa, who did not seem to be thriving under the Doctor's care.

The bulletin board was the object of uneasy curiosity. It had bloomed out in a number of boldly printed notices, each printed separately and posted flat with thumbtacks.

Sorebelly cannot afford to buy a ticket to the Captain's party because he is already afraid he cannot pay his bar bill, yet he sits drinking brandy after brandy. Long life to his ulcers!

"What indecency!" exclaimed Frau Baumgartner, warmly taking her husband's arm. "Don't pay any attention, my dear!" for she was touched at the grief in his face. He smiled bravely at her, blowing his nose and wiping his eyes as they walked on, Frau Baumgartner silently and deeply wishing the cruel words were not true. "They have said worse about others," she reminded her husband, who tried to appear consoled.

Herr Löwenthal read: *If a Jew is invited into the society of human beings he would do better to take advantage of his opportunity. It may not happen twice.* He wrote carefully on the margin with a thick pencil: *What human beings?* and strolled on looking very pleased with himself.

"This is what I mean," David said to Jenny, glancing over the morning display of insults. "Look! *The American artists so-called are afraid if they take their noses out of their sketchbooks, someone will discover that they draw caricatures for each other because they can't read."*

"Somehow that doesn't get to me as much as they hoped," said David. "My feelings are not really hurt."

"Mine aren't hurt, either," said Jenny. "Let's make a few caricatures of them and post them here."

"Why?" asked David. "It would just be a nasty row. What's the point?"

"It's just the kind of row I'd like to make," said Jenny.

"Well, leave me out of it," said David. "It's not worth it."

Jenny's temper began rising in her like a newly lighted bonfire. "Passive resistance," she said, contemptuously. "Superior silence. Toploftical reserve. Stiff upper lip. Turn the other cheek but with dignity, mind you. Don't let them ever dream we are too yellow-livered to answer back. Just don't look now and they'll get tired of spitting in our eye. Never let it be said —"

David turned on his heel as squarely as a soldier on parade drill, and walked away from her. Jenny clenched her eyes tight, drummed both feet on deck, and screamed after him: "Coward, coward, coward, you always were — coward, coward!"

She then opened her eyes and there was Wilhelm Freytag standing not ten feet away, watching her with a real sparkle of interest. Jenny tried to change her scream into a peal of merry laughter, but Freytag was not deceived. He came straight to her and looked very closely into her eyes, smiling handsomely.

"But you are wonderful," he said, "I never imagined you had so much fire in you. I thought you were a self-possessed, cold sort of girl. Tell me, what does a man have to do to get you into this state?"

Jenny said, "You'll not believe me, but David does *nothing*; nothing, he won't talk, he won't stay to listen, he won't answer, he won't give in, ever, he won't believe anything I say, he won't —"

"If he won't, he won't, Jenny," said Freytag, very gently reasonable. "Didn't your mother tell you that?"

"Nobody told me anything that was of the least use," said Jenny, all at once feeling quite restored and good-humored. "And I wouldn't have listened if they had."

"Will you listen to me?" asked Freytag. "Would you like some coffee?"

"Not particularly," said Jenny, "I'd like some company."

"Anybody special?" he asked, full of self-confidence. She walked along beside him without answering, and he saw by the guarded look on her face what she thought of that gambit. This made it easy for him to decide again that she was not an attractive girl, or at least not to him, and apparently, not to her young man, either. A girl in her situation hadn't got any business being so stiff-necked and hard to handle.

Herr Rieber and Lizzi stopped to laugh again at the funny things those Spaniards had posted against other people, and saw this: *If the pink pig would stop guzzling beer and ogling the peahen, he might be a brighter social asset on this voyage.* Scribbled next to this in red crayon were the words *¡Arriba España! ¡Arriba la Cucaracha! ¡Mueran a las Indiferentistas — !*

"But what has that to do with us?" asked Lizzi, trembling with anger. "What do we care for their savage politics?"

Dr. Schumann entered the bar for his eleven-o'clock glass of dark beer. One of the Cuban students was fastening a new notice to the board, with little Concha standing by watching. The Doctor paused, put on his spectacles and read: *The fake Condesa with her glass jewelry and bead pearls loves to dance, but does not like to pay the piper — a typical anarchist attitude. Perhaps her devoted doctor should change her prescription from drugs to a ticket for the Captain's party.*

Dr. Schumann blinked, his face contracted as if dust had blown in his eyes. He pinched the slip of paper off the board and carried it between thumb and forefinger to the corner table where the dancers were seated at coffee. "I suggest," he said with the careful firmness he would use with a patient who might be a homicidal maniac, "that this is carrying your stupid comedy a little beyond bounds. I advise you to change your methods, and your manners, if possible, at least for the rest of the voyage." As he tore the notice into strips and placed them on the table, he looked into the half-circle of staring, hard faces with an impression that he was gazing into eyes that had got misplaced: they belonged to some species of fierce beast peering out of a cave or ready to leap in a jungle, prowling and sniffing for blood; the same expression, only older, more intensely aware and ready, that had dismayed him in the eyes of Ric and Rac. Not one of them spoke, and moveless as lurking wildcats, they did succeed in staring Dr.

Schumann down. Involuntarily his glance flickered aside. He spoke sternly: "Be good enough to drop this nonsense."

A chilling burst of laughter followed him down the deck. Dr. Schumann, not intimidated but repelled and indignant at the immunity of such insolence, reflected on the so-called lighter side of life, the merrier arts and their practitioners; cabarets and beer halls where one went in relative innocence for a pleasant evening of listening to popular music, watching the pretty young dancers, drinking a little wine or beer, clinking the glass with one's wife across the table — how had it happened that this side of life was almost entirely the work of such creatures as these, a criminal league organized and managed by the lowest of the criminal world? Yes, even the outdoor, health-giving sports? They were all run by the same people who dealt in drugs and packaged sex and murder and every possible sort of monstrous cheat and forgery. The gauzy glittering surface of gaiety lay lightly over the foulest pools of evil. Yet how dull life would be without the dancing and the music and the drink and the lovemaking and all that ecstatic confusion! God bless the comedians, just the same — are we not all sinners?

He knew well that the next time that gang of hoodlums chose to put on their dancing dress and bring out their instruments to sing and dance and clatter and strum in their enchanting way, he would be there; he would not be able to resist, he would drift into their rhythms without a thought or care for what they were in truth, for in truth what were they? He would take for truth only what they appeared to be at that moment, when they had no more humanity than a flock of bright-plumaged birds, just a pretty sight provided for his enjoyment. Dr. Schumann had always loved the circus, the music hall, the cabaret, or any little half-lighted cellar full of queer goings-on. As he grew older his sense of professional gravity, of obligation, had restrained him. Often his wife, who seemed a more severe character than she was in fact, would persuade him in his moments of fatigue: "Come along, my dear, let's go to see the vaudeville. We need a change!" And she was always right. Dr. Schumann admitted, but only to himself that if hyenas were beautiful and could sing and dance, he would forgive them for being hyenas. But would they ever forgive him for being human? And then, who was he to presume to offer forgiveness even to the least of God's creatures? And what indeed *was* he? He loved La

Condesa because she was perverted, strayed, a taker of drugs, a woman who lived outside religion, outside law, outside morality, who was beautiful, willful, and he had no doubt, a born liar. In what way had he tried to help her? He had subdued her, caged her, shut her off from those ambiguous students — even at moments half believing the scandals about them that seeped like filth under the surface of the ship's talk; not by any medical means or by human sympathy, but by abuse of his power, and by using against her the vice that harmed her most — drugs.

Dr. Schumann faced an aspect of his character he had not suspected until that hour. He had lived on flattering terms with the delusive wickedness of his own nature; comfortable in the doctrine that no man may be damned except with his own consent, and that man's desire for redemption is deathless as his own soul; and when he does evil he knows what he is doing. How could he have wronged that unhappy creature so, when he had believed he meant only to help and comfort her? He was so horrified his words of denial took shape, sound, he could hear himself speaking within his skull. "No," he was saying, "I did not harm her, I did what I could in an emergency. Father Garza assured me that what I have done was not wrong. That I must treat her severely as a responsible doctor towards an incorrigible patient . . . 'Otherwise in one way and a dangerous way you are yielding to her seductions,' Father Garza said. . . ."

He was not consoled or reassured, and knew that he could never be by any means he was able to imagine now. She was a burden on his conscience he was condemned to carry to his death. He gave a great deep-drawn sigh, but not of resignation, and said most cheerfully, "*Grüss Gott*" to that poor wretch Herr Glocken, who was strolling along by himself as usual, with a face more desolate than ever. "How are you this morning?" Dr. Schumann asked, rashly.

Herr Glocken brightened at this combination of human kindness and no doubt professional medical interest. "I am not feeling very well," he said, eagerly. "I have a kind of strangling feeling in my chest, all the time."

"What are you doing for it?"

"Well, nothing much," said Herr Glocken. "It just came on lately."

"Maybe you'd better come down to my office and let me look at you," said Dr. Schumann, his mind clearing a little at the prospect of serious work. Herr Glocken looked amazed and pitiably hopeful. "Now?" he said, unbelievingly.

"Now," said Dr. Schumann.

Herr Glocken needed not only materia medica, his soul was shattered. Lola had come towards him, swinging her skirts, her left hand spread on her hip. She looked down smiling, holding out her right palm to him like a gypsy fortuneteller. "Cross my palm with silver, little man," she said, "and I promise you a ticket with a lucky number, that will win you a beautiful lace fan to take home to your pretty German sweetheart!"

Her Glocken shuddered and could not control the convulsion of pain and horror in his face. He turned his head away and closed his eyes. She bent over him intently and struck at his hump cruelly with her sharp fingers. "For luck, that's the only thing you're good for!" she said, then whirled on her heel to join the others, waiting nearby. They closed about her silently and drifted along together, lighting cigarettes.

The next morning, there was another bit of paper tacked on the wallboard in the bar: *If you are a hunchback, symbol of every kind of degeneration, you may be excused from behaving like a normal human being.*

Herr Glocken, who had been seen to smile with deep satisfaction over some of the other bulletins aimed at other victims, stood motionless reading the dreadful words over and over; then, after a quick glance around him, he snatched the shabby little scrap and crumpled it in his pocket, then walked on, face raised, hands clasped and dangling below his knees in the back, his thin legs carrying him safely out on deck, where no one had witnessed his humiliation. The passengers, whoever they were, had always each one taken pains to treat him well, to greet him and give him the time of day. They now greeted him again kindly, smiling over their morning cups of broth, noting in a brief incurious glance his face passing their line of vision stiffened in its look of perpetual grief and pain. They observed him without thinking of him, the moment he had passed they forgot him with the easy indifference of those who view a misfortune from which they feel themselves in no danger. They need never hate or fear him, his disease was not contagious, his bad luck was strictly his own; "But how terrible," said little Frau Schmitt to Frau Rittersdorf, "how fortunate I feel when I see him!"

Frau Rittersdorf responded with the look described by many of her former suitors as "cryptic," lifted one corner of her mouth, wrinkled her nose a trifle, and wrote rapidly in her red leather book: "Query, whether it would not be a benefit to the human race if there were a well-enforced law providing that all defective children should be given the blessings of euthanasia at birth or as soon afterwards as it might become evident that they are unfit? Let me think seriously about this, and read all the arguments in favor of it. I have never heard one against it that seemed to me at all valid." She closed the book, which now had very few remaining blank pages.

Amparo, seeing Jenny enter one of the small writing rooms alone, bore down upon her under full power, stepped before her without hesitation and spoke abruptly as one who had no time to waste: "You have not yet bought a ticket for the raffle — why not?" Her voice and manner were so righteously censorious Jenny was almost thrown off guard. Amparo stood solidly fixed, waiting, right hand extended holding a bit of cardboard, head up, left hand flattened on hip, toes turned out as if she were about to begin a dance. Jenny's refusal to admit the existence of the woman now turned to a deep resentment that somehow she must be dealt with and disposed of, unpleasantly — a nonexistence not to be ignored. She said, with a good sharp voice and a stare she hoped was as steely as the other's: "I shall not buy a ticket and I do not wish to be annoyed about it." She stepped in turn around Amparo, whose gaze held and followed her own. A thug's eye if ever I saw one, Jenny decided, and wondered what character her own expression might suggest to an observer uninstructed in the meaning of the situation. "Let me alone," she said furiously.

Amparo slapped her inner thigh and whirled about. "No money, no man, and nothing *here*," she said, slapping herself again, "*Jesús!*" and went her way superbly.

Jenny, who felt she had escaped from a real hold-up, pistol and all, had no vanities that Amparo could have recognized. After her first brief anger, she went looking for David to tell her little story, and rounding the bow from port to lee, she saw David, back to the sea, elbows on the rail, seeming to lean away from Lola, bending towards him, her face almost touching his. David did not seem unhappy, he was looking Lola straight in the eye and smiling, a watchful little smile, but pleased, too — Jenny, whose first impulse was to interfere, or, as she said, "rush to the rescue," had leaped forward one step, then slowed down at once and strolled past, pretending not to see the absurd tableau at the rail. She saw that David was not saying much, but he was keeping his hands out of his pocket, too; yet she did not quite trust him, and resolved clearly that if he should buy one of those ridiculous pieces of pasteboard, she would lay hands on it, tear it into bits and cast it into the sea. She passed by resolutely not giving the pair a glance. But soon David was beside her, and said, "I think we're through with that question. It's all settled that I am a man with no mother, no entrails, no human feelings; in Lola's country they keep creatures like me in cages —"

Jenny laughed and David joined in. "Oh that isn't so bad! Amparo told me I had no money, no man, and nothing here," and unselfconsciously as a cat washing itself, Jenny slapped herself high up on the inner thigh. David turned instantly so bright a scarlet his eyeballs flushed too, and he said quite desperately, "Jenny *angel*," with such violence the words sounded like a curse, "do you ever think how you *look?*"

She studied his face silently, in a smiling sort of detached wonder — "I never saw you actually bare your teeth, before," she said. "We used to have a horse that was always trying to bite people, and you looked just like him there for a second — I could hardly believe my eyes —"

"I can hardly believe mine, some of the things you do," said David, getting hold of his temper heroically. When Jenny began ridiculing him she was out of control and reckless.

"I think it is a wonderful gesture," said Jenny. "You used to think it fun when two Indian women started a fight over a man, trailing their skirts and stomping nearer and nearer each other, all slit-eyed and showing their teeth, slapping themselves there, right in the middle, each one bragging about what she's got that the other hasn't —"

"Yes," said David, in spite of himself, "and the man they're fighting over just stands there looking like a fool —"

"Why, David! I always thought he looked proud and fatuously pleased and full of curiosity as to which one would get him — how would you feel if I got into a catfight with, let's say, Mrs. Treadwell over you?"

David broke down and laughed nearly aloud over this notion. "Like a fool, of course," he said.

"I can't see why," said Jenny. "Those women are proving to the world he really is a man worth having, they don't tear each other's hair and eyes out and skin each others noses for a dildo. And the other men all stand back respectfully pretending they're not there, but they don't miss a lick. And the women all huddle together staring, their mouths moistened, and they give each other warning hard looks as if to say, 'Look out, take care!' and the whole air around is so thick with sex you can lean against it — you see, David?" cried Jenny as if she had explained everything to him and proved something on her side. "You should have seen that Amparo. She was wonderful. I had to see if I could do it too!"

David said clearly and flatly, "You don't have to prove anything to me, Jenny angel." He took her arm and they moved to the rail, and their blood surged up so hotly between them, they leaned together there speechless and breathless, feeling as if their flesh melted and fused where they touched each other.

Denny went by at speed as if he were really on his way somewhere, flung up his arm at David and Jenny, calling out excitedly, "Landfall, landfall, this evening, the purser told me!"

The news had got about, though it was not unexpected. Mrs. Treadwell and the Baumgartners and the Lutzes came on deck with their fieldglasses, and other passengers began borrowing them for long staring at sea and sky. The Cuban students hung cameras around their necks, made a procession blowing tin bugles, shouted *"Arriba España — Mueran los Anti-Cucacheros!"* ("Up Spain — Death to the Anti-Cockroach Party"), then quite suddenly settled down to chess in a corner of the barroom. The bulletin boards were swept clean of landlubbers' irrelevant doings, and curt, sparsely scattered notices informed the passers-by that land had been sighted — the *Vera* was approaching Santa Cruz de Tenerife, the first island of the Canaries for eastbound ships. Other scraps were forthcoming in rather a grudging tone in language suitable to those persons ignorant of their whereabouts and the seagoing tongue. They expected to dock early in the morning, all ashore for the day who wished to go, the ship would sail again at half-past four. It was Wednesday the ninth of September, two days before the full moon. Frau Schmitt remarked this on a calendar in one of the writing rooms, and said thoughtlessly to Mrs. Treadwell: "The first quarter was on Wednesday the second. That was the night Echegaray was drowned."

Mrs. Treadwell, standing at a table turning over the pages of a fashion magazine, said absently without raising her eyes: "How long ago that seems."

Ric and Rac, on their routine patrol of the ship, found themselves at the end of a long corridor, empty except for that crazy woman with the necklace Lola and Amparo were always talking about. She was all in flimsy white and her feet were bare. She came along slowly, with her eyes half closed, and Ric said, pretending terror, "It's a ghost!" Their eyes met once, they seized each other's hand and dug their nails in, waiting to see what would come up, what they might do. As La Condesa approached with a slow, weaving step, they both saw in the same glimpse that her pearl necklace had loosened itself, had slid down her front and caught in a pleated fold of her sash, where it hung at full length, gently swaying outward and falling back with her step. She was quite near before she noticed them, and waved them out of her path with an absent-minded circling of her hand outward. Instead of turning back, or falling to one side, they rushed past her jostling her rudely, and Ric being nearest snatched the necklace as he went, stuffing it down his collar as they careened for the deck. La Condesa, at the sharp jolt of their passing, put her hand to her throat and knew at once they had taken her pearls. She spun round and ran after them until the ship's rocking brought her to her knees; and there she sat back on her heels, holding her throat with both hands until the stewardess found her. While putting her back in bed, the stewardess said, in the hard voice of one who has gathered desperate courage: "*Meine Dame*, I will not serve you any longer if I can help it. You are going to do yourself harm and I shall be blamed."

La Condesa said: "Do what you like. But meantime, send for the purser. Those children have snatched my pearls."

The stewardess said, "Where? When?"

"In the corridor where I was walking, just now."

"I hope *meine Dame* will pardon me, but I must tell you, you were not wearing your pearls today, not since early morning. I noticed this and thought it strange when I asked to be absent for a few minutes. You were not wearing your pearls, *meine Dame*. They are in this room and will be found."

La Condesa said, "The curse of my whole life has been that I must always deal with fools. Go and bring the purser. And wait until I ask you for your opinion."

Elsa, walking with her father and mother, almost collided with Ric and Rac, who seemed to be more in flight, or pursuit as it might be, than usual. They dodged the Lutzes, but not quite enough; Ric jogged Mrs. Lutz's left elbow and hit that mysterious nerve that makes one shudder all over. Mrs. Lutz seized him instantly by the arm, all her maternal instincts for discipline of the young aroused. "Someone must teach you a little decent behavior," she told him in her German-Mexican Spanish. "I will begin." She slapped him soundly, and he scuffled so energetically the necklace dropped out of his shirt. Rac sprang to retrieve it, brought it up dangling in her hands. Herr Lutz then tried to seize her, but she escaped and ran to the rail, climbed up and dropped the pearls into the sea. Mrs. Lutz released Ric, who joined Rac at the rail.

Little Frau Schmitt, wandering about rather aimlessly, worrying about her husband, or rather, about his body and how it was faring in his coffin in the hold, noticed the rather agitated scene a little farther down the deck, but when she saw the twins, she asked herself no questions. Trouble went where they were, confusion and ill doings. Possibly it had something dimly to do with the will of God, His great mysterious plans. But what were they throwing overboard now? She greeted the Lutzes pleasantly as she passed, noticing they looked somewhat flushed and disheveled, but, as Frau Schmitt was learning on this ship the great lesson life had been preparing for her all this time — and to think she had never once suspected what it would be! — she must be quiet, keep to herself, express no opinions, bear no witness, carry no tales, make no confidences, nobody cared, nobody cared, there was nobody — this was the unbelievable thing!

All her resolves about standing up to Frau Rittersdorf had come to nothing. Frau Rittersdorf pushed her toilet things to one side and said, "Please keep your things out of my way!" and she, Frau Schmitt, had tucked them into one small space on the dressing table. She said once, trying to sound firm, decisive, "I do not like the porthole open at night." "Well, I *do*," said Frau Rittersdorf, and the porthole stayed open. Frau Schmitt took a long breath, and wondered what those children had thrown overboard, though it was none of her affair.

The stewardess asked the purser to go to La Condesa. He went and listened to her story, noted her drugged speech and manner, decided the whole thing was a dream, and sent for the Doctor. Dr. Schumann believed what she told him, and explained to the purser that he understood her temperament and that her fantasies did not take such forms. He advised the purser to report the theft to the Captain, who would no doubt order a search and investigation. The purser took the liberty of informing the Captain, who was much put about with this latest piece of awkwardness on his ship, that though Dr. Schumann took the lady's word for it, he, the purser, did not. The Captain at once ordered a search, a good thorough one, the criminal might have accomplices in the steerage, and meantime he would be pleased to ask Dr. Schumann a few questions.

Dr. Schumann asked La Condesa: "Are you sure? It *was* the children — ?"

She took his hand between hers and held it loosely, stroking the fingers, and said, "You are no better than the purser! What a question."

"Do you always get up and wander about by yourself this way?"

"Whenever the stewardess goes, yes."

"Tell me," he said, anxiously, "if your pearls are not found, what will you do?"

"I still have the emerald," she said, "and a few other little things." She touched her forehead to his for a moment, then drew back smiling. "What can it matter now? What I love about this is, you are thinking about me — you are troubled, you would help me if you could! But you can't," she told him, in triumph. "Nobody can."

A cabin boy brought him a message from the Captain. Dr. Schumann rose and kissed her hand. "Where are you going?" she cried in distress. "Don't leave me!"

"I am going to help the Captain look for your necklace," he said, "and I could wish you might stay here quietly and I could know you were safe. Please can you not do this?"

"For you," she said, "for you, and for nobody else."

"There goes La Condesa's doctor," said Herr Lutz. "Let us ask him if she has missed her pearls."

Frau Lutz said, "You will only go making trouble for yourself, only you can be so indiscreet! How do we know they were pearls? They could have been beads, for all we know."

Herr Lutz said, "There was a diamond clasp on them. And hidden in his blouse?"

"How do you know they were diamonds? Where could he put things except in his blouse?"

Herr Lutz drew a deep breath and expelled it in a sigh of monstrous despair. "Look, my poor wife, stay where you are while I speak to the Doctor." Going straight towards Dr. Schumann, and cutting across his path, he brought him to a pause, and spoke only a few words. Dr. Schumann nodded very gravely, and went on.

The search for the lost pearls turned out to be a rather cut-and-dried affair: the four staterooms of the zarzuela company were turned out rather thoroughly, a few suspicious characters in the steerage, known to be antireligious, were harried about enough to make them sullen and insolent, even the fat man was hauled up to sit in his bunk while three sailors searched the mattress and inside the pillow cases. He snarled bitterly, "What are you looking for?" One of the sailors said, "You'll know if we find it" and left him dangling so, cursing luxuriously.

The purser sent for Lola and Tito, but as all the dancers had been turned out of their cabins by the sailors making the search, they went in a body to the purser's door, where all but Tito, Lola, Ric and Rac were turned away and asked to wait outside.

The purser asked without ceremony, "Are these your children?" glancing from Lola to Tito to the twins, who stood back huddled together shoulder to shoulder facing out like wild cattle in danger. His look was a mixture of repulsion and incredulity — surely these creatures could not really exist. But yes, there they stood, their snake eyes glittering. He turned back to the parents.

"Of course they are ours," said Lola. "Whose do you think they are?"

"You might be glad if they were somebody else's before this is over," said the purser. He bawled suddenly at Ric and Rac: "Did you steal the lady's necklace?"

"No," they said in one voice, instantly.

"What did you do with it?" asked the purser, keeping his voice harsh and loud. "Answer me!"

They stared at him in silence. Lola took Ric by the nape of the neck and shook him. "Answer!" she said, fiercely. The purser noticed that her face had gone a strange yellow, her lips were pale, she looked ready to faint. In truth, Lola had not known why the sailors were searching the ship. The zarzuela company had planned to rob La Condesa, but not until the last moment, perhaps as she left the ship or just afterward; and here these unspeakable brats had ruined everything. The purser might have doubts, he might just be trying the old game of scaring somebody into confession by surprising and bullying them, but she, Lola, knew already that the worst was true — Ric and Rac had done it, no matter what it was, and they had almost caused her to show fright before that fat pig of a purser. "*Jesús!*" she said devoutly under her breath. "You wait!"

Ric said very clearly and deliberately, "I don't know what you are talking about," and Rac nodded her head at him, not at the others.

The purser said to Tito and Lola, "Let them alone until later. If you do not know, really do not," he said, insinuatingly, "I will tell you," and he did tell them the fragments that had been assembled about the incident — what the Doctor had heard from La Condesa, what Herr Lutz had told him first, and later, unwillingly, Frau Lutz and even Elsa — yes, it was a necklace in Rac's hand and she had thrown it overboard. Lola and Tito had no trouble expressing horror and dismay, as well as their belief that it could all be a mistake, and a hope that their accusers could be proved in the wrong; and a severe promise to question the children further in private and to find out the truth. The purser did not for a moment believe anything but that they were doing a fair job of acting, but not good enough to fool him.

"Do what you please," he said, dismissing them coldly. "We will go on with our investigation."

The sailors were gone from the cabin when Tito and Lola returned, having put back everything in decent order; but they found waiting there, crowded together in silence, Amparo and Pepe, Manolo and Concha, Pancho and Pastora; they rose in silence and converged upon the pair, who were each holding a twin by the arm, high up near the shoulder. Their breaths were hot in each other's faces. "What is it?" whispered Amparo. "Is it about us? Those students say so, but nobody will tell us anything."

"Get out of my way," said Lola, "let me alone." She elbowed her way into the cabin and sat down on the end of the divan with Ric held firmly between her knees. Tito stood by holding Rac.

Lola said, "Now tell me," and wrapping her legs around him, she took both of his hands and began pressing the finger nails down bitterly, one at a time, steadily and coldly, until he was writhing and howling, but she only said, "Tell me, or I'll turn them backward, I'll stick pins under them! I'll pull your teeth out!"

Rac began to struggle in Tito's hands and scream incoherently, but she did not confess. Lola began turning Ric's eyelids back with thumb and forefinger, so that his screams turned from pain to terror. She said, "I'll tear them out!" and Manolo lowered his voice to a croak: "Go on, give it to him, don't let up!" The others kept moving restlessly, calling out to her in a ragged echo not to stop, but to go on, make him tell.

At last Ric collapsed between her knees, his head rolling back helplessly in her arms, tears flooding, strangling, crying, "You said they were only beads, not worth the trouble. Only beads!"

Lola abandoned him at once, adding a slap in his face for good measure, and rose up in fury. "He is an idiot," she said, "why do we keep him? I will leave you in Vigo," she told him, "and you can starve!"

Rac shrieked at this, jerked and bounded in Tito's grasp, until he flailed her head and shoulders with his fist, but she still cried out: "Me too! Leave me, too. I won't go with you — I stay in Vigo — Ric, Ric," she squealed like a rabbit in the teeth of the weasel, "Ric, Ric —"

Tito let go of Rac and turned his fatherly discipline upon Ric. He seized his right arm by the wrist and twisted it very slowly and steadily until the shoulder was nearly turned in its socket and Ric went to his knees with a long howl that died away in a puppylike whimper when the terrible hold was loosed. Rac, huddled on the divan nursing her bruises, cried again with him. Then Manolo and Pepe and Tito and Pancho, and Lola and Concha and Pastora and Amparo, every face masking badly a sullen fright, went away together to go over every step of this dismaying turn of affairs; with a few words and nods, they decided it would be best to drink coffee in the bar, to appear as usual at dinner, and to hold a rehearsal on deck afterwards. They were all on edge and ready to fly at each other's throats. On her way out, Lola paused long enough to seize Rac by the hair and shake her head until she was silenced, afraid to cry. When they were gone, Ric and Rac crawled into the upper berth looking for safety; they lay there half naked, entangled like some afflicted, misbegotten little monster in a cave, exhausted, mindless, soon asleep.

PART III

The Harbors

For here have we no continuing city . . .
SAINT PAUL

In the evening, late, with the reflected sunlight still faintly green and golden in sea and sky, the voyagers' long day's waiting, hovering and staring at the horizon was rewarded with a distant sight of Tenerife, a jagged, rock-shaped, rock-colored fortress of an island rising abruptly from gray water, misty at the base and canopied with sagging violet clouds.

David spoke quietly to Jenny after a long silence together leaning on their arms at the rail so as not to disturb the gentle mood between them; the deep shining satisfaction in his face surprised her. "That's my notion of Spain," he said, "that's my kind of country. Toledo, Avila, not Sevilla. Orange groves and castanets and lace mantillas — not for me!"

"They're got them in Spain too, though, for those who prefer them," said Jenny, tenderly, "but no, not for you, David darling. Granite and sand and faces of the finest Spanish leather, and bitter bread, and twisted olive trees — where even the babies are so tough they won't wear diapers. I know that is really your idea of heaven, isn't it?"

"Yes," said David stoutly, "something tough and grand — Toledo steel, and granite, and Spanish leather, and Spanish pride and hate, and Spanish cruelty — they're the only people who know how to make an art of cruelty . . . I'm sick of things all runny at the edges. . . ."

"Couldn't there be something between a runny edge and a knife-edge?" asked Jenny, hearing herself sound wistful and hoping David did not notice. "There are palms and flowers even in Tenerife, I'll bet you anything, and a lot of people who are very soft on each other; and the boys serenade the girls on moonlight nights just as they do in Mexico — you'll hate it!"

He said nothing more, gave her a blue-eyed look that she loved, and that quieted her entirely, because no matter what came up for them to fight about, she still believed that she was willing to make peace with him on his own terms, if only she could find out what they were.

The gulls came out to meet them and circled about screaming furiously, pumping their stiff mechanical wings and turning their wooden heads as if on hinges to eye the scene severely, falling like stones to the waves, snatching at lumps of galley refuse.

"Same old story," said Herr Lutz, pausing alongside, "all looking for something to eat, and they don't care where it comes from."

"It will be nice, hearing the last of *him*," whispered Jenny, hopefully.

In the morning, the engines gave three loud thumps, and stopped. Jenny put her head out, and there at her very porthole was Santa Cruz de Tenerife, a jagged long rock indeed, sown with palms, smothered in bougainvillea, the flat square houses perched and huddled on cliff-steep levels hacked out as with chisels. The wharf was on a wide beach, the longshoremen were gathered and ready, a small crowd waited without much expectation. Two policemen came among them and began to wave them back towards either side of the wharf, until there was a wide path opened between them. Jenny heard the anchor going down. By the time she reached the deck, the gangplank was settling into place. Almost everybody was there before her, she observed, and nearly all in festive, going-ashore dress. The breakfast bugle sounded, but almost nobody stirred from the side; a loud gruff voice, the purser's maybe, began bawling good advice through a megaphone: "First-class passengers will please be so good as to go to breakfast, which is now waiting for them. In any case, will the ladies and gentlemen of the first class be so good as to clear the decks: a part of the passengers of the third class are now about to be disembarked from the main deck. Attention! First-class passengers will please be so good . . ."

They began straggling away reluctantly, David among them; Jenny started towards him, but was intercepted by Wilhelm Freytag, who gently put out an arm to bar her way. "This should be something to see," he said. "Who wants breakfast?" David does, thought Jenny, watching him disappear. "Let's go over here," said Freytag, taking her elbow, "where we can see them start up."

The people in the steerage who were about to go were gathered at the foot of the steep iron stairway, packed solidly together, their lumpy sack bundles on their shoulders, the smaller children riding above them, all the faces turned upward waiting for the signal that would bring them to the wide freedom of the upper deck, for the blessed word that would give them permission to cross the gangplank and set foot once more on their own earth. Every face wore its own look of private expectation, anxious joy, tranced excitement; and as they stood each body inclined, straining upwards in perfect silence and stillness, their breathing made a small moaning sound and there was a tight trembling of the whole mass. A short young fellow with black-jawed blunt easy-going features, a wild shock of hair, his bare feet clutching into the steps, rushed uncontrollably up the stairs to the rail of the upper deck and poised there on his spread toes, his gaze soaring out from him like a bird to the little towns lying at the foot and climbing up the sides of the stony island. Oblivious, smiling, the round instinctive eyes filled with tears. Even as Wilhelm Freytag saw him and envied him his homecoming, even as Jenny said, "It must be wonderful to cry for joy!" a young officer dashed at the man as if he would strike him, stopping short three feet away, mouth open and square and noisy with outraged authority.

"Get back *down* there, you!" he shouted, but the man did not hear. "Get back *down!*" bawled the officer in an indecent fury, his bad Spanish almost failing him, his face turning purple. Mrs. Treadwell, passing the door on her way to breakfast, paused to glance at him with some curiosity. Yes, no doubt about it, that was her young dancing partner who had practiced such downright pretty manners. She went on, one eyebrow slightly raised. The man at the rail blinked, heard and understood at last, and turned upon the frantic officer the same tender smile, the bright film of water covering his eyes; still smiling, he turned obediently as an unoffended dog and dived back down into the crowd, swinging his hemp bundle. Even before he had turned about again, the officer leaned over and shouted at the waiting people: "Come on, you, come on up, hurry up there, get on up here and get off this ship! Don't crowd, come three abreast, come on, get off, get off!" As he heckled and nagged, several sailors below herded the crowd and urged them on.

The young fellow leaped ahead instantly and led the people upward. They approved of his boldness, and they had found new heart. They scrambled and stumbled and shoved each other about in good-tempered play, laughed aloud in a ragged chorus of free voices calling out jokes and catchwords to each other, no longer oppressed and intimidated, but home from exile, back to the troubles they knew, in their own country where a man's life and death were his own business. They ignored the little yelling angry man with the purple face and the comic Spanish;

nothing he could do, or say in any language, could make any difference to them any longer; they could hardly wait to leave his ship. They turned back and shouted blessings and farewells to those left behind, who shared their joy and shouted back hopefully.

Seven women who had borne children during the voyage came up slowly in a group, some of them supported by their husbands or leaning upon other women, carrying their young in tightly wrapped bundles. They were flabby and pale, some of them with brassy spots on their foreheads and cheeks, their bellies still loose and soft, with their milk staining the fronts of their faded clothes. Their older children, with sad, disinherited eyes, clung determinedly to their skirts. A boy of about twelve years with a fierce, burning smile turned about as he reached the upper deck, and saw them.

"*Olé, Olé,*" he called out, raising a clenched fist and shaking it in the air. "We are many more than when we started!"

One of the mothers lifted her worn dark face and called back in triumph, "Yes, and men, too, all of them!" A great rollicking torrent of laughter rolled through them all. Shouting they rose and poured like a tidal wave upon the deck, spreading, forcing the officers and the other passengers back to the rail and within doors, thinning out in good order at the gangplank and flowing off the ship without a backward glance. The officer turned aside, his face writhing with nausea. He looked straight into the eyes of Dr. Schumann, on his way to say good-by to La Condesa and to help prepare her to go ashore. "God, how they stink," he said, "and how they breed — like vermin!"

Dr. Schumann said nothing, and the young officer calmed down a little, interpreting the Doctor's absent glance as sympathy. The Doctor watched two sailors helping the fat man up the steps. He was wearing the same cherry-colored shirt he had come aboard in at Veracruz, but he was dazed and leaned heavily on his escorts. Dr. Schumann had been down to change the dressing and re-bandage his head, and the wound was doing very well. No doubt he would recover and get into more mischief. As the man passed he looked out from under his huge helmet of surgical dressings directly at Dr. Schumann, but gave no sign of recognition.

Dr. Schumann noticed as he turned the knob of the door that his hand was bloodless, the veins a sunken greenish tracery. He felt weak and tired and wished he had stopped for coffee. He found La Condesa dressed and ready, even wearing a tiny rosy velvet hat with a short, coarse-meshed black veil over her face, lying almost flat as if posing for her effigy, ankles crossed, handbag on one arm, a pair of short white leather gloves in her left hand. She turned her head towards him slightly and smiled. The stewardess, who had long since made up her mind about the odd goings-on between this pair, who were certainly old enough to know better, bowed with an air of great respect to the Doctor, and swiftly closing the small hand valise she had been packing, left at once. The rest of the luggage had been taken away, the lights were turned off, and the place was altogether empty, gray and desolate.

He stood beside her with such grave, rueful depths of concern in his face, she shrank from him with the slightest quiver of her eyelids, and asked with an edge of fright in her voice:

"Have they come for me?"

"Yes, they are here. No, please listen. The Captain and I have talked with them to find out their orders for you. They have been instructed. They will not touch you, or even come near you. They are only to be at the foot of the gangplank — don't look around you, you need not even see them — to make certain you leave the ship, and that you are on the island when the ship sails again. . . ."

"When the ship sails again," she said, "just to think, for me this voyage will have ended."

"You have nothing at all to fear," he said, taking her wrist and feeling for her pulse. Even now he refused to doubt that he had done, not right, perhaps — who could be certain of that, ever? — but the only thing possible. La Condesa drew back her hand and said, "Oh, what can a pulse matter now? That is all over too. You may say I have nothing to fear — how easy for you, who are going home! But I am going to be a prisoner here. Never think once I am left here at their mercy they won't put me in a dark dirty place by myself."

He sat on the side of the bed and held her hand firmly. "You are not going to be a prisoner except on this whole island," he told her. "A most beautiful place, and you may live where and how you choose in it."

"As I choose?" she said, her voice rising but not in a question. "Alone? Friendless? Without a *centavito*? Without my children, not even knowing where they are? And how shall they ever find me? Oh, my friend, have you gone mad with virtue and piety, have you lost your human feelings, how can you have forgotten what suffering is?"

"Wait," he said. "Wait."

He brought out the needle and the ampule and prepared deliberately to give her another *piqûre*. She watched him, not with her familiar expression of clever mischief, but passively, her eyes scarcely moving to follow him. She sat up in silence and took off her jacket, unbuttoned the cuff of her shirt and rolled the sleeve up for herself very slowly and said with a short intake of breath as the needle pierced the flesh, "Ah . . . how I shall miss this! What shall I do without it?"

"You are to have it when you need it," he reassured her. "I am giving you a prescription and a special note to show to whatever doctor you choose there. I believe any doctor will accept it. I do not think you will be allowed to suffer."

She took his hand between both of hers and clung with imploring inquiry: "Why will you not tell me what it is? Or better, give it to me and let me use it for myself — I know how to use a needle."

"I don't doubt it," said Dr. Schumann, "but I cannot. You are much too reckless, I can't trust you — remember? You told me so yourself."

"That was *then*," she cried, gaily, putting on her jacket again. "I am altogether changed now, as you see — reformed by your good example!" She put her feet over the edge of the bed and sat beside him. "Tell me something," she said, "you know we shall never see each other again. Why then may we not talk like friends, or even lovers, or as if we two were meeting again on the other side of the grave. Ah come, let's play that we are two little winged, purified souls met in Paradise after a long Purgatory!"

"But you have told me you do not believe in the other side of the grave," said Dr. Schumann, smiling, "much less in souls and Paradise."

"I don't, but it shall make no difference — we shall meet there just the same. But why not tell me something now?"

She leaned towards him until he felt her light breath and asked very simply without any special feeling in her voice:

"Did you come in here late last night and kiss me? Did you put your arms around me and almost raise me up from my pillow, and call me your love? Did you say, Sleep, my love, or was I dreaming? Tell me . . ."

Dr. Schumann turned towards her and took her deeply in his arms, and laid his head on her shoulder and drew her face to his. "I did, I did," he groaned, "I did, my darling."

"Oh why?" she cried, "Why, when I didn't know waking from sleeping? Why did you never kiss me when I could have known surely, when I could have been happy?"

"No," he said, "no." He raised his head and folded his arms around her again. She began to sway a little, from side to side, as if she were rocking a cradle; then releasing herself very gently and sitting back from him with her hands on his shoulders she said, "Oh, but it was only a dream then — oh, do you know what it is, coming so late, so strangely, no wonder I couldn't understand it. It is that innocent romantic love I should have had in my girlhood! But no one loved me innocently, and oh, how I should have laughed at him if he had! . . . Well, here we are. Innocent love is the most painful kind of all, isn't it?"

"I have not loved you innocently," said Dr. Schumann, "but guiltily and I have done you great wrong, and I have ruined my life. . . ."

"My life was ruined so long ago I have forgotten what it was like before," said La Condesa. "So you are not to have me on your mind. And you must not think of me as sleeping on stone floors and living on bread and water, for I shall not ever — it is not my style. It is not becoming to me. I shall find a way out of everything. And now, now my love, let's kiss again really this time in broad daylight and wish each other well, for it is time for us to say good-by."

"Death, death," said Dr. Schumann, as if to some presence standing to one side of them casting a long shadow. "Death," he said, and feared that his heart would burst.

"Why of course, death," said La Condesa as if indulging his fancy, "but not yet!" They did not kiss, but she took his hand and held it to her cheek a moment. He trembled so he could hardly write the prescription and the note he had promised. He opened her handbag and tucked the papers inside. They did not speak again. He walked to the gangplank with her, and handed her the small valise. She did not raise her eyes. He watched while she stepped into an elegant white caleche on the wharf, drawn by an inelegant shaggy small horse, and then noticed the two quite ordinary-looking men who took the next available equipage and drove away slowly after her, at a discreet distance.

"Have you any plans?" Freytag asked Jenny as they lingered while the students formed a line and went leaping down the gangplank shouting the chorus of "Cucaracha."

"Aren't they tiresome!" said Jenny, watching them. "No plans at all. I'm waiting for David."

"I'll be getting along, then," said Freytag, easily, "maybe we can all meet somewhere for a drink on the island."

"Maybe." His retreating straight back and manly stride reminded her of an actor, a good-looking leading man used to taking the stage whenever he appeared. He veered expertly around a straggling little crowd of frowzy-looking persons, men and women with a child or two, coming on board with odds and ends of stuff to sell, bits of linen and silk, clumsy small objects not worth a glance. A very dark young gypsy woman stepped before Jenny as if she had been looking for her to give her good news. "Stop," said the gypsy, in Spanish, "let me tell you something strange." She came so close Jenny smelt the pepper and garlic on her breath, the weathered animal reek of her skin and great gaudy red and orange petticoats. She took Jenny's hand and turned the palm upward. "You are going to a country that is not for you, and the man you are with now is not your real man. But you will go soon to a better country, and you will find your man. You will be happy in love yet, don't be troubled! Cross my palm with silver!" She held Jenny's hand firmly, her eyes were shrewd and impudent, she smiled with her teeth closed.

"Go away, gypsy woman," said Jenny, in English. "You don't know enough. You've got a one-track mind. I don't want any other man, the very notion gives me the horrors. I'll stick by the trouble I know. There are going to be a lot of other things much more interesting in my life than this man, or any other man," she assured the gypsy with the utmost seriousness. The gypsy stared, her eyes glinting with suspicion; she held Jenny's hand, refusing to go without her coin. But their hands had changed positions — Jenny was now holding the gypsy's palm upward examining it studiously. "Those are the things I'd like to hear about! Now as for you," she added in Spanish, "you are going to take a long journey and meet a dark man . . ." The gypsy snatched her hand away violently and stepped back.

"What are you saying to me?" she asked in a fury.

"I was telling your fortune, free," said Jenny, in Spanish, putting a one-dollar note in her hand. "You are born lucky."

"*Valgame Dios,*" said the gypsy, suddenly mild, crossing herself. Her dark fingers closed over the crumpled paper, and instantly, a look of complete contempt, triumph, a quite astonishing play of hatred, twisted her mouth and paled her skin under its patina of dirt. As she spun away with a wide swing of her many ruffles, she flung back over her shoulder a word Jenny did not understand, except by the tone and look. She called back clearly in her best Spanish, "And you, too!" with all confidence.

"Do you really know what she called you?" asked David, materializing at her side.

"Something apt, something appropriate, no doubt," said Jenny. "Anyway, she got it back."

"Must you go on brawling with gypsy women?" asked David, though without curiosity. "Did you pick up any new tricks?"

"Wait and see," said Jenny merrily. "Mind your own business." In dead silence they walked down the gangplank, just behind the Huttens and Bébé, just before Elsa and her parents, the Baumgartners with Hans following closely. Herr Freytag had disappeared, Mrs. Treadwell, wearing an enormous flat black hat, and carrying of all things a parasol, stepped into a second waiting caleche and was carried away as if for good. The students piled into a larger conveyance, in a tangle of arms and legs, their heads clustered like a nest of noisy birds.

The Spanish company went off together in an unusual silence, eyes fixed ahead, faces closed and hard. Ric and Rac, still looking somewhat battered, lagged and sulked. The women all wore widely fringed, large black silk embroidered shawls, the children wore short jackets with deep pockets, the men wore, for the first time during the voyage, quite ordinary sack suits except they were somewhat too snugly fitted. They all managed without any trouble to look most disreputable. Once on the dock they closed ranks and walked away up the stony street towards town as if they were late for an appointment.

Following them closely, each one intent on his own interest in their movements, Hansen and Denny found themselves jostling elbows somewhat at the gangplank. "There they go," said Denny, spiteful and baffled, trying to keep ahead of Hansen, who just the same shouldered past him rudely with thunderous brow, bawling: "Is it your business? Why not they go where they please?"

Keep your shirt on, you big bastard, said Denny to himself, and aloud: "Dirty work at the crossroads, I bet," but without contending further for the right of way. The big Swede looked like a tough customer, no use tangling with him, anyway not now. He tried to pick out

Pastora from the huddle of dancers, who were keeping well ahead of the crowd now straggling through the dock; by the time Denny and Hansen reached shore, they had vanished.

The steerage passengers left on the ship, those who would go ashore at Vigo, crowded to the rail and leaned at ease, watching intensely but without envy their shipmates on the dock being rounded up and counted once more by the officials who had come to take charge of them. On the upper deck Johann wheeled his uncle's chair near the gangplank, steadied it against the rail, and tried with flickering vision and leaping heart to pick out Concha from the black-shawled dancers as their graceful backs swayed and retreated. He fetched from his depths such an explosive breath of despair, Herr Graf roused and spoke: "What is your trouble, dear boy, are you in pain?"

Johann kicked the near wheel of the chair, jarring the sick man, who flinched and groaned loudly, glancing about him to call any chance passer-by to witness the behavior of his shameless nephew. "It's none of your business," said Johann, also glancing around and speaking in a low voice. The silence of the nearly deserted ship in harbor disturbed them, as if a protective wall had been torn away. Dr. Schumann, walking slowly, hands clasped behind him, meaning to go to his cabin but dreading to be there, stopped a moment beside them. "You are looking very well, this morning," he said to Herr Graf. "I hope you are enjoying your voyage."

"My soul is at peace," Herr Graf assured him, a little sulkily, "here, or anywhere. It does not matter where I am."

"That is most fortunate," said the Doctor, amiably, "most enviable."

"It is a question of God's grace," said Herr Graf, whose grudge against doctors and surgeons was soundly based on professional jealousy, the inspired knowledge that they were standing in his light, preventing his free exercise of God's will in the matter of the cure of souls and bodies. "What good is all your materia medica if the soul is sick?"

Dr. Schumann said mildly, "That is one of materia medica's thorniest problems. For myself, I try to do my human part, and leave the rest to God," for he always gave a respectful answer even to the most afflicted minds and misguided beliefs; and at this moment his own suffering in his own guilt drew him slowly into a vast teeming shapeless wallow of compassion for every suffering thing, a confusion so dark he could no longer tell the difference between the invader and the invaded, the violator and the violated, the betrayer and the betrayed, the one who loved and the one who hated or who jeered or was indifferent. The whole great structure built upon the twin pillars of justice and love, which reached from earth into eternity, by which the human soul rose step by step from the most rudimentary concepts of good and evil, of simple daily conduct between fellow men, to the most exquisite hairline discriminations and choices between one or another shade of faith and feeling, of doctrinal and mystical perceptions — this tower was now crumbling and falling around him, even as he stood beside the little dying fanatic gazing up at him with a condescending smirk on his exhausted face.

Miracles are instantaneous, they cannot be summoned, but come of themselves, usually at unlikely moments and to those who least expect them. Yet they make use of some odd assistants, and the Doctor's rescuing miracle took advantage of Herr Graf's all-too-human glance meant to tell the Doctor what a poor, inadequate, ill-informed and poverty-stricken sort of Christian he was, and the message went home like an arrow. The Doctor suffered the psychic equivalent of a lightning stroke, which cleared away there and then his emotional fogs and vapors, and he faced his truth, nearly intolerable but the kind of pain he could deal with, something he recognized and accepted unconditionally. His lapse into the dire, the criminal sentimental cruelty of the past days was merely the symptom of his moral collapse: he had refused to acknowledge the wrong he had done La Condesa his patient, he had taken advantage of her situation as prisoner, he had tormented her with his guilty love and yet had refused her — and himself — any human joy in it. He had let her go in hopelessness without even the faintest promise of future help or deliverance. What a coward, what a swine, Dr. Schumann told himself, calmly, bathed in the transfiguring light of Herr Graf's contempt; but not only, not altogether, if he did not choose to be!

With a pleasant "Good morning" he dispersed the hovering miasma of theological discussion with Herr Graf and went to one of the writing rooms, where he wrote a short letter to La Condesa, which he entrusted to the purser, who would know how to convey it to the care of the right police agent. Dr. Schumann wished to convey his respects to Madame, he gave her his own office address, in his home city, with his telephone number, the address of the International Red Cross headquarters in Geneva, with an earnest request that Madame write to him at once and let him know where a letter might find her at all times. He renewed his anxious inquiries for her health, hoped for a reply to the ship before it would have sailed at four o'clock. He signed himself her assured and devoted servant. He then made a round of the sick bay, where he found two sailors, neither of whom needed further attention, and a tour of the steerage, where a newly born baby's navel showed faint signs of infection. This occupied him for a few minutes, cleansing, anointing, and binding, but at last the day was on his hands, and he did not know what to do with it. He walked slowly around the deck, noting with some relief that Herr Graf had disappeared with his bad-tempered nephew; but walking tired him. At last he gave way, and returned to his cabin to rest. Lying there, in his habitual posture of early medieval effigies, feet crossed, hands crossed over his midriff, his perverse infatuation began to fade, and with it his distrust and hatred of his love — it had been only a long daydream. A warm surge of human grief for that creature who was doomed maybe beyond his or any human help filled him like a tide body and mind, bringing its own healing. What nonsense to say anyone was doomed until his last breath! Gently, clearly, steadily, his long plan of reparation unfolded in its simple, sensible, practical perfection; he was to provide for her and see that she was cared for and protected, that medical treatment should be available: she was to be watched and guarded and saved from her own suicidal romantic folly. It would be a blameless charity which could call for no explanation, could be carried on at a distance, and his wife need never know. He thought of his wife with habitual fondness, of her known strength, always the same, her unexpected and constantly changing weaknesses and whims. She was the center, the reason, and the meaning of his marriage, around which his life had grown like an organism; she was not to be disturbed for anything. He would make his reparations for the wrongs he had done, in silence, as part of his penance. Dr. Schumann, soothed, eased, felt himself blissfully falling asleep in the divine narcotic of hope, and relief of conscience.

He waked to the familiar creaking, pounding, shouting commotion, rolling and heaving of the old *Vera* getting out to sea again, and lay quietly a few minutes enjoying the absurdity of his situation, the combination of homely domestic muddle and the rigors of nautical discipline on an old tub like this, where God knows, anything could happen. The Doctor felt refreshed, full of a gentle, smiling delight. He looked out of his porthole and saw the island at a little distance, already shrouded in mist, its scattered lights twinkling like Christmas candles.

His darling was there, and she would know by now that she was not alone, not deserted, not left to her fate, the wayward little soul who should never have been treated with severity. He would feel better to know she was on that island for a while, until he found a way to have her set free; meantime, why had the steward not brought him her answer to his letter? He would go up. Indeed the dinner bugle was sounding; in the Captain's absence the Doctor should always appear at the table. He stopped by the purser's office to inquire about a message. The purser of course was already at his dinner, but the young assistant had been instructed and had an answer for Dr. Schumann. The police agent, he said carefully, standing very straight, had delivered the Herr Doctor's letter to Madame. She had read it there in his presence, and the police agent said he would be pleased to wait for an answer.

Dr. Schumann took a short step forward and extended his right hand slightly curved. "Where is it?" he asked, his voice contracting.

The assistant purser spoke his piece as if he had memorized it. "Sir," he said, "Madame thanked the police agent, and said there was no answer."

"David darling," said Jenny, "let's be tourists again. Oh look, look," she said in rapture, "at all the things here we never saw before."

"Such as . . . ?" asked David idly, without turning his head. "Palms, you mean? Burros? Red tile roofs? Barefooted, unwashed peasantry? We had all that in Mexico, we'll have all that in Spain . . ." They found themselves again in their most familiar difficulty, being quite unable to agree what to do next. They were sitting on a bench on the edge of a small plaza halfway up the hill beside the stony ascending narrow street shaded with palm and mimosa.

"Well, camels, you idiot," said Jenny patiently, "for example. Camels with great loads on their humps and barefooted unwashed peasantry with *turbans* driving them."

"Just variations on a theme," said David. "Why don't we sit here and let the scenery pass us?"

Jenny would not have this for a moment. She was restless and looking, David knew, for something besides scenery. She sat stiffly forward on the bench, her eyes roving, feet planted exactly for a straight leap up and away on a second's notice, and leap she did, waving her hand and calling out, as if they were old friends and delightful company, to sad Elsa and her dull parents laboring up the path towards the market center of town. Elsa waved back sedately. Herr and Frau Lutz waggled their heads with solemn faces, for Frau Lutz was not reconciled to Elsa's view that Jenny behaved like a nice woman in the cabin. Jenny said briskly, "All right, David, you stay here and sprout mushrooms; I'm off with the raggle-taggle gypsies O!" David was left to mull over in his mind again the fact, the incomprehensible fact, that Jenny at times seemed to prefer any company to his own.

A small procession traipsed past him, Jenny and the Lutzes, Freytag and Mrs. Treadwell a few paces back, followed at a short distance by Fräulein Spöckenkieker and Herr Rieber, randy and rowdy as usual, swinging hands and cackling. The Baumgartners lagged somewhat, with Hans between them. The bride and groom walked rather far back, arms around each other, their bowed heads touching, their faces in a trance of sensual bliss. David felt a violent surge of sexual envy; they were always so discreet, and obviously they believed they were not seen; but they were in full honeymoon swing now, that was plain. The bridal shyness was little by little being overcome; they both had circled eyes, the bride had a rash on her cheek. If they stayed on deck in the morning, they fell asleep in their chairs, hands clasped. They disappeared in the afternoon, and showed up for dinner exhausted, silent, faces closed and secretive except for their eyes when they exchanged glances. . . .

David stood up suddenly, shaking his head, going hot all over with a rush of blood to all his vital strategic points — his nerve centers raged and his mind was a reek of spermy violent images and sensations which he loathed for the pleasure they gave him. He stepped forward, meaning to follow Jenny. The bride and groom saw him then; their arms dropped away at once, the bride slipped her hand into the crook of the groom's elbow, and they walked by rather stiffly.

David felt like a fool. He had unfathomable contempt for all those unsavory imaginations roused to concupiscence by sexual scenes, music, certain words or reading matter, by dancing, by dirty stories — the peepers, the eavesdroppers, the feelers, the footie-players, the neckers, the strip-tease chasers, or just the daydreamers who could bring it on by sitting still and staring into space. His own method had been clear-cut, at least. When the fit took him, he had gone out and found an object. Once or twice he had tried the risky business of having a regular girl in the mining camp. But that could get very sticky in no time at all; he wondered at women. There wasn't a whore on earth, he was willing to bet, who didn't believe that some fellow would come along, fall in love with her, and take her away to a life of luxury, or at least idleness. Some of them even dreamed of marriage — it had been known to happen. A little grubby half-Indian girl with black finger nails and lice in her beautiful thick glossy hair had attracted him. He put kerosene in her hair (she distrusted the stuff, did not know how to apply it) and then had heated gallons of water in a pot in his narrow, walled patio, and had given her a good scrub from head to foot, outside in the sunshine, including hairy parts and fingernails. He had finished the job by showering her with his West Indian bay rum. After having prepared the dish so carefully, he found his appetite gone. He ended by giving her five pesos and sending her away, to her entire mystification. While she was putting on her petticoats, she asked him matter-of-factly, "Why do you not marry me? I would make a good wife — I know how!" He explained that he was not ready to marry yet, and she went away quite cheerfully confident, but from her look and manner it was clear she regarded him as a species of eunuch or one of those foreigners with strange tastes, for she said as she went: "When you feel like a man, you let me know!"

Well, what a roundabout his mind had gone to get out of this mess. He waited until the bride and groom passed, and fell in to the straggling pilgrimage. He could not help but notice that Jenny was now walking with Freytag and Mrs. Treadwell, and he was offended when Jenny suddenly jumped for joy and pointed excitedly ahead. Everybody paused and turned their heads. So did David and he saw something strange and new and beautiful; after that day, he would not see it again, or ever forget it.

A young slender girl, limber and tough as a ballet dancer, in a short tight black dress showing her bare brown legs, her head swathed in a small square black shawl with a tiny hat no larger than a doll's resting on her forehead, secured somehow under the knot of her covered hair, hurled herself across their path and leaped up the rocky incline ahead of them, turning sharply to the left on a narrower path, sure-footed as a deer and as wild. On her head she carried a great flat tray loaded with battered metal water cans, and under this weight, in her worn tennis shoes, she went at flying speed uphill, in a half-run with rigid shoulders, raised chin and extravagantly swaying hips, her arms spread like wings.

Looking about them, the travelers saw that the girl was not alone.

From all directions in every place for the rest of the day, they saw the water-carriers, up and down the island, young beautiful girls with fine noses and tender mouths, and the wonderful Spanish pale cream skin. A few older women, perhaps as much as thirty, still had this beauty of athletes in training— "It would kill two longshoremen in a week," remarked Freytag, admiringly, after watching them run so endlessly and apparently without effort or fatigue. "They *can't* last long."

All the strangers were enchanted, they wanted it explained. There was, they might have known, no mystery to it. They hailed in a common cause the first Islander they saw passing, a rough-haired man, barefooted, with his cotton drawers rolled to the knees, a large shapeless bundle on his back, and Herr Professor Hutten questioned him about this phenomenon. The Islander began, as he always did, for he made a business of meeting boats, and he knew these foreigners well, by remarking simply that those girls were very respectable young persons employed in making an honorable living. He was familiar with the strange views of tourists, and not only the men, on the subject of the conduct of young women in foreign lands. He could not however after long experience overcome his amazement that boatload after boatload of tourists passing through could never understand the simple, natural, everyday task of young girls carrying water. It was part of woman's household work through all ages, who else would be supposed to carry it? They were all under the strict family rule young girls must observe . . . They were employed by the company that controlled water-carrying, they wore a uniform, of course. At this point he always ran again into the one thing they wanted to know — what, what was the meaning of that little black doll hat every girl wore flat on her forehead just under her tray? This he did not know, nobody knew; it was not a question any Islander had ever been heard to ask. It was a custom, nothing more. A part of their dress. If a girl did not wear that hat, she would not be allowed to carry water. It was all so simple, yet they could never understand it. And when Freytag asked the inevitable question: "Why are they all so beautiful?" the rough-haired man was happy to give his familiar answer — "We have no choice on this island. We take what God sends. All our girls are beautiful and chaste."

This was invariably received with respectful silence.

The Baumgartners with Hans, Freytag and Mrs. Treadwell, the Lutzes and Jenny, the Huttens, who had overtaken them, and Herr

Glocken, wearing his red necktie, were now clustered around the Islander. Tourists, therefore barbarians all, the Islander knew them well, and offered to show them the sights, with appropriate histories, at so much a head. This was the last thing anybody in the group wanted, so they scattered somewhat and walked on at discreet distances from each other, but all in the same direction and bound, sooner or later, to meet in the same places on pretty much the same errands. Herr Glocken had straggled along hopelessly, but in the pause made up his lost time. He waved genially to David as he went past, flashing his painful smile. "Hurry!" he called, helpfully. "You'll be left!"

David followed along, keeping them in sight but not trying to overtake them. He thought with some satisfaction how grotesquely out of place everybody looked with their makeshift shore clothes and wrong kinds of shoes. All sizes and shapes; even Jenny looked awkward in that sagging hopsack bag she insisted on wearing all times and places, on the grounds that it was hand-woven. If she could see herself! It took this kind of perfectly clear air, the palm shade and the dappled sunlight along the crooked narrow old streets, for they were coming near the town, to show them up in their awful dullness, Jenny among them. Father Garza and Father Carillo flapped by in their billowing soutanes and old-lady shoes with elastic sides; their flat-topped side-rolled hats stiff as boards over their grim faces; striding like ostriches they caught up to and passed the strolling sight-seers.

David meditated a little on his situation, and admitted that it looked hopeless — yet had it ever been anything else? He had never been anywhere but that he wanted to be somewhere else; never in any kind of fix that he wasn't planning all the time to get out of it. He had never known a girl he could trust, and Jenny was the last straw. But he couldn't hate her — or not just yet, or not except in fits and starts. Whatever their feeling for each other had become, it could even now be a kind of love, he supposed, but if it was, they'd both be better off without it . . . How better, or in what way, he had no idea. As if it mattered. Having arrived at this tolerable mood, he set out in haste and caught up with Jenny, took her arm, greeted Freytag and Mrs. Treadwell and some of the others as he passed them, and unfolded his plan of action: "Jenny angel, let's look for a nice little joint and drink the wine of the country, with those red bull meat sausages? I'm hungry, let's eat and then go looking around."

Jenny said, "Let's go," and gave a little skip. They put on such a burst of speed they left the others at a safe distance, and came into one of the small plazas of shops and wine rooms. Trying to choose, for they all looked and smelled much alike, they lit on a sign over a door, *El Quita Penas*. "That's ours," said Jenny, "come along, David darling, let's forget our troubles." As they took the little table near the small dark window, they saw the zarzuela company entering the plaza on the other side. They streamed into a doorway festooned with embroidered silk shawls and lace-trimmed linen and swooped upon the merchandise displayed, while Ric and Rac fumbled and pulled and hauled at the rolls of stuff on the counter outside the shop. The shopkeeper rushed out to shoo them away, and back to keep an eye on her customers. David said, "It looks more like a raid than a shopping expedition," and Jenny said, "It probably is a raid —" but they spoke idly and went on sampling the Canary wines from the barrels along the wall: along with a very copious, savory platter of Spanish peppers and sausage, they tasted Malaga, Muscatel, Malavasia, an Islands brandy called Tres Copas, and afterward with their coffee an orange liqueur which reminded them distantly of Curaçao. Denny came in, greeted them almost fondly, and sat down with them as if he had been invited.

"God, I'm bushed," he began. "I've been nearly all over this island at a dead run. You know those girls with water cans on their heads? Well, one of them give me the eye, can't tell *me*, I'd know the kind if she was wearing mule's harness — so I took out after her, thinking she meant to let me know she was knocking off soon and would be ready for a — for —" he swallowed and looked at Jenny, "for a little sociability, and honest to God, she went stomping up and down those rocky ridges and paths like a mountain goat, and every once in a while she'd come to a house, and practically without stopping, she'd hold her tray steady and bend her knees and a woman would come out and lift off a can of water, and put on an empty, and away she'd go buckety-buckety, me trailing after with my tongue hanging out. A couple of times she doubled on her tracks and passed me, and every time she'd give me that look — she didn't smile, she just sparked her eyes at me. . . . What's that you're having?" he asked David. "Get me some, will you? I can't talk the lingo, I don't know the names — and finally I figured she was about through, couldn't have anything but empties by now, so I followed her on down a good ways, and there she came to a kind of long shed full of barrels — great big water kegs they were, and there were a lot of the girls sitting round resting, and a lot more were getting fresh cans set on their trays. My girl wasn't resting though. She got a fresh trayful and went by me like a runaway wildcat and this time she just cut her eyes at me and said '*Vaya, vaya!*' . . . I know what that means. The old runaround. Well, I looked over the situation down near the waterworks, and decided it was no deal . . ."

"Just as well," said David. "Wait till your luck changes."

"Look at that Pastora, now," said Denny, holding up his glass for another Malaga. "This stuff's too sweet, ain't there any hard liquor?"

"She's right across the street, in that shop," said Jenny, encouragingly.

"Let her stay there," said Denny, "For the time being. I don't mean look at her actually. Right now I wouldn't care if I ever saw her again. I'm beginning to think Spanish women are just plain skittish," he said, "you can't seem to get 'em to keep still long enough to get anywhere . . ."

"Well, you've seen the sights," said Jenny, "so David and I are going out to be tourists for a while." David paid in American money, and received a handful of Spanish coin.

"You'd better hurry out and spend that," said Denny. Waving his glass to signal a third drink, he said almost plaintively, "What's the name for brandy? I wish you all wouldn't go off and leave me here by myself. I'll get into some kind of a mess. I don't feel good. If I get a few more drinks I'm liable to go out and beat the pants off that Pastora —"

"Unless she beats you first," said David, cheerfully, "she's tougher than she looks and has a tough gang with her."

"Why don't you pick on a Guardia Civil?" asked Jenny, who had noticed a great burly pair of them, at the wharf, in their varnished cocked hats and tight uniforms, looking solid as walnut. "Why do you want to pick on a girl?"

Denny unexpectedly showed logic and even dimly, remotely, some hint of a deep-buried sense of justice, even morals, even to strain a point, ethics. Or at least, common sense.

"Because she's the one I'm mad at," he said, simply. "What did the Wardia Civeel ever do to me?"

Jenny gave him a deep, friendly smile, which faded instantly when she remembered he might take it as an illicit invitation, but said, "How right you are! David, did you hear that? Mr. Denny has just uttered a most important rule from the code of honor."

"No . . . what is that?" asked David uneasily, but Jenny was quite harmlessly silly, after all. "Why, don't fight with anybody you're not

mad at," she said. "Don't get your grudges crossed . . . use your judg-
ment." They both waved a hand to Denny as they went. He was
frowning into his half-filled glass. He wondered if that sassy piece was
poking fun at him. Well, it would be a hot day in January when he'd
make a pass at *her*.

Frau Rittersdorf, somewhat uneasy at being alone at a table under a
tree in a strange place — in spite of a surly old man setting a cup and
a ragged cotton napkin before her, and the greasy smells pouring out of
the barracks-like house, she could hardly call it a café — pulled her
rose-colored scarf a little over her eyebrows, flattened her notebook be-
side her coffee, and wrote: "The innumerable heterogeneous elements
so freely mingled on that ship naturally have brought on a series of
most sinister occurrences, the logical consequences of such lack of dis-
cipline, the insolence of the lower classes when allowed the least shade
of liberty —" She read this sentence over and decided that her indigna-
tion had got the upper hand of her style, and the paragraph was getting
away from her. She drew thin lines through each sentence, not enough
to conceal it but only a reminder that she had rejected it, yet kept it as
a disciplinary example of something to avoid in the future. She began:
"They are all over the shops, everywhere, like a pack of invading rats. I
have watched them, and I know they are stealing right and left. I can-
not quite make out the objects, nor precisely their method, but then I
could not come close enough for a clear view. I feel they carry a kind
of pestilence with them, they shed around them the true metaphysical
odor of evil." Frau Rittersdorf paused to read this sentence with sur-
prise and delight. Where had it come from? Was it hers? Had she read
it somewhere? She could not recall ever having had such a thought,
but then, certainly she had never heard anyone say such a thing. In-
deed, was there such an odor? She had always adhered to the maxim
that dirt is misplaced matter. It offered a powerful scientific argument
for keeping the inferior orders in their place. This did not answer her
questions but it brought her around to her subject again. The zarzuela
company, as well as a number of other persons in first class on this voy-
age, were most certainly misplaced matter, and the consequences were
beginning all too obviously to be seen. . . .

"The unhappy Condesa," she wrote, "where is she now, abandoned, a
prisoner on this Island of the Dead?" Frau Rittersdorf raised her chin
and swung a glance in a half-circle, taking in quite a busy scene, men,

women, children of all ages, an assortment of domestic animals, obviously going about their particular business, full of unimaginable interests. *What* had such poor shabby tired-looking beings to live for? This was her great question, could they be called alive at all?

A woman sitting on the ground, not ten feet away, with her baskets of wilting market stuff around her, laid her baby in her cradle of a lap between her crossed knees, and put him to her great naked breast with its brown nipple big as a thumb, while she ate voraciously of onions, tomatoes, sausages, apricots, all wrapped in a disk of tough half-baked unleavened bread. The baby suckled and kicked in bliss, she put her food down now and then to wait upon her customers, they holding their woven palm leaf bags to receive the vegetables, she counting out change from the small flat basket beside her. Frau Rittersdorf was so revolted by the spectacle she was unable to take up her pencil. The baby was fat, and should obviously have been weaned months ago. The woman's neck, face and hands were like old leather, all her side teeth were gone, she mangled and tore her food with her front teeth, yet ate like a wolf. The baby climbed out of her lap, and stood up. He wore a single dirty shirt that reached barely to his navel. He squared himself off on his feet and spread legs, his infant male tassel rose and pointed acutely skywards and a very energetic spout of water ascended in a glittering arc, pattering in the dust not three feet from Frau Rittersdorf's immaculate light-colored shoes and gossamer stockings. She was so startled she almost cried out, but stood quickly, backing away and drawing in her skirts. The mother did not understand either her movement or her stare, for she reached out and patted her baby encouragingly on the back, with utter love and tenderness, while the baby finished his proper business with deep-breathed joyous noises of satisfaction. The mother pulled him back and covered his adorable shame with her bare hand, smiled gaily at Frau Rittersdorf and called out with pride. *"Es hombre, de veras!"* — He's a man, all right! — as if that explained everything and made it a happy secret among women. Frau Rittersdorf gathered up her things and walked away in a chill of horror as if a bony hand reached out of the past clutching her coldly and drawing her again into the awful wallow of ignorance and poverty and brutish living she had escaped oh barely — barely! The dirt-floored hut of her grandparents, with the pigpens and the cattle stalls and the chicken roosts all opening into the one room where the whole family lived: the dull mean village cottage of her shoemaking father and her seamstress mother, who felt they had risen high in their world; their ambition for her to become a teacher in the village school — Oh, oh, oh, cried the whole frightful memory, not only in the voices and faces of those dead and gone people she had tried all these years to forget, to deny; but the very animals, the smothering walls and the dirt floors and the stinking shoe leather, the taste of lard on the slice of sour bread she took to school with her — the very bread itself, all rose again out of that deep pit in which she had buried them, and one was as alive as the other; in a terrible voiceless clamor they cried and lamented and accused her, soundless as screams in a nightmare. The floors, the pigs, the bread, her grandfather and grandmother, her parents, all cried in the same voice the same terrible words she could not understand, though she knew what they meant to tell her. Frau Rittersdorf stood swaying somewhat, her right hand flattened on her forehead. The old man in the dirty apron spoke to her politely, holding out his hand. "Oh yes," she said, "I owe you something," and carefully she counted the exact sum into his palm in Spanish coin that she had got from the ship's exchange, with a few coppers over. There was a roaring in her ears, and the ground under her swayed like the deck of the *Vera*. "I must be having an attack of some kind," she said aloud, in German, and the waiter answered agreeably, "*Si, si, Señora, naturalmente!*" which struck her as being rather uncalled for. As she walked, she recovered rapidly; still she was puzzled as to what exactly had happened to her. She decided to go back to the *Vera*, and have lunch there. As she picked her way carefully over the stones, she saw Señora Ortega with her nurse and baby leisurely rolling along (with not a care in the world, on her way to Paris and her husband, a successful diplomat!) in one of those rather absurd but chic miniature conveyances called a caleche, or they could be chic if they had proper horses and drivers. She realized she was tired, and might hail one for herself. An uneasiness about the expense halted her. Such extravagances, she foresaw, would be preparing for her an old age of loneliness, a servile existence in middle-class houses, a superannuated governess on board and keep with an occasional holiday tip, putting up with insufferable children in common families no young, able woman would look at. . . . If Otto could have dreamed she would be left to such a fate, would he have gone with never a thought of her to a hero's death? What had he left to her? An iron cross and his dress uniform and sword. If it had not been for his parents' leaving her his modest inheritance, where would she be today? But oh, Otto, Otto, if you could see me now, if you could have dreamed what was to become of me, oh surely you could not have thrown away your life for nothing.

She was greeted pleasantly by a young officer or two. On her way down to her cabin she met Frau Schmitt on her way up, carrying her knitting. "Back so soon?" Frau Rittersdorf asked. Frau Schmitt said gloomily, "I saw enough, just the same."

Frau Rittersdorf meant to go on, but this remark stopped her in her tracks.

"There was, then, something to see?" she asked, in the tone of condescension Frau Schmitt found so infuriatingly unanswerable.

"For those who can see," she said, "there was something." Feeling a touch light in the head from such boldness, she did not wait for Frau Rittersdorf to rally, but went on her way to the peace and comfort of the empty lounge.

Frau Rittersdorf did not overlook this saucy speech of her cabin mate, but decided to ignore it for the moment. She had crossed some line in her thoughts she had not known was there, but already she had left it behind, and she was strangely easy as if her mind had thrown off some great load that had been exhausting and hampering her all this time. . . . She opened her handbag, took out her passport case, searched its compartments for a moment with two fingertips, and brought out a small photograph of her husband in a flat silver frame. Ah no — he was not like that. His splendid image in her imagination got a blow as always at sight of this rather staring, lifeless army photograph, no light, no color, the clear eyes empty, cold as agates. No, no — never again, never again. She replaced the picture and put her handbag away. She would forget this hero who had forgotten her, had left her to whatever fate might come — what a selfish cruel thing to do to a wife who adored him! No no. She would forget, and she would find another husband, a real one this time. . . . When this stupid voyage was over, she would stay at home where she belonged, she would be among her own people, the kind of men who would appreciate her qualities. . . . Names and faces began to drift into her mind. She opened her notebook and began to write them down. . . . "First things first," she gently admonished herself. Her imagination began wandering over a new, springlike landscape, full of likely encounters with eligible persons, some known, some unknown, all delightful encounters full of possibilities. Scenes began to enact themselves before her eyes. Don Pedro intruded at one point, but was instantly rejected, and the charming pantomime of herself in an endless promenade with ever-changing partners went on and on while she brushed her hair hundreds of strokes, not counting. She forgot about lunch. She had been rather dreading her welcome at home, among her friends and her husband's family after what they must regard as her failure in Mexico: for her Mexican circle had been painfully eager to keep them informed of every stage of her romance with Don Pedro — yes, even to the last . . . and then, there was always the haunting shade of Nemesis who would materialize, one fine day, on her doorstep in the shape of some clumsy oaf of a relative, a nephew, a second cousin, looking for the fabled member of the family who had got an education and gone out in the great world and become no doubt rich and would be glad to help them do as much. Her fears had lessened as time passed and no one came, but the danger was real, just the same. She pored over her red and gold address book, turning the pages slowly, marking a name here and there: circumstances change, so do telephone numbers: people find new homes, and hearts new dwelling places too; she must not expect miracles, but just the same, she would write half a dozen discreet notes to older admirers she felt she could trust to be pleased to hear from her again, and there was one in Bremen: to him she would announce the ship, the date, the place, the hour of her arrival, and unless she had lost her womanly intuition altogether, he would be at the shipside to greet her, yes, even with flowers as in a happier time.

"Why David, I hadn't realized," said Jenny, when they were safely out in the open. "How on earth do you put up with that fellow in your cabin?"

"It isn't my cabin, altogether," said David, reasonably.

"Don't split hairs," said Jenny, "you know perfectly well what I mean. It's an outrage."

"That's what I thought too, at first. Now it's just a bore. But he was really on his best behavior just now. I was surprised."

"Exhausted after the chase maybe," said Jenny. "Let's look for something to buy. We didn't buy a thing in Cuba. What kind of tourist is that?"

"What do you want?" asked David, as they walked towards the row of shops on the far side of the plaza.

"I don't know, let's give each other a present." Something of the charmed mood of Havana was in them both again; they caught hands for a moment, and peered into the doorways of shops. "No baskets," David said, and "No dolls and animals," said Jenny, as they passed, "no pottery, no jewelry, yet, David, it should be a piece of a native or local art, shouldn't it?"

"Maybe," said David doubtfully, "but no sandals, no leather or woodwork."

"No lace or embroidered linen?" asked Jenny.

"Not for me," David assured her, firmly.

"Let's not think about it," said Jenny, rather wearily, "let's just go on looking around now and then, and see what happens."

Suiting their actions to her words, they looked around, and saw what happened. Mrs. Treadwell and Wilhelm Freytag, stepping out of a shop two doors away, wiggled their fingers in greeting and David, to his surprise, wiggled his fingers back at them with no reluctance whatever. Freytag asked, "Where are they? Did you see them?"

"He means our friends the zarzuela company," said Mrs. Treadwell, also with unusual animation.

"They're in there," said Jenny, pointing, "or were, a few minutes ago. Why?"

"They promised to buy the prizes here in Santa Cruz, remember?" Freytag asked David. "Well, they're picking them up at a great rate — it's something worth seeing!"

"Let's see it then," said David, but as they moved to enter the shop Ric and Rac rushed forth, and their elders followed them in a gracefully composed group, chattering freely among themselves, turning as one body to their right away from their observers, moving swiftly to a shop three doors away, and swarming in, the children running ahead.

The woman whose shop they had just left came outside to give her opinion of them. "Look out for your back teeth!" she shouted to the listening air. "Count your fingers! That kind don't come to buy!" With a grieving face and shaking hands she sorted over her tumbled disordered merchandise, then spoke dolefully to the Americans: "Pure linen," she told them, "real lace, all hand-embroidery, fine beautiful things, cheap . . ." but it was plain she had no hope, her luck was gone for that day, she made no real attempt to attract them. She was too distressed trying to find out what had been stolen from her.

Jenny and David, Freytag and Mrs. Treadwell entered the next shop after the dancers. Pepe, on guard at the door, stepped aside bowing slightly. The shopkeeper was waiting on Frau Schmitt, who was looking for real linen handkerchiefs, with a plain black mourning border. The sudden entrance of this mixed mob of strangers, whom she divided at a glance into respectable and lowlife, unnerved her. She had shown Frau Schmitt box after box of perfectly correct mourning handkerchiefs, but they were all too large or too small, too thick or too thin, the black borders too narrow or too wide, all too expensive or too cheap. In a panic she gathered up the handkerchiefs and spoke shrilly to Frau Schmitt: "Señora, I can do nothing for you! Nothing! Nothing!" for she saw in despair that the respectable strangers were standing back, and the thieving flock of crows was descending upon her.

Frau Schmitt, shocked, deeply hurt at such a change of manner, backed away, and saw with happy surprise her shipmates — not the Spaniards, she did not count them — the odd Americans, odd but nice, after all. She could not help but remember Herr Scott and his good feeling for the poor little woodcarver in the steerage — it was all very well to be stern and cold and right about everything, as the Captain most certainly was, but it was also touching to be human, to love one's fellow creature, to have mercy on the poor and the unfortunate. In a single thought, she was glad to see Herr Scott's face here in this unfriendly spot, even if it was like a wax face with blue marble eyes. The young woman with him she could not understand, the widow she did not trust, and Herr Freytag had most surely done wrong to pass himself off as a Christian when he was in fact married to a Jew . . . "Yet, oh God," said Frau Schmitt plaintively, and made the sign of the Cross with her thumb and forefinger, "what shall I do? Die of my loneliness?"

She moved nearer the group, and they all spoke to her, and smiled, so that she stood near them, and they all saw the same thing, each with his own different way of seeing. The zarzuela company went through their well rehearsed act with their unswerving attention to the business of the moment, with the same bold contempt for the bystander they had shown on board ship, and it was like a play: Amparo and Concha went to one side of the shop, calling to the shopkeeper, distracting her attention by holding up objects and asking the price loudly, both at once. Manolo joined Pepe outside. Pastora and Lola kept up a noisy conversation on the other side of the shop with

Pancho and Tito, now and again flurrying their way across to the shop-keeper, carrying some object, turning her eyes from Amparo and Concha, whom she rightly suspected as the ones worth watching. But the whole company was in constant movement, all over the place, running to the door to show Manolo and Pepe what they were thinking of choosing and asking their advice, then back to the shelves to pull down and scatter more stuff and turn it over. Ric and Rac bustled about, always at their best when playing in a show, begging and tormenting: "Please, Mama, buy me this, buy me that," brandishing whatever they had been able to pick up. Stern Lola then would threaten to smack them, order them to put everything back where they found it, and in a few minutes, sure enough, the whole company surged out of the narrow door, bitterly protesting there was nothing in the place worth having after all, or that they would never pay such bandit prices! This shopkeeper too was left in her little corner burning with helpless fury, all her goods in such disorder she would spend hours searching and folding and counting before she might miss what had been stolen.

It went on, in other plazas, with other witnesses. Herr Professor and Frau Hutten met them piling out of a little cubbyhole jeering and taunting a wild-eyed little man who cursed them for thieves. They laughed their bloodcurdling laugh, and flaunted on. Frau Hutten said to her husband, "They are just the same as they are on the ship! Is there nothing we can do? Where are the police? The Guardia Civil? They look so very able. Where are they? Should we not call them?"

Herr Professor Hutten gave her arm an affectionate squeeze; no doubt about it, what he had found most endearing in her, that quality which outlasted youth, beauty, slenderness, blue-veined breasts, hollow, sweet-smelling armpits and a firm rosy chin was this: her eternal female imbecility of faith that there was a power in this world existing solely for the purpose of rushing infallibly when called upon to the rescue of the innocent and oppressed . . .

"Call the police," she said, the dear idiot.

"Listen, my love," he said, "this is not any country we know, and its customs are strange to us. They cannot like us, we are from another country and speak another language —"

"We speak Spanish as well as they do, and maybe better," said Frau Hutten, with girlish vanity. Her husband made love to her often now, she was confident as a bride with him. Ever since the night the poor

Basque had been drowned rescuing Bébé, her husband had seemed restored to his first manhood again. It made her feel like a young woman, too: she was beginning to look at herself, and to plan what she must do to keep herself attractive; the first thing, to grow thin. The streaks of gray in her hair must be tinted. Her husband would undoubtedly find a professorship in a good German college. She would demand that he have a secretary to free her from the slave-work of research, typing, correcting proofs, the whole tedious existence of a professor's wife. She would save herself for love.

"You are right," she said, taking his arm, "it is not our affair, not in the least."

Frau Schmitt followed Herr Freytag and his friends a few steps into the street, but stopped when she heard him invite his party for a drink. All too obviously she was not included, in fact they seemed to ignore her. It was not of course, could not be, that they intended a rudeness to her; they were lighthearted careless people, thinking only of themselves. Frau Schmitt had her proper pride and it never failed her when she needed it most: wounded she might be, newly widowed and tender, but she would die rather than force her presence where it was not wanted. She returned to the ship after stopping to buy a little sack of candied fruits. She ate morsel by morsel as invisibly as she could, knowing well that only persons of inferior breeding would be seen eating in the streets. She could only hope she was not seen.

Herr Glocken, looking about vaguely for some article of attire to brighten up his shabby suit, fingered with envy the wide scarlet waistbands to be worn only by male dancers, the delightful white pleated bosoms, the coquettish narrow collars of shirts made for bull-fighters. The neckties seemed to be either narrow black strings, or so gaudy they could only be intended for masquerades or other fancy dress events. He fingered covetously a fine silk scarf in his favorite color, bright red, and was gathering courage to ask the price, knowing without asking that he must not afford to buy it, when the shopkeeper, a woman riddled with anxiety, spoke to him kindly: "Come inside — I have much better things inside, not expensive —"

Herr Glocken was not such a fool as to think her hardbitten face had a trace of coquetry. She wanted something, but what? Then he heard the all-familiar hateful sounds of the zarzuela company, and the woman said urgently: "Come inside, please. Help me watch them!" He followed her not so much to be of help as for protection, and he backed his hump against the folds of shawls and mantillas.

He saw that the woman was shrewd and wary. She greeted the invaders with a bitter voice, and commanded them all to stay out but one, one only, whoever they chose to come in and buy. As if she had not spoken they rushed and crowded into the little cubby, began pulling at things and asking prices, arguing among themselves. Concha saw Herr Glocken trying to hide. She called in delight, "Oh, look, here is our little luck piece!" and flew to touch his hump. Then each in turn added to the confusion by struggling to reach him. He defended himself by backing more deeply into the shawls and flattening his hands on his shoulders. But they touched him anyway, anywhere they could reach, slapping him sharply with open palms, until he could bear no more. In a panic he broke through and got to the open air, where Ric and Rac, on guard, shrieked and chased him to get their share of good luck, too. Blindly he careered into the Baumgartners, and just beyond them, the Lutzes. Mrs. Lutz again rose instantly to her duties as a mother: all in a breath, she tripped Ric with her foot and sent him sprawling, seized Rac by the arm, smacked her most satisfyingly, and spoke sternly to Herr Glocken: "Why did you not defend yourself? What were you thinking of?"

Herr Glocken, much grieved and ashamed, said meekly, "I did not think. It was like getting caught in a hornets' nest."

They went nearer the shop but did not venture in. The Spaniards were everywhere, the shopkeeper could not watch them all at once, she could not drive them out because they did not listen, but finally Lola, to fix her attention, with immensely prolonged haggling and fast talking and high contempt for the object, bought with hard money a small square of embroidered gauze with lace. Meantime the children had got back to their station; the desperate shopkeeper, wedged in a corner, shouted to them all to get out. Even as Lola handed over the money, and the woman was counting change, they all surged out into the street, and very plainly the watchers saw that the shapes of the company were all lumpy in odd places, and from under Amparo's black shawl there dangled the fringed corner of a pure white one.

They dashed across the plaza and hailed a large open conveyance drawn by a big sad bony horse. The women and children piled in upon one another first; Manolo, Pepe, and Tito squatted on the steps and Pancho crowded in beside the driver. "Hurry," he said, "hurry, we are late!"

"For what?" inquired the driver. "Look, Señor, this carriage is for six persons, you are ten; you will pay me for ten. I charge by the passenger."

"That's mere robbery," said Pancho, "I will not pay it."

The driver drew his horse to a stop. "Then all must get out," he said convincingly. Lola leaned forward and said, "What are we stopping for?" an edge of panic in her voice.

"We are being robbed," said Pancho, though without much force.

"Tell him to drive on, drive on!" screamed Lola. "Goat, mule! Drive on."

Pancho said, "Who are you talking to? Shut your big mouth!"

Tito said, "Listen, Pancho, you're not talking to Pastora. Lola's running this, don't forget. Get on there now . . ." and he said to the driver, who seemed to have gone to sleep along with his horse, "How much do you want?"

The driver roused to full life instantly and named his price. "And I want it in hand, now, Señor," with the self-possession and readiness of a man long experienced in human trickiness. "Now," he said, without lifting the reins, holding out his hollowed hand so that whoever had the money could put it where it belonged. Tito paid.

The Lutzes and the Baumgartners had wandered about, enjoying such pastimes as the island afforded, including the sweet heavy aromatic wines of the country, so festive and so soothing. Herr Baumgartner had taken two or three more than he should have, and had bought a bottle of Malavasia, promising his wife he would drink it instead of brandy. They now being chance-met at this place, Mrs. Baumgartner remarked that it seemed to be a fate that they were not to be free of those sinister characters the dancers for a moment — they had spoiled the voyage until now and they would go on spoiling it to the end . . .

"No, they leave at Vigo, thank God," said Herr Lutz, "and so do the rest of the steerage people."

"It will be a pleasant ship then," said Frau Baumgartner to Frau Lutz.

"I cannot think improvement will go so far as that," said Frau Lutz, quelling all hope, "but we have the right to expect at least decency. Those creatures," she said, bobbing her chin towards the old carriage lumbering away like an overcrowded bird's nest, "should be left here in jail, if there were any such thing as justice —"

"Instead of that poor Condesa," said Herr Baumgartner. "I am sure she was an innocent afflicted lady, suffering and not strong enough to bear her pains without the relief of drugs —"

"I never approved of that woman," said Frau Lutz. "I cannot find one argument in her favor, still I think it injustice that she should be punished for her faults — not that she doesn't deserve it — but that these worse criminals than she should escape without a scratch . . . Well, what do you expect of this world?"

Herr Glocken, who dimly resented Frau Lutz's tactless intervention in his favor, saving him but making him ridiculous, spoke up to get the talk down to facts. "They were stealing everywhere today, they have been cheating on the ship all the time — that raffle! — those children, those little monsters, stole La Condesa's pearls and threw them overboard —"

"It was never proved," said Herr Lutz. "It is not known whether they were real pearls, even — nor whether the object thrown overboard was her necklace or a string of beads —"

Frau Lutz broke into cold indignant speech. "My husband is very nearsighted," she said, "or at least, he does not see well. He cannot possibly know what went on when those children collided with us on deck. . . . I did see, and I do know, and it was a pearl necklace with a diamond clasp, and those unnatural children stole it and the girl threw it into the sea. That is all," she said, with sarcasm. "All. It is by no means enough to disturb anyone, we are wrong to concern ourselves with such peccadilloes —"

Herr Lutz rebuked his wife by speaking in turn to the others as if she were not present: "My poor wife has the highest principles, and no misdeed is too trivial not to call for hanging at least; I have never known her to overlook the slightest fault in anybody's character but her own, and it is no good to tell her that no matter what appearances may be, what circumstances may indicate, we must not rely on them as positive evidence, no, not even in the lightest cases —"

Frau Lutz spoke up firmly: "Elsa! You saw it too, did you not?" Elsa, who had stood silent and lumpish, looking away from her elders and hardly listening, started and answered instantly, "Yes, Mama."

Herr Baumgartner roused and reached to Herr Lutz to shake his hand, saying, "But you talk like a lawyer, like a good defense man, it is rare to find a layman who has any grasp at all of the great principles ruling evidence, that crux of all legal procedure . . . Congratulations! Did you ever read, perhaps, for the bar?"

"No, but I have good friends in the profession. In my business, I have needed them. They gave me good advice."

Herr Glocken was suffering from his sense of failure, of having run away when he should have stood his ground, to witness the zarzuela company do their thieving, to denounce them, to have seen them all arrested and dragged away to the *juzgado* — and instead of this heroic conduct, he had run, cravenly. He had let that Frau Lutz even defend him from children — children; what humiliation! He had then seen the dancers leaving with their loot, and so had all the others, and yet they stood there, gossiping all around the subject and never once admitting guilt or complicity. . . .

"We should have done something, that I know," he said to them all, and they all looked down at him with varying degrees of condescension.

"Can you think of anything?" asked Herr Lutz. "In my business, we take no notice at all of petty pilfering, what we lose on one customer we make up on another. We have a budget for replacing all sorts of portable objects — you'd hardly believe what magpies tourists are; it does not matter how respectable they look. So I do not take it seriously —"

Herr Lutz glanced at his watch and then at the sun. The great dark clouds were rolling up again from the east, just as they had yesterday. The others glanced too at their wrists and Mrs. Baumgartner said, "It is late. If we walk, we may miss the ship."

"It will wait for us," said Herr Lutz. But in all of them, the fog and glow of the wine they had drunk seemed to fade. Each face showed uneasiness to the others, and in a mild state of common panic, they hailed a caleche, and drove in unexpected state to the very foot of the gangplank, which was indeed prepared for rising. They scrambled up out of breath with only minutes to spare and joined the other passengers, who were lining up to witness the commotion of sailing. There were rumors of rising seas outside the harbor. The band started playing, "*Adieu, Mein Kleiner Garde-Offizier!*" and the shoals of Syrians prowling the docks trying to sell sheepskin rugs and opium scattered away.

As the strip of water widened between pier and ship, with Santa Cruz at the right distance taking on again its first beauty, the zarzuela company huddled at the rail in silence but with intent bristling attention, watching a frantic weeping woman on shore who shook her fists screaming desperate curses and accusations at the upper deck of the moving ship. One of the invincible-looking Civil Guards left his patrol partner to quell this unseemly disturbance. He turned the woman round by her shoulders and marched her briskly out of sight of the foreign ship and its passengers. It was part of his duty to guard against such bad propaganda. This kind of behavior gave the town an inhospitable appearance. "Keep away from here," he instructed the woman, harshly. She covered her head with her shawl and went away without looking back.

Jenny and David rested their elbows on the rail and Jenny said, "That's one station past. Now — David, I'm going to try for a French visa at Vigo —"

"If we stop at Vigo," said David.

"There's talk now that they will stop. All those dancers . . . and then I'll leave the ship at Boulogne."

"If we stop there," said David.

"We're going to stand out and a tender will come for us," said Jenny. "We'll make it."

"Who said so?"

"The purser."

"Who are we?"

"Mrs. Treadwell, and I, and those silly students. Oh David, do please come with me. It makes me sick even to think of your going on. What will you do in Spain by yourself?"

"What will you do in Paris?"

"That's a question," she said. They strolled around to the other side of the deck. "We're setting out tonight off the coast of Africa . . . there was nothing new or strange in Santa Cruz, was there? It could have been Mexico, crooked old streets and the sound of Spanish and the little markets and the colors of the plaster — but did you notice how it seemed strange in the new part of town where the real interna tional business is? Did you notice that brass plate on the brick wall saying here is a branch of the Bank of British West Africa?"

"Why, no," said David. "What about it?"

"Just for a second, I felt far from home, in a strange, strange land, and I didn't want to be there."

"Where is home, Jenny angel?" asked David, with the always unexpected tenderness that could dissolve her at her highest melting point; her eyes glistened, she blinked at him and smiled carefully.

"I don't know," she said, "I still don't know, but it is very far away." They leaned together and rubbed cheekbones and nuzzled a little and then kissed. David said in an offhand, take it or leave it tone, or even somewhat as if he did not expect to be heard, "We'll get French visas at Vigo and we'll get on that tender outside Boulogne harbor, and we'll land in Paris next day. I'm through with the argument, Jenny."

"Would you like me to cry on your neck, rubbing my nose on your necktie and dribbling tears down your collar, darling? I don't care who sees us," she said, wrapping her arm around his neck, nudging under his chin with the top of her head.

"Stop it, Jenny," said David, "where do you think we are?"

She straightened up and took her powder case out of her pocket. "We'll go to Spain a little later," she promised, "to Madrid and Avila and Granada and everywhere there is. David, if you want, let's go to Spain first and *then* to Paris . . . really, darling, I don't mind. I shan't care where we go, after this. Let's land at Gijón? And go on to Madrid."

Anger came up in David as if it had been patiently ambushed nearby waiting to be recalled to its natural place. It was her old trick of holding out until he gave way, then turning on him suddenly by yielding everything, pretending it was what she really wanted all along, leaving him bare and defenseless. But first he must give way. "I'll stop if you will . . ." "I'll do anything you want if you'll do what I want *first* —" Now having won, again, she was all for giving him the victory, for showing him how easy it was to be generous, to drift along with him in happy agreement — everything she should have done from the beginning without all this pull and haul. Now, of course, she was all set to take over the Spanish trip, to manage everything, starting with Gijón, a port he had never for a moment considered as a landing place. My God, now it was all to do over again, in a kind of reverse. His silence worried Jenny.

"David?" she asked, leaning gently and speaking in her "melted" voice. "What do you think? Wouldn't it be nice to go somewhere we'd never even thought of going, and just stroll through the country until we got to Madrid?"

David said, "Why Madrid, particularly? I hadn't thought of Madrid. I should like to stay along the coast awhile — Santander, maybe, or San Sebastián, or up to the French border, to Irún —"

"Well," said Jenny, feeling chilled, "anywhere you like."

"You seem to forget we're going to Paris," said David, "Spain's out, remember? We're going to Paris together, and then we'll see —"

Jenny turned upon him a severe, censorious face, not angry, nor wounded, nor intimidated, nor resentful — just a regard of critical disapproval, and she spoke evenly in her normal voice raised to the *n*th, David thought with a sour little humor.

"I wish you'd just make up your mind *once*, David, just once, and then *keep* it made up until we could get one thing finished, or one thing decided, or just even — well, this is like all the times you walked me two miles to a certain restaurant for dinner at nine o'clock, and then changed your mind at the door, and walked me off somewhere another mile, and more than once we wound up eating green tamales out of a tin boiler on a street corner . . . and is this whole trip going to turn out like that, too? Why don't we just jump overboard now and call it a day? David, what do you *want?*"

David let her words pour over his ears like rain off a tile roof. When the fishwife streak in Jenny's nature took hold, and her entire being fused all its elements into pure mindless femaleness condensed into words having no thinnest thread of a hold on reason, David's central knot of tension loosened, he felt pleasantly released from the burden of taking her seriously, of trying to answer, to explain or placate: any quarrel lost its edge, any queston of love its meaning; no man owed one iota of his manhood, one moment of attention, one shred of consideration to a woman who was all the same as jabbing him with a hatpin. With relief he saw Jenny, that so-special creature, the woman like no other woman, merge into the nameless, faceless, cureless pestilence of man's existence, the chattering grievance-bearing accusing female Higher Primate. Jump overboard? What for? He noticed that the waves were rising, the boat was beginning to plunge a little. That was a speech silly for Jenny even when she was talking like a woman.

"My mind *is* made up," he said. "You weren't listening, Jenny angel.

We are going to Paris, and that is settled, once for all." It seemed as good a place as any to run through this business and make an end of it — Berlin, Madrid, Paris, what would be the difference? "Let Spain alone for a while. It's time to begin arranging France."

"You arrange it," said Jenny, as amiably as if she had never spoken a bitter word. "We'll see what happens at Vigo." Then she said almost shyly, "You are a dear love not to take me up when I fly off the way I did. David, I don't expect you to believe it, but I'm perfectly happy — perfectly. Please don't think about what I said —"

"I won't any more," David said reassuringly, with good-tempered malice spreading like an inner smile all through him.

The dinner bugle sounded, but they delayed a few minutes. The ship was leaving the harbor, and the sea was so wild the pilot launch was almost swamped. The man at the wheel was drenched and had hard work to stay on board.

The pilot came down the rope ladder like a spider dropped down his web, and swung into the launch, which almost capsized. He took the wheel and nosed her away. After a good sharp tussle, the engine died. For a moment the pilot stood there, steadying the wheel, looking up at the tall bow of the ship louring over him. Jenny said, "Oh David, *look* at him!" She leaned far out, took off her square red scarf and waved at him in great circles until she caught his attention. He removed his sober pilot's hat with a beautiful sweep and waved back. David clenched the rail with both hands and leaned away, arms stiffened to the shoulders. He shuddered. Jenny lingered, her scarf dangling, her face softened and full of gaiety and tenderness. David took her arm and drew her away.

"Let's wait and see how he does," she said, but David had had enough of Jenny for one day. "He'll do very well, and now it's dinnertime," he told her, and she came along with one of her rare entirely fraudulent but well-played acts of complaisance. It usually meant she had thought of something else to do later that would amuse her more.

Jenny, tilting her first glass of wine towards David's, felt, she could not say why, that she was having the loveliest, most charming time of her life. David was somewhat wrapped up in himself about something, the ship was rolling with long, swooning swoops enough to chill the pit of her stomach, yet she was not chilled. The same tables were occupied by the same passengers, yes, nearly all of them present, looking much the same. She was sober, so it wasn't that delightful maze of Canary wine. The zarzuela company came in a little late, and seated themselves in silence with frowning faces; even Ric and Rac were not showing their usual spirits. Jenny said to David: "I heard they beat those children terribly about the pearl necklace — they beat them senseless. But they seem to be all right, don't they?"

"Who told you?" asked David. "I didn't hear about it."

"Wilhelm Freytag," said Jenny, "and the purser told him. And those students followed La Condesa to the little hotel where she went, and then took a carriage load of flowers from the market and stood them up against the walls under her window and got the servants to hang them on her balcony. But she would not come out, she would not speak to them."

"Who told you this?" asked David.

"Freytag," said Jenny, "while we were walking up the hill and you were lurking along behind."

"Lurking," repeated David, thoughtfully. Then he asked, "How had Freytag learned that, so soon?"

"One of the secret police who saw it came back to the ship before we left."

"I give up," said David, "I can't see where there was time for all this."

"There was, though," said Jenny, "it did happen."

David changed the subject. He observed the Spaniards with some curiosity. They were eating quite seriously without talk and hardly raising their faces, taking large mouthfuls.

"They might as well be Germans," said David, "but I suppose an afternoon of shoplifting makes you hungry."

Jenny poked lightly at the wilted lettuce leaves before her. "Wouldn't you think they could have got some fresh salad on the island?"

"Typhoid, maybe, or cholera," said David in a verbal shorthand, not to delay his mouthful of *Eisbein mit Sauerkohl und Erbsenpuree* to say nothing of a stack of fried onions.

"Fuddy-duddies," said Jenny, whose life in Mexico, far from intimidating her on the subject of germs, had given her a hearty contempt for foreigners who boiled everything they ate or wore, and missed all the lovely fruit and the savory Mexican food from the steaming clay pots in the Indian villages. Now she was not hungry, or not for all this substantial, overfilling stuff. She wondered again at David's appetite that never failed no matter what, like a particularly voracious bird rearing up its gaping beak with blind punctuality to swallow what-ever was dangled before it. At least, he had fairly good manners; he did not wolf or gulp or gobble or crunch or talk with his mouth full. Those stingy old aunts may have starved him out but they had taught him how to eat civilly what little they gave him. Still it was astonishing; he went on methodically reducing his plateful of food to the bare surface, then he took more. He could not leave a crumb or morsel of anything before him, and this was not only at breakfast, lunch, and dinner but midmorning broths and teatime sandwiches. Yet when his eyes strayed looking for another mouthful, downward and sideways, his eyelids had a pathetic, famished tightness, his mouth opened slightly in a spurious air of neglected orphanhood that hardened Jenny's heart every time she saw it. Her joyful mood turned into mischief and she began revising David's personal history. A changeling, of course, that is what he is. Those playful little pixies came and stole a mother's own boy out of his cradle and left one of their monsters instead. You've got all the signs, my poor David. That child eats and eats and never gains an ounce and is always starving; no matter how much he is loved he can't love back again; he can't feel pain either in himself or for others; he can't cry for anything and he doesn't care how much trouble he makes for everybody; and he takes all he can get and he never gives anything, and then one day, he disappears without a word, he just goes. "That is what becomes of those no-good fellows," said the old Scots nurse when Jenny was six. "And so many poor mothers think their willful boys have run away to sea, or gone to roam the world in India or Africa, or the wild deserts of California, and they wonder, poor souls, after all they have done for the ingrates. But they don't know they've been warming a viper all that time — no, and those creatures aren't anywhere in human life any more, they've gone back to their own Bad People, and forever after they help to steal children and put changelings in their places!" A question occurred to Jenny at last, but years afterwards when it was too late: "What did they do with the children they stole?"

The steward took up David's plate at last and set down a huge apple tart covered with whipped cream. "I'm *famished*," he said to Jenny in friendly confidence, squashing into the mess with his fork.

What did they do with the children they stole?

Jenny glanced around and said, "Everybody looks tired. It's just the same as we were in Veracruz, or in Havana. We all remember we're strangers and don't like each other. We're all on our way somewhere else and we'll be glad to see the last of each other. God, I'd hate to think I'd ever get even a postcard from anybody on this ship again, as long as I live!"

David speared another forkful of apple tart. "You mean even Freytag?"

Jenny put down her idle fork and picked up her napkin and dropped it. "All right, David. Sleep well. Good night," she said, blazing. She rose with her flying lightness as if she had springs instead of muscles and took off at top speed in her tight little walk but as if she were on skates. . . . David finished his dessert and drank his coffee.

The voyagers straggled out of the dining room and took a turn or so about deck and disappeared. Portholes were darkened early. The Captain on the bridge swallowed his bismuth and went to bed, abandoning the fiction that he and not the second mate was getting the ship to sea after the pilot left. The purser doing his paper work sent for coffee and cake, nodding and waking as he ate. Dr. Schumann, as if walking in his sleep, made a round of the steerage, treated the baby with the infected navel, gave paregoric to a man with cramps, dressed the cut forehead of a man who had taken part in the steerage brawl, and did what he could to pass the hours of this disastrous night, as he felt the sea and distance and time itself piling up between him and the island he would never see again, had not in fact seen at all, except as a steep road from the dock with a small white carriage climbing away slowly taking with it all the vanities and illusions of his life. Father Garza could say as much as he liked "Deal with her as with a scarlet woman, an incorrigible heretic, do not set foot in her snares," but these words changed nothing, meant nothing. He walked around the deck and waved a greeting to the ship's band, folding up for the night after a token tune or so; stepped round the sailors who had the ship to themselves, such healthy fine young animals, with not a shaky nerve among them, lucky dogs; in the whole crew there was not a sick man among them except the boy with the floating kidney, who still presided over the deck games, and seemed to be no worse for it, though no attention had been paid to Dr. Schumann's recommendations for his treatment. Dr. Schumann resisted his impulse to ask the boy how he was getting on, and barely glanced in passing, without his habitual twinge of commiseration, at the handsome young man, a perfect specimen of pure mindless well-being, wheeling the crotchety little dying man for a last breath of evening air. Noticing again the sulky, scowling face secure in its instinctive self-righteous resentment, Dr. Schumann felt the swift sting of a strange envy of that preposterous cruel innocence.

They seemed to be setting out along the coast of Africa, Herr Glocken decided, following the end of his finger across the map of an atlas he picked up in the library. He was troubled with his recollections of the day just past in Santa Cruz, not the town nor the people in it, but himself and his own unhandsome part in events witnessed by passengers who would be sure to despise him for lack of presence of mind, for cowardice, even. The very shape of the word in his head gave him cold shudders. He ached steadily all over, in his veins and in his bones, his teeth throbbed, and a double dose of his medicine did very little to ease him. He ate his dinner to keep up his strength and went to bed early to be free of his cabin mates for an hour. He tucked himself in on his side under his blanket, doubled the pillows under his head, and opened his big flat unwieldy book full of facts that might help put him to sleep. "Latest maps," the foreword announced, ". . . all countries . . . all states . . . the heavens . . . voyages of discovery . . . statistical information on oceans, lakes, rivers, islands, mountains and stars . . ." Herr Glocken could see plainly on his map under his finger that indeed even now the ship must be reeling along the indifferent coast of Africa that had no port on that shore. What was the difference to him where he was, or what doing? He fell asleep.

David sometime later found him there breathing slowly, the light still on, the open atlas spread over his face. David removed the book and turned out the light without disturbing him. He then remembered seeing Denny in the bar, by now so sopped in alcohol David half expected him to ignite spontaneously every time he lighted a cigarette. No such luck, though; he would come in late falling over everything in the place, stinking and sweating and mumbling; on second thought, David drew Herr Glocken's curtain close, turned on the light again as a guide to Denny, went to bed and drew his own curtain. The very top of his mind seemed to be the only part of it that was working at all, or at least, any voice he could hear, and that kept stupidly repeating like a parrot: "To hell with it. Jump ship. Just get off at Vigo and keep going. Jump ship. To hell with it. . . ." The clamor went on until it came to him that he might as well be counting sheep. He counted sheep slowly and breathed very deeply at the same time, an exercise his mother had taught him at five years, when songs and bedtime stories could not quiet him any longer. The old trick worked again, good as new; he waked next morning much refreshed to Denny's loud yawns and groans, Herr Glocken's pleadings for someone to give him a glass of water, and the peremptory call of the breakfast bugle.

Jenny woke early and looked out of the porthole for news of the weather. The sky was pale, sunless, the water was gray and silver-speckled for the first time. She was chilled and pulled on a sweater when she dressed. The ship had crossed some line in the night, it was not summer any more, but early fall.

Elsa opened her eyes and stretched and got up to the porthole to breathe in the dampness with delight. "Oh, look," she said, in gentle wonder, "oh, it is like Europe now, all misty and dim and soft, I remember it now. It is like coming home already. It seems strange I ever lived in Mexico. . . ."

"But Switzerland is all sunlight and color, or so I have heard?" remarked Jenny. "I thought they had nothing but sunny weather. And snow. All the travel folders say so."

Elsa brought her head in and around from the porthole. Her ungirlish face was softened in a near-smile, not very becoming, perhaps, but a change from her habitual bewildered sadness.

"Oh no," she said with a queer earnest pride, "in St. Gallen we have fogs and rain like anywhere else. Oh," she breathed out despairingly, "maybe it will be better there."

The bulletin board once again bristled with seagoing information: ship departures and arrivals, maritime strikes and other disturbances in world ports; troubles in Cuba, troubles in Spain, troubles in Germany, knots, latitudes, longitudes, sun risings and settings, phases of the moon, today's prophecies of weather for tomorrow; besides the games and horse races and moving pictures and the ship's pool; and an announcement by the zarzuela company that the long-awaited gala evening in homage to the honored Captain of the *Vera* would take place this very evening, with a dinner, music, and dancing, a brilliant performance of comedy by the members of the zarzuela company, hosts of the evening; and a final drawing of numbers for the splendid prizes offered to the fortunate holders of tickets for the raffle. Fantasy costumes and masks. Seating arrangements at all tables to be changed for the sake of festive novelty. A few tickets remained unsold; Doña Lola or Doña Amparo would be happy to oblige whoever wished to purchase. A special view of the prizes would be offered at the morning refreshment hour in the bar. All cordially invited.

Several of those who had been targets of rude remarks on this subject now drifted by with wary side glances — Herr Glocken, the Baumgartners; Herr Rieber, taking advantage of Lizzi's absence, no telling what those guttersnipes might think of next; and even Freytag, moved by curiosity only, stopped to read.

"Quite a change of tone," he remarked to the next comers, Frau and Herr Professor Hutten, "sinister, I should say. Isn't it a little late for them to be practicing manners on us?"

"*Good* manners, yes," said the Herr Professor, carefully, "after all the other kinds they have been giving us. But a change for the better, I should say dear sir, even if only superficial, temporary, and for unworthy motives —"

"What other kind could they have?" asked Freytag, feeling cheerful all at once. There was something about the way the Herr Professor took on any subject or situation, on a moment's notice, poured it into the mold of his own mind and handed it back to you all in one piece, without a seam, that put Freytag in a good malicious humor. It took genius to be such a bore as that.

Frau Hutten signaled to Bébé by a small pull on his leash. Her husband took the hint and they went on to the bar. Frau Hutten could hardly wait to see what those thieving dancers had managed to bring on board. She was not the only one. Lola and Amparo, looking remarkably fresh and somewhat less scornful than usual, stood on each side of a narrow trestle table with a kind of display rack above it, a makeshift got up for them by the barkeeper and the commissary stores man together, and they had a quite presentable show of loot; somewhat on the feminine side, perhaps, as if meant for women to win for themselves or men to win for them. "It's all right if you like lace," David said to Mrs. Treadwell, and she smiled vaguely as she passed and said, "I do like lace usually, but not today." There were a number of fine carved tall tortoise-shell combs, an assortment of lace tablecloths, a gauzy black lace mantilla, a large white embroidered shawl, bright-colored scarfs, a rather coarse lace bedspread, an assortment of black and white lace fans, two ruffled petticoats, and a length of airy white embroidered linen. Frau Schmitt could not decide whether this linen was meant for altar cloths or petticoat ruffles. In any case, she refused to covet it, or even to admire it, for it was stolen, and those people should be denounced and punished. But who would denounce them? And to what authority? Who would listen to her? She had troubles enough, griefs enough, she could not bear the thought of one more snub or piece of neglect from anybody about anything. This was a terrible, evil world and she was helpless in it. She reached out and rubbed the linen tenderly between thumb and forefinger. "Beautiful, beautiful," she said in German to Amparo, almost under her breath. Amparo instantly extended her right hand full of tickets and pulled one from the pack with her left. "Four marks," she said, as if Frau Schmitt had asked for one. "Wait," said Frau Schmitt, rather breathlessly, fumbling in her change purse.

Denny, a good deal the worse for wear, had nonetheless succeeded in overtaking Pastora for a moment. They were at a table near the bar. He was drinking restorative beer, she was sipping a cup of coffee and watching him acutely over the rim of her cup. He later reported to David that he never had really caught on to what they were up to, but Pastora made it all sound like good clean fun — "just a regular *baile*," he said, "sounds like one of these hoedowns the greasers are always having around Brownsville. Well, let's go. Anyhow, I'm collecting off that gal tonight or I'll damn well know why not." Meantime, he decided to lay off the liquor, take a good sleep and get himself in shape for the hoedown.

Herr Baumgartner's favorite theory was that a social occasion was a sacred duty, to be performed as well as one was able no matter what one's private condition of mind or body. His parents had observed this at first with some approval as the normal fun-loving spirit of childhood, later with some dismay as they saw that he would leave any family task undone, all study hours neglected, all household rules ignored, even defied, to run after the most trivial fleeting pleasures, often in most undesirable company. Frau Baumgartner, after long experience with her husband's vagaries, agreed with his parents that there was an incurable streak of frivolity in him. In spite of all, she had never succeeded in refraining from wifely warnings and cautions, not against innocent pastimes, who could disapprove of those? but the late hours, the drinking, the prolonged card games with inevitable loss of money; all the male amusements of the *Turnverein*, bowling, singing half the night, steins in hand; running off to the street fairs with a set of cronies to shoot at clay targets and make himself sick on Mexican food, bringing home an armload of trashy dolls and vases and mechanical toys too childish even for Hans, who dutifully pretended to be pleased with them. Ah well, she had done what she could, and yet — was it her fault that her husband, who loved her, she was sure of it, who had been so delightfully merry-hearted in their first years together — who, she could never deny, had been until late years a devoted husband, father, provider — was it her fault that he could not find any satisfaction in the joys of home, the gentle domestic habits, the company of his dear family? She began to fear that she would never know.

She was therefore not surprised, but unpleasantly impressed, when in midafternoon he began rummaging in the crowded cabin, fishing out oddities of costume suitable for Mardi Gras or shipboard parties. He tried on her red and white plaid jacket, which sat on him with just the right misfit for comic effect. "What are you doing?" she asked, knowing the answer before he spoke.

"But I cannot understand!" she cried. "What have we to do with those terrible people, who cheated us out of our money and then stole everything they could lay hands on in Santa Cruz . . . we saw them. Why, why should you go to their party?"

"It is a party, just the same," said Herr Baumgartner, seriously, tying on the shaggy whiskers that had frightened the little Cuban girl. "I feel we should not be skeletons at the feast. At least the children should be allowed a little enjoyment." He smiled at Hans, whose face was shining happily as he watched his father's preparations. "*They* are innocent," he said unctuously, "why should we punish them for the guilt of their elders?"

"What innocent children?" asked Mrs. Baumgartner, with a severe glance at Hans, who winced. "Innocent? You mean those criminal twins who threw poor Bébé overboard and caused that poor steerage wretch to be drowned? Do you mean them, too?"

"Why not?" asked Herr Baumgartner, with the irrelevant piety his wife always found so exasperating. "God must be their judge, not we. It is not even proved that they did it, you know."

"Not proved!" said his wife, purposely keeping her voice down. "What proof was needed? Who else on this boat, who in the wide world but that pair would have been capable of such a thing? Oh, but *you* are the innocent one, after all."

"I hope I have managed to preserve a little of that blessed quality after all these years," said her husband smugly, putting on a huge red papier-mâché nose by means of wire hooks over his ears. "What I am doing is quite simple. I shall get some toys for the children, and try to amuse them a bit — that is all. But my dear, I wish you would be a little kinder sometimes about these happy little occasions."

"I don't mean to be unkind," she said, stricken, "it is just that sometimes I do not quite understand . . ."

"Please dress up a little," said her husband, "wear your pretty Bavarian peasant dress you used to wear to our parties in Mexico. Do that for me," he wheedled, his eyes glazed with tenderness over the clownish red nose.

"I'll think about it," she answered, and her husband understood at once that she would do it. Hans, sitting by with a large paper cowboy hat on and a small drum hanging around his neck, waited patiently as always for the dispute to end and the next thing to begin. When his father said, "Now, my Hans," he leaped up and took a step towards the door. His mother's voice with the familiar warning note in it chilled the back of his neck and stopped him in his tracks.

"Come and kiss me," said his mother. This done, he and his father escaped together, his father frowning as if he had a stomach ache again. Before they appeared on deck, Herr Baumgartner paused, and fished out of his back pocket a paper brownie cap given him by a steward, and pulled it down over his ears.

"Now," he shouted gleefully, bending down to Hans's face, "tell me, what is my name?" And he did a hop-skip-jump sort of dance in a circle.

"Rumpelstilchen!" shouted Hans, at the top of his voice.

"Right!" bawled his father heartily, and they hurried forward, feeling that the party had already begun.

Jenny sat on the edge of her chair in the late afternoon light, sketching a sea gull in flight, from memory. She had filled several pages, everything from a half dozen hasty dashes that might be a bird of some sort in flight to a tight drawing of a sea gull's head encased in a design of feathers that resembled chain armor. Everything wrong, as usual. David sat near, reading *Don Quixote* again, perhaps for the dozenth time — "Nothing like it to warm up your Spanish," he said; his sketchbook tied with a tape was propped beside his chair. Since she had made the scene about showing him her drawing, he no longer sketched in company with her, and never asked to see what she was doing. Jenny pretended not to notice, wondering how long he would hold out.

"I think I'll go now, time to change," she said. "The steward may be able to get me an extra shower."

David without raising his eyes from his book inquired carefully: "Are you really going to dress for this fool party?"

"No, *change*," said Jenny, "I always do, every evening. Hadn't you noticed?"

Herr Baumgartner appeared at the head of his parade, twirling a stick like a drum major, doing the goose step, the children goose-stepping after him in shrieking disorder. The commissary had distributed trumpets, drums, matracas, whistles, which they rattled, struck, beat, blew as they pleased. Hans marched beside his father, the small Cuban boy and girl came after, and Ric and Rac drew up in the rear, knocking dried gourds together and beating a drum, with a strange look of almost childish pleasure in their faces. Jenny stood smiling as they approached, and applauded lightly. Herr Baumgartner glared at her over his false nose and called out with joyless vehemence: "Why don't you join us? Why don't you help?"

"You don't need it," answered Jenny, but she followed them, just the same, and David held his breath for fear she would break into a goose step; she was more than capable of it, she could not be depended upon one minute not to make a holy show of herself. He had a horror of female clowns, and it came over him miserably in moments like this that Jenny had more than a streak of low comedy in her nature. He watched her disappear into the bar in the wake of the miniature carnival, still walking sedately but clapping her hands in marching time, for Hans and Herr Baumgartner were now singing breathlessly, "*Ist das nicht ein gulden Ring? Ja, das ist ein gulden Ring . . .*" while the twins and the Cuban children simply shrieked more or less in rhythm. They marched around tables swinging their legs straight up and out, the drinkers seizing glasses out of the way as they passed.

Herr Baumgartner stopped singing long enough to admonish the gathering to right and left, with his anguished frown and grieving voice: "Why don't you join us? Why don't you help?" and though the little merrymakers were favored with the kindly glance and sweet smile customary to such occasions; the all-too-brief joys of childhood were of course sacred, no matter how boring they could be, sometimes; yet nobody stirred from his place, nor turned his head after them when the disturbance passed. Herr Baumgartner concealed his despair, and went stamping out on deck, keeping up the spine-shattering goose step he had loathed all through his military service. He led them once around, and turned them loose near the bar, where each child might find his family — except Hans, who was sent back to his mother as if he were being punished for something. He went, carrying his toys, ready to cry; what had happened, what had he done? The other children separated at once without a word or glance exchanged, each hugging his loot, and forgetting Herr Baumgartner instantly. Herr Baumgartner wanted only to be forgotten, and to forget: he longed only for privacy, invisibility, and a bottle of brandy. Failing all, he asked for a stein of beer, and sat over it with a face of guilty apology, not daring to drink brandy until his wife came; she had made him promise solemnly he would never again drink except when she was with him. After a few minutes' brooding, he remembered to take off his whiskers and nose and brownie cap. When his wife joined him, with Hans, just before dinner, wearing her lacy headdress with ribbon streamers, her ruffled blouse and abundant skirts, freshly powdered and smelling of *eau de lilas*, he set down his third stein of beer and leaned toward her gratefully. "My Greta, how lovely you are — my same little girl. You have not changed since our wedding day! All these years —"

"Ten," she said, with good-tempered abruptness, "and you are very forgetful. You promised not to drink except —"

"Ah," he said, jovially, for his stomach was eased and warmed, "I thought that meant only brandy!"

"No," she answered, "nothing was said about brandy. You were never to drink alone!"

He chose to be whimsical. "Not even lemonade? Not water? Coffee?"

"Nonsense," she said, a little edgily. "You are talking like a lawyer. We both know what you promised. And I do wish you wouldn't wear my jacket. You are stretching it out of shape. I do not think a man should wear women's clothes, even in a masquerade." She looked around uneasily, but the bar was nearly empty. "People talk," she said.

"I'll find something else," said her husband, miserably.

"Why?" asked his wife. "It's too late now — everybody has already seen you . . . I think I'll have a beer, too."

Hans sat elbows on table, chin in hand, waiting until one or the other of them would remember to ask for his raspberry juice.

Freytag went in, thinking of a bath and shave, and found Hansen, half dressed, sprawling in the upper berth with his bare feet dangling.

"What's the matter? Seasick?"

Hansen's great worried face hung out over the edge. "I, seasick?" He seemed ready to take offense. "I was born on a fishing boat."

After this personal confidence, if it was that, he rolled back and gazed upward. "I am thinking."

Freytag stripped off his shirt and started the warm water in the hand basin.

"I am thinking," said Hansen, "about all the things people everywhere do to make each other miserable —"

"What was your mother doing on a fishing boat?" asked Freytag. "I thought no woman was allowed to set foot —"

"It was my father's boat," said Hansen, gloomily. "Look, the big trouble is, nobody listens. People can't hear anything except when its nonsense. Then they hear every word. If you try to talk sense, they think you don't mean it, or don't know anything anyway, or it's not true, or it's against religion, or it's not what they are used to reading in the newspapers . . ."

At this point Freytag stopped listening and devoted his whole attention to brushing lather on his face. Balancing expertly with the roll of the ship, he proceeded to shave himself with a straight razor, a feat of which he was proud. If any witness remarked on this, he was certain to say it seemed to him the only way to get a real shave. Not once during the entire voyage had Hansen noticed Freytag's way of shaving; he rubbed on readymade lather out of a tube and scraped his cheeks and chin briskly with a small safety razor, and appeared to be quite unconscious that there was more than one way of shaving. When next Freytag heard Hansen's voice he was saying: "No. They won't. In France, for example — all the bottles, white wine, red wine, pink wine, everything but champagne — the bottles have shoulders, no?"

"Quite," said Freytag, rolling up his socks and putting them in a brown linen bag with the word WÄSCHE embroidered in green.

"But now, you go to Germany — yes, just barely across the line, not even to Germany, just to Alsace — and what do you find? All the bottles without shoulders, bottles like bowling pins!" His wrathful voice shook Freytag's nerves.

No wonder people don't listen, he thought unkindly. What is it now, I wonder — that Spanish woman or Herr Rieber, or what? For he had discovered about Hansen something he had surmised a good while ago about most persons — that their abstractions and generalizations, their Rage for Justice or Hatred of Tyranny or whatever, too often disguised a bitter personal grudge of some sort far removed from the topic apparently under discussion.

This elementary fact of human nature came to him as a personal discovery about others, he did not once include himself in it. His own plight was unique, peculiar to himself, outside all the rules. His feelings about it were right beyond question, subject to no judgments except his own, and not to be compared for a moment to such shabby little troubles as Hansen's.

"It is such things," said Hansen, "men insisting to make bottles with shoulders on one spot; and not fifty feet away, on the other side of a purely imaginary line which would not exist except for the stupidity and greed of mankind, just to show their independence they make bottles without shoulders!"

Freytag felt patience settling and weighing down his spirits like a fog. "But the line is not imaginary, it is there to define something, to give shape to an idea, to express the language and ways of a certain kind of people . . . look," he said, with a glance at the knotted, impenetrable face above him, "nobody fights about the shape of a bottle. They fight about the differences in their minds that shaped the bottles differently in the first place. . . ."

Hansen sat up and roared: "But yes, yes, that is just what I am trying to tell you. That is what I am saying."

"I didn't quite catch that," said Freytag, folding his razor.

"Naturally not," said Hansen, his face so closed in despair his rudeness gave Freytag no offense. "Nobody listens."

Hansen sat up, put on his socks and shoes and hurled himself out of the berth, reached for his shirt hanging on the top bar, and said: "All is crooked, everything — look at these Spaniards! You know they are whores and pimps, nobody wants their party — but here we are, we all pay and we all go, like sheep! They blackmail, they cheat, they lie, they steal from everybody all over Santa Cruz, everybody sees, knows — what do we do? Nothing. And that poor fat man below — what was his crime? He said the word *Freedom* in front of a priest! So — then they break his head open and sew it up again so it cannot be said they did not take care of him, yes, even such an outcast as him. Religion and politics — what did I tell you?" His hoarse dull bellow rose almost intolerably.

"Ah, yes, so you did," said Freytag amiably, thinking what a restful cabin mate Löwenthal might have been if only he could have disposed of that Rieber, whom nobody wanted. Yes, even Rieber himself might be preferable to this obsessed suffering man. Suffering should be strictly private, he decided; it was part of the human privilege for a man to enjoy his own afflictions without having them mixed with someone else's — above all, he knew of nothing worse than to be offered sympathy for the wrong reason from someone who had no right to offer any sympathy at all. He was of course thinking of Jenny, who took the high ground that racial prejudice or any sort of prejudice was the symptom of psychic and moral disease, especially anti-Semitism, which was inexcusable and unpardonable on any grounds. He had been strongly tempted to interrupt her rhapsodic little homily by saying, "Why, I know lots of people who don't care for Jews, but you couldn't call them anti-Semitic — they're some of them very fond of Arabs!" She would never understand his joke on the precise meaning of a word, and it would be merely silly to shock and offend her. She was pleasant to dance with, and it was rather piquant, the way a curious innocence, naïveté, a priggish little moral earnestness rose now and then to the surface of her light chatter, like cloudy bubbles on a pool, causing you to wonder what strange fish swam below, or what drowned thing was sending up gaseous signals from the bottom. Mary would size her up in a glance, and dispose of her in a phrase — some shrewd and murderous flick of the tongue that need not be in the least true, or even near the mark, but it would be deadly and would make him ashamed of his interest in such a girl. Mary would never hear of Jenny — why should she? As he knotted his tie, he began to feel a tingle of excitement that rose to exhilaration, as if it were Mary he would find when he went on deck; as if the ship were even then being warped into the dock and Mary was there on the pier waiting for him, already looking for him with her field-glasses. His fantasy so lifted his spirits, so carried him away, that not until he was brushing his hair full speed with the pair of English whale-bristle brushes Mary had given him for his birthday did he realize that Hansen had fallen silent, and hastened to try to give him some sort of decent attention.

"They were certainly wrong to bash his head in," he said, carefully, "but I'm not so sure he deserves much sympathy. There must be something wrong with a fellow who will make a row at a funeral, and after all, of a poor workingman like himself. But you'd think he'd want to pay a little respect to the dead, wouldn't you —"

"Always the same," groaned Hansen, seizing the top of his hair with both hands for a moment, "respect for the dead, never for the living!"

"Let's go up and have a drink," suggested Freytag as a way out.

Hansen dropped his hands and shook his head. "I don't want a drink," he said, as self-centered and frank as a five-year-old. Freytag heaved a deep breath as he stepped outside, and shook his shoulders as if the Old Man of the Sea were clinging to them.

Mrs. Treadwell, her narrow hand on the rail, descending the stairs towards the dining salon, observed critically her reflection in the broad looking glass on the landing. Her gilded sandals exposed her toes with bright red varnished nails. Quite a good figure, she decided again, if a little on the flat side, and not such a bad head. She wished there were not those lines from nose to mouth, deeper on the right side, or that small shadow of a fold under the chin. With those away she would have nothing to worry about for a long time; but they were there, and to stay and to grow deeper, and to be joined by other shadows and folds and lines marking every step of the long solitary journey towards old age. Forty-six is the second awkward age. Which would turn out worse, to be fourteen, not child, not woman; or as she was now, not young, not old? What is expected of me now, I wonder, she asked herself as she had done at fourteen, almost in the same bewilderment. I still dance as well as I did, still ride, still swim, still like doing most of the young things I did like — still, still — what a terrible word. She had dressed herself carefully for a possible evening of a kind of enjoyment; she longed to be merry and light-hearted indeed, but how could she be since there was no one to be lighthearted with? A pink-faced young officer or two would spin her around sedately a few times at arm's length, but she loved dancing so much a dull partner was sometimes better than none. I wish one of those good-looking gigolos would ask me to dance, but of course none of them will, the little pests. They'll go on dancing and quarreling and making love to their sluttish girls — they're young, at least, and that's what's wanted. With a thin line forming between her eyebrows, a new one she had first noticed a few days before, she paused before the looking glass on the landing and examined her face sharply under the harsh light. It was true, she was old, she had not been young for years and she had not known it, nor feared it, nor even thought of it; now seeing herself clearly and without mercy, the way others must see her, it was bitterly obvious and impossible to believe. Her age seemed something temporary, outside of herself, a garment she could put off at will, a mask painted on her face that she could by some simple magic wash away at any moment in her bath. Oh dear God, I'll be paying gigolos to sit with me in night clubs if I don't take care. Soon there won't be anybody left of my charming friends to send me flowers and dance with me and take me to the theater. I'll be sitting by myself at corner tables or on terraces and a creature with waved hair and a border-line eye will come smirking up: "Dear Madame, will you be pleased to dance?" and I — no, I'll never, never never! I'm going to grow old gracefully as they used to warn me I must — in those days when I knew I was going to be young forever — with a fine false front of dignity. Nobody is going to suspect that I am that unfortunate girl who couldn't grow up, that under my sober old-lady skin I am hiding carefully my sixteen-year-old heart. That's going to be my own dreary business. The first thing I must do in Paris is to get everything new and more suitable to my years. Her thin light pleated gown, rose-red, with a wide gilded leather belt, falling smoothly from her bare shoulders over her sharp little pointed breasts neatly sustained by a harness of lace — all very pretty, but none of it matched her face, she noticed for the first time. Should I wear more black, I wonder? And if I painted my toenails green, would anybody really care?

Such a profound melancholy fell upon her spirits at this point, she had half a mind to turn back and change to an ordinary gown. David Scott, who had been following her, overtook her and stopped to speak, and to gaze at her with that pleased, approving glint which she knew well in the eye of a man and never tired of seeing. "You are looking wonderful," he said, in exactly the right tone; and this was so extraordinary, coming from him, Mrs. Treadwell took his arm and smiled at him with great confidence and charm. "You are simply a dear to say so," she told him and they walked on together. She noticed that his black knitted tie was a little crooked, his linen suit slightly rumpled, but no matter. She rested her fingertips on his forearm and kept step with him, reassured and consoled by his attractive unequivocal male presence.

"I thought, though," said David, "we had all agreed to ignore this party."

"Well, it is a party, after all," said Mrs. Treadwell, "no matter how it happened. I mean to dance a little, I should like to drink champagne, and I shan't mind in the least pretending that I feel a little better than I do — at least, now. Something even halfway pleasant, or just funny, you know? absurd — may happen. Think of those slummy dancers giving a party for anybody! Suppose they did steal the prizes and pick pockets besides? I didn't give them a penny, and neither did you. Why should we miss the show, if there is going to be one?"

"Oh, they'll get away with it," said David. "They always do."

"I get so tired of moral bookkeeping," said Mrs. Treadwell, gently. "Who are They? Why does it concern me what They do?"

David, chilled to the marrow at this hateful indifference, tightened his arm and drew it to his side impulsively. She lifted her fingers from his sleeve at once and dropped her hand to her side, and said, "For me *They* are just Others who bore me, or behave stupidly to me — anything of that kind. These Spaniards — what do I care what they did, or what they may do? They dance well, they are good-looking in their savage unkempt style, let them be amusing at least! What else are they good for? But even they make it sound dull with their horrid little unkind notices about people. . . ."

"It's a form of blackmail," said David, "and it nearly always works." He glanced at Mrs. Treadwell, whose attention had wandered. They were coming into the crowd entering the dining room, and she nodded lightly in several directions — to Freytag, who nodded back without smiling; to the young Cuban pair with their two children; to the bride and groom, who did smile; to the purser, who beamed at her with his broadest smirk; to anybody and everybody, David noticed, without appearing really to see anyone. She behaved in fact like Jenny, except that Jenny was looking for something, a response of some kind, almost any kind at all, always either a little too hard or too soft, with no standards that he could understand or believe in. An intense resentment against Jenny rose in him when he saw her at work trying to undermine him, to break down by any means his whole life of resistance to life itself — to whatever environment or human society he found himself in. He preferred Mrs. Treadwell's unpretentious rather graceful lack of moral sense to Jenny's restless seeking outlaw nature trying so hard to attach itself at any or at all points to the human beings nearest her: no matter who. It was just that he could not endure promiscuity. He almost forgot the woman beside him in the familiar hatred of Jenny which moved all through him in his blood; then he saw her standing near the wall below, waiting for him, looking upward, very beautiful in one of her plain white frocks that looked well at any time of day. She had the severity and simplicity of a small marble figure, smooth and harmonious from head to foot, no rouge or powder visible, no varnished nails, fresh and sweet as a field of roses: she was smiling at him, and he smiled back, with such a deep intake of breath that Mrs. Treadwell, glancing down, nodded to Jenny, then turned back to David. The whiteness and tightness of his face and the blaze of his eyes astonished her. "There she is," he said, and with the barest bob of his head to Mrs. Treadwell, he left her and leaped down the stairs while even then Jenny was coming towards him.

Herr Rieber had not for a moment given up his notion that he was still going to find ways and means to seduce Lizzi successfully and thoroughly. "Sometime, someday, somewhere, somehow," he sang to himself silently the refrain of his favorite popular song; but no, it must be done on the boat, tonight or never. Once he set foot in Bremerhaven there would not be a moment to spare; he was in fact to be met at the pier by several of his employees. He would be able to do no more than bid Lizzi the most amiable of farewells — amiable but formal, of course, and final — as he put her on the motor coach for Bremen. Since that unfortunate evening of the dog, Bébé, and all the confusion that followed, he had been able only once to entice Lizzi to the boat deck again; and that time she had been all modesty and reserve, refusing to allow him even to touch her in any way that mattered, until at last he had thought of a new strategy — that of humility and childish gentleness. He laid his head in her lap and called her his little lamb. She stroked his brow a few times, as if she were thinking of something else. As indeed she was. She was wondering why, in all this whirligig, Herr Rieber had never once mentioned marriage. Not that she wished to marry him — far from it. For a permanent settlement, and she had resolved that her next settlement should be permanent, wedlock locked and double-locked, secured with the iron bolts of premarital financial contracts, she looked, materially speaking, considerably higher than Herr Rieber. Still, it would never do to let any man run away with a situation, whatever it was; it must be clearly understood always — and not just by implications, hints, threats, glances, by mute understandings, but plainly in so many words — that she was a woman of the marriageable kind, and any amorous frolics with her were only preliminary to a possible march to the altar. Every other man she had known unfailingly pronounced the magic word "marriage" before ever he got into bed with her, no matter what came of it in fact. This one had not, and until he did, well! so far and no further.

Herr Rieber had not mentioned marriage to her, much as he might have liked, for the simplest reason in the world — he had a wife from whom he was legally separated, who refused to divorce him, was blameless herself in any lawful sense so that he could not divorce her. He was supporting her and three children, a family of four who detested him and whom he detested, who would hang on him leeching his blood for life. Oh what had he done to merit such a fate? Yet there it was, and Lizzi must never learn of his embarrassing predicament; it would be an intolerable affront to his pride. Besides, he was certain she would never understand, and why should she? Ah, the fine tall creature who moved like a good racing mare, oh, for a nice soft bed in a quiet hotel in Bremen even for a night and a day before he must go on. No such hope. It must be here and now, during the party those impudent guttersnipe Spaniards were so unaccountably giving "in honor of our Captain" — honor, indeed!

He went on a tour of the boat deck, selected a likely spot, indulged again in his day dream that after plenty of champagne and tender words, after long waltzing to soft music on deck, she would be melted and oozing like hot cheese on toast. He would then persuade her to take a walk in the beautiful soft night — the nights were growing a little cooler and windier — and the deed could be done in a twinkling, while everybody else was dancing on the lower deck or drinking in the bar. Such was his eagerness by now he even feared an unmanly incontinence at the great moment, but even the thought was too great a shame to face. In his imagination it all was as easy and uninterrupted and blissful as the happy ending in a child's story.

He had scrubbed and polished himself until he appeared to be lacquered, and with his playful mood at top peak he was wearing a white baby bib, and a frilled baby cap sitting on his bald head with strings tied under the chin. Leaving a solid wake of Maria Farina cologne, straight as a homing pigeon he bored his way through the crowd of confused dinner guests looking for places to sit, for the seating arrangements had all been changed about, with the usual place cards but no one knew where to look for his own. Stewards hovered being helpful and people followed them about blindly.

The one thing certain, common knowledge to all, was that the Spanish company were to be seated at the Captain's table, and none of his original guests went near it. Herr Rieber lowered his head and charged through a group and took Lizzi by the elbow, who screamed with delight at his baby cap. She was wearing a long green lace gown and a small green ribbon eye-mask, and wanted to know at the top of her voice however he had managed to recognize her! Herr Rieber pushed her firmly towards a table for two under a porthole. "We'll sit here, no matter what!" he cried recklessly and burst into song in a high tenor: "Sometime, someday . . . !"

"Somewhere, somehow!" Lizzi joined in, off key two tones above him. They bent towards each other until their noses almost touched and sang the whole chorus into each other's mouths. "Bring champagne instantly," he commanded the nearest steward, drawing out a chair for Lizzi himself. "At your service, *mein Herr*," said the steward, who did not belong at that table. He disappeared at once and did not return.

"Champagne, champagne!" shouted Herr Rieber into the air. "We want champagne!"

"Sometime, someday," sang Lizzi, and they were both overcome with enjoyment of her wit. They noticed that the Baumgartners, she in Bavarian peasant costume, he with his chalked clown face with false nose and movable whiskers, were observing them with particularly unfestive, censorious faces, their mouths prim and down at the corners, eyes glancing sidelong. The Cuban medical students came leaping in a line singing *"La Cucaracha,"* all wearing matelots and caps with red pompoms. They rushed upon their own table as if taking it by storm, and were prepared to defend it from a siege. The bride and groom, dressed simply as usual, went quietly to their own table, removed the cards and placed them on the table next to them, and sat smiling gently at each other. They opened the small packets beside their plates, unfolded the gilded paper hats and the noise-making devices and laid them aside. A bottle of wine was set before them, and they touched glasses before they drank.

A large square hand with fingers the same thickness from one end to the other, a rude-looking thumb attached to a palm powerfully secured to a muscular wrist covered with a thatch of hair that gleamed red under the table light, reached over Herr Rieber's shoulder and plucked the place card from its metal holder.

Herr Rieber's skin crawled coldly and colder still when a familiar voice brayed reverberating, outlandish, altogether repulsive German: "I am sorry to trouble you, but this is *my* table," and coming around where he could face Herr Rieber, Arne Hansen brandished the card under his nose. Back of him stood Herr Glocken, wearing a single large colored quill pen in his hair; his pink necktie flourished the words *Girls, follow me!* painted on it. Hansen picked up the second card from before Lizzi's plate and brandished that. "Can you not read?" he asked. "This says *Herr Hansen* and this *Herr Glocken.* So, I do not understand why . . ."

Lizzi reached out and struck him lightly on the forearm. "Oh, but dear Herr Hansen, do try to understand —"

"Please," said Herr Rieber, pulling himself together, the top of his head bedewed with large clear drops that shortly began to join and run, "please, Fräulein, this is for me to settle . . ."

"There is nothing to settle," bawled Hansen in his unmodulated voice heavy as a club, "nothing but that you find your own table and leave me mine!"

"Herr Hansen," said Herr Rieber, swallowing violently and shooting his chin out of his collar, the baby cap bobbing, "I cannot overlook your rudeness to a lady. Please meet me on the main deck."

"Why should I meet you anywhere?" bellowed Hansen, staring down at him overpoweringly. "I ask you for my table, you make trouble about that?" and he gave Lizzi a look of contempt that scalded her. She rose with her knees shaking and implored Herr Rieber, "Let us go, let us go," and walked away so swiftly he had to run to overtake her. "Find us our table," he shouted to the nearest steward, almost as ferociously as Herr Hansen. The steward said instantly, "Come with me, *mein Herr,* — never was there such confusion in this salon." But he seemed to recognize Herr Rieber, found their table quickly, pulled out Lizzi's chair, and said briskly, *"Jawohl!"* to Herr Rieber's demand: "Champagne, at once!"

"He *insulted* me," said Lizzi in a small whimper, and lifting her mask she dabbed at a tear. Herr Rieber had never seen her in such a mood. He was delighted in spite of its cause.

"Don't think of it again, he shall pay for it," he declared stoutly, mopping the top of his head and running his handkerchief inside his collar. "Let us not have our evening spoiled by such a lout!"

"He is always claiming your chair — remember that first day? I knew then he was a low person. He is a Bolshevik I think, from his talk . . ."

"Ha!" said Herr Rieber. "I threw *him* out that time! This is his revenge." The thought restored his good humor. "Now I shall make him sorry for this!"

"What will you do?" asked Lizzi in delight.

"I'll think of something," he answered her, beaming with confidence.

They watched furtively under their eyebrows halfway across the room while Hansen put on the red cocked hat at his plate, glanced around him sourly, and took it off. That hunchback Glocken was grinning like a gargoyle. He would have been glad of a fight, no doubt — he would be in no danger! "Will you look at that nasty dwarf," she said, as the champagne was being poured. "Why are such horrors allowed to live?"

"That is a great question," said Herr Rieber, beaming at her and mounting one of his favorite subjects. "As publisher my aim is to direct the minds of my readers to the vital problems of our society. I have lately got a doctor to begin a series of articles, very learned, very scientific, advocating the extermination of all the unfit, at birth or as soon as they prove themselves unfit in any way. Painlessly, of course, we really wish to be merciful to them as well as to everyone else. Not only defective or useless infants, but the old as well — all persons over sixty, or sixty-five, perhaps, or let us say, whenever they lose their usefulness; in bad health, exhausted, a drain upon the energies of the gifted, the young and strong of our nation — why should we handicap them with such burdens? The doctor is preparing to present this thesis, with the strongest arguments, examples and proofs drawn from medical research and practice and sociological statistics. Jews too, of course, and then all persons of illegitimate mixtures of race, white with colored of any kind — Chinese, Negroes . . . all such. And for any white man convicted of serious crime — well, as for him," he twinkled at her mischievously, "if we do not put him to death, at least the state shall make certain he does not bring any more of his kind into the world!"

"Wonderful," sang Lizzi in rapture, "then we would not have that dwarf around, nor that dreadful little man in the wheel chair either — nor those Spaniards!"

"And a good many more besides! To our new world —" said Herr Rieber, lifting his glass to hers, his spirits rushing back so merrily in his vision of the glorious future he almost forgot that no amount of extermination of the kind of people he didn't like could possibly include the one he liked least — Arne Hansen, who was himself one of the strong, the healthy, the useful, the powerful, the man who knew how to defend himself, who would always, ever and anywhere, find the chair marked with his name and take it, or take it anyhow, as he had done with Herr Rieber's plainly marked deck chair. That hairy paw, fit to grapple a lion, that jaw with the big square teeth —

Herr Rieber shuddered abruptly. Such thoughts could ruin everything — let it all go until tomorrow. He gulped his champagne as if it were the first swig from a stein of beer. Lizzi tossed hers down too, and he poured again at once, and ordered another bottle. The great evening was begun at last, and where might it not end? Herr Rieber was certain that he knew.

The purser, dodging and striking at the colored balloons floating in his path as if they were perhaps horseflies, halted at Mrs. Treadwell's table with a bottle in one hand and two champagne glasses in the other. "We Germans, *gnädige Frau*," he began, weightily, "are not allowed any longer since that war to use the word *champagne* to describe our German bubbling wine — not that we wish to do so. But I shall be happy if you will permit me to offer you a glass of our noble *Schaumwein*. I myself after many years' comparison am not able to distinguish between this and the very finest *Moët Chandon* or *Veuve Clicquot*."

"Naturally not," said Mrs. Treadwell, consolingly. "Do sit down, I'll be delighted. Have a chair brought, please." The purser stood, holding his bottle uncertainly, a faint mistrust of her cordiality blowing like a small cold draft through his congenitally clouded mind. He set it on the table though, and motioned to a steward to bring the chair.

Jenny and David sat at their own table watching the joyless, agitated scene, noting certain absences — Dr. Schumann, Wilhelm Freytag. Jenny had seen Freytag in the bar a few minutes earlier, where dinner was being served him at a small table. He stood up, bowed and called out to her, "May I have the first dance this evening?" "Yes," she called out without pausing, smiling back at him. She felt for the first time that the evening might not be a total loss. Pleasantly excited, she reached up and struck lightly at a balloon floating over her head.

"There," she said, "David darling, that is my contribution to this wild, wild evening." For when she saw David's face as he came down so swiftly to join her, with Mrs. Treadwell lingering so as not to come near them, she knew he was in love with her again, or trusted his feelings for her, or perhaps even believed for a moment in her love for him — no matter what, the blessed reconcilement was occurring again; and she felt such a warm surge of delight in him she had by internal violence to restrain herself from ruining everything by saying something hopeless and unanswerable, such as — "Oh, David darling, *why* can't we . . . *why* don't we, or why do we, or what shall we do or say or where shall we go, and why, why, when we have this, must we make each other so unhappy?" She kept silence and smiled at him, her eyes glimmering. David reached over and touched her hand. "Jenny angel, you're looking lovely, you really are," he said seriously as if he did not expect her to believe it. But she did, she believed it with all her heart, and saw him transfigured as he always was in these mysterious visitations of love between them — reasonless, causeless, having its own times and seasons, vanishing at a breath and yet always bringing with it the illusion that it would last forever. . . .

"You're looking wonderful too," she said.

Herr Löwenthal, alone at his table, his absurd paper bonnet askew above his censorious face, chose for his festive dinner schmalz herring in sour cream, buttered beets, boiled potatoes, and Münchener beer. The rather careless movements of the steward's hands caused him to glance up. He caught the brief shadow of a look he knew too well, a secretive, repelled, contemptuous amusement, ridiculing not only Herr Löwenthal personally, his whole race and religion, but his wretched dinner as well, symbol of his condition in life, his place as pariah in a swinish Gentile society: this dinner he had been forced to select carefully, even though it was not clean but only permissible, from a garbage heap of roast pork, pork chops, ham, sausages, pig's knuckles, lobsters, crabs, oysters, clams, eels — God knows what filth — until even nearly starved as he was, his stomach turned at the mere sight of the words on the card.

As the steward, a mild-looking young fellow, whose dislike of Jews was so ingrained, so much a habit of his second nature he was quite unconscious that it showed in his face, was about to pour the beer, Herr Löwenthal almost shouted, "Stop! That is not what I ordered . . . take back that bottle and bring me a stein of draft Münchener!"

The young man said, "I am sorry, *mein Herr*, but we have no draft beer left, and no dark beer at all. Only light beer, in bottles."

"Then in such a case, you tell me before, and I do the ordering," said Herr Löwenthal, furiously. "Do you pay for this beer, or do I? Who drinks it, you? What kind of place is this that you can change the order without telling the customer? Do you want I should report you to the head steward?"

The steward appeared unmoved at this threat. "As you please, *mein Herr*," he said in a respectful tone, and Löwenthal saw the shadow of that look again, undisguised this time — the upper lip curled ever so slightly, the naturally insolent blue eyes wandering for a second.

"Well, what are you waiting for?" demanded Löwenthal in fresh rage. "Pour it out, pour it out and bring me another!" He pushed his glass towards the edge of the table. The steward poured the beer, made a few ritual passes above the table as if refining his services, and went away swiftly. Herr Löwenthal then remembered his comic hat, snatched it off, crumpled it in his fist and kicked it under the table. He ate his potatoes and beets in chunks, piling herring and sour cream on them, the food sticking in his throat so that the beer could hardly wash it down. He had made a tour of the ship with some other passengers, and the sight and smells of the galley had sickened him. He remembered it again with loathing, the dirty cave below decks where everything was all the same as cooked in one pot; it was no good trying to keep clean, to eat decently, the way they handled the stuff it was dirty anyway from the start, enough to poison a man. He could not swallow another mouthful yet he was bitterly hungry. When the young steward came back with his second bottle of beer, he pushed away his plate and said: "Take this swill away and bring me a couple of hard-boiled eggs, and another bottle of beer."

For dramatic effect, the zarzuela company delayed their entrance until everyone else was seated. The Captain, who knew nothing of this strategy, took his place at his accustomed hour. Glancing round at the empty chairs surrounding him, he proceeded to order his dinner without delay. The decorations reminded him of grave ornaments in peasant churchyards. The center was a large mass of red cotton roses, mixed with shiny tinfoil foliage and lace paper flowers of an unknown species. A stuffed dove with a few feathers missing was perched beak downward on a stick above the floral arrangements, carrying around its neck a placard bearing in multicolored crayon the single word "*Homenaje.*" The Captain leaned forward in idle curiosity, even amusement at this childish display, and drew into his nostrils an almost lethal cloud of synthetic rose scent. Sitting back and turning his head aside, he breathed out as long as he could, then began to sneeze. He sneezed three times inwardly, one forefinger pressed firmly to his upper lip as he had been taught to do in childhood, to avoid sneezing in church. Silently he was convulsed with internal explosions, feeling as if his eyeballs would fly out, or his eardrums burst. At last he gave up and felt for his handkerchief, sat up stiffly, head averted from the room, and sneezed steadily in luxurious agony a dozen times with muted sounds and streaming eyes, until the miasma was sneezed out, and he was rewarded with a good nose-blow. This cleared his head, but further dimmed his view of this ill-advised, extremely dubious occasion, unlike any he had known in his whole experience. With his own hands, at arm's length, he shoved the pestiferous homage clear across the table from him. The dove fell off his perch and the Captain did not notice. He glanced at his watch, and it was almost a quarter of an hour past the precise moment when his soup should have been set before him. The Captain had not been kept waiting, not even in his own house, since he became Captain. He began to brood in ruffled, glaring, swollen immobility, extremely resembling an insulted parrot. His dignity demanded that he begin his dinner at once as a rebuke to their impudence, and to further ignore as far as he was able the presence of these guttersnipes from Granada, or wherever they came from. He glanced about him until his eyes rested coldly on several members of his scattered dining circle — the Huttens and Frau Ritters-dorf sat together, eating already, indifferent to the goings-on around them. That Rieber fellow and that Lizzi were behaving like monkeys as usual, waving glasses at each other. Little Frau Schmitt was sitting with the Baumgartners — at least he had been spared *their* company! He could not say he regretted the absence of any one of them, but he resented the reason for their absence. It was his due right and privilege to protect himself against the tedious society of his table, voyage after wearisome voyage of it; he could and did retreat to the sanctuary of the bridge, where he saw only subordinates, who would not dream of speaking until they were spoken to; who did as they were told instantly in silence as matter of course. That was his true world, of unques-tioned authority, clearly defined caste and carefully graded privilege, and it irked him grievously to be forced to concern himself with any other. He knew well what human trash his ship — all ships — carried to and from all the ports of the world: gamblers, thieves, smugglers, spies, political deportees and refugees, stowaways, drug peddlers, all the gutter-stuff of the steerage moving like plague rats from one coun-try to another, swarming and ravening and undermining the hard-won order of the cultures and civilizations of the whole world. Even on the surface, where one might expect at least the good appearance of things, what moral turpitude showed itself, given opportunity. He knew too well the respectable father of a family, or the trusted wife and mother, traveling alone for once, taking a holiday from decency as if they were in another country where no one could find out their names; as if a ship were merely their floating brothel!

His stomach burning, he dabbled in his thin soup, afraid of his food which had a way of turning and rending him. So — these Spaniards were no news to him even before he picked up the gossip and rumors about them from his table guests. It had all been abysmally beneath his notice, they were so obviously pimps with their prostitutes dis-guised as dancers in order to get proper passports, up to their shady tricks night and day. Anything would do, from scrounging money from passengers to stealing right and left from shops in Santa Cruz — he understood now the meaning of that howling leaping madwoman on the pier as the ship drew away; and the only question was, how had they managed to blackmail so many people, how had they got themselves seated at his table, where they had no right on earth to be, and what criminal effrontery had given them the notion in the first place? And what — this was the painful question, not to be answered: what had he been thinking of, to let such disorder thrive under his very eyes, and to consider it of no importance, something for the women to gossip about?

He resisted an impulse to leave the table then and there. It would be better to stay, to observe them further, to let their impudence run its course, and to chastise them publicly with his contempt at the right moment. The one thing necessary with such people was to control them, to keep them firmly in their place. Once you allowed them the smallest impertinence, they would edge in and crowd you out like that camel who got his nose into the Arab's tent, and after that, there was only one course to take: they must be put down with fire and sword.

The Captain was fascinated by American gangster films full of gunfights, raids on night clubs, wild motor chases between police and bandits with screaming sirens and spouting machine guns; abductions, roadside murders, bullet-riddled bodies streaming blood sprawled about the streets, with only now and then at long intervals a lone gangster being led to the death chamber in the last scene. He now entertained himself with dreaming, as he sometimes did, that he was turning one of those really elegant portable machine guns on a riotous mob somewhere, always from a splendidly advantageous position, swiveling it in a half circle, mowing them down in rows. At this point there was some confusion in his mind, though not enough to interfere with the enjoyment of his fantasy; for though he could not imagine himself as being on any side except that of established government, he had in fact noticed that it was nearly always the gangsters who were shown operating the machine guns. There was no good reason why this should be so, and it was a state of affairs which could only exist in a barbarous nation like the United States. It was true that all the Americans were devoted to crime and criminals, to indecent dancing and drug-taking in low Negro jazz cellars, a debased people who groveled in vice, and left their police to depend mostly on tear gas bombs, or hand grenades or revolvers, all more awkward and less effective than machine guns. Even supposing that an American policeman might possibly be an honest man, though very unlikely, why put him at such a disadvantage? If it had not been for the constant gangster warfare among themselves, killing each other off in great numbers, they might easily have taken the country over entirely, years ago! But it was common knowledge that American gangsters and police were in close partnership, one could not thrive without the other. The leaders on both sides divided the power and the spoils, and they took in everything, from highest government posts to labor unions to the gayest night clubs and even the stock market, the food crops — yes, and the international shipping, God knows! All all was one vast gangster's paradise, where only petty criminals and stupid policemen and decent workmen got killed or beaten and cheated. Besides the moving pictures which told him all this, the newspapers every day told him the same. In a word, the whole country was run by mobs of gangsters, there was not a single law in the land that they could not break as they pleased, and not a single man who would have dared to oppose them.

The Captain, from his eminence of perfectly symmetrical morality, a man who steered by chart and compass, secure in his rank in an ascending order of superiors so endless the highest was unknown, invisible to him, took deep pleasure in his apocalyptic vision of the total anarchic uproar of the United States, a place he had never seen, for no ship of his carried him into any port more interesting than Houston, Texas, with its artificial canal in a meadow in a part of the country far removed from any marks of civilization. It was narrower and duller than the river Weser that took him into Bremerhaven.

He reveled secretly in the notion of lawless murderous fury breaking out again and again at any time, anywhere — in some place he could not even fix on the map, but always among people whom it was lawful to kill, with himself at the center, always in command and control. Nothing worthy of his hopes of violence had ever occurred, not even in the war, where his part had been useful, honorable, if inconspicuous, as he was bound to admit, and altogether lacking in opportunities for him to exercise his real talents. This fate seemed to dog him: competent as he was to deal with the largest disorders and insubordination, here on his ship he dealt with silly rows, headcrackings in the steerage, a gang of petty knaves making themselves a nuisance: beneath his notice, yet he must deal with them.

He brooded on his vanished Germany, the Germany of his childhood and earliest youth, the only Germany whose existence he admitted in his soul — that fatherland of order, harmony, simplicity, propriety, where every public place was hung with signs forbidding this or that, guiding the people so there could be no excuse for anyone making a mistake; whoever did so disobeyed clearly with felonious intent. This made the administration of justice more swift and certain than in other countries. Set the very tiniest sign saying *Verboten* at the edge of a grass plot, and even a three-year-old boy who could not read should know better than to put his toe over the edge. He had not known, or perhaps had been guilty of inattentiveness to signs, because in childish ignorance or carelessness, he had put his toe over the edge of the grass plot near the little sign, and his father, who had taken him for his morning stroll in the park, had whipped him with his walking stick until his back was welted blue all over then and there, on the very spot, so that the lesson might sink not only into the culprit's mind, but furnish a public demonstration of the discipline parents should practice on their young. . . .

The Captain shuddered, leaped out of his revery, glanced at his watch and said to the steward, "Pour my wine please, and bring the fish."

At that moment the Spanish company erupted into the dining room in the full uproar of their professional native dress and arts, and bore in procession towards the Captain to the rhythmic strains of a popular bullfighter's entrance march, played on two guitars by Tito and Manolo to the light flutter of castanets on the fingers of the ladies, whose brilliantly smiling faces were masks in black, white and red. They wore flimsy red and white figured cotton gowns with long ruffled trains. High tortoise-shell combs filled out in front with cotton roses and draped with short black lace mantillas adorned their shining black hair. They glittered with sequined fans, jingled with necklaces, earrings and bracelets of colored glass and ornaments of gold-colored metal; their skirts, shorter in front, showed their beautiful ankles and feet in black lace stockings and red satin high-heeled slippers.

The men wore their uniforms of tight high-waisted black trousers, wide red sashes and short black jackets, their thin black dancing pumps with flat ribbon bows. Ric and Rac wore their bullfighter and Carmen costumes, a little disheveled from pulling each other back by clutching hair or garments, each wanting to go first in the parade.

The whole company circled around the table in a bright carnival of bowing and strumming and clacking and whirling, every face fixed in an intent smile. The Captain, monumentally remote, rose and returned the greeting with deadly courtesy. They responded as to an enthusiastic audience. At last the stewards pulled out the ladies' chairs, and they settled with excited little cries, like crows to a cornfield, Lola at the Captain's right hand, Amparo at his left; the others found their places at the much extended board and there at last after their long bitter fight, they found themselves seated at the Captain's table, the high place they were determined to be even if only once in their lives, and not only to be there, but to prove their right to the place they had won. Their smiles faded, their eyes were hard, glittering, savagely triumphant as they glanced around at the other passengers, some of whom were still pretending to ignore them. Let them! Not for a moment did they forget the point of their victory. They had come to do honor to the Captain, and they did him honor at length and in profusion. As food was set before them, grew cold and was taken away, except for Ric and Rac, whose appetites never failed, they rose in turn with lifted glasses and made speeches, each expressing in a slightly different arrangement of florid phrases the burning hope that this beautiful occasion would serve to bring those two great martyred countries, Spain and Germany, closer to each other, that the old splendid order might be restored — the Spanish monarchy, the German Empire, in all their glory!

The Captain began to squirm slightly as oratory piled upon oratory; when the political trend of their words became clearer, he turned pale with rage. He had never ceased to mourn the Kaiser; he loathed with all his soul the debased pseudo-republicanism of defeated Germany, and was shocked to discover that this ragtag bobtailed lot were claiming as it were relationship with him, calling themselves Royalists; they were toasting a high glorious cause to which by the very nature of things they had no right to adhere — they were only to live under it, as under the whip of their master. Royalists? How did they dare to say the word, much less call themselves that? They were the beggars whose place it was to line the streets and cheer when royalty passed, to scramble for the money thrown at the cathedral door after royal weddings, to dance in the streets at fairs and pass the basket afterward.

The Captain could hardly find the will to raise his glass, he felt he would choke if a drop of wine passed his lips in such infamous company. He suspended it a few inches above his plate with a nearly imperceptible flourish, nodded stiffly without looking up and set it down again. The zarzuela company rose stormily as if in a delirium of admiration, crying, "Long live your mother!" at which indecent familiarity the Captain blushed in deepest resentment. His mother had been dead for more than twenty years, and he had not liked her much when she was alive. As his invaders closed in upon him, leaning in until the beads of black wax on the women's eyelashes, the almost liquid oiliness of the men's hair, the intolerable stench of their perfumes, seemed to be rubbing off on his skin, tainting him forever, his grudging pretense of acknowledgment vanished altogether. His face grew sharper and dryer, he sat back with his hands on the arms of his chair. His former guests began to suffer for him, and their eyes began to meet from their scattered places in the salon, with a kind of unanimous agreement among them, for the first time: even Lizzi and Frau Rittersdorf shook their heads and frowned together, even the purser and Dr. Schumann, who had come in late, exchanged looks of disapproval. The young Cuban married pair, who had put their children to bed after an early supper, invited the Mexican diplomat's wife, little Señora Ortega, to join them at the table assigned to them, since she had been turned away from her own, and they were all looking for respectable company in the emergency. They watched the performance of the dancers around the Captain's table for a few minutes. The young husband remarked: "It is most inappropriate. When I bought those tickets for their raffle, I had no notion they were planning such impudence as this!"

"It makes one almost ashamed of being Spanish, doesn't it?" asked Señora Ortega, well aware of what the Spanish of Spain, even the lowest of them, thought about the Spanish of Mexico and Cuba . . . mongrels speaking a parrot Spanish, their veins rotted with Indian and Negro blood. "These are lower than Indians," she said.

"Ah well," said the young man, "they are only gypsies, from Granada."

"I was told," said his wife, "that they are even worse than gypsies — they are Spaniards calling themselves gypsies."

"Yes, and behaving like it!" said Señora Ortega. "But how I pity that poor Captain, and I never expected to feel sorry for him! I have always found all Germans very unsympathetic. After knowing so many Germans in Mexico, I say often to my husband, 'Oh, please be careful and never get yourself sent to Germany!' "

"My great-grandfather was a German, a businessman of Havana," said the young Cuban wife, rather unpleasantly.

"Oh," said Señora Ortega, dismayed. "I'm *so* sorry." They went on with their dinner in silence.

At the Captain's table, Lola took charge of the ceremonies by right. She turned, her eyes blazing with fury, and brandished her wine glass in all directions like a weapon, calling out in her deep voice: "Silence! I wish to propose a toast! To the eternal friendship of our two great nations, the Kingdom of Spain and the Empire of Germany, and to the great leaders who are restoring order and government to these countries in distress! *Viva!*" and *"Viva! Viva!"* shouted the others, in chorus, drinking down their wine. The Captain did not move, and not a glass was lifted except their own. Then Lola shouted again, her voice brassy with rage: "And to all selfish, obstructive, inhuman people who refuse to contribute their share or take part in this occasion meant to do homage to courage, to leadership, to nobility of mind and heart, to — in short — to *you*, my Captain," she said, bowing towards the Captain with her most brilliant smile, "to all who have tried to destroy the joy and beauty of this homage, eternal shame and confusion and dishonor!"

All the dancers, even Ric and Rac, shouted *"Viva!"* and swallowed their wine. The Captain, his head buzzing, not sure whether a toast or a curse had been proposed, for or against whom, rose and flung his napkin. The Cuban students at once leaped up waving large goblets of red wine, shouting cheerfully, "To eternal confusion! To dishonor! To shame! *Viva las Vergüenzas! Viva la Cucaracha!*" and they burst noisily into their song about the unhappy cockroach and her many privations. All over the salon voices joined in, a large untidy bawling at first which at once settled into a chorus, hands clapping, feet patting: *"Cucaracha, cucaracha, ya no puede caminar, Porque no tiene, porque no tiene, Marihuana para fumar!"* The Captain inserted his fingers into his collar as if he were being strangled, spat out the words "Thank you, thank you" between his teeth, and strode out of the salon charging blindly between tables.

The dancers ignored the situation, and all else except their chosen object; they trailed after him still crying *"Viva! Viva!"* though quite drowned out by the rowdy singing. At the head of the stairs they looked in vain for him; he had eluded them, had taken to the bridge like a fox to his burrow, and was not seen again for twenty-four hours.

Jenny broke down as David knew she would, and began swaying and patting and clapping her hands with the rest, singing at the top of her voice about the cockroach, going straight ahead from bad to worse, for each verse was a little more ribald than the one before, and

Jenny sang them as they came, until people at nearby tables began staring. She was the only woman singing. "My *God*," he said at last, in despair. "Do you know what you are saying?"

Jenny went on beating time hand and foot. "Of course, I do. If you like, I'll sing it in English. Please, David, I can't help it. I'm just as much a prisoner in myself as you are in you. I think this whole thing is wild, and everything about it is crooked, we both know it; but I don't understand why, if you know it is all so wrong, you didn't do something about it — why didn't you let me speak to the police, or tell one of the shopkeepers in time? We saw these people stealing right and left."

David said shortly, "It was none of our business."

"Well, then, what makes you so self-righteous about it? Why do you sit and sulk?" asked Jenny, quite reckless in her impatience.

"This is none of our business either," said David, a traplike finality in his tone. Jenny drank her wine and watched passengers straggling slowly in the wake of the dancers. "Well," she told him, "have a merry evening. I am going to dance with the first man that asks me!" And left him alone to the dessert and coffee.

The band leader had been well instructed by Tito and Lola; he was to play alternate German and Spanish dance music until time for the drawing of tickets for the prizes. After that, he could play what he chose; he was given five tickets for his obliging consent to this, and had already set his heart on the white embroidered silk shawl for his girl in Wiesbaden. As the zarzuela company with their followers appeared, he struck his favorite "Tales from the Vienna Woods" with great spirit. At the first sound of the music, a faint spark, a firefly gaiety, played through the crowd lighting each face with a wavering, hopeful smile. The Spanish company led the way, paired off and swung into step as their feet touched the deck, stepping out rhythmically pair by pair, matched like slender porcelain figurines alike in their practiced grace, serpent-litheness, thin-boned, smooth narrow heads, fine feet and hands. They seemed to be a beautiful, evil-tempered family of brothers and sisters, their hard eyes and bitter mouths denying their blithe motions. Several German pairs followed — Frau Rittersdorf with a young officer, the Baumgartners, sad-faced, Elsa and her father, Herr Rieber and Lizzi — they all looked rustic and awkward and mis-matched beside the Spaniards — their bodies all shapes and heights and widths, their faces nondescript, their coloring lifeless; nothing but a common heaviness proclaimed them as members of the same nation; that, and a certain fitful, uneasy vivacity as if practicing social graces not quite their own. The Spaniards did not favor them with so much as a glance, and the Germans could not take their gaze from the Spaniards. As they watched, first to one and then another came a vague impression that shortly settled into a disturbing certainty; the zarzuela company was no longer dancing a pure, classical Viennese waltz, with their birdlike lightness; they were — yes, no doubt of it — doing an imitation — an insulting parody, of the German style of waltzing.

Mrs. Treadwell, with her young officer, noticed this most amusing bit of comedy, and laughed merrily together as they moved into the dance. Jenny and Freytag saw it too, at the same moment. Jenny said, "Oh how cruel and funny!" and Freytag said a trifle grimly, "It's almost too true to be funny, I think," and swung her firmly into step. Within a turn or two, it became impossible for them not to see clearly that the zarzuela company was now giving imitations of them — and it was further impossible for any of them to deny that they were as comic as those public figures of fun, Lizzi and Herr Rieber. Pepe and Amparo had become perfect impersonators of Mrs. Treadwell's mincing, arm's length style, her wooden young partner; Manolo and Concha did a wicked imitation of Herr Freytag's somewhat muscular aggressiveness and Jenny's abandoned, swooning manner, head thrown back loosely. Pancho and Pastora had from the first stuck firmly with their parody of Herr Rieber and Lizzi, Pancho bouncing like a rubber ball, Pastora turning on an axis like an animated flagpole.

"No, really," said Jenny, stopping abruptly, "that is too much. Those people are really insufferable . . . I don't want to dance any more."

"Neither do I," said Freytag. "Let's make a tour of the ship. Let's see what makes it run. I'm bored with this."

Mrs. Treadwell danced with her officer once, declined Denny's invitation, who thought she would do to pass the time until he could catch Pastora, and accepted the fat purser's, who walloped with astonishing speed three times around the narrow dance floor with his partner streaming from his clasp like a scarf, then halted suddenly, blowing and snorting, his face a rich red-violet, his eyes closed, until Mrs. Treadwell, alarmed, asked if there were anything she could do?

"Yes," he gasped, "you may sit with me and have some more *Schaumwein*."

But providentially her good-looking, gold-braided young officer intervened, and with a deferential bow to the purser, took her away again. He had a smooth fair face with no expression at all, she observed, none. He was as sleek, neat, immaculately correct and inhuman-looking as if he were poured into a mold. He danced with waxlike smoothness, with small even steps accommodated to hers, holding her at an unfashionable, formal distance, as if he had been trained at her own dancing school. "Why, he's young enough to be my son," she could not help thinking, "and he reminds me of my grandfather." She decided this was no real drawback, settled into the leisurely spin of his style and began to enjoy the floating lightness and the pleasant male nearness, no weight and no burden but only a presence. She closed her eyes a moment and danced in lulling darkness, with a diffused tenderness for this wraith who guided her with light fingers at waist and palm, the lover who had danced with her in her daydreams long before she had danced with any man. Opening her eyes, she found him watching her face with a peculiar intentness unexpected and disturbing. Was it her imagination, instructed in the ways of the lurking animal, was it her own seeking eyes? Or was it really a goatish gleam? — for as her glance met his, his eye became bland, distant, even maybe a touch bored, and he said, "Let's leave this to those ruffians. Wouldn't you like to make a little tour of the ship? It's a kind of custom on gala evenings."

Mrs. Treadwell, remembering all the voyages she had made in all sorts of ships to how many ports, had never yet on the most gala of evenings made a tour of any ship. It was hard to imagine anything more boring, perhaps; she smiled at her escort, slipped her hand into the crook of his elbow, and set out for new, if not amusing, sights.

When the music changed to a rumba, the Cuban students moved in a body to take the Spanish dancing girls for partners — it was a gaudy race in which each one claimed the girl he reached first. The two left out turned at once to look for other possibilities; one seized Jenny as she was leaving the dance with Freytag, and the other, smiling and humming the tune, slipped an arm around Elsa and took her hand, and she found herself in a daze looking into the eyes of her love, the stranger, the beautiful merry one for her. No, it could not be — yet he

4 3 4

was still smiling, frowning a little, and she felt his arm tugging at her waist as she stood planted like a tree, unable to move a muscle. "Oh no, come now," he said, in very civil persuasive Spanish, no argot at all, "we are going to dance."

Elsa stood immovable. "I can't," she whispered in a small child's voice, frightened. "No, no, please — I can't."

"Naturally you can," he assured her lightly, "anything with legs can dance!" And he performed the feat of dancing in one spot while embracing a motionless form too weighty to push from its foundation. "You see?"

"Oh, no," cried Elsa in despair, "I never learned how!"

He dropped his hands and stood back and she saw with terror a look of serious distaste in his face. *"Perdoneme!"* he said and turned swiftly away as from something extremely unpleasant, and as she stood there, was gone, without looking back. Oh, and he would never look back. In a few seconds he was dancing with Mrs. Treadwell, who left her officer for a brief turn with this diverting creature out of a carnival, and Elsa felt her heart break quite finally. She wished to go at once to bed, and cry as much as she wanted, but first she must tell her father and mother, or they would be looking for her. They were playing checkers in the salon. "No, Elsa," said her mother, "if you go to bed so early, you will not sleep well. Why aren't you dancing?"

"I don't feel like it, Mother," she said, so desolately both her parents gave her looks of intimate sympathy and understanding. "Ah well," said her mother, so knowingly that Elsa blushed for shame, "you are wise to be quiet. So just sit here and play checkers with your father, and I will go on knitting, and we will have a nice evening together after all this hubbub and foolishness."

Elsa, feeling her doom in her, where before she had only feared it, in some terrible future, smiled blindly at her father, and began her play.

Arne Hansen, sitting in a deck chair with a bottle of beer on the floor beside him, his big shoulders hunched and his eyebrows in a tangle over the bridge of his nose, watched Amparo dance first with Manolo and then with one of those crazy students, and she had not given him a glance all evening. When the third tune struck up, a German waltz, he lumbered over to her, standing near Manolo fanning herself. Manolo discreetly evanesced from the scene, and Hansen took her firmly by the elbows, his favorite clutch when dancing. Amparo wasted no words. She wrenched free violently, dropped her fan, which he did not notice. She bent to pick it up while he was lunging towards her a second time, ground her heel cruelly into his foot, and rising abruptly, cracked him under the jaw with the top of her head, closing his mouth so abruptly he bit his tongue, which bled.

"Now, see what you do," he said, accusingly, getting out a large handkerchief and collecting bright red spots on it, dabbing and dabbing.

"Let me alone, then!" cried Amparo in pure rage. "This one evening I will not lug your stinking corpse around everywhere I go. I am working, it is nearly time for the raffle, you go and sit over there and drink your beer and keep out of the way."

"I bought four tickets," Hansen reminded her, feeling in his shirt pocket and bringing out his stubs.

"Yes, four, you cheap bastard," said Amparo, deliberately. "Four!" and she spat just past his left sleeve.

"You'll take back that word," said Hansen, with sudden dignity. "You'll be sorry you did that." He returned to his chair and ordered two more bottles of beer.

Her student no sooner had grasped Jenny's waist and hand than he began manipulating her, whirling her around, tossing her out to arm's length and retrieving her on the beat, closing in and embracing her hotly, throwing her away again carelessly, until she almost expected to be seized by the legs and spun around head downward. She protested, out of breath. "I'm an infighter," she told him brightly, "I like to slug it out toe to toe. All these acrobatics — what for?"

He was delighted with the compliment. "Ah," he said unexpectedly in a species of English, "you like? So?" and he began winding her up as if she were a top.

"No," said Jenny, "no," and she broke away, laughing of course. "Too much!" She waved him good-by merrily, merrily, both of them laughing, and ran to Freytag.

He favored her with a very German, superior smile, saying: "Tell me, you should know this, do all women prefer thugs, and *maquereaux*, and guttersnipes at heart? What is this strange feminine taste for lowness? *La nostalgie de la boue?*"

"Low?" said Jenny, puzzled. "Mud? He's just a noisy middle-class medical student, he could be a bore, but what's low about him?"

"He was dancing with you without respect, as if he were making fun of you," said Freytag, bluntly.

"He may have been," she said, simply. "That's his affair, not mine."

"Have you no pride?" he asked severely, for he was tired of trying to understand this strange girl who seemed to lack everything he required in a woman and yet disturbed him almost constantly with a sexual desire unlike any he had known — pure lust without one trace of warmth or tenderness. He did not even like her.

"Not much," she said. "Are you trying to pick a quarrel with me? Don't do it. I have enough of that already."

Freytag, reflecting that this was indeed a bad start for an evening of which he had some hopes, changed his tone at once. "Don't mind me," he said, "I am perhaps just a little jealous. Let's dance again before we start our ramblings, what do we care what those funny Spaniards think?"

David finished his dessert, drank his coffee with a liqueur and a cigarette, then wandered leisurely out to the bar, rather hoping that Jenny might notice his entire composure. She was not in sight, though, so he joined William Denny in the bar, where the Baumgartners were already installed without their child at a small table. The Huttens were sharing a bottle of wine at another, Bébé, apparently completely recovered from his misadventure, lying near their feet.

David wondered now and again at the way he and Denny had settled down into the limited but satisfactory relationship of fellow drinkers. He decided that Denny could drink with anybody or alone, it made no difference; but David, whose main trouble was that he did not really like anybody except Jenny now and then, and Jenny less and less every day, was at ease with Denny because, so far as David could see, Denny did not exist at all; at least, as nothing more than a bundle of commonplace appetites and cranky local prejudices. He had tried him out and there was nothing to him. They sat and drank each in his own silence so far removed and so unrelated to each other it had the look of companionship.

Over their fourth whiskey, David remarked in a sluggish tone, his tongue a little thick: "Ev'ry time I look out there, I see her going by with Freytag. Now, there she goes again," he said, waving his hand loosely, "there she goes."

Denny leaned sidewise from his stool, he bulged towards David, his face full of conspiracy. "I don't want to get personal," he said earnestly, "I never mix in anybody's business, understand, but if that bitch belonged to me, I'd break every bone in her. Not that it's any of my business, understand, but believe me you're gettin' a raw deal."

His moony expression of solicitude touched David, who felt at once a responsive glow of benevolent feeling not exactly for Denny but for the words. "Oh, that's all right," he said, "I know what you're up against, too. That Pastora. We're just two shipwrecked mariners in the same lifeboat," he said, genially. Inside him the thin sharp wires were twanging, snapping, letting go one at a time, he was getting easier under the ribs, he wasn't even annoyed with himself to hear himself talking like a fool to Denny, who talked like one all the time; in fact, he enjoyed it. "We all have our troubles," he told Denny, expansively. "You'll find a way out."

"I'm tryin' to find a way *in*," said Denny, lewdly. "The way out's easy. I don't mind tellin' you, she got a lot more out of me than I meant to give her, she's a slick worker; and now she's tryin' to give me the runaround. Well, there's goin' to be a showdown tonight, this here very night, I'm tellin' you. It's not goin' to be any trouble, no trouble at all for anybody but her," he said. "I just mean to show her, like I told you, that's all."

David thought this over carefully. "Well," he decided, sympathetically, "with a woman like that, no wonder you eat yeast."

Denny was bewildered but not offended. "What's yeast got to do with it?" he inquired. "Who said yeast?" He began pushing David about somewhat at arm's length, urgently. David leaned back out of his range. "Go on," said Denny, "are you a man, or a mouse? Go ahead. Now is your time. Knock her front teeth out."

"Pastora?" asked David. "Why don't you? That's your job."

"Yeah, well —" said Denny, doubtfully. "No, not exactly. I aim to give her a little more time to do the right thing. I'd like her in good condition," he said, thoughtfully. "I wouldn't want her all bunged up . . . what I always say is, better the man, worse the bitch trouble. That's me. But you've *had* that Jenny, and I'd put her out of circulation if she belonged to me."

David focused his nearsighted eyes with some effort upon the face sagging near him and said distinctly, because it now occurred to him that Denny was getting extremely personal, "Well, she doesn't belong to you," and added, with a stroke of lightning revelation, "She doesn't belong to anybody, not even to herself." He heard this with some astonishment, then felt instantly he had crossed a line into a new truth and was even then looking back calmly on old false hopes. His brief flash of elation sank again into gloom as the dancers passed the barroom door again, revolving swiftly — among them, Pastora with her student, Jenny with Freytag. He rapped on the bar and pushed their two glasses forward. "The same," he said. "Oh well, so long as they keep passing we know where they are."

"Yeah, and what they're doin'," said Denny, leering with such abandon his face went all out of shape.

The bride and groom, arm in arm, paused in their after-dinner stroll on the lee side away from the dancing, stood back to allow the surly blond boy to pass with the sick man in the wheel chair, the ghostly little dying man drooping among his rugs and blankets, turning the leaves of a small Bible with tremulous fingers. As he neared them, he lifted exalted eyes and raised a shaking hand towards them reaching to touch the bride. Her husband felt her shudder deeply and shrink against him. "God bless your marriage and make it fruitful," said Herr Graf. The groom said, "Thank you, sir, thank you," for he was bound to pay the respect due to age, and they remained motionless until the boy, ignoring them with a furious face, had pushed the chair safely past them. The bride still trembled a little, and leaned closer to her husband. "Oh, it sounded like a curse," she said. "Oh, he almost touched me!"

Her husband said in his new tone of husbandly fondness, indulgence, reassurance and guidance, delicious to them both: "You know perfectly there is no such thing as a curse. Besides, what could harm us? He is only a poor dying man — after all, he wished us well. It is a sad thing to be old and sick . . ."

The bride, who was gentle-hearted, repented at once of her uncharitable feelings, and being honest, she knew they were caused by her horror of age and ugliness and sickness and her fear of them, and her greater fear of death, which was the only alternative, the one possible escape from them. Feeling rather sensible and calm, and joyously well and immortal, she said in a dreaming voice, "I hope we die young." Her husband, in the privacy of the bow, slipped his arm around her and gave her a little shake. "Die young? We'll never die. We're going to live together until the end of the world!" They laughed together for happiness, without a trace of irony, and kissed hastily and guiltily, for fear they might be seen.

Johann had been so late for dinner the salon was almost deserted, he missed the balloons and the paper hats and all, and nobody came to sit with him. He was late because his uncle had chosen to have a coughing fit that almost strangled him. Johann had given him smelling salts to breathe, had washed his face in cold water, and sat fanning him with a folded paper, hoping he would die. Instead he had come around rather strongly, and demanded to be bathed and dressed, fresh from the skin out, demanded that Johann sit with him and help him eat his dinner, and insisted on being taken for an airing on deck afterwards — the old hypocrite, pretending he wanted fresh air when what he really wanted was to watch the dancing and hear the music and talk about how sinful it all was. By the time Johann finished his hurried dinner and got on deck, Concha was already dancing. She wiggled her fingers at him over her partner's shoulder and gave him a look that would melt stone; but Johann still knew that without money he would never be any nearer her than he was then. When she saw him again, wheeling his uncle on the margin of the party, she was with another partner, and this time she looked at his uncle, crossed herself, made an obscene sign against the evil eye with her right hand, and went on.

Johann was slowly coming to a most desperate resolve — money he would have, he would not put up another day with this selfish greedy old man who pretended to be such a saint and was pure devil. He would end this slavery, he would free himself no matter how — this is the end, the end, he said, and each time the thought repeated itself in words he got again a shock of fright that almost stopped his heart; yet he would do it. He would ask his uncle once more for the money he owed him — no more than he would have to pay a servant; if he refused, why then — then he would search the cabin, he would find it. He believed his uncle kept his wallet under the mattress at the head of the bed. He would wait until his uncle slept, he would give him a sleeping powder, he would find the money and take it —

He turned the wheel chair abruptly into the doorway and started for the cabin.

"Where are you going, nephew?" asked Herr Graf, rousing with a groan.

"Where do you think? Back to that filthy hole. It is time for you to sleep!"

"Turn back, Johann. I do not want to sleep." As the wheels bumped roughly from step to step downward, Johann stubbornly silent, Herr Graf added: "God is good, but He is also just. I say again, I leave you to Him, Johann."

"You'd better," said Johann contemptuously, "it's all you can do."

When he shoved the wheel chair roughly through the cabin door, the sickly shaded light burning day and night and the profuse loathsome smells accumulated there almost broke the spirit of his resolution; he was suffused from head to foot in a slow sweat of terror. Not daring to hesitate an instant, he spun the chair around and crouched as if he would spring at Herr Graf, almost choking on his words. "Now you will give me some money, or I'll — where is it? Where do you hide it, you old miser? I give you one more chance! Where is the money?"

"Not so loud, Johann. I do not want strangers to know your disgrace. I expected this," he said calmly, through the bubbling of phlegm in his throat. "This is your next step towards damnation. The money is where it should be . . ."

"Give it to me!" shouted Johann desperately. "Give me only a little, but I must have it. I will take it, I will kill you if you don't give me the money!" and he raised his hands together fingers curved like talons as if they would close around his uncle's throat.

Herr Graf without moving his head fixed his gaze in Johann's eyes, lifting both hands, palms outward. He spoke just above a whisper with laboring, scanty breath: "Don't do it, my Johann, my dear child. You will be found out. They will put you to death. Beyond that, Johann, after your miserable end here, there is God's judgment."

"Damn God's judgment," said Johann raging, but retreating a step, his fists clenching, "don't talk that rot to me any more. Where is the money? Where is the money?"

"Be a thief if you must, Johann, but not a murderer. I beg of you, not for my sake — do you think I am afraid of death? but for your own, don't be either. Don't throw your life away, my child. Why can't you be patient just a few days longer, when you have so many years to enjoy after I am gone?"

Johann's fury and fright broke in him like a burst artery. His face crumpled, his chin shook, his eyes filled and flooded over on his cheeks, his mouth drew together convulsively in the center and opened at the corners, in a frenzy he shouted and sobbed until his words were almost smothered in his throat: "I don't want to kill you, I don't want to rob you, why do you drive me to it? Why can't you treat me like a human being, Uncle? What harm did I do you? Give me a little money," he wept, inconsolably, "that is all I want! I won't kill you — I want only to be free!" He was sitting huddled over the edge of the divan, mopping his face with his soiled handkerchief and blowing his nose. His uncle watched him, shaking his head sorrowfully.

"There is no such thing as freedom, Johann," he said, with a long broken sigh, "no such thing. If there were, how could you hope to gain it this way?"

"I want to buy a bottle of wine!" cried Johann, in a passion of renewed rebellion. "I need some decent clothes, you keep me looking like a beggar! I want to dance and be young while I'm young, I have the right to live. Just because you are going to die — is that any reason you should take me into the grave with you?"

Herr Graf said, "I wanted only to save your soul, Johann. You are dear to me."

Johann felt himself melting, giving way, losing the fight, betrayed by this sly attack on his blind side, that side of his human feeling that was famished for love and blinded with the anguish of being forever outside of life, always left out of things, never being able to take part, to give his share, to be one of his own kind: he struggled and thrashed within himself trying to find the very words he needed to explain to this old man, to placate him if possible, to get what was needed from him, without hurting him, without stealing, without killing him, damn him! "My soul is my own," he said sulkily, almost in his normal voice.

"No, it is not," said his uncle calmly, "and that is a stupid thing to say. But I cannot contest with you any longer. I shall let you go." He motioned towards his bunk. "There," he said, "reach under the mattress, back near the wall, and give me my wallet."

Johann, shocked by this sudden victory, fumbled among the blankets with uncertain hands, ashamed and humbled and resentful. He brought it out and handed it to Herr Graf, who opened it at once, reached into a certain compartment without hesitating, and without counting gave a generous sheaf of notes to Johann, a terrible smile on his suffering face.

"For your good, I should have done otherwise, perhaps," he said gently, "but no gift is good unless given with a blessing," he said. "Bless you. Johann, you should have known I am not afraid of death. I do not give you this for fear that you may take my life. I do it because I am afraid you may otherwise become a murderer. These are two quite different things, Johann. This is yours and I am no longer your guardian. Take it freely and go your ways, my child."

Clutching the solid roll of money he believed could buy him everything he wanted, Johann blurted helplessly, baffled and bewildered by his uncle's determination to keep him forever in the wrong, "Uncle, you treat me like a servant, but you wouldn't dare cheat a servant as you cheated me!"

"I never mistook you for a servant, Johann. Don't attempt to justify yourself in such a dishonest way . . . and now, please help me to go to bed, for I am very tired."

Johann stuffed the money in his inside jacket pocket, and went about his duties with a smoldering face. "And give me a sleeping draught, please," said Herr Graf. Watching him drink it, Johann was moved with pity. He fought this new strange feeling as he undressed the little skeleton carefully as he had been taught, without immodest exposure in the change from dress to nightgown, lifting the arms one at a time and laying them down gently, pulling the gown over the swollen knee joints and lifting the limp body in his arms as if it were a child's, straightening the limbs, and tucking in the blanket lightly. "There you are," he said, in a husky voice. "Thank you, thank you always," said his uncle. "Now I can rest."

Johann stood over him hesitating, then said, "Uncle, thank *you*. I will do better, I promise —"

"No promises, please," said Herr Graf, lifting a hand and smiling his frightful dying smile. "Alas, my needs have not changed. I must still be a burden to you until the end of the voyage. I must live, Johann, to see Germany once more. Be patient."

"Uncle, you will not be a burden," said Johann eagerly. Herr Graf looked for the first time into a candid, friendly face, strangely a *forgiving* face, so transformed he could hardly recognize his hard-hearted sister's hard-hearted child. "Good night," he said, as Johann dashed for the door and paused to look back for an instant to say "Good night, Uncle, and sleep well."

Herr Graf closed his eyes and let the blessed narcotic take its way in the slow blood and the pained nerves — ah, to close his eyes and extinguish breath, to conjure a lightless world, no, a universe of darkness, that would be pure bliss. O, God, darken the sun and the moon, put out Your planets as I would blow out candles. Drop from Your great nerveless hands darkness and silence, silence and stillness, stillness of dust buried under dust, the darkness and silence and stillness of the eyeless deeps of the sea. Heal my sorrows in your darkness, O God, I am blinded in your light. Remember me for one merciful moment, answer my only prayer: live and be in Your own Being and rule in Your light for all eternity, but let me go — let me go. Do not deny me the gift of Your divine silence, Your eternal darkness. O God, let me die forever. . . .

Johann as he neared the end of the long dim passageway could already hear the music, and voices, and the sound of the sea. He lingered a moment at the bottom of the stairs, confused and melancholy, his nerves still raw from the punishment they had received, deep in his mind a lingering resentment, a sense of being wronged still, in some way that could never be made up to him. He resisted the softening of his heart towards his uncle, though he could not deny it. He argued with himself that his uncle had done for him only what he should have done long ago, and without waiting to be asked, much less threatened. Johann thought almost in despair, "I'll never get rid of this — never —"

Running his hand into his jacket pocket to touch the roll of money, he straightened his shoulders and, with an unpleasant apprehensive sinking in the pit of his stomach, set out to look for Concha.

He had not far to look; there she was, idling with Amparo and Tito near the piano, where a small covered basket with the raffle tickets had been set up, and the prizes were on display — the lacy feminine assortment of tablecloths, scarfs and fans, and the two ruffled petticoats, of flimsy red cotton edged with coarse white lace. His heart gave such a jolt he stopped short for an instant, then moved to the open deck where she might notice him. She did not, but went on holding one of the petticoats before her, kicking lightly under the ruffles. It was Tito who saw him first. He gave Concha a discreet sign, at which she handed the petticoat to Amparo, wiggled her fingers at Johann, and walked to meet him, face very serious, hand lifted, her hips swaying in that rhythm he had heard her call the *Meneo*. Once when they were walking together, she took his hand and placed it on her side at the waist, just above the hipbone, and said: "Feel that? Only Spanish women move like that. It is called the *Meneo*. Feel? I am not a gypsy, you know that? I am real Spanish, and this is the sign." He had been set on fire by the delicate side-to-side rocking of the hips, perfectly natural, in the bones not in the muscles, so she insisted. "You are doing it on purpose," he accused her, but she said seriously, "No, I was born that way. You hear what they say, my hipbones? They say *Meneo, Meneo,* all by themselves."

He stood waiting for her to come all the way to him, still doubtful, still shaken by his bitter victory over his uncle, with something very like terror in his blood as he realized what he had done and what he now faced. Their glances locked as she neared, and were fixed unsmiling until she was under his very chin, looking up, no coquetry, no trickiness at all in her eyes. He even thought he saw anxiety in them. He was in such a rigorous tremor of excitement he hardly dared to speak for fear his voice would betray him, but she did not hesitate. Setting her hand over his heart she spoke at once: "Did you do as I told you?"

He frowned and said in a bullying tone: "Did you think I would? Do you take me for such a fool?"

Her hand dropped away. *"Valgame Dios,* so you haven't got it." Her despair infuriated him.

"Of course I've got it," he boasted angrily without shame, "and I didn't even steal it, either."

Concha flung herself upon him and attempted to leap into his arms. He seized her by the waist and swung her above his head and set her down again still without smiling.

"Let's dance," she whispered, nipping the lobe of his ear with her smooth white teeth, "I don't care what you did! And let's have some champagne," she added, as they turned slowly together, not dancing, in time to the music. "Remember? You promised."

He tightened his grip around her ribs until she could hardly breathe. "We're going to bed," he told her, "now. Remember? Now, while everybody is out here. Where's your cabin?" Concha said, "Don't be such a German!" as he marched her across the deck more like a police officer than a lover.

"What do you expect me to be?" he asked, but not as if his mind were on the question.

"Well," said Concha, uneasily, "look —" and he could feel resistance in her whole body through the slight yielding arm. "Look then, if you are going to be like this, I'll show you my cabin when you show me your money. How do I know you are telling me the truth? Manolo would kill me . . . how do I know?"

"You'll know," he said. "Just wait." Now he was sure, there was nothing to worry about, he had the winning card in his pocket. His face cleared and grew amiable, he gave her a warm little squeeze that could almost pass for tenderness.

"Well," said Concha, her doubts vanishing also, "if you fool me, I'll kill you." She nuzzled under his arm.

"You think so?" said Johann, with lordly indulgence. "Try it." He drew her swiftly in front of him, stopped in the dim passageway and closed his hands lightly around her throat. "Like this?"

Concha shuddered with pleasure and smiled up at him without a shadow of uneasiness, and said, "No, not like that. Another way. Better." They laughed in each other's faces and went on, his arm around her shoulders.

"Here we are," she told him, opening the door and going in first to turn on the light. She expected an onslaught, a violent blind fumbling brutality such as she knew too well from the inexperienced and overwrought; or worse even, panic and impotence and the fury of impotence or its deathly despair, which she must coddle and flatter and persuade away without seeming to, for men in such disgrace with themselves were likely to turn resentful, unmanageable, even dangerous, blaming her and wanting revenge for their outraged male pride. She was on guard, ready for anything; but he just stood there looking at her expectantly, all shining and golden-haired. She had a weakness for blond men, and this one had turned eager and warm and simple; he put out his hand and stroked her smooth black hair and said in German, "Beautiful, beautiful."

She laughed with relief to find that everything would be easier than she had thought, took his hand in both of hers and said, "Come in, don't be strange, you are with me — we are going to be gay together." She drew his head down and kissed him, then began to loosen his tie, saying, "And you must help me undress, too. It is more fun to do everything together. Tell me darling, am I your very first girl?" He nodded, and blushed, then gathered himself together and said, "Why do you say that?" Concha sheered away from the subject. "Do you love me, ah, well — do you love me just a little?"

"I don't know," he said, hoarsely, wrapping himself around her so resolutely she could hardly get his shirt off him. He began to pull at the front of her dress to get at her breasts. "Wait," she said, "are you going to let me be very nice to you?" and she wriggled out of her shabby little black frock, dropped her colored silk petticoat and was naked. "I am a very bad girl," she said, teasing, "you'll see." He did not seem to hear her, and he did not need any blandishments.

Herr Rieber sent beer once more to the band, and called for "Tales from the Vienna Woods" for the fourth time. The music, the *Schaumwein*, the starry sky, Lizzi in a tender promising mood whirling in the waltz almost caused him to forget future pleasures in the wanton luxury of his present delights. His bib worked round under his ear, his baby cap slipped to the back of his neck, he had not a care in the world. His wide tireless smile showed the tip of his wet pink tongue, when now and then he smacked his lips over the sweet morsel of his joy. Taking a fresh grip on Lizzi's waist and hand, he pressed his hard little stomach against her and burst wordlessly into high tenor song. "La dedada, la dedada, la de da, de daa!" sang Herr Rieber, frisking like a faun, turning lightly on his toes gazing up in ecstasy at Lizzi, who answered at once "La dedada," like Echo herself. He felt he was a faun, a fleet prancing faun deep in the forest glade, stamping a pattern of cleft flowers into the leaf mold under his sharp little polished hoofs; with the winds moaning like violins in the treetops, the sweet voices of birds calling la de da to each other among the branches where the harp strings were sighing, and the nymph waiting for the young goat-boy, half god, light on his hoofs and ready to leap the likely, long-legged creature in the green gown who loved a good caper! Ah, lade-dada, de da, sang the young faun at the top of his voice in a panic rapture as he spun wildly on the very tiptoe of his sharp hoofs, while the nymph, leaning backward from the waist, whirled so steadily her lace skirts rose and spread out slowly upward at the back like an opening fan.

Hansen, sunk in his chair, nursing his bottle of beer, glared at them from under his frown clutched hard over his nose. They had passed him several times, and the last time they came so near Lizzi's skirt brushed his knees, an outrage so bitter he resolved that, if she did it again, he would put out his foot and trip her up and send the pair of them sprawling. As they careered towards him again more wildly than ever, he gathered himself and put a foot forward in readiness. Lizzi's flying skirts brushed his face this time, he blinked and flinched, and

Herr Rieber's boot came down grinding cruelly into his toes. Her Hansen, with a subterranean rumble of groans, rose instantly, opened out to his full height and brought his beer bottle down forcefully on Herr Rieber's naked defenseless skull. Herr Rieber stopped dead in his tracks looking immensely surprised. The glass shattered and a long, bright red track appeared at once on his head and began streaking and trailing downward rapidly.

"You see?" inquired Herr Hansen sternly as if he had proved something beyond argument. "You see?"

The blow knocked Herr Riber still deeper into his fantasy. He bleated like a goat, "Baaah, meeeeh!" and charged Herr Hansen, butting him accurately in the sensitive midriff just where the ribs divide. Herr Hansen doubled over deeply and fought for breath. Before he could recover it, a matter of seconds, Herr Rieber charged again. "Baaaah, meeeeeh!" he bawled and butted with all his might, leaving untidy red smears on Herr Hansen's shirt front.

"Just stop that now," gasped Herr Hansen, his chest heaving. He caved in once more, and pushed Herr Rieber's face away with the flat of his hand. "Just you now, you *stop* that!"

Herr Rieber threw the hand off and drew away for a third charge. The trap drummer pushed his paper hat off his forehead and grappled with Herr Rieber, who looked confused and did not resist. The violinist laid a gently restraining hand on Herr Hansen's arm and was shaken off like a kitten. When the music stopped so suddenly, the Cuban students, dancing with the Spanish girls, crowded about to see the show, and when they saw Herr Rieber's blood-festooned head, they shouted, *"Que vive la sangre! Viva la barbaridad!"* Frau Rittersdorf and the Huttens had been sitting together not so much as spectators as living models of decorum publicly rebuking an indecorous spectacle. They now rose ostentatiously though nobody noticed, and took themselves away. Frau Rittersdorf said, "We shall do very well if we reach port alive!" a conclusion so obvious the Huttens thought it not worth answering.

Lizzi stood staring, her hand over her mouth, her forehead wrung with shock. The violinist patted her on the cheek. "So, so," he said soothingly, and at this gentleness she woke to a sense of her disaster. Little fine wrinkles leaped about in her face, she turned from him and ran blindly, bent forward, hands up, palm outward, uttering the shrill cries of an anguished peahen. The violinist followed swiftly and said,

"Fräulein, let me help you if I can. Don't try to go by yourself." She hunched her shoulder away from his hand, and broke into shrill laughter and tears. She moved past Herr Rieber without a glance at him, and he did not see her go, or remember her. Herr Hansen walked away alone, his arms folded tightly across his stomach. The trap drummer stayed firmly by Herr Rieber, who was plainly dazed. Both Rieber and Hansen stopped abruptly, some distance apart, and leaned over the rail. They stood back after some moments of agitation, wiped their faces and went on weaving with the rise and fall of the deck.

The violinist by then regretted his gallant attempts to aid a distressed female who showed nothing but the most shameless ingratitude, who would scream "Don't touch me!" as if she were being raped, every time he tried to take her arm and guide her. Yet she was staggering all over the passageway, from side to side, bumping into the walls, and God knows she was the ugliest woman he had ever seen. Yet, slave to his decent upbringing and perhaps his natural good temper, he persisted, keeping a brave face to the business, and did succeed at last in landing his nuisance at the right door, where he knocked as loudly as he dared, and waited.

Denny struggled up from his bar stool for the first time that evening, and said, "I've got business. I'm going to cut in on Pastora. I see her buzzing around with one of those Cubans. She's going to do some tall explainin' now — little she knows!"

David, who had been benumbed for some time without having enjoyed any of the progressive pleasures of getting drunk, now felt detached enough to offer good advice to Denny, who was so obviously born to do the wrong thing no matter what he did: "You ought to have started earlier, maybe. You've lost control. You won't be able to gauge distance or pull your punches. Remember, it's dangerous to hit a woman *any*where, even when you're sober. They're all over soft spots, they can't take it."

"This one will," said Denny, firmly. He tottered, held on to the bar with his left hand, hit himself in the stomach with his right, and gave a loud belch. As if this had a steadying effect, he walked a fairly straight line towards the dancers. David followed along, hoping to see Denny snubbed properly. Not at all: the Cuban student surrendered all claim to his partner at once. Before she could refuse and take flight, Pastora was hedged in Denny's arms; while they wobbled about in a series of ellipses, Pastora held him away by both his elbows, and Denny hung on around her shoulders in gruesome silence, breathing a miasma of mingled unclean fumes into her face. "Let me go, you smell like a buzzard!" Pastora was crying out, turning away and struggling. Altogether, a most unpromising situation, David was pleased to see. With a cheerful heart he wished Denny a fine busy evening bringing Pastora under, and all the bad luck in the world at it.

He had troubles of his own, and as he had begun to do lately, when the whiskey, as he hoped, had cleared his head and taken the edge off his anxieties, he wondered at his lack of self-respect, letting any woman, and above all a woman like Jenny, weigh on his mind and hound his feelings day and night and interfere with his plans and side-track him into places he had never meant to be, and corner him with unfair arguments and work on his weaknesses with her tears and her lovemaking, upset his work and drive him to drink — simply no end to her bitchery — what in God's name could he have been thinking of? Here he was, getting drunk every day simply to get away from her and the thought of her, and what had come of it? What had become of Jenny? For the girl he thought he knew had disappeared so entirely he had almost to believe he made her up out of odds and ends of stuff from his own ragbag of adolescent dreams and imaginings. Of course, it was time he grew up. There never was, there couldn't possibly be, any such living girl as he had dreamed Jenny was. . . .

His drunkenness almost bowled him over. He leaned on the rail holding his head, and though his knees shook under him, and his gorge rose as it did too often even under less provocation, his heart and his will hardened as if they had separate lives of their own not subject to the caprices of alcohol. "Darn you, Jenny angel, I give you up. I won't fight with you any longer. It's not worth it. I can't live like this." When he heard his own voice he glanced about in dismay, but no one was near. Jenny's bright voice spoke up with its unbearable gay mockery: ". . . and the Emperor Cuautomoc then spoke to him from his pit of fire and asked, 'Think you that I am on a bed of roses?'" She had already said that a long time ago when he did not take her seriously; when he let her know she was causing him distress and making him unhappy, she had always answered in some oblique way that she was unhappy too, and it was his fault, and it was her belief that if they tried hard enough, they were bound to be blissful together. But she never said how they were to try, nor who should begin.

Pastora, with a face of fury, passed him in full flight, her ruffled skirts and black lace mantilla flowing backward; with a glance over her shoulder she dived through the nearest door. Denny, far off his center of gravity, approached more slowly but in earnest pursuit. He blinked at David and rounded on him confidentially: "She thinks she's goin' to get away," he said easily, "but there isn't any place on this ship she can hide. I'll get her, don't worry."

David said, "Maybe you ought to wait now until morning, you'll be in better shape," but Denny shook his head obstinately and said, "No, tonight's the night." He hobbled on with a good deal of waste motion, but made it safely to the doorway where Pastora had disappeared, leaned against the jamb for a few seconds, and went on. David wandered without plan, meeting strayed revelers whom he saw through a mist — Mrs. Treadwell with that solemn young officer; poor Elsa being escorted probably to bed by her parents; Dr. Schumann, who appeared to be walking in his sleep: they swam past him, and from the other side of the ship floated the strains of that never-ending bore of a waltz, "Tales from the Vienna Woods." At last he admitted where he was going, and who he was looking for and what he expected to find; he was beyond feeling, his nervous system felt dead, yet he was in anguish, a distress so deathlike it gave him a shock of fright, he really feared for the first time in his life that he might be going to die. There was nothing for it, though, but to keep going, up one flight of steps after another, to the boat deck, there to circle about warily and stealthily until he found them there together, and they were not even trying to hide. With a scalding shock in his blood as if he had not known all along they would be there, his search ended. They were huddled together on the deck, backs against a funnel, their knees drawn up, heads bowed thoughtfully, turned to each other, their foreheads touching, their bodies infolded, and fitted together smoothly. The twilight of the moon in a drift of cloud shone on Jenny's frost-white face, the look of one suffering in her sleep on her closed eyes and mouth. Freytag was holding her firmly and easily, his arms completely around her, her folded hands held in one of his rested on her closed knees turned helplessly towards him.

David's hands and feet turned cold, his nose grew thin and white and pointed downward, the nostrils working — he could feel it changing shape, drawing in upon itself in utter repulsion. A frightful confusion of simple jealousy, human outrage, pure disgust, a freezing hatred of

Jenny set up their clamor in him at once. Yet he could not tell which was the more loathsome to him, the scene itself and its meaning, Jenny's face of shameless, painful rapture, or Freytag's self-possession, his easy, familiar hold on her, his control, the kind of professional expertness of a born handler and trainer of women.

This was what David, then and afterwards, could not endure; very murder rose in his soul at the sight of Freytag's amiable, composed face, with its rather pleasantly elated look. Obviously he was waiting for Jenny to move into another phase of her desire, with his attentive help, and to declare herself first, before he closed with her. They might have been in a tower or on an island, in their absorption with themselves. Freytag raised his forehead from Jenny's, and spreading one hand upon her hair, he held her head back, turned her face up to his, studied it with quiet interest for a few seconds, then kissed her deliberately with the utmost luxury on the mouth. Jenny stirred and seemed to try to bury herself in his arms. He gathered her to him fully, competently, without haste or excitement, and began straightening out her legs, until he lay at full length beside her, moving his hand over her breast.

Still watching her face, he shifted his shoulder easily and covered her upper body with his, and there he stopped, and put his cheek to hers as if listening to her breathing. Then he turned away, and lay beside her, cradling her head on his arm, and he laughed, a very odd small laugh, under his breath, all to himself. He shook her head a little, kissed her, drew her up sitting, and tried to raise her to her feet. "Shame on you, you wench!" he said, in the utmost good temper. "Imagine passing out at a moment like this!" Jenny moaned, and said, "Oh, let me alone. Leave me here!"

"You know I can't do that," said Freytag in a tone very like brotherly annoyance. "Now stand up, Jenny, don't be tiresome."

David, standing frozen there in the shadow of the funnel, now turned in an utter horror of humiliation and tiptoed down the steps, his head roaring like a seashell.

In the bar, Herr Baumgartner, his clown make-up streaked, his whiskers on the floor under his chair, fumbled for the stem of his liqueur glass, jostled his coffee cup and spilt coffee on his napkin. Using the napkin as a handkerchief, he wept in silence, wiping his mouth, eyes and forehead distractedly. His wife watched him with eyes like agates, and spoke in a lowered, hardened voice: "Everybody is very carefully not looking at you. So after all I suppose you are not making a show of yourself in public."

He swallowed his Benedictine, his expensive, festive after-dinner treat, in one gulp without tasting it. Reaching over the stack of saucers between them, he touched the back of her hand with a forefinger, tapping lightly. She could see only one blurred hopeless eye behind the napkin, and the tremulous corner of a mouth full of unspoken reproaches. "*Mein Liebchen*," he said, "have you forgotten? We have been married ten years today."

"What is there to remember?" she asked him unforgivingly. "What has it been? A hell, a little hell on earth from the beginning."

"No," he said, "not from the beginning. That is not true —"

She hurried on, fiercely determined to deny everything but her unhappiness, unable, unwilling to remember anything but disappointment. "Don't tell me I don't know what it has been! Oh, aren't you ashamed of the life you have made for us?"

He covered his face again and groaned through the cloth. "Yes, yes, I am ashamed, I am always ashamed. But I am dying, Gretel, you know I am dying with these ulcers, maybe cancer, how do we know? I am dying and what do you care, what have you ever cared . . . ?"

"If you stopped this swilling day and night you would be well," she told him, leaning nearer. "You want to be sick, you want to make me wretched, you want to ruin all our lives — I understand you now. You hate me. You do it to spite me . . ."

Herr Baumgartner straightened his shoulders, drooped again, swayed, braced his fists on the table. "Very well," he said, "that is the last straw. Think what you please. I am finished, I have lived too long already — not another hour of this torment. I am going to kill myself."

"Of course," said his wife, freezing with anger and fright, "now begin that again! Well, just how and when do you propose to end your life this time? I should like to know your plans for once."

"I shall jump overboard in this next minute," he said, gulping his coffee. "That will be —" He smashed the cup down so violently it shattered and several persons glanced about, glanced instantly away again. He caught every eye as it turned and gave a stagy hoot of joyless mirth. "That will be the safest way!"

"Yes," she said, taunting him, "you will make a big disturbance and be rescued like Bébé —"

"Or maybe like the Basque," he reminded her.

"Bah!" she said. "You make me sick!"

He saw with dismay that she was simply and purely angry, that she was taking this merely as another quarrel, but he had gone too far to draw back; he must persist until he had driven her to believe in the seriousness of his threat and to take action to prevent him from carrying it out, as a wife should do.

Frau Baumgartner almost read his thoughts. She saw him waiting for her next move, a wicked childish calculation in his gaze, trying to measure the limits of her resistance, to break her down into pleading until he would at last consent, for her sake, to live. Instead, she folded her arms and leaned back and said wearily, "You will never do anything, so stop talking nonsense. I am tired of this, I am going to bed and you may stay here as long as you please."

He leaped up blindly at that and took long strides towards the nearest door before he looked back. His wife had not unfolded her arms, and she was not watching him. When he looked back again from the deck she had left the table and was walking in the opposite direction from him, the gaudy streamers of her peasant's headdress fluttering.

Benumbed from the shock of this treachery, this desertion, the last thing in the world he could have expected from her, he tottered out and lagged along the rail, his eye roving, looking for her to appear presently from almost any direction; she surely meant only to punish him for a few minutes, then she would come round from somewhere to intercept him, to prevent him, to plead with him, to bring him to reason as she had so often tried to do. Waiting, he stopped short, holding his head, elbows at rest, trying to pretend that he really meant to jump. Gazing into the steeply rising and falling sea, staggered by the unruly heaving of the deck, he shuddered in bitter horror at his vision of himself, poised upon the rail for one split second over the frightful depths, leaning forward with the leaning of the ship, falling in a curve, head downward, just at the the very split second Gretel should come running with her arms stretched towards him, hands clasped, imploring, "Oh, nonono, waitwait my love forgive me!"

He fell back in such terror he almost lost his balance, and nearly collided with Mrs. Treadwell, who was walking with that boyish-looking young lieutenant Herr Baumgartner had noticed with her before. They were laughing merrily and zigzagging with the roll of the deck, his arm around her.

"Pardon, pardon," he said, recovering his foothold, bowing from the waist and attempting to click his heels. They nodded and turned their distant eyes upon him, waved their hands lightly and went on, utterly indifferent to his sufferings, coldly careless that he was on the point of ending his miserable existence — worse still, unable even to imagine such a disaster! — with no more pity and humanity in them than his heartless wife. He returned to the side, took a good grip, and contemplated the waters again, and his situation, somewhat more calmly. So it was with him, here and now; he had come to this, and what a fool he had been to expect better! It was a tragic thing when a man was abandoned in his despair by the wife he had loved and trusted and given the best of everything, the wife he had depended upon to appreciate his devotion, to respect the nobility of his motives, to sustain his courage by her loyalty, to be indulgent of his weaknesses whatever they might be, for what man was altogether free of them? giving him freedom in all things while at the same time maintaining the restraints, appearances, and disciplines of daily life — what else was a wife for? Yet here he stood alone in the damp windy chill of midnight at sea in September, on the point of suicide; and she had not lifted a finger to save him. In fact, she had jeered at him, and mocked him onward.

Ah, it was the end. He could not endure it. No, and he would not either. What madness could have come over him that he had even for a moment dreamed of leaving his innocent, promising son, his only child, an orphan, and so badly provided for, after all. His insensible mother would certainly marry again, and leave her child to the tender mercies of a stepfather as she had left her husband to the cruel sea. In a new wave of fright and fresh outrage, but with a new resolution too, he began a long, dim struggle back to his cabin, with no clear plan in mind, but a fixed idea that seemed to be rooted somewhere in his vitals that now was the time to settle certain accounts, long overdue, with the female viper he had warmed in his bosom all these calamitous ten years.

Frau Baumgartner opened the door to her cabin noiselessly, and shaded the wall light with her palm as she turned the switch. Hans was in bed, as she had left him. He opened his eyes and blinked at her, smiling. She sat on the side of the bed and with a shake in her voice she could not control, asked him: "Were you asleep? Dreaming?"

"A little," he said shyly. "I listened to the music a long time."

"Did you say your prayers?"

"I forgot," he said anxiously, afraid of a scolding. Instead she smoothed his hair and kissed him. "We'll say them later," she told him. "Would you like to hear a story?"

Hans sat up instantly happy and wide awake. "Oh, you haven't told me a story since we came on this ship!"

"Poor child," said his mother, reaching for her knitting bag, and sitting near him again. "What do you want to hear?"

"Hansel and Gretel," he said at once. "I'd like that."

"You're getting to be a big boy for such a childish story," she told him, controlling her trembling fingers and getting the knitting started.

"I like it though, still," he said a little timidly. "Is that my sweater you're making?"

"Yes," she said, "and I mean to finish it before we get to Bremerhaven. I simply cannot worry any more about anything." After a short uneasy pause while he watched her face to find out what she meant, she smiled at him and began: "Once upon a time there were a little brother and sister who lived in the Black Forest. His name was Hansel — Hans, like you; and hers was Gretel, like me; and one day they were wandering in the woods, picking flowers, when there came an old witch . . ."

Her voice steadied itself and smoothed out into the gentle drone that lulled Hans to sleep as if it were a rocking cradle; when she came to the part where the dear little brother and sister were stuffing the wicked old witch into her own blazing oven, Hans's eyelids were fluttering in vain efforts not to close, but at last he gave way and to the howling of the doomed witch he drew a soft deep breath and turned his head on the pillow.

Frau Baumgartner shaded the light with a small scarf, her eyes already running with tears. She sat down again and began to knit blindly, counting her stitches. If it took all night, she was going to sit there knitting and waiting for her husband.

When he opened the door wide and swung in, he could hardly believe what he saw there, yet it was all too clear. He had not known what he meant to do or say, but when she raised her stubborn face and stared at him unrepentantly, he raised his right arm. She dodged violently to one side, but the tears burst again down her cheek before the flat of his hand struck it like a wooden paddle. It was a light spanking blow that did her no harm, but in getting up from her chair she staggered and fell, striking her cheekbone on the washhand stand. Hans woke cowering and cringing; he covered his eyes with his crossed arms and shrieked. The ship was rolling so heavily Frau Baumgartner was awkward trying to get off the floor, and her husband took her hands and helped her. "Knitting!" he shouted at her as he raised her up, in a frenzy of grief, all anger forgotten. "Oh, how could you? Knitting with me about to destroy myself! Oh God, what does a man do with such a woman?"

"I don't care!" she cried with terrifying obstinacy. "I don't care! Look at your poor child," she said, "you are frightening him to death. What will become of him if he sees us like this? Shame on you!"

The father turned upon his son, arms outspread to embrace him. Hans implored with his hands spread before him, "No please Papa don't hit me!" This was the cut that went to Herr Baumgartner's marrow. He dropped on his knees beside the bed, drew the sobbing child to his breast murmuring tenderly, "Papa's poor little boy, poor good little child, I wouldn't harm a hair of your head. How could you think I would hurt you?" Hans stiffened and turned his head rigidly from the stink of the breath blown in his nostrils, his mouth tightly closed, feeling with horror his father's clammy warm tears joining his own on his face. His mother came silently, her weeping finished, a big blue bruise already forming on her cheekbone. She spread her arms around her son and husband and said in a most loving voice, "Look, Karl — this must stop. We are wrong to torment him like this with our troubles. He will be sick. He will never forget. Karl, try to forgive me. I am sorry." At once he straightened and turned about, drew her towards him almost over Hans, who leaned out as far from between them as he was able. "My sweet Gretel," he said, "I am sorry too. My heart is broken!"

"Oh no, no," she said, dismayed. Melted with tears and surprised by rising sensuality, they began to fondle not each other but the child between them; their newly roused passion for each other poured back and forth over and through him like a wave. Hans threw himself sidewise trying to break out of the prison of their arms. They then recollected themselves, and let him go. He hunched back in his bed against the wall and tried not to see them. His mother's headdress had fallen and lay underfoot, its ribbons crumpled and streaked by their bootsoles. She stopped to pick it up, his father lurched forward to hand it to her. They rose together, then sat down again, their arms about each other. "Oh, oh, oh," his mother kept whispering in a breathless voice, hiding her face in his father's shoulder as if she wished to be smothered. "Oh, oh . . ."

When she raised her head, her wandering eyes rested on her little boy, his head turned away, hands hanging. He looked like any other lost unhappy neglected child, a foundling in the room not sure of his welcome. Without moving, for her husband's face was now buried on her shoulder, she spoke to Hans in her familiar maternal voice: "Wash your hands and face, my son, you'll feel better — hurry now, in warm water, not cold. It is late for you to be awake. We must all go to sleep now, to sleep."

Hans rose, and began to wash his face timidly, fumbling with the wet washcloth, eyelids lowered as if he were ashamed to be seen in his nightshirt, washing before these strangers. In soundless wretchedness, with a pitiable mouth, he dried his face and hands and crawled into bed, pulling the covers up to his chin.

His mother approached him again, gently. "Ah, never you mind, my dear little one. Go to sleep to sleep — everything is over, nothing bad has happened. Sometimes we are crossest with the ones we love best. Say your prayers, little love, good night."

She was smiling vaguely not exactly at him, but at something she was thinking about. His father came also and kissed him with a wet mouth on his cheek. "Good night, my little man." They turned out the light and began to undress rapidly. He could tell by the sounds.

In the dark, he lay still, arms folded tightly over his chest, knees stiff, his stomach a hard knot, hearing in the narrow bed a few feet away his father and mother moving, turning, the sound of bedclothes being drawn up, pushed back; the gentle rustle and hiss of their whispered secret talk, shallow irregular breathings, and his mother's slow measured broken sighing — "Oh, oh, oh . . ." as if she were in pain; and his father's breathing "Sh-sh-sh —" suddenly ended by a long low groan. Something horrible was happening there in the dark, something frightful they were keeping from him — he strained his eyes staring, but there was only a wall of pure blackness mingled with the sounds of struggle. It was not even sound, but a feeling of commotion as if they might be struggling — and yet, maybe not, for his heart was beating so hard and so loudly it deafened him for a while; when his ears cleared again there was nothing to be heard. Then he heard his father asking tenderly in a slow whisper: "How do you feel? Are you happy?" And his mother's drowsy murmur, "Oh yes, yes, yes — yes."

The little boy's muscles and nerves and even the ends of his fingers and the roots of his hair let go all at once, all over, all through him, as if the thousand sharp cords binding and cutting him everywhere had broken all at once. A long yawn of delicious sleepiness flowed in him like warm water. He flung himself loosely on his side, nearly face downward towards the wall; his hands and feet and the back of his neck felt easy and soft, he fell asleep blissfully drifting from cloud to cloud all by himself into that soft darkness without sound and without dream.

Mrs. Treadwell and her young officer were joined by other junior officers who seemed to be taking them in on a drinking party, while making a round of the ship. She remembered afterward that she had been rather gay all over the place — first in the bake shop helping some very polite lads make rolls. Her party looked in on the galley, the bar, the officers' mess, all four decks, the engine room, and no matter where they were, trays of drinks followed them. She was offered, and accepted, cognac, Chartreuse, port, Amer Picon, Rhine wine, and German champagne. At one point they met up with the purser, who got the surprise of his life when Mrs. Treadwell greeted him as a boon companion and kissed him fondly. He returned the compliment with a hearty smack on her cheek, and a shrewd look into her eyes. "So," he said, indulgently, and trundled on, with the junior officers in his wake. Her partner of the evening appeared to expect her then to kiss him; she asked him why. He said it was not a thing one gave reasons for. Mrs. Treadwell thought it much the better idea to wait until tomorrow and see then how they both felt about it. He could not conceal his horror at such a point of view. "That is simply terrible!" he said, severely.

"I suppose so," said Mrs. Treadwell. "I am sorry." The charming young man looked very sulky, and Mrs. Treadwell noticed for the first time that he had a flashlight with him. He directed the ring of light at Mrs. Treadwell's feet, lighting her way, and they descended the narrow steps in silence, he holding her arm firmly. "I do not believe you are sober," he informed her at last, "on the bridge you offered to steer the ship. No harm done of course — but I think it is the first time such a thing ever happened to the Captain."

"He must lead a very sheltered life," said Mrs. Treadwell, "poor man." They strolled along the main deck, passed the dancers and the music, noticed Lizzi and Herr Rieber still waltzing, and towards the bow, that wretched Herr Baumgartner seemed to be being sick at the rail. He turned a face of despair towards them, almost an appeal for help. They passed, the young officer now supporting Mrs. Treadwell with an arm around her waist.

"He seems awfully sick, somehow," said she, "perhaps dying. He says he is dying, of something very painful."

The young officer said flatly, "I don't believe it at all. He just likes to drink all the time and keep himself sick. . . ."

Mrs. Treadwell said quite soberly "You don't believe then that people get sick and die some times just naturally? Of some disease they can't help?"

She noticed for the first time the cocky set of his white cap, farther to one side than was usual. He spoke up promptly in an intolerant voice: "Of course. But why should anyone claim special consideration merely because he happens to be dying? We are all sick," he said dogmatically, and the stoic mask of self-pity covered his features for an instant. "We are all dying, only not at the same pace . . . well, is that anything to get excited about?"

"I am not at all excited about it," said Mrs. Treadwell, a little on the defensive side, "but you seem to be."

"I am never excited, never," he told her, with a tremor in his voice that could mean anger, "it is simply that I who live a life of endless discipline have no patience with all the stupid muddle caused by such people as he, who do not know how to live!"

"Do you know?" asked Mrs. Treadwell gently, stopping and raising her face to his so that their glance met steadily. "Tell me." It occurred to Mrs. Treadwell that this was an odd conversation in the light of what she saw at once was going to happen. He enveloped her wholly, waist, shoulders, arms, brought her instantly under control and kissed her violently on her mouth, which was still open in speech. Mrs. Treadwell shuddered at the same unpleasant sensation of being bitten, of the blood being drawn by suction to her mouth that had revolted her in the past, and she drew away, turned her head outward, refused, and defended herself by a passivity that dismayed and enraged him.

He drew his head back, lifted his elbow and swept her hair back with his forearm, and she saw the sweat standing on his forehead. "I have been looking at you, thinking about you, for a long time," he said, harshly. "You never noticed me, no not even when we danced — why not? Now you will not kiss me — why not? . . . Do you want me to beg you? to say I love you? I never knew what people meant by that word."

"Don't say it, don't say it, I cannot bear the sound of it . . ."

His face, manner, mood, all shifted with the same violence, from erotic impetuosity to sheer pettiness. "Then why did you come with me, why did you encourage me to kiss you?"

Mrs. Treadwell drew away altogether, stood back facing him. "And now for the first lovers' quarrel," she said outrageously and laughed with a somewhat extreme amusement. What a young face he had; she saw him as if for the first time — smooth and lineless, clear features, tightly drawn, with angry vanity in the set of the mouth, a burning uneasiness in the eyes.

"I do not deserve for you to laugh at me," he said, with a dignity that carried his resentment past its crisis. He offered her his arm again but as if he did not wish to touch her. "Thank you for a very pleasant evening, Madame, and I shall be happy to see you to your door."

"Oh thank *you*, but it isn't at all necessary. Please don't trouble, I can go the rest of the way by myself."

He clicked his heels, bowed sharply from the waist, made a fine swift about face, and marched straight back towards the dancers. Mrs. Treadwell took time to admire him, thinking that the masculine passion for physical discipline of all sorts had its points — he was undoubtedly as drunk as she was, and yet, here she was, skipping and leaping down the perilous slopes from main deck to B deck, where on the last step but one she caught her sandal on the metal-edged tread and tore the heel off. It rattled down before her as she stood a moment, balancing herself on one foot. A young steward who was polishing shoes rose, came forward, picked up the heel, and spoke with high good manners, holding out his hand; "If you please, *meine Dame*, allow me to repair it for you." Mrs. Treadwell, with a wave and a smile, bent her knee, raised her foot and offered him the slipper, which he removed; she then went hippety-hop down the corridor, now and then stopping to raise her skirts and try a good high kick, straight up, toe pointed. What an absurd evening, and how pleasant to know it was over. She liked the young steward's shadowy face and tactful gestures: if everyone were like that, how much more possible life might be.

Lizzi would be dancing and then lurking about in corners with her pet pig, until any hour at all. Mrs. Treadwell leaned very close to the looking glass and studied her features thoughtfully, and began to amuse herself with painting a different face on her own, as she used to do for fancy dress balls. She drew long thin very black eyebrows that almost met over her nose and ran back over her temples almost into her hair. She covered her eyelids with bluish silver paint, weighted her lashes with beads of melted black wax, powdered her face a thick clown white, and at last drew over her rather thin lips a large, deep scarlet, glistening mouth, with square corners, a shape of unsurpassed savagery and sensuality. She brushed her black hair sleekly from her forehead, and moved back a few steps to admire the effect at the right distance. Yes, it would have done very nicely — she could have worn a mantilla and comb and gone to the party masked as one of the zarzuela company — Amparo perhaps. Why hadn't she thought of it? Because it would have been dull, and the evening would have ended just as it did, no matter what.

Mrs. Treadwell was nearly through her third round of solitaire, cards spread on her small game board, at the dressing table before the looking glass, where now and again she might glance at her strange assumed face, which no longer amused her but seemed a revelation of something sinister in the depths of her character. Mrs. Treadwell had, to begin with, hardly suspected she possessed a character in the accepted sense of the word, and had never felt the lack of one. It was rather late perhaps to discover there were depths in her, where were hidden all sorts of unpleasant traits she would detest in anyone else, much more in herself. She sighed and pushed the cards together without finishing the game, and rummaged in her dressing case for her sleeping tablets.

The door flew open and Lizzi fell in, went to her knees and up again in a sweeping movement, her features distorted, her speech incoherent and full of tears. A thin, chronically worried-looking young man just behind her let go her arm a moment too soon for fear of being dragged with her into a ladies' cabin. He could not conceal his astonishment at Mrs. Treadwell's face in its bizarre disguise; at first glance he had mistaken her for one of those Spanish dancing women, at second he knew better and was mystified. He stepped back and stood in shadow outside the door. "*Meine Dame,*" he began, and swiftly gave Mrs. Treadwell a brief account of events. Lizzi, far gone in hysteria, wrapped her arms around her head and swayed to the rhythm of sobs and hiccups. "I must leave her to you, pardon, *Meine Dame,*" said the young man, "I am in the band and must get back to my place at once."

"Thank you," said Mrs. Treadwell with extreme sweetness, closing the door. Lizzi moaned luxuriously, now lying at full length on the divan, and kept it up to intolerable lengths. "Oh, the brute, the savage, the beast," she repeated monotonously. Mrs. Treadwell repressed her airy impulse to ask, "Which one of them?" as she helped Lizzi get out of her dress and into her nightgown. She even picked up and put away tidily those garments steaming with body heat and the dreadful stale musky scent. She then remembered her sleeping tablets and swallowed two. Lizzi's abjectly suffering face on the pillow turned to her, the eyes like a beaten dog's, the forehead glistening with sweat. "Oh," said Mrs. Treadwell, full of remorse and gentle feelings, "you need those, too." She brought water and the sleeping pills, and Lizzi took them in silence. "There," said Mrs. Treadwell, simply as one friendly woman to another, "That should settle something for tonight, at least."

"Oh, but tomorrow!" sighed Lizzi brokenly, calming a little.

"Tomorrow? Let it come!" said Mrs. Treadwell. "At least tonight will be over!" She was quieted and easy, her lightness of heart might almost have been happiness, only of course that would be absurd. What was there to be happy about? She moved about rather unsteadily, not noticing that she was walking with one high-heeled sandal and one bare foot. Lizzi, soothed and wearied, forgot her troubles long enough to stare at Mrs. Treadwell's face. "But whatever for?" she gasped. "Whatever — what did you do to yourself?"

"I was putting on a mask," Mrs. Treadwell explained reasonably. "A mask for the party."

"But you're late," sang Lizzi, weeping again, "the party's over!"

"Yes, I know," said Mrs. Treadwell, thinking that Lizzi was already coming back in her old ghastly style, and would soon be the same bore as ever. She felt she must be entirely drunk, for Lizzi's high voice came to her full of echoes as if she were calling down a well: "Oh what shall I do now? Oh everything is so changed. Oh, I wish never to see him again . . . Oh dear, Mrs. Treadwell, can you tell me how I could have been so deceived? I never loved him, I see it now!"

"How does one know these mysterious things, always so sure, first one thing and then another?" asked Mrs. Treadwell, amiably detached and smiling, dressing gown in hand. She spoke apparently to the ceiling, for her eyes were raised as if she expected to see an answer written there. "How do you know what you feel?"

She lowered her eyes slowly without curiosity and listened a moment to a clamor at the door, a ferocious beating and kicking, and drunken shouting. She moved nearer, recognized Denny's voice: "Listen, Pastora, let me in there, you filthy little —" Mrs. Treadwell's ears shuddered, but she listened to Denny's thick-tongued descriptions of the Gothic excesses he intended to commit upon Pastora's person, of which rape would be the merest preliminary.

Lizzi sat up covering her ears and screaming, "Oh no, no, no, this is the last straw . . . No, no, I do not deserve this . . . No, I will not have this, no no, no . . ."

"Oh, please," said Mrs. Treadwell, carefully. "He is not talking to you. He is not talking to either of us. He is talking to himself. Lie down and be quiet."

She took her time, put a wet cloth on Lizzi's forehead, rearranged her as if she were a jointed doll, then went to the door, walking hippity hop, and stood there a moment, hand on the knob. Quite suddenly, she snatched the door back wide. Denny, surprised, swayed backward a step, then surged forward and seized the front of her gown, wrung it into a rag and said, "Come out here, you whore," almost formally as if he were delivering a message from someone else. "Come out here now, I'm goin' to break every bone in you." He gave a twist to her front, which wrenched her breast so painfully she almost went off balance.

She seized his wrist with both hands and said earnestly, "You are terribly mistaken. You'd better look again!"

"Who are you?" he asked dimly, then: "Jesus, what is this?" leaning over to examine her face under the paint, blowing a pestiferous breath in her face. "Oh, come on, come on, you can't fool me."

Mrs. Treadwell braced herself against him and pushed him in the chest with more force than she knew she had. He tottered back limply, taken off guard, staggered against the opposite wall, slid along it sideways as he fell in a confusion of grunts, arm-waving, thumpings, scrapings and sprawlings. Mrs. Treadwell watched him in motionless amazement, unable to believe that her unpremeditated little gesture had accomplished so much. He lay still. Mrs. Treadwell knelt near him and felt his head and neck with the tips of her fingers, not being willing to touch him further. There seemed to be nothing broken; though his neck felt loose, that might be only natural. He was breathing loudly with his mouth open, his eyes rolled up between his half-closed lids. His tongue moved to the edge of his lips, he seemed to be forming a word, Mrs. Treadwell doubled her fist and struck him sharply, again and again, in the mouth, on the cheek, on the nose. The blows hurt her hand and seemed to make no impression on Denny. He moved as if he might get up. Feeling her sandal under her, she took it off and held it firmly by the sole and beat him in the face and head with the heel, breathlessly, rising on her knees and coming nearer, her lips drawn back and her teeth set. She beat him with such furious pleasure a sharp pain started up in her right wrist and shot to her shoulder and neck. The sharp metal-capped high heels at every blow broke the skin in small half moons that slowly turned scarlet, and as they multiplied on his forehead, cheeks, chin, lips, Mrs. Treadwell grew cold with fright at what she was doing, yet could not for her life stop herself. Denny stirred and groaned bitterly, opened his eyes for one glimpse, then amazingly opened them wide, struggled until he sat halfway up, fell back again, crying out in his nightmare in a strangled voice, "Pastora, Pastora!"

Mrs. Treadwell got to her feet, feeling that not Denny, but she, had been averted from a shocking end. She swayed in drunkenness and exhaustion, balancing on one foot while she put on her sandal; there was just time for it before the steward appeared at the head of the passageway. She motioned to him anxiously and he hurried to her as if she were the injured one, though he saw instantly at a distance the crumpled form at her feet.

"*Meine Dame,*" he inquired with real anxiety, "you are not hurt? The gentleman," he glanced downward, "he did not . . . ?"

"Oh, no," she said vaguely, "nothing of that sort." The boy knelt beside Denny, who had relapsed into stupor. Mrs. Treadwell recognized the boy to whom she had given her other sandal. "I was in my cabin," she said, with blameless candor. "I heard cries, I heard someone fall . . . he seemed to be calling for someone, I couldn't hear . . . I came to see if I could help . . ." Her voice faded into a bewildered child's, her mouth trembled. "I was frightened," she added, clearly, with perfect truth.

"Don't trouble yourself, *meine Dame,*" said the boy. "I will look after this. It is not serious," he said, scrutinizing the bleeding little half-circle wounds all over Denny's features. "It is just that the gentleman is a little — perhaps . . . not quite . . ."

"I'm sure of it," said Mrs. Treadwell, with a deprecating smile, taking her hand from her forehead in a small, round defensive motion. "I'm very grateful to you, and sorry for your trouble. Good night."

Lizzi had pulled the sheet over her head, and peered out at Mrs. Treadwell like a timid furry beast from its nest. Mrs. Treadwell's smile still lingered on her lips if not in her eyes. She was very reassuring. "He is gone. It was nothing, just a mistake. He knocked at the wrong door, that was all. He knows it now."

"I wish I were dead, just the same," whimpered Lizzi. "Life is unbearable, don't you find?"

Mrs. Treadwell laughed outright. "Nonsense," she said, handing Lizzi a glass of water and a third sleeping pill. "I think it is wonderful." She swallowed another herself, and smiled delightedly at her hideous wicked face in the looking glass. In her joy and excitement, she snatched off her bloodstained sandal and kissed it. Leaning over Lizzi on the divan, who asked dreamily, "What are you doing now?" she tossed it through the porthole. "*Bon voyage*, my friend," she said, and to Lizzi peremptorily, "Go to sleep at once, or I'll give you a whole handful of sleeping pills!" She stood over her threateningly. Lizzi in her daze was flattered by all this attention, mistook it for an unsuspected softheartedness in this difficult stranger, dropped away into a light snore.

Mrs. Treadwell washed her disfigured face lavishly, slapping on warm water, anointing, patting, restoring herself to a semblance she recognized. Blissfully she sang a tuneless song under her breath as she tied her Alice in Wonderland hair ribbon and slipped into her white satin gown with the bishop sleeves. She was just folding herself into bed like a good little girl who has finished her prayers when a discreet knocking at the door brought her out again. The young steward stood there at attention, bowing. He handed her the sandal with the heel nicely replaced. "With your permission," with deep respect and an expression that was too near a knowing smile to match his words, "*meine Dame*, your sandal."

She took it by the sole firmly as if it too were a weapon. She thanked him gently, modestly, standing there before him quite unconcerned in her nightgown. His eyes flickered over her once, up, down, sideways, and he resented what he saw. To her he was just a servant, a nothing, something that came when it was called and did whatever she demanded. He leaped away down the passage wishing there were some way to get even with her — to make trouble for her, standing there smirking like a cat as if he didn't know how that stupid Herr Denny had got those heel marks in his face. Served him right!

He made the gesture of spitting, but he did not spit — he would have had to clean it up.

Mrs. Treadwell went again to the porthole over the spraddled form of Lizzi, and cast the second gilded sandal after its mate into the sea. She leaned forward a moment to breathe blissfully the damp fresh wind, to hear again the surge of the waves rolling up in great round hills, under the black-blue sky scattered with immense stars. She remembered how once she had sat for her portrait to a young painter in a tall old house near the Avenue Montaigne, and as the evening came on, he went down all those flights of stairs and brought up bread and cheese and cold beef and a bottle of wine for their supper. Afterwards, he held the creaky ladder for her while she climbed and put her head through a tiny open skylight in the roof; and she saw the glimmering lights of Paris coming on slowly, and above, the clear darkening blue sky with the stars coming out, one by one. It was the middle of May.

As the evening wore on, Dr. Schumann emerged for a walk and a look around him, but wearied soon of the disturbances and disorders taking form and breaking like waves, the monotonous barbarous beat of the music, and the inevitable results of an evening of gaiety on shipboard. The Spanish dancers, he noted, remained sternly sober, and kept their minds on business. They still had some business to transact, though the possible audience appeared to be thinning out in all directions. One or two of the young officers were still dancing occasionally with the Spanish girls, and the students were indefatigably athletic as usual, performing a comic version of a Basque male square dance; but several of the other men were miserably drunk — such as Herr Denny, having a violent argument with the zarzuela dancer called Pastora. Dr. Schumann considered seriously what means might be used to control such people, or at least, their language and behavior in public; that fellow should not be allowed to use such language on deck even to such a woman as she; but it was not his affair, thank God. Nearly every woman still visible showed signs of having been recently in tears, or a temper, or both, and some of them were none too sober, either. He retired to his quarters, where he might be found if needed, and almost at once a cabin boy came with a message that he was wanted in Herr Rieber's cabin. He went at once, oppressed with weariness, and found Herr Löwenthal, drowsy, indignant, reeking of beer, wringing out towels in cold water and laying them on top of Herr Rieber's head.

"Bottle fighting," he said, "like in the lowest places. Come in, Doctor. And now tell me, Doctor, can anybody show me a place on this ship where I can go to get rid of this fellow, who makes nothing but trouble for me every day? What did I do I deserve to get stuck with him when I'm nearly asleep after a hard day?"

He dipped another towel in the washhand stand, wrung it out and slapped it down on Herr Rieber's head. "Is there any way I can lose him?"

Dr. Schumann said, "Wait, I'll look at him. It's a pity, I'm afraid there's no place to put him. I'll get the steward to nurse him."

"Nurse?" groaned Herr Löwenthal. "Is it that bad?"

Dr. Schumann took a brief look at the wound under his flashlight, mopped the skull with alcohol, gave Herr Rieber a *piqûre* at the top of his forehead, and took seven neat stitches in a row on his scalp. He tied a line of small black silk stitches, snipping them off so that Herr Rieber appeared to be growing an extra row of eyelashes on his head. Herr Rieber squeezed his eyelids together during this operation but was otherwise motionless. Dr. Schumann then gave him a *piqûre*, and sent for the steward to undress him and put him to bed. Herr Löwenthal was very near complete demoralization. "My God, my God," he kept muttering to himself under his breath, until Dr. Schumann said, "He'll sleep a long time. I think you don't have to worry about him any more. But if you need me, call me." He heard the croak of exhaustion in his voice as he pronounced the ritual words.

He was no sooner in bed and settling into sleep than he was called again by the cabin boy. This time it was Herr Denny, the young Texan; he had got into an encounter with mysterious forces which left his face from forehead to chin a lumpy, discolored mass of ugly-looking little cuts and bruises, full of dried blood and already swelling.

Herr Glocken was shaking and fluttering in helpless fright. "I sent for you, Doctor, what could have happened to him? Two stewards brought him, and said they found him so, and one of them said he knew what had happened, he had seen it before, these were heel marks from a woman's slipper!" He fluttered and nattered at Dr. Schumann's elbow, who was giving his patient an antitetanus *piqûre* as a beginning. He washed the battered face carefully with alcohol and said, "Yes, or it could have been a tack hammer. There must have been metal caps on them." Dr. Schumann had seen such wounds before, too, and of course, he decided at once, the sharp talons on that Spanish dancer's slippers would exactly fit any and all of these wounds.

"What could have happened, Doctor?" gibbered Herr Glocken, and his self-pitying face added plainly, "*Why* must such things always happen to me? What am I to do now, with no one to help me?" And he implored, "Doctor, you know I am not well. Don't leave me here alone with him! Confidentially, dear Doctor, he is a species of monster, certainly not quite human, I have seen and heard him. What can I do?"

Dr. Schumann smiled at him very frankly and said, "You are one of the few sober passengers I have seen this evening. Why not go looking for Herr David Scott and bring him back to help you? But I think you will not need it. Herr Denny will sleep, never fear. Good night."

Herr Glocken followed him out, but took his forlorn way up deck alone, and Dr. Schumann went at once, fearing he might collapse before he could reach the porthole in his cabin for a breath of air while he took his crystal drops. In that moment, when he truly expected death, he looked upon all these intruders as his enemies. Without exception, he rejected them all, every one of them, all human kinship with them, all professional duty except the barest tokens. He did not in the least care what became of any one of them. Let them live their dirty lives and die their dirty deaths in their own way and their own time, so much carrion to fill graves. He crossed himself and folded his arms and lay still breathing carefully, turning his head slowly from side to side, denying his own bitter thoughts even as they rose and flowed again painfully all through him as though his blood were full of briers.

The blessed medicine worked its spell again. In his waking sleep La Condesa's face floated bodiless above him, now very near, peering into his eyes; then retreating and staring and coming again in ghostly silence. The head rushed away into the distance, shrunken to the size of an apple, then bounded back, swollen and white like a toy balloon tossed upward by a hand, a deathlike head dancing in air, smiling. Dr. Schumann in his sleep rose and reached up and out before him and captured the dancing head, still smiling but shedding tears. "Oh, what have you done?" the head asked him. "Oh, why, why?" not in complaint, only in wonder. He held the head tenderly between his spread palms and kissed its lips and silenced it; and went back to bed with it, where it lay lightly on his breast without smiles or tears, in silence, and he slept on so deeply he did not know it was a dream.

At eleven o'clock, the band played "*Auf Wiedersehen*" and disappeared, all except the pianist, who held a ticket for the raffle. The Spanish company started their show, with the gramophone going at top voice. They first did a bolero, with Ric and Rac taking part; when in the dance they came face to face, they searched each other's eyes fiercely threatening murder. The medical students sat in a shallow ring near them, clapping their hands and shouting "*Olé*" at the right moments. The expected audience however had all but dispersed; those who stayed or wandered by and wandered back were not ticket-holders. Arne Hansen, after disposing of Herr Rieber and disappearing to change his bloodied shirt, was back in his chair with a bottle of beer beside him. He seemed calm enough, his eyes were closed, and one might have thought he was asleep, except that at intervals he would reach for his beer and take a good swig. Now and again he sat up, motioned to a deck steward, and uttered one word: "Another." Amparo decided prematurely that she need not expect any more trouble with him for the evening.

Frau Schmitt, clutching her ticket, sat timidly on the edge of a deck chair near the band. Frau Rittersdorf, passing, said, "Good night. I wish you luck!" If she had stuck needles in her Frau Schmitt could not have been more injured. Herr Löwenthal, who had spent the earlier part of the evening in the writing room smoking, drinking beer and addressing postcards to family, friends and business associates to go by airmail from Southampton, avoiding his cabin for sheer detestation of Herr Rieber's presence, had given up and gone down to his quarters just in time to receive Herr Rieber's battered person. He was now back on deck and meant to stay there until the last light was out. He had even a notion to stow himself away on the leather couch in the writing room. His stomach was turned for good, he would not pollute his nostrils with the breath from that pig. Nobody could force him: he would sleep on deck first. He would go down to the steerage — there was plenty of room there now, on deck anyway. He stood at the rail, arms folded, brooding, his cigar shooting sparks into the wind, and stared with pure unappreciation at Amparo's expert performance of a dance she announced as a Cachucha, a dance he had never seen, would not care if he never saw again, and he wondered what any man in his right mind could see in a woman like that no matter what she was doing. He had heard plenty of times that shicksas were good stuff if you took them in the right way, that is, you didn't have to think of them as people, the same as Jewish, only just live meat, but he never had been able to buy that argument. . . . He presently went in the bar, asked for a stein of beer and a piece of cheese, returned to the writing room and enjoyed his snack. He turned off the light and stretched out on the leather sofa. Oi, oi oi; this was peace and quiet, the first he'd had on the voyage.

A steward pulled naggingly at his sleeve. It was daylight and the steward remarked, "You must have gone to sleep, sir," with the chilly resignation of a man who cannot afford to despair of clearing up one more little area of disorder in self-perpetuating chaos. Herr Löwenthal, instantly wide awake, sat up, scrubbed his face swiftly with the palm of his hand, planted his feet on the floor and asked with sarcasm, "What do *you* think?" The steward spun away with an angry jerk of his shoulders, at which Herr Löwenthal, who delighted in forcing unwilling service from any kind of subordinate, bawled, "Hey, boy!" meaning to order a pot of coffee. He noted with satisfaction the purely automatic pause in the steward's stride, but the man in the servant conquered, and the man fairly burst from the room as if devils were after him.

Herr Löwenthal, feeling sodden and lumpy, went back to his cabin to wash and change before breakfast. He supposed he would have to go on doing that, but never again would he sleep in the place — nothing could force him. He found another steward and Dr. Schumann already there, fussing over Herr Rieber, who was installed in the lower berth without so much as an if-you-please to Herr Löwenthal, the lawful occupant, who took in the state of affairs with instant rage which he betrayed only by the slight shake in his voice. "He is welcome to my bunk, Doctor, so long as he has got it already. I wouldn't want it, I got no further use for it."

That pig Rieber kept his eyes shut but his lids were working, pretending he was asleep, or sick or couldn't hear, it didn't matter which, he was pretending and it was enough to drive an honest man crazy. As if a little crack with a bottle could hurt a skull like that. Dr. Schumann nodded and spoke absently as he changed the dressing, spreading a nasty smell of iodoform around. "Well, no, I suppose you haven't," he said. "There is always the divan, anyway."

A deep slow swelling soundless howl rose and echoed and died away in Herr Löwenthal's soul. It was a howl and a song with words. "Take my table, take my bed, take my blood, grind my bones, God curse Them what do They want more?" In his fury he shouted so loudly close to Dr. Schumann's ear, the Doctor jumped and almost dropped the gauze he was winding around Herr Rieber's brow. "Careful, will you?" he snapped, but Herr Löwenthal's voice drowned the words. "Maybe I want my bed for myself, Doctor? Maybe for once I should like to come back somewhere and not find somebody pushing me out? Is there a law saying I shouldn't have what I paid for? How is it you can come in here as if he owned the place and take my bed just because he is drunk and I am not? Doctor," he said, his speech trailing off in a tone of pathos, one righteous man appealing to the sense of pity and justice in another, "Doctor, I want to know these things — you tell me!"

Dr. Schumann, deeply repelled by this show of selfishness and bad temper, as if his disgusting patient were not trial enough, asked coldly: "Is it such a martyrdom as all that to give up your bed to someone who needs it, especially since you have another as good? I shall have him put on the divan if you wish, but the ship is beginning to roll heavily and there is less danger of his falling out here."

So I can fall out until all the Jews go back to Jerusalem, what of it? It is only my head is cracked, who cares? Aloud he said in a luxury of contempt: "Let him have the whole stinking place, I got no use for it!"

Dr. Schumann said with weary scorn: "Thank you," at which Herr Löwenthal gave a loud spluttering puff of air from his pouched lips, and got out into the passageway before he really said what he thought about that kind of thanks.

The Captain invited Dr. Schumann for mid-morning coffee on the bridge, and opened the conversation at once. "I have had the reports of various officers in line of duty," he said, stretching his wattles and tucking them in his collar again, "and beyond the sheer impudence of the thing, beyond their total ignorance of any forms of social decency, those disorderly dancers seem to be quite a common sort of petty criminal, too, of the pilfering and pickpocket order. This has been an unusually eventful voyage —"

"It is a disaster," said Dr. Schumann, making no attempt to conceal his weariness or his indifference to the whole sordid affair.

"That is not a word we use at sea for anything less than the loss of a ship," said the Captain, tempering his austerity with a thin smile. "An old sea-dog," he said, leaving Dr. Schumann to infer which sea-dog he meant, "knows what danger and disaster really are, and could never mistake the misdemeanors of a load of passengers for anything serious. They do not know how to behave on a ship —"

"Nor on land, either, some of them. But there are still some very decent persons on board."

The Captain almost smirked at this opportunity handed to him as if on a tray. "I shall be more than pleased if you will show me one," he said, with unctuous enjoyment. Dr. Schumann decided to appear somewhat amused. "It is difficult," he agreed, "on short acquaintance and in a trying, unfamiliar situation. Very few persons show up at their best."

This required no answer. The Captain went on: "I am told La Condesa's pearls were stolen — unhappy lady! I began to think at last that her mind was not exactly —" He touched his forehead lightly with an index finger.

"It is possible," said Dr. Schumann, to end that topic. "We do not know whether the pearls were stolen or not. La Condesa said the children snatched them from her. Her nurse the stewardess said La Condesa was not wearing her pearls that day. The children threw some object overboard. There were two witnesses, Herr and Frau Lutz, but unfortunately they do not support each other's testimony. Nothing is proved."

"The trouble with this sort of thing," said the Captain, raising a hand and keeping silence while the young steward standing out of earshot came forward and poured more coffee, "the trouble is, when a man, any sort of man," he added generously, "not just a naval officer, finds himself embroiled in a low kind of women's gossip, it is an affront to his self-respect to have to deal with these things on their natural debased level. I was told the Spanish company robbed many shops in Santa Cruz, and that many of those you call decent persons among the passengers witnessed this. No one interfered or took steps to prevent this on the scene?"

"Several passengers, not women," said Dr. Schumann, "have agreed among themselves this morning that what they saw looked very dubious indeed, they had well-founded suspicions, but after all, no proof. At no time did anyone feel it was his business to interfere or even to take particular notice."

"That was very prudent," said the Captain, dryly. "Tell me, how are your casualties getting on? The young fellow whose name I do not remember, who seems to have been attacked by someone wielding an unorthodox weapon, perhaps a tack hammer or a woman's shoe heel?" Dr. Schumann saw the glint of gallantry in the Captain's pale eyes. "I should imagine there are the usual number of shipboard romances with their inevitable disappointments and dramatic scenes," he said, with relish. "Is the young man recovering?"

"He'll live," said Dr. Schumann, "and so will all the others. There is again the question of who committed this thoroughly mischievous act. The young man himself insists it was a girl called Pastora, one of the Spanish company. But a steward has defended this girl, says she is innocent — a strange word to use about any of that troupe — and that he is certain it was done by a woman wearing a mask, so that he did not recognize her. That was all he knew."

"As for the incident on deck when Herr Rieber got his scalp scratched?"

"That is the only perfectly clear incident we have. Herr Hansen has, throughout the voyage, showed himself consistently as a man of unstable temper and eccentric views, and for his own reasons he broke his beer bottle over Herr Rieber's head when Herr Rieber was dancing harmlessly with a lady —"

"Lady —" echoed the Captain thoughtfully. The word hung between them like a drift of vapor. Dr. Schumann proceeded without a pause: "Everybody knows this and it seems to be the one thing everybody does know. All the rest is a very sordid little sort of tempest in a teapot . . . a trivial mystery."

"La Condesa was the mysterious one," said the Captain. "That beautiful lady should never have been left on that barbarous island alone. No matter what she did. No lady could do enough harm politically to deserve such a sentence. By the way, you were her physician and in her confidence, what *did* she do?"

"I don't know," said Dr. Schumann, rather bluntly.

The Captain's chin retreated, his neck stiffened, his face turned slowly a dark red. "I have thought as much from the beginning," he said with rancor. "It is a pity she did not respond better to your treatment. Indeed, I gather that her condition worsened very much in your hands . . . well, Dr. Schumann, flesh is grass, no? A doctor cannot afford to let his failures weigh upon his mind!"

Dr. Schumann stood up suddenly in the middle of this speech, and at the end, took his leave with a stiff bow, noting the signs of the Captain's wrath and chagrin, but with such a stinging anger in himself it crossed his mind only a good while later that the Captain's blood pressure was apparently rather high.

Denny's loud groans and threats of revenge on Pastora had been quieted by Dr. Schumann's needle, but his swollen lips and end of his nose just visible in a swathe of bandages big as a large pumpkin emitted burbles and rattles and snorts for the rest of the night. David stood swaying, legs wide, feet rocking, trying to keep his balance and to take in the meaning of the squalid disorder in the cabin. Herr Glocken was almost entirely demoralized, and tearfully begged David not to go to sleep, and not to let him, Herr Glocken, go to sleep either. Life was too dangerous on board this ship, nobody was safe, the innocent and the guilty were threatened alike, and the innocent first —

"Not always," said David, with a flapping gesture full of drunken portentousness towards Denny.

"Always," said Herr Glocken, obstinately.

"Have it your way," said David, struggling to the bunk by the wall, falling into his pillow face downward and letting his drunkenness take charge of him. He sank through qualmy waves into bottomless deeps of drowning and yet could not drown. Nightmare closed around in whirling flame and orange flashes of dreadful shapeless visions with crazed eyes and stretched silently screaming mouths. He rolled face up and opened his eyes on the low comedy of his surroundings and heard himself say loudly, "I'm ready for the nut-hatch!"

"What? What is that?" Instantly Herr Glocken responded. "Don't turn out your light. Don't go to sleep!"

"All right," said David, "I won't. But you go to sleep. It's all over anyhow. Nothing more can happen."

"Oh, how do we know?" moaned Herr Glocken, but in a few minutes David saw that he was asleep. He slept also at last, for an hour, and woke in the horrors of headache fit to crack his skull, a leaping gorge, blazing thirst, and a stomach so estranged it refused to harbor its only friends, aspirin and cold water.

Denny was awake again, too, this time merely groaning at intervals, begging for water, but unable to lift or turn his head to drink it. David said, "Just keep still for God's sake and open your mouth as much as you can, and I'll pour a little and you swallow!" This was done with much commotion and spilt water and sounds of choking from Denny, with Herr Glocken pleading, *"Bitte, bitte, bitte*, my medicine, Herr Scott, please my medicine, I am late with it, *bitte* —"

David gave him his medicine, swallowed more aspirin, and while he washed lightly at the stand and changed his clothes, he asked Denny whatever had happened to him. Denny's beaten mouth moved and he told the story of his afflictions, or rather his version of them, slowly in a vocabulary that astonished even David, who thought he knew all the words and most of their meanings. He almost lost track of the events in his fascinated attention to the language, but the name Pastora did emerge from the depths of boiling pitch.

"Are you sure?" asked David. "Last time I saw her she was running from you like a rabbit, way ahead, too —"

"I finally got to her cabin," said Denny in a low hoarse voice, "and she came right out and lit into me with an ice pick. I bet her pimp put her up to it. I bet he was right there back of her —" His mouth pouted and twitched at the corners. "She already had my money," he whispered, "all the hell she was going to get. I guess they figured it all velvet and no wear and tear —"

David left the cabin without waiting for more, pretending that he didn't hear Herr Glocken pleading earnestly that Herr Scott should not leave him alone. "Let him get out on deck by himself," David decided, "I'm through." Hunched and sick, he found his table. For once he was not hungry but drank coffee, hoping for Jenny and fearing she would not come, glancing around in spite of himself every time someone entered, hating the very thought of seeing her and hardly able to endure his waiting for her. At last he felt he had something to say to her that she would not be able to answer. Would she dare to say to him again, *"It wasn't love, David* —" Well, this time he didn't care what it was. It was the end for him and he was going to walk off the ship at Vigo.

When he glanced about again, Jenny was there, coming towards him. He was so blinded with excitement he could not see, until she was quite near, that she was pale, exhausted, her eyes swollen; but she was freshly washed and smelled of roses, her smile was quite frank and friendly if a little shamefaced. She seated herself, shook out her napkin and said, "Lord! that was heavy going last night, wasn't it? I've never been so absolutely blotto in my life. What happened to the raffle, I wonder? Finally? Or to anything else? David darling, you look downright done in. What became of you?"

She had not looked straight in his eyes, in spite of her smile; she now asked the steward for orange juice and coffee and toast and jelly and milk, then said, "Heavens, it's just force of habit. I can't eat anything! Is coffee all you're having, too?"

David said in a crackling voice, "Look here, Jenny, what are you up to? What are you trying on this time? Pretend you don't remember? Well, you never believed me when I told you that, and now I don't believe you."

"That's fair enough," said Jenny, "but now I do believe you, because I don't remember one single thing after a lot of dancing and scurrying around the ship with Freytag and drinking a lot, and then I woke up this morning with a crashing head in my own chaste narrow bunk with Elsa lying there staring at me across the cabin, and the minute I opened my eyes she asked, 'How do you feel now?' I was delighted to tell her I felt simply immeasurably awful and it seemed to cheer her up."

David saw that she was really uneasy and kept a cold steady eye upon her as she rambled along, but interrupted to ask: "You don't remember?"

Jenny said, "I am trying my best to tell you that for the first time in my abandoned career, I don't remember a thing after a certain point. We joined up for a while with Mrs. Treadwell and her little powder puff of an officer, and we were all over the ship and we seemed to drink everything in sight, but I can't remember how I got back to my cabin. Oh," she said painfully, drooping her face into her hands.

"Are you sure you went to your cabin at all?" asked David with a scorching smile.

"I woke up there, if that's any proof," said Jenny, feeling a chill in her spine, for David was about to tell her something she did not want to hear, and her blood knew what it was. "Why?"

"Why, nothing," said David. "This alcoholic blank *is* convenient, isn't it?"

"Why, no," said Jenny, drearily, "not if you've been trailing me around again and peeping. What was it? What did I do?"

He turned his head away and his profile was one tight small secretive smile. "Ask Freytag," he said, watching acutely her pallor taking on faint greenish shadows.

Jenny knew that expression in his face too well, and resented it again. "I'll do that, later," she said. "There's no hurry." The anger in her voice didn't match the tears slowly filling her eyelids. More tears, yes, she could draw them at will — this time they wouldn't work. "Don't cry, Jenny, or not before people. They'll think I've been beating you —" he said. "You do cry so nicely, but it's a little late for that now. We've crossed a line, it's all over, why can't we say so and let go?"

"Haven't we been doing that, letting go little by little, all along?" asked Jenny, her tears drying at once and her face beginning to glow pinkly with anger. "Does it have to be a wrench? Do we have to break bones? I wish we could let it come of itself when we are really ready for it — when it won't hurt so much! We'll get used to it gradually —"

David flared up in turn. "What exactly am I supposed to get used to? Seeing you sprawled flat on your back in a fairly public place, the boat deck? And the only reason you stayed nearly faithful to me is that you were too drunk to be interesting to your seducer, after all." He poured another cup of coffee and said, "Let's drop this subject. I'm sick of it already."

Jenny took a good swig of too hot coffee, gasped a little and said, "You are a monster, did you know that, you monster?"

"Are you still drunk?" asked David in something like triumph. "Sometimes when I thought I was sobered up and could face the mean trivialities of real life again, one cup of hot coffee would slam me back into the ditch, I'd have to crawl out once more through the slime and weeds —"

"You're pleased with yourself, aren't you?" asked Jenny accusingly. "You're glad this happened, aren't you? You were really hoping all along for something like it, weren't you? I'd give a good deal to know what you really have had in mind all this time — not that it concerns me."

"It did concern you," said David in a new tone, as if he were talking pleasantly with a stranger, "but you are right. It doesn't now."

Jenny stood up calmly, her face quietly intent, but David saw her hands shaking. "I'm sorry," she said, "but I must run away now. I've got a question to ask somebody."

"I've told you already." David raised his voice a little, but did not glance at her again as she went. He poured more coffee, and said to the waiter, "I'll have scrambled eggs and ham now, thank you."

Mrs. Treadwell and Herr Freytag greeted each other pleasantly on a morning stroll around the deck and agreed that breakfast together in the open air would be a very nice way to dispel the lingering miasma of last night's uproar. They were both clear-eyed, in amiable mood and inclined to smile at each other when some specially used-up-looking reveler strayed by their chairs. They exchanged one or two universal if minor truths — pleasure was so often more exhausting than the hardest work; they had both noticed that a life of dissipation sometimes gave to a face the look of gaunt suffering spirituality that a life of asceticism was supposed to give and quite often did not. "Both equally disfiguring," said Freytag. "The real sin against life is to abuse and destroy beauty, even one's own — even more, one's own, for that has been put in our care and we are responsible for its well-being —"

Mrs. Treadwell turned her dark blue eyes on him in faint surprise. "I never thought of that," she said. "I just thought beauty was a phase of living and would pass with everything else in time —"

"Maybe," said Freytag, "but that is not the same as hurrying to kill it, do you think?"

"Maybe not," said Mrs. Treadwell, watching Jenny Brown coming towards them slowly, head towards the sea, hands crossed and folded at the wrists. She passed without seeing them, all pallor and melancholy. "That poor girl," said Mrs. Treadwell, rather idly, turning to Freytag. He started so sharply the things on his tray rattled, he gazed after the retreating Jenny, and his dilated pupils turned his gray eyes to black fire. Mrs. Treadwell instantly was warm with embarrassment, as if Freytag had spoken some dire impropriety: he simply had no reserve, no dignity. It did not matter what kind of thing existed between him and that girl, it was so weak of him to let every feeling he had show in that way. She carefully avoided facing him. It was like that other morning when the talk about his wife came up; like the time he had picked the quarrel with her in the writing room. Mrs. Treadwell set her tray carefully on the deck between their chairs, alighted feet together, and rose as if she were getting out of a motor car.

"Why are you going?" asked Freytag simply as a small boy.

"My cabin mate is not well, I promised to help her."

"Isn't that the screeching hag who made all the trouble?" asked Freytag with a writhing mouth. Mrs. Treadwell walked away. Freytag got up and went in the opposite direction, looking for Jenny. He did not find her after a half hour's search.

As Mrs. Treadwell neared her own door, the door of the cabin next hers was opened, and the Baumgartner family emerged, the little boy in front with his timid hangdog air. Herr Baumgartner held the door for his wife and stepped aside for her with an almost theatrical show of deference on his weak-mouthed, self-pitying face, with its beaten look of guilt. His wife passed him like a stranger, yet her perpetually grieved air was now touched with shame, the silence among the three was like some burdensome secret they were carrying together. Mrs. Treadwell opened her door and, halfway in, said hastily, "*Grüss Gott* —" over her shoulder, then closed the door, and Lizzi, pushing the ice cap off her brow, said plaintively, "Please, what is it now?"

"Nothing," said Mrs. Treadwell. "Is there anything I can do for you?"

"I would like another sleeping pill," said Lizzi, drearily. "Tell me, did you hear anything new upstairs? What happened to the party?"

Mrs. Treadwell handed her the pill and a glass of water. "There are rumors," she said, "not very interesting. There was almost nobody at the raffle, and one of those twins drew the tickets out of an open basket, and the Spanish company won all the prizes except a little white shawl for the pianist and a pair of castanets for one of those Cuban students. . . . I only overheard this — some of the Germans talking, those Huttens and others. Nobody told me anything directly. Now then," she ended amiably, "will you go to sleep again?"

"I think so," said Lizzi, almost entirely chastened. "You did not hear any word of Herr Rieber?"

"He is resting," said Mrs. Treadwell, "and I hope you will too."

Out she went near desperation, but managed to make her way to the small writing room, where almost no one went these days, without a glance or greeting for anyone. She sat there alone reading stale magazines until the luncheon bugle sounded. The exact vision of the Baumgartners' faces would not leave her. It was plain they too had suffered some sort of shabby little incident during the night. Mrs. Treadwell did not even wish to guess what it might have been. That sad dull display of high manners after they had behaved no doubt disgracefully to each other and their child was intended no doubt to prove that they were not so base as they had caused each other to seem. That dreadful little door-holding bowing scene had meant to say, You can see, can't you, that in another time or place, or another society, I might have been very different, much better than you have ever seen me? Mrs. Treadwell leaned back and closed her eyes. What they were saying to each other was only, *Love me, love me in spite of all! Whether or not I love you, whether I am fit to love, whether you are able to love, even if there is no such thing as love, love me!*

A small deep wandering sensation of disgust, self-distaste came with these straying thoughts. She remembered as in a dream again her despairs, her long weeping, her incurable grief over the failure of love or what she had been told was love, and the ruin of her hopes — what hopes? She could not remember — and what had it been but the childish refusal to admit and accept on some term or other the difference between what one hoped was true and what one discovers to be the mere laws of the human condition? She had been hurt, she had recovered, and what had it all been but a foolish piece of romantic carelessness? She stood up to take a deep breath and walk around the stuffy room. All morning long she had been trying in the back of her mind to piece together exactly what had happened last night to her, and what she had done. The scene with that young officer was clear enough. She remembered Herr Baumgartner hanging over the rail looking sick. Lizzi was delivered to her hands later, when she had been amusing herself painting her face; and then —

No good putting it off any longer. She could not find her gilded sandals when she was putting her things in order. There were small random bloodspots on the lower front of her nightgown. And as she walked, she remembered, and stopped, clutching a chairback, feeling faint. Walked again, then left the room and set out to look for Jenny Brown. She should know everything about it, being the "girl" of that rather self-absorbed young man, Denny's cabin mate. . . . Mrs. Treadwell remembered very well what had happened, what she had done; she wanted a few particulars of the damage she had caused, and above all to learn whether her enemy had recognized her.

Jenny Brown was reading the bulletin board. A ragged-edged imitation of an ancient proclamation announced: *The victims of last night's violence and bloodshed are resting quietly. The suspected criminals are under surveillance, not yet apprehended, but an early disclosure of some interesting identities is expected.* Signed: *Les Camelots de la Cucaracha.*

For the rest, news from the faraway world mentioned the shipping strike, the number of ports tied up, the number of men involved, the amount of wages lost, the many millions of money lost to the shipping business, and no end in sight; the situation in Cuba was not improving, all attempts at a settlement between factions had failed; unemployment was world-wide and growing worse, a real threat everywhere; yesterday's ship's pool, so much, had been won by Herr Löwenthal; the horse races would begin at two o'clock, and whoever had lost a gold-banded fountain pen with the initial R engraved on it, please call at the purser's office.

Mrs. Treadwell said to Jenny: "But no bulletins about the casualties in last evening's engagement. I wonder how they are doing."

Jenny said: "It seems to have all been very gay. That dancer called Pastora is said to have attacked that William Denny with an ice pick. And that long-legged Swede hit that Herr Rieber over the head with a beer bottle. These are notes I have just picked up in my travels around deck."

Mrs. Treadwell suddenly and surprisingly laughed out — not a loud laugh or an empty one — a small rich trill of merriment, pure pleasure; Jenny was so taken with the sound she laughed too, in a small shaken voice; she had not expected to feel like laughing about anything, and now she laughed without knowing why.

"So it was that little dancer, after all?"

"That's what he says, and I'd think he should know," said Jenny, and they went on with light laughter in their voice, quite blithe and ruthless, perfectly frank in their delight that the insufferable fellow had got his comeuppance.

"It nearly restores my faith in life," said Jenny. Her face then changed, instantly, became pale and anxious once more. Mrs. Treadwell saw Freytag coming towards them, and without any sign of uneasiness, she drifted away in her strange motionless walk as if she did not use the ordinary human muscles. Jenny stood until Freytag came straight towards her and waited until he spoke. He leaned very close and said gently: "I've been worried about you."

Jenny said, "Don't, please."

He said, "I've been looking for you all over. Where were you?"

Jenny said soberly, "Oh, here and there. No one can get really misplaced for long on this ship. . . . Oh, I can't bear it much longer. Oh, I want to leave at Vigo, but I haven't got a visa for Spain."

"Stop saying 'Oh,'" said Freytag, soothingly. "Things aren't so bad as all that. You haven't got anything to be sorry for."

"Oh, what do you know about it? Tell me, tell me, what happened — ?"

"If you could see your face!" he told her. "Jenny, you're such a strange sort of girl. You'd think you'd just been sentenced to death. Listen to me," he said, familiarly as a brother. With something of a brother's impersonal touch he took her elbow lightly and steered her out to deck center and strolled along with her. "You'll not believe this maybe, but nothing, nothing, absolutely *nothing* happened, we were both too drunk, I'm very sorry to say; I was good for nothing and you were — well, not there at all, on the moon, I should say; and Jenny, it was perhaps a little dull and certainly absurd and nothing for either of us to think about again. Do you hear me?" he said, leaning forward and peering into her face. She stopped short, and to his astonishment, laughed with convincing merriment. "How idiotic!" she said. "Nothing, after all. For all the trouble you've made me, I should have had *something* out of it! Something more than just trouble! *You* needn't think of it again, but David will for the rest of his life. He saw us last night — saw something that about finished him, I think . . ."

"So long as he goes prowling and spying on you," said Freytag, boldly, "anything he sees will be too good for him."

After a long pause, Jenny took a few slow steps ahead of him. "I deserve that," she said flatly. "Good-by." Her face was anything but repentant-looking and the manner of her leavetaking was, to say the least, he observed wryly, not humble. He did not cast off at once the tingle of annoyance and curiously wounded feelings her sudden snub left in him. Even after he reminded himself again that she was not really attractive, a little nobody not worth a man's attention, just a moody, shallow neurotic American girl pretending to herself she was an artist to give herself false importance — the whole series of belittling tags seemed inadequate to his sense of injury, his desire for revenge of some kind on her. His grudge against Mrs. Treadwell for her inconsequent gossip with Lizzi had quite vanished — indeed he had a slight new grievance against Mrs. Treadwell because she had not once made the smallest gesture towards advancing their dubious entente, thus denying him the satisfaction of putting her off in the little ways he knew, just enough to whet her appetite for conquest but not enough to discourage her. He had been rather pleased at her readiness to have breakfast with him again as if their first had made a light bond between them; and she had ended by walking away rudely, as rudely as Jenny, after all, though she did seem to be of a somewhat better class; well, maybe American women are all of them rude. He shook his head as if that might scatter his uncomfortable thoughts, and tried to think of Mary, but the nearer he came to her bodily, the more dimly her image flickered in his mind. What was there to think of? She was Mary, she was there, waiting, they would take up their life together just where they had set it down — no, they had never set it down anywhere, this separation was nothing, a mere interruption of habit, of custom, of the good warm dailiness of marriage, as if marriage could be in any way changed or affected by absences from each other. He drew a deep breath and sighed loudly.

In the bar Herr Hansen was bowed over a stein of beer like a man looking into an open grave. The Spanish company sat around a table with coffee cups before them, Ric and Rac clawing into the sugar bowl; they were all silent and sulky-looking and concerned only with themselves. Their affairs with this ship and its passengers were ended, they were finished with all on board, they had no need to express their hatred and contempt any more. They looked a little dull and melancholy in their sullenness, as if their victory had cost more than it was worth, and had exhausted them. Freytag passed on through the bar without stopping when he saw who was already there: no beer could do him any good in such company.

Jenny returned to her cabin, and there was Elsa on the divan, hands flattening a book on her knees. "What's that you're reading?" asked Jenny, washing her hands for lack of something to do.

"The Bible," said Elsa, distantly, without raising her eyes.

"Have you had breakfast?"

"Yes," said Elsa, "and those Spaniards were already there, and when we passed them my mother said, loud enough for them to hear, 'Look out for your wallets!' but they pretended not to hear. My poor father, I felt sorry for him, he said in a low voice making a joke, I think, that my mother would get him stabbed in the back if she said such things to that kind of foreigners, and my mother just said loudly in Spanish that thief was too good a word for them after all the names they called other people. I thought I would just die," she added suddenly. Without warning she closed the Bible and fell sidewise on the divan and stretched out, crying deeply with tears rolling into her hair.

"It's no use," she babbled, "nothing helps. I can't find anything in it that tells me how to live when I am so ugly and stupid and nobody wants to come near me, nobody can dance with me! Once my mother made me try to play the piano. I took lessons years and years, but anybody could play better than me, nobody wanted to hear me —"

Jenny offered her a clean handkerchief and said helplessly, "Elsa,

Elsa, it's not so bad as all that! Here, take this. Let's wash our faces and go up on deck. We're coming into Vigo soon, and we'll all go ashore and those wretched dancers will stay there, and everything will be better then."

"No, no," said Elsa, "I am not going. You go."

Johann woke from his short heavy sleep warm and eased all over; he stretched and yawned and rolled like a cat, making luxurious noises in his throat. He had come in just before daylight decently quiet but not guiltily, not cautiously; his uncle was awake, and did not question him, but asked only for a glass of water. Now he was sleeping well, comfortably composed, with a peaceful reconciled face, his eyelids tightly folded, his wax-yellow skin smoothed out and cold-looking. In panic Johann laid his palm near the mouth and nostrils to feel if there was still breath; then to the heart, his hand shaking. "Uncle!" he called loudly. "Wake up!" His uncle opened his eyes, gave a little melancholy sound of protest, and said, "No, why must you wake me? I did not sleep until very late."

Johann snatched back his hand and stammered a confused apology. His uncle did not reply, but closed his eyes again. Johann waited uncertainly for some sign of life, trying to remember his promises, fighting down resentment and impatience mixed with fear of that deathly presence — why could he not draw his last breath and make an end of this dirty job? "Uncle." He spoke more sharply than he intended. "Would you like a wash and some breakfast now? Tell me!"

His uncle opened his eyes and said, "Yes, Johann, your task is what it was yesterday. Do the necessary things, as before. But first, kneel down here beside me, and let us say a prayer together." Johann knelt and bowed his head in a rebellious silence, and did not join in when his uncle began, "Our Father . . ." Concha would be waiting for him, she had promised to spend the afternoon alone with him. His clasped hands doubled into fists over his mouth, he was almost blind with the bitter rapture of lust that struck him like a blow from an unknown source, with a violence not of pleasure but like a mortal sickness or other disaster he had not dreamed of, and no one had warned him. "And deliver us from evil —" said his uncle. "Amen." Johann blundered to his feet and began getting the morning sponge bath ready, silent, back turned to the cabin, hot with defensive outrage that his own uncontrollable body had so nearly put him to shame before that pious old hypocrite who would pretend to be shocked and would give no matter what to have just a flash of such feelings again. As he went on with the work he calmed down quite well, even felt a little remorse for thinking rude things of his poor wretched burden, and at last, when the steward brought the breakfast tray, he made a very creditable show of disappearing reluctantly. Once outside the door he went leaping like a stag, whistling *"Das gibt's nur einmal, das kommt's nicht wieder —"*

Lizzi finally got up and ventured on deck. She lay in her chair, shawled and muffled like an invalid, drinking hot broth. She was quite silent, and for the rest of the voyage sat or walked alone, had food brought to her cabin, her face melancholy and confused as if she could not see well, or had just received painful news. Mrs. Treadwell observed silence with her, and they lapsed rather comfortably into their natural relation of strangers, as separate as silkworms in their cocoons. Yet moved by some impulse, perhaps of vague mischief, Mrs. Treadwell brought Lizzi an orange from the breakfast table, and remarked: "Herr Rieber was up and about this morning. He seems to be doing very nicely."

Lizzi inserted a thumbnail in the orange peel and pulled off a section as if she were flaying something that could scream. "Let him," she remarked, sinking her teeth into the fruit.

At Vigo the harbor was filled with anchored, idle ships standing bows pointed outward. The steerage passengers again crowded upon the main deck and were herded down the gangplank first. The bride and groom, her hand on his arm, went ashore for good and disappeared without a single word of farewell to anyone. The Cuban family with the small girl and boy nodded and bowed to several of the officers as they went. David and Jenny set out together as they had finally agreed, to get visas for France. They went down just behind the Spanish company, who without a glance, not even a frown, towards their recent accomplices, the medical students, streamed off, loaded again with their parcels now containing their loot from Tenerife, chattering like blue jays, looking and behaving quite as they had when they boarded ship at Veracruz. The weather was wonderfully warm and tender, and they went at once to a small shaded park nearby, where they occupied a half dozen benches and seemed for the first time at ease with themselves.

Jenny and David, in a pleasant moment of truce, went to the French

consul, an earnest bearded young fellow of the utmost gravity of man-
ner, and were told with gestures of regret that he had not the faculty
to grant visas to persons in transit. He went to the door with them, still
expressing sympathy in a stern uncompromising voice. Jenny held her
head while David took her elbow and led her down the steps. "Let's go
to Spain?" she said, woefully. "No," said David. "Do you know where
we are going first?" They passed the little park again, and the zarzuela
company were still sitting, very quietly for them, as if they were waiting
for something to happen. Jenny and David sat on a bench some distance
from them, and for no reason, David took his wallet out and looked at
his passport and ticket. "To Bremerhaven, that's where," he told her,
at the same moment that he discovered that his ticket read "South-
ampton."

"Good God," he said simply. "Let's go." They hurried back and ran
to the purser, who already had prepared to put David aboard the
British tender at Southampton, a notion that filled David with acute
horror. The purser made a few small grumbles in his mustaches about
people who were always changing their minds in mid-ocean, refusing
utterly to grant that the mistake was not the passenger's. Jenny wanted
to argue the question, but David marched her out firmly, though he
could not prevent her thanking him much too warmly as they went.
"It's the Captain who needs to make up his mind," said Jenny, and
they exchanged the familiar bits of rumor drifting from ear to ear;
someone had heard the Captain swear repeatedly that once that cursed
steerage was emptied at Vigo, the next harbor would be Bremerhaven.
He would not stop at Gijón, nor at Boulogne, and if he pleased, not
at Southampton. His contention, so the gossip ran, was that his was a
German ship sailing through enemy waters, and his duty was to get
her into home port safely without international incident. Wilhelm
Freytag had been looking forward to seeing the last of those Cuban
medical students at Boulogne, to say nothing of Mrs. Treadwell. Yet
even as it was, the ship seemed nearly deserted. No one except David
Scott and Jenny had gone ashore — the passengers had been warned
to stay on board unless they had urgent business ashore, for it was
necessary for the *Vera* to get out of the harbor before nightfall, whether
because of port regulations, or the weather, or the shipping strike, the
announcer did not say. David learned from the purser that the fare
was the same for all ports from Vigo, and that from there the Captain
could put them off where he liked, or take the whole lot to Bremer-

haven and, said the purser kindly, "Our good Captain is not in the mood to have his orders questioned by anyone. However, in any case, I am sure we will not stop at Southampton."

"Well, I'll be going on to Bremerhaven, anyway," said David, and Jenny said instantly, "Yes, and then we can get our visas for Spain!"

David said nothing. They went on deck together, in the oddly changed mood of tenderness they were arriving at as if they were two strangers discovering something lovable in faces they were seeing for the first time. David's fury had melted at white heat all his habitual views and impressions and feelings about Jenny, and these began to flow and mingle and form again into quite different shapes, so new, so unexpected, David seemed a stranger even to himself; and whatever Jenny he thought he had once known, she had vanished. Silently he watched her turn into someone else, someone he did not know, maybe would never know, yet this new creature before him was certainly one he had created for himself, as he had created the other, out of stray stuffs of his own desire. They leaned together and their hands slid along the rail and took gentle hold. Jenny said, "What are we doing, venturing out into this livid world without our keepers? — I don't know who to curse this time, that little worm of an agent in Mexico who told me I could get a French visa in any port, or the purser, who assured us in Veracruz, while it still wasn't too late, that the ship would not stop at Boulogne, but never mind, just go to the French consul at Vigo, the old liar said —"

"I don't mind at all," said David, "I don't care where we land, just so we do land, sometime or other, in the same place. That's the way I really feel, Jenny angel, and I wish you'd stop fretting."

"Or maybe I should just curse myself," said Jenny, in mock resignation, snuggling her face for a moment blissfully on his sleeve. "David, darling, when you're like this, I could creep back inside and be your rib again!"

"I like you better the way you are," said David. And his mind added, Even if I can't keep you from creeping off into corners with other men . . . one day this won't matter either, it will help finish things off. He changed the subject.

"We are certainly not loitering in port," he said, "and the pilot is going with us all the way to Gijón."

Jenny said, "I wonder if the pilot at Tenerife got back all right?"

David said, "Pilots always do."

Between Vigo and Gijón the famous weather began to whip up. The waters rolled and whirled upon themselves and piled up in spiteful green mountains opening suddenly to another abyss. The *Vera* almost lost her head at the mere approach to the Bay of Biscay. Jenny could not sleep, but sat at her porthole until nearly morning, watching the great *faros* along the coast flaring and turning and flaring. Spain was the most beautiful coast she could even imagine: after the solid promontory of rock, a great table rising out of the sea, further along the hills were like low mounds of greenest moss, then again the rocks thrust up like furious fists, but softly colored as agate and jade and coral, with the great ill-humored clouds louring above them. "What was wrong with me?" she wondered. "It should have been Spain all along. We'll go straight to Spain," she assured herself firmly, watching the turning lights flashing across the tumbling waters, hoping she would never forget them. Now and then the *Vera* would rear like a giant shied horse, give a loud frozen roar with all her machinery and plunge head-on once more.

At Gijón, coming into harbor, hearing yelps outside, Freytag put his head through the porthole to take a glimpse of the new scene. The *Vera* was turning very slowly. Half a dozen launches were circling round filled with yelling enthusiasts, all waving colored scarfs, nearly all standing up at their own peril in their bounding little shells. Again there was a long row of Spanish ships backed neatly into docks like parked motor cars. Here, he noted later on the bulletin board, a strike of longshoremen had been added to the general strike, so no cargoes would be unloaded here on this account. The air was gray and heavy, and Freytag observed that the effect of the shouting welcoming people swaying in their little boats, getting in the way, only added confusion, not gaiety. The ship began her wild plunging again almost before she was out of the harbor, and Dr. Schumann remarked to Herr Professor Hutten that it looked like a good classical kind of crossing, he expected to give out a good many sedatives, and it was a relief to have all those steerage people safe on land. Herr Professor Hutten improved the moment and asked for a few cachets of something to help his wife sleep.

Then, after all, the ship did stand out from Boulogne, at midnight, foghorn bellowing, the half-empty ship lighted with sailors bustling and scurrying. Jenny leaped into a long coat over her gown and slipped into shoes without stockings and hurried to the side. A small shadowy French pilot boat eased up to the gangplank on the lower deck, its small bell going *twing-twingtwing,* and leaning out Jenny saw the six Cuban students, silent for once, leap to the narrow deck. Mrs. Treadwell followed, holding out her hand towards one of the officers for help; she seated herself with her back to the ship she was leaving. The Mexican diplomat's wife went next, with the Indian nurse carrying the baby. The officer took the child from her arms, and Jenny saw her narrow naked feet as she stepped into the wet slippery little boat. Jenny listened with pleasure to the sharp quick nasal speech in French voices, and she watched with something near an anguish of longing to be there, as the little bell went *twing-twing* and the pilot boat moved slowly out of the circle of ship's light, and moved, glimmering faintly in its own thrifty light, towards the blessed shores of France, towards the beloved City of Light — when would she come there? Jenny put her head down on the rail and broke into tears, then ran wildly down to her cabin. Elsa was at the porthole, but drew her head in and asked at once in concern — "Why, what has happened?"

Jenny hung up her coat and took a handkerchief out of the pocket. "Oh nothing! Don't trouble . . . it's just my turn now!"

At Southampton, no tender came out to meet them, just a cutter carrying the revenue and other necessary officers. No passenger came on or left there. Jenny could laugh then at her heart-jolting vision of David, keeping a stiff upper lip and a thoroughly dissenting eye, being borne away to the shores of England, a place where neither of them had ever dreamed of going. A scruffy neglected-looking little boy carrying an armload of newspapers came on deck, but when David and Jenny tried to buy one from him, they could not understand one word he said, and the little boy knew no word of their language. They had only German money, and when David placed a half dozen marks in his hand, he regarded them with gloom and distrust, though he did not give them back, nor would he give them a newspaper, either.

"What language does this boy speak?" David asked a young officer passing by.

"English," said the officer, curtly without pausing. "Nonsense!" said Jenny, to the back of his head.

The British officers, at the Captain's invitation, seated themselves around a table on the sunny side of the bar, temporarily closed. Jenny wandered in and sat within hearing distance quite purposely, though David refused to stop with her. But the officers were disappointingly silent for some time, unfolding and looking at their various documents, passing them around, signing something. One of the British officers asked the Captain kindly to explain a puzzling entry on a certain page, and his forefinger jabbed the place rather abruptly. Then glancing around and seeing Jenny, he dropped his voice, the half dozen heads leaned towards each other, and there followed to Jenny's chagrin a pantomime of bad temper and disagreement. The Captain's face was scarlet, he was awkward, baffled, fuming, even his wattled jaw puffed up over his collar, his eyes turned bloodshot. The young Britishers were quite self-possessed, they sat back with their chins up and their hands properly disposed and stared down their noses at the German making a holy show of himself, managing to put him in the wrong by their very postures of righteous ease. Jenny was pleased to observe that the British really behaved the way they were said to, in newspapers and novels. They were behaving as if they thought this was a social occasion and some low uninvited person had managed to get in and commit a nuisance.

The Captain raised his voice. "Of course, the French, the Americans, the British, they have everything, they can do as they like, it is only the Germans who need not expect any justice, or rather, even decency at this point."

"I did not make this ruling," said one of them, in a chilling voice, "I am only here to see it carried out." He frowned severely, and Jenny noticed that the more severely he frowned, the more helplessly he blushed with some deep inexpressible embarrassment.

"Of course," said the Captain huffily, "we are all martyrs to our duty, who does not know that? But is it a state of affairs that we may not even complain of?"

There followed a stiff silence. One of the British officers reached out and touched the papers. "We may as well get on with this," he said to the others, and after that they spoke only to each other and not once to the Captain.

"I'd give anything just to know what they were arguing about," Jenny said to David later.

"Something dull, no doubt," said David.

"I wish I knew what that little boy was trying to tell us," said Jenny.
"He was trying to sell us a newspaper," said David.
"Oh, all right," said Jenny. "All right, all right."

The last part of the voyage was quiet and pleasant enough, the few survivors agreed among themselves: even Herr Löwenthal, noting all the vacant chairs in the dining room, suggested to his steward that perhaps Herr Freytag could have a whole table to himself, now. The steward was happy to inform Herr Löwenthal that Herr Freytag had thought of that for himself and the change had been made. William Denny got up and took the bandages off his head without telling Dr. Schumann, who promptly put them back on again, but allowed him to go down for his meals. His one slowly burning resentment was that Pastora had, after all, got clean away, had nearly got clean away with murder. "These little head wounds are very chancy," said Dr. Schumann. "Why do you suppose I gave you a tetanus shot? Do please let me handle this."

"That Pastora ought to be sent to the clink for life," said Denny, "and given the hell of a beating before she got there."

Dr. Schumann, deeply offended by the generally coarse low nature of his patient, said very coldly: "It was not Pastora. It was Mrs. Treadwell, that modest and gentle lady whom you somehow succeeded in exasperating beyond bounds."

Denny was so shocked he could only give a long low whistle that ended "*Jeeeeee*-sus! For a fact? How did you know?"

"A young steward told me."

"Which one?" insisted Denny, sitting up suddenly.

"That I cannot tell you," said Dr. Schumann. "This episode is now in the category of things past, and you will do much better to chalk it up to Experience. Good morning. I will see you tomorrow." He closed his black satchel and left, feeling a real glow of some kind of malicious satisfaction mixed with moral unction: for once justice was being done in the most roundabout and no doubt reprehensible way, but it did Dr. Schumann's heart good to see it at work.

When the ship passed the Isle of Wight, Jenny was enchanted with the fairy-looking castle standing in a greensward the color of an emerald, surrounded by small tender woods, and the grass shaven neatly to the very edge of the sea. As they passed so near to the shore, she believed she was deceived again in her sense of smell, which often brought her strange improbable whiffs of cross currents of air. Now she smelled herbs and freshly cut grass and grazing cows.

"Yes, yes," said Elsa, almost happily, "it is true. I have passed here this is the fourth time and there is always that lovely smell. When I was little I thought maybe heaven would be like that."

The passengers began to be restless and inert at once; the daily games ceased, some of the moving pictures were being shown for the second time, they lolled on deck or in their cabins, and began packing and repacking their luggage and worrying about their belongings in the hold. By the time the *Vera* went through the lock and emerged into the narrow River Weser, Lizzi was still refusing to return to the Captain's table when she learned that Herr Rieber was back in his accustomed chair. She brooded on the way Mrs. Treadwell had simply picked herself up and left the cabin as if she were going to take a turn on deck, and had said no farewell — not even a little simple *"Grüss Gott,"* which costs nothing. When she was in her deckchair, which she had caused to be moved far away from Herr Rieber's, she closed her eyes and pretended to be asleep when she saw him trotting by — what a little pig, after all, with that big piece of tape and lint on his bald head . . . what a disgusting life it was!

The Captain, Herr Rieber, Frau Rittersdorf, and the Huttens, with Frau Schmitt and Dr. Schumann, sat at their table nearly in silence, for they all felt that any topic they had in common would lead to awkward or trivial gossip. And they were no longer interested in anything the others had to say — their minds were closing in and folding up once more around their own concerns, their only common hope being to leave that ship and end that voyage and to take up their real and separate lives once more. Yet at the very last dinner together, they drank each others' healths and gave each other friendly looks, and Herr Professor Hutten said warmly, "At last we are nearing home, and we are, after all, all good Germans together. Let us thank God for his blessings."

There at last they faced another port town, with its cluttered docks and warehouses crowding down to the water, full of floating harbor filth around the familiar line of idle empty ships waiting like others in harbors all over the world for the strike to be settled. Again small craft full of people waving scarfs and shouting welcomes circled about playfully and got in the way.

Bremerhaven! And the old *Vera* safe in harbor, among a fleet of others like her, battered rusty tired veterans coming in from all the seas, always the long way round, carrying the scars of their hard voyages with their untidy cargoes and middling people in the anxious middling way of life, who were not traveling for pleasure. Yet from every ship the flags were flying and dipping in courtesy to the harbor and all in it, the little bands on every deck were playing their hoppity tunes, the crews and the officers were at their stations, all paint-fresh, fit and ready, in good discipline. On the *Vera* the passengers lined up as near to the gangplank as they could without disorder or crowding. They were indeed all Germans and together, except for the three Americans, who stood together somewhat back and apart. Eyes met eyes again vaguely, almost without recognition and no further speech. They were becoming strangers again, though not suspicious and hostile as at first. It was a pleasant indifference to everything but the blessed moment of escape to life once more. For a moment all the faces were raised, eyes searching out the roofs of the town, filled and softened with generous feelings — their hearts beat freely and their stomachs trembled with the illusion of joy; all mysteriously entranced as if they approached a lighted altar, they prepared to set their feet once more upon the holy earth of their Fatherland.

The day was dark and cold, with lightly floating snow. The family groups drew together, the tall golden-haired Johann with his dying uncle in the wheel chair, who opened his eyes now and again and looked about him; the Baumgartner child in the orange buckskin leather *charro* dress shivered in it instead of sweating. Elsa, wearing a wooly white coat, her white beret covering her hair, clutched her small traveling bag to her, and repeated patiently, "Yes, Mama," or "No, Mama," to every question her mother asked her, sometimes twice over. "Elsa, did you pick up all your hairpins and safety pins, did you leave any handkerchiefs, have you got all your stockings together? Did you leave your nail file and scissors? In underwear you started out with six of everything, I hope we reach home with that number . . . besides sweaters —"

Herr Lutz said jocosely, "You have not said exactly how many hairpins, Elsa. Twenty-seven, maybe?"

"Oh, Papa," she said gratefully, "I'm sure I brought everything."

"Of course you have, my dear little girl. Now we are going home and you should be happy."

"Yes and thank God," said Frau Lutz, glad to shift the ground of argument, since she plainly was losing. "And the rest will be on land, in our own compartment, on a European train, like a real family once more and none of this promiscuous mingling with low types we cannot avoid. Ha!" she said in gloomy triumph, "This will be my last voyage. There is no sea where we are going to live, Elsa."

"No, Elsa," said her father, "and no ships. And no iodine or salt: You buy salt with iodine in it from the pharmacist. Otherwise you'll have goiter."

"Oh for shame!" cried Frau Lutz. "How can you say such things? Elsa, your father is making one of his jokes —"

"How many of your relatives in St. Gallen have goiter?" asked Herr Lutz, reasonably. "There was Aunt Fike, and Aunt Wilhelmina, and Uncle Wolfgang and Cousin August, and your own sister Lotte, and your grandfather on your mother's side —"

"Stop!" cried Frau Lutz, nearly beside herself. "Slander your own family, not mine!"

"It is no slander," said Herr Lutz. "Elsa, what are you looking for? Who do you see?" For he noticed that while they were talking her eyes roamed slowly, steadily, furtively under her half-closed lids, her head turned ever so slightly, and he had never seen an expression like that on her face. As a father, he did not approve and he was disturbed. Elsa flushed darkly and put her hand over her mouth. "Nothing, no one," she said in such confusion he said nothing more. At that moment Herr Hansen lunged by, his face in knots, and he threw Elsa a glance as he went, the glance of a wandering eye that is seeking nothing, and yet for Elsa the blow was as cruel as if he had intended it. He had always looked at her as if she were thin air or a blank wall. She flinched, and her father said, "That was never the man for *you*, my dear." Her mother was shocked into agreement. "The idea," she said in derision. "Whoever thought so, for a minute?"

Hateful as Herr Hansen was to her, yet he had been crazed about that terrible Amparo, and he had smashed that horrid Herr Rieber for some good reason, she was sure, so he was a man of strong feelings, only he had never treated her as if she were human; what did she care? Yet she did care. She did not really want anything from him, no not even a look. It was her student she would remember all her life, stand-ing there on deck with the music playing and his arms around her, with his smiling questioning face and his coaxing voice — and still she could not dance. She drew such a deep breath she felt she must explain it. "I am only tired," she told them. "I am not sick, Mama."

Freytag moved away from the German group and approached Jenny and David, who stood hand in hand near Denny, who was picking silently at bits of tape and cotton covering the heel cuts all over his face. Freytag stopped before them and held out his hand to Jenny, who took her hand out of David's and gave it to him with a gentle pressure. She smiled, but he saw her eyes grow very dark and excited. "Good-by," said Freytag, his own gray eyes clear and pleasant. "I hope you will like it here."

David offered his hand and Freytag gave it a good manly shake. Their eyes met, and though their faces were entirely impassive Jenny saw a curious expression pass between them — the merest flicker of a glance like light on water, but it chilled her blood. It was the wordless affirmation of pure male complicity, complete understanding from far depths of instinctive being, safe from all surface movements and per-plexities of events, sympathy and a secret alliance, from which she was excluded by natural law, in their unalienable estate of manhood. Jenny trembled so violently that David said, "Are you cold, Jenny angel? Let me help you." He took her coat off her arm and held it for her to put on. While he did this, he nodded to Freytag, who was going towards the gangplank.

"Good luck," he said, and Freytag answered with a wave of his hand.

"Just to think, it's all over," said Jenny. "Soon it will be only a dream. Why did I come here?"

"Because you wanted to go to France and I wanted to go to Spain, wasn't that it?"

"I am a sleepwalker," said Jenny, "and this is a dream."

"Dreams are real too," said David, "nightmares, everything."

"David, we aren't going to spend our lives together, why are we going on with this?"

"Don't you remember? We aren't ready yet." He stood beside her and took her hand again, quite composed and certain of his own mood. He watched her eyes beginning to glisten, and he became very touched and gentle with her as he did sometimes when she wept on his account.

The sight of her weakness and defeat gave him pleasure like no other.

"Do you know," he said, falsely, "maybe we shall never leave each other. Where could we go?"

"We'll think of somewhere," she said, "let's wait."

"Here we go talking again," said David. "Let's think of something pleasant."

"You think of something, David darling," said Jenny, "something wonderful."

David leaned with great discretion and a very straight face and whispered, "Tonight in Bremen we'll sleep in the same bed for a change." Jenny made a slight purring sound at him, and he watched her face grow radiant.

The band played *"Tannenbaum"* at last, and kept it up until the gangplank was down, and the passengers began to descend rapidly and silently. As the musicians were wiping the mouthpieces of their instruments, wrapping up their drums and putting away their fiddles, their mouths were wide with smiles, their heads towards the dock, towards the exact narrow spot where the *Vera* had warped in and cast her anchor. Among them, a gangling young boy, who looked as if he had never had enough to eat in his life, nor a kind word from anybody, and did not know what he was going to do next, stared with blinded eyes, his mouth quivering while he shook the spit out of his trumpet, repeating to himself just above a whisper, *"Grüss Gott, Grüss Gott,"* as if the town were a human being, a good and dear trusted friend who had come a long way to welcome him.

Yaddo, August, 1941
Pigeon Cove, August, 1961